REMEMBRANCE, HISTORY, AND JUSTICE

REMEMBRANCE, HISTORY, AND JUSTICE

Coming to Terms with Traumatic
Pasts in Democratic Societies

Edited by
VLADIMIR TISMANEANU
and
BOGDAN C. IACOB

Central European University Press
Budapest–New York

© 2015 the editors

Published in 2015 by

Central European University Press

An imprint of the
Central European University Limited Liability Company
Nádor utca 11, H-1051 Budapest, Hungary
Tel: +36-1-327-3138 or 327-3000
Fax: +36-1-327-3183
E-mail: ceupress@press.ceu.edu
Website: www.ceupress.com

224 West 57th Street, New York NY 10019, USA
Tel: +1-212-547-6932
Fax: +1-646-557-2416
E-mail: meszarosa@press.ceu.edu

ISBN 978-963-386-092-2 (hardback)
ISBN 978-963-386-101-1 (paperback)

LIBRARY OF CONGRESS CATALOGING-IN-PUBLICATION DATA

Remembrance, history, and justice : coming to terms with traumatic pasts in
democratic societies / edited by Vladimir Tismaneanu and Bogdan C. Iacob.
    pages cm
    Includes bibliographical references and index.
    ISBN 978-9633860922 (hardbound : alk. paper)

1. Europe, Eastern—Politics and government—1989– 2. Collective memory—Europe, Eastern. 3. Memory—Political aspects—Europe, Eastern. 4. Democratization—Social aspects—Europe, Eastern. 5. Europe, Eastern—Historiography—Social aspects. 6. Europe, Eastern—Historiography—Political aspects. 7. Social justice—Europe, Eastern. 8. Post-communism—Europe, Eastern. 9. Fascism—Social aspects—Europe, Eastern. 10. Dictatorship—Social aspects—Europe, Eastern. I. Tismaneanu, Vladimir. II. Iacob, Bogdan.

DJK51.R46 2015
323.4'90947—dc23

                                2014046041

Printed in Hungary

Table of Contents

Part Two
HISTORIES AND THEIR PUBLICS

Part Three
SEARCHING FOR CLOSURE
IN DEMOCRATIZING SOCIETIES

VLADIMIR TISMANEANU and BOGDAN C. IACOB

Introduction

Polish journalist Ryszard Kapuściński once wrote that "when thinking about the fall of any dictatorship, one should have no illusions
that the whole system comes to an end like a bad dream. A dictatorship ... leaves behind an empty, sour field on which the tree of thought
won't grow quickly."[1] The twentieth century has left behind a painful
and complicated legacy of massive trauma, monstrous crimes, radical social engineering, and collective/individual guilt syndromes that
were often the premises for and the specters haunting the process of
democratization in the various societies that emerged out of these profoundly destructuring contexts. More often than not, the past appears
as a devastated landscape full of corpses, dashed illusions, failed myths,
betrayed promises, and unprocessed memories. Over a decade into the
twenty-first century, the historical experience of the previous one is still
fundamentally shaping how we envisage our contemporary world at
personal, local, national, continental, and global levels. The burden of
authoritarian pasts brought whole societies into international conversations about their histories. Identities are essentially defined by dual processes of remembrance and historicization of large-scale state sponsored
violence. Policies of transitional justice have increasingly acquired a
transnational character. Since the late 1980s, there has been a prolifera-

---

[1] Quoted in Adam Hochschild, "Shadowlands. Marci Shore's 'Taste of Ashes'," *New York Times*, April 26, 2013 (http://www.nytimes.com/2013/04/28/
books/review/marci-shores-taste-of-ashes.html?pagewanted=all&_r=0, last
accessed April 30, 2013).

tion of truth commissions across very diverse geographical areas. In the former socialist bloc, there appeared a plethora of "Gauck-type" agencies for keeping secret police files or institutes of national memory dealing with the traumatic legacies of either the communist period or the entire totalitarian experience (i.e., fascism or Nazi occupation). Many times these institutions are the result of emulation and dialogue with earlier similar incarnations in other countries. All in all, the underlining presupposition that defines this culture of remembrance, historicization, and justice, which has consistently developed in over two and a half decades, is that long-term, state-endorsed amnesia ultimately subverts and even delegitimizes post-dictatorial democracies.

In post-authoritarian societies, responsibility, empathy, tolerance, trust, and also reconciliation are essentially dependent on confronting the penumbra of one's recent past. In struggling to explain and understand the consequences of radical evil and the pathologies of political extremism, both history and memory find themselves pushed to the limit. From the Holocaust to the Gulag, from genocide to sociocide, from ethnic cleansing to apartheid, from mass murder to crimes against humanity, the twentieth century forced us to find new ways to confront and remember shattered pasts. Far from having this experience now behind us, the latter stays with us. We have yet to learn all of its lessons. This volume is a collective effort to analyze how the interplay between memory, history, and justice generates insight that is multifariously relevant for comprehending the present and future of democracy without becoming limited to a Europe-centric framework of understanding.

This book is structured with three complementary and interconnected trajectories: the public use of history, politics of memory, and transitional justice. Subsequently, the contributors deal with trauma and the reconstitution of democratic communities, with the multiple publics of historical inquiry in the context of a shift from authoritarianism to pluralism, with the competing narratives resultant of the process of *Aufarbeitung*, and last but not least, with the juridical and investigative efforts to acknowledge and punish the crimes and abuses of the past. One can hardly complain that there is a scarcity of scholarship in the general topics discussed here. We believe, however, that *Remembrance, History, and Justice* is innovative from the point of view of its thematic, methodological, and geographical breadth. Additionally, it brings together an eminent group of authors, who have had a significant presence in and impact on local and international debates on the very topics discussed in the current pages. Finally, the chapters also rely on extensive contextualization and engagement with the scholarship of the politics of memory, transitional history, historiography of the twentieth century, and comparative politics across multiple area of studies, including: the European Union, former Soviet space, Western Balkans, Latin America, South Africa, East Asia, and, to a limited degree, the Middle East.

The volume combines case studies with more extensive transnational and comparative approaches. It brings together historiography with memory studies, intellectual and legal history, and political analysis with theoretical insight. It integrates local and regional experiences with traumatic histories into a global structure that offers the possibility of more general conclusions about the legacy of a century touched by the "reek of cruelty." The authors situate the process of coming to terms with the past (communism, fascism, authoritarianism, failed democracies) in Eastern Europe (including the Western Balkans) and the former Soviet space within the larger context of discussing the memory and history of postwar periods. There are several case studies dealing with Russia (David Brandenberger); Poland (Andrzej Paczkowski); Romania (Alexandru Gussi, Raluca Grosescu and Raluca Ursachi, Cristian Vasile, and Bogdan C. Iacob); Yugoslavia (Vladimir Petrović); Bulgaria (Nikolai Vukov); Lithuania (Leonidas Donskis); and Moldova (Igor Caşu). They are further contextualized and assessed by way of comparison, as other contributors discuss them in regional and European environments (see chapters by Timothy Snyder, Vladimir Tismaneanu, and John Connelly). This allows for the expansion of the discussion, as countries such as Ukraine and Belarus are taken into account. Additionally, the volume features the German case prominently, as authors examine both experiences of working through the past, that is, the Nazi and the communist ones (Jeffrey Herf and especially, Jan-Werner Müller). This *exemplum* is a recurrent theme in a large number the texts because "with its postwar and postcommunist experiences with undemocratic regimes and their injustices, Germany offers an imperfect but incredibly important model for reckoning with the demons of the twentieth century."[2]

---

[2] The editors owe this truly pertinent remark to one of the two anonymous peer-reviewers of the volume.

At the same time, the European overview is compared with other cases of post-authoritarian transitions such as those in Latin America (Eusebio Mujal-Leon and Eric Langenbacher), South Africa (Charles Villa-Vicencio), East Asia with a focus on Japan (Daniel Chirot), and the Middle East (Jeffrey Herf). Even though Europe remains the setting for the historical framework discussed in this volume, the comparisons with non-European contexts serve the purpose of globalizing the narrative and investigation, while also de-parochializing the insights on the burdens of post-dictatorial experiences. The result is a clustered, big picture of practices of remembrance, reckoning, and historiographical reevaluation. Ultimately, *Remembrance, History, and Justice* distinguishes itself from most of the existing literature through its diversity and comprehensiveness.

The book stands out within current scholarship because of the cascade of interrelated themes tackled by its contributors. All authors point to the recent surge, as compared to larger post-dictatorial timelines, to confront guilt, responsibility, and trauma in the cases discussed. Another highly salient issue underlined by many of the contributors is the internationalization of judicial and historical accountability practices. Several chapters examine extensively the relationship between collective/individual memories and state narratives about the past, indicating the complexities of the inevitable cleavages or probable consensus between social and political vectors of remembrance. A factor that is widely stressed is the role of delegitimizing authoritarian politics and agents (successor elites still entrenched in undemocratic ideological stances) in facing up to dictatorial legacies. A related, important theme is the destructuring effect of the politicization of memory and history on post-traumatic communities. Some of the authors also discuss the multiple mechanisms of accountability (trials, truth commissions, state apologies, legislation, and so on) and their connections to existing horizons of expectation in the various societies under scrutiny. The volume stresses the difficulty of establishing a culture of remembrance as older historicizations and commemoration regimes come into conflict or are replaced by novel historical and communal discourses about authoritarian experiences.

An additional crucial subject is the criteria for evaluating and/or comparing processes of working through the past. The contributors advocate complementing the findings in national cases with inquiring about their relevance in regional, continental, and global frameworks. In this way, coming to terms with a problematic and painful period in a country's history is not only de-ethnicized, but also it is not taken as a bloc. By the latter we mean that its features (specificities or similarities) can be identified and taxonomized in accordance with dominant motifs in international discussions about processing dictatorial legacies, with evolving ideas about justice and reparation, or with contemporary problems faced by democratizing societies (of which some are in transitional phases). A by-product of such a reading is that issues such as post-memory, post-modernity, deprivation (political, economic, or anamnestic), and nostalgia are better perceived as they reflect phenomena that go beyond local challenges. Historian Marci Shore rightly wondered: "Was it possible to restore human dignity through truth, if arriving at truth involved gazing anew through old peepholes?"[3] Indeed, historical reckoning is greatly dependent on altering and adjusting the means, vocabulary, and references we employ in novel representations of suffering and responsibility that overcome silence, cynicism, amnesia, or recoil.

Some of the most important questions *Remembrance, History, and Justice* tries to offer pertinent answers to are: How do memory and memorialization shape political communities? What are the relationships between memory, commemoration, and state-controlled rituals? To create and foster legitimacy, authority, prestige, and influence, what resources are mobilized, when, and by whom? Under what conditions can anamnestic solidarities ensure the experiential continuity from a generation that lived through trauma to the one that only learns about it? How can one avoid cultivating memories that deliberately forgot the suffering of whole collectivities who at one point had been destined for extermination? What is the political, social, and cultural reality captured by the term post-dictatorial, if any? How can postmemory be constructed, developed, and directed in a democratically-minded direction, rather than perpetuating discourses of rancor, vindictiveness, and resentment? Is there a way to create a common European memory of the twentieth century? After all, the foundations of the European Union project were set up by individuals deeply affected by the totali-

---

[3] Marci Shore, *The Taste of Ashes: The Afterlife of Totalitarianism in Eastern Europe* (New York: Crown Publishers, 2013), xii.

tarian cataclysms whose main concern was to preempt and prevent the re-enactment of such dismal scenarios.[4] If so, how does it compare with the memories and histories of other regions of the world? What are the lessons of the *travail de mémoire*, the transitional justice, the historiography and experience of authoritarianism in Latin America, South Africa, East Asia, or the Middle East, and how can they be accommodated with the European stories?

The two editors did not seek a unitary argument or a communion of standpoints among various authors on the topics analyzed. For instance, there are some differences, though not considerable, in the way the German case is interpreted in various chapters; or for that matter, among contributors discussing Poland, Romania, and Russia. However, we firmly believe that diversity of topics, cases, *and* of explanations is perhaps the most vital attribute to a comprehensive, nuanced, and complex understanding of the phenomena and events that are the focus of this book. Ultimately, such multiple readings prove predominantly complementary rather than contradicting, and this is one of the main accomplishments of *Remembrance, History, and Justice*.

The volume opens with Timothy Snyder's contribution on the evolution and challenges of commemoration and mass killing in Europe. His chapter identifies one of the crucial issues that is recurrent throughout many of the chapters, namely, the difficulty in studying the history of the twentieth century, while the horrors are stilll being commemorated. Developing on the findings of his path-breaking *Bloodlands*, Snyder shows the fundamental interrelatedness and multilayeredness of mass murder in Eastern Europe between 1933 and 1948. This situation shows an intricate web of traumatizing memories that often are in conflict with established postwar practices of commemoration or which, in the past years, have become victims and subjects of competitive martyrologies. His prospective solutions are fundamentally based on the idea of integration of Eastern Europe into the history of twentieth-century Europe, and of the comparativity of mass murder while keeping in mind the uniqueness of the Holocaust. Timothy Snyder nicely anticipates some of the analyses developed in several of the other chapters of the book.

---

[4] Jan-Werner Müller, *Contesting Democracy: Political Ideas in Twentieth-Century Europe* (New Haven and London: Yale University Press, 2011).

Part one of the volume discusses the relationship between the politics of memory and the process of democratization. The contributions that it comprises are fundamentally comparative providing an impressive geographical scope for the overview of the topics analyzed. The first of these texts is Dan Chirot's counterpoising of practices of memory work in Europe with those in East Asia. The sociologist states that an unwillingness to recognize the dark side of one's national history is, after all, the rule rather than the exception. His review of World War II memories in South Korea, China, and particularly Japan shows a persistent acrimony in Southeast Asia in terms of assuming responsibility for both atrocities and collaboration with their perpetrators. However, when this picture is compared with evolutions in Europe, both in the West and in the former socialist bloc, he underlines the rather spotty record of most of these countries in admitting their ultranationalist and anti-Semitic policies. His final remark that history is mostly meant to serve the present rather than the past is echoed across the entire volume. In this context, it is up to scholars to accelerate the process of recognition, admission, and therefore reconciliation by providing the raw materials that honest intellectuals and political leaders will use when they finally come to accept the necessity of facing the past. Chirot's text stands out also because the author reminisces about his experience as a young Jewish child struggling with his family to survive in wartime Nazi occupied France.

The next contributors, Eusebio Mujal-León and Eric Langenbacher, draw their theoretical insight on collective and post-authoritarian memories by discussing the cases of Germany, Spain, Chile, and Argentina, which they then test in the Cuban context. The latter is perceived as a revolutionary project losing its vitality/legitimacy and is expected to be either replaced or transformed. One important factor in the evolution of politics of memory is in the nature of the authoritarian regime. The more radical a regime, the greater its capacity and will to destroy all memories, except for those partial and partisan, which the regime subscribes and seeks to implant. The second is the degree and responsibility for trauma. The last factor that they point to is that the international dimension matters in the recovery of memory or in support of democratization processes. Historian Jeffrey Herf revisits the main theses from his influential book *Divided Memory* and then tests his conclusion against the fascinating case study of the Grand Mufti of

Jerusalem, Haj Amin el-Husseini. He had been a collaborator with the Radio Division in the German Foreign Office during the Nazi regime, but in the postwar period, he became a member of the leadership in Palestine without being forced to change his views; he continued to combine anti-Zionism with visceral hatred of the Jews. Herf remarks that in the aftermath of gross human rights violations, there is tension between rapid democratization and judicial reckoning. In his view, the evolution of memory politics in Germany shows that where elements of the old regime persist and where foreign occupation has not taken place, as is the case in most post-dictatorial settings, the ability of the successor democracy to explore the traumatic past has been much weaker. However, by bringing into the discussion Husseini's case, he insists on the vital importance of the complete delegitimation of anti-Semitism and of the support for anti-democratic politics for allowing the possibility of coming to terms with the past. Similar to Chirot, Herf concludes that Germany was an exception because foreign powers and past democratic traditions eventually tipped the balance in favor of memory, despite the existence of widespread cynicism, opportunism, hypocrisy, and amnesia in the postwar period.

The last chapter in this section adds an additional facet to Herf's general observations. Romanian political scientist, Alexandru Gussi, underlines the connection between deliberate politics of forgetting and biased politics of memory in post-communist Europe and the collective feelings of frustration among individuals living in this region's societies. He shows how the instrumentalization of the past subverted the moral weight that collective remembrance could potentially carry after 1989. Ultimately, Gussi's conclusions remain within the interpretative framework of the other contributors in the section: politics of memory are an integral part of democratization, but the latter process neither guarantees nor presupposes a genuine confrontation of the past. But the consequences of institutionalized amnesia or selective remembrance are dire on the long term, as they conceal societal tendencies that can severely subvert the very building of democracy.

This insight is the stepping stone for Part Two of the volume, which discusses the relationship between the historicization of the past and the dynamics within different publics directly affected or involved in the process of dealing with past. Vladimir Tismaneanu's opening contribution is an essay that fulfills a double function. On the one hand, it is an evaluation of the process of confronting the communist past in Romania from the point of view of the existing literature on politics of memory and truth/expert commissions. On the other hand, the account is also biographical, as it is based on his experience as chair of the Presidential Commission for the Analysis of the Communist Dictatorship in Romania (PCACDR). The political scientist perceives PCADCR, its report, and the condemnation act from the point of view of moral justice and of epistemic renewal in contrast to pre-2006 state-sponsored and institutionalized politics of amnesia. Tismaneanu, however, goes on to present the way the Romanian case is different from the German *Enquete-Kommission* and the South African Truth and Reconciliation Commission (TRC). He considers that the PCACDR's Final Report was a history lesson during which the "truth" about the communist totalitarian experience was publicly acknowledged. He ends with an exposé on the developing framework of European remembrance based on collective continental traumas and the negative lessons and *exempla* provided by various national histories from the former socialist bloc.

David Brandenberger discusses the politics of history textbooks in Russia and the activity of the Commission to Counter Attempts to Falsify History at the Expense of Russian Interests. The chapter examines the circumstances under which new state-endorsed textbooks of Russian history emerged and the extent to which they have succeeded in catalyzing a new official line on the past. He concludes that the efforts to impose a new state-historiographical orthodoxy have enjoyed a rather mixed record of success. However, the long-term effects of the impact of the textbooks and of the Commission's pronouncements remain significant in oblique and indirect terms.

Part Two of the volume ends with Jan-Werner Müller's assessment of the two processes of coming to terms with the past (Nazi and communist) in Germany. The author first overviews the reasons behind claims that both "coming to terms with the Nazi past" and "overcoming the legacies of the GDR" might have been failures after all. He then engages this phenomenon of tortured self-criticism by reconstructing some recent debates in Germany. In analyzing the criticisms of the *Bewältigung* of the Nazi past, the author argues that some critics of this process correctly point to the fact that guilt has strangely turned into pride. This chapter points out a recurring theme in this volume, namely the criteria for evaluating the success or failure of specific aspects of the process of dealing with the past. Müller concludes that the appraisal of the German case of remembrance can only be perceived as a problem because the German culture of remembrance is highly developed and firmly grounded in the country's political. He does, however, point to the danger of remembrance degenerating into a kind of routine. He believes that the latter can be countered only by persevering in conscious and reflective interaction with institutionalized memory.

Part Three of *Remembrance, History, and Justice* encompasses studies that deal with specific mechanisms for confronting the past: trials against those responsible for politically-motivated crimes under communist regimes and truth or expert commissions. Even though the chapters are case studies, taken together they provide a larger picture of the challenges facing the employment of distinct institutional and juridical instruments in the process of coming to terms with the past. This is the reason why the editors employed the term closure, though it is used in a significantly diluted sense. A final decision in court or a report of a Commission should theoretically allow the completion of a certain stage in the endeavor of reckoning. But as these chapters show, more often than not, such mechanisms themselves have questionable dynamics and are far from truly bringing about closure. The first three chapters in this section start from the same premise: trials against former leaders of a dictatorial regime are symbolic moments in the founding of a new democratic order. However, as Paczkowski pertinently demonstrates, prosecution against perpetrators from the communist regime (in his case, the Polish one) has been slow, unconvincing, and of little effectiveness. One explanation for this reality is the negotiated nature of the transition from communism to pluralism. Another is the unwillingness of the leftist part of the opposition and its intellectual milieu to pursue a "settling of the accounts" with the past. Paczkowski presents a detailed historical account of the legal and institutional tribulations of the various attempts to prosecute crimes from the communist period (and sometimes the Nazi occupation). He then focuses on the activity of the Institute of National Remembrance (Instytut Pamięci Narodowej, IPN) concerning legal accountability for the martial period in the context of a public opinion divided on the appropriate manner of dealing with these years. He emphasizes two topics that are directly tied to this larger debate: conspiracy theories concerning the persistent influence of ex-communists in present-day Poland and the alleged collaboration of Lech Wałęsa with the secret police.

The next text in this section deals with the history, avatars, and consequences of the various trials against either former leaders of the Romanian communist regime (e.g., Nicolae and Elena Ceauşescu or the members of the last Politburo) or generals involved in the repression of demonstrators during the revolution of 1989. Two Romanian political scientists, Raluca Grosescu and Raluca Ursachi, discuss the relationship between the procedural profile of these juridical events and their connection with post-communist politics and the dynamics of symbolic narratives relating to the local, violent, and bloody events of December 1989. The contributors conclude that the examination of the epistemic dimension of the Romanian Revolution trials opens the possibility to identify the narratives they put in circulation about the events of December 1989, the values they promoted, and the extent to which they were used politically during the transition. They state that these legal events did not contribute to elucidating historical developments, but to the contrary, they misrepresented them, subsequently distorting history. Their remarks are similar to Paczkowski's observation that during the trials in Poland, usually only marginal perpetrators were convicted (or even brought to court), as important communist decision makers are yet to be held legally accountable for their abuses while in power. Romania stands out because, as Lavinia Stan showed, it "conducted the second largest number of court trials related to the recent past, a veritable 'justice cascade' in the region."[5] Paradoxically, as Grosescu and Ursachi show, this situation compromised the validity of the process of transitional justice and its significance for historical reckoning.

Vladimir Petrović also focuses on a trial of a former head of state, namely that of the former Serbian leader Slobodan Milošević in front of the International Criminal Tribunal of the former Yugoslavia. He stresses that the reading of the impact of this momentous juridical process in the building of an international framework of accountability for national politicians involved in crimes and massive abuses has been significantly hampered by its premature end due to Milošević's death.

---

[5] Lavinia Stan, *Transitional Justice in Post-Communist Romania: The Politics of Memory* (Cambridge and New York: Cambridge University Press, 2013), 30.

Petrović underlines that as the Milošević trial moves from the legal field to join the ongoing memory wars over his role in the Yugoslav wars, its achievements ought not to be measured solely from the point of its procedural outcome. Despite the protracted and almost unmanageable nature of the proceedings, the trial produced a massive body of evidence, inspiring further proceedings on both the international and national level.

The next three chapters in this section bring into discussion a second mechanism of institutional coming to terms with the past—truth or expert commissions. Charles Villa-Vicencio provides an analytic and informative account of the Truth and Reconciliation Commission in South Africa, while also looking into the aftermath of the activity of this body. Like Tismaneanu's chapter, Villa-Vicencio's work is also important from a biographical point of view—Villa-Vicencio was the Commission's National Research Director. He first looks into the context of the South African political settlement, culminating in the 1994 elections, presenting the specific circumstances that set the ground for the Commission. He then examines the nature, structure, and functioning of the Commission itself. Villa-Vicencio also dwells on the unfinished work of the Commission that is centered on issues such as prosecution of perpetrators, reparations for victims, and reconstruction of society. He concludes that the process of healing the deep wounds of the past in South Africa is inevitably interlinked with overcoming and alleviating current societal disparities and cleavages.

The remaining two chapters examine the role and functioning of expert commissions in Romania and Moldova. Both are also insider accounts, as their authors were directly involved in the activity of these bodies: Cristian Vasile was scientific secretary of the PCACDR, while Igor Caşu was vice president of the Commission for the Study and Evaluation of the Communist Totalitarian Regime in the Republic of Moldova (CSECTR). As Caşu notes, the Romanian Commission was, to a certain extent, a model for the Moldovan one. If one is to put together the two accounts and that of Tismaneanu (who references the German Bundestag Commissions as the main inspiration for the Romanian one), we notice a pattern of transnational institutional emulation/transfer that underlines that current processes of dealing with the past cannot be limited to their national environments. This point reinforces another phenomenon stressed by most authors in the volume: the gradual and arduous construction of a common culture of remembrance in Europe.

Cristian Vasile's work complements Tismaneanu's contribution, as the author provides additional details about the specificities, dynamics, and difficulties of the PCACDR and of the background of its most important members. He also offers extensive information on the implementation of the recommendations of the Romanian Commission concerning access to the archives, legal measures, education, commemoration, and so on. One conclusion that he draws is that the PCACDR was an independent, nonpartisan body where the authors of the various sections of the Commission's Report interacted with each other on the basis of dialogue and consensus. Moreover, Vasile also stresses the Commission's role in bridging dissension between Romanians and minority groups (especially Hungarians) on contested topics concerning the communist past and its efforts to demythicize the history of the Romanian Orthodox Church between 1945 and 1989. He ends by stressing the fact the Commission was a crucial step in the acknowledgment and identification of the responsibility of communist leaders and institutions for the crimes perpetrated between 1945 and 1989.

Igor Caşu's study adopts a different angle for contextualizing the Moldovan Commission. The first part discusses the evolutions and specifics of the nationalities policy in the Soviet Union, with a particular focus on the case of Moldova. He points out that Moldova acquired a special status once Romania itself was Sovietized in the sense that the Soviet Union had to develop policies that could institutionalize and consolidate sharp distinctions between the populations of the two communist countries. The result was strong cultural, social, and economic discrimination of the ethnic Romanians in Moldova. This was also the background for the protracted processes of rehabilitation of the victims of communism and of acknowledgment of the crimes committed in Moldova. Caşu refreshingly chooses to examine these phenomena across the 1990–1991 divide, thus presenting their evolution from the Soviet into the post-Soviet period. The Commission for the Study and Evaluation of Communist Totalitarian Regime in the Republic of Moldova appears as the culmination of a gradual development toward a minimal consensus on the importance of discussing the trauma of the past. However, Caşu concludes by warning that in Moldova, because of its specific history within the Soviet Union, the process of coming to

terms with the past is in danger of being ethnicized, as either Romanians or Russians often tend to claim a monopoly of victimhood. This
remark echoes similar points made by Snyder, Tismaneanu, and Chirot, who list among the most problematic elements of the mis-memory
of the past the tendency to blame other national groups or countries
for one's own responsibility for crimes and collaboration in their per-
petration.

Part Four of *Remembrance, History, and Justice* concentrates on the
competing narratives regarding the troubled pasts in Eastern Europe.
Two chapters discuss the issue from the point of view of the connection between national evolutions and international milieus, while the
other two are case studies. Echoing some of the innovative insights of
his influential volume, *From Enemy to Brother*,[6] John Connelly contends that if anti-Judaism was a pillar of a Christian belief system up
to World War II, then researchers need to treat seriously the factors
that supported that belief, and investigate the processes that allowed
for such a pillar to be removed without upsetting the entire edifice.
Connelly provides an account of the evolution of the Catholic Polish
Church's position toward the Jews in parallel with the development
of a new Catholic vision about Jews, founded on essential documents
such as the Vatican II document *Nostra aetate*. Despite several similarities between the ideas advocated by certain liberal Polish Catholic
circles and the Vatican's new thinking inspired by witnessing the Holocaust, Connelly stresses that the latter rather originated with German,
French, and American theologians. He nevertheless underscores that
statements made by Pope John Paul II (Karol Wojtyła) inspired a set
of "Notes on the correct way to present Jews and Judaism in preaching
and catechesis of the Roman Church," released in 1985. He concludes
that the continuing difficulties in Catholic attitudes toward the Jews
can be countered by an emphasis on dialogue and empathy rather than
through theological overconceptualization.

Leonidas Donskis offers a reassessment of some of the cultural
debates in the Baltic countries from the point of view of the challenges of the post-modern and post-totalitarian era. He contends that

---

[6] For more details, see John Connelly, *From Enemy to Brother: The Revolution
in Catholic Teaching on the Jews 1933–1965* (Cambridge: Harvard University
Press, 2012).

many of the problems in the region, and Eastern Europe in general, are rooted in the fact that the countries included in it squeezed two centuries of uninterrupted European history within two-and-a-half decades of "transition." He perceives this part of Europe as a laboratory of change and a vast area of the side effects and damage inflicted by modernity on the world. According to Donskis, the disparities of the hypermodernization of countries such as Lithuania led to a dangerous fragmentation of the society. Such a situation opens the possibility for the development and consolidation of nondemocratic values and projects, which are defended within the European community on the basis of claims of national sovereignty. These remarks are similar to a point made in the volume by Snyder and Tismaneanu, who state the EU accession of Eastern European countries might have actually worsened the possibilities of accountability in terms of illiberal tendencies both in politics and in collective narratives about the past. One of the solutions proposed by Donskis to this unexpected postaccession development is the reaffirmation of the *critical* role of intellectuals in Eastern Europe. The author concludes that the current memory wars in the Baltic countries, despite the legitimacy of their attacks again current Russian revisionism, have taken a dangerous turn because of the tendency for competitive martyrology that is manifest among many of the actors involved.

The last two contributions in *Remembrance, History, and Justice* are case-studies on how reckoning with the past in Romania and Bulgaria has been partially (if not entirely) highjacked by cultural and political wars. Bogdan C. Iacob adds to the volume's examination of the Romanian case in two respects. He offers a detailed analysis of the contents of the PCACDR's Final Report (from now on, referred to as the Report) while also engaging the existing international scholarship on the activity of the Commission and on the condemnation of the communist regime in Romania. He then examines some of the local critical reactions to the Report, as he assesses cultural and ideological attitudes toward the process of coming to terms with the communist past. Iacob remarks that, in the post-December 2006 period, communism (taken generically, as regime, ideology, or experience) has ceased having value as a subject in itself. The debates about communism have often served as a pretext to disparage persons, institutions, and opinions in the present. Not surprising, in significant areas of the public sphere, there is a scarcity of further problematizations of the communist historical experience along the directions signaled by the Commission's Report. Iacob concludes that working through the communist past in Romania is suffering from a case of arrested development. Nevertheless, he perceives the current situation as the expression of a difficult and protracted discursive process centered on the meaning of the past for Romania's present and future that is essential to bringing a long-awaited political consensus about the post-communist liberal democracy.

Nikolai Vukov echoes some of the general comments previously made. Vukov provides a comprehensive account of the tribulations of the process of dealing with the communist past in Bulgaria from the early 1990s until the present. The author argues that in the first decade of post-communism, commemorative acts concerning the victims testified to the entering of public memory in the political discourse and to its transformative potential after decades of silence. In the later years, however, they gradually started to illustrate the penetration of politics in public commemorations, and the increasing disengagement of Bulgarian society from memory's politicization. Vukov concludes that a noticeable contemporary avoidance of traumatic references to the communist past coupled with revisionist tendencies generated a new gap in the negotiation between still vivid individual and still precipitating collective memories. Similar to Iacob, he emphasizes the persistence of poverty in historical reckoning from the point of view of unmastered responsibilities (individual, moral, or legal). More than two decades removed since 1989, the public sphere in Bulgaria and Romania has yet to comprehensively engage in truth-telling and recognize the importance of a culture of contrition about the national experience of communism.

Returning to a more general evaluation of the topics approached in *Remembrance, History, and Justice*, one needs to point out that all of the authors start from the premise of the twentieth century as a time of fundamentally overlapping and interconnected violent, traumatic, and guilty pasts. Furthermore, most of the contributions adopt a vision of a continuous history of the last century that is suspicious toward the use of a past in order to reject, obstruct, or negate another. There are two contention points to this story: that of justice, and, subsequently, that of reconciliation. This volume extensively shows that we can only partially claim success in solving the puzzle of how to legally pursue the perpetrators of some of the most horrendous crimes of the twentieth century and particularly of the past fifty years. There have been various solutions such as: international and national trials, lustration, reparations, and negationism, but there are still only limited exemplary cases where those responsible for crimes against humanity or blatant violations of the basic human rights were convicted. Closure via didactic justice has not yet been reached. Inevitably, one wonders, especially in several of the case studies discussed, whether these countries can truly achieve reconciliation in the absence of didactic justice? Are truth-telling and critical historicization enough for accomplishing the necessary anamnestic solidarity vital for democratic, post-authoritarian consensus? Despite offering extensive, comparative, and interdisciplinary analyses of these questions, covering a geographical area from Europe to South Asia and from Russia to South Africa, *Remembrance, History and Justice* can hardly offer definitive answers. In the end, any discussion of the problems raised in processes of historical reckoning, legal accountability, and collective remembrance more often than not remains open-ended. To paraphrase Jan-Werner Müller in this volume, any final pronouncements on these developments' failure or success depends both on the criteria of comparison and on the existing horizons of expectations.

Maybe the most significant insight of the volume is that we should approach with lucidity and restraint teleological readings of the transition from dictatorship to democracy, and the triumphalist claims that the past can be made okay. Trauma must be worked through, authoritarian legacies should be confronted, and guilt and responsibility ought to be processed in frameworks of accountability. But liberal democracy remains a contested and fragile construct that is stabilized and perpetuated only through persistent and pervasive cultures of remembrance and contrition, which counterbalance possible relapses into problematic pasts or contemporary forms of left/right wing extremisms. Many of the cases analyzed in the book are countries that in spite of inherent problems and crises did manage to pass important thresholds in coming to terms with their own histories and in synchronizing with larger democratization trends.[7] Nevertheless, in most of them, there remain

---

[7] See for example, Tomas Kavaliauskas, *Transformations in Central Europe Between 1989 and 2012: Geopolitical, Cultural, and Socioeconomic Shifts* (Lanham, MD: Lexington, 2012).

landscapes still haunted by collective neuroses and populist, atavistic anxieties. In the context of the economic crisis and with the duress of shifting geopolitics, in Europe and across the globe, we witness the second life of fantasies of salvation,[8] of exclusionary, vindictive, and potentially disastrous myths of political redemption. In-depth knowledge about the wreckage of the twentieth century, of its dreams of total power, exterminism, and discrimination and about the mechanisms that allow the working through of such legacy are essential correctives to the radical appetites of contemporary times.

The editors wish to dwell a bit in the history of this volume. The book includes the proceedings of the conference "Remembrance, History, and Justice. Coming to Terms with Traumatic Pasts in Democratic Societies" (November 11–12, 2010). The event was part of a multiyear project (started in 2007) coordinated by the Center for the Study of Post-Communist Societies at the University of Maryland (College Park) in collaboration with the Romanian Cultural Institute. The endeavor aimed to provide, by means of reflecting on watershed moments of post-1945 history, an overview of the global dynamics characteristic of the twentieth century and its lessons and impact upon the twenty-first century. A second aim of the series of conferences was to offer a forum for young Romanian scholars to present their scholarship and to join international debates with important names in the field. These exchanges would encourage the synchronization of local research with larger academic evolutions abroad. This is why each of the volumes published by CEU Press comprises a cohort of texts about Romania or by Romanian authors.

The conveners of the conference were H.R. Patapievici, who until summer 2012 was president of the Romanian Cultural Institute (RCI), Vladimir Tismaneanu, professor of politics at University of Maryland, and Christian Ostermann, director of the Cold War International History Program at the Woodrow Wilson International Center for Scholars. The editors would like to express their gratitude to H.R. Patapievici and Mircea Mihăieş, who until 2012 was the RCI's vice president. They enthusiastically embraced the idea of a series of conferences on seminal political-intellectual issues in Washington DC,

---

[8] Vladimir Tismaneanu, *Fantasies of Salvation. Democracy, Nationalism, and Myth in Post-Communist Europe* (Princeton: Princeton University Press, 1998).

with the purpose of strengthening and developing the already existent connections between the Romanian scholarly community and American academia.

However, Romanian politics caught up with this initiative. In the summer of 2012, Mr. Patapievici and Mr. Mihăieş resigned in protest over drastic budget cuts and strong ideological pressures on the RCI's programs. The new leadership radically changed the institute's strategy and espoused a parochial approach to Romanian culture and international dialogue.[9] Inevitably, this extraordinary project of transatlantic scholarly cooperation that began more than five years ago came to an end. Despite its abrupt termination, it did meritoriously generate five elite conferences[10] that brought together some of the most important scholars in the field of twentieth-century history and comparative politics. The events were the foundation upon which the current book series published by CEU Press was created.[11] The tumultuous events that affected the project had an impact on the progress made in putting together the present volume, delaying its publication. Nevertheless, the research timeline in some contributions extends up to 2014. In order

---

[9] For more details on these events, see Vladimir Tismaneanu, "Democracy on the Brink. A Coup Attempt Fails in Romania," *World Affairs*, January/February 2013, 83–87.

[10] The fifth conference was "Ideological Storms: Intellectuals and the Totalitarian Temptation" (November 14–15, 2011, Washington DC). In the summer of 2012, just before Mr. Patapievici and his team were forced to resign, the preparations for the last conference in the series were almost finalized. It was planned for mid-November. Its title was "Dreams of Total Power: Dictators and Dictatorships in the Twentieth Century." As the entire project collapsed, the event was cancelled. On March 14, 2013, the conference did take place, in a limited format, at Boston College. This was possible because of the enthusiastic and generous support of the Clough Center for the Study of Constitutional Democracy and its director, professor Vlad Perju. For more details on this event see http://www.bc.edu/content/bc/centers/cloughcenter/events/f2012-s2013/0318-dictators.html.

[11] The previous volumes in the series are: Vladimir Tismaneanu. (ed.), *Stalinism Revisited: The Establishment of Communist Regimes in East Central Europe* (New York/Budapest: CEU Press, 2009); Vladimir Tismaneanu, (ed.), *Promises of 1968: Crisis, Illusion and Utopia* (New York/Budapest: CEU Press, 2011); and Vladimir Tismaneanu and Bogdan C. Iacob, *The End and the Beginning: The Revolutions of 1989 and the Resurgence of History* (New York/Budapest: CEU Press, 2012).

to maintain the original coherence and thematic focus of *Remembrance, History, and Justice*, the editors were weary of the trap of permanent revisions based on current events that took place during the publication process.

A few additional acknowledgments need to be made. We are grateful to Annette Wieviorka and István Rév, whose contributions greatly enriched the discussions and debates during the conference proceedings. The editors would also like to thank Christian Ostermann (director of the History and Public Policy Program at the Woodrow Wilson International Center for Scholars) and Jennifer Long (former program coordinator of the Center for Eurasian, Russian and Eastern European Studies at Georgetown University) for their significant and enthusiastic support in the organization of the five conferences in the project. Last, but not least, Gail Kligman, Marc Howard, Karol Sołtan, and Bartłomiej Kamiński were superb discussants for the events' panels. The editors would also like to thank Adam Volo Tismaneanu for his contribution during the preliminary editing of the manuscript of this volume. Vladimir Tismaneanu expresses his gratitude to the Department of Government and Politics at the University of Maryland for its continuous support and encouragement regarding this project. Bogdan C. Iacob expresses his gratitude to Imre Kertész Kolleg in Jena and the Center of Advanced Studies in Sofia, ideal academic environments where he could continue his work for the present volume. The editors are thankful to CEU Press for showing unwavering interest in the completion of the present volume and in the continuation of the series.

Part One

POLITICS OF MEMORY AND CONSTRUCTING DEMOCRACY

TIMOTHY SNYDER

European Mass Killing
and European Commemoration

The history of mass killing and the commemoration of that history are two separate subjects.[1] I would like to divide this chapter between these two topics, emphasizing that they are different, and, at the very end, I will make some modest suggestions about how they ought to be brought together. So, this is an essay about the last twenty years of my own work, which involved an attempt to bring together German and Soviet policies of mass killing in Eastern Europe in the volume *Bloodlands*. At the same time, the past two decades was a rich period of commemoration of Soviet and German crimes in a region where I was working. This is something we have all experienced, as we try to work on the history of the twentieth century, while simultaneously around us that history is being commemorated.

I am going to begin with reflections about the killing itself, and then move to a kind of analysis of why commemoration, or to put it in a way which is almost oxymoronic, satisfactory commemoration, has been so terribly difficult in the region we are concerned with in this volume. I want to be clear about something right away: in the first part of the chapter I will be discussing the history of deliberate mass killing, that is to say policies by which leaders deliberately killed large numbers of people. This is distinct from the history of the camps, although

---

[1] The text is based upon of the author's keynote lecture at the conference, "Remembrance, History, and Justice. Coming to Terms with Traumatic Pasts in Democratic Societies" (November 11–12, 2010, Washington DC). This version is revised by the author.

it is related. It is distinct from demographic analysis of losses, which is a rather vague term used a lot, which includes children who might have been born had something terrible not happened. There are other matrixes that one could use; I just want to be clear that what I will be talking about is mass killing.

What I noticed in the years while I was working on the subject is something rather striking, that throughout all the space and time when the Nazi and the Soviet systems functioned, the huge majority of the deliberate killing happened during a specific time and place. That period is between 1933 and 1945, when both Hitler and Stalin were in power, and the place is what I call in the book the bloodlands, namely Ukraine, Belarus, Western Russia, most of Poland, and the Baltics. The regimes taken together deliberately killed about 17 million people. Of these 17 million, 14 million were in the bloodlands, in this time and place; the density of this horror inspired me to choose this as the premise for the book.

I would like to emphasize that in my mind, and I realize there is some disagreement about this, the numbers are extremely important. If we agree, as I guess we all do, that the difference between zero deaths and one death is very significant, and we do not have to think very long to agree about that, then we also have to agree that the difference between 700,000 and 700,001 deaths is equally significant. I am not going to claim that we will ever know these numbers with that kind of precision. What I would say, though, is that numbers are important, because every big number is a multiple of one, and although we can never reach perfection, I think we ought to be as careful with these big numbers, as we would be with small numbers, and to care about them for the same reasons that we care about the small numbers, only more so.

So, when you look at history in this way, when you take this time and place as your platform, as your premise, what do you find? You find the following six or seven major events that comprise the total of 14 million deliberate killings. The first is the deliberate famine in Soviet Ukraine in 1933, and then the Great Terror of 1937 and 1938. In general, what you see when you look at this period is that Soviet killing dominated in the 1930s. Then, there is a period between 1939 and 1941 when the Soviets and the Germans were allies, and they were killing in much the same way and at much the same rate. And then, there's a period from 1941 to 1945, when almost all of the deliberate killing is done by the Germans. So this period begins with a Soviet action—a distinct Soviet action—that has something to do with Germany in the sense that Adolf Hitler refers to it in his electoral campaign in the spring of 1933. Nevertheless, the famine in Soviet Ukraine was a result of the Soviet policy of collectivization that we now know was deliberately manipulated in the summer and especially the fall of 1932 so that 3 million people in Ukraine would die. The record of Stalin's correspondence over this period and the record of Politburo meetings during this period are clear enough for us to know that Stalin knew what would happen and pursued policies such as blockading settlements, taking meat, and closing the borders of the Soviet Ukrainian Republic knowing it would lead to massive deaths. In fact, the way that he and Kaganovich discussed it makes it clear that they knew what was coming. And one of the reasons why they knew it, by the way, was because of what had just happened in Kazakhstan, where a famine had killed an even larger number of the population in 1930 and 1931. Often the way this argument is presented is as follows: if Kazakhstan happened, then there must not have been something particular about Ukraine. I see this in exactly the opposite way: precisely because Kazakhstan happened, in 1930 and 1931, the Soviet leadership knew what a combination of policies would bring about in 1932 and 1933 and pursued them deliberately. And, to be absolutely clear about this, the food which was exported would have saved almost all of the Ukrainians plus others who died in 1932 and 1933. Access to grain stock piles would have saved almost all of them. Simply not fulfilling requisition targets would have saved almost all of them. So, this was a deliberate policy and it also—to be clear—had a political backdrop and rationale. The political rationale involved imagined plots by Ukrainian nationalists, who had supposedly taken control of the Ukrainian branch of the Soviet Communist Party in league with Polish spies and others. So there was a political rationale, there is clear documentation of knowledge, and there is advanced knowledge of what would happen if these policies were pursued.

The second stage of the killing in the bloodlands is that of the Great Terror in the Soviet Union, where, as we now know, 682,691 people were recorded as having been executed. We now know a great deal about the terror that we did not know twenty years ago. What has not happened is that this particular knowledge has not worked its way into the general discussion that we have about the Soviet Union. The numbers are smaller than people had generally thought, the figure I just gave—roughly 700,000—added to the other recorded killings in the 1930s and 1940s, can get you up to a figure of about 1 million deliberate executions, but not much higher than that.

The other thing that we now know about this period in Stalinism is that parts of the great terror that were visible, the show trials and, to some extent, the executions of officers, which intelligence agents at the time had an idea about, are only the tip of the iceberg and not representative of the totality of the event. Party members and military officers were indeed affected in the tens of thousands, but other groups, identified as kulaks or as national minorities, were affected in the hundreds of thousands. In particular, the clarity with which the Great Terror targeted particular ethnic minorities has only been reached in the last twenty years. The Estonian, Finish, Latvian, Polish, German, Korean, and also Caucasian and Central Asian actions deliberately signaled out national minorities. About 250,000 people were killed predominantly because of who they were rather than anything they did. The methods for finding people were often as simple as looking through local records for a certain kind of last name. The largest of these was the Polish action in which 110,000 people were shot—essentially for being Poles—the charge being that they were Polish spies. I worked on this from the other end, and I do not believe a single person who was executed was actually a Polish spy. That is, I have a sense of who the Polish spies in the Soviet Union were at the time, it would be senseless to deny that another sovereign power did not have spies in the Soviet Union. But the Soviets managed to kill 110,000 people without executing a single one of them. That is what happens when ethnic criteria motivate mass killing.

The next stage in the killing in the bloodlands was when the Soviets and the Germans were allies, between 1939 and 1941. From the broad point of view of European history, this period is important, because it is when both the Soviets and the Germans were expanding territorially: the Soviets more modestly trying to invade Finland, incorporating Eastern Poland and Northeastern Romania. The Germans were much more ambitious, invading western Poland, the Low Countries and France, beginning the Battle of Britain, fueled by the way, with oil from the Soviet Union. In terms of our subject of deliberate killing, this is a period when 200,000 people were killed, roughly in equal numbers by the Soviets and the Nazis. During this period the two were targeting the same kinds of groups, coming from different sorts of analysis: one racial and the other class. Both the Soviets and the Germans came to the same conclusion that the way to destroy, in the German case, or dominate, in the Soviet case, Poland, was to remove the group which both of them called the intelligentsia. *Intelligenz* in German, *intelligentsia* in Russian—there are long debates about where that word came from—but what I find interesting is a kind of convergence between those who destroyed and those who were destroyed. It was this group, this intelligentsia, the educated classes that were the most important. The profiling was so similar that in the number of cases that we now know about, one brother was killed by the Germans and one brother was killed by the Soviets, or one sister was killed by the Germans and another sister was killed by the Soviets, precisely because Moscow and Berlin were using the same kind of metric.

The next stage is the most dramatic, between 1941 and 1945, when the Germans betrayed their Soviet allies and invaded the Soviet Union. In order to understand what comes next, one has to have a sense of the scale of destruction which was envisioned by the Germans for the invasion of the Soviet Union, which was, in fact, far greater than anything the Germans managed to achieve, unthinkably horrible as that was. These plans imagined not only the elimination of all of the Jews who fell under German rule, which was a goal from the beginning, but also the starvation of some 30 million inhabitants of the Soviet Union after a victorious war. By the way, that would have meant the death of about three quarters of the Jews in the Soviet Union, who lived in the cities, which were targeted to be starved and then razed to the ground. The general notion of this plan, which was called the Hunger Plan, was that Soviet modernization, that is, all of the building of cities, the urbanization, all the development that took place in the 1920s and 1930s, especially under the first Five Year Plan, had to be reversed. The people who came into Soviet cities were to be killed by hunger, the cities themselves were to be removed, progress was to be undone, and this was to become a kind of German agrarian paradise. That was the foundational idea. The other plan, which is worth recalling, was something called *Generalplan Ost*, which was a postwar colonization scheme that envisaged a very large number of people, how many depends on what premise you start with, but somewhere between 30 and 50 million, to be forcibly deported across the Urals, enslaved, assimilated, or killed. So this was the vision of the Germans, and these were their plans, in the spring of 1941. They aimed at a transformation that is almost unthinkably murderous and unthinkably radical. These ideas to demodernize the Soviet Union and the racial and imperial assumptions with which the Germans entered the Soviet Union are necessary to understand some of the policies that followed. The most dramatic of these were the starvation of Soviet prisoners of war. About 2.6 million Soviet prisoners of war were starved to death in the camps, victims who are largely forgotten. Another half million Soviet prisoners of war, predominantly though not entirely Jews, were also shot at this time. The starvation siege of Leningrad was not just a military contingency; it was consistent with Hitler's desire for that city to be destroyed. Smaller starvation policies were pursued with Kiev and Kharkiv, as such cities were not meant to exist by the end of the war.

When the Germans invaded the Soviet Union, they also intended to eliminate its Jews, but they were not quite sure just how this could be achieved. They had considered a number of deportation plans for the Jews of Europe, none of which had proven practical: to Madagascar, to a reservation in Poland, to the Soviet Union (which of course declined). Now the idea, such as it was, was to forcibly deport Jews to Siberia. But what emerged instead was mass killing. The most important policy, within the years 1941–1945, although it is important to note that this is hard to put under one heading, is the policy that we describe as the Holocaust. It begins with shooting campaigns of Jewish men of military age in the East, after the invasion of the Soviet Union, which quickly became the destruction of women and children, then the elimination of whole communities. By the end of 1941, some 1 million Jews are already dead in the Soviet Union, most of them by gunfire; some of them by gas vans using a technology which had earlier been used on the handicapped. The Holocaust then shifts both in technology and geography, even as the shooting continues in the East and claims a total of about 2.6 million lives. Death facilities using carbon monoxide are built in occupied Poland: Bełżec, Sobibór, Treblinka, Chełmno (a slightly different initiative), and Majdanek. The final stage of the killing that is very familiar to us is Auschwitz; Auschwitz is a bit atypical and is very important because one in six Jews who were murdered died there. It is atypical in the sense that many Soviet Jews, who were the second largest group of Jews killed in the Holocaust, did not die in Auschwitz; they died in the killing fields. Polish Jews, who were the largest group of Jewish victims, died in significant numbers in Auschwitz, around 200,000, but they were mainly murdered at other killing facilities. Auschwitz is special because Auschwitz was the gathering point for Jews in Southern and Western Europe, and Hungarian Jews, in 1942 through 1944, especially in those last two years. That is a main reason why it is remembered. The other reason is that it was simultaneously a death facility and a concentration camp. The concentration camp had many survivors, the death facility did not, but the concentration camp survivors were able to recall and tell others about Auschwitz. It is much harder to recall Treblinka, Sobibór, Belzec, and Chelmno because the total number of survivors from those places is somewhere under a hundred.

The final policy that needs recalling, which is actually related to the Holocaust, is the German policy of "reprisals." In occupied Belarus, well over 300,000 non-Jews were killed in what we categorize as "reprisals" for partisan actions. By the late stages all the women and children were shot, and then the men were taken as forced laborers in the Reich. The way that the Germans carried out reprisals involved herding people into barns, burning them, and performing mass shooting over pits. This policy was the same in terms of what was going on with the Jews. In fact, the same police units and security divisions would kill Jews one day and partisans the next day. In many cases, in their own records, they did not even bother to distinguish between them, which means that the records of these two events blurs together.

So, when you take all these events together, from 1933 to 1945, you reach a total of about 14 million people who were deliberately killed. People were deliberately killed in other policies, but these major policies embrace almost all of the numbers. The people in question were Jews, Ukrainians, Belarusians, Poles, Russians, and others. If you add people who were killed in the bloodlands but did not come from the region, the largest group would be the Hungarian Jews. There was a distinct, but related event, in a neighboring territory, which was the murder of Romanian Jews that claimed another 300,000 lives. If you add the horrible suffering of the Gulag and the concentration camps, you add a few more million lives, but you do not change the basic geography of where and how the killing took place. Most of the civilians who died were not killed in camps; most of them never saw a camp.

I hope I have succeeded in showing you not only the depth of the destruction and the horror, but also, and now I am changing subjects, some of the reasons why this catastrophe might now be difficult to commemorate. The most obvious point is the simplest one and I am going to try hard to make it clear: we do not control time; people who commemorate do not control time. Commemoration is an attempt to fix an event at a certain point and describe it in such a way that it will be remembered in a certain way for the future. However, there is never any possibility of a fresh start. You're always commemorating it some distance in time from the events. The current post-communist commemoration of the events that I am talking about, which took place between 1933 and 1945, begins in 1989, after forty-five years of already existent traditions of commemoration. This in itself is a normal situation of any act of commemoration, as the latter develops upon earlier strata of memory practices. When I speak of these traditions of commemoration, I am not trying to say that they are historically false. In each case, in different balances, they weld together historical truth with commemorative success.

One of these commemorative traditions is what you might think of as the "liberation from the West": the Americans landed in Normandy and ended evil in the world; I am simplifying it a bit, but not too much. This is a view which is very powerful in the United States. In more sophisticated versions it also has a great deal of power in the UK. We see it repeated not only in film, but also in commemorations of Victory in Europe Day (V-E Day). There are a lot of problems with this, obviously. One of them is its particular connection, in the last 15 years or so, with the Holocaust. The idea that we landed in Normandy and somehow that had something to do with ending the Holocaust is, I think, something which many if not most Americans have come to believe. There are two fallacies in this narrative: the first is that we had no Jewish motive at the time; we took little action to save Jews during World War II, aside from a warning in late 1942 and Roosevelt's War Refugees Board in 1944; we did not liberate any of the places where Jews died in large numbers. The second is that, at a different level, the Allies, in order to defeat the Germans, relied on the Soviet Union, which at the moment when we sealed the alliance had killed more people than the Germans had. Now, the Germans changed that over the course of the war, becoming the most murderous regime in the history of the world, even as we fought against them. All this is important, because it keeps the American contribution in perspective, but also reminds us of the moral compromise which was at the heart of the victory.

Another narrative, equally powerful in a different part of the world, can be called "liberation from the East." This account goes as follows: the Soviet Union modernized itself and strengthened itself in the 1930s. It succeeded in liberating most of Europe, on the basis of heroic efforts. Again, this has a certain core of truth, but there are some problems with it. The modernization of the 1930s involved starving millions of people to death. The terror involved shooting hundreds of thousands of people. In neither case is it at all clear that this prepared the Soviet Union in a material way to win the war. The idea that it all somehow makes sense because the Soviets won the war is appealing, but I do not think it is actually very convincing. The scenario also overlooks that the Soviet Union was one of the initiators of World War II in Europe. The war in Europe might perhaps have begun in some other way, but the way that it did in fact begin was with an alliance between the Soviet Union and Nazi Germany. This narrative tends to overlook the Soviet crimes that led to deaths, which were then counted in the total number of losses that the Soviet Union suffered. In post-Soviet times, a new problem with this narrative is that in today's Russia the distinction is not often made between the Soviet Union and Russia. So most of the losses, but also most of the fighting done by soldiers, was not done by Russians, it was done by Soviet citizens. Russia suffered horribly—the territory of today's Russia—in the war, incomparably greater than any Western territory, but far less than Belarus or Ukraine, or for that matter, Poland. The greatest victim group on Soviet territories was the Jews. And so the conflation between Russia and the Soviet Union allows for both martyrdom and the triumph to be reapportioned in a way which is, in fact, inaccurate.

The final narrative or tradition of commemoration is that of the Holocaust. Now, the history of the Holocaust by 1989, and I would say even more since 1989, has established certain important facts and I by no means wish to diminish them. It established the numbers and Raul Hilberg was very close to being correct about the total numbers more than forty years ago. It established very precisely the victim group and how the Jews were different from other victim groups. It showed that the Germans meant to eliminate all the Jews and by the end of the war were tempted to kill every Jew who was under their control, anywhere they lived, and that makes the Jewish case different. It established, to a great degree of accuracy, the methods by which Jews were killed. All this historic narrative has improved with time and the last twenty years of scholarship on the Holocaust has been remarkable.

However, there are certain problems with the way that we have studied the Holocaust in the West, which has made commemoration in the East a bit harder. The first is that in general, and by that I mean about 99 percent of the time, we approach Holocaust history with the sources that were left by the perpetrators. This is appropriate if you are trying to establish their motives, and the debate about the German motives and the timing of their decisions has been one of the most impressive debates in the history of historiography itself. However, that optic leaves out the terrains where the Holocaust took place, which the Germans themselves understood very imperfectly. It also leaves out the majority of the victims, 97 percent of whom could not have left a trace in German because they did not know the language.

The second problem with the Holocaust tradition, as we know it, is the over-identification with the West. The victims whom we do know well, for example, Anne Frank or Victor Klemperer, are atypical victims. They belong to relatively small groups of Jews, whose chances for surviving in the German case, although it might seem ironic, were far greater than the chances for survival of Jews elsewhere. There is also the epistemic irony that the less deadly the Holocaust was, the more likely we were to learn something about it, because there could be survivors who could leave us with memoirs, recollections, or novels. The more deadly the Holocaust was, the harder it is for us to find things about it. This is consistent, all of it, with the image that had been consolidated by 1989, of Auschwitz as the center of the Holocaust, which again, is an important part of the truth. But there are at least two other things which you have to add, namely the carbon monoxide killing facilities in Poland and also the killing fields from the Eastern-occupied Soviet Union to get a more complete picture. Those things are generally left in the shadow of Auschwitz, although in each case there were more victims from more typical groups of victims.

What this means is that by 1989 the countries where Jews actually lived in large numbers, which are the countries where the Holocaust took place, were far less present in the commemoration of the Holocaust than they were in its history. Why is that? Is it because all of the places where the Holocaust actually took place fell behind the Iron Curtain? They became something which was called Eastern Europe. They were studied within a Cold War framework or within a national framework, but for most people in the West they simply lost a great deal of the palpable reality they had before World War II. And so they came to be defined, in so far as they were thought of at all, in terms of these horrible terrains, these cities, these killing fields, these death facilities where the Holocaust took place. I do not want to overstress this point, but it seems to me that the fact that these countries came to exist chiefly in that capacity in the Western imagination makes it difficult for various kinds of commemoration later on.

Another source of difficulty lies in the contradictions of democratization and commemoration, which I would like to stress, are more complicated here than they might have been elsewhere. For example, in the case that I am referring to, one has this overlap of two different things that became the object of commemoration. In all of these countries you have an overlap of historical experience with both Nazi and Soviet power. So try to imagine how complicated this is, just structurally. You have one system that is in power for forty-five years. It ends, and then, in some sense, you want to commemorate the suffering at the hands of that system—communism. But before that system, there was a bloody occupation during World War II, and you would also like to commemorate that, perhaps differently, perhaps for different constituents. Making matters worse, that first period of suffering, under German occupation, has already been commemorated by the second system, the communist system, and any way you choose to commemorate it, you are in some sense working with or against the way it has already been commemorated. Then on top of it all, if I have not already lost you, you cannot actually distinguish in some of these places between one period of Nazi and one period of Soviet domination, because during the war itself, you very often had both experiences.

Sorting all this out would be incredibly difficult, in the best of circumstances. I would note that the positions that East European countries find themselves in are very hard to sort out within the frameworks which we offered them, after 1989, the frameworks of commemoration: liberation for the West, liberation for the East, and liberation from the Holocaust. Each of these has a certain amount of purchase, and the Holocaust, I believe, has the most, but none of them can actually capture this complicated position that East Europeans, including East European Jews still in these countries, found themselves in. On this basis, let me try to run through briefly some of the problems that particular countries have found themselves in and the commemoration situation generally in some specific cases.

These are the special cases: Ukraine, Belarus, and Poland—the countries that are at the center of what I am calling the bloodlands. I am going to leave out Russia because David Brandenberger's chapter covers this case, and the Baltics, because Leonidas Donskis discusses the topic extensively. In any event, these three countries are the core of what I am calling the bloodlands and most of the killing took place in these countries, so what has happened?

Ukraine, if you look at the history, is the country that between 1933 and 1945 suffered the most losses of deliberate killing, at least 7 million people through famine, Soviet terror, Soviet citizens dying in German prisoner war camps, and the Holocaust. There is nothing comparable to that in any European country, and not surprisingly, it has been very hard to find some kind of stable commemorative tradition. There are two very powerful and rival stories of the war. One of them is a version of liberation from the East, where the Red Army drives out the Germans. That is, understandably, the dominant story for most Ukrainians. There is an alternative story, which involves resistance to Soviet power by the Organization for Ukrainian Nationalists, because the latter did, in fact, resist with great persistence the Red Army. Tensions do exist, however. For example, in the summer of 1941, the same people who were involved in this resistance in many cases were then involved with the German police and took part in the execution of Jews. So then, there were those problems, which, of course, the other Ukrainian tradition of commemoration is very happy to note. That nationalist tradition of course records that the Red Army brought back a system that had killed millions of Ukrainians.

The consequence of all this is that you have had radical oscillations in memory policy in Ukraine. There is nothing that could really compare to this that has not involved a revolution. So, for example, the *dead* Joseph Stalin was convicted of genocide along with a handful of other people, in early 2010, in the Ukrainian court of appeals. A few days after that happened, the very crime for which he was convicted, which was genocide in regard to the case of the famine, was removed from the presidential website entirely, because the president who supported this decision lost elections and another who did not agree to it won them. Within another few weeks, you have a a new statue of Stalin being erected in an Ukrainian city, and then, a few weeks later, a communist is put in charge of the Ukrainian Institute of National Remembrance. Up until now, including the Yuschenko regime, there has been a kind of pluralism in Ukraine, which meant that various kinds of positions could at least be articulated. That pluralism has recently come under serious threat, which is unfortunate.

The second very important case and perhaps the most complicated one is Belarus. I said that Ukraine was a territory that suffered the most in the 1930s and 1940s. The territory of Europe that suffered the most during the war itself was Belarus. It suffered directly from the Holocaust, suffered disproportionately from the mass murder of Soviet prisoners in German camps, and it also disproportionately experienced the policy of "reprisals." Although Serbs and Poles also suffered, Belarusians were hit hardest of all because of this policy of the Germans. Belarusians, for the most part, believed that they are alone with this history of suffering, and they are right. How many of us have even heard of Stalag 352, Maly Trostenets, Operation Hermann, or even the Battle of Bagration, which was arguably the decisive battle in the war? The first three are events which claimed huge numbers of innocent civilian lives and which simply have not found their way even into the historical discussions of the war. Yet, these are things which Belarusians remember and commemorate.

What dominates in Belarus is a version of liberation from the East due to Alexander Lukashenko, who himself was raised in the 1970s, which was the time when the Soviet version of liberation from the Germans became so popular and widespread that it turned into something which was taken for granted. What is interesting in Belarus today is the extent to which Lukashenko is trying to pass on that very narrative to the next generation, and he might as well be successful. Perhaps the most palpable and ridiculous instance of this situation is that of his illegitimate son, Kolya, who is ten years old and whom Lukashenko has mentioned as his preferred successor. Kolya, on the relevant days of commemoration, wears a tiny military uniform. It is absurd enough that Lukashenko pretends to have—he was born in 1954—liberated the Soviet Union, but the implication that his ten-year-old son liberated the Soviet Union is taking the whole thing to another level. In this narrative of liberation from the East, there is very little room for the Holocaust. Belarus is one of the very few countries where you can even compare non-Jewish to Jewish losses during World War II, in absolute numbers, not in proportions. Nevertheless, the Holocaust is a crucial event in Belarus. The way that this works is that Jewish citizens are counted as Belarusian citizens, just as they used to be counted as Soviet citizens. Therefore the Holocaust is molded into a larger story of the suffering of Belarusian civilians, which has enough appeal that most people would simply accept it. This is done explicitly. Lukashenko has a court historian who postulates his verdicts on these issuses. One of his verdicts is that it is unjust to take into account ethnicity when counting victims of the war. Of course, once you say that, what you are saying, in fact, is that it is unjust to actually distinguish the Holocaust from other traumatic events.

The other important thing about the way this narrative functions is that it is anti-Western. It is much more anti-Polish than it is anti-German, because it is more convenient to be anti-Polish than to be anti-German. What it does is that it presents Belarus as being in a sort of vanguard of protecting civilization. This is a kind of Western narrative *à rebours*: the barbarians were in the West and we in Belarus are the ones who were protecting Russia from the aggression of the West. This particular story makes it very hard to imagine that the Byelorussian foreign policy could change any time soon. However, I would point out that there are weaknesses of this commemorative policy and that a better discussion of history might exploit them. I will try to get to that in the conclusion.

The third case is Poland. Between the 1930s and 1940s, Poland suffered in numerous ways, some of which were forgotten. Even Poles sometimes do not remember the Polish action of 1937–1938. There is no commemoration of this in Poland, even though four times as many people were killed as in the Katyn massacres. From 1939 to 1941, there was social decapitation, which I mentioned earlier. Then there was the Holocaust, which touched above all Jews who were Polish citizens. There were reprisals; at least 120,000 Polish civilians were killed during the Warsaw uprising, there were concentration camps, and forced labor, and so on. What has Polish memory policy been like? I cannot really summarize. There have been a couple of unusual bright moments. One was the Polish-Ukrainian discussions about ethnic cleansing in the 1990s, where a historian from each side had to give a paper under the same title. This meant that each of them used the sources that he knew the other was going to use. The consequences were that the papers ended up being much more reasonable and (more) scholarly than one might have expected. You had nine volumes of publications, which was, in fact, quite an accomplishment.[2]

The other high point of Polish commemoration was the debate after the publication of Jan Gross's book, *Neighbors*, about Jedwabne, which led to the densest discussion of the Holocaust which has ever taken place in any country. It is often compared to the *Historikerstreit,* but the degree of social participation and influence seems to have been much greater. It led to a huge jump upward in general Polish knowledge about the Holocaust, including subjects that have little to do with the actual events at Jedwabne—for example, Poles being able to say where Treblinka was and what Treblinka meant.

The problem (there were many others, but I am going to focus on one for our purposes) with both of these discussions—about Ukrainian-Polish ethnic cleansing and about Jedwabne—is what I would call *agency inflation*. In both of these cases, Ukrainians and Poles (in the first case) tended to talk about World War II as though it were chiefly about Ukrainians and Poles, and as though Ukrainians and Poles had more to do with what actually happened than in fact they did—which is perhaps inevitable within a framework of the national history. In national history you tend to shift from being an agent to being a victim, but when you are a victim, you want to be an agent as much as you can. The same holds for the Jedwabne debate. It was incredibly important when Jan Gross pointed out that Poles had killed Jews and this led to other important research. But, as German historians have pointed out since, this was part of a larger policy of self-cleansing which the Germans were carrying out, using locals. While Polish participation is incredibly

---

[2] Published by Karta as *Polska-Ukraina: trudne pytania.*

important morally, the debate lost some of the larger framework, which is important if one is to understand the true horror of it all.

Poland is also exemplary of a particular problem which has spread throughout Eastern Europe and that is the problem of the memory ministries. These are extremely well-funded government institutions that were charged with functions which perhaps do not all go together nicely: control of critical archives, prosecuting criminals, lustration, and also public education. Arguably, it might be a good idea to separate some of these functions, because when they are together in one institution, as they are in the Polish model, and then in the Ukrainian model (which is a kind of cousin to the Polish one), one creates endless possibilities for abuse. This even applies in scholarly terms and I will give an example of this: After Jan Gross published his book *Neighbors*, there was a two-volume publication by the Polish Institute of National Remembrance (IPN), which was the best treatment of the subject.[3] It was excellent in terms of documentation and analysis. It brought to light and confirmed a number of cases similar to Jedwabne. That, in my view, was the high point. However, a few years later, as IPN leadership changed as a result of a new government coming into power, Jan Gross wrote another book called *Fear*. The reaction of IPN was preemptive. A Polish book came out ahead of the publication of Gross's book, with a preface which misled readers about what the subject of Gross's book was going to be about, let alone what actually happened during the 1938 pogrom at Kielce.

There have also been other strange features. For example, I fondly remember when a friend and colleague from Poland wrote to me and said, "I am looking forward to sharing a prison cell with you and with other friends because a law has just been passed about defaming the Polish nation." It turned out that if you claimed that any representative of the Polish nation had been involved in either National Socialism or communism, you committed a crime. A prosecutor actually planned to make a case against Jan Gross. Fortunately, that never came to anything.

Something which is particular about Poland and distinguishes this country from Ukraine and Belarus, is what one might think of as—for lack of a better word—normality. This is a country of economic success, which has joined the European Union (EU). But what normality has

---

[3] Under the title, *Wokół Jedwabnego*.

brought with it were a couple of strange consequences. One of them is a new generation. We now have a young generation of Poles who, in many cases, are not that concerned with the past in so far as the past is a way to get rid of those annoying people above them, who might have some dealings with the communist regime, which, of course, everybody over age 45 did, in some way or another, because it was a communist system. But young people, who often thirty years ago would have been the very people who would have joined the Party for opportunistic reasons, are now very much in favor of lustration for the same opportunistic reasons that would help them clear out the people who were above them. So, that is something which comes with normality.

Another paradoxical situation couched as normalcy is that joining the EU leads to greater irresponsibility in commemoration policy. Here is why: when a country is trying to join the EU, it is necessary for it "to be good"; it is necessary not to have scandals about, for example, the Holocaust, at least not to react to the scandals in a way which is going to make your candidacy look worse. I am simplifying somewhat, but this is the general drift of things. However, once you are actually within the EU, you can do whatever other members do and treat history entirely as your own internal affair. Therefore, your scandals can become national or local, and it does not matter, you are not going to be expelled from the EU for your history discussions any more than Portugal or Greece are going to be expelled. So, ironically, the level of Polish discussion of difficult historical events has decreased since 2004 when Poland joined the EU.

To sum it up: what then are the limits of commemoration, of the event of mass killing, which I tried to describe? Obviously, if I am correct to say that it is fair and reasonable to describe European mass killing as this one long event with certain important episodes such as the Holocaust, then we have to observe that nothing like this has been commemorated. There is not even vaguely this kind of transnational commemoration, or even commemoration of events, as opposed to selected groups of victims. Why is that? There is the problem of the outside narratives that existed—liberation from the West, liberation from the East. The Holocaust offered some but limited help to countries who were trying to pursue national commemoration policies. There is also another problem which is a little bit more subtle since it is an absence: there has not been, after 1989, a second wave of Ger-

man commemoration of another group of German victims. The Holocaust commemoration narrative in Germany has become, if anything,
crisper in the last twenty years. However, the turn that has been made
in Germany was more toward "We have our groups of German victims
now. And we would like to have it discussed in some way." This point
has been formulated more or less politely and more or less correctly.
There has not been a move to integrate or to add, for example, the
Soviet prisoners of war. Now, of course, educated Germans—very educated Germans—know that 3.1 million prisoners of war were deliberately killed by the Germans, but that group has not been brought into
a larger German story. Polish victims, too, are, to a large extent, not
brought in or added to this story. Had that happened in the last twenty
years, I think it would have been easier to commemorate in Eastern
Europe, but it has not really happened.

Another thing that has not happened is that rather than Russia
developing a Russian historical policy, Russia has unsurprisingly modified Soviet narratives. If Russia had pulled back in, and concerned
itself with events that took place on the terrain of the Russian Federation, Ukraine, Belarus, and Poland would have had an easier time, but
it has not happened. Russia, predictably, has instead worked within
the framework of the Soviet narrative of the war, though it modified it
in certain ways. But the fact is that there is a kind of a modern matry-
rological imperialism going on—in typical official Russian proclama-
tions, the victims who are discussed lived well beyond the territory of
today's Russian Federation. This makes it hard, because you have victims who have been claimed by numbers of states at the same time. If
everyone in the German-occupied Soviet Union was a "Russian" victim, we get some strange consequences. For example, a victim of the
Holocaust in west Ukraine could be simultaneously claimed by four
different states, counting four different ways: Israel, obviously, but
also Poland, since the person was a prewar Polish citizen; Ukraine,
since the land in question is now Ukraine; and Russia, since the territory in question was annexed by the Soviet Union after the invasion of
Poland in 1939.

I would like to conclude by making some recommendations, not
about what East Europeans should do, because I think that is too easy,
but about what people in the West might do to make commemoration
policies a little bit less unsatisfactory. The first is—this is where I say

my word of thanks—to the Romanian Cultural Institute, the Romanian Embassy, and to Vladimir Tismaneanu and Bogdan Iacob personally, for organizing a conference of this sort. In general, money which is available for commemoration is not used for multinational conferences: the fundamental problem is that commemoration is always national. I only mentioned the word "Romania" in this text once, now twice, and I am not going to mention it again. I think it is very important that discussions of memory and history take on a multinational framework, as this one has done.

A second recommendation: I think it is very important that, within the next twenty-five years, the United States and the EU members bring Belarusian and Ukrainian elites, historians, and others, through educational institutions and allow them to go back, or encourage them to go back. There is no perverse incentive here, by the way, because there is very little chance that Belarus and Ukraine are going to join the EU in the next couple of decades, so that process that I have mentioned about Poland is not going to happen. In the meantime, that will, at least, multiply perspectives.

A third item which Western institutions could do would be to recognize the existence of memory ministries as a phenomenon, just as we recognize the existence of say, police forces, and think about how they might be coordinated. International policing is coordinated. There is no reason why international memory work might not be coordinated. For example, it would be a good thing if Polish historians working in the Polish memory ministry and Czech historians working in the Czech ministry, and so on, spend one year in each other's institutions. They would learn languages; they would break out of national frameworks; they would get to know other scholars. A much more ambitious plan of this sort would have them rotating through the United States Holocaust Memorial Museum in Washinton, DC or Yad Vashem in Israel. I would point out this kind of rotation of cadres, which would freshen up the discussion on what happened in Eastern Europe immensely, would cost almost nothing. The EU could just spend a few hundred thousand dollars a year to finance post-docs or other programs, the condition of which being that you leave your own ministry for another. Everyone could profit from that and it would do a great deal, over the next generations, to make these discussions more realistic and fresher.

A fourth thing that we can do, and here I am following Omer Bartov in an important article he wrote in 2008,[4] is to regard the Holocaust, among other things, as an event in East European history. We should do this for a number of reasons, one of which is because it is just correct. The Eastern part of Europe was the region where the Holocaust took place; it is where most of the victims lived. But there are other reasons which have to do with commemoration. One of these is that if one learns local languages, and sadly, Yiddish is an exception, then you are suddenly in contact with these countries' historians in a way that you would not be otherwise. If you start to treat the East European Jews as the central object of your scholarly concern and write about the Holocaust, you are then embracing East Europeans. In other words, you can go through the *Ostjuden*, who are often not attended to with the kind of detail one would hope, to the other *Osteuropäerin*. You go through the Eastern Jews to East Europeans. Once you're working on Eastern Jews, then you've already started working on Eastern Europe. That can enable you in all kinds of ways to address other problems of commemoration. The obvious example is bringing into the discussion difficult issues such as collaboration, but in general, it would create a situation in which West and East could talk to each other much better. I think the Holocaust divides Western historians from East European historians to a large extent, but it need not.

My final point is that if we are going to keep pace with historical discussions in Eastern Europe, if for no other reason, we have to drop the taboo on comparing Nazi Germany and the Soviet Union in so far as anyone believes in it. There are a number of good reasons to overcome this taboo. One is that it never really made any sense. If I say to you that you cannot compare Nazi Germany and the Soviet Union, I am issuing a comparative judgment. Once I say that, all I have said is "I have compared the two and I would prefer that you do not and I have the microphone." It has no other logical content besides that one. The other reason we should abandon the taboo is that when we enforce it, we are denying the experience of Jews and others. Almost everyone who lived and suffered under one regime had some kind of contact with the other regime, precisely because the zone I am talking

---

[4] Omer Bartov, "Eastern Europe as the Site of Genocide," *Journal of Modern History*, vol. 80, no. 3 (September 2008), 557–593.

about—where most of the victims died—is a zone where both powers ruled. Most of the victims, at some point in their lives, even if their lives ended very quickly, had an occasion to think about which regime was better and what one should do. This is at the heart of the history of the event and comparison runs through the primary sources, Jewish and otherwise. These people were condemned to compare.

Another reason why I think it is important to compare is that if you do not compare you cannot make a convincing judgment about the singularity of the Holocaust. I think once you have gone through the other German and Soviet crimes, then you are in a position to talk about the singularity of the Holocaust in a convincing way. If you do not do that it is going to be very hard to convince East Europeans, or, in the long run, anyone else. My own book makes the most radical case for the singularity of the Holocaust ever made, precisely because all of the other German and Soviet policies are in view.

Additionally, if we retreat to a discussion of the Holocaust which relies only on the Germans and is focused on the West, we then drift away from the East European historians, including those who have bad intentions, who talk about the Holocaust in different ways. There is no contact, no way to refute them. If we do not learn East European languages and talk about the Holocaust in ways that account for ongoing discussions in East European historiographies, in a comparative context, then we do not know the things that local historians know, for better and worse, and they are going to dominate the discussion about these things.

The original question of my paper was the relationship between history and commemoration. At the very most, I think the kind of conservative approach to history that I have recommended could place some limits on some of the worst kinds of commemoration; it could make it a little bit less unsatisfactory. The paradox of this is that the only way that history could work is if we continue to think of it precisely as history, rather than as a policy of memory.

DANIEL CHIROT

Why World War II Memories Remain So Troubled in Europe and East Asia

German and Japanese attitudes toward the atrocities their nations committed during World War II are often contrasted as if they were completely different, but that is both too simple and somewhat misleading. Nevertheless, as I hope to show, one must start with the observation that the dichotomy has considerable merit. Then I will explain why, for the rest of Europe, recognition of what actually happened during that awful period has been quite similar to Japan's evasiveness, at least until quite recently, and to a considerable degree, even now in parts of Eastern and Central Europe. This will lead me to conclude that an unwillingness to recognize the dark side of one's national history is, after all, the rule rather than the exception.

A few years ago, Germany introduced a new schoolbook about the Holocaust for thirteen- and fourteen-year olds. It is a "comic" (or better, graphic) book, that is, a series of illustrations in which the characters speak in "bubbles." The topic is hardly comic, as it features the life a German Jewish girl saved from death when a kind policeman intercepted her as she is about to get home from school. He tells her that her parents have been arrested, and that she should flee. She never sees her parents again, and survives Nazism to tell her grandchildren what happened. This is meant to get children to identify with the complexities of moral choice and personal responsibility when faced by the nightmarish regime that ruled their country from 1933 to 1945.[1] It is

---

[1] Michael Kimmelman, "No Laughs, No Thrills, and Villain All Too Real," *New York Times*, Feb. 27, 2008. sec. B–1, 6.

hard to imagine a Japanese school assigning a book that would be so emotionally troubling to children of that age, or one that would call for so much open discussion about a terrible episode in their country's history.

It is not that there are no Japanese eager to face their brutal World War II record, particularly on the left and in the Japanese Teacher's Union. Yet, it is still possible for right-wing nationalist Japanese, including members of the parliament, to force the banning of a film about the Yasukuni Shrine. Right-wing threats can also force the cancellation of a meeting of the Teacher's Union by a hotel where it was scheduled.[2] Clearly, if there were no tolerance for this kind of intimidation by Japan's leaders and public opinion, it would not occur. Germany also has right-wing extremists, but they are considered marginal, and such kinds of repressive occurrences are completely unthinkable in today's Germany.

It is well-known that in the case of Germany, the Holocaust has been widely taught in schools for a long time, and that the public airing of films and television shows over at least the past three to four decades has deeply marked German thinking. The introduction of more personal, child-oriented graphic textbooks is meant to make children think yet more deeply about how they would react, not to soften or evade German guilt. West Germans recognized their guilt after World War II, promised never to do it again, taught their children about the horrors of the Holocaust, made those Germans who resisted Hitler heroes, and have long been accepted as reformed, good Europeans. This fact is reflected in (the now unified) Germany's schoolbooks that downplay nationalism in favor of appreciation of a "more globalized and diversified world."[3] Germany's attitude has contributed greatly to European unity. Japan, on the other hand, has generally been evasive about its brutality and is now still being accused

---

[2] Justin McCurry, "Far Right Closes Yasukuni Screening in Tokyo," *The Guardian*, March 19, 2008 (www.guardian.co.uk).

[3] Yasemin N. Soysal, Teresa Bertilotti, and Sabine Mannitz, "Projections of Identity in French and German History and Civics Textbooks," in Hanna Schissler and Yasemin N. Soysal (eds.), *The Nation, Europe and the World* (New York: Bergham Books, 2005), 13–34.

by the countries it victimized, particularly Korea, and most stridently, China.[4]

It is not that Japanese schoolbooks tell lies, but rather that the subject of the war has not been strongly taught, and this has produced a public that generally denies Japan's guilt.[5] This makes it possible for many, perhaps a substantial majority of the Japanese, to believe that the war their country conducted was a noble effort to free Asia of European colonialism, and that in the end they were victimized rather than having been the victimizers. South Korea, China, Japan, and Southeast Asia may be increasingly economically interdependent, but in some ways the acrimony over war memories seems to be undiminished.

While some Germans have sought to portray themselves as victims rather than perpetrators of the war, or as defenders of European Civilization against "Asian" (by which they really meant Russian!) barbarism, this has not gained wide acceptance in Germany. The issue was fought out in a very public way in what was called "the historian's conflict" *(Historikerstreit)* in the 1980s.[6] In the end there has been no revival of any major effort to exonerate the Nazis, least of all at the elite level. Even the racist skinheads who sometimes use Nazi symbols are no more than marginalized, angry, anti-immigrant, lower class youths with virtually no major political or intellectual support.[7]

All this is true; however, the major comparative book on the subject by Ian Buruma is much too sophisticated and subtle to fall into the trap of presenting so simpleminded a contrast.[8] It shows how

---

[4] Yinan He, "Remembering and Forgetting the War: Elite Mythmaking, Mass Reaction, and Sino-Japanese Relations 1950–2006," *History and Memory*, Vol. 19, No. 2 (Fall/Winter), 2007, 43–74 and Yinan He, *The Search for Reconciliation: Sino-Japanese and German-Polish Relations Since World War Two* (New York and Cambridge: Cambridge University Press, 2009).

[5] Hiroshi Mitani, "Writing History Textbooks in Japan," in Gi-Wook Shin and Daniel Sneider (eds.), *History Textbooks and the Wars in Asia: Divided Memories* (London: Routledge, 2011), 193–207.

[6] Charles S. Maier, *The Unmasterable Past: History, Holocaust, and German National Identity* (Cambridge: Harvard University Press, 1988).

[7] Gordon A. Craig, *Politics and Culture in Modern Germany: Essays from The New York Review of Books* (Palo Alto: Society for the Promotion of Science and Scholarship, 1999), 339.

[8] Ian Buruma, *The Wages of Guilt: Memories of War in Germany and Japan* (London: Jonathan Cape, 1994).

complicated a story both German and Japanese postwar behavior and attitudes really have been, and how in both cases, they have hardly remained frozen. There have been many strands of opinion in both cases, and some attitudes have changed over time. Furthermore, once the entire story of World War II in Europe is examined, the problem becomes far more complex, and far less dichotomized, because in Europe, too, it has taken many decades for reality to be faced, and that process is far from complete to this day.

Looking into more detail at German memories of the war as a single trajectory toward repentance and admission of wrongdoing runs into several problems. The first of these is that the German story is very much embedded in all of Europe's interpretation of what happened. For a long time, until some ten to twenty years ago, depending on which European country we are talking about, this was the most troubling aspect of how World War II was remembered. The countries occupied by Germany in Western Europe, without exception, constructed stories that blamed everything bad on Germans and a fairly small number of virtually criminal and deviant collaborators. It was more complicated in Central Europe and the Balkans where the Germans had various allied states (Hungary, Croatia, Slovakia, Romania, and Bulgaria, along with Italy that occupied parts of the Balkans) and also deliberately exacerbated ethnic tensions in mixed areas, but the stories put forward were rather similar. Where the Soviet Union set up communist regimes in the East after the war, not only Nazi Germany, but also the local "reactionary bourgeoisie" and upper classes were blamed. In all cases, however, the guilty were said to be either outsiders or a relatively small number of treacherous locals who were quickly disposed of after the war. There was therefore no perceived need for any general national self-examination, much less repentance for wrongdoing in either Western or Eastern Europe, except among Germans.

This story, that the Germans and small numbers of domestic collaborators were the only responsible ones, is mostly a postwar fabrication. It neglects not only the fact that there were many violent, large-scale reprisals after the war against those suspected of collaborating with Germans, but that in many cases once that was settled, the much larger number of collaborators and fascist sympathizers who survived faded into the background and it was forgotten how much help the Germans really had received.[9]

The most important country occupied by the Germans in Western Europe was France. France abjectly surrendered in 1940 when it could have continued to fight from its protected colonial holdings in North Africa. Then, the collaborationist, pro-German Vichy government of Marshal Pétain was both popular and almost wholly supported by the French civil service, police, and military. The now famous speech transmitted from London on the BBC by General Charles de Gaulle after the French surrender in 1940, urging France to fight on, was heard by almost no one at the time, and only tiny numbers of French officials, either from France itself or from the unoccupied colonies spread throughout the world, rallied to his cause. The only important colonial governor to join de Gaulle's Free French was also the Black Caribbean French high civil servant, Félix Éboué, governor of Chad, whose dislike of racist ideologies convinced him to abandon Vichy. The only two generals to join de Gaulle from the colonial forces were immediately pushed out of their positions.[10] De Gaulle himself at the time was a fairly obscure brigadier general who had been quickly brought into the last wartime cabinet as a junior minister because he seemed to be the sole French officer to understand the importance of tank warfare. Now, his BBC speech of 1940 is widely memorialized as the start of a resistance movement, but in fact, there was no resistance until a year later when the French communists turned against Germany at the time Hitler broke his treaty with Stalin and invaded the Soviet Union in June 1941. Even then, the resistance did not gain much strength until 1943 when, after German defeats in North Africa and at Stalingrad, and after the United States began to actively fight in North Africa and then Italy, it became evident that Germany was going to lose the war. In fact, after France's surrender in 1940, French

---

[9] István Deák, "Introduction," in István Deák, Jan T. Gross, and Tony Judt (eds.), *The Politics of Retribution in Europe: World War II and Its Aftermath* (Princeton: Princeton University Press, 2000), 3–14.

[10] Charles de Gaulle, *The Complete War Memoirs of Charles de Gaulle*, translated by Jonathan Griffin and Richard Howard (New York: Carroll & Graf [First French edition 1954], 1998), 86 and 108.

industrial production, largely for the benefit of the German war effort, actually increased.[11]

It was not until the screening of the 1969 documentary movie *The Sorrow and the Pity*, a lengthy set of interviews with surviving French participants in the war, both as collaborators with Germans and in the resistance, that the full extent of cooperation with the Nazis, and the early weakness of the resistance began to be publicized. Serious historical examination of how thoroughly France supported the collaborationist Vichy regime for some years after the 1940 defeat, and how that very regime is what made resistance so weak for so long had to wait until the 1980s. In fact, one of the first major examinations of the disgraceful anti-Semitic laws and arrest of Jews by Vichy was the work of a Canadian and an American historian, Michael Marrus and Robert Paxton, whose 1981 work, *Vichy France and the Jews*, was quickly translated into French.[12]

The situation varied from country to country, but generally, local authorities and elites worked with Germans quite cooperatively except in cases such as Poland and the Soviet Union, where the population was automatically condemned to eventual enslavement by Nazi racial policies, and where officials, intellectuals, and potential leaders were specifically targeted for annihilation. Germany never had enough soldiers or police in most of the countries it occupied to effectively control them alone. Most occupied European countries, and even supposedly neutral Spain contributed volunteer soldiers to fight with the Germans on the Eastern Front against the Soviets.[13] On top of this, Germany's allies, Italy, Finland (which did not participate in the Holocaust and was involved only because it had earlier been invaded by the Soviet Union), Hungary, Romania, Bulgaria, and the puppet states of Croatia and Slovakia were mostly cooperative, and only Croatia (as part of Yugoslavia) produced an early resistance of any sort. Though the communists later publicized stories of partisan resistance to pro-German

---

[11] Julian Jackson, *France: The Dark Years 1940–1944* (Oxford: Oxford University Press, 2001).

[12] Michael R. Marrus and Robert O. Paxton, *Vichy et les Juifs*, translated by Marguerite Delmotte (Paris: Calman-Lévy, 1981).

[13] Stanley Payne, *Franco and Hitler* (New Haven: Yale University Press, 2008).

governments, these were largely myths. In Bulgaria, for example, a meaningful partisan movement sprang up only a few months before the arrival of the Soviet army in the summer of 1944, and the same was true for Hungary, while in Romania it was the king who overthrew the pro-German dictator Antonescu in August 1944 and turned the country over to the invading Soviet army just as it was entering Romania.[14] Austria, which managed to have itself defined after the war as the first victim of German aggression because it was annexed by Germany in 1938, was actually largely pro-Nazi.[15] In occupied Greece, the small and rather ineffective resistance was bitterly split between communists and anti-communists, while collaborators helped the Germans and Italians keep control. At the end of the war, as Greece was liberated by the British, a civil war broke out between the communists and conservatives, so that ultimately most of the collaborators were enlisted in the anti-communist cause. As Mark Mazower has observed, to this day Greeks have not integrated a realistic appraisal of what happened into their national consciousness.[16]

The communist version of what had happened during the war was also taught in East Germany, so that blame was assigned to West Germany where the old order had supposedly survived. East Germany had no need to confront Nazism, leaving its people unprepared for the new world in which they found themselves after reunification in 1990.[17] The same story of communist partisan activity was put forward by communists in Western Europe, especially in Italy and France where there were very large communist parties after the war.

---

[14] Richard J. Crampton, *A Concise History of Bulgaria* (Cambridge: Cambridge University Press, 2005), 175; István Deák, "A Fatal Compromise? The Debate over Collaboration and Resistance in Hungary," in Deák, Gross, and Judt (eds.), *The Politics of Retribution in Europe*, 39–73.

[15] Steve Beller, *A Concise History of Austria* (Cambridge: Cambridge University Press, 2006), 231–248.

[16] Mark Mazower, *Inside Hitler's Greece: The Experience of Occupation, 1941–1944* (New Haven: Yale University Press, 1993) and Mark Mazower, "The Cold War and the Appropriation of Memory: Greece After Liberation," in Deák, Gross, and Judt (eds.) *The Politics of Retribution in Europe*, 212–232.

[17] Tony Judt, "The Past Is Another Country: Myth and Memory in Postwar Europe," in Deák, Gross, and Judt (eds.), *The Politics of Retribution in Europe*, 307–308.

Communists did play an important role in the resistances in these countries, but similar to France, it was not significant until 1943 and by then communists were far from being the only participants. The same thing happened in Italy. It was only after Mussolini's overthrow in 1943, followed immediately by the seizure of most of Italy by German troops, that resistance began.[18] In other words, as in most of Europe where there either were governments allied to Germany or puppet regimes beholden to the Germans, it was only the decisive turn of events against Germany that unleashed major resistance.

For decades after World War II, Germans' acceptance of their guilt allowed the rest of Europe to evade this truth, namely that they had been mostly quite willing to help the Nazis, and closed their eyes to gruesome German brutality as long as it seemed that Germany was winning. In official histories and books what were often minor acts of resistance, or tardy ones that became effective only from 1943 on, were played up, collaboration by broad swaths of officialdom was overlooked, and the need for any kind of remorse or apology to the many victims, including, of course, Jews and Roma, were not part of remembrance.

France was a major example of this. As it was being liberated some 10,000 supposed collaborators were murdered in spontaneous local vengeance killings, but once the state got control of the situation, it jailed a few thousand collaborators, freeing and forgiving most of them after a few years except for a small number who were executed. The ugly reality of what had really happened was replaced by the carefully fostered myth that most of France had nobly resisted and was antifascist.[19] German acceptance of guilt made this evasion by everyone else much easier. Very similar stories about resistance sprang up throughout most of the Continent, even where they were mostly fabrications.

The second, somewhat related problem with the simple contrast between the European and Asian memories of the war is that most of the Central and Eastern European countries, where the worst abuses and the most killing took place, evaded responsibility even more than Western Europe. In part this was because of the communist interpre-

---

[18] Maria Wilhelm, *The Other Italy: Italian Resistance in World War II* (New York: Norton, 1988).

[19] Michel Dobry (ed.), *Le mythe de l'allergie française au fascisme* (Paris: Albin Michel, 2003).

tation of fascism and Nazism as a class phenomenon, the last gasp of a historically condemned bourgeois order. Thus, the ultranationalism and ethnic hatreds that had so troubled this part of Europe even before World War I, and only grew worse between 1918 and 1939, were brushed off as yet another manifestation of the evils of the corrupt old order, now replaced by healthy socialism. The problems of ethnonationalist conflict were swept under the rug, even though that had been part of the background cause of the rise of fascism and the early success of the Nazi occupations throughout almost the entire region.

By the time communists took power in Eastern Europe after the war, many ethnic problems actually had been settled either by the Nazis (the extermination of most of the large Jewish minorities), by the movement of borders after 1945 and mass exchanges of population, and by the largest example of ethnic cleansing in European history when ethnic Germans were expelled from Poland and Czechoslovakia or internally displaced in the Soviet Union. Some 11.5 million Germans whose ancestors had been living in these regions for centuries were forced out. Perhaps over a million died.[20]

Little of this violent history got incorporated into the official record. In Poland, the bulk of the genuinely large resistance had actually been anti-communist and nationalist. This was, of course denied by the communists. At the same time, the suffering of the Jews during the war, Poland's long standing anti-Semitism well before 1939, and the continuing violent anti-Semitism after the war were also played down to the point of being practically ignored.[21]

One of the most unfortunate aspects of these fabrications was that even in the case where there was the most genuine, strong communist resistance movement, Yugoslavia, the story was overused and eventually lost its power as communism's legitimacy faded. Josip Broz Tito,

---

[20] Norman Naimark, *Fires of Hatred: Ethnic Cleansing in Twentieth-Century Europe* (Cambridge: Harvard University Press, 2001), 14 and 108–138; Timothy Snyder, *Bloodlands: Europe Between Hitler and Stalin* (New York: Basic Books, 2010), 313–337.

[21] Jan T. Gross, *Polish Society Under German Occupation: The General-Gouvernement, 1939–1944* (Princeton: Princeton University Press, 1979) and "A Tangled Web: Confronting Stereotypes Concerning Relations Between Poles, Germans, Jews, and Communists" in Deák, Gross, and Judt (eds.), *The Politics of Retribution in Europe: World War II and Its Aftermath*), 74–129.

the leader of the communist partisans during the war, and Yugoslavia's dictator until his death in 1980, based much of his reputation and his party's legitimacy on the partisan myth that all good Yugoslavs had joined together to fight the bourgeois, treacherous domestic fascists, and foreign invaders. Here we have a perfect example of why school-books are not necessarily effective if they tell a story that loses credibility. In fact, the Yugoslav war from 1941 to 1945 was a complex combination of a struggle against German and Italian occupiers as well as a very nasty, multisided civil war between the country's various ethnic nationalists. It is true that Tito's communists worked hard to overcome ethnic divisions, but the partisan story repeated endlessly in classrooms and in state propaganda did not make people forget the bitter ethnic divisions that had also existed. By emphasizing the myth of class unity over ethnic division, Tito's state failed to explain the troubling past. Already by the time of Tito's death, ethnic strains were evident, and in the 1980s they grew out of control. In the 1990s, they exploded into a tragic war that killed hundreds of thousands and broke the country apart into its various ethnonationalist groups.[22]

The third problem with the easy dichotomy contrasting "good" Germany and a reconciled, harmonious Europe to "bad" Japan and a troubled East Asia has already been mentioned, but needs more explanation. In Europe, the Jewish problem was for the first couple of postwar decades relegated to obscurity, even denial, and in some cases this lasted well into the 1990s. This was true even in Germany where, according to Buruma, the full extent of the nightmare was not quite recognized by the general public until the showing of an American television drama on the Holocaust in Germany in 1979. *Der Spiegel*, a leading West German newspaper commented at the time: "An American television series, made in a trivial style, produced more for commercial than for moral reasons, more for entertainment than for enlightenment, accomplished what hundreds of [German] books, plays, films, and television programs have failed to do in the more than three decades since the end of the war: to inform the Germans about crimes against Jews committed in their name, so that millions

---

22 Misha Glenny, *The Balkans: Nationalism, War and the Great Powers, 1804–1999* (London: Penguin, 2000), 570–593 and 622–662.

were emotionally touched and moved."[23] Aside from being well produced, the American television show featured an assimilated middle-class family that was not obviously Jewish in any way, and perhaps this is what so startled the Germans.

As a French Jewish baby who was hidden with his mother and grandmother during the war in a small village, and as a professional social scientist, I recall thinking in 1979 that this show was too smooth, and not nearly horrible enough. But that may have been the secret of its success in the United States and especially in Germany. It was easier to identify with the family portrayed than with the skeletal, dying concentration camp prisoners one sees in documentaries and pictures. In any case, after this, West German (but not East German) textbooks placed increased emphasis on Nazi crimes that killed some six million Jews. Furthermore, the number of monuments and museums featuring the persecution of Jews under Nazi rule has proliferated so that now German guilt is very solidly established. New generations come out of school aware of how xenophobic ultranationalism and racist theories resulted in such a catastrophe.

What most of the rest of Europe failed to do for a long time, however, was to admit that the Germans could never have killed so many Jews without the help of the countries they had occupied and to which they were allied. In the few cases where local authorities resisted German demands very few Jews were caught and killed. So, for example, Bulgarian public and church opinion protected Bulgarian Jews in Bulgaria proper, but not in the parts of Greece and Yugoslavia occupied by the Bulgarians during the war. There, Jews were turned over to the Germans.[24] The same was true of Hungary where the administration of Admiral Horthy turned over Jews in the countryside and particularly in the parts of Transylvania it had occupied. Elie Wiesel, probably the most famous of all Holocaust survivor writers, was from that Transylvanian Jewish community, almost all of whom died in the Nazi camps. Only in the summer of 1944 did Horthy stop these operations and thus protected and"saved" Jews in Budapest.[25]

---

[23] Buruma, *The Wages of Guilt*, 88.
[24] Crampton, *A Concise History of Bulgaria*, 171–173.
[25] Deák, "A Fatal Compromise," 64–67.

Romania's pro-German wartime dictator, Marshall Antonescu, had no qualms about slaughtering Jews in Bessarabia (today's Republic of Moldova) and in Romanian Moldova where local anti-Semitic feelings were high. Those farther south and particularly Jews in Bucharest, however, were more protected because they were thought to be economically useful, and there most survived.[26]

Yet, to this day the full extent of these countries' complicity in the Holocaust, and in cases such as Romania and Hungary, the nature of their particularly vicious native fascist movement remain poorly known and not widely taught in schools. What remains part of the general perception is the help they gave to some selected portions of their Jewish populations, not what happened to the majority of Jews.

In Romania recognition of what had happened to the Jews was partially exposed right after the war but then erased from public discourse. By the time the communist regime was overthrown at the end of 1989, few Romanians had much of a sense of how increasingly racist, xenophobic, and stridently anti-Semitic the atmosphere had been in the 1920s and 1930s, and how viciously cruel the Antonescu regime had been from 1940 to 1944, when it was replaced to try to mollify the invading Soviet army. There was almost no serious Romanian scholarship on that period until the 1990s. On the contrary, by the late communist period, the regime had begun rehabilitating Antonescu, portraying him as a dedicated, honest, and reform-minded nationalist rather than as member of the anti-Semitic Iron Guard. It even provided material support for an American scholar, Larry Watts, to spread this story. After the fall of communism, he continued to receive ample help from the Romanian military, which was intent on proving that Antonescu was a hero.[27] Indeed, when the proceedings of the communist-led trial of Antonescu that resulted in his execution in 1946 were published in Romania in 1996, he was again made out to be a

---

[26] Radu Ioanid, *The Holocaust in Romania: The Destruction of Jews and Gypsies Under the Antonescu Regime, 1940–1944* (with a Foreword by Elie Wiesel) (Chicago: Ivan R. Dee, 2000) and Dennis Deletant, *Hitler's Forgotten Ally: Ion Antonescu and His Regime, Romania 1940–1944* (Basingstoke: Palgrave Macmillan, 2006).

[27] Larry Watts, *Romanian Cassandra: Ion Antonescu and the Struggle for Reform 1916–1941* (Boulder CO: East European Monographs, distributed by Columbia University Press, 1993).

noble, heroic figure.[28] Only more recently has some Romanian scholarship exposed the deep roots of the nasty ideologies espoused by much of Romania's intellectual and political elite in the pre-World War II period and during the war itself, and of course by Antonescu.[29]

What made this evasion of how much of a role Eastern and Central European xenophobia, anti-Semitism, and general racism contributed to the Nazi Holocaust easier had something to do with the fact that a disproportionate number of the communist cadres right after World War II were Jewish. This was partly because communist parties were originally very small except in Czechoslovakia and Yugoslavia, their leaders consisted largely of marginalized minorities. Later, Jewish communists became some of the main victims of the purges in Eastern Europe as Stalin set out to destroy what was left of Jewish life in the Soviet Empire. All this contributed, first, to a systematic downplaying of the Holocaust, and then it contributed to a lasting anti-Semitism that blames Jews for their countries' misfortunes. It will take a long time for such popular misconceptions to go away.[30]

Nowhere is this more evident than in Poland where Jan Gross's best selling 2001 book, *Neighbors*, caused a sensational debate to break out. Gross, a Polish-American historian at Princeton University, documented how in 1941 in a Polish town that was half Jewish and half Christian, the Christians turned on their 1,600 Jewish neighbors and slaughtered almost all of them – beating them to death, herding them into buildings and burning them, hunting them down in the fields as they tried to escape, all without any prompting by the Germans who were occupying the area but not that particular town. Only seven Jews survived. Poland had generally portrayed itself solely as a victim of the Germans, and therefore free of any possible guilt. Indeed, Poles

---

[28] Marcel-Dumitru Ciura, *Procesul Mareşalului Antonescu: Documente* (two volumes, with a Foreword by Iosif Constantin Drăgan) (Bucharest: Saeculum I.O. and Europa Nova, 1996).

[29] Vladimir Solonari, *Purifying the Nation: Population Exchange and Ethnic Cleansing in Nazi-Allied Romania* (Baltimore: Johns Hopkins University Press, 2010).

[30] Judt, "The Past Is Another Country," in Deák, Gross, and Judt (eds.), *The Politics of Retribution in Europe*, 312–313; George Schöpflin, *Politics in Eastern Europe 1945–1992* (Oxford: Blackwell, 1993), 42–43; Yuri Slezkine, *The Jewish Century* (Princeton: Princeton University Press, 2004), 313–314.

were deemed part of an inferior race by the Nazis, their intellectuals and leaders were killed in large numbers, and every effort was made to wipe out Polish culture. They, along with Yugoslavs, proportionately suffered the highest casualties in Europe during the war. Yet, Poland was also one of the most anti-Semitic countries in Europe, and some Poles helped the Germans round up Jews. Some others Poles did hide Jews or help them, but most did not, and in some cases, as in the town Gross studied, they took the initiative in killing Jews. Gross's book woke the country up to what had really happened, but it was also bitterly attacked by Polish nationalists, and by many parts of the Catholic Church, which is particularly powerful in Poland. Even Lech Wałęsa, Poland's heroic anti-communist leader and its first post-communist president accused Gross of just being another greedy Jew spreading lies to make money. Still, the book finally led to an official apology by the Polish government, and a new monument being put up to commemorate the massacre described by Gross. Subsequently, in 2006, Gross published a new book, *Fear*, in which he described how some of the few surviving Jews (over 85 percent of the roughly 3 million Polish Jews were killed) who returned to their homes after World War II were set upon by Christian Poles and massacred. This produced another burst of nationalist outrage in Poland, where the debate about the whole issue remains bitterly divisive. It is not just in East Asia that descriptions of massacres that took place more than 60 years ago are still contentious and subject to nationalist distortions.[31]

In Lithuania, once home to a Jewish community of some 160,000 (7.6 percent of the population, the second largest percentage of the population that was Jewish after Poland) some two-thirds were wiped out. Lithuania had traditionally been quite anti-Semitic, like its neighbor, Poland, and there were many Lithuanian collaborators who helped the Nazis between 1941 and 1944. During the time from World

---

[31] Jan T. Gross, *Neighbors: The Destruction of the Jewish Community in Jebwadne, Poland* (Princeton: Princeton University Press, 2001); Jan T. Gross, *Fear: Anti-Semitism in Poland After Auschwitz* (New York: Random House, 2006); David Engel, "On Continuity and Discontinuity in Polish-Jewish Relations: Observations on *Fear*," *East European Politics & Societies*, vol. 21, no, 3 (Summer 2007), 534–548; Martin Gilbert, *Jewish History Atlas* (New York: Macmillan, 1969), 85–88.

War II until 1991 when Lithuania was under Soviet communist rule, collaboration with the Germans was officially deemed to have been a "bourgeois nationalist" phenomenon, though the killing of Jews itself was downplayed. It is no surprise, then, that the period since independence in 1991 has seen a confused conflict between various political factions over what happened. This is complicated, as elsewhere in Eastern Europe, by the fact that Jews are often blamed for having worked with the communists. Because Lithuania from 1939 to 1941, and then again after World War II was subject to murderous repression and mass deportations of its citizens by the Soviet Union, the myth that confounded "Jews" with "communists" made it difficult to come to grips with what had happened during the German occupation. It is only now that some efforts are being made to clarify the historical record, but it will take a long time before this gets absorbed into school teaching or general public perception.[32]

In Austria, also, the fact that in 1938 the population and state officials rallied to the Nazi cause and instituted large scale expulsion and killing of the substantial Jewish population has been, until recently, largely overlooked except by a few scholars. A bitter joke about Austria is that they are the world's best propagandists as they have convinced the world and themselves that Ludwig van Beethoven (who was born in what is now Germany) was actually an Austrian (he worked and died in Vienna) while Hitler (who was born in Austria) was a German. Austria's former president Kurt Waldheim, who had previously served as the United Nations' Secretary General before returning to Austria to run for president, was exposed as a significant participant in Nazi war crimes in the Balkans during the war, against Greek Jews and Yugoslavs. Both the American and Soviet intelligence services knew this before he became United Nations Secretary General, but both countries had backed him for this post, perhaps because they felt that he could easily be blackmailed and would therefore be more compliant. The deceitfulness of his public biography was only openly revealed after his UN term, while he was running for Austria's

---

[32] Gilbert, *Jewish History Atlas*, 85–88; Saulius Suziedelis, "The Perception of the Holocaust: Public Challenges and Experience in Lithuania," *EES News*, January–February 2008 (Washington, DC: Woodrow Wilson International Center for Scholars, East European Studies Center), 7–10.

presidency. This, however, had little impact. The Austrians still chose him as their president.[33]

In the Soviet Union, official anti-Semitism blocked out most of the story of the persecution and destruction of Jews. After the war, Stalin became increasingly anti-Semitic, and this remained part of a policy of discrimination until the fall of Communism in 1991. Even now, however, Russian anti-Semitism is too omnipresent to produce much official acknowledgment of the massive suffering of Jews during the German occupation, and school books that are not even willing to admit anything close to the full extent of Stalin's own crimes are hardly likely to dwell on the unfortunate situation of the Jews during and after World War II. Though Hitler's crimes are taught in Russian schools, what happened to the Jews is not.[34]

Nor has this kind of evasiveness been limited to the Soviet Union, Central, or Eastern Europe. Few French Jews would have been sent to concentration camps without the cooperation of the French police and denunciations by French citizens. To be sure, about three-quarters of French Jews survived, a higher number than in countries farther east, and a much higher proportion than in the Netherlands. This was partly because France was relatively large, and the Germans had few occupying troops to devote to running it. At the same time, this very fact meant that it would have been easier for the French to protect all of their Jews, and in parts of France that were more left-wing, as well as in more Protestants towns and villages (Protestants are only about 3 percent of France but have played a disproportionately large role in the economy and politics), Jews were better protected than in right-wing areas. Where local authorities did not cooperate with orders from the Germans and from the Vichy government to turn in Jews, relatively few were caught.[35] In my family's case, we were in a strongly social-

---

[33] Richard Mitten, *The Politics of Anti-Semitic Prejudice: The Waldheim Phenomenon in Austria* (Boulder: Westview, 1992).

[34] Amir Weiner, *Making Sense of War: The Second World War and the Fate of the Bolshevik Revolution* (Princeton: Princeton University Press, 2001), 114–126; Robert Maier, "Learning about Europe and the World: Schools, Teachers, and Textbooks in Russia after 1991," in Schissler and Soysal (eds.), *The Nation, Europe and the World* (New York: Bergham Books), 138–162, particularly, 142.

[35] Marrus and Paxton, *Vichy et les Juifs*, 191–196, 325–339.

ist village in Vichy France, but near the border of the part of France directly occupied by the Germans. The socialist mayor, Anatole Ferrant, provided us with false papers and ration tickets. On the other hand, the Jews and others fleeing the German zone who sometimes wound up in the same village would be put up in the local hotel only to be picked up the next day by the police. Presumably, unlike with us, village people did not feel any personal connection to these strangers, and were less sympathetic to their plight. After the war, France compensated few of its Jews whose property had been looted during the war, mostly by other Frenchmen, and it was not until July 1995 that a French president apologized for what had happened. Now it is all different, and in Paris there are plaques commemorating the arrest of French Jews, as well as a new Holocaust museum in what used to be the old Jewish quarter of the city. But it took a long time for this to happen.[36] France only began to include materials on the Holocaust in its schools in the late 1970s, and the way to best do this remains a subject of controversy. In February 2008, President Sarkozy suggested that every child in school be assigned the biography of one of the French Jewish Holocaust victims, a proposal that was widely deemed excessive, though it was admitted that it was necessary to somehow revive the study of this topic to make it more relevant.[37] This shows once more that it is Germany that has taken the lead in treating the subject, and that other European countries lag behind. The controversy raised by the French president's remarks shows also how much the contestation over memories now more than sixty-years old remains alive.

The Netherlands, Buruma's home country, also had a somewhat darker record than most of its citizens were willing to acknowledge after the war, when everything was blamed on the Germans and the small domestic Dutch Nazi Party. Anne Frank, the most famous of all Holocaust victims, was turned in by Dutch neighbors. While the majority of the Dutch did not like the German occupation, and local Nazis were a minority, there were enough willing collaborators to run

---

[36] *Le Monde*, "Une dette imprescriptible," *Le Monde*, July 18, 1995 (www.lemonde.fr); Shmuel Trigano Shmuel, "Que faire avec l'indemnisation des spoliations," *Le Monde*, March 2, 2000 (www.lemonde.fr).

[37] Stéphanie Le Bars, "Le projet de parrainage d'enfants de la Shoah contesté," *Le Monde*, February 16, 2008 (www.lemonde.fr).

a dependent Dutch civil service. Partly because of this, but also largely because of the Netherlands' small size, over 70 percent of the 140,000 Dutch Jews were killed.[38]

Almost everywhere, including in Denmark, a country that saved most of its Jews by shipping them off to neutral Sweden, resistance to German occupation only developed to a significant degree in 1943, when Germany started to lose its war, and also began to use harsher occupation measures to obtain labor and resources.[39] Policy toward Jews was largely a secondary consideration for most Western Europeans during the war. Though Jews had made up less than 1 percent of any West European country before the war (most European Jews lived in the East), there was generally enough anti-Semitism to make most people in the occupied countries indifferent to their fate, or in the case of many officials, to cooperate with German orders.

Compared to countries farther east, and also to Russia, Western Europe has finally admitted that it was not just Germans who committed crimes, but this has taken decades of work by historians, filmmakers, and organized efforts to bring about such recognition. In all these cases, it took a new generation that came to the fore 25 years after the war to start the process of admission. Their elders preferred to forget as much as possible, and to keep quiet, except for the communists who distorted history to vilify their bourgeois enemies in order to better conceal communism's own crimes. That has not yet happened in the eastern parts of Europe even though the overwhelming majority of Jews killed were in the East, in what Timothy Snyder has called "the Bloodlands."

The contrast between Germany and to some extent (belatedly) with much of Western Europe and Japan or East Asia in general, therefore, stands. But the reluctance of almost all of Europe to face its nationals' participation as well as the widespread feigned ignorance and indifference to the horrors that occurred during and right after World War II should serve to remind us that there is nothing easy about confronting

---

[38] Peter Romijn, "'Restoration of Confidence': The Purge of Local Government in the Netherlands as a Problem of Postwar Reconstruction," in Deák, Gross, and Judt (eds.), *The Politics of Retribution in Europe*, 180 and 190; Raul Hilberg, *Perpetrators Victims Bystanders: The Jewish Catastrophe 1933–1945* (New York: Harper-Collins, 1992), 209–211.

[39] Marrus and Paxton, *Vichy et les Juifs*, 325.

such moral evil. Europe's admissions of guilt and acceptance of historical truth did not surface quickly, the process of reconciliation with the
past remains problematic, and it has barely begun in some countries.

If we turn back to Germany itself, a fourth problem appears in
the effort to explain the contrast between its behavior and Japan's. It is
obviously true that West Germany's acceptance of its guilt contributed
to the reconciliation with the rest of Europe, while Japan's stubborn
tendency to generally evade the issue has continued to sour relations
with its neighbors despite the development of close economic links.
German willingness to shoulder the blame allowed other European
countries to look away for a long time from their widespread cooperation with the Germans during the war, but over time, after decades,
it also facilitated their gradual if belated coming to terms with their
own role. At least this has been the case in Western Europe, and it is
starting to take place, though unevenly, in Eastern Europe as well. But,
after all, why did Germany itself behave so differently than Japan?

Perhaps, as some suggest, this has something to do with a difference between German and Japanese cultures, with the former being
one that emphasizes "confession" while the latter stresses "guilt" and
"shame." Ian Buruma correctly dismissed this as a rather dubious,
shallow explanation.[40] Even if one were to try to delve more deeply
into the differences between the two cultures, it would be very difficult
to prove that this played a major role because there is a far more obvious and convincing explanation. The key is the international situation
in which Germany and Japan found themselves by the end of 1945 and
in the years immediately following the war.[41]

France, humbled and in terrible economic shape by 1945, was,
nevertheless, the most powerful country on the West European mainland (excluding, of course, island Britain), and the French wanted to
see Germany dismantled and permanently crippled. The other formerly occupied West Europe countries were bitterly hostile to Germany as well, and deeply embarrassed about the fact that so many
of their countrymen had collaborated with the Germans. The United
States and the Soviet Union, however, did not want to fragment Ger-

---

[40] Buruma, *The Wages of Guilt*, 116.
[41] Robert Dujarric, "Retour sur un japon conquérant," *Le Monde*, December
25, 2007 (www.lemonde.fr).

many into little pieces. Stalin hoped to be able to milk postwar Germany for reparations that his country desperately needed, and the United States, along with Britain, understood that a punitive peace after World War I had set the stage for Hitler's rise, so they did not want to repeat the same mistake. The creation of an occupied but economically more united Germany served their purposes better than the kind of revenge France wanted.[42]

As the Cold War developed, and especially in 1948, with strong Communist parties in France and Italy, and the final, complete subjugation of Eastern Europe by the Soviets, the Americans began to think of West Germany as a possible bulwark against communism. But without French and general West European acceptance of West Germany as a legitimate, trustworthy state, it would have been impossible to construct a strong, united North Atlantic Treaty Organization (NATO), and probably very difficult to bring about the kind of West European economic recovery able to dampen pro-communist sentiment where it was already strong. It took years of difficult negotiations and the participation of some farsighted French and German statesmen to bring reconciliation about, but helped by the dire international situation and American pressure, it happened. France and Germany began to take steps to cooperate economically, first in the coal and steel industries, and then more broadly. Maurice Schumann and Jean Monnet of France led the way, starting in 1950, in changing French attitudes. In West Germany, the elderly Konrad Adenauer had become head of his country. Adenauer had a history of being friendly to France and Britain in the early 1920s, when he was mayor of Köln. Jailed several times by the Nazis, he had barely survived the war, but as the leader of the new Christian Democratic Party he was also fervently anti-communist. He was therefore receptive to overtures from France. A patient, diplomatic, and generous America greatly helped the process along. What was required was for West Germany to make it clear that it would not fall back into the same aggressive ultranationalism that had dominated it in the first half of the twentieth cen-

---

[42] Frank Giles, *The Locust Years: The Story of the Fourth French Republic 1946–1958* (New York: Carroll & Graf, 1991), 99–102; Julian W. Friend, *The Linchpin: French–German Relations 1950–1990* (Westport: Praeger, Washington Papers 154, Center for Strategic and International Studies, 1991), 12–16.

tury.[43] Franco-German friendship and mutual confidence thus grew, and became the basis of a united Europe, first through the Common Market, and then eventually in the European Union. This alliance remained the bedrock of European unity, even after the collapse of East Germany and its reunification with West Germany in 1990.[44]

Part of the bargain was that Germany had to educate its young differently than in the past. German schools changed the way they taught history, and with the rise of new postwar generations, attitudes changed. Programs were set up in the 1950s and 1960s to exchange high school students between the two countries. Those who took part in these exchanges still remember them as being among the more significant events of their youth. A German friend born just after the war told me how he was sent on such an exchange program and met his first love, a French girl his age. She had to keep it a secret for fear that if her father found out she was involved with a German he would kill both of them. To these youths, this made no sense at all, but that was how some in the older generation that had actually experienced the war still felt. In France, also, the teaching of history changed, though much more slowly. Since the mid 1980s, French textbooks have gradually shifted away from a nationalist perspective toward a more pan-European and even global emphasis, whereas in Germany the process began earlier and has gone much farther.[45]

Nothing like this was either necessary or even possible in East Asia. First of all, the Americans agreed to maintain the Japanese Emperor (something that would have been totally unthinkable with Hitler, even if he had not committed suicide) in order to better control Japan, so it became far easier for the Japanese to evade the issue of responsibility.[46] Just as important, the countries that had been occupied by Japan had almost no say at all in determining Japan's fate. China was embroiled in civil war until 1949, and then, especially in 1950, China became a direct enemy of the United States. Korea

---

[43] Friend, *The Linchpin*, 16–25.

[44] Friend, *The Linchpin* and Friend, *Unequal Partners: French–German Relations 1989–2000* (Westport: Praeger, Washington Papers 180, Center for Strategic and International Studies), 2001.

[45] Soysal, Bertilotti, and Mannitz, "Projections of Identity," 18.

[46] Buruma, *The Wages of Guilt*, 172–176.

was weak and divided, and after the Korean War, it was in ruins.[47] In Southeast Asia the main issues were a set of anticolonial wars and the dissolution of the French, British, and Dutch Empires. Influencing policy toward defeated Japan was neither possible nor particularly important.[48]

Thailand skillfully extricated itself from its wartime association with the Japanese and became pro-American. Perhaps only someone born in France still notices that the Victory Monument in Bangkok celebrates a Thai victory over the French in Laos in 1941, at a time when French Indochina was dominated by the Japanese and France itself was helpless.[49]

In short, there were no hostile Asians the Japanese needed to placate or listen to until much later when a recovered South Korea and an emergent China began to make demands for apologies. By then, the pattern of Japanese denial had been fixed for a long time. To be sure, Japanese leftists did seek to expose their country's brutality and aggression during the war, but they tacked this on to a strong anti-Americanism unlikely to win much sympathy from the United States. The dominant Japanese conservatives were, at first, very much the same elites who had run Japan before and during the war, except for a few top people who were purged, and today's elite made its way in the same Japanese conservative circles that ruled in the 1950s and 1960s. So, there is little pressure for Japan to change, and since both the Japanese left and right can agree that they were the innocent victims of the nuclear bombings and Western aggression, the situation has not changed much.[50] This is all the more so because China and South Korea have been perfectly willing to cooperate economically with Japan, even as they complain about its refusal to make official apologies or change its textbooks.

---

[47] Bruce Cumings, *Korea's Place in the Sun: A Modern History* (New York: W.W. Norton, 1997), 185–298.

[48] Gerhard L. Weinberg, *A World at Arms: A Global History of World War II* (Cambridge: Cambridge University Press), 534.

[49] Daniel Fineman, *A Special Relationship: The United States and Military Government in Thailand, 1947–1958* (Honolulu: University of Hawaii Press, 1997); Nigel J. Brailey, *Thailand and the Fall of Singapore: A Frustrated Asian Revolution* (Boulder: Westview, 1986), 91–94.

[50] Buruma, *The Wages of Guilt*, 295–296.

Finally, there is the question of collaboration. In Europe, as the Germans took the blame for what had happened, it was easy for a full generation to evade the fact that so many other Europeans had helped the Nazis. By the time this began to change in the 1970s and 1980s, West European unity was a solidly established fact, and few felt endangered by the gradual admission in other countries that they too may have been partially at fault. But what about in East Asia? How many Koreans worked willingly with the Japanese? To what extent have Koreans faced up to this? Undoubtedly, the fact that Park Chung-hee, the long time military dictator of South Korea, was trained as a Japanese military officer and had once taken a Japanese name kept South Korean complaints about Japan to a minimum during his rule, and probably also helped South Korean economic cooperation with the Japanese.[51] There were many Chinese who also worked with the Japanese, but during Mao's rule, this was mostly blamed on bad class elements as in communist Eastern Europe. Thus, the early postwar decades put little pressure on Japan itself to apologize. As post-Mao Chinese reforms weakened the legitimacy of socialist ideology, and the Communist Party replaced this by emphasizing nationalism, however, hostility toward Japan and the cultivation of memories of Japanese atrocities came to the fore once more in the 1980s and 1990s.[52] This is something a poorly educated Japanese public and its conservative politicians have had a hard time understanding or accepting because, unlike in West Germany there was so little pressure to face the facts in the immediate postwar decades.

To conclude, much of the difference between the Japanese and German way of understanding their nations' behavior during World War II is due to their very different geopolitical situations after the war. It hardly seems necessary to invoke deep cultural differences. Also, within Europe, it was Germany, or rather West Germany that stood out in admitting its fault. It really had little choice. Other countries,

---

[51] Cumings, *Korea's Place in the Sun*, 349–356.

[52] He, *The Search for Reconciliation*, Chapters 2 and 3. Also, Chang Jui-te, "The Politics of Commemoration: A Comparative Analysis of the Fiftieth Anniversary Commemoration in Mainland China and Taiwan of the Victory in the Anti-Japanese War," in Diana Lary and Stephen MacKinnon, (eds.), *Scars of War: The Impact of Warfare on Modern China* (Vancouver: UBC Press, 2001), 136–160.

most of whom had significant numbers of collaborators, and some of whom had quite terrible records of ultranationalism and vicious treatment of their Jews were very slow to admit this to themselves and to the rest of the world. Seen in that light, it begins to seem that the Japanese public's reluctance to face the past, and its continuing view of Japan as victim rather than as an instigator of morally repugnant aggression, is normal. That is what is to be expected of those not forced to admit to wrongdoing. There is nothing uniquely Japanese about this.

We should not be surprised by this conclusion. White American Southerners long evaded, and to some extent still fail to come to grips with the fact that they did not fight a bloody civil war for "states' rights" but to preserve slavery. The Russian government today is busy trying to get Russians to forget how cruel and needlessly bloody Stalin really was. The Turkish government denies that its Ottoman predecessors conducted a genocide against Armenians, though historians have more than adequately documented what happened. The Catholic Church has spent decades trying to avoid admitting the sexual scandals that have besmirched its reputation, though when forced to do so, it has relented somewhat. West Germany, on the other hand, had little choice, and that opened the way for those Germans who really were repentant to gain the upper hand. In other cases, when enough time has passed, and the threat of retaliation no longer exists, sometimes the truth can become widely accepted, as long as it does not threaten the existence and legitimacy of the nation or any major institution. Because after all history is always meant to serve the present rather than the past, we should not expect too much more. But we should also remember that as professional scholars some of us can help accelerate the process of recognition, admission, and therefore reconciliation by providing the raw materials that honest intellectuals and political leaders will use when they finally come to accept the necessity of facing the past.

EUSEBIO MUJAL-LEÓN and ERIC LANGENBACHER

Post-Authoritarian Memories in Europe and Latin America

I. Introduction

Over the last decade and a half, academic attention has grown considerably in two closely related yet rarely connected areas. On the one hand, the field of transitional justice has looked at the importance of various judicial, bureaucratic (lustration) and political (truth and reconciliation commissions) processes aimed at confronting legacies of authoritarian persecution and repression. Authors often contest the overriding goals of such measures, yet most agree on the importance of providing a modicum of justice for those who suffered previously, as well as prospectively rebuilding social and political trust and legitimacy in the new liberalized and/or democratic order. Moreover, many writers emphasize the role of transitional justice in changing mindsets and constructing a democratic political culture.

Another set of scholars have studied the dynamics and impact of collective memories.[1] They argue that such shared interpretations of existentially important historical events are a core component of collective identity, and thus, of political culture. Memories may either support or undermine a particular regime and may aid or hinder elites and the power that they wield. Certain kinds of memories often result from

---

[1] A great number of terms currently circulate—social memory, historical memory, historical consciousness, myth, and so on—all of which have their advocates. We do not delve into these debates in this chapter, and use the term "collective memory" or just "memory" to refer to the phenomenon unless explicitly stated otherwise.

and simultaneously support transitional justice measures—in short, memories can affect the likelihood that the system and political culture will democratize successfully.

In this chapter, we delve into the conceptual dynamics behind the notion of collective memory, which has gained less attention among social scientists than transitional justice has, and which has rarely been explicitly connected to the literature on democracy and democratization. We discuss what post-authoritarian and democratic memories look like with the aim of identifying relevant variables and patterns. A brief examination of Germany, Spain, Chile, and Argentina shows that a two-step process is involved and that the timing of the process is greatly affected by the nature and circumstances of the transition and the international environment or Zeitgeist. The chapter concludes with some thoughts on the case of Cuba and what analysts might expect as the revolutionary project loses its vitality/legitimacy and is either replaced or transformed.

II. Defining Collective Memory and Its Emergence

Collective memories are intersubjectively shared interpretations of a poignant common past—often some kind of traumatic event—with a high degree of affect.[2] They are a kind of interpreted knowledge, what James Wertsch calls "mediated narratives,"[3] simultaneously determined publicly, but ultimately subjective in that they are lodged in individuals' minds. Any objective or public "text," narrative, symbol, or memorial is ultimately meaningful only insofar as it becomes relevant in the mental structures of individuals. Collective memory matters because it is a primary means by which the past affects political culture—the inherited sets of beliefs, practices and traditions, and especially values

---

[2] See Maurice Halbwachs, *On Collective Memory* (Chicago, IL: University of Chicago Press, 1992); James W. Pennebaker, Dario Paez, and Bernard Rimé (eds), *Collective Memory of Political Events: Social Psychological Perspectives* (Mahwah: Lawrence Erlbaum, 1997).

[3] James V. Wertsch, *Voices of Collective Remembering* (New York: Cambridge University Press, 2002).

of a given group that provides a sense of identity and subjective order that generates meaningful action.[4]

Memories also constrain, by creating taboos and cutting off certain paths of action—what is remembered presupposes that something is also forgotten. Moreover, collectivities—like individuals—can only accommodate a finite number of memories and there are ever-present processes of prioritization, filtering, and removal, exacerbated by the intrusion of more recent historical events and the memories based on them. Some actors or groups will benefit from a specific memory; others will benefit from forgetting. Thus, it cannot be assumed that collective memories will retain emotional intensity and political cultural influence in perpetuity. Memories must be actively created, re-created, and defended from these tendencies or explicit strategies of forgetting and supersession.

Nevertheless, there is ample evidence for the longevity and intergenerational transference of collective memory (e.g., Northern Ireland, Serbia). Historical events and the memories based on them also engender path-dependent effects on institutions and behavior—for example, the extreme reluctance of postwar German policymakers to support the use of force abroad or sensitivity of Israeli policymakers to perceived existential threats. Another factor facilitating the continual re-creation of memory over generations is the institutionalization of an infrastructure of documentation, commemoration, and civil societal organizations that are dedicated to keeping the memory alive.

With the aim of achieving more analytical precision, authors have differentiated among (sub)types of collective memory. James Young, for example, speaks of collected memories: "the many discrete memories that are gathered into common memorial spaces and assigned common meaning. A society's memory, in this context, might be regarded as an aggregate collection of its members' many, often competing memories." Jeffrey Olick distinguishes collected and collective memories with the former denoting the aggregation of individual experiences in a society operative at the mass level and the latter a kind of "general will" produced by elites. Even more useful is Aleida Assmann's typology of communicative, generational, collective and cul-

---

[4] Jeffrey Alexander and Steven Seidman (eds.), *Culture and Society: Contemporary Debates* (New York, NY: Cambridge University Press, 1990).

tural versions of shared memories, whose societal breadth, institutionalized depth and longevity vary.[5]

Elite agents, who represent and advocate specific memories, are
crucial for their construction, dissemination, and defense from com-
petitors. Such privileged interpreters and socializing agents include
politicians, journalists, religious and societal leaders, artists, teachers,
intellectuals, and so on. Especially central for memory issues is the
agency of a "critical community,"[6] a politically and morally engaged
elite motivated by the existential gravity of the events on which the
memories are based. Such elite actors advocate, justify, and validate
a politically acceptable memory regime, the "public transcript" of
memory.[7] How these leaders interpret, package, and assert meaning,
as well as the various lessons and values they connect to the memory
greatly influence average citizens.[8] Conversely, key elite interpreters
also respond at times to the memories and opinions from below (collected memories), either from individuals or from particularly aware
and interested groups whose memories and interpretations these actors
aggregate and represent.[9] Finally, although memories can differentiate
groups in unexpected ways, there is often a left right partisan politics
of memory with the left usually advocating for more memory and the
right for less.

---

[5] James Young, *The Texture of Memory: Holocaust Memorials and Meaning*
(New Haven, CT: Yale University Press, 1993), ix; Jeffrey Olick, "Collective
Memories: The Two Cultures," *Sociological Theory*, vol. 17, no. 3, (1999):
333–348; Aleida Assman and Ute Frevert, *Geschichtsvergessenheit—Geschich-
tsversessenheit: vom Umgang mit deutschen Vergangenheiten nach 1945* (Stuttgart: Deutsche Verlags-Anstalt, 1999).

[6] Thomas Rochon, *Culture Moves: Ideas, Activism and Changing Values* (Princeton: Princeton University Press, 1998).

[7] James C. Scott, *Domination and the Arts of Resistance: Hidden Transcripts*
(New Haven: Yale University Press, 1990).

[8] This point is made more generally for public opinion by John Zaller, *The
Nature and Origins of Mass Opinion* (New York: Cambridge University Press,
1992).

[9] There may be a gap between the public transcript or elite discourse and a
hidden, mass one. Such a disjunction, as in the larger political culture model, is one potential source of change when some members of the elite shift
their conceptions to better represent or correspond to popular discourses
(See Scott above).

Because memory influences culture, and, in turn, culture affects political institutions, policies, and behavior, it matters immensely what memories circulate publicly, how they are framed, and which ones emerge to actually influence outcomes. Actors seek as much acceptance as possible for their views and are therefore incentivized to increase the breadth and deepen the intensity with which memories are held. The ultimate goal is to achieve maximum soft or discursive power; to make the preferred memories a taken-for-granted background consensus, orthodoxy, or Gramscian cultural hegemony—understood as "maximally institutionalized norms."[10]

There are at least seven interrelated factors that can explain why and how memory comes to the fore in some countries and not in others, as well as why memory emerges at a specific point in time. The first is the magnitude of the historical trauma. Events like the Holocaust in which half of world Jewry was murdered, the genocide and ethnic cleansing of the Armenians in Turkey during and after World War I (1 to 1.5 million deaths out of a prewar population in the Ottoman Empire of 2 million); the 15–20 million Soviet citizens that perished during Stalin's reign before World War II,[11] and the 40 million Chinese who died during Mao's time in power are illustrative of such traumatic events. They have the societal breadth necessary for a given memory to achieve the possibility of hegemony—"collective memories are most likely to be formed and maintained about events that represent significant long-term changes to people's lives."[12]

The second set of factors that explain the emergence of memory come from the vast corpus of psychological and psychoanalytic literature about coming to terms with the past. To simplify, successfully working through a trauma to regain a semblance of normality or health entails discourse (Breuer and Freud's "talking cure") and especially

---

[10] Robert Bocock, *Hegemony* (London, UK: Tavistock Publications, 1986), 11; See also David Laitin, *Hegemony and Culture: Politics and Religious Change Among the Yoruba* (Chicago, IL: University of Chicago Press, 1986); Ian Lustick, *Unsettled States, Disputed Lands: Britain and Ireland, France and Algeria, Israel and the West Bank* (Ithaca, NY: Cornell University Press, 1993).

[11] See Timothy Snyder, *Bloodlands: Europe Between Hitler and Stalin* (New York: Basic Books, 2010).

[12] Pennebaker et al, *Collective Memory of Political Events*, 17.

recognition by a collective entity such as a family or the nation that it is more than an individual tragedy, that it has provoked a deep lesion in a broken community. Such insights are the very motivation behind truth and justice commissions in many places, and provide much of the justification behind various monetary compensation or reparation agreements that recognize the harm inflicted.[13]

A third variable relates to the existence of mechanisms that allow the memory to be absorbed by a given population, as well as individuals to disseminate and construct the memory. As Wertsch writes: "Instead of being grounded in direct, immediate experience of events, the sort of collective memory at issue . . . is based on textual resources provided by others."[14] A modicum of development, education and democracy is necessary: literacy and at least a nascent press, civil society and educational system are preconditions for collective memory. There must be committed and visible leaders (a critical community) to construct the "textual resources" and share them with others in the group.[15]

Fourth, collective memory may be delayed if the victimized or their representatives are not present in the post-traumatic political system and if they do not feel safe enough to speak up. Memories of the Holocaust in postwar West Germany, the Armenian genocide in Turkey, or Japanese atrocities against other Asian civilians during World War II (in contrast to the internal victims in the South American cases), were impeded by the (relative) absence of the victimized groups in those countries. The impetus had to come from outside and such an exogenous critical community had to struggle for voice and allies within the political system, a real challenge before the pervasive globalization and "mediatization" of the last twenty years. More generally, there must be some basic freedoms and liberties (press, speech, organization) to make such individuals and their mission possible—as well as public spaces, civil society, in which to exercise voice. Of course,

---

[13] See Theodor Adorno, "What Does Coming to Terms with the Past Mean?" in G. Hartman (ed.), *Bitburg in Moral and Political Discourse* (Bloomington, IN: Indiana University Press, 1986); Dominick LaCapra, *Representing the Holocaust: History, Theory, Trauma* (Ithaca, NY: Cornell University Press, 1994).

[14] Wertsch, *Voices of Collective Remembering*, 5.

[15] See James W. Booth, "The Unforgotten: Memories of Justice," *American Political Science Review* 95 (4) 2001, 777–792.

there are recursive interactions among factors: an operative civil society is necessary to gain voice, empowerment and memory which, once spurred, can further reinforce and strengthen civil society and interpersonal trust.

Fifth, the traumatic events or episodes must have concluded and the actual perpetrators must have passed from the scene (e.g., the death of Franco or Mao). There must also be a degree of openness, freedom, and liberalization in the political system. Yet, even when the events have ended and the political system has opened up—some democratic consolidation has occurred so that the return of the perpetrators and their regime is considered unlikely—it usually takes years for the affected individuals to feel secure and trusting enough of the political system to voice their pain and demands for restitution in public. Also salient in this context is the extent to which the society was complicit with or supportive of the outgoing regime and its crimes— the more pervasive the complicity, the longer it will take for victims to come forward.

The type and nature of the transition from the authoritarian system and the relative strength of incumbents and opposition during and after this process are the sixth factor. Memory discourses will be more constrained (also because the requisite security that victims and their representatives need to advocate for more open memory discourses will not be operative) where the transition takes the form of a "transplacement" or through a pact/agreement that allows authoritarian incumbents to retain more power and influence (reserve domains or authoritarian enclaves), as compared to a more radical process of replacement or "revolution." Examples of this type of partial change in which previous incumbents retain a degree of power (or at least assurances that they will not be prosecuted) include Chile and Spain. Nevertheless, the likelihood of strong push-back by the vanquished may be greater in a replacement scenario if transitional justice measures and memory construction are deeper and quicker (e.g., Argentina in the late 1980s).

A seventh and final set of factors that affects the delayed emergence of memory and processes of working through a past is connected directly to the post-transition adoption of strategies emphasizing silence toward the past and reintegration of those previously compromised. Memory must wait for those who constructed this period of silence to also lose legitimacy and ultimately power—examples are the passing of Konrad Adenauer in West Germany and the retirement of Carlos Menem in Argentina. There is also a dimension of generational replacement, with the entry onto the political scene of younger, less compromised, or less invested cohorts who are willing to investigate the past and let memory emerge. This arguably happened with José Luis Rodríguez Zapatero in Spain and Néstor Kirchner in Argentina, though the magnitude of the trauma also appears to be a factor in this context: the greater the trauma, the sooner the emergence of memory. Moreover, whether individuals were victimized by civil strife or by foreign aggressors matters. In Spain, the two sides in the Civil War were broadly balanced and trauma was perceived to have been reciprocally inflicted—a situation that probably delayed the emergence of memory and highlighted generational change as a necessary condition for the emergence of a new memory environment.

One exception to these dynamics is certain truth and reconciliation initiatives, where such discourses of the oppressed occur almost immediately. Specific circumstances can also speed up the process, including the presence of an international "guarantee" of democratic stability such as in the former Yugoslavia, and differently, international anti-apartheid opinion toward South Africa, or of relatively evenly balanced groups of victims and perpetrators as in Spain. Many countries that went through a traumatic past had a brief flourish of memory and working through the past (the Nuremberg Trials, the Tokyo Tribunal, the *nunca mas* report in Argentina) around the moment of transition to democracy (resembling Truth and Reconciliation Commissions), which was then followed by an "institutionalist" period of silence (see next section). Most of these trials or commissions focused on very specific and demonstrable criminal acts, as opposed to the broader issues of societal culpability and regime support, and many were limited to prosecuting top decision makers so as to limit the likelihood of a societal backlash (e.g., resentments created over the trials of low-ranking East German border guards in the 1990s).

In sum, the emergence of memory is based on the interaction of multiple factors: a degree of freedom to enable voice and dissemination, the magnitude of the trauma/event, the degree of relative power, the nature of the transition and the strategies employed in the initial post-transition years. This combination of factors helps to account for many cases of memory surfacing years after the end of the un-free regime: from the well-studied cases of postwar Germany (repression and silence in the 1950s, discursive opening in the 1960s, memory boom from the mid 1980s onward); to the unexpected cases such as Spain, which needed twenty-five to thirty years after Franco's death to begin to confront the memory of the civil war; and in Latin American cases like Chile and particularly Argentina—where the return of memory over the last decade has largely been dependent on the partisan balance of power and the ascendance of left-wing Peronists around Néstor and Cristina Kirchner.

The following table (Table 1.) summarizes the relevance of these factors in four important cases of post-authoritarian memories:

TABLE 1.

	Germany	Spain	Argentina	Chile
Previous Regime Type	Totalitarian	Proto-Fascist/ Authoritarian (post 1945)	Military Authoritarian (with a totalitarian edge)	Military Authoritarian
Magnitude of crimes/trauma	High (20,000,000+ killed)	High (500,000 killed)	Medium (13,000+ killed)	Medium (3,000 killed)
Years after transition before emergence of memory	20+	25-30	15-20	10+
Type of transition	Replacement (externally imposed)	Pacted	Replacement	Pacted
Authoritarian enclaves	No	Some	Some	Yes
Predominantly internal victims	No	Yes	Yes	Yes
Degree of societal complicity	High	High	Low	Medium
Initial flourish of memory	Yes	No	Yes	No

	Germany	Spain	Argentina	Chile
Early institutional-ist strategies	Yes	Yes	Yes	Yes
Critical community	External, after 1960s internal; initially leftist	Weak, after 2000s leftist	Strong (especially from Peronist Left)	Weak/medium
Generational change important	Yes	Yes	Partially	No/partially
Internal presence of victims after transition	No	Yes	Yes	Yes
Strength of civil society and media	Strong by late 1950s (10 years after transition)	Strong from early 1980s (7 years after transition)	Strong (immediately)	Strong by mid 1990s (7 years after transition)
Length of Dictator-ship (years)	12 (+ 4 occupa-tion; GDR 40)	38 (1939–1977)	7 (1976–1983)	17 (1973–1990)

III. Memory and Democracy

Numerous authors have alluded to the connection between memory and democracy. When referring to the deepening democratization of West Germany in the 1960s and 1970s, Jeffrey Herf writes that "daring more democracy required more memory and more justice."[16] Memory often emerges as part of the public coping process in the context of a free, pluralist regime that has reached a degree of consolidation and institutionalized stability. Memory flourishes in this setting because transparency is central to legitimacy and because democracies are by definition transparent and quasi-therapeutic political systems. As

---

[16] Jeffrey Herf, *Divided Memory: The Nazi Past in the Two Germanys* (Cambridge, MA: Harvard University Press, 1997), 7.

Michael Mann puts it: "(R)egimes that are actually perpetrating murderous cleansing are never democratic, since that would be a contradiction in terms."[17] But what is this connection with democracy?

Anne Sa'adah has provided one of the most powerful explanations for the emergence of memory and the innate connection between memory and democracy. She argues that after a traumatic episode or experience with a human rights-violating regime, most countries initially pursue minimalist "institutionalist" coping strategies aimed at reestablishing "thin" trust-as-reliability (the new regime will not be overthrown, the trauma will not begin again). This is achieved by "letting the past be" and reintegrating individuals compromised by the previous regime, although the immediate prosecution of top decision makers and blatant murderers is common. Sa'adah shows how pervasive such strategies were in places like postwar West Germany, post-Vichy France and the newly independent United States. Timothy Garton Ash once called this the "Spanish approach" (contrasted with the German model) and notes how widespread such strategies have been in post-communist Eastern Europe.[18] As Sa'adah suggests, however, a "thicker" trust-as-trustworthiness is eventually necessary, one that requires maximalist "culturalist" discursive processes, where memory both emerges and is central to the production of such reconciliatory trust.[19] Yet, achieving the "thin" version of trust is what helps to increase the relative position of the victims, finally empowered to push the "thicker," more therapeutic version that they need. Moreover, only democracies (or highly liberalized authoritarian systems) have the civil society that makes memory discourses and elite agency possible. Finally, democracies require (a degree of) transparency and the lack of discursive limitations. Thus, it would be impossible to prevent the emergence of memories under democratic circumstances without jeopardizing the legitimacy and stability of the democratic regime itself.

---

[17] Michael Mann, *The Dark Side of Democracy: Explaining Ethnic Cleansing* (Cambridge, UK: Cambridge University Press, 2005), 4.

[18] Timothy Garton Ash, "Trials, Purges or History Lessons: Treating a Difficult Past in Post-Communist Europe," in Jan-Werner Müller (ed.), *Memory and Power in Post-War Europe: Studies in the Presence of the Past* (Cambridge, UK: Cambridge University Press, 2003).

[19] M. Anne Sa'adah. *Germany's Second Chance: Trust, Justice and Democratization* (Cambridge, MA: Harvard University Press, 1998).

Moreover, only liberal democracies allow the presence of multiple memories. Their very essence is that, just as there are many interests to reconcile in the present, so there are different memories regarding the past. There is no teleological unfolding in a democracy because there are many pasts and the future is unknown. Autocracies have a fundamentally different approach, though the intensity and exclusivity of the vision vary depending on the nature of the regime. The more radical and totalitarian, the more thoroughly exclusivist is the vision—not only about the past (there can be only one valid interpretation of the past under such circumstances), but also about the future. This exclusivist element is the key to differentiating democratic and nondemocratic memory regimes.

Indeed, all political systems have memory regimes. Despite the attention memory has received in the postwar German case, for instance, it is often forgotten that the Nazis fostered, abused, but also greatly benefited from a strong collective memory—Germany's "internal defeat" or "stab-in-the-back" (purportedly by socialists and Jews) in World War I. Mussolini's Italy, Imperial Japan, the Soviet Union, authoritarian regimes in the Balkans and communist China are similarly all examples of state-constructed (Wertsch) collective memories, obviously and often very effectively supporting the stability of dictatorial rule.

The dynamics of memories and memory regimes discussed above are agnostic toward regime type and can be operative in all cases. In unfree systems, elite agency—in the state, party, or authoritarian coalition—and validation of public transcripts of memory are extreme. There can be extensive competition over acceptable history and memories at least within the ruling class. The crucial variable is the availability of a meaningful structure with which an individual can explain and thus work though a trauma. All of the examples cited provided very powerful and accessible meanings, usually some kind of nationalist affirmation (even in the communist cases) that sanctified war and justified repression and control. Indicative are the terms used in these regimes. The Soviet Union (and now Russia) referred to World War II as the "Great Patriotic War" and the communist regime in China deems the period 1937–1945 the "Chinese People's Anti-Japanese War of Resistance," the "Anti-Japanese War of Resistance," or the "Eight Years' War of Resistance." Decades of research on nationalism as a kind of secular or political religion, replete with evocative memories have strongly substantiated just how effective and legitimating such doctrines are.[20]

Unfree (exclusivist) political systems impose severe limits on memory. Autocratic elites only foster collective memories that are based on the search for and identification of enemies harming the self. The "Other" here could be an external foe, such as Nazi Germany invading the USSR or the Japanese in China, or a "vanquished" internal foe, such as a previous regime or a "ruling" minority, such as the Chinese in Indonesia. It bears repeating that the interpretation of historical events embedded in these kinds of memories, is so tendentious that the best descriptive term is not collective memory, but myth. These myths focus solely on "heroic triumphs" (some factual, others fictional) for which the regime takes credit. On the other hand, autocratic regimes neither admit nor foster memory of traumas they themselves have unleashed on their citizens (Mao, Stalin, Franco). Instead, they constantly blame others—enemies, fifth columnists, external powers, "vermin," "worms," and so on.

Under these circumstances, the processes of working through the past that occur under unfree regimes are necessarily partial—or implemented in a fashion that only serves to impose a single explanation and/or excludes and delegitimizes any alternative remembrance—so that the overall legitimizing and therapeutic function of memory ranges from nonexistent to minimal. Of course, more "honest" alternative memories do not so simply dissipate and are often maintained in the private sphere. Such family memories constitute a nascent counternarrative to officially sanctioned memories and are potentially destabilizing forces. There may also be institutions (churches) and diasporic or exile communities that serve as depositories of these alternative memories. Unfree regimes place such a focus on education to implant their own hegemonic discourse and to eliminate other discourses.

We do not question the existence of hegemonic discourses under any regime, but in democratic ones these can be challenged, amended, even overturned. Exclusivist memory regimes struggle against alternative explanations because their very legitimacy depends on a specific

---

[20] See Emilio Gentile, *The Sacralization of Politics in Fascist Italy*, (Cambridge, MA: Harvard University Press, 1996

reading of history. Such regimes actively endeavor to censor and pre-vent the emergence of such counter-memories (discursive coercion that often further fuels counter-memories) and generally such regimes must be wary of having too much memory, as it necessarily begs questions the regime will not or cannot answer. The rulers of China have learned this lesson in the recent past. They had facilitated a wave of anti-Japa-nese protests in 2004–2005, trying to use the nationalism unleashed as a tool for relegitimization of communist rule in an increasingly plural-istic, capitalistic, and unequal country. Yet, they soon learned that the energies, precedents, and organizational networks produced could be and were turned on the regime itself—leading to the cessation of offi-cial anti-Japanese rhetoric.[21]

Thus, memory indeed can arise in both free and unfree politi-cal systems. Yet, political and discursive dynamics, constraints and sheer self-interest mean that memory discourses in unfree systems are extremely tendentious and partial. The public spaces (civil society), elite actors and necessary discourses (legal, therapeutic) simply cannot exist, so working through processes are never complete and traumas linger (often eventually delegitimizing the regime itself). At a mini-mum, although memory can be present in unfree systems, it can never flourish because it is inevitably partial and cannot correct itself. There may not be an exclusive connection between memory and democracy, but both phenomena do share elements of debate, pluralism, transpar-ency and self-correction.

Finally, we must also mention international factors. Often ignored as more generally in the literature on democracy and democratization, they may not be central, but they are certainly relevant—especially where domestic actors are weak or still traumatized. In many cases, the "critical community" and impetus for memory construction comes from the outside. Seminal examples are Jewish communities espe-cially in the United States and Israel that (for various internal reasons) became vociferous advocates for Holocaust memory in Germany, and the Armenian Diaspora in the West pushing Turkey to come to terms with the 1915 genocide. Returning exiles—many of them embedded in university and intellectual circles in those countries that took them in

---

[21] Joseph Kahn, "China Is Pushing and Scripting Japan Protests," *New York Times*, April 15, 2005.

(Sweden in the case of Chileans)—have played a similar role in post-authoritarian South American cases.

The international Zeitgeist also matters. The 1950s and 1960s, for example, witnessed the ascendency of anti-communist mind-sets for many policymakers. Given the resonance or at least the ambivalence toward the communist alternative among many intellectuals at that time, policymakers were wary of advocating too much democracy because they feared that the foes of capitalism might be empowered. Only after the 1970s (coinciding with the Third Wave of democracy) and especially after the demise of the Soviet Union, did liberal democracy become the "only game in town." Accompanying this ideational triumph of liberal democracy (and the many governmental and non-governmental institutions that made democracy promotion major policy goals), was a human rights and international law discourse that supported transitional justice and transparent memory construction efforts in many countries. "Thicker" globalization has also increased the pressures for transparency and enhanced communication, both of which have aided the memory construction processes.

Furthermore, ever since the "Third Wave" of democracy crested in the late 1990s, "democratic fatigue" arguably has set in, as well as the partial rehabilitation of non-democratic alternatives (e.g., China, Russia) and the strengthening of hybrid authoritarian regimes. Many observers no longer consider the proliferation of democracy, human rights, and the rule of law to be inevitable. As revealed by the varied responses to the post-2010 "Arab Spring," many international actors are also less consistent in their pronouncements and policies. There appears to be a new-found sense of realism and a reprioritization of stability over democracy (e.g., Egypt). These subtle shifts in the Zeitgeist (either globally or regionally) create a less salubrious context for actors advocating democratization, memory, or transitional justice.

So far in this chapter, we have discussed cases where the recovery of memory and implementation of transitional justice have accompanied a transition to democracy. We have argued for a connection between these processes, though we also recognize the varying degrees of "exclusivism" depending on regime type. This is not the place to emphasize how totalitarian and authoritarian regimes are in many ways different—the former atomize, remake and seek total control over society, while the latter prefer demobilization and pursue a strategy of cooptation. The differences between the regime types are real enough. There is quite a range between the Holocaust and the extermination strategy of Nazi Germany that took tens of millions of lives, the civil war and post-civil war repression in Franco's Spain during which 500,000 are thought to have died, and the more recent Argentine and Chilean cases where estimates of those murdered or "disappeared" were 15,000 and 3,000, respectively.

But, there are commonalities between the German and Spanish experiences, as well as certain parallels with the Argentine and Chilean cases. They all involved breakdowns of democracy and civil strife where the objective (and not just of the winner, but sometimes of the loser or losers) was the destruction of the other. Thus, Juan Linz and Alfred Stepan referred to Argentina as a "hierarchically led military regime . . . with a totalitarian edge."[22] The Franco regime lasted nearly 40 years, but the worst atrocities occurred during the Civil War (1936–1939) and in the years immediately following it. In Germany, the emergence of democracy and the beginning of the process of recovery of a more plural memory (in its thin version) came after the violence of the Weimar and Nazi eras and what many consider to be a long European civil war (1914–1945). Although the Federal Republic of Germany underwent its transition to democracy in the late 1940s and 1950s, the Spanish transition would not come until three decades later, with the Argentine and Chilean ones to follow in what became the Third Wave. Nevertheless, the deeper version of democracy and memory would take much longer in all cases. In our analysis, we have emphasized the affinity between democracy and inclusionary memory regimes, and we have also followed Sa'adah in distinguishing between minimalist "institutionalist" coping strategies of the early phase of the transition and the deeper, more robust strategies that emerge when (multiple) memories are recovered and reestablished, and in their interaction produce more complete and less illusory (albeit still strongly debated) versions of the past, while also correspondingly enhancing reconciliatory trust.[23]

---

[22] Juan J. Linz and Alfred Stepan, *Problems of Democratic Transition and Consolidation: Southern Europe, South America and Post-Communist Europe* (Baltimore, MD: Johns Hopkins University Press, 1996), 190.

[23] Lily Gardner Feldman, *Germany's Foreign Policy of Reconciliation: From Enmity to Amity* (Lanham, MD: Rowman and Littlefield, 2012).

❖

We are now ready to apply some of the "lessons" learned both from our theoretical discussion and our analysis of the cases we have considered above to Cuba. This more speculative exercise analyzes the obstacles and prospects for the recovery of memory (and democracy) there. In so doing, we shall consider the nature of the incumbent Cuban regime and discuss how the variables we examined earlier might apply to this case. The variables highlighted in this section differ somewhat from those we have previously discussed in the context of post-transition cases because of the resilience of the Castro regime in Cuba. Hence, we emphasize both the historical and memory discourses that have been articulated by the regime as well as the societal actors (such as the Catholic Church) that may play a crucial role in the post-Castro era.

IV. Memory and the Cuban Future

Memory is how we remember and interpret the past—it also provides a guide and justification for how to act in the future. Moreover, how the claim to memory and the past is expressed tells us a great deal about political intentions and perspectives. The following quotations exemplify how Fidel Castro has laid claim to the mantle of the "Revolution"—the century-long struggle for independence that he asserts culminated with his January 1959 seizure of power and in whose name he subsequently embarked on the radical transformation of Cuban society.

> "The Republic was not freed in 1895 . . . . The Revolution did not take place in 1933 and was frustrated by its enemies. (This time) we can say—and it is with joy that we do so—that in the four centuries since our country was founded—this will be the first time that we are entirely free. . ."[24] (January 3, 1959)

> "(T)here has only been one Revolution in Cuba—the one which Carlos Manuel de Céspedes began on October 1968. . . . (It is)

---

[24] http://lanic.utexas.edu/project/castro/db/1959/19590103.html.

the result of 100 years of struggle . . . Marxism-Leninism . . .
came to complete the arsenal of the country's revolutionary and
historical experience . . . (to allow us) to become a single force.
. . . For when we say people we are talking about revolutionary
people; when we talk of people willing to fight and to die, we do
not think of the worms, nor the handful of rascal groups which
we see. We are then thinking of those who have the legitimate
right to call themselves Cuban."[25] (October 11, 1968)

"And so there is an enemy that can indeed be called universal.
And if ever in the history of mankind there was really a universal
enemy, an enemy whose attitude and whose acts are of concern
to the whole world, and in one way or another perpetrate aggression against the whole world, that really universal enemy is Yankee imperialism."[26] (January 13, 1968)

These citations capture the essence of Castro's all-encompassing and
exclusivist vision of collective memory and provide the meta-historical
justification for the imposition of a totalitarian regime in Cuba after
1959.[27] It is a political and moral vision that weaves together nationalist and Marxist narratives—two (apparently contradictory) traditions affirming a teleological unfolding that only the enlightened few
can identify and for whom it serves as a guiding light. This vision has
a totalitarian logic that is premised on permanent struggle or revolution; the process needs enemies just as much as it needs heroes. As
Castro declared in January 1961, several weeks before the U.S.-spon-
sored Bay of Pigs invasion: "The Revolution needs to do battle. Battle
is what makes revolutions strong. . . A revolution that is not attacked
might not be a true revolution in the first place. Moreover, a revolution that did not have an enemy before it would run the risk of falling
asleep, of weakening itself. Revolutions need to fight, revolutions need
to do battle; revolutions, like armies, need to have an enemy in front of

---

[25] http://lanic.utexas.edu/project/castro/db/1968/19681011.html.
[26] http://lanic.utexas.edu/project/castro/db/1968/19680113.html.
[27] The discussion in this and subsequent paragraphs draws on Rafael Rojas,
      Isla sin Fin—Contribución a la Crítica del Nacionalismo Cubano (Miami, FL:
      Ediciones Universal, 1998), 73–104.

them in order to become more courageous and self-sacrificing!"[28] In this pugilistic worldview, "worms" (this is a translation of the epithet *gusanos* that was used indistinguishably against exiles and/or those who opposed the regime) and "rascals" join the "universal enemy" (Yankee imperialism) as subjects to be extirpated. Speaking of these "worms" in 1962, Fidel Castro said: "What do the ones who left signify? It is the same thing as squeezing a boil. Those who have left are the pus, the pus that was expelled when the Cuban Revolution squeezed the society. How good the body feels when pus is eliminated!"[29]

Just as there was no alternative to one-party rule and the ruthless suppression of enemies and "worms," there was no possible interpretation of Cuban history other than the one Castro insisted had been inexorably unfolding since the first nationalist insurrection in 1868. In collective memory, he transformed the heroes of Cuban independence—Carlos Manuel de Céspedes, José Martí, and Antonio Maceo—into men whose views were compatible and bonded with his own, their sacrifices intelligible and given meaning because they unfolded into his own victory. The only trouble with this approach is that these men were neither Marxist nor imbued with a totalitarian vision. For example, Martí was a complex thinker whose brilliance as a political strategist, Lillian Guerra has rightly noted, came from his ability to forge a discourse of social unity at a time when "Cubans had drastically, almost irreconcilably, different ideas of what Cuban society should be like after the (revolutionary) war."[30] Martí was a nationalist who stood and warned against U.S. imperialism, but beyond a commitment to a republican form of government, he did not advocate any specific political or economic model. He was certainly not an advocate of a centralized and intolerant political order; and, during his many years in exile in the United States, he displayed a pluralist outlook and

---

[28] Cited in Lillian Guerra, "'To Condemn the Revolution Is to Condemn Christ': Radicalization, Moral Redemption, and the Sacrifice of Civil Society in Cuba, 1960," *Hispanic American Historical Review* 89 (1), 91.

[29] Quoted in Tom Gjelten, "Cuban Days: The Inscrutable Nation," *World Affairs* (Summer 2009) from a speech to Cuban intellectuals in 1962. See http://www.worldaffairsjournal.org/article/cuban-days-inscrutable-nation.

[30] Lillian Guerra, *The Myth of José Martí—Conflicting Nationalisms in Early Twentieth-Century Cuba* (Chapel Hill, NC: University of North Carolina Press, 2005), 6.

worked with people of many different points of view who were, none-theless, working toward an independent Cuba.

Historians will long debate why, in the years after 1959, so many Cubans abandoned their sense of political restraint and turned themselves over to Fidel Castro's oversized and quixotic vision of creating the New Man and scaling the heights of communism, all within the span of a generation. Certainly, Cuba was a country whose sense of nation and statehood developed late (compared to other Latin American countries) and was accompanied by a deep sense of nationalist grievance against the United States. Cuban nationalism did not develop until the late nineteenth century, and when the opportunity for national independence finally came, it arrived stillborn. The Cuban War of Independence that began in 1895 became the Spanish-American War in 1898—the change in name indicated whose narrative emerged victorious at the turn of the century. Truncated sovereignty—in the form of the Platt Amendment that was included in the 1901 Constitution and gave the United States the right to intervene militarily on the island at its discretion—and a rapidly expanding U.S. economic presence followed. If limited sovereignty marked the post-independence period, so did the emergence of a limited, if not defective democracy.[31] For the first decades after independence (1902–1933), Cuban politics was dominated by *caudillos* and traditional landed elites. The Revolution of 1933 overthrew President Gerardo Machado and ushered in a new period marked by the abrogation of the Platt Amendment (1934) and the establishment of a new Constitution (1940) as well as the emergence of modern political parties and an incipient civil society. The Constitution of 1940 was a progressive charter that in many ways resembled Germany's Weimar Constitution (1919) and ushered in a period of democratic institutional development.

Just as Weimar would come to be regarded as "the republic without republicans, the democracy without democrats," so the post-1940 Cuban transition to liberal and constitutional democracy found its path beset by numerous problems. Its politics was marked by patholo-

---

[31] For analysis of the interplay between Cuban nationalism and U.S. expansionism, see Louis A. Pérez, *The War of 1898: The United States and Cuba* (Chapel Hill, NC: University of North Carolina Press, 1998) and by the same author, *On Becoming Cuban: Identity, Nationality, and Culture* (Chapel Hill, NC: University of North Carolina Press, 2008).

gies of political violence, venality, and rampant corruption. Intellectual elites lamented these developments, expressing growing concern and frustration over the failure of the national project to congeal. Fulgencio Batista severely wounded the democratic republic with his February 1952 *coup d'état*, and Castro, whose insurrectionary movement (the 26th of July Movement) had claimed the restoration of the Constitution of 1940 to be its objective, killed it once he seized power.

Fidel Castro came to believe (and, in any case, so justified his rule) that there was some unfolding logic to these events—one that made his January 1959 seizure of power inevitable and desirable. Few would argue with the proposition that Cuban society, like so many others in the twentieth century, had a sensibility supporting nationalist discourse and had elites who were extravagant in its use. The final stanzas of the national anthem declare that "to die for the *patria* was to live" and the purported degeneration of the Cuban nation was a favored topic of the Cuban intellectual elite. Nevertheless, whatever nationalist sensibility may have existed in Cuba and despite the depth of outrage over the existence of a corrupt elite, there was no pre-determined path that led either to the collapse of the older order and the rise of Castro or to his adoption of a radical, totalitarian path. Whatever totalitarian intentions Castro harbored, he kept them to himself during the guerrilla insurgency, preferring instead to condemn the illegality of the Batista coup and to emphasize his commitment to support the restoration of the 1940 constitution.[32] Few imagined the radical turn that events would take after 1959.

Castro moved quickly to fill the vacuum left when Batista fled the country on New Year's Eve of 1958. Within the first two years, the new regime had consolidated control and embarked on a radical agenda focused on the radical overhaul of Cuban society. Repression, mobilization, and militarization were evident in all aspects of Cuban life—they included summary executions and sham trials, as well as the organization of production brigades in agriculture to sending high school and university students into the countryside in literacy campaigns. The emblematic spokesman for this effort to remake Cuban society was Ernesto (Che) Guevara. His essay, "Socialism and Man in

---

[32] See, for example, Fidel Castro's "History Will Absolve Me" speech from October 16, 1953. http://www.granma.cubaweb.cu/marti-moncada/jm01.html.

Cuba"[33] stressed the need to apply "incentives and pressures of a certain intensity . . . not only on the defeated class but also on individuals of the victorious class." Expressing the totalist mind-set, he went on to insist: "New generations will come that will be free of original sin . . . Our task is to prevent the current generation (of youth) . . . from becoming perverted and from perverting new generations. . . . Youth . . . is especially important because it is malleable clay from which the new person can be built with none of the old defects." He was invariably unapologetic about the need to employ violence. Addressing the United Nations General Assembly in October 1964, he declared: "We must say here what is a known truth (that) we have always expressed before the world: firing squad executions, yes, we have executed; we are executing and we will continue to execute as long as is necessary. Our struggle is a struggle to the death."[34]

The post-1959 drive to create a New Man and abolish capitalism fragmented and traumatized the Cuban nation. Over the next fifty years, the country suffered a demographic hemorrhage as successive waves of immigrants left the country.[35] Nearly 15 percent of the population (in 2012 it stands at 11.3 million) emigrated, and many more would have otherwise abandoned their homeland, if they could have. More than 250,000 persons are on the waiting list for visas in the U.S. Interests Section in Havana. The outflow intensified after the disintegration of the Soviet Union and the onset of a severe economic crisis. Between 1994 and 2009 more than 500,000 Cubans left their homeland—a statistic that did not include those who departed illegally.[36] Neither did this total include the thousands who surely perished

---

[33] See the full text of Ernesto Guevara, "Socialism and Man in Cuba" (March 1965) in http://www.marxists.org/archive/guevara/1965/03/man-socialism. htm.

[34] See his December 1964 speech to the United Nations General Assembly in http://www.marxists.org/archive/guevara/1964/12/11.htm

[35] For a thorough and insightful account, see Silvia Pedraza, *Political Disaffection in Cuba's Revolution and Exodus* (Cambridge: Cambridge University Press, 2007.

[36] Haroldo Dilla Alfonso employs data from the National Statistics Office (ONE) in "Hemorragia demográfica," *Cuba Encuentro*, 11 July 2011, http://www.cubaencuentro.com/opinion/articulos/hemorragia-demografica-265215.

while trying to cross the perilous Florida Straits on flimsy rafts.[37] In January 2013, the Cuban government loosened restrictions for those who wished to travel abroad with the result that in the first ten months of the year more than 226,000 Cubans left the island (compared with more than 176,000 during the same period a year earlier).[38] The new policy aimed to diminish popular displeasure with previous tight exit controls and formed part of more general effort to "normalize" Cuban society. Another objective was to palliate domestic unemployment and potentially increasing remittances from abroad. The changes were unlikely immediately to stanch the flow of those who sought to leave the island permanently. Only the prospect of sustained economic growth would eventually have that effect. Earlier in this chapter we emphasized that societal traumas must eventually be confronted in the process of recuperating memory and democracy. How long a given regime has been in power matters in this regard, especially if the perpetrators of such traumas are no longer on the scene. The totalitarian experience has had profound political, social, and economic consequences for Cuba. But it is perhaps in the spiritual or psychological sphere where the impact has been most severe. Fear, distrust, and intolerance pervade the Cuban nation, and this condition reaches deep into both those in exile and on the island. It is a condition that Archbishop Pedro Meurice of Santiago de Cuba perceptively described in May 1998 as the "anthropological lesion"[39] that Cuba had suffered over the preceding five decades.

Conditions were particularly harsh during the first years of the revolutionary government. Summary executions, sham trials, and lengthy prison sentences served under horrific conditions became the norm. British historian Hugh Thomas estimates 5,000 executions took place between 1959 and 1970, while another source estimates that between 7,000 and 10,000 people were shot and another 30,000 imprisoned

---

[37] See Stephanie Courtois et al., *The Black Book of Communism: Crimes, Terror, Repression* (Cambridge, MA: Harvard University Press, 1999), 657, the estimation is that 30,000 people have perished in the Florida Straits.

[38] See http://america.aljazeera.com/articles/2013/10/28/cubans-travelingoverseasinrecordnumbersofficialssay.html

[39] See Archbishop Meurice's Commencement Address at Georgetown University in May 1999 at http://college.georgetown.edu/43702.html.

during the 1960s.[40] In the early and mid 1960s, the new government faced insurgencies in various parts of the country, waging an especially harsh campaign against peasants (the so-called *lucha contra bandidos*) who took up arms in the Sierra del Escambray and in Pinar del Río province. The revolutionary government also organized military-style campaigns to transform education, health, and agriculture. As part of its strategy to erode parental authority and old values, the government dispatched middle and high school students to work and participate in literacy campaigns in the countryside for months at a time.

Beginning in the early 1960s, nearly all independent organizations disappeared and/or were systematically brought under state control. Only the Catholic Church and several other religious organizations survived, even though severe pressures were brought on them. The labor movement lost its autonomy, and the government organized the ubiquitous *Comités de Defensa de la Revolución*, neighborhood commit-tees, which kept tabs on neighbors and collaborated closely with the security services.[41] During the mid 1960s, the government also estab-lished many labor and reeducation camps (called *Unidades Militares de Ayuda a la Producción*, UMAP) where it sent those deemed unreli-able or unfit for the revolutionary project. From late 1965 through mid 1968, nonconformists and clergy of various denominations (including Jaime Ortega, Archbishop of Havana from 1981) as well as homosexu-als were sent to these camps. Persecution of the latter was especially intense with one regime intellectual declaiming: "We are not talking about persecuting homosexuals but of destroying their positions in society, their methods, their influence. Revolutionary social hygiene is what this is called."[42] Estimates of how many people were interned

---

[40] Stéphane Courtois et al., *The Black Book of Communism: Crimes, Terror, Re-pression* (Cambridge, MA: Harvard University Press, 1999), 664.

[41] A sympathetic observer of the Revolution, K.S. Karol observed that the CDRs were "appendices of the security services." See his *Guerrillas in Power: The Course of the Cuban Revolution* (New York: Hill and Wang, 1970), 457. For a perceptive analysis, see Josep Colomer, "Watching Neighbors: The Cuban Model of Social Control," *Cuban Studies* no. 31 (1999), 118–138.

[42] Lilian Guerra, "Gender Policing, Homosexuality and the New Patriarchy of the Cuban Revolution, 1965–70," *Social History* no. 35, 280–281.

in the UMAPs range from between 20,000–30,000 to as high as one-third of the adult population.[43]

Perhaps the most nefarious of the laws the Cuban government employed to establish its control over society and to stifle dissent and opposition has been the *Ley de Peligrosidad Social* (whose origins dated back to the Spanish colonial order) under which an individual could be arrested not for what s/he actually did but rather for his/her "special proclivity to commit crimes, demonstrated by conduct that is observed to be in manifest contradiction with the norms of socialist morality." Under its rubric the state could impose "pre-criminal measures" (including surveillance and re-education programs for those whose "dangerousness" may include "failing to attend pro-government rallies, not belonging to official party organizations, and simply being unemployed."[44] Given such legal latitude and the absence of an impartial system of justice (what might otherwise be termed rule of law), it should come as no surprise that Cuba has one of the highest per capita incarceration rates in the world. The Cuban government does not release official data on the number or conditions of the prisoners it holds; neither does it allow international observers to visit its jails. The unofficial Cuban Human Rights Commission estimated there were 100,000 inmates in more than 200 prisons and labor camps,[45] while the 1995 UN Human Rights Commission and described what it called the "precarious living conditions

---

[43] Norberto Fuentes, *Dulces Guerreros Cubanos* (Barcelona: Editorial Seix Barral, 1999), 300–303 is the source for the lower figure. Robin D. Moore, *Music and Revolution: Cultural Change in Socialist Cuba* (Berkeley, CA: University of California Press, 2006) provides the higher one (251–252). Eventually Fidel Castro apologized for regime policies toward homosexuals, though he never went into detail about what had transpired. See http://latindispatch.com/2010/09/01/fidel-castro-apologizes-for-treatment-of-gays-during-the-revolution.

[44] See the article entitled "Cuba – A Way Forward" by Daniel Wilkinson and Nik Steinberg writing in the *New York Review of Books* (May 27, 2010). http://www.nybooks.com/articles/archives/2010/may/27/cuba-a-way-forward/?pagination=false.

[45] Nancy San Martín, "Cuba's Prisons May Hold 100,000," *Miami Herald* (September 22, 2003) cites the unofficial Cuban Commission on Human Rights.

in prisons."[46] Another estimate published by the International Centre for Prison Studies of Kings College estimated the prison population at 60,000 (or 531 per hundred thousand), thus giving Cuba the fifth highest such population in the world.[47] Over the past five decades, Amnesty International, Human Rights Watch and other human rights organizations have systematically decried the inhuman conditions in Cuban prisons. Those who have spent time in these jails have described the apalling conditions, the cramped spaces, contaminated food, unsanitary conditions, and rampant diseases that political prisoners (and others) have endured. Even as recently as November 2009, Human Rights Watch had this to say about the penitentiary situation in Cuba:

> Conditions for political prisoners and common prisoners alike are overcrowded, unhygienic, and unhealthy, leading to extensive malnutrition and illness. Political prisoners who criticize the government, refuse to participate in ideological re-education, or engage in hunger strikes or other forms of protest are routinely extended solitary confinement, beatings, restrictions of visits, and the denial of medical care. Prisoners have no effective complaint mechanism to seek redress, granting prison authorities total impunity. Taken together, these forms of cruel, inhuman and degrading treatment may rise to the level of torture.[48]

Looking forward and after decades of immobility, we can begin to see the blurry outlines of change in Cuba. Following Samuel Huntington, we identify three phases to the evolution of the single-party Cuban state. There was a first phase of instauration (1959–1970), a second phase of consolidation (1970–1990) and a more recent phase of adaptation (1990–until present). This latter phase began with the disintegration of the Soviet Union and included in more recent years (after July 2006) a transition from the charismatic leadership of Fidel Castro to a more

---

[46] UN Human Rights Commission, "The Situation of Human Rights in Cuba" (October 24, 1995).

[47] *World Prison Population List* (8th edition, 2010) edited by Roy Walmsley at Kings' College (London).

[48] "New Castro, Same Cuba" Human Right Watch (November 2009), 10. See http://www.hrw.org/sites/default/files/reports/cuba1109web_1.pdf.

collegial and institutionally focused approach of his younger brother, Raúl. This adaptive phase of the Cuban Revolution has involved a slow and fitful transition that may eventually culminate in the emergence of an authoritarian regime.[49] Among the most significant initiatives Raúl Castro has announced are: (1) shrinking the size and scope of the state, while enhancing its administrative efficiency and maintaining its control over the strategic sectors of the economy; (2) transforming state enterprises into autonomous holding companies that would no longer receive state subsidies and whose survival would depend on their ability to increase productivity and generate profits; and (3) increasing opportunities for self-employment (*cuentapropismo*) with the goal of spurring agricultural production and providing additional jobs for those state workers (more than 1.3 million of them) whom the government has announced will be laid off over the next several years. So far, however, neither political opening nor liberalization has accompanied these reforms, and it is doubtful there will be significant political reforms, at least while the original revolutionary generation remains in power and, probably, even longer. If fully and successfully accomplished, however, these economic reforms could significantly reduce the weight of the Cuban state and eventually create the conditions for the emergence of private property and a "social market" economy, while also providing space for the development of civil society. Success on the economic front will also be crucial if those who succeed the Castro brothers are to reconstruct the atrophied social compact on the island and lay new foundations for the frayed legitimacy of the regime.

Earlier in this chapter we emphasized the existence of a vibrant civil society as a crucial element in the recovery of memory and as a force for democratic change. Over the past decade, Cuban civil society has not quite "resurrected" (in the evocative phrase of Enrique Baloyra),[50] but neither has it remained immobile. Multiple civic networks and associations have developed, but it is by no means easy

---

[49] For a discussion of the economic reforms and changes within the Cuban elite since Raúl Castro ascended to power, see Eusebio Mujal-León, "Survival, Adaptation, and Uncertainty: The Case of Cuba," *Journal of International Affairs* (Fall/Winter 2011) 65 no. 1, 149–168.

[50] Enrique Baloyra, "Socialist Transitions and Prospects for Change in Cuba" in Enrique Baloyra and James Morris, (eds.), *Conflict and Change in Cuba* (Albuquerque: University of New Mexico Press, 1993), 38.

to "disentangle" what are "oppositional, dissident, and non-oppositional sectors and activities."[51] That acts of civil disobedience have multiplied over the past decade provides clear evidence of incipient political awakening, if not contestation,[52] but for the most part human rights groups and opposition organizations still face daunting obstacles in their quest to connect with and engage ordinary citizens. There is also much associational activity on the island that does not fit neatly into extant categories about civil society because few groups and networks are independent. Most continue to depend on the Cuban state, even while seeking margins of autonomy from it. Even where they are critical of economic and social conditions, however, they are not necessarily calling for regime change. As befits a country in the midst of transformation from a highly personal and state-centric system (Raúl Castro has emphasized the need to "institutionalize" regime and dismantle "senseless restrictions"),[53] the situation is complex and contradictory.

In addition to his economic reforms, the younger Castro has loosened cultural and social controls, tolerating a surprisingly lively debate to emerge in journals and blogs, ranging from Catholic Church-sponsored journals like *Espacio Laical* and *Palabra Nueva* to the website *Havana Times*, the nonconformist *Generación Y* and the critical but regime-supportive magazine *Temas*. At the same time, repression and harassment of dissidents continues with the *Brigadas de Accion Rapida* and government-organized *grupos de repudio* beating and threatening peaceful demonstrators whose only crime it is to call for peaceful political change.

Perhaps one of the most important developments since Raúl Castro took power have been his overtures to the Catholic Church (long one of the advocates of national reconciliation and dialogue) and the corresponding willingness of Church leaders to engage the regime,

---

[51] Margaret Crahan and Ariel Harmony, "Does Civil Society Exist in Cuba?" (posted on the Cuban Research Institute website), 4.

[52] For an excellent account, see Xavier Utset, "The Cuban Democracy Movement: An Analytical Overview," 16 June 2008. Available at *http://cubainfo. fiu.edu/documents/* Utset%20Cuban%20Democracy%20Movement%20 June%202008.pdf.

[53] See Raúl Castro's speech to the National Assembly in February 2008 at http://embacuba.cubaminrex.cu/Default.aspx?tabid=7239.

while pressing for deeper changes. Church-State relations eventually improved to the point that at the Sixth Communist Party Congress in April 2011, Raúl Castro specifically thanked the Church and Cardinal Archbishop of Havana Jaime Ortega, for their contributions to "national unity" by helping to negotiate the release of political prisoners. By implicitly inviting the Church to join forces in a new national compact, Raúl Castro acknowledged how much Cuban society had changed in the preceding two decades, while also signaling that, in order for the regime to successfully relegitimize, it needed to broaden its base of support and make peace with the only major independent civil society actor on the island. For its part, the Church was also engaged in a delicate balancing act, serving at once as companion, critic, and competitor to the regime. Which of these roles would predominate in the years to come became an even more open question with the election of Pope Francis in March 2013 and the impending retirement of Cardinal Ortega. A new pastoral letter ("Hope Does Not Disappoint") issued by the Cuban bishops in September 2013 suggested the Church might adopt a firmer position in favor of political change. Calling Cuba "a pluralistic society, the sum of many Cuban realities . . . with all their differences and aspirations," the text called for "the right to diversity in thought, creativity and the search for truth," concluding that "from (this) diversity comes the need for dialogue" and a quest for "national reconciliation." The Cuban Catholic Church is much weaker than its Polish counterpart was in the days of Solidarity, but its national scope and organization (and its emphasis on dialogue and reconciliation) make it the only actor (civic or otherwise) capable of standing up to or negotiating with the Cuban state. Over the past half century, the Cuban Church has proven its resilience. It is also an important reservoir of counter-memories and a strong advocate of national reconciliation. Whatever spaces it conquers will only enhance the capacity of Cuban society to recover its multiple memories and undertake its reconciliation.

Another important actor and agent for counter-hegemonic history and memory discourses is the Cuban Diaspora. Cuba remains a fractured nation cleaved by separation and conflict, internal and external exile. More than a million Cubans live in the United States. Many of them have maintained close links with relatives on the island. Recently, the Obama Administration has lifted many of the restrictions on family visits and remittances. Approximately 300,000 Cuban-Americans visited in 2010, and estimates are that at least 475,000 visited in 2012.[54] These visits will encourage dialogue and reconciliation between the Cuba of the island and its exiled and immigrant brothers and sisters. The Diaspora is one of the most visible dimensions of the Cuban tragedy, but it has also provided fertile ground for maintaining memories of the past and developing alternative views of Cuban history.[55] These will be important to the national conversation about Cuban identity that will surely flower over the next decade.[56] As change deepens in Cuba and relations between Cuba North and Cuba South (Havana is the political capital of the island, while Miami has been the epicenter of economic wealth) improve, so will relations with the United States enter a new phase. Normalization of U.S.-Cuba relations would do more than end fifty years of political and diplomatic confrontation between the two neighbors. It would also encourage Cubans to examine their past with greater objectivity and build their common future without the polarizing presence of the United States in their polity.

There is no crystal ball that can foretell the Cuban future. The old order is exhausted, and the generation of historic leaders will eventually pass from the scene. The future course of events will depend on two crucial factors—whether the successor generation within the regime is able to maintain its unity and whether autonomous actors in civil society can gain enough ground to be able to negotiate a transition with the incumbent elite. Broadly speaking, there are four possible pathways from the current regime: (1) immobility; (2) economic reform without much, if any *political apertura*; (3) *ruptura pactada* with significant political reform; and, (4) collapse. Of these options, the most improbable are the extreme scenarios of immobility or collapse. Raúl Castro has opened the gates to change, and though this might not lead to democratic transformation, his economic reforms point at

---

[54] http://www.miamiherald.com/2011/08/14/v-fullstory/2359558/many-cubans-living-abroad-cant.html#ixzz1g9nXCT8Z.

[55] Rafael Rojas, "Dilemas de la nueva historia," *Encuentro* (Madrid), 153–157.

[56] For an early effort to discuss this issue and link it to the emergence of democracy in Cuba, see the "Task Force on Memory, Truth, and Justice" (of which one of the authors of this chapter took part) in Marifeli Perez-Stable, *Cuban National Reconciliation* (Latin American and Caribbean Center of the Florida International University, 2003).

the very least in the direction of "market socialism" characterized by the emergence of new capitalist elite and rising social and economic inequality. In short, a new regime will emerge. This leaves us with two possible change scenarios. One entails controlled reform from above and the emergence of a post-communist capitalist elite (mostly drawn from military entrepreneurs but also including princelings or the children of prominent historical figures) that continues to preside over an autocratic system. This might not be the exact equivalent of a Thermidorean phase, but it would entail the dramatic decline of the original state-centric and totalitarian vision and the emergence of greater social space from which civil society organizations could begin the arduous process of the reconstruction of memory and history. The final scenario would involve a *ruptura pactada* where change is accelerated, and the incumbent elites lose ground more rapidly, even if assurances are provided. If those assurances are not provided, the incumbent elites will have far less incentive to negotiate their exit. This is the clear lesson from the experience of Spain and also Chile.

The path to democracy and the full recovery of memory and history is likely to be long—as the German case exemplifies. The *ancien régime* may not last, but neither will it be easily replaced—the weight of the past is too great; the lesions inflicted on Cuban society, too deep. Healing those wounds will require time, not just for the recovery of trust, history and memory, but also for the reestablishment of a sense of national community and shared identity. If the experience of the other cases we have considered in this paper is indicative, the construction of "thick" memory (to use Sa'adah's evocative phrase) as well as democracy will take considerable time to develop reliable foundations.

V. Conclusion

This overview of the dynamics between collective memory and democratization generates several concluding thoughts. First, the nature of the regime matters. There is an affinity between democracy and memory because democracy facilitates the restoration and continual correction of memory, akin to why emphasis on procedure is not trivial or "thin." Concern with procedure reflects a broader set of notions about how actors seek political "truth" and the optimal regime. On one side is revealed truth (or myth) that is only accessible to those who can interpret reality correctly. On the other side is the view that memory is never complete, never ideal. Rather, it is in a constant process of reassemblage with which democracies deal better than other types of totalitarian or authoritarian regimes. Democracies have mechanisms for self-correction—whether this has to do with power or its ideational expression, memory. The give-and-take that produces the most complete and honest version of memory (which includes respect for others and the possibility that your version, though true, may not be the sum total) is least likely under foundational/ totalitarian regimes. The more radical a regime, the greater its capacity and will to destroy all memories, except for the partial and partisan one to which the regime subscribes and seeks to implant. Related to this, the route to memory passes through the type of transition: no transition (change so things do not change); *reforma*; *ruptura pactada*; or collapse.

Second is the degree of and responsibility for trauma. The recovery of memory and the pursuit of justice are the only ways to heal the "anthropological lesions" that society and polity suffer. These processes take time, perhaps more time depending on the degree of the injury and subsequent trauma. Memory cannot be restored quickly because only when there is a deep sense of trust and community can real memory (one that is at once apparently complete but also open to reinterpretation) be restored. We would argue that one element that will complicate both democratization and the restoration of memory in the case of Cuba—unlike the other four cases briefly examined previously—is the absence of a sense of community and agreed-upon national identity.[57]

Moreover, it matters a great deal whether responsibility is singular or shared for the trauma. The more one side is responsible (or viewed as such) the greater the likelihood the search for culprits will be swift. If responsibility is shared, then there is often a willingness to let bygones be bygones or, at least, to develop a case of collective amnesia. This is also true when, as in the case of the Spanish Civil War, the memory of the past is so alive that elites (and society) wish to avoid

---

[57] See the seminal article by Dankwart Rustow, "Transitions to Democracy: Toward a Dynamic Model," *Comparative Politics* (2) 3 (April 1970), 337–363.

its reenactment. It also matters whether the victims and/or their representatives are present. The victims may be dead or no longer present in the community (e.g., Germany). Or, if enough time has passed, the victims may be forgotten.

Third, the question must be posed whether collective memory is contested. It is difficult to agree on a memory if community does not exist. Totalitarian regimes with their foundational enthusiasm are about the creation of a new community, new men and women, or, in the Guevara metaphor, had to be cleansed of (political) original sin. Regimes embarked on foundational ventures seek to destroy the past, its memories and its rationales. Such regimes exercise extraordinary control over information, education, and history—thus making the recovery of alternative narratives all the more difficult. Paradoxically, this power (as East Germany amply demonstrated) is quite brittle. Perhaps one key (and, again it relates to Cuba) is whether the regime has captured the narrative of building the nation.

Finally, the international dimension matters—both in terms of Zeitgeist, and in terms of the capacity/interest of external actors to become involved in the recovery of memory. The ideational Zeitgeist may be analyzed in terms of its international and regional dimensions with the latter perhaps more significant than the former. External actors may be energized or rendered more passive by this Zeitgeist; their activities may elicit approval or criticism. The difference between solidarity and interference on this score is in the eye of the beholder. International factors may not be (though they occasionally are) determinant, but they are not irrelevant—either in the recovery of memory or in support of democratization processes.

Jeffrey Herf

Divided Memory Revisited: The Nazi Past in West Germany and in Postwar Palestine

The following paradox, illustrated most famously by the transition from the Nazi regime to that of the Federal Republic of Germany, is central to issues of memory and justice in the aftermath episodes of massive state organized crimes. On the one hand, only a liberal democracy based on the rule of law, checks and balances of power, an independent judiciary, and the basic principle of the dignity and rights of all individuals is able and is interested in bringing perpetrators of war crimes and crimes against humanity to justice based on the rule of law. Only a liberal democracy and its stress on the principles of openness and transparency places value on examining the inconvenient truths about a nation's past. Yet, on the other hand, liberal democracy by definition empowers the people and allows them to be citizens who choose their government in free elections. The resulting governments, or at least some part of their parliaments thus always have representatives who speak for voters who are deeply opposed to efforts to look closely at the criminal past or to bring those responsible for past crimes to justice or even to define these actions as criminal. As a result, the norm of democratic governments that follow episodes of gross human rights violations follows the dictum I expressed in *Divided Memory*, in 1997, according to which there is a tension between democratization, and certainly rapid democratization, and judicial reckoning. Daring more democracy quickly brought less, not more, justice precisely because some part of the now empowered people has the democratic right to oppose such reckoning.[1]

---

[1] Jeffrey Herf, *Divided Memory: The Nazi Past in the Two Germanys* (Cambridge, MA: Harvard University Press, 1997).

This norm was evident in the American South following the collapse of the Reconstruction governments after the Civil War.[2] It has been the norm in the democracies that have followed communism, in post-apartheid South Africa, in the democracies in Chile and Argentina after the dictators as it was in the "Vichy Syndrome" in postwar France and its variations in Austria. In each of these cases, both elites and popular supporters of the old regime were able to prevent a full and rapid judicial reckoning with the traumatic past. Indeed, before the Holocaust and the genocides of the latter half of the twentieth century, there is a good case to be made that what Winston Churchill, in a speech in Zurich in 1946, called "sacred acts of oblivion" had been the norm in European history since the Treaty of Westphalia advocated a "perpetual Oblivion, Amnesty, or Pardon of all that has been committed since the beginning of these Troubles," that is, the beginning of the Thirty Years War."[3] The primacy of memory over forgetting is thus a relatively recent phenomenon and an understandable one in response to the extremity of the Holocaust and other horrors in Europe's twentieth century.

As has been often noted, in its first decade, the new West German democracy also followed this pattern where compromised elites and their supporters were able to delay and frustrate calls for judicial reckoning.[4] The West German (and Japanese) case differed from these others case in three ways. First, there was an unconditional, unambiguous Allied military victory and complete and total defeat in 1945 after six years of war and 5.3 million German military and 600,000 civil-

---

[2] See David Blight, *Race and Reunion: The Civil War in American Memory* (Cambridge, MA: Harvard University Press, 2002).

[3] For the text of Churchill's Zurich speech see http://www.churchill-society-london.org.uk/astonish.html. On the norm of forgetting in the service of future peace see the third clause of the Treaty of Westphalia of 1648. It begins by stating: "That there shall be on the one side and the other a perpetual Oblivion, Amnesty, or Pardon of all that has been committed since the beginning of these Troubles. . . ." at: http://avalon.law.yale.edu/17th_century/westphal.asp. For a helpful discussion of the balance of memory and oblivion in the Western tradition, see Helmut König, *Politik und Gedächtnis* (Göttingen: Velbrück Wissenschaft, 2008).

[4] See Norbert Frei, *Adenauer's Germany and the Nazi Past: The Politics of Amnesty and Integration*, trans. Joel Golb, (New York: Columbia University Press, 2002); and *Vergangenheitspolitik: Die Anfänge der Bundesrepublik und die NS-Vergangenheit* (Munich: C.H. Beck, 1996).

ian deaths. It was followed by an Allied occupation that lasted for four years during which there was no national German government as well as a massive program of de-Nazification and extensive trials for war crimes. Last, there were surviving anti and non-Nazi political traditions that were able to return to German politics after 1949. Most dictatorships, including the Soviet Union and those of the former communist states of Eastern Europe, have not been ended by military defeat and foreign occupation. As a result the elites of the old regimes and their public supporters are in a far stronger position to resist efforts at judicial or other forms of reckoning with the past. Seen from the perspective of what should have been done, the West German record falls short of the demands of justice. Viewed in this comparative perspective, the West German case presents us with more judicial reckoning and more frank assessment of the criminal past than any of the other of the transitions from dictatorship and gross injustice to democracy from the American South after the Civil War to the post-communist regimes of recent years in Europe.[5]

The shortcomings of West German justice in the 1950s have been well documented. Yet both the Allied occupation era and the continued Western Allied presence in West Germany in the 1950s ensured that the Nazi party was destroyed and that it was prevented from reentering West German politics. No advocate of Nazism in any form found success at the national level in West German politics after 1949. To be sure, there were former members of the Nazi regime and Party who became local mayors, police chiefs, and even a governor or two. Within the functional elites of the West German government, most recently noted in a study of the Foreign Office, there was a remarkable level of continuity of personnel.[6] In the 1960s, the NPD, a neo-

---

[5] A discussion of the transitions from dictatorship to democracy in Chile and Argentina, and from apartheid to a nonracial democracy in South Africa is beyond the bounds of this paper. In the former two cases old elites persisted but elements of judicial reckoning emerged as well. In South Africa, the Truth and Reconciliation Commission also offered a middle solution that combined elements of the imperative to remember with avoidance of judicial reckoning.

[6] Eckart Conze, Norbert Frei, Peter Hayes and Moshe Zimmermann, *Das Amt und die Vergangenheit: Deutsche Diplomaten im Dritten Reich und in der Bundesrepublik* (Munich: Karl Blessing Verlag, 2010).

Nazi party, almost received enough votes to get into the West German parliament. Yet for the major parties, especially the major conservative parties, the Christian Democratic Union (CDU), and the Bavarian based Christian Social Union (CSU), advocacy of Nazism, Nazi ideology, or radical anti-Semitism was unacceptable.

The election of Kurt Georg Kiesinger as West German Chancellor in 1966 most famously illustrates this point.[7] Kiesinger was the Director of the Department of Radio Policy in the German Foreign Office in the Nazi regime from 1943 to 1945. It was an office that oversaw the production of massive amounts of Nazi propaganda broadcast via short-wave radio to many countries in many languages.[8] Kiesinger's reentry ticket into West German democratic politics was a change of heart, however cynical or sincere that led to public support for the values of liberal democracy. In his case, a mix of cynicism, opportunism, and reassessment contributed to his support for democracy. He left Nazism behind.

By contrast, Haj Amin al-Husseini, the Grand Mufti of Jerusalem who spoke on Nazi radio, returned to Egypt, Lebanon, and to a leading role in Palestinian politics in 1946 without having to repudiate or revise any of the views he expressed in wartime Berlin. In Husseini's case, the reentry ticket to being elected President of the Palestine National Council in 1948, and then playing a leading role in the war against the Jews in Palestine of that year did not require any reassessment or change of his support for Nazism during the war. On the contrary, as the leader of the Muslim Brotherhood, Hassan al-Banna, pointed out in 1946, it was Husseini's support for Hitler's war against the Allies and the Jews that endeared him to the Brotherhood, as well to his supporters in Palestine. With a mix of oblivion about the facts of his Nazi collaboration as well as admiration for it, his Arab supporters held him in high esteem precisely because he did not change his views after the Third Reich was defeated and continued to combine his anti-Zionism with visceral hatred of the Jews.[9]

---

[7] Phillip Gassert, *Kurt Georg Kiesinger, 1904–1988: Kanzler zwischen den Zeiten* (Munich: Deutsche Verlags-Anstalt, 2006).

[8] On Kiesinger's role see Jeffrey Herf, *Nazi Propaganda for the Arab World* (New Haven: Yale University Press, 2009), 39.

[9] See the extensive discussion of Husseini's role during the Nazi years and his political welcome in the Middle East after World War II in Herf, *Nazi Propaganda for the Arab World*, esp. xii–xv, and 233–260.

In historical scholarship and political debate, the Federal Republic of Germany or West Germany, remains the paradigmatic case of a democracy that engaged in *Vergangenheitsbewältigung,* that is, to "come to terms with" a traumatic past. It is not an exaggeration to say that *Vergangenheitsbewältigung* was one of the preeminent preoccupations of West German intellectual and less so political life in the decades following World War II and the Holocaust. In the remainder of this chapter I want to discuss how West German democracy remembered and forgot the crimes of the Nazi regime. I then want to examine how the reception of Nazi collaborators in the Middle East after World War II sheds interesting light on issues of memory and justice in West Germany. In the midst of a broad popular desire to avoid discussion of the crimes of the Nazi regime, a tradition of public memory emerged in parts of the political and intellectual establishment of the Federal Republic.[10] West German Chancellor, Konrad Adenauer, the Federal President, Theodor Heuss, and the leader of the Social Democratic Party, Kurt Schumacher took the lead as founding fathers who established the contours of public memory of the crimes of the Nazi era by the early 1950s. In the midst of silence, Heuss and Schumacher in particular, offered speech and public memory of crimes. In view of the absence of an indigenous revolution before 1945 and, on the contrary, the tenacity of the German armed forces up to the end of World War II, the emergence of any memory of the Holocaust in the postwar years, rather than complete silence, requires explanation.

There were several reasons that any memory at all became a part of West German politics, however marginal at times. First, unconditional victory on the battlefield combined with the Allied occupation, meant that there would be no repetition of a stab in the back legend that plagued the origins of the Weimar Republic. The Allied occupation the destruction of the Nazi by bringing the leaders of the regime and Party to trial and purging government, politics and business of those most closely linked to the Nazi regime. The postwar purge of about 100,000 officials of the Nazi regime was extensive, far more so than popular terms such as "whitewash" or "amnesia" implied. The

---

[10] See Herf, *Divided Memory.* On German military and civilian deaths in World War II see Rüdiger Overmanns, *Deutsche militärische Verluste im Zweiten Weltkrieg* (Munich: R. Oldenbourg Verlag, 2000).

International Military Tribunal in Nuremberg and successor trials revealed the crimes of the regime to a very broad public. Among modern dictatorships, only Imperial Japan came to a similar end.[11] Those four years of Allied occupation from 1945 to 1949 were one indispensable precondition for subsequent developments. Indeed, the contrast between the American South after slavery when the U.S. government withdrew troops and ceased supporting the Reconstruction government with the Allied occupation of Germany after Nazism reminds us that Allied power, the absence of democracy—rule by will of the people—and, national sovereignty in occupied Germany were preconditions for memory and justice. In both cases, the Federal Republic after 1949 and the American South after the collapse of the Reconstruction governments, the rapid return of democracy and expression of a popular will stood in the way of a fuller reckoning of past injustice.

The postwar trials left behind a massive documentary record of the files of the Nazi regime that confirmed the facts of the criminal past. After Nuremberg, in both West and East Germany, and in unified Germany, there were politicians and voters who avoided discussion about the Holocaust or claimed it was not unique to German history. But denial of the basic facts presented in the Nuremberg era trials never extended beyond extremist fringe parties. Public debate was about how and why the Holocaust occurred but not whether the Nazi regime in fact murdered approximately six million of Europe's Jews or engaged in aggressive wars. In the year following the end of World War II, the Western allies indicted over 90,000 Germans on charges related to crimes committed during the war. In the period from 1945 to 1989, about 6,500 convictions were delivered by Allied and West German courts. Of them, about 80 percent or 5,025 were rendered by the Western allied occupation courts between 1945 and 1949. In the occupation era, American courts convicted 1,517 persons of whom 324 received the death penalty and 247 life sentences. British mili-

---

[11] On postwar Japan see John Dower, *Embracing Defeat: Japan in the Wake of World War II* (New York: Norton, 1999). Also see essays by Franziska Seraphim, Ishida Yuji and Yagu Kunichika in Crhistoph Cornelißen, Lutz Klinkhammer and Wolfgang Schwentker (eds.), *Erinnungskulturen: Deutschland, Italien und Japan seit 1945* (Frankfurt am Main: Fischer Taschenbuch, 2003); and Franziska Seraphim, *War, Memory and Social Politics in Japan, 1945–2005* (Cambridge, MA: Harvard University Press, 2006).

tary courts convicted 1,085 persons, 240 of whom received the death penalty. French courts convicted 2,107 people, of whom 104 received the death penalty. In 1946–1947 alone, the United States delivered 3,914 people being sought for trial in sixteen European countries, two-thirds of them to France and Poland.[12] To be sure, many perpetrators escaped justice. Yet viewed in comparative perspective of other efforts to come to terms with criminal dictatorships, the Nuremberg era stands out as the most consequential such effort of modern history. Victory, occupation and Allied judicial proceedings convinced a majority of German voters that the National Socialist regime had, indeed, committed massive criminal acts. In so doing, these trials and internments of former Nazi officials did much to destroy the moral legitimacy of Nazism and fascism in postwar West Germany and in Europe and to reinforce the case for a turn to liberal democracy.

As the German political theorist Hartmut König has pointed out, the postwar West German experience represented a break from a conventional wisdom about memory after trauma, one that had been expressed by Thomas Hobbes and at the time by Winston Churchill and de Gaulle.[13] The norm in European history had been to opt for Churchill's "sacred acts of oblivion," to let bygones be bygones and draw the famous line under the past so that a new start could be made. In view of the enormity of Nazism's crimes and the extensive number of persons who perpetrated them this conventional wisdom, rather

---

[12] See Frank M. Buscher, *The U.S. War Crimes Trial Program in Germany, 1946 to 1955* (New York: Greenwood Press, 1989); Jörg Friedrich, *Die kalte Amnestie: NS-Tater in der Bunderepublik* (Frankfurt am Main: Fischer, 1984); Albrecht Götz, *Bilanz der Verfolgung von NS-Straftaten* (Cologne: Bundesanzeiger, 1986), 29; Klaus Dietmar Henke, "Die Trennung vom Nationalsozialismus: Selbstzerstörung, politische Säuberung, 'Entnazifizierung,' Strafverfolgung," in Klaus Dietmar Henke and Hans Woller (eds.) *Politische Säuberung in Europa: Die Abrechnung mit Faschismus und Kollaboration nach den Zweiten Weltkrieg* (Munich: Deutscher Taschenbuch Verlag, 1991), 21–83; Clemens Vollnhals, *Entnazifizierung: Politische Säuberung und Rehabilitierung in den vier Besatzungszonen, 1945-1949* (Munich: Deutscher Taschenbuch Verlag, 1991). On war crimes trials in Europe outside Germany, see Norbert Frei (ed.), *Transnationale Vergangenheitspolitik: Der Umgang mit deutschen Kriegsverbrechen in Europa nach dem Zweiten Weltkrieg* (Göttingen: Wallstein, 2006).

[13] Helmut König, *Politik und Gedächtnis* (Weilerswist: Velbruck Wissenschaft, 2008).

than facilitating democracy, would have undermined its legitimacy from the outset. In addition, from the Allies perspective, the popularity of Hitler and the Nazi regime in significant parts of the German population up to May 1945 cast doubt on the very value of democracy in Germany. If, after all, the Germans had celebrated Hitler, was there not a significant risk that a German democracy might return to Nazism? The Western Allied presence made democracy in West Germany less threatening both to Germans and to their European neighbors than would have been the case without American, British, and French military presence. One of Konrad Adenauer's most famous campaign slogans of the 1950s was "no experiments." The presence of the Western Allies had the function of making sure that however experimental West German politics became, it remained within clearly defined limits.

In addition to Allied unconditional victory followed by occupation, "multiple restorations" of previously defeated, anti- or non-Nazi political traditions which had survived in foreign or "inner emigration" were a third factor that contributed to the emergence of critical postwar memory. The fact that the Third Reich was destroyed after "only" twelve years in power facilitated the return of democracy in its wake. All of the leading political figures of early postwar political life in West and East Germany—Konrad Adenauer, Kurt Schumacher, Theodor Heuss as well as Walter Ulbricht—came of political age between 1900 and 1930. They experienced Nazism, World War II, and the Holocaust in their mature, not their young and formative years, and interpreted it after the war on the basis of long-held beliefs. The power or "hegemony" of the victors lay only partly in the ability to impose their own interpretations on the Germans. It also lay in the ability to encourage some to speak and discourage or repress other, in this case, Nazi voices. The Allies helped them to bring about "multiple restorations" of the political traditions which Nazism had crushed, including communism, Social Democracy, liberalism and a chastened and Westernized West German conservatism.[14] The resulting language or political culture of both West and East Germany was thus less the result of a zero hour or tabula rasa than of a mixture of the victors' efforts to lend support to advocates of these preexisting ideological outlooks. The

---

[14] On multiple restorations, see Herf, *Divided Memory*.

power of the occupiers lay less in creating wholly novel ideas about democracy and the rule of law in West Germany or anti-fascism and communism in East Germany than it did in lending support to German actors who expressed such views.

The key figures of the formative years were the following: Konrad Adenauer (1876–1967), the leader of postwar Christian Democracy and Chancellor of the Federal Republic of Germany from 1949 to 1963, who had been Mayor of Cologne from 1917 to 1933. Kurt Schumacher (1895–1952) the leader of postwar Social Democracy, who had served as a member of the Reichstag in the Weimar Republic. Theodor Heuss (1884–1963), the first President of the Federal Republic, who had worked as a journalist, professor of politics, and was active in liberal politics in the Weimar years as well. Ernst Reuter (1889–1953), the Mayor of West Berlin during the crucial early years of the Cold War, who had been a Social Democratic politician in Weimar; after being held a prisoner in a Nazi concentration camp, he went into political exile in Ankara, Turkey. The communist leadership in East Germany also came of political age before 1933 and drew on an intact German political tradition. Walter Ulbricht (1893–1973), the effective head of the East German government was born in 1894. Otto Grotewohl (1894–1964), co-chair of the Socialist Unity Party, and Wilhelm Pieck (1876–1960), a comrade and friend of Rosa Luxembourg and first President of the German Democratic Republic, were born in 1894 and 1987, respectively. Paul Merker (1894–1969), a leading figure of the German Communist Party since 1920 whose unsuccessful efforts to raise the Jewish question in East Berlin led to his political downfall in 1950 was also born in 1894.

From May 6, 1945, two days before the Nazi surrender, until his death at the age of fifty-seven on August 20, 1952, Kurt Schumacher urged his fellow Germans to face the facts about the mass murder of European Jewry. Among postwar German political leaders, he was the first to emphatically support *Wiedergutmachung* or financial restitution to the Jewish survivors of the Holocaust, and to support relations with the new state of Israel. A democratic socialist, Schumacher believed that overcoming the Nazi past meant breaking with German capitalism. Yet, his Marxism notwithstanding, Schumacher stressed that Nazism had been more than a plot by a small group of capitalists and Nazi leaders. He recalled that it had a mass base of support, that the

Germans fought for Hitler to the bitter end, and that the Nazi regime was destroyed only as a result of Allied arms. He offered a novelty in the history of Social Democracy, namely a vision for the present and future that drew heavily on memory of the crimes and tragedies of the recent past rather than on an optimistic view of the laws of history pointing to a brighter future.

Schumacher rejected the idea of a collective guilt of the German people because doing so neglected the anti-Nazi resistance, and, by dispersing guilt so widely, it aided those who had committed crimes escape justice. If all were guilty, none were responsible. Schumacher was blunt in his criticism of German passivity in the face of Nazi criminality. In 1945, he said that the Germans knew what was taking place in their midst. They "saw with their own eyes, with what common bestiality, the Nazis tortured, robbed, and hunted the Jews. Not only did they remain silent, but they would have preferred that Germany had won the World War II thus guaranteeing them peace and quiet and also a small profit." They had believed in dictatorship and violence, and thus were occupied by others after 1945. "This political insight," he said was "the precondition for a spiritual-intellectual and moral repentance and change."[15] In his postwar speeches, Schumacher supported the removal of former Nazis from positions of power and influence; the continuation of war crimes trials; payment of financial restitution to Jews; and honesty about the crimes of the Nazi past. Yet, in the inaugural election of 1949, the West Germans by a narrow margin opted instead for Adenauer's very different view of the relationship between democratization, and the Nazi past. During the 1950s, Schumacher's views on these issues were echoed by Social Democratic leaders such as Ernst Reuter, the Mayor of West Berlin, and Carlo Schmid, the parliamentary leader of the Social Democratic Party in the Bundestag.[16]

The distinctive West German government tradition of public remembrance of the crimes of the Nazi past began as elite tradition that sounded a soft dissonant note in the larger West German silence.

---

[15] Kurt Schumacher, "Wir verzweifeln nicht!," May 6, 1945 in Willy Albrecht (ed.), *Kurt Schumacher: Reden-Schriften-Korrespondenzen, 1945–1952* (Berlin: J.H.W. Dietz, 1985), 217; cited in Herf, *Divided Memory*, 245.

[16] On Ernst Reuter and Carlo Schmid, see Herf, *Divided Memory*, 300–312.

Its founder was then Bundespräsident Heuss.[17] In articles and speeches during the occupation era, Heuss had articulated the importance of clear and honest memory of past crimes.[18] From 1949 to 1959, he used the platform of the office of *Bundespräsident* and its insulation from electoral politics, to urge Germans to remember the crimes of the Nazi era, especially the Holocaust. To his critics, he was the cultured veneer of the Adenauer restoration, and an advocate of eloquent memory separated from politically consequential judicial reckoning. Yet in speeches about German history, extensive private correspondence with Jewish survivors, resistance veterans, and West German, and foreign intellectuals, Heuss forged a tradition of political recollection that would eventually contribute to broader public discussion and action. His most important speech regarding the Nazi past, "No One Will Lift This Shame from Us," was made during the memorial ceremonies held at the former Nazi concentration camp at Bergen-Belsen on November 29–30, 1952.[19]

The memorial in Bergen-Belsen was also important because for the first time after 1949 a representative of Jewish survivors, Nahum Goldman of the World Jewish Congress, spoke alongside an official of the West German government.[20] Goldman described the destruction of European Jewry in detail and recalled "the millions who found their tragic end in Auschwitz, Treblinka, Dachau, and in Warsaw, and Vilnius and Białystok and in countless other places."[21] In this very Western ceremony during the Cold War, Goldman drew attention to the Eastern geography of the Holocaust. In so doing, he implicitly pointed out that the geography of memory did not coincide with the fault lines of the Cold War in the West. The Holocaust had largely taken place

---

[17] On Heuss on the Nazi past see Herf, *Divided Memory*, 226–239 and 312–331.

[18] For some of Heuss's occupation era speeches see *Theodor Heuss: Aufzeichnungen, 1945–1947* (Tübingen: Rainer Wunderlich Verlag, 1966).

[19] Theodor Heuss, "Diese Scham nimmt uns niemand ab!" *Bulletin des Presse-und Informationsamtes der Bundesregierung*, December 2, 1952, 1655–1656.

[20] Theodor Heuss, "Diese Scham nimmt uns niemand ab: Der Bundespräsident sprach bei der Weihe des Mahnmals in Bergen-Belsen," *Bulletin des Presse- un Informationsamtes der Bundesregierung* Nr. 189, (December 1, 1952), 1655–1656. For some of his speeches as *Bundespräsident* and for an abridged version of the Bergen-Belsen address see *"Das Mahnmal,"* in Theodor Heuss, *Der Grossen Reden: Der Staatsmann* (Tübingen: Rainer Wunderlich Verlag, 1965), 224–230.

[21] Ibid., 1–2.

in a part of Europe that during the Cold War was "behind the Iron Curtain." Goldman's recounting of the Holocaust inevitably called to mind German aggression on the Eastern Front during World War II, an invasion which eventually led to the presence of the Red Army in the center of Europe in May 1945. Heuss's speech, "No One Will Lift This Shame from Us" was the most extensive statement to that date of national West German reflection on the mass murder of European Jewry. It was broadcast on radio, and was the subject of reports in the West German press, especially the liberal press.[22] Heuss included among patriotism's virtues a willingness to honestly face an evil past rather than seek to avoid doing so by pointing to misdeeds of others. Following Heuss' Bergen-Belsen speech, the memory of the Holocaust became a part of official West German political culture.

More than any other West German political leader, founding Chancellor Konrad Adenauer shaped West German policy toward the Nazi past. In his speeches as the leader of the Christian Democratic Union between 1945 and 1949, Adenauer asserted that Nazism was the result of deep ills in German history and society including Prussian authoritarianism; the weakness of the individualism, Marxism, an ideology of racial superiority which filled the vacuum left by the erosion of the dignity of all human beings grounded in Christian natural right. For Adenauer the antidote to these ills was democracy resting on the basis of Christian natural right, and the belief in the dignity and value of every individual that flowed from it.[23] (His belief in the importance of a Christian religious revival did not include an interrogation of the place of anti-Semitism in Christian theology.) Paradoxically, Adenauer's pessimism about the breadth and depth of Nazism's

---

[22] Theodor Heuss, "Diese Scham nimmt uns niemand ab!," *Bulletin des Presse-und Informationsamtes der Bundesregierung* Nr. 189 (December 2, 1942), 1655–1656.

[23] On Adenauer's interpretation of Nazism, see Herf, *Divided Memory*, 209–226. For texts of his postwar speeches, see Hans-Peter Schwarz (ed.), *Konrad Adenauer: Reden, 1917–1967: Eine Auswahl* (Stuttgart: Deutsche Verlagsanstalt, 1975). Also see Henning Köhler, *Adenauer: Eine politische Biographie* (Frankfurt am Main: Propyläen, 1994); and Hans-Peter Schwarz, *Konrad Adenauer: Der Aufstieg, 1876–1952* (Stuttgart: Deutsche Verlagsanstalt, 1986).

roots within German history and society led him to advocate reticence about a sharp confrontation with the past lest this lead to a nationalist and anti-democratic backlash. Instead, he adopted a strategy of democratization by integration of former and hopefully disillusioned followers of Nazism even including government officials who had served in the Nazi regime. He combined this view with reluctance to discuss the crimes of the past and support for amnesty for many convicted of crimes. As early as spring and summer 1946, Adenauer told audiences in his election speeches in the British zone of occupation that "we finally should leave in peace the followers, those who did not oppress others, who did not enrich themselves, and who broke no laws."[24] For Adenauer, liberal democracy in post-Nazi Germany could not be established against the will of the majority. He did not want to risk offending the will of crucial minorities who could make the difference between electoral victory and defeat.

The result was a tension between the early emergence of democratic politics in post-Nazi Germany, on the one hand, and the desire for clear memory and timely justice, on the other. West German politicians seeking to win elections in the postwar decade were seeking the votes of citizens many of whom were emphatically opposed to timely trials for war crimes and crimes against humanity. Paradoxically, daring more democracy at an early point also meant achieving less judicial reckoning. With the term *Vergangenheitspolik* or "politics about the past," the German historian Norbert Frei has described the connection between the emergence of West German sovereignty and democracy, on the one hand, and opposition to the de-Nazification measures of the occupation era.[25] There was, he wrote, a compelling case that a broad consensus existed within the postwar West German establish-

---

[24] Konrad Adenauer, *"Grundsatzrede des 1. Vorsitzenden der Christlich-Demokratischen Union für die Britische Zone in der Aula der Kölner Universität,"* in Hans Peter Schwarz (ed.), *Konrad Adenauer: Reden, 1917–1967: Eine Auswahl* (Stuttgart: Deutsche Verlagsantalt, 1975), 92.

[25] See Norbert Frei, *Adenauer's Germany and the Nazi Past: The Politics of Amnesty and Integration,* trans. Joel Golb (New York: Columbia University Press, 2002); and German original, *Vergangenheitspolitik: Die Anfänge der Bundesrepublik und die NS-Vergangenheit* (Munich: C.H. Beck, 1996); and Herf, *Divided Memory,* 288–297.

ment in favor of amnesty and integration of ex-Nazis.[26] From 1949 to 1954, when democratically elected German politicians first had a chance to act, they passed "a series of parliamentary initiatives, legislative acts, and administrative decisions aimed at the 'vitiation' of the de-Nazification measures of the occupation era." The result was "both an annulment of punishments and integrative measures on behalf of an army of millions of Nazi Party members. Virtually without exception, these people regained their social, professional, and civic, but not their political status," a status which they had lost in the course of de-Nazification and internment after the war.[27] The grand bargain of West German democratization via amnesty and integration entailed letting bygones be bygones in exchange for willingness by those left in peace to support or at least not attack the new democratic political institutions. The result were striking continuities of personnel in important government ministries such as the foreign office, executive offices in industry, the universities, judiciary, medical profession and other parts of the West German establishment.[28] Amnesty and integration for all but the unreconstructed was a formula which linked democratization with silence about Nazi era crimes in the crucial early years. As the philosopher and social theorist Theodor Adorno wrote in 1959, repression of the Nazi past was far less the product of unconscious processes or deficient memory than it was "the product of an all too wide awake consciousness."[29]

---

[26] On the opposition of West German leaders to continued de-Nazification efforts, also see Thomas Schwartz, *America's Germany: John J. McCloy and the Federal Republic of Germany* (Cambridge, MA: Harvard University Press, 1991). On the Catholic Church and the amnesty issue, see Suzanne Brown-Fleming, *The Holocaust and the Catholic Conscience: Cardinal Aloisius Muench and the Guilt Question in Germany* (Notre Dame: University of Notre Dame Press, 2006).

[27] Frei, *Adenauer's Germany and the Nazi Past*, xii.

[28] From the large literature on continuities of personnel and rapid changes of allegiance from Nazi Germany to the Federal Republic, see Hans-Jürgen Döscher, *Verschworene Gesellschaft: Das Auswärtige Amt Under Adenauer zwischen Neubeginn und Kontinuität* (Berlin: Akademie Verlag, 1995); Steven Remy, *The Heidelberg Myth: The Nazification and Denazification of a German University* (Cambridge, MA: Harvard University Press, 2002).

[29] Theodor Adorno, *"Was bedeutet: Aufarbeitung der Vergangenheit?,"* in *Theodor Adorno: Gesammelte Schriften*, vol. 10, no. 2 (Frankfurt am Main: Suhrkamp,

By the late 1950s, it became apparent to leaders in the West German parliament and to several prosecutors at the state, that a very large number of persons suspected of having participated in the Holocaust and other war crimes remained at large. As a result in 1958, the Central Office of the Land Judicial Authorities for the Investigation of National Socialist Crimes was established in the town of Ludwigsburg. In the 1960s, the Bundestag held the first of widely discussed debates about extending the stature of limitations on crimes of murder as a result of which it was finally abolished in 1979.[30] Fritz Bauer, the attorney general of the state of Hesse, directed the efforts that led in 1964 to "the Auschwitz Trial" of guards at the former extermination camp.[31]

The 1960s did witness greater discussion of Nazi era crimes. Yet it was not, as has sometimes been claimed, the era in which the memory of the extermination of European Jewry emerged on a broad scale in West German politics and intellectual life. In 1969, Willy Brandt's *Neue Ostpolitik* brought increased attention to the war on the Eastern Front as did his famous gesture of kneeling at the memorial to the Jews of the Warsaw Ghetto. Yet *détente* was more about improving relations with the Soviet bloc countries than about recovering the memory of the Holocaust. The emergence of the new left in the universities in the 1960s inspired Marxist discussions about fascism and capitalism more than examinations of the particularities of the Holocaust. In 1965, the West German historian Andreas Hillgruber broke new scholarly ground in Germany by placing racial anti-Semitism in a central place in his examination of Hitler's war strategy. In 1969, in separate works, Karl Bracher and Eberhard Jäckel wrote specifically about the

---

1977), 555–572. See also Theodor W. Adorno, "What Does Coming to Terms with the Past Mean?" trans. Timothy Bahti and Geoffrey Hartman, in Geoffrey Hartman (ed.), *Bitburg in Moral and Political Perspective* (Bloomington, Ind., Indiana University Press, 1986), 114–129.

[30] See Herf, *Divided Memory*, 337–342; and Helmut Dubiel, *Niemand ist frei von der Geschichte* (Munich: Carl Hanser, 1999), 79–182.

[31] See Rebecca Wittmann, *Beyond Justice: The Auschwitz Trial* (Cambridge, Mass: Harvard University Press, 2005); and Devin Pendas, *The Frankfurt Auschwitz Trial, 1963–1965: Genocide, History and the Limits of the Law* (New York: Cambridge University Press, 2010).

link between Nazi anti-Semitism and the Final Solution of the Jewish question.[32]

Though historians, prosecutors, and producers of television documentaries had examined the Holocaust since the 1960s, it was first in the 1980s that the Final Solution of the Jewish Question in Europe, by then widely known as the Holocaust, became a topic of debate and discussion in a broad public extending beyond the political, judicial, and intellectual elites.[33] The radical left had marginalized it in the "red decade" of the late 1960s and 1970s, compared nuclear deterrence to a "nuclear Auschwitz" in the early 1980s and made antagonism toward Israel one of its defining features. Indeed, the leftist terrorist organizations made common cause with Palestinian terrorists who were attacking Israel as well as Jewish persons and institutions

---

[32] See Karl Dietrich Bracher, *Die Deutsche Diktatur: Entstehung, Struktur und Folgen des Nationalsozialismus* (Cologne: Kiepenheuer and Witsch, 1969); Andreas Hillgruber, *Hitler's Strategie: Politik und Kriegführung, 1940–1941* (Munich: Bernard and Graefe, 1965); Eberhard Jäckel, *Hitler's Weltanschauung: Entwurf einer Herrschaft* (Tübingen: R. Wunderlich, 1969). On Hillgruber's place in the Historikersstreit, see Charles Maier, *The Unmasterable Past: History, Holocaust and German National Identity* (Cambridge, MA: Harvard University Press, 1988. On the reluctance of West German historians of the 1950s and 1960s to explore the Holocaust, see Nicolas Berg, *Der Holocaust und die westdeutschen Historiker: Erforschung und Erinnerung* (Göttingen: Wallstein, 2003). Also see Lucy Dawidowicz, *The Holocaust and the Historians* (Cambridge, MA: Harvard University Press, 1981). Despite these important works, the major scholarly works that examined either the specific governmental institutions in the Nazi regime that implemented the Holocaust or that explored the intellectual and cultural roots of what became genocidal anti-Semitism were almost all written by Israeli, British, or American scholars. They included, among others, Norman Cohn, *Warrant for Genocide: The Myth of the Jewish World Conspiracy and the Protocols of the Elders of Zion* (London: Eyre and Spottiswooode, 1967); Raul Hilberg, *The Destruction of the European Jews* (Chicago: University of Chicago Press, 1961); George Mosse, *The Crisis of German Ideology: Intellectual Origins of the Third Reich* (New York: Grosset and Dunlap, 1964); Leon Poliakov, *Harvest of Hate: The Nazi Program for the Destruction of the Jews of Europe* (Syracuse: University of Syracuse Press, 1954).

[33] On the efforts of West German television documentary producers, especially since the 1960s, to examine Nazi crimes and the Holocaust see Wulf Kansteiner, *In Pursuit of German Memory: History, Television and Politics After Auschwitz* (Athens: Ohio University Press, 2006).

in Europe.[34] In the mid 1980s, conservative intellectuals also began to obscure its historical distinctiveness by comparing the Holocaust to other episodes of mass murder and inhumanity, such as the Soviet Union's Gulag.[35] On May 5, 1985 U.S. President Ronald Reagan and West German Chancellor Helmut Kohl visited a West German military cemetery in Bitburg, where members of the Waffen SS were buried. Three days later, on May 8, 1985, the fortieth anniversary of the end of World War II, *Bundespräsident* Richard von Weizsäcker delivered a speech to the West German parliament that placed the memory of the Holocaust in the center of West German memory of the crimes of the Nazi era. The Weizsäcker speech and the enormous outpouring of support and enthusiasm with which it was greeted by elites and the public indicated that the memory of the Holocaust would not succumb to oblivion, that efforts to marginalize or repress it had failed, and that it remained an enduring aspect of West German official understanding of the Nazi era.[36]

---

[34] On West German leftist antagonism to Israel see Jeffrey Herf, "An Age of Murder: Ideology and Terror in Germany," *Telos*, No. 144 (Fall 2008), 8–38 and "1968 and the Terrorist Aftermath in West Germany" in Vladimir Tismaneanu (ed.), *Promises of 1968: Crisis, Illusion, and Utopia* (New York/Budapest: CEU Press, 211), 371–385; Martin W. Kloke, *Israel und die deutsche Linke* (Frankfurt/ Main: Haag and Herchen, 1994); Wolfgang Kraushaar (ed.), *Die RAF und der linke Terrorismus* (Hamburg: Hamburger Edition, 2006; "*Wann endlich beginnt bei Euch der Kampf gegen die Heilige Kuh Israel?: München 1970: über die antisemitischen Würzeln des deutschen Terrorismus* (Hamburg: Rowohlt, 2013).

[35] From the now growing literature on the bizarre aftereffects of the Holocaust on the radical left in the 1960s, see Wolfgang Kraushaar, *Die Bombe im Jüdischen Gemeindehaus* (Hamburg: Hamburger Edition, 2005). On the use and misuse of the memory of Auschwitz by the left during the debate over intermediate range nuclear weapons in Europe, see Jeffrey Herf, "The Nazi Past and the Nuclear Present," in *War By Other Means: Soviet Power, West German Resistance and the Battle of the Euromissiles* (New York: Free Press, 1991), 185–192. On the *Historikersstreit* of the 1980s, see Maier, *The Unmasterable Past: History, Holocaust and German National Identity* (Cambridge, MA: Harvard University Press, 1988).

[36] On Bitburg and the Weizsäcker speech, see Herf, *Divided Memory*, 350–359. For documents of the Bitburg controversy and the English text of Weizsäcker's speech, see Geoffrey Hartman (ed.), *Bitburg in Moral and Political Perspective* (Bloomington: Indiana University Press, 1986). For the German text, see Richard von Weizsäcker, *Von Deutschland aus: Reden des Bundespräsident* (Berlin: Siedler Verlag, 1985), 11–35.

Beginning in the first months after the end of World War II and continuing in the seven decades since, there were always German voices seeking "finally" to put the past behind and forget about the Holocaust. With the collapse of communism in 1989 followed by German unification, some observers expected that these voices would achieve their long sought goal in the midst of a wave of nationalist triumphalism. While controversies continued about the issue, in 1995, the parliament of a then unified Germany declared January 27th, the day in 1945 that the Red Army liberated the Auschwitz-Birkenau death camp, to be a national day of remembrance for the victims of Nazi persecution and genocide. In 1999, the same parliament agreed to build a memorial to the murdered Jews of Europe within walking distance of the Bundestag and the Chancellor's office in Berlin, the new national capital.[37] While the bulk of major works of historical scholarship on the Holocaust continues to be written outside Germany, significant works making original contributions have appeared from German historians who came of age since the 1970s. As unique as the Holocaust is in history, so too is the West German and now German tradition of public memory of the most criminal and barbaric period of Germany's past.

Historians of postwar Europe such as Tony Judt and Henry Rosso have drawn our attention to what Russo called "the Vichy Syndrome" in various national forms.[38] It was the tendency to present the nation as virtuous, filled with heroic resisters and anti-Nazis or with realistic politicians only a few of whom collaborated with Hitler and did so not out of ideological conviction but from a desire to prevent even worse things from taking place. The recent scholarship indicates that such notions were a chapter in the longer history of acts of oblivion which bought social peace at the price of mythologizing the past. Yet another aspect

---

[37] For documentation of the extensive debate that took place in Berlin and elsewhere regarding the memorial, see the comprehensive (1,298 pages) collection by Ute Heimrod, Günter Schlusche and Horst Seferens (eds.), *Das Denkmalstreit–das Denkmal? Die Debatte um das "Denkmal für die ermordeten Juden Europas": Eine Dokumentation* (Berlin: Philo Verlagsgesellschaft, 1999).

[38] Tony Judt, *Postwar: A History of Europe Since 1945* (New York: Penguin, 2005); Henry Russo, *The Vichy Syndrome: History and Memory in France Since 1944* (Cambridge, MA: Harvard University Press, 1994).

of the Europe after Nazism which has received less scholarly attention deserves mention. It is that Nazism remained defeated and that no major national politician emerged who sought to restore fascism and Nazism to a postwar European country. Those who had been in the Nazi regime and Nazi party but who wanted to pursue professional careers in public life understood that they could not do so if they publicly expressed support for Nazism or anti-Semitism. As the example of Kurt Kiesinger indicated, former members of the Nazi regime could reenter public and professional if they offered compelling evidence of what Jerry Muller aptly described as "de-radicalization," that they had abandoned Nazism and were committed to liberal democratic institutions.[39]

A comparison of the postwar careers of the above mentioned Kurt Kiesinger and Haj Amin al-Husseini sheds interesting light on the contrasting reentry tickets into public life in postwar West Germany and postwar Arab and Palestinian politics. After World War II, Kiesinger spent several months interned by the Allies. In 1948, a denazification court, perhaps unaware of the activities of the Radio Division in the Foreign Office, acquitted him of involvement in war crimes. He was one of the thousands of former Nazi officials and party members who were subsequently able to reintegrate into West German society and public life with remarkable, indeed, unseemly, haste. After the war, Kiesinger changed his political opinions. He quickly discovered the blessings of liberal democracy, the Western Alliance and the containment of communism with a timely mixture of opportunism and disillusionment. His election to the German parliament—only four years after the Nazi regime was defeated—began a political career at national, state, and again national level that culminated in his election as the chancellor of the Federal Republic of Germany in 1966. Yet despite the skepticism that his rapid and timely postwar political transformation arouses, his subsequent political success presupposed abandonment of his convictions of the Nazi era. When he was elected West German Chancellor in 1966, Nazism was a part of his biography, not his present political views.

The same was not the case for Husseini. Unlike his former associate in the Nazi propaganda offices, Husseini did not change his views. Moreover, he did not have to change them as a precondition for con-

---

[39] Jerry Muller, *The Other God That Failed: Hans Freyer and the Deradicalization of German Conservatism* (Princeton: Princeton University Press, 1987).

tinued political prominence. Upon his return to Egypt in 1946, Hassan al-Banna, the leader of the Muslim Brotherhood described him as "this hero who challenged an empire and fought Zionism, with the help of Hitler and Germany. Germany and Hitler are gone, but Amin Al-Husseini will continue the struggle."[40] In the postwar decade following the end of World War II, Husseini remained the most important leader of the Palestinian national movement. From 1946 on, after Husseini's return to the region, the Arab Higher Committee functioned again in Palestine. In the words of Edward Said, the AHC was "chaired by Palestine's national leader, Haj Amin al-Husseini." Under his leadership, this organization "represented the Palestinian Arab national consensus, had the backing of the Palestinian political parties that functioned in Palestine, and was recognized in some form by Arab governments as the voice of the Palestinian people, until the Palestine Liberation Organization acquired its representative character."[41] In 1948, the Palestine National Council meeting in Gaza, unanimously chose him to be its president, putting him at the head of the leading organization of Palestinian nationalism and the precursor to the Palestinian Liberation Organization, which was founded in 1964. Husseini rejected all efforts to reach a compromise with the Jews in Palestine and played a central role in organizing armed units to engage in what he called the "holy jihad," his term for the Arab war on the new state of Israel in 1948. Husseini's political preeminence and his ascendency over moderate Palestinians constitute powerful evidence that at very least his partisanship for Nazism and his much broadcast hatred for the Jews and Zionism during World War II did not disqualify him from continued participation in political life. The ideological fusion between Nazism and Islamism, to which he contributed before and during World War II, had a second life in the Middle East. From the 1930s to the 1950s, Husseini's hatred of the Jews remained at the core of his world-view.[42]

In postwar Europe, despite many myths regarding who did and did not support and oppose Nazism and fascism, and despite a postwar era in which too much was forgotten and too many criminals escaped timely judicial reckoning, Nazism and the Jew-hatred from which it was

---

[40] Herf, *Nazi Propaganda for the Arab World*, 243–44.
[41] Ibid., xii.
[42] Ibid., 241–244.

inseparable ceased to be dominant factors in the mainstream of European politics. Husseini's prominence indicates that his support for Hitler's Germany and his radical anti-Semitism did not have a comparable disqualifying impact in parts of Palestinian and Arab politics after 1945. He and his apologists excused his hatred of the Jews as being an apparently justified response to the creation of the state of Israel in 1948, to the Zionist project as a whole, and to imperialism and colonialism more generally. They refused to acknowledge that the ideological synthesis between Nazism, Islamism, and radical Arab nationalism that he helped to broadcast over Nazi radio during the World War II remained intact as he won the support of a significant part of the Palestinian and Arab sentiment. Rather, the slogans of anti-imperialism facilitated the survival, in a different political and cultural context, of the fusion of Nazism and Islamism he helped to shape in wartime Berlin.

The following conclusions are in order: First, the reason that discussion of the crimes of the Nazi regime—and of the nature of the East German dictatorship—was more extensive than in other post-dictatorial or post-traumatic settings was that in both cases, the old regime was overthrown. Other governments, in the first case foreign and in the second case the German government, made it their policy to examine the crimes of the old regime. Where elements of the old regime persist and where foreign occupation has not taken place, as is the case in most post-dictatorial settings, the ability of the successor democracy to explore the traumatic past has been much weaker. Second, liberal democracy was both a precondition for any serious reckoning with the past and a restoration for the rule of law. Yet it also empowered those who preferred strategies of oblivion. Elections, especially close elections, gave power to voters and lobbies who opposed coming to terms with the past. Forced to choose between such reckonings and wining votes, politicians often sought the votes. However, the establishment of liberal democratic ideas and institutions created the necessary preconditions for a reckoning, especially as the compromised generations left the scene of public life. Third, despite the presence of the oblivion, forgetfulness, and mythmaking, Nazism and fascism ceased to have a prominent place in postwar European politics. Scoundrels and chameleons survived but not as Nazis and public anti-Semites. Their cynicism and opportunism, as de Gaulle, Adenauer, and Churchill understood, were also elements that made liberal democracy possible in postwar

Europe. In this sense, the postwar era in Europe bears comparison to previous postwar eras in which acts of oblivion were part of the political agreements that facilitated peace more than justice. Yet amid the forgetfulness, Nazism remained on the extremes and the margins.

Husseini's prominence in Arab and Palestinian politics illustrates that this extent of delegitimation of anti-Semitism and Nazism did not take place to the same extent in Arab and Islamist politics after 1945. Others such as Sayyid Qutb, Hassan al-Banna and the Muslim Brotherhood and the traditions of postwar Islamism also offered vehicles for continued expression of the radical anti-Semitism of the Nazi era. Egypt and Syria became safe havens for former members of the SS. The lines between anti-Zionism and anti-Semitism became hard to distinguish in the propaganda of the Arab secular nationalist governments as well.[43] Despite postwar Europe's paucity of short-term memory and the mythmaking of the postwar years, it would not have rewarded an unreconstructed advocate of Nazism's radical anti-Semitism such as Husseini's with the political success and prominence he enjoyed in the early postwar years in Egypt, Lebanon, and Palestine before 1948. Postwar Europe had no shortage of shortcomings regarding its treatment of the Nazi past. Anti-Semitism did not disappear. Antagonism toward Israel did become an important element of parts of mainstream politics. Yet the persistence of elements of mid-twentieth century Europe's hatreds of the extreme right amid anti-Zionist Arab nationalist and Islamist ideologies in the Middle East after 1945 reminds us about one of most important and taken for granted accomplishments of the victors of World War II and then of the postwar European leaders. It was that Nazism ceased to be a major element in the mainstream politics of Germany and Austria, the countries from which it had emerged.

---

[43] See, for example, Paul Berman, *Terror and Liberalism* (New York: W.W. Norton, 2003); Matthias Küntzel, *Jihad and Jew-Hatred: Nazism, Islamism and the Roots of 9/11* (New York: Telos Press, 2009); Robert Wistrich, *A Lethal Obsession: Anti-Semitism from Antiquity to the Global Jihad* (New York: Random House, 2010).

Alexandru Gussi

On the Relationship between Politics of Memory and the State's Rapport with the Communist Past

Introduction

Over the past twenty-five years, the debate about the communist past in Eastern Europe became largely a discussion about the debate itself. In this chapter, I will argue that, in the immediate aftermath of the events of 1989, the main concern of the public actors was not to clarify the nature of the old regime, but to assess its specific elements, to condemn and/or to forget them. Such processes were perceived to be the perquisites of embarking on the project of building a new democratic state.

From the very beginning, many politicians and analysts confused the social necessity of memory, but also of forgetting, with the political use (if not manipulation) of these natural feelings. Subsequently, more often than not, the need to achieve political power and to have access to material resources overshadowed the interest for a sustained archeology of the past. Nevertheless, the narratives of the communist past[1] remained an essential element for the understanding of political

---

[1] I analyze the narratives of communist past and the political use of memory of the communist period as part of the relation between political identities and the political discourse on the recent past inspired by works like Henry Rousso, *Le syndrome de Vichy 1944–1987* (Paris: Seuil, 1987) and Marie-Claire Lavabre, *Le fil rouge. Sociologie de la mémoire communiste* (Paris: Presses de la FNSP, 1994). For the theoretical approach, see also Serge Berstein, "Introduction. Nature et fonction des cultures politiques" in Serge Berstein (ed.), *Les cultures politiques en France* (Paris: Seuil, 1999), 7–31, Henry Rousso, "La Seconde Guerre Mondiale dans la mémoire des droites françaises" in Jean-François Sirinelli, *Histoire des droites en France*, vol. 2, (Paris: Gallimard, 1992), 550–660.

cultures in post-communist Europe.[2] I state in this work that the new identities of political parties, civil society, intellectual circles and various schools of thought, and even of new nation-states after 1989 have been fundamentally rooted in the discursive and representational processing of the communist (and not only) past. From this perspective, the attitude toward the past was inextricably linked with the gradual development of democracy and pluralism.[3] We can say that remembering the communist historical experience was a ritual that could "serve political organizations by producing bonds of solidarity without requiring uniformity of belief."[4]

At the same time, it was almost impossible to depoliticize the question of the totalitarian legacy. Across the entire former socialist bloc, deliberate politics of forgetting and biased politics of memory contributed, in different ways, to collective feelings of frustration among individuals living in post-communist societies. Resentment, however, fluctuates along a wide array of social categories, from victims of the communist regimes to collaborators of the various secret police agencies. Regardless, if one was a perpetrator, fellow traveler, a bystander, or a member of those sections of the population that were subject to direct and targeted repression, everybody needed to understand, in different ways obviously, what kind of historical and political experience they have been through. Though motivations might be in radical contrast, all members of a former communist society revealed a certain urge toward some kind of closure.

---

[2] For Vladimir Tismăneanu, "Left, right, center: all these notions have strange and elusive meanings under post-communism. Using interpretative Western paradigms would simply create false analogies and would explain little, if anything." See Vladimir Tismaneanu, "The Leninist Debris or Waiting for Perón," *East European Politics and Societies*, vol. 10, no. 3, (Fall 1996), 504–35,.

[3] For Geoffrey Pridham, "National identity expresses a basic form of collective experience, while parties are important as agents for transmission, but also transmogrification of historical memories" in Geoffrey Pridham, *The Dynamics of Democratization: A Comparative Approach* (London and New York: Continuum, 2000), 35.

[4] David I. Kertzer, *Rituals, Politics and Power* (New Haven and London: Yale University, 1988), 67.

The political instrumentation of collective memory undermined a significant part of the moral weight that the recourse to such mechanism potentially brings forth (on this, see Grosescu and Ursachi's contribution). Consequently, those societies judged the communist past almost exclusively from the perspective of the political and economic context. In this aspect, one could categorize post-communist states on the basis of the relationship between their capacity to condemn the totalitarian past and the swiftness of their transition toward a democratic regime.[5] My hypothesis is that the countries where the successor parties were not defeated in elections in 1989 or 1990, as it was the case in Romania,[6] Bulgaria,[7] and some other Balkan and ex-Soviet states,[8] these heirs of the former Communist parties were able to "dissolve" into the State and maintain a more or less covert control over administrative structures.[9] Subsequently, the alternation to power, when such successor parties ultimately lost elections, could not change fundamentally this legacy of communist bureaucratic "conversion" originating in the early post-communist period. In other words,

---

[5] For Vladimir Tismaneanu "the new radical-authoritarian trends (often disguised as pro-democratic) in Russia, Ukraine, Bulgaria, Romania, Slovakia, and elsewhere, lingering reflexes and habits inherited from Leninist and pre-Leninist regimes authoritarianism continue to exist: intolerance, exclusiveness, rejection of all compromise, extreme personalization of political discourse, and the search for charismatic leadership. These Leninist psychological leftovers can be detected at both ends of political spectrum," Vladimir Tismăneanu, "Leninist Legacies, Pluralist Dilemmas," *Journal of Democracy*, October 2007, vol. 18, no. 4, 34–39, 35–36.

[6] For Romania, see Alexandru Gussi, *La Roumanie face à son passé communiste: Mémoires et cultures politiques* (Paris: l'Harmattan, 2011), 45–142.

[7] For Bulgaria, see for example, Rumyana Kolarova and Dimitr Dimitrov, "Bulgaria," in Jon Elster (ed.), *The Roundtable Talks and the Breakdown of Communism* (Chicago and London: University of Chicago Press, 1996), 178–212; and Marta Touykova, "The Genesis of a Successor Party in Bulgaria," *Raisons politiques*, no. 3, August–October 2001, 127–38, 130.

[8] For post-communist Russian Federation, see Kathleen E. Smith, *Mythmaking in the New Russia: Politics and Memory in the Yeltsin Era* (Ithaca and London: Cornell University Press, 2002).

[9] In this sense, we can say that some state institutions acted as forms of counter-power, a role which the state may have in another context, as pointed out by Jean Louis Quermonne, *L'appareil administratif de l'Etat* (Paris: Seuil, 1991), 10.

the democratic transition was often hindered by the interest of the ex-Communists to block the access of anti-communist and democratic forces to real power over the State structures.[10]

The assessment laid out above is obviously more of a background generalization. There is, of course, no uniform pattern. However, in the countries quoted above, when compared with Central European states, we can notice, at the very least, various symptoms of this feeling of lack of control of non-communist political leaders over state structures. In the Romanian case, two such developments are highly relevant for my present analysis. The first is the political instability that goes as far as claiming a coup d'état. The second is the lack of a minimum consensus on condemning the crimes of the communist state (on this also see Vladimir Tismaneanu's and Bogdan C. Iacob's chapter).[11]

One recent example, far from anecdotal, is provided by Vladimir Tismaneanu, who pointed out that the recent law which makes August 23th the Day for the Commemoration of the Victims of Fascism and Communism, and December 21th the Day of the Victims of Communism in Romania was simply ignored in 2013 by public authorities, even though it touched on an issue that was apparently on the public agenda at the time of its issuance. It seems that the blame could be laid exclusively on a lack of political will or on the continuity of the communist state. After twenty-five years, state bureaucracy is far from monolithic, and the continued existence of the networks formed before 1989 can only partially explain what is going on. Our interest, how-

---

[10] Romania is notorious in this matter; according to Emil Constantinescu, the first president who represented a political alliance different from the successors of the communist party: "we won the elections, but not the power." He was expressing at the time a feeling that I believe may be generalized across various former communist countries. On this issue see Alexandru Gussi, *La Roumanie face à son passé communiste*, 213–228.

[11] In Romania, the 2006 condemnation of the crimes of Communism was challenged by the Social Democratic Party, in spite of the fact that the latter never accepted the idea of any form of continuity with the Communist Party. Moreover, as Cristian Vasile shows in this volume, Mircea Geoană, then chairman of the SDP, initially supported the idea of nominating Vladimir Tismăneanu as head of a commission to analyze the communist regime. See "Rezoluția Congresului Extraordinar al PSD în legătură cu folosirea trecutului ca armă politică din 10 decembrie 2006," www.psd.ro, December 12, 2006.

ever, focuses upon the relationship between the society that tends to see the state as a whole, and the reality of that state, which, in relation with the past, becomes plural, we could say even contradictory. That is because there seem to be several policies of memory that are applied, based on narratives about the past that contradict each other. From this point of view, the analyses that do not start from the tension that exists within state structures between differing narratives on the communist past end up exaggerating the significance of an official discourse on the past, a discourse which cannot be reduced to a single narrative of the past. In fact, in Romania, one cannot talk about a coherent official discourse about the communist period. Such situation defies expectations of the state producing an official history that it subsequently imposes upon society. Within this logic, we can better understand the fact that there are collective frustrations among those segments of society which expected justice from the post-communist state.

Many researchers interested in the dynamics of post-communist societies notice such widespread dissatisfaction within significant sectors of a traumatized society.[12] Eastern European societies discovered the limits of the break from communism, and the lack of feasibility of lustration laws against the background of constitutional considerations intrinsic to the establishment of a rule of law. Similar reactions were triggered by the reality of the inability to implement measures concerning transitional criminal justice, that is, the difficulty in condemning those responsible for the crimes perpetrated throughout the existence of communist regimes.[13]

The rule of law is based on the principle of nonretroactivity and this became one of the main obstacles for anyone willing to legally condemn former communist perpetrators. The latter, that is the victimizers and not the victims, benefited from the democratic principles against which they themselves fought their entire lives. After 1989, they reported a final victory against their adversaries. Craig Calhoun excellently diagnosed this phenomenon when he remarked that former com-

---

[12] For specific examples, see the country studies in Lavinia Stan (ed.), *Transitional Justice in Eastern Europe and the Former Soviet Union: Reckoning with the Communist Past* (New York: Routledge, 2009).

[13] See Raluca Grosescu and Raluca Ursachi, *Justiția penală de tranziție: De la Nurnberg la postcomunismul românesc* (Iași: Polirom, 2009).

munists understood that they "can use the language of democracy to ensure their future right to participate in the government, while invoking liberalism's limitations on state powers to safeguard themselves against future retribution."[14]

Social frustration is also a result of the lack of coherence of the anti-communist political leaders, who excelled in making glowing promises and in setting high expectations by invoking political reform built on moral grounds.[15] Upon coming into power, these elites inevitably broke their promises, thus seriously subverting the democratic frameworks of responsibility and of institutional accountability. Under these circumstances, one general phenomenon that can easily be noticed is that the past was selectively used as a weapon against adversaries, while simultaneously functioning as a mechanism to protect one's supporters.[16] Unsurprisingly, such political instrumentation of the pre-1989 period contributed to an ever-ascending spiral of collective frustration.[17] Subsequently, nostalgia, on the one hand, anger, on the other hand, placed great strain upon the very legitimacy of post-communist regimes.[18]

In the public space, one can notice the coexistence of two opposing and separate types of discourses. First, there are narratives of indictment,

---

[14] Quoted in Lavinia Stan, "Poland" in Lavinia Stan (ed.), *Transitional Justice in Eastern Europe*, 68.

[15] For example, historian James Mark underlined that "the impulse to remember only developed with the growing perception in the mid-1990s that the former system had not in fact been fully overcome." See James Mark, *The Unfinished Revolution: Making Sense of the Communist Past in Central-Eastern Europe* (New Haven/London: Yale University Press, 2010), xiii.

[16] For Vladimir Tismaneanu, "Critical intellectuals may insist on the need for moral clarity, but the political class remains narcissistically self-cantered and impervious to the injunction to live in truth." Tismaneanu, "Leninist Legacies," 35.

[17] For a comparative analysis of the complex relationship between criticism against post-communist regimes and the attitude toward the Communist past, see Sergiu Gherghina, "Attitudes Towards the Communist Past in Five Central and East European Countries," *History of Communism in Europe*, vol. I, 2010, 167–181.

[18] For a study on lustration impact, see Cynthia M. Horne, "Assessing the Impact of Lustration on Trust in Public Institutions and National Government in Central and Eastern Europe," *Comparative Political Studies*, vol. 45, no. 4, 2011, 412–446.

which condemn the crimes of communism. Second, there is nostalgia, which goes so far as to use artifacts for advertisement on prime-time commercial television (for example, the region-wide trend to employ in advertisement some "classic" products from the "beautiful years" of the 1970s and 1980s). However, it is remarkable that we cannot find a correspondence between the pluralism of narratives of the past produced by the State and those most visible in the public sphere. Below I will try to present an explanation for this phenomenon.

In almost all post-communist countries one can notice the widespread expression of nostalgia toward communism that is not, at least for the moment, a political one, but rather a social one.[19] At the same time, nostalgia is also an intergenerational experience of selective, subjective bits of personal memory, which usually manifest themselves in the absence of a canonical condemnation of the totalitarian past. One cannot predict the effect, if any, of this nostalgia, when it comes to its appropriation by the political structures. Political scientist Grigore Pop-Eleches recently concluded that "to the extent that civic participation deficit is driven by the experience of having lived through communism, we have no reason to expect it to persist beyond the current generations."[20] Protests such as those in Sofia and Bucharest in 2013 seem to prove Pop-Eleches right. This is significant because we are talking about precisely the generations that have produced a new type of social nostalgia. Additionally, polls indicate that in Romania, for instance, *ostalgia* is low among the youth. The more "classical" nostalgia is stronger than ever among the generation which is over sixty years of age. The tension between generations is an important element that can potentially explain, to a certain extent, the difficulty of producing social or political consensus around some form of relating to the communist past.

In Romania, the twenty-year anniversary of the collapse of communism can provide an excellent exemplification of the above-mentioned ambivalence, rooted in both the political elites' incapacity to

---

[19] For this observation, see Dominik Bartmanski, "Successful Icons of Failed Time: Rethinking Post-Communist Nostalgia," *Acta Sociologica*, vol. 54, no. 3, 2011, 213–231.

[20] Grigore Pop-Eleches and Joshua A. Tucker, "Associated with the Past? Communist Legacies and Civic Participation in Post-Communist Countries," *East European Politics & Societies*, Special Section "Democracy in Central and Eastern Europe: The State of the Art," February 2013, 27, 64.

adopt coherent policies in reference to pre-1989 times and the society's inability to own up to its past. The anniversary could have been highlighted and celebrated at the official level, but it actually passed with a whimper, as officials chose not to dwell on the significance of the 1989 revolutions and the breakdown of state socialism. They appeared hampered by an embarrassment with their own past, which they once invoked with great zeal. Simultaneously, civil society commemorated the collapse of communism in its own way. Conspiracy theories were embraced with enthusiasm across the entire media spectrum.[21] The symbols of the anti-communist revolution simply lost their power. How can one explain this transformation? Is this not, in the context of the economic crisis, a clear manifestation of the rejection of the post-communist establishment?

In the Romanian case, the explanation can only start from the degradation of the significance of the December 1989 moment in society's eyes. As far as this historical experience is concerned, one can point to a revolutionary form of change, but there was a visible continuity both in the state bureaucracy and the political elite as well. This contrast is widely discussed by the contribution of Raluca Grosescu and Raluca Ursachi in the present volume. The first dimension of the fall of communism, the revolutionary one, is visible because it granted legitimacy to the new rulers in 1989–1990, and for the new regime overall. At the same time, it also obscured the dimension of continuity with the communist past. In this context, the two and a half decades that have passed since 1989 can be described as a long and successful challenge to the revolutionary dimension; the strengthening of the dimension that highlights continuity. The central element here is the contrast between the two dimensions, which leads to a sharp decline in the capacity for granting legitimacy that the 1989 moment had. The process of degradation undergone by the revolutionary moment's symbolic image can be considered the outcome of twenty-four years or so of collec-

---

[21] In their article published in this volume, Raluca Grosescu and Raluca Ursachi identify "four narratives on the nature of the Revolution and its violent repression." In addition, there is a veritable ritual related to television broadcasts deconstructing the 1989 moment. Most of the guests invited either have a negative image in the academia or they are not professional scholars. For details, see Bogdan Murgescu (eds.), *Revoluţia română din decembrie 1989. Istorie şi memorie* (Bucureşti: Polirom, 2007), 205–212.

tive *travail de mémoire*. We may even say that partisanship has affected the significance of December 1989 to the point that it turned from the symbol of a break with the communist past into the paradoxical icon of continuity with it.

The Paradox of the Relation of Post-Communist States with the Recent Past

The paradoxical relationship with the past appears to have originated in the following situation: after 1989, the pluralist discourse coexisted with institutional and cultural mechanisms marked by the totalitarian experience. This tension was projected in the political sphere by roughly two camps that are in a competition on the basis of their sharply contrasting attitudes toward the communist past. After 1990, the State needed to build a form of negative legitimacy against its Communist past. It was also a way of taking distance that was considered necessary for post-communist states in order to gain credit in the eyes of the West.[22] This attitude toward the past also contributed to the birth of civil society inside the countries in Eastern Europe. Accordingly, many states formally declared themselves to be non-communist and democratic without, in fact, taking seriously widespread concern for policies aimed at removing communist state institutions. The identity of the new states was decisively shaped by their acceptance or rejection of a certain political memory. This is evident in the case of states belonging to the sphere of influence of the former Soviet Union.[23]

Simultaneously, the main political parties, whether anti-communist or simply ex-communist, had to respond to the same injunction:

---

[22] As Katherine Verdery emphasized, "In Eastern Europe, rewriting history has been perhaps unusually necessary because of powerful pressures to create political identities based expressly on rejecting the immediate past. The pressures came not just from popular revulsion with communism, but also from desires to persuade Western audiences to contribute the aid and investment essential to reconstruction," Katherine Verdery, *The Political Lives of Dead Bodies. Reburial and Postsocialist Change* (New York: Columbia University Press, 1999), 52.

[23] Kathleen E. Smith, *Mythmaking in the New Russia: Politics and Memory During the Yeltsin Era* (Ithaca and London: Cornell University Press, 2002).

to define themselves as post-communist and anti-totalitarian entities. In the background, of course, lay the question of a genuine separation from totalitarianism—at stake was the overcoming of Communist experience. Initially, this was presented as a national objective, publicly proclaimed by all ex-communist actors.[24] As the immediate aftermath of communism's collapse passed, the political debate mainly concentrated on the practical and symbolic ways of implementing such a program. After twenty-five years, one can legitimately wonder to what extent the political and social cleavage with the past was truly radical, as long as the goals of post-communist transitions were similar, while only the timing and the style of the political and social actors were different. Furthermore, if one is to adopt a panoramic view of the entire former Socialist bloc, the homogeneity of the trajectories of the post-communist states is striking. One cannot fail to notice that the methods used by the main political forces at the level of their social and economic policies were also quite similar. At least two inevitable questions beg answers: Was the rift over the past only artificial? Did it come about from a symbolic need?

It is true that sometimes the politics of memory were different, but again—looking at the big picture—we do not see great, unassailable differences in the respective relationships that societies from Central and Eastern Europe have with their communist past. The idea of the end of history, the attraction of and for the Western model, in parallel with the complete demise of the communist societal model, were such powerful realities in 1989 that, across the entire region, pluralism could come about as a result of the competition between political parties that either opted for a narrative centered on the truth about the past (or the need for revenge) or for official amnesia out of the fear of the removal of communist heritage. Consequently, the relationship with the past in its every aspect (condemnation, nostalgia, or reaction against too much of either) remained one of the main sources of mobilization in these countries. It is central to the definition of political identity, individual affect, and societal symbols.

---

[24] For G. Pridham, "the presence of regime alternatives to democracy depends very much on perceptions of the authoritarian past. Historically based anti-authoritarian attitudes continued to delegitimize a possible return to non-democratic rule," Pridham, *The Dynamics of Democratization*, 226.

Compared to the German model of uncompromising condemnation of the Nazi past or the Spanish model of consensual oblivion,[25] the countries in Eastern Europe provided a new blueprint, structured on a top-down trajectory of *instrumental cleavage*. The latter was based on an impossible compromise (or consensus) over the past. The impossibility of compromise also functioned as one of the primary mechanisms that produced and legitimated ideological pluralism. The paradox lies in the fact that the ideological consensus over the type of future society makes impossible the consensus over the means of condemning the old society.

In addition, because the "capitalist" model that everyone aspired to fundamentally excluded any form of anti-communist revolution or violent removal of communism, post-1989 parties did not have to take into account the risk of violence in the process of system building because apparently there was none, maybe with the exception of Romania and Albania. The risk of violence being low, both in terms of removal of communism and possible return to communism, political parties took extensive liberty in using and manipulating the politics of memory. Subsequently, society saw its grieving and mourning being confiscated by various political actors and by the State itself. The past (or better said, the memory of it) then almost exclusively began to be perceived as an instrument for amassing partisan majorities of different political coloring. The result was that the State seemed to lose its credibility in facing the past, maybe with the exception of some moments of apparent consensus in some of the countries of Eastern Europe.

The above situation was a direct result of the encounter between the ruins of a type of totalitarianism that lasted over forty years with the ideal of a liberal democracy, for which Western institutions did not have a pre-prepared "recipe" for the East. At the same time, the West (either the European Union or NATO) had no intention of encouraging the so-called Nuremberg of communism. Furthermore, decades of

---

[25] For a broader comparative perspective, see Paloma Aguilar, Alexandra Barahona De Brito, Carmen Gonzalez-Enriquez (eds.), *The Politics of Memory: Transitional Justice in Democratizing Societies* (Oxford: Oxford University Press, 2002).

Soviet hegemony and the resilience of Leninist legacies[26] limited the emergence of genuine internal resources, able to define the problems of the past in the terms of the rule of law.

The fall of communism was an event lived simultaneously in the West and the East of Europe. This simultaneity produced the illusion of the existence of comparable mental patterns and even the idea of a common memory. But memories were very different and they continue to remain so until present. These realities generated the fact that international justice did not work in the case of post-communism. It was considered that there were European courts and rules applicable. However, these courts defend the fundamental principles of liberal democracy. Therefore, individual responsibility and nonretroactivity could be used as arguments against the logic of lustration, inside and outside the judicial system. Europe seemed to tell its East to forget the past, to ignore the possibility that the democratic identity of post-communist states could be founded on the condemnation of the crimes against humanity from their recent past.[27]

Since the 1990s, the pro-democratic circles in the region regarded Western Europe as a political and social model, as well as a pressure factor for the democratization process and guarantee for the stability of the political regime. The entry of the ex-communist states in the European Union validated this strategy, but that did come at a steep price. The cost was that the political balance artificially maintained with the purpose of achieving EU accession was broken in the immediate aftermath of ending this stage of post-communist evolution. With external political pressure lessened, the limits of democratization become apparent, especially at the level of the political sphere and in reference

---

[26] On Leninist legacies in Eastern Europe see Kenneth Jowitt, *New World Disorder: The Leninist Extinction* (Berkeley: University of California Press, 1992), Anna Grzymała-Busse, *Redeeming the Communist Past: The Regeneration of Communist Successor Parties in East Central Europe* (Cambridge: Cambridge University Press, 2002), or Grzegorz Ekiert and Stephen E. Hanson, *Capitalism and Democracy in Central and Eastern Europe: Assessing the Legacy of Communist Rule* (Cambridge: Cambridge University Press, 2003).

[27] On this issue see John Gledhill, "Integrating the Past: Regional Integration and Historical Reckoning in Central and Eastern Europe," *Nationalities Papers*, vol. 39, no. 4, July 2011, 481–506 and Grosescu and Ursachi, *Justiția penală de tranziție*, 68–106.

to state institutions. In this respect, the continuous crisis experienced by Romania after 2007 can hardly be considered an exception.

The Romanian Case—Exception or Blueprint?

Romania is one of the most representative examples among Eastern European countries where the political use of the past played an essential role in the development of political pluralism and of civil society. Moreover, the reality of a profoundly unassumed communist past generated a deep feeling of frustration. This remains true despite the presence of public gestures along the path of overcoming earlier state politics of amnesia, such as the presidential condemnation of the communist regime in 2006.[28] Even as the Romanian state admitted the crimes of the former dictatorship, the absence of coherent policies toward the past only augment preexisting resentment or nostalgia (on this issue see Tismaneanu's and Iacob's chapter). We can also notice an exacerbation of the initial frustration coming from the great expectations fueled by the revolutionary form of the regime change. This horizon of anticipation was unmet by the political power after 1990 due to continuities at the level of elites, state institutions, the judiciary, or the military. However, the question that I am asking is whether the Romanian case can be a paradigmatic example, which illustrates certain characteristics of post-communist democratization that maybe manifested themselves in other countries, but at a lower intensity or in a more diluted fashion.

It is already commonly agreed in the scholarly literature that one should take into consideration the specific nature of the local dictatorial regime in order to understand the specificities of various countries after 1989. In some cases, including the Romanian one, the transition to the rule of law was done without a radical reform of the judicial system. More often than not, one of the reasons behind such continuity was exactly the intention of avoiding the possibility of judging the crimes of the former regime and of postponing indefinitely the act of

---

[28] See Bogdan C. Iacob and Cristian Vasile in this volume. See also, Cosmina-Tanasoiu, "The Tismaneanu Report: Romania Revisits Its Past," *Problems of Post-Communism*, vol. 54, no. 4 (July-August 2007), 60–69.

truth-telling[29] in relation to the past. To this end, it is significant to look at the observation made by Raluca Grosescu and Raluca Ursachi in this book. They show how the politicization of the justice system dramatically diminished its capacity of clarifying responsibility for the crimes perpetrated in December 1989.

Simultaneously, one cannot overlook the instrumental nature of the position adopted by political elites toward the communist past throughout Eastern Europe. The most obvious proof for this state of facts is the failure to enforce the laws aimed at the removal of communism or at dealing with the traumas of state socialism. The implementation of such policies was avoided even by the leaders and the parties claiming to be anti-communist.[30] I believe that this phenomenon can also be tied to the issue of representation that is arising every time the past is invoked. More than twenty years after 1989, it has become increasingly difficult to say who represents whom in terms of the relationship between political actors and the partisans of pro-active politics of memory. However, one should wonder whether, back in the 1990s, representation based on attitudes toward the past was as clear as we have grown to believe. It is doubtful that even then there was no direct connection between the social and the political dimensions constructed upon the cleavage about the communist past.[31] The two elements did exist, but a clear cut link between them is debatable.

All things considered, the last statement does not mean that the memory of the communist past was any less valuable in transitional dynamics. As I mentioned earlier, political and civic identities have been built on memory as a pillar of individual and collective significations. It does allow us, nevertheless, to reassess the extent to which this process that included turning the victims into instruments in political and cultural struggles had positive effects not only on what some people called "the trial of communism," but also on the pace of democratization itself.

---

[29] Priscilla B. Hayner, *Unspeakable Truths: Facing the Challenge of Truth Commissions* (New York: Routledge, 2002).

[30] Alexandru Gussi, *La Roumanie face à son passé communiste*, 213–228.

[31] See also Daniel-Louis Seiler, "Peut-on appliquer les clivages de Rokkan à l'Europe centrale ?" in Jean-Michel De Waele, *Partis politiques et démocratie en Europe centrale et orientale* (Brussels: Editions de l'Université de Bruxelles, 2002), 115–144.

I therefore argue that only by starting from revisiting our understanding of the evolution of the issue of representativeness can we properly understand the failure to enforce a politically acknowledged judicial amnesty instead of a de facto one. This type of de facto amnesty is indeed rather inconspicuous, but it is also fairly obvious, thus producing social frustration. It also erodes the credibility of the State and of political parties, which, in spite of their anti-communist discourse, have been heavily involved in preserving de facto amnesty of the communist past.[32]

What one should not forget though is that the rift over memory gave the former communist parties the opportunity to reinvent themselves. Subsequently, these parties could target two large population categories. On the one hand, there was the part of the population fearing rapid changes. On the other hand, there was the former bureaucratic apparatus (which was defined by continuity) that still needed the political levers to block the advocacy for lustration. We can wonder whether, from this perspective, the ex-communist parties were not perhaps closer to that part of society they claim to represent from the point of view of their attitude toward the communist past than the anti-communist parties in relation with their electorate. And this raises questions about the resources and the importance of the anti-communist political culture in post-1989 Eastern Europe.

In this sense, the Romanian case is interesting because it presents us with a clear split, after 1996, between the instrumental-political dimension, represented by political parties in the Democratic Convention, which won the parliamentary and presidential elections in November that year, and civil society organizations, some of which were part of the Convention (e.g., the Civic Alliance and the Association of Former Political Prisoners). Soon after the Democratic Convention got into power, the civic elements denounced the divorce between the anti-communist discourse and the practice of governing. Taking into account such context, one can identify two types of anti-

---

[32] The fact that they disappeared, as was the case with the Romanian Democratic Convention and with the National Peasant Christian Democratic Party, raises the issue of pluralism and of the democratic process being reversible, as long as other parties do not take over their message in favor of the development of civil society.

communism: the one that turns the past into an instrument used to achieve political goals, and the one that wants to use political power in order to implement certain policies of memory.[33] The failure of the latter, despite the fact that it managed to have a significant impact on shaping democratic political cultures in the countries of the former socialist bloc, was important both for "freeing" anti-communist parties from their social base and for understanding the role of the state institutions that were constructed after the collapse of communist regimes.

The opposition that developed in Romania in the first seven years of post-communism was based on the confusion at the core of the anti-communist discourse between challenging the party in power (National Salvation Front, Social Democratic Party) and condemning the continuity of a State heavily dependent on its Communist legacies. After this period, the anti-communist discourse in the civic and political sphere became the main anti-legitimacy discourse aimed against all political powers, a narrative that was at once pro-democratic and delegitimizing for the new regime and the institutions of the state overall. The importance of this discourse is shown, as Vladimir Tismaneanu points out in this volume, by successfully pushing the body politic to form the Presidential Commission for the Analysis of the Communist Dictatorship in Romania.

The cleavage over the past is not only political and social. It is also a rift at the level of state institutions, which remain profoundly marked by the totalitarian pattern. Beyond the political leadership, the majority of post-communist states went through a period of denial of the past. At the time, the State was organized like a fortress in order to resist the assault of the anti-communist actors. Telling the truth about the past was presented and perceived as a threat against the *national interest* as it was defined by the very state structures that invoked it.[34] It is no surprise then that some post-communist states, such as Romania or Bulgaria (not to mention Russia or other ex-Soviet states), produced and encouraged a political culture that ignored the challenge of the totalitarian past. From this point of view, in many cases, the post-commu-

---

[33] Alexandru Gussi, *La Roumanie face à son passé communiste*, 201–212.

[34] See Alexandru Gussi, „Construction et usages politiques d'un lieu de mémoire. La Place de l'Université de Bucarest," *Revista Română de Ştiinţe Politice-Studia Politica*, vol. II, no. 4, December 2002, 1057–1091.

nist State was not neutral, and therefore it could not provide a coherent policy of memory. Instead, it preferred to encourage oblivion in order to ensure continuity. The logic of the State fortress transformed even the imperative of a judiciary independent from political parties into a legal system that cannot guarantee the rule of law.

Under the circumstances, it becomes obvious that as long as the cleavage over the communist past remains a central issue of social and political dissent, the notion of truth remains politically contingent. Moreover, the struggle for the recovery of traumatized memory and for the condemnation of the crimes of communist regimes remains trapped into an endless loop of de facto amnesty. At the same time, as long as important political actors identify with continuities of the totalitarian period into the present post-communist States, and as long as these continuities are noticeable and regarded as illegitimate by a part of society, telling the truth as part of a neutral discourse will not be credible or perceived as legitimate. Within such arrangement, the memory of the communist past will remain a potential weapon against the democratic legitimacy of the ex-communist States.

Conclusion

In this chapter I analyzed how the State can tell the truth in Eastern Europe, and the conditions for the politics of memory to become neutral in the context of the resilience of a cleavage about the communist past in the political sphere and within society. These questions can hardly be considered rhetorical. I argue that the answer can be found in revisiting our established perceptions about the part played by the communist past in the process of democratization during the last two and a half decades. The split caused by the memory of the pre-1989 dictatorships lays at the core the new democratic States. Moreover, the attitude toward the communist past remains the identity principle of many political parties competing for electoral and structural dominance. This situation cannot be reconciled with the affirmation of the impartial liberal State. In the rare moments when the institutions of the State want a nonpartisan form of condemnation of the totalitarian past, as in 2006 Romania, it is still regarded by society as an ideological projection of a group of interests, not of the society as a whole.

The post-communist state does indeed preserve in its relationship with the citizenry something of the systemic attitudes from before 1989. The State is not acknowledged as a neutral actor on the political scene. This genuine difficulty of present day liberal democracies in Eastern Europe, though sometimes exaggerated at the level of the public opinion, is mainly the result of the absence of a consensus on the nature and role of the past in the current political and social establishment.

In addition, the present analysis has concentrated on those dimensions of Romania's case which may make it significant for several states in the former Communist bloc, especially those of which we can talk about a significant continuity at the level of state structures. In Romania, it can be concluded that there are two distinct pairs of competing narratives of the communist past. One is produced by some state institutions and the political elite; the other one is the product of civil society. The great difference between them has to do with the fact that, on one hand, the former have in common the fact that they attempt to consolidate the legitimacy of the post-1989 state, of the present political regime, by either condemning the crimes of communism or by attempting to grant different value to some portion of the past. On the other hand, the second pair of narratives, produced by society, uses either an anti-communist discourse or forms of nostalgia in order to challenge the legitimacy of the post-communist state and of the present political regime. This is a remarkable phenomenon by which the classical conflict between the positive and negative perspectives of the recent past is substituted by a conflict revolving around the post-communist State and the transitional regime. The positive or negative attitudes toward the past thus become secondary. The central position is taken by the role that discourses about the past have in granting or removing legitimacy to the political regime and to its institutions.

Part Two

HISTORIES AND THEIR PUBLICS

Vladimir Tismaneanu

Democracy, Memory, and Moral Justice

In January 2007, Romania acceded to the European Union (EU), a few years after having entered the North Atlantic Treaty Organization (NATO). This was a watershed in Romania's history, a significant moment in the history of Eastern Europe, and a test for the EU's commitment to accepting problematic candidates as long as they have complied with the major accession requirements. Sometime ago, in a controversial article published in the *New York Review of Books*, the late Tony Judt argued that the real test for the EU was Romania's accession, considering its pending structural problems. The piece generated anger among Romanian intellectuals and produced reactions both pro and con.[1] Nevertheless, one cannot deny the nature of the difficulties with which Romania is faced, among them that of an unmastered past. This article proposes to document and critically examine, in a comparative perspective, Romania's efforts to confront and judge its communist past. The starting point for the analysis is the country's decision to work through its communist past, a late decision that came about in

---

[1] Tony Judt's article "Romania: Bottom of the Heap," *New York Review of Books*, November 1, 2001, came out in Romania in a volume edited by Mircea Mihăieş, including various polemical responses by influential Romanian intellectuals—see Tony Judt, *Romania: la fundul grămezii. Polemici, controverse, pamflete* (Iaşi: Polirom, 2002); see also Tony Judt's discussion of Eastern Europe in his masterful *Post-War: A History of Europe Since 1945* (New York: Penguin, 2005). I discussed the moral and political dilemmas of decommunization in *Fantasies of Salvation: Nationalism, Democracy, and Myth in Post-Communist Europe* (Princeton: Princeton University Press, 1998).

a convoluted fashion. Still, once the process started in late 2005 and early 2006, it gathered a tremendous momentum and resulted in a categorical state condemnation of the communist dictatorship as illegitimate and criminal.

The questions I try to answer with this chapter are as follows: Why did Romania engage so late in the effort to face up to its communist past? What were the main obstacles that prevented this historical catharsis for almost seventeen years after the December 1989 revolution? Why did this catharsis occur precisely in 2006? How does Romania compare to other East European countries in terms of mastering its dictatorial past? What political and cultural conditions explain the resurgence and intensification of the anti-communist sentiment after a long period of relative indifference or even torpor regarding this topic? At the same time, I also wish to explain the *coincidentia oppositorum* of the efforts to "condemn the condemnation," the common front in negating the Final Report of the Presidential Commission for the Analysis of the Communist Dictatorship created by unrepentant radical left-wingers, fanatical nationalists, national-Stalinist nostalgics, and Orthodoxist fundamentalists.[2] In short, I consider that it is crucial to identify the political and cultural forces that seem to have invested themselves into the subversion of the process of decommunization in Romania. Going beyond various subjective stands, resentment, or personal vanities (from people such as the former president Ion Iliescu, who most of his life was a Leninist apparatchik), one needs to emphasize that this offensive against the process of working through the past has structural motivations that are deeply rooted in the mentalities of communist times that have survived in the transitional Romanian political culture. This mind-set preserves the elements of an ideological syncretism that I have previously labeled as the fascist-communist baroque. The public sphere is still haunted by unprocessed memories, the refusal by some intellectuals to acknowledge the magnitude of the anti-Semitic massacres, and even efforts to present Ion Antonescu as a hero of sorts. Negationism is present also in attempts to present the communist regime, especially the Ceaușescu period, as an expression of national affirmation.

---

[2] For an extensive discussion of the various groups involved in this "front" see the contributions in this volume by Cristian Vasile and, especially, Bogdan C. Iacob.

Decomunization is a complex process that comprises political, juridical, and moral elements. The process of therapy through knowledge, what I would call exorcising the spectres of the past by way of accessing nonmythicized truths, is the royal path in achieving such a goal. Furthermore, I contend that decommunization and defascization must be inextricably linked if Romania is to participate in building what German political scientist Claus Leggewie defined as a shared European memory.[3] William Faulkner's famous line from *Requiem for a Nun* certainly applies to the haunted lands where communism once held sway: "The past is never dead. It's not even past." A major source of frustration and discontent in the region and especially in Romania is the widespread belief that ex-communists have been too successful at blunting genuine efforts to reckon with the past.

It is important to point out that the belated nature of Romania's decision to confront its communist totalitarian past was predominantly the consequence of obstinate opposition to such an undertaking from parties and personalities directly or indirectly linked to the *ancien régime*. The elections of November and December 2004 resulted in the victory of an anti-communist coalition and the election of Traian Băsescu as the country's president. In spite of political rivalries and the disintegration of the initial government coalition, both the National Liberal and the Democratic Parties understood the importance of coming to terms with the past. Especially after January 2006, the liberal prime minister, at the time, Călin Popescu-Tăriceanu (then head of the Liberal Party), and President Traian Băsescu (linked to the Democratic Party) have championed decommunization. At the other end of the political spectrum, in an effort to boycott these initiatives, former president Ion Iliescu and other leaders of the Social Democratic Party (in many respects still dominated by former nomenklatura figures) allied themselves with the ultrapopulist, jingoistic, and anti-Semitic "Greater Romania Party," headed by the notorious Corneliu Vadim Tudor, a former Ceaușescu sycophant. The condemnation of the communist dictatorship has become one of the most hotly debated political, ideological, and moral issues in contemporary Romania.

---

[3] Claus Leggewie, "Seven Circles of European Memory," *Eurozine*, 20 December 2012 (http://www.eurozine.com/articles/2010-12-20-leggewie-en.html).

Unlike Germany, where a parliamentary consensus (minus the radical left) allowed for the relatively peaceful activity of the Enquete Commission headed by former dissident pastor Rainer Eppelmann,[4] the Presidential Commission for the Analysis of the Communist Dictatorship in Romania (PCACDR—from now on the Commission), which I chaired, was continuously attacked from the extreme left, the nationalist right, and Orthodox clericalist and fundamentalist circles. The inconsistent institutional backing for the PCACDR led some to argue that this Commission was merely a presidential initiative, implicitly allowing them to paint it as a form of political partisanship. Such a characterization is utterly mistaken: the Commission was mandated by the Romanian head of state and it was the result of the successful pressure from below exercised by the most important organizations and representatives of Romania's democratic civil society. The Commission and its Report are the products of a collective civic effort officially endorsed by the Romanian state.

As its chairman and coordinator, I witnessed the historical event on December 18, 2006, when the Romanian President, Traian Băsescu, presented and adopted before the Parliament the conclusions and proposals of the Commission's Report. The behavior of those present could be divided into two categories: those who acted like hooligans, vehemently denying the importance and legitimacy of official reckoning with the communist past; and those who, imbued with the solemnity of the event, reacted in a dignified manner. The next day, in an interview with the BBC, the president insisted that the hysteria of the crypto-communists and the nationalists was no reason to be deterred from continuing along the line of working through Romania's traumatic dictatorial past. On the contrary, their attitude was a sign that the path chosen was the right one, from an academic and moral point of view. A functional and healthy democratic society cannot endlessly indulge in politics of oblivion and denial. Though some have argued along these lines, I do not believe that a collective com-

---

[4] For a detailed description of the prerogatives of the Enquete Commission in Germany, see Hermann Weber, "Rewriting the History of the German Democratic Republic: The Work of the Commission of Inquiry" in Reinhard Alter and Peter Monteath (eds.), *Rewriting the German Past* (New Jersey: Humanities Press, 1997), 157–173.

municative silence [*kommunikatives Beschweigen*] about the past can enable post-communist countries to evolve into functioning democracies.[5]

Reconciliation remains spurious in the absence of repentance. In the short term, the politics of forgetfulness (what former Polish Prime Minister Tadeusz Mazowiecki once called "the thick line with the past") can have its benefits if one takes into account the newly born and fragile social consensus. In the long term, however, such policies foster grievous misgivings in relation to collective values and memory, with potentially disastrous institutional and psychoemotional consequences. Pastor Joachim Gauck, chair of the authority dealing with the Stasi (East German secret police) files, argued that "reconciliation with the traumatic past can be achieved not simply through grief, but also through discussion and dialogue."[6] In this sense, Charles Villa-Vicencio, one of the main members of South Africa's Commission for Truth and Reconciliation, defined reconciliation as "the operation whereby individuals and the community create for themselves a space in which they can communicate with one another, in which they can begin the arduous labor of understanding" painful history. Hence, justice becomes a process of enabling the nation with the aid of a culture of responsibility.[7] Communism wished to strictly and ubiquitously control remembrance. It detested the idea of emancipated anamnesis, so it systematically falsified the past. Until 2006, Romanian democracy had been consistently deprived of truth-telling in relation to its troubled twentieth century past.

The new identity of a post-authoritarian community can be based upon negative contrasts: "on the one hand, with the past that is being repudiated; on the other, with anti-democratic political actors in the present (and/or potentially in the future)."[8] A new "anamnestic soli-

---

[5] Herman Lübbe first employed this term in 1983 in order in reference Federal Germany's transition the democracy after 1945.

[6] Joachim Gauck and Martin Fry, "Dealing with the Stasi Past," *Daedalus* vol. 23, no. 1, *Germany in Transition* (Winter 1994), 277–284.

[7] Charles Villa-Vicencio and Erik Doxtader (eds.), *Pieces of the Puzzle: Keywords on Reconciliation and Transitional Justice* (Cape Town: Institute for Justice and Reconciliation, 2005), 34–38.

[8] Jan-Werner Müller, *Constitutional Patriotism* (Princeton/Oxford: Princeton University Press, 2007), 97–119.

darity" would be based upon the ethical framework circumscribed by both the knowledge of the truth and the official acknowledgment of its history. The destructive power of silence and of unassumed guilt would thus be preempted. This way, according to German political scientist Gesine Schwan, the fundamental abilities and values of individuals are nourished so that to sustain their well-being, social behavior, and trust in the communal life. The moral consensus over a shared experience of reality is preserved making possible the democratic existence of the specific society.[9] In this context, the priority of transitional justice becomes the "deep healing" of society: "the quest for a new quality of life and the creation of a milieu within which the atrocities of the past are less likely to recur in the future."[10]

The condemnation of the communist regime in Romania can be integrated, from a historical standpoint, into the space circumscribed by two factors that marked the post-1989 period. On one hand, Ion Iliescu, who, during his three mandates (1990 to 1992, 1992 to 1996, and 2000 to 2004) practiced what Peter Schneider coined for East Germany as a "double zombification": the two totalitarian experiences that plagued Romania's second half of the twentieth century officially were another country after 1989. This was also a regrettable characteristic for the Democratic Convention during the Emil Constantinescu administration from 1997–2000. Only after his own scandalous comments on the Holocaust in Romania that provoked a strong reaction both in diplomatic and international academic circles did Ion Iliescu create, in 2004, the International Commission on the Holocaust (ICHR) in Romania, chaired by celebrated writer and Nobel Peace Prize laureate Elie Wiesel. The objective of this mis-memory of the totalitarian experience in the country was indeed the fuel of the legitimization discourses of the post-communist political establishment, of the original democracy designed by Iliescu and his acolytes in the first post-communist years.

---

[9] Gesine Schwan, *Politics and Guilt: the Destructive Power of Silence*, trans. Thomas Dunlap (Lincoln/London: University of Nebraska Press, 2001), 54–134.

[10] Charles Villa-Vicencio, "The Reek of Cruelty and the Quest for Healing: Where Retributive and Restorative Justice Meet," *Journal of Law and Religion*, vol. 14, no. 1 (1999–2000), 172–175.

But why, under Constantinescu, the first president of Romania that was not representing successor parties of the communist one, was it not the hour of decommunization? Leaving aside explanations tied to his personal hubris, I believe that sometimes distance in time can help. In May 2012, in Brazil, President Dilma Rousseff created a truth commission to investigate human rights abuses, including those committed during military rule.[11] This is just another example that it is never too late. In 2011, a museum about the Trujillo times was opened in the Dominican Republic.[12] But there is an additional, generational element of significant importance and here I am anticipating my analysis below. Many people, both critics and researchers of the Commission and of its Report, often forget that in 1996 there were very few, if any, young Romanian historians or political scientists with a Western background who could do what the members and experts of the Commission achieved in 2006. The decade that passed between Constantinescu's election and Băsescu's condemnation of the communist regime worked in favor of the strengthening of the epistemic reform in Romanian historiography.[13] The average age of the Commission's experts was thirty. Ten years earlier, under Constantinescu, the average age of the same individuals was twenty. Most of them were still deciding on their scholarly trajectories, if at all. But by 2006, they either held or were on their way to receiving Ph.D.s either in Romania or at Western academic institutions. They had been equally socialized in the existing international debates on communism and exposed to the incremental nature of Romanian academia, which was seriously marked by its involvement in the regime's politics and policies. In this sense, there was a consensus among most of the experts and members of the Commission that self-serving narratives of perpetual victimization need to be demystified.

---

[11] See "Brazil Truth Commission Begins Abuse Inquiries," *BBC News*, 16 May 2012 (http://www.bbc.com/news/world-latin-america-18087390) and Paulo Cabral, "Brazil's Truth Commission Faces Delicate Task," BBC Brasil, 16 May 2012 (http://www.bbc.com/news/world-latin-america-18073300).

[12] Randal C. Archibold, "A Museum of Repression Aims to Shock the Conscience," *New York Times*, September 12, 2011 (http://www.nytimes.com/2011/09/13/world/americas/13trujillo.html?_r=0).

[13] For a review of the state of Romanian historical studies at the end of the 1990s, see Bogdan Murgescu, *A fi istoric în anul 2000* (Bucharest: Editura All, 2000).

More generally speaking, I think that the rise of a new generation of social scientists—I include historians in this category—has already resulted, especially in the past six to seven years, in a different perspective on the nation than the one embraced by the more traditionalist interpretations. These younger historians, political scientists, philosophers, and anthropologists contributed to the writing of the Final Report as a modern, rigorously scholarly document. Between 1945 and 1989, authoritarian myth-making has obfuscated the necessary *Vergangenheitsbewältigung*. More diluted, but similarly pervasive practices perpetuated after 1989. Generally speaking, most troubling in post-communist societies is precisely the excruciating need to prolong an indulgence in self-pity, myth-making, and a failure to address the wrongs of the past in a demystifying way. It would be hard to deny that the new democratic narratives amount to a repudiation of the belief systems, which are rooted in a self-serving, mendacious rendering of the main events and meanings of the continuum of dictatorship from the late 1930s until 1989.[14]

I would like to return to the second factor that played into the condemnation of the communist regime. Throughout the years, there were the constant attempts from civil society to speed up the process of decommunization. The latter is defined by several original movements: the Timişoara proclamation in March 1990 that advocated lustration and the June 1990 student protest movements spearheaded by the Civic Alliance. Also encompassed within this framework are various attempts to rehabilitate certain periods of Romanian communism, along with campaigns aimed at recycling aspects of the country's authoritarian past (e.g., numerous initiatives to "restore the name"

---

[14] For example, historian Maria Bucur judiciously pointed out the ambivalence of the ongoing search for a historical truth about the World War II: "The world of post-communist democracy is proving, however, far more complicated and nondemocratic when it comes to remembering the war dead than political elites would want. How these commemorative discourses change in the next few years will attest to what extent remembering Europe's world wars can become a nonantagonistic local and continental effort. For now, the tension between these two levels of framing the tragedy of World War II leaves little room for imagining a space for reconciliation." See Maria Bucur, *Heroes and Victims: Remembering War in Twentieth-Century Romania* (Bloomington: Indiana University Press, 2009), 17.

of pro-Nazi Marshal Ion Antonescu or to sanitize the murderous history of the fascist Iron Guard[15]). In contrast, there were attempts at a "memory regime," that is, an effort to recuperate "a shattered past" (Jarausch), in addition to movements that demanded other sorts of clarifications—particularly legal ones on the basis of the gradual opening of the *Securitate* archives and of other institutions that had a crucial role in the functioning and reproduction of the regime—and obtaining moral and material compensations for suffering inflicted by the twentieth-century totalitarian experience in Romania. The essential obstacle to any democratic endeavor to work through the communist past lies in the fact that even though knowledge of the truth is gradually developed, it does not translate into an officially sanctioned acknowldgement of its history.[16] In other words, institutionalized amnesia could be fully overcome only by an institutionalized memory of the communist dictatorship.

In 1997, a person who was the child of deportees during Stalin's Great Terror (and spent his youth drifting from one orphanage to another) asked his interviewer the following question: "How can someone be a victim of a regime that has not been officially declared criminal?"[17] Regardless of the civic initiatives and the scholarly production that stressed, documented, and detailed the communist government's criminality *(Regierungskriminalität)*, there had been no state

---

[15] See my Romanian language volume *Spectrele Europei Centrale* (Bucharest: Polirom, 2001). I extensively discuss this interesting process of recycling (neo/proto/crypto) fascism by means of integrating it into the identitarian discourse legitimizing the communist regime. In the "Lessons of Twentieth Century" chapter I argue that "the Ceaușescu regime was, at its most basic level, a very interesting mix that brought together both the legacy of militarist authoritarianism from the 1941–1944 period, which was celebrated in a myriad ways, and the degraded mystic inspired by the extreme-right, which was grafted upon the institutional body of Romanian Stalinism." (246–247).

[16] Andrew Rigby, *Justice and Reconciliation: After the Violence* (Boulder: Lynn Rienner, 2001), 82.

[17] In *Algemeen Dagblad*, November 1, 1997: 1–2 *apud* Nanci Adler, "In Search of Identity: The Collapse of the Soviet Union and the Recreation of Russia," in Alexandra Barahona de Brito, Carmen González-Enríquez, and Paloma Aguilar, *The Politics of Memory Transitional Justice in Democratizing Societies* (Oxford: Oxford University Press, 2001), 289.

admission of misdeeds and any recognition of wrong doing. According to the Iliescu paradigm, the communist regime had been delegitimized and condemned by the 1989 revolution; no further public inquiry and statements were necessary. To paraphrase Tony Judt, the mis-memory of communism nurtured a mis-memory of anti-communism. And indeed it seemed to succeed: as the process of the society's normalization progressed, decommunization gradually faded into the background. First and rather controversially in Poland, and then in Romania, it came back to the forefront of civic and political agendas. Traian Băsescu, during his electoral campaign in 2004, neither placed decommunization prominently in his platform nor pretended to have been a victim of communism.[18]

However, the specific dynamics of Romanian politics and the mobilization of civil society acted as catalysts for a strong return into the public debate of topics related to the communist dictatorship. In March 2006, the Group for Social Dialogue (a major civil society organization of some of the country's most famous intellectuals) as well as the leaders of the main trade unions endorsed an Appeal for the Condemnation of the Communist Regime, launched by prominent Civic Alliance personality Sorin Ilieşiu. This accelerated the process by which the Romanian state finally took an official attitude toward its traumatic past. In April 2006, convinced by now of the urgent necessity of such an initiative, President Băsescu decided to create the Commission. His position at the time, and during the entire period of decommunization, proves the importance of political will and determination in the attempt to initiate and sustain a potentially centrifugal endeavor. President Băsescu entrusted me with selecting the members of the Commission. In so doing, I took into account the scholarly competence and moral credibility of the people invited to join this body. Among the Commission members figured well-known historians, social scientists, civil society personalities, former political prisoners, former dissidents, and

---

[18] Born in 1951, Traian Băsescu graduated from the Naval Institute in Constanţa and spent most of his life under communism as a sea captain for the Romanian commercial fleet. After 1990, he became a member of the Petre Roman government, minister of transportation, then mayor of Bucharest and head of the Democratic Party. In 2004, he won the presidential election against former prime minister and social democratic leader Adrian Năstase.

major figures of democratic exile. President Băsescu charged the Commission with the task of producing a rigorous and coherent document that would examine the main institutions, methods, and personalities that made possible the crimes and abuses of the communist regime. In addition to its academic tasks, the work of the commission was meant to pass moral judgment on the defunct dictatorship and invite a reckoning with the past throughout a painful, albeit inevitable, acknowledgment of its crimes against humanity and other forms of repression. This was a revolutionary step in Romanian post-communist politics: neither ex-communist president Ion Iliescu nor anti-communist president Emil Constantinescu had engaged in such a potentially explosive undertaking. The Romanian case seems to validate Michael Ignatieff assertion that "leaders can have an enormous impact on the mysterious process by which individuals come to terms with the painfulness of their societies' past. Leaders give their societies permission to say the unsayable, to think the unthinkable, to rise to gestures of reconciliation that people, individually, cannot imagine."[19] By creating the Commission, the Romanian President did institutionalize a fundamental tool of transitional justice despite its nonjudicial truth-seeking nature. He offered mandate to an organizational structure that in the former socialist camp comes closest to a Truth Commission: the *Enquetekommission*.

The PCACDR was the first such state body created in the countries of the former Soviet bloc. The only precedent could be found in unified Germany, where the Bundestag created, between 1992 and 1998, two successive Enquete Commissions that investigated the history of the SED (Socialist Unity Party) Dictatorship and its effects on German unity.[20] At the end of the mandate of the second Enquete Commission, on the basis of its activity and practice, a foundation was established: the Stiftung zur Aufarbeitung der SED-Diktatur (June 5, 1998). The creation of the German commissions represents, however, a different situation under circumstances of unification, institutional absorption, and value transference on the West-East axis. There are nevertheless a series of similarities between the Enquete Commissions

---

[19] Michael Ignatieff, *The Warrior's Honour: Ethnic War and the Modern Conscience* (London: Chatto & Windus, 1998).

[20] A. James McAdams, *Judging the Past in Unified Germany* (New York: Cambridge University Press, 2001).

and the PCACDR, particularly in what concerned the mandates. Both the Romanian and the German mandates understood the analysis of communist pasts along the lines of the study of the structures of power and mechanisms of decision-making during the history of the regime; the functions and meaning of ideology, inclusionary patterns, and disciplinary practices within the state and society; the study of the legal and policing system; the role of the various churches during the various phases of state socialism; and finally, the role of dissidence, of civil disobedience, and, in Romania's case, of the 1989 revolution. Both in Romania and Germany, the commissions were meant to provide evaluations related to problems of responsibility, guilt, and the continuity of political, cultural, social, and economic structures from the communist through post-communist periods. The overall purpose of both bodies was to establish the basis for what Avishai Margalit called an ethics of memory.[21] The PCACDR activity was generally guided by Hannah Arendt's vision of responsibility and culpability: "What is unprecedented about totalitarianism is not only its ideological content, but the *event* itself of totalitarian domination."[22]

The difference between the German and Romanian commissions is that the Enquete Commissions of the SED Dictatorship and the subsequent foundation were created in a unified Germany with the massive support of the Bundestag, under circumstances of thorough delegitimation of the communist party and state, and in the context of a national consensus regarding the criminal nature of the Stasi. In contrast, in Romania there was a flagrant absence of expiation, penance, or regret. Without such premises, any act of reconciliation draws dangerously close to whitewashing the past. I agree with political scientist Lavinia Stan who stressed that "the country's bloody exit from communism and the revolutionary leaders' decision to summarily try, condemn, and kill Ceaușescu took the forgive-and-forget option off the table."[23] The situation was made worse as Ion Iliescu and the par-

---

[21] Avishai Margalit, *The Ethics of Memory* (Cambridge: Harvard University Press, 2002).

[22] Hannah Arendt, *Essays in Understanding 1930–1954* (New York: Harcourt Brace, 1994), 405.

[23] Lavinia Stan, *Transitional Justice in Post-Communist Romania. The Politics of Memory* (Cambridge/New York: Cambridge University Press, 2013), 30.

ties that were successors of the communist one entrenched amnesia in state institutions, policies, and in public opinion. They avoided genuine legal accountability for those involved in crimes and abuses from 1945 until 1989.[24] It would have been unrealistic to expect a conciliatory position toward the Commission's activity and Report on the side of the politicians who had legitimized themselves through obscuring truth-telling about a traumatic and guilty past.

Reconciliation is not and must not be bound to the premise of moral absolution. For example, two historians who had made their careers during communist times, Dinu C. Giurescu and Florin Constantiniu, were invited to be members of the Commission. They refused. Later, CNSAS (National Council for the Study of the Secret Police Archives) would reveal documents that showed their extensive association with the activity of the *Securitate* either in domestic academia or in the regime's cultural diplomacy. After the condemnation speech, both were very vocal critics of the Report, as they promoted normalizing narratives toward the Ceaușescu regime. I believe that James Mark's criticism according to which the calls from the left for a Reconciliation Commission were ignored overlooks the complexity of the commitments and biographies of the actors involved in the debate, especially between 2005 and 2007. Many of the critics of the Report had yet to confront their personal responsibilities from the communist period. The opposition to the Commission was often rooted in individual unmastered pasts.[25]

The transition from an illegitimate and criminal regime to democracy and a culture of human rights is, to paraphrase Charles Villa-Vicencio, a process in situ, it implies a series of compromises and negotiations. However, the act of healing a community must not be confused with the moral consensus about the traumatic past. The historical justice and the shared memory provided by an Enquetekommission opens the path to post-transitional political realignment. The conclusions of President Băsescu's speech condemning Romania's communist regime evoke this path of overcoming the past:

---

[24] For example, she the pertinent analysis in Gorsescu and Ursachi's article about the trials of the Romania revolution in this volume.

[25] See James Mark, *The Unfinished Revolution. Making Sense of the Communist Past in Central-Eastern Europe* (New Haven/London: Yale University Press, 2010), 37.

We thought that we could forget communism, but it did not want to forget us. Thus, the condemnation of this past arises as a priority of the present, without which we shall go on bearing something like the burden of an uncured disease. The memory of the crimes committed by the communist regime in Romania helps us to move forward with more decisive steps, to achieve the changes that are so necessary, but it also helps us to appreciate the democratic framework in which we live. . . . We have escaped the terror once and for all, we have escaped the fear, and so no one has the right to question our fundamental rights any longer. *The lesson of the past proves to us that any regime that humiliates its citizens cannot last and does not deserve to exist.* Now, every citizen can freely demand that his inalienable rights shall be respected, and the institutions of state must work in such a way that people will no longer feel humiliated. . . . *I am sure that we shall leave behind us the state of social mistrust and pessimism in which the years of transition submerged us, if, together, we make a genuine examination of the national conscience. All that I want is for us to build the future of democracy in Romania and our national identity on clean ground* [original emphases, n.a.]. [26]

The replacement of a criminal regime with a democracy founded on justice, tolerance, trust and truth can reach a positive outcome only through the assumption and disclosure of individual and political responsibilities, only with a social rebirth founded on real, systematic reform.

In Germany, the parliament's mandate was the obvious sign of a political consensus over the necessity of mastering and overcoming the totalitarian past. At the same time, it also meant a serious commitment on the part of the state for purposes of investigating and researching the complexities of the communist phenomenon in the country. In Romania, the Commission lacked legislative backing and had minimum financial support, its members working mostly pro bono. The

---

[26] The Message of the President of Romania, Mr. Traian Băsescu, addressed to Parliament on the occasion of the presentation of the Report of the Presidential Commission for the Analysis of the Communist Dictatorship in Romania (the Parliament of Romania, December 18, 2006) in Vladimir Tismaneanu et al., *Raport Final—Comisia Prezidențială pentru Analiza Dictaturii Comuniste în România* (Bucharest: Humanitas, 2007), 18.

parliament proved to be a site of outward and tacit opposition and subversion to the president's initiative to investigate the history of the communist regime. Moreover, various political factions promoted institutional parallelisms by continuous fueling of opposite, nostalgic, and even negationist interpretations from budget-dependent bodies such as the Institute of the Romanian Revolution (chaired by Ion Iliescu) or the Institute for the Investigation of Totalitarianism (created in the early 1990s and dominated by nationalist politicians and historians). Therefore, the Commission did not have the infrastructure, the resources, and the consensus for a countrywide, state-supported campaign for implementing the Report (with its conclusions and policy recommendations). The permanent squabbles between parties and their representatives and the strong negationist trend characterizing Romania's political realm prevented the Report and the PCACDR from having a structural impact similar to that of the Stiftung zur Aufarbeitung der SED-Diktatur.

Political scientist, Lavinia Stan, invoking data from opinion polls released in the aftermath of the condemnation speech, especially between 2010 and 2012, stated that despite the fact that the Commission "informed the society about communist crimes, but at the same time the number of Romanians knowledgeable about the past did not significantly increase..."[27] Despite my own misgivings toward the absence of greater institutional and financial support for the promotion of the Report's findings and of its recommendations, I would be restrained toward such sweeping conclusions. First and foremost, the dissemination of the Commission's work is very difficult to quantify. I believe that one ought to pursue a study of the number of references to the condemnation speech and the Report's content in the mass media or public debates, and in scholarship concerning the communist period. Second, some of the same opinion polls used by Stan *did* employ the essential terminology of the condemnation speech. For example, in September 2010, respondents were asked "In your opinion, was the communist regime in Romania illegitimate, in the sense that it reached power and maintained it through falsifying the will of the majority of its citizens?" Forty-two percent answered "yes," 31 percent "no," and 27 percent "I do no know/I do not wish to answer." In the same poll, at the question "was the commu-

---

[27] Stan, *Transitional Justice in Post-Communist Romania*, 130.

nist regime in Romania a criminal one," 41 percent said "no," 37 percent "yes," and 22 percent answered "I do not know/I do not wish to answer."[28] I think these numbers, along with those of other opinion poll from the past years, reveal a sharp division within the Romanian population with a view to the communist historical experience. As I will discuss next, I doubt whether knowledgeability is the crux of the matter, but rather the conflicting memories about overlapping pasts that comprise not only crimes and abuses, but also survival, self-fulfillment, and individual involvement in the regime's existence over four decades.

In a sense, the Commission comes close to the commissions for truth and reconciliation created in countries such as South Africa, Chile, Argentina, and Rwanda. The PCACDR had the features of a Truth Commission as identified by Priscilla Hayner: it focused on the past, it investigated patterns of abuse over a period of time, rather than a specific event; it was a temporary body which completed its work with the submission of a report, and it was officially sanctioned, authorized and empowered by the state.[29] There are two main elements that distinguish it from cases such as South Africa or Germany: the absence of a parliamentary mandate meant that it had no decision-making power and no subpoena prerogative; and, it did not rely on the collection of testimonies from the victims of the communist regime. It took on the mission to provide the scholarly evidence for its conclusions and recommendations. This did not entail though that the voices of those who suffered were to be blocked behind a pseudo-Rankean analysis of *wie es eigentlich gewesen*. The PCACDR main objective was to impose the primacy of an ethical framework that went beyond the traumatic experience that could be recorded by means of historical positivism. The introduction of the *Final Report* clearly states its purpose:

> The condemnation of the communist regime is today first of all a moral, intellectual, social and political obligation. The Romanian democratic and pluralist state can and must do it. The acknowl-

---

[28] For the results of the opinion poll in September 2010, see http://www.iiccr. ro/ro/sondaje_iiccmer_csop/. The same link provides information on similar opinion polls from December 2011, May 2011, and November 2010.

[29] Priscilla B. Hayner, *Unspeakable Truths: Facing the Challenge of Truth Commissions* (New York: Routledge, 2002), 14.

edgment of these dark and tragic pages of our national recent history is vital for the young generations to be conscious of the world their parents were forced to live in. Romania's future rests on mastering its past, henceforth on condemning the communist regime as an enemy to human society. If we are not to do it today, here and now, we shall burden ourselves with the further complicity, by practice of silence, with the totalitarian Evil. In no way do we mean by this collective guilt. We emphasize the importance of learning from a painful past, of learning how was this possible, and of departing from it with compassion and sorrow for its victims.[30]

The project and activities of the Commission benefited from the previous experience of the International Commission on the Holocaust (ICHR) in Romania. The main difference between the two endeavors is that the proceedings of the ICHR could not be perceived, as in the PCACDR's case, as a direct threat or involving a personal stake in contemporary society and politics, since the three historical groups involved in the Holocaust (the victims, the perpetrators, and the bystanders) had mostly disappeared. As far as the communist past is concerned, many of the perpetrators, victims, and witnesses of or bystanders to the regime's crimes are still alive and involved in societal dynamics, some of them even holding seats in the Romanian parliament. The moment on December 18, 2006, when exponents of the radical left and right booed President Băsescu's presentation of the findings of the Commission, demonstrated that a genuine democracy cannot function properly in the absence of historical consciousness. An authentic democratic community cannot be built on the denial of past crimes, abuses, and atrocities. The past is not another country. It cannot be wished away—the more that is attempted, the more we witness the return of repressed memories. For example, consider the recurring efforts to prosecute former Mexican president Luis Echeverría for his involvement in 1968 student killings.[31] For the first time in post-1989

---

[30] Vladimir Tismaneanu, et al., *Raport Final* (Bucharest: Humanitas, 2007), 35–36.

[31] James C. McKinley Jr., "Federal Judge Overturns Ruling Against Mexico's Former President in 1968 Student Killings," *New York Times*, 13 July 2007 (http://www.nytimes.com/2007/07/13/world/americas/13mexico.html?_r=0).

Romania, the Commission rejected outright the practices of institutionalized forgetting and generated a national conversation about long-denied and occulted moments of the past (including instances of collaboration and complicity).[32] One of its significant accomplishments is that it simultaneously represented state authorities and important sections of the civil society in making public and admitting *truths* that broke a hegemonic dominance of partial, mediated, and mystified knowledge about the communist past.

In January 2007, President Băsescu visited the Sighet Memorial (a museum dedicated to the victims of communism) in northern Romania. This institution, because of poet Ana Blandiana and writer Romulus Rusan's dedication and because of the diligence of historians from the research center affiliated with the memorial, is the most important *lieu de mémoire* dealing with Romania's tragic communist past. By January 2007, immediately after having posted the Commission's Report on the president's website, there were some reactions which signaled what I consider a false problem. It has been argued that the PCACDR document exonerates certain political figures murdered by communists, but who themselves could hardly be considered democrats. The Commission aimed at a synthesis between understanding the traumatic history through an academic praxis that presupposes distance from the surveyed subject and empathizing with the people who suffered from the crimes and abuses of the dictatorship. The commission pursued a reconstruction of the past along the dichotomy of distance-empathy, focusing upon both general and individual aspects of the past. The Report's transgressive intentionality lies in the facts[33], in the more or less familiar places

---

[32] See Bogdan Cristian Iacob, "O clarificare necesară: Condamnarea regimului comunist din România între text și context," *Idei in Dialog* no. 8 (35), August 2007, 12–15; no. 9 (36), September 2007, 37–39; no. 10 (37), October 2007, 33–34; no. 11 (38) November 2007, 21–22. By the same author, see also, "Comunismul românesc între tipologie și concept I-II," *Idei in Dialog*, no. 4 (43), April 2008 and no. 5 (44), May 2008, and Cosmina Tanasoiu, "The Tismaneanu Report: Romania Revists Its Past," *Problems of Post Communism*, July August 2007, 60–69.

[33] See A.D. Moses, "Structure and Agency in the Holocaust: Daniel J. Goldhagen and His Critics," 218, *History and Theory*, vol. 37, no. 2 (May 1998), 194–219. Dominick LaCapra similarly points to the distance-empathy synthesis, as valid method of approaching recent history, in his argument for reconstruction and electivity on the basis of fact within a democratic value sys-

of Romanian's communist history. The Commission first identified victims, regardless of their political colors, for one cannot argue that one is against torture for the left while ignoring such practices when it comes to the right. The militants of the far right should have been punished on a legal basis, but this was not the case for the trials put forth by the Romanian Communist Party (RCP). The communists simply shattered any notion of the rule of law. The Report identifies the nature of abuses and its victims, though it does not leave aside the ideological context of the times. For the Commission, the communist regime represented the opposite of rule of law, an *Unrechtsstaat*. However, any attempt at "discovering" a Bitburg syndrome[34] in the body's document is a malevolent, biased statement more than a pointed academic argument.

The PCACDR was "a state, public history lesson" during which the "truth" about the communist totalitarian experienced was "officially proclaimed and publicly exposed," that is, acknowledged. It was an exercise of "sovereignty over memory,"[35] an attempt to set the stage for resolving what Tony Judt called the "double crisis of memory":

> On the one hand cynicism and mistrust pervade all social, cultural and even personal exchanges, so that the construction of civil society, much less civil memory, is very, very difficult. On

---

tem: A reckoning with the past in keeping with democratic values requires the ability—or at least the attempt—to read scars and to affirm only what deserves affirmation as one turn the lamp of critical reflection on oneself and one's own." Dominick LaCapra, "Representing the Holocaust: Reflections on the Historians' Debate," 127, in Friedländer, *Limits of Representation,* 108–127. See also Dominick LaCapra, "Revisiting the Historians' Debate: Mourning and Genocide," *History and Memory,* 9 (12), 1998, 80–112.

[34] Geoffrey Hartman, *Bitburg in Moral and Political Perspective* (Bloomington: Indiana University Press, 1986), Charles S. Maier, *The Unmasterable Past: History, Holocaust, and German National Identity* (Cambridge, MA: Harvard University Press, 1988).

[35] I am employing here the concepts developed by Timothy Garton Ash and Timothy Snyder in Timothy Garton Ash, "Trials, Purges and History Lessons: Treating a Difficult Past in Post-Communist Europe" and Timothy Snyder, "Memory of Sovereignty and Sovereignty over Memory: Poland, Lithuania and Ukraine, 1939–1999" in Jan-Werner Müller (ed.), *Memory and Power in Post-War Europe: Studies in the Presence of the Past* (Cambridge: Cambridge University Press, 2002).

the other hand there are multiple memories and historical myths, each of which has learned to think of itself as legitimate simply by virtue of being private and unofficial. Where these private or tribal versions come together, they form powerful counterhistories of a mutually antagonistic and divisive nature.[36]

The post-1989 practice of state-sponsored amnesia created two main dangers: the externalization of guilt and the ethnicization of memory. As both Dan Diner and Gabriel Motzkin argue, the process of working through the communist past raises a crucial problem: "How can crimes that elude the armature of an ethnic, and thus long-term, memory be kept alive in collective remembrance?" The domination and exterminism of a communist regime generally affects all strata of the population, terror and repression are engineered from within against one's people. Therefore, "the lack of specific connection between Communism's theoretical enemy and its current victims made it more difficult to remember these victims later."[37] When no *Aufarbeitung* takes place, the memory field is left for "alternative" interpretations.

On the one hand, the evils of the regime are assigned to those perceived as *aliens*: the Jews, the national minorities, or other traitors and enemies of an organically defined nation. Such line of perverted reasoning unfolded immediately after my nomination as Chair of the PCACDR. I became the preferred target of verbal assault, including scurrilous slanders and vicious anti-Semitic diatribes, targeting the commission's president.[38] The Commission itself was labeled as one made up of foreigners *(alogeni)*. Entire genealogies were invented for various members of this body, all just to prove the fact that the "real perpetrators" are forcing upon the nation a falsified history of its suffering. Upon delivering the condemnation speech, the president and some

---

[36] Tony Judt, "The Past Is Another Country: Myth and Memory in Post-War Europe" in Jan-Werner Muller, *Memory and Power*, 173.

[37] See Dan Diner, "Remembrance and Knowledge: Nationalism and Stalinism in Comparative Discourse" and Gabriel Motzkin, "The Memory of Crime and the Formation of Identity" in Helmut Dubiel and Gabriel Motzkin (eds.), *The Lesser Evil: Moral Approaches to Genocide Practices* (Portland: Frank Cass, 2003), 197.

[38] See my books *Democraţie şi memorie* (Bucharest: Curtea Veche, 2006) and *Refuzul de a uita* (Bucharest: Curtea Veche, 2007).

members of the Commission were showered with threats and imprecations by the representatives of the xenophobic and chauvinistic Romania Mare Party. Unfortunately, as an indication of the deep-rooted malaise of memory in Romania, very few members of the Parliament of the other mainstream parties publicly objected to this behavior (Nicolae Văcăroiu, then President of the Romanian Senate, did nothing to stop this circus). A further proof of narrow-mindedness came a few months later, when a critic of the Report found no qualms in stating that: "if it weren't for the stupid, but violent reactions of nationalists, extremists, etc., the Report would have passed almost unnoticed by the public opinion that counts, the one from which one can expect change."[39]

In reality, however, such utterances are indicative of a very interesting, though worrisome, post-condemnation phenomenon: the argumentative coalition against the Report of a self-proclaimed "new left" with the national-stalinists (those who perpetuate the *topoi* of the pre-1989 propaganda or those who are nostalgic for Ceaușescu's "Golden Age"), and with the fundamentalist orthodoxists. Such alliance can be explained in two ways: first, these are the faces of resentment, the people who were forced to confront their own illusions and guilt or those who stubbornly refuse to accept the demise of Utopia (what in Germany fell under the category of anti-antiutopianism); second, these are those for whom, mostly because of ignorance, dealing with the communist past can be resumed to mechanical instrumentalization, for whom this redemptive act is a "strategic action." The result of their mainly journalistic flurries is one that does not surprise the sober observer: a countertrend of *malentendu* revisionism that does represent, because of its promise of facile remembrance, a latent danger for continuation of the strategy of legal, political, and historical *Aufarbeitung*.[40]

Another peril of a mis-memory of communism is the development of "two moral vocabularies, two sorts of reasoning, two different pasts": that of things done to "us" and that of things done by "us" to "others."[41] Tony Judt sees this practice as the overall postwar European

---

[39] Ciprian Șiulea, "Imposibila dezbatere. Incrancenare și optimism in condamnarea comunismului," *Observator Cultural*, July 5, 2007, no. 385.
[40] For an extensive analysis of this phenomenon, see Bogdan C. Iacob's contribution in this volume.
[41] Judt, "The Past Is Another Country," 163–166.

syndrome of "voluntary amnesia." In Romania, its most blatant manifestation was the denial of the Holocaust, of the role of the Romanian
state in the extermination of the Jews.[42] As in the case of Poland, the
myth of "Judeo-Bolshevism," frantically embraced and disseminated
by the far-right is directly linked to widespread propaganda-manufac-
tured misperceptions about alleged Jewish overwhelming support for
the Soviet occupiers during the period between June 1940 and June
1941. I agree with Maria Bucur that: "The most important consideration in rethinking the periodization of World War II, however, per-
tains to how historians interpret the meaning of specific actions and
words. Periodizing the war strictly from June 1941 to October 1944
allows one to easily avoid discussing the important anti-Semitic policies and pogroms experienced by Jews in Romania between the fall of
1940 and the summer of 1941. It also excludes the violence that took
place in northern Transylvania in the fall of 1940. Not extending the
war beyond 1944 places the experience of violence between November
1944 and the 1950s into a context that is circumscribed to Cold War
politics. But the Cold War on the ground was not a mere projection of
the Soviet desire for power and control in Romania."[43] In other words,
the origins of the violent confrontations and social tensions in post-
1944 Romania cannot be disassociated from the major ethnopolitical
disruptions during World War II, including the genocidal actions of
Ion Antonescu's fascist regime against Jews and Roma. It took a long
time for Romanian historians to even admit the existence of a Holocaust in Romania. Politically the recognition came in 2004 with the
ICHR, but similarly to the PCACDR, its findings were not consistently
and convincingly taken up into policies aimed at a widespread and
thorough coming to terms with this traumatic and guilty past.

Another manifestation of the syndrome can also be found in
relation with the communist past. One of the master narratives after
1989 was, because of the Soviet imposition, the regime was not part

---

[42] An account of this phenomenon is the chapter "Distortion, Negationism,
and Minimalization of the Holocaust in Postwar Romania" of the Final Report of the International Commission on the Holocaust in Romania. The
English version of this document can be found at http://www.ushmm.org/
research/center/presentations/features/details/2005-03-10/.

[43] Bucur, *Heroes and Victims*, 200.

and parcel of the national history. It was a protracted form of foreign occupation during which the population was victimized by foreigners and rogue, inhuman, bestial individuals. This discourse was and is based upon the topical trinity of *they and it vs. us*. In later years it went through finer qualifications: on the one hand, the 'High Stalinism' period (roughly 1947–1953, with maybe the added value of 1958–1962), the so-called haunting decade, was blamed on the 'Muscovites' (mostly Ana Pauker, Vasile Luca, Iosif Chişinevschi) and, sometimes, but in a redemptive key on Gheorghiu Dej as well (who also wears a historiographical cap of national awakener on the basis of his later years in power). On the other hand, the Ceauşescu period is seen as one of patriotic emancipation and self-determination from under the Kremlin iron heel. The distortions of such "healthy path" are mostly blamed on Ceauşescu's personality cult. It is no surprise that in some quarters, his execution was seen as the end of communism, of its evils and/or legacy. The overall conclusion of such normalizing gymnastics was similar to the previously discussed issue: the criminality of the regime lay in its antinational past, while its development of the Nation's interest and being can be separated from the degeneration of its leaders.

I believe that one of the most important achievements of the Commission's Final Report, in terms of what Claus Offe called "politics of knowledge," was the denunciation of the country's communist totalitarian experience as "(national) Stalinist." That is, the regime was Stalinist from the beginning to the end and it also experienced a hybridization of an organic nationalism with Marxist-Leninist tenets. The document's "Introduction" clearly states the thesis: "tributary to Soviet interests, consistent with its original Stalinist legacy, even after its break with Moscow, the communist regime in Romania was antinational despite its incessant professions of national faith. . . . Behind the ideology of the unitary and homogenous socialist nation lay hidden the obsessions of Leninist monolitism combined with those of a revitalized extreme right endorsed by the party leaders."[44] In other words, there was a continuity between the first and second stages of Romanian communism, which shattered the historiographical consensus that the Ceauşescu regime

---

[44] *Raport Final*, 32 and 767.

was fully nationalist compared to the first stage and therefore salvageable on grounds of national interest, pride, and loyalty.

I consider that there is an overlying conceptualization of memory in the pages of the Report, one that puts together what Richard S. Esbenshade identified as the two main paradigms in Eastern Europe, shaped before and after the fall of communism, for the relationship between memory and communal identity. On the one hand, there is the "Milan Kundera paradigm," according to which "man's struggle is one of memory against forgetting" (that is, instrumentalized amnesia vs. individual, civic remembrance). On the other, there is the "George Konrad paradigm," where "history is the forcible illumination of darkened memories," presupposing a "morass of shared responsibility." In bringing together these approaches, the Commission attempted to answer to Tony Judt's "double crisis of history" in former Eastern Europe.[45] As the reactions to the Report show, the formation and employment of a society-wide "critically informed memory" (Dominick LaCapra) is challenged by widespread cynicism and distrust for all sociopolitical levels and by multiple historical myths, anxieties, expectations, illusions, and memories (developed during the communist period as resistance to the ubiquitous ideological discourse of the RCP dictatorship) that claim legitimacy because of their private and unofficial character.[46] In a sense, throughout a large part of Romania's twentieth century history, "time itself was hurt" (R.J. Bosworth). Dealing with both the communist and fascist past (and implicitly Romania's responsibility for the Holocaust) must become a factor of communal cohesion as it imposes the rejection of any comfortably apologetic historicization.

The Report's conclusions postulate the moral equivalence of the two extremisms that caused such trauma: "the far left must be rejected as much as the far right. The denial of communism's crimes is as unacceptable as the denial of those of fascism. As any justification for the

---

[45] Richard S. Esbenshade, "Remembering to Forget: Memory, History, National Identity in Postwar East-Central Europe," *Representations*, 49 (Winter 1995), 72–96. I also dealt with this topic in detail in *The Crisis of Marxist Ideology in Eastern Europe: The Poverty of Utopia* (New York and London: Routledge, 1988).

[46] See István Deák, Jan T. Gross, and Tony Judt (eds.), *The Politics of Retribution in Europe: World War II and Its aftermath* (Princeton: Princeton University Press, 2000).

crimes against humanity performed by the Antonescu regime ought not to be tolerated, we believe that no form of commemoration of communist leaders/representatives should be allowed"[47] One of the essential dilemmas of the twentieth century was, to paraphrase Raymond Aron, the relationship between democracy and totalitarianism. This issue remained vital up until today; the struggle between democracy and its enemies is far from over. Communism and fascism were not regimes of opposite nature. They were embodiments of different types of totalitarianism, as novel political systems that came about in the second decade of the last century with roots in the nationalism and socialism of the nineteenth century. They were facets and dimensions of human existence under the attempted total control of a political entity that had not existed before in history and which was undergoing constant development.[48] With this in mind, I believe, and the Commission was imbued with such an approach, that one needs to take into account a moral imperative that reflects the comprehension of the tragic experience of the twentieth century. In the context, opposition to any form of totalitarianism is fundamental.

Subsequently, the main instrument for the process of mastering the past, employed by the Commission, was the deconstruction of the ideological certainty established by the communist regime upon which the latter founded its legitimacy and that it creatively instrumentalized in its attempt to encompass the *entire* society. From the appearance of antifascism to the discourse of the "socialist nation," the *topoi* (traditional theme or motif) of Romanian Stalinism permeated public consciousness, simultaneously maiming collective memory and significant chunks of the country's history.[49] The post-1989 period in Romania was dominated by an absence of expiation, of penance, or of a mourning process in relation to the trauma of communism. Therefore, reconciliation was impossible, for it lacked any basic truth value.

---

[47] *Raport Final*, 637.

[48] For more on the comparative analysis of communism and fascism, see Vladimir Tismaneanu, *The Devil in History. Communism, Fascism, and Some Lessons of the Twentieth Century* (Berkeley/London: University of California Press, 2012).

[49] Lavinia Stan correctly underlined that in Romania "the nature of the communist past led to a preference for truth and justice—at the expense of reconciliation." In Stan, *Transitional Justice in Post-Communist Romania*, 28.

Taking into account all of the above, it can be argued that the condemnation of the communist regime was based upon a civic-liberal ethos and not, as some commentators stated, on a moral-absolutist discourse, as legitimization for a new power hierarchy in the public and political space. Though he does not make this remark approvingly, James Mark is correct to state that the Commission promoted an interpretation of history that was rooted in counterpoising liberal democracy with a dictatorial criminal past. According to him, "it was this vision of democracy—as the rule of law and this as shield for the individual from the abusive state—that would provide the template for the Presidential Commission's liberally framed condemnation of Communism."[50] But, as Bogdan C. Iacob judiciously stresses in his chapter of this volume, considering Romania's continuum of authoritarianisms, such a choice is a positive and refreshing departure in both the representation of the past and in local historiography.

In the following lines, I will provide an extensive quote from President Băsescu's December 18, 2006 speech to clarify the conceptual and discursive complex that lies at the core of the communist regime's condemnation. During a joint session of the Romanian parliament, President Băsescu accepted the conclusions and recommendations of the PCACDR's *Final Report*. His address became an official document of the Romanian state, published in the country's *Official Monitor*, no. 196, on December 28, 2006.

> As Head of the Romanian State, I expressly and categorically condemn the communist system in Romania, from its foundation, on the basis of dictate, during the years 1944 to 1947, to its collapse in December 1989. Taking cognizance of the realities presented in the Report, I affirm with full responsibility: the communist regime in Romania was illegitimate and criminal. . . . In the name of the Romanian State, I express my regret and compassion for the victims of the communist dictatorship. In the name of the Romanian State, I ask the forgiveness of those who suffered, of their families, of all those who, in one way or another, saw their lives ruined by the abuses of dictatorship. . . . Evoking now a period which many would wish to forget, we have spoken both of the past and of the extent to which we, people today, wish to go to the very end in

---

[50] Mark, *Unfinished Revolution*, 39.

the assumption of the values of liberty. These values, prior even to being those of Romania or of Europe, flow from the universal, sacred value of the human person. If we now turn to the past, we do so in order to face a future in which contempt for the individual will no longer go unpunished. This symbolic moment represents the balance sheet of what we have lived through and the day in which we all ask ourselves how we want to live henceforward. We shall break free of the past more quickly, we shall make more solid progress, if we understand what hinders us from being more competitive, more courageous, more confident in our own powers. On the other hand, we must not display historical arrogance. My purpose is aimed at authentic national reconciliation, and all the more so since numerous legacies of the past continue to scar our lives. Our society suffers from a generalized lack of confidence. The institutions of state do not yet seem to pursue their real vocation, which relates to the full exercise of all civil liberties. . . . Perhaps some will ask themselves what exactly gives us the right to condemn. As President of Romanians, I could invoke the fact that I have been elected. But I think that we have a more important motive: the right to condemn gives us the obligation to make the institutions of the rule of law function within a democratic society. We cannot be allowed to compromise these institutions. They cannot be allowed to be discredited by the fact that we approach them with the habits and mentalities of our recent past. . . . The condemnation of communism will encourage us to be more circumspect towards utopian and extremist projects, which want to bring into question the constitutional and democratic order. Behind the nostalgic or demagogic discourses, there lies more often than not the temptation of authoritarianism or even totalitarianism, of negation of the explosion of individual energies, of inventiveness and creativity which has taken place since December 1989. We have definitively escaped terror, we have escaped fear, in such a way that no one has the right to bring into question our fundamental rights.[51]

---

[51] The speech given by the President of Romania, Traian Băsescu, on the occasion of the Presentation of the Report by the Presidential Commission for the Analysis of the Communist Dictatorship in Romania (The Parliament of Romania, December 18, 2006), www.presidency.ro.

The above excerpt indicates several directions along which the meaning of the act of condemning the communist regime was drawn. First of all, this initiative is a fundamentally symbolic step toward national reconciliation by means of clarifying and dealing with the past. Only in this way can Romanian society overcome the fragmentation typical of the "legacy of Leninism."[52] President Băsescu advocated a reinstitutionalization freed from the burden of the party-state continuities and the possibility for laying the foundation of a "posttotalitarian legitimacy."[53] It is his belief that only in such fashion can one develop the not-yet-attained national consensus. Two years later, in 2008, at the launch of the first volume of documents of the Commission, he stated that the condemnation speech broke, once and for all, with the continuity with the postwar state, which was born by way of the forceful creation of the puppet government of Petru Groza on March 6, 1945 and through the arbitrary abrogation of the Romanian monarchy on December 30, 1947. In his reading, the revolution of 1989 marked the collapse of the communist dictatorship, but not the final and definitive end of the communist state. The restoration that followed, not so velvet in Romania if one takes into account the bloody repression of the protests in June 1990, aimed to hinder such a total break with the institutional communist past.

The process of *Vergangenheitsbewältigung* that was initiated by the Commission set up criteria of accountability fundamental to the reenforcement and entrenchment of democratic values in Romanian society. For, as Jan-Werner Müller argued, "without facing the past, there can be no civic trust, which is the outcome of a continuous

---

[52] Kenneth Jowitt defined Eastern Europe as a "brittle region" where "suspicion, division, and fragmentation predominate, not coalition and interrogation" because of lasting emotional, ethnic, territorial, demographic, political fragmentation form the (pre-)communist period. See "The Legacy of Leninism" in *New World Disorder: The Leninist Extinction* (Berkeley: University of California Press, 1992). For a discussion of this thesis, see also Vladimir Tismaneanu, Marc Howard, and Rudra Sil (eds.), *World Order After Leninism* (Seattle: University of Washington Press, 2006).

[53] Bogdan C. Iacob, in the first article of his series in *Idei in Dialog*, argued that the nature and profile of the condemnation of Romanian communist regime comes close to what Jan-Werner Müller coined as the *Modell Deutschland*. See Jan-Werner Müller, *Another Country: German Intellectuals, Unification, and National Identity* (New Haven/London: Yale University Press, 2000), 258.

public deliberation about the past."[54] Following upon Ken Jowitt's footsteps, I consider that the fundamental Leninist legacy in Eastern Europe was total fragmentation of society, the break of the civic bonds and consensus necessary for a healthy, democratic life. The tumultuous post-1989 years in Romania are the perfect proof for this thesis: sectarian interests, widespread authoritarian tendencies within the public and political spheres, anomie, and so on, were all rooted in forgetting. The Commission did not find new truth, but it lifted the veil of denial over those truths that were widely known but stubbornly unacknowledged. In a country where the legal measures against the abuses perpetrated during the communist years are close to nonexistent and where the judicial system is rather weak and corrupted, it can be said that the Commission created the future prospects for justice.

The Report, besides its detailed accounts on the functioning of the various mechanisms of power and repression, also named names; it listed the most important people who were guilty for the evils of the regime. It did not stigmatize any group, its purpose was not inquisitorial; but it engaged in a truth-telling process essential for understanding the nature of responsibility for crimes and suffering under communism. In Priscilla Hayner words: "where justice is unlikely in the courts, a commission plays an important role in at least publicly shaming those who orchestrated atrocities." It revitalized the principle of accountability, fundamental for democracy's survival.[55] Considering the present political environment in Romania, I can only reiterate Chilean President Patricio Aylwin dictum upon the creation of the Retting Commission: justice as far as possible (*justicia en la medida de lo posible*). The moral-symbolic action is after all one of the four types of retributive justice (the others being the criminal, the noncriminal,

---

[54] Jan-Werner Müller, "Introduction: the Power of Memory, the Memory of Power and the Power over Memory" in Jan-Werner Müller (ed.), *Memory and Power*, 33–34.

[55] Priscilla Hayner makes a very convincing argument about the ways in which the activity of truth commissions can supplant for the fallacies and impotence of the judicial process, about the means by which a commission's activity and results can become the foundation for future legal action against abuses of the past. See Hayner, *Unspeakable Truths*, 82–87.

and the rectifying aspects).[56] Naturally, in the following years there has been an immense background of expectation which, given the political situation in Romania, has only partly been satisfied. Legislative incapacity and lack of any will to take responsibility for the past on the part of the majority of the political class have produced regrettable confusion as to the purpose, functions, goals and mandate of the Commission. For example, even an insightful analyst such as Lavinia Stan argued that "the Commission led to no reforms meant to strengthen the legal system, although the evidence it amassed did not represent 'inconsequential truth.'"[57] Considering the mandate and the reactions to the Commission from important parties and political actors in Romanian Parliament, it would be unrealistic to expect the body to have such a transformative immediate impact on the local legal system. In his book Pieces of the Puzzle, Charles Villa-Vicencio enumerates bluntly the possibilities and impossibilities of a Commission for Truth. On the one hand, such a commission can

> break the silence on past gross violations of human rights; counter the denial of such violations and thus provide official acknowledgment of the nature and extent of human suffering; provide a basis for the emergence of a common memory that takes into account a multitude of diverse experiences; help create a culture of accountability; provide a safe space within which victims can engage their feelings and emotions through the telling of personal stories without the evidentiary and procedural restraints of the courtroom; bring communities, institutions and systems under moral scrutiny; contribute to uncovering the causes, motives, and perspectives of past atrocities; provide important symbolic forms of memorialisation and reparation; initiate and support a process of reconciliation, recognizing that it will take time and political will to realize; provide a public space within which to address the issues that thrust the country into conflict, while promoting restorative justice and social reconstruction.

---

[56] McAdams, *Judging the Past*.
[57] Stan, *Transitional Justice in Post-Communist Romania*, 131.

However, a Commission for Truth does not have the capability to

> imposing punishment(s) commensurate to the crime(s) committed; ensuring remorse from perpetrators and their rehabilitation; ensuring that victims will be reconciled with or forgive their perpetrators; addressing comprehensively all aspects of past oppression; uncovering of the whole truth about an atrocity or answering all outstanding questions in an investigation; allowing all victims to tell their stories; ensuring that all victims experience closure as a result of the process; providing adequate forms of reconstruction and comprehensive reparations; correcting the imbalances between benefactors and those exploited by the former regime; ensuring that those dissatisfied with amnesties or the nature or extent of the amount of the truth revealed will make no further demand for punishment or revenge." [58]

Authors such as James Mark and Lavinia Stan consider that the PCACDR was a history and not a truth commission.[59] Indeed, the Romanian case is not a textbook truth commission. However, the body did fulfill most of the above functions of a truth commission listed by Villa-Vicencio. PCACDR did not have the time and the institutional bedrock upon which to rely in order to grant the victims the possibility to testify of their suffering and trauma. But, as mentioned earlier, it did include the point of view of the Association of Former Political Prisoners, which triggered criticisms related to the employment of the AFPP's formula "the communist genocide in Romania." In this sense, the Commission did provide an extent for the victims to "own" the truths that it told about the crimes and abuses of the *ancien régime*. Only the inability of the local state institutions prevented the development of outreach programs that would further alleviate the victims' suffering. In fact, it could be argued that under the umbrella of the Institute for the Investigation of Communist Crimes and the Memory of Romanian Exile, which I chaired as president of the Scientific Council from March 2010 until May 2012, such assistance was and still provided by offering expertise

---

[58] Villa-Vicencio, *Pieces of the Puzzle*, 92–93.
[59] See Stan, *Transitional Justice in Post-Communist Romania*, 112–115 and Mark, *The Unfinished Revolution*, 32–33.

on individual cases concerning imprisonment, executions, homicide, and repression brought forward by victims and/or their families. I would contend that PCADCR was a truth commission in the specific political, institutional, and public context of post-communist Romania.

Another issue that I wish to discuss is whether the project of the condemnation of the communist dictatorship falls in the category of what Adam Michnik called the "mantra of anti-communism." In some of his writings, Michnik noted quite a few similarities between some forms of anti-communism, especially in Poland, with the former anti-fascism of the Comintern and post-1945 periods. He saw both as mere forms within which a deeper structure, focused upon political bickering and neoauthoritarian tendencies, is hidden. According to him, "Anti-communism, like antifascism, does not itself attest to anyone's righteousness. The old lie—the lie of communists settling scores with fascism—has been replaced by a new lie: the lie of anti-communists settling scores with communism. . . . Communism froze collective memory; the fall of communism, therefore, brought with it, along with a return to democracy, paratotalitarian formations, ghosts from another era. . . . The debate about communism has thus become, through blackmail and discrimination against political enemies, a tool in the struggle for political power."[60]

In Romania, the condemnation of the communist regime has taken place with a consistent view to reconciliation, consensus, reform, and working through the past. It did not serve either as a weapon of President Băsescu against his enemies or as a means of rehabilitating any xenophobic and/or antidemocratic, procommunist movements (as in the case of Poland with Roman Dmowski's ultranationalist Endecja). Starting in late April 2006, some sections of the Romanian mass media indulged in an abuse of Michnik's ideas. Many individuals with hardly liberal-democratic pedigrees, such as former president Ion Iliescu, former prime minister Adrian Năstase, and Social Democratic Party ideologue Adrian Severin, used the principles professed by former Polish dissident Michnik to justify their lack of penance,

---

[60] Adam Michnik, "Mantra Rather Than Discourse," Peace and Mind Symposium, *Common Knowledge* 8:3, 2002, 516–525. Also, Adam Michnik, *Letters from Freedom*, trans. by Jane Cave, with a foreword by Kenneth Jowitt (Berkeley: University of California Press, 1998).

their amnesia, and their opportunism.[61] They missed (or conveniently ignored) the fact that Michnik's positions originated in his weariness toward neo-Jacobin radicalism and vindictive rigorism, especially when they are advocated by those who never uttered not even a word against communism before the collapse of the system (or, even worse, they enthusiastically collaborated and compromised with it). Michnik is profoundly concerned about *les enragés*, whom he suspects of double moral standards, Phariseism, and even of irresponsible adventurism. Michnik however does not oppose, in my reading of his writings, the idea of moral justice. And, he is, without a doubt, an irreconcilable adversary of amnesia. The Romanian philosopher, Horia-Roman Patapievici, offered a superb interpretation of Michnik's thought:

> The unpopular ethical choices made by Michnik reveal the imprisoned comrade who never betrayed his friends. Those who experienced the penitentiary colony of communism know that only one thing can save you from treason: love. A love greater than any idea. In the name of this love did Michnik take the liberty of provoking those who transformed into occupation the act of confusing *la revanche* (maybe entitled) with justice (maybe justified). He chose the most difficult path because, and one fells it in his every line, because he loved too much.[62]

I consider that Michnik endorses an anti-utopian, anti-absolutist, anti-monopolist position toward the past; a humanist perspective, rational, and empathic toward the victims. He has no illusion that, at the end of the day, we do have to distinguish between truth and lie, good and evil, freedom and barbarism. He once wrote in 2009 that "we believe that communism was a falsehood from the beginning. We try, though,

---

[61] Adam Michnik was shocked upon being informed that his ideas on "Bolshevik-style anticommunism" (which cannot be understood without the context of the Polish debates and without taking into account the post-1989 tribulations of Solidarity) were invoked by various former nomenklatura members in Romania, with the purpose of blocking the clarification of the past (personal conversation with Adam Michnik, București, Romania, June 9, 2007).

[62] Horia-Roman Patapievici, "Adam Michnik și etica iubirii," *Evenimentul Zilei*, Joi, 25 iunie 2009. A longer version of the text was published in *Idei în Dialog*, 1 iulie 2009, as "Confruntarea cu trecutul: soluția Michnik."

to understand the people who were engaged in communism, their heterogeneous motivations and their biographies, sometimes heroic and
tragic, always naive and brought to naught. We do this, driven perhaps
by a conviction hidden somewhere in our subconscious that it's necessary to distinguish the sin from the sinner: the sin we condemn—the
sinner we try to listen to, to understand."[63]

The reverberations of the past are part of contemporary polemics
and define competing visions of the future. It is quite often in relation to the past, especially a traumatic one, that political actors identify
themselves and engage in competitions with their opponents. Reviewing Jan T. Gross's book *Fear*, David Engel wrote,

> Unless Polishness, whatever its constituent characteristics, is
> transmitted from generation to generation through mother's
> milk, as it were, nothing that Gross or anyone else might say
> about any part of the Polish community in 1946, 1941, or any
> other year more than six decades in the past *necessarily* reflects
> upon any part of the community today. It can do so only to the
> extent that the present community continues to affirm the values
> implicated in past events. Thus *Fear* or any other work of history
> can legitimately be neither offered nor read as a vehicle for con-
> temporary self-examination except insofar as it prompts contem-
> poraries to question strongly whether they remain committed to
> those values.[64]

The post-communist debates on the past should be seen as indicators
of contemporary ideological cleavages and tensions, confirming Jürgen
Habermas's analysis of the public use of history as an antidote to oblivion, denial, and partisan distortions: "It is especially these dead who
have a claim to the weak anamnestic power of a solidarity that later
generations can continue to practice only in the medium of a remem-

---

[63] Marci Shore, *The Taste of Ashes: The Afterlife of Totalitarianism in Eastern
Europe* (New York: Crown Publishers, 2013), 343.

[64] See David Engel, "On Continuity and Discontinuity in Polish-Jewish Relations: Observations on Fear," *East European Politics and Societies*, vol. 21,
no. 3,(Summer 2007), 538–539. See also Jan T. Gross, *Fear: Anti-Semitism
in Poland after Auschwitz—An Essay in Historical Interpretation* (New York:
Random House, 2006).

brance that is repeatedly renewed, often desperate, and continually on one's mind."[65]

The Report's approach to the category of *perpetrator* is focused on three types that have been consistently ignored by those who blame the document for a so-called blanket condemnation. According to Cosmina Tănăsoiu, one can identify those "guilty for the thousands of dead and deported" (i.e., top Party officials, cabinet ministers, police commanders, high-level magistrates), those "guilty for the annihilation of diaspora dissent" (i.e., the heads of the external services of the secret police and counter-intelligence), and those "guilty for the indoctrination of the population" (the largest category, ranging from Party members and cabinet ministers to writers and poets)."[66] Additionally, the Report signals out those who were responsible, after 1989, for the manipulating and forging the truth in order to preserve their power and continue, by means of an "original democracy," the fateful structures and the interest groups dominant during the last decade of the party-state rule. I think that this last section of the third part of the Report, is fully justified by the specific post-1989 history of Romania, one marred with moments of critical, managed anarchy (the miners' trips to Bucharest and the pyramidal financial schemes), by the quasi-bankruptcy of the market economy, and by infrastructural retardation. The part of the Report that analyzes the events, the meaning, and the aftermath of the 1989 Romanian revolution concludes:

> During the first years in power, Ceaușescu's successors defended their hegemonic positions through manipulation, corruption, and coercion. But, we should not confuse this with an attempt to reinstate communist rule. [...] The Revolution from below was accompanied by a re-grouping of the nomenklatura, which succeeded in taking power by means of backroom negotiations led by people and groups from the secondary ranks of the old regime (the party, the Union of the Communist Youth, the secret police, the army, and the attorney's office) Based on these observations we can conclude that the phenomenon of "continuity" was a seri-

---

[65] See Jürgen Habermas, *The New Conservatism: Cultural Criticism and the Historians' Debate* (Cambridge: MIT Press, 1989), 233.

[66] Cosmina Tănăsoiu, *The Tismaneanu Report...*, 65.

ous obstacle on the path to establishing a genuine democratic political community. The old Leninist habits continued to inspire the new rulers to an intolerant, paternalistic, and authoritarian behavior.[67]

Consequently, it can be argued that the individual and his inalienable rights were the main reconstitutive focus of the Report. The members of the Commission refused the principle of collective guilt and/or punishment. The question that none of the political actors in Romania wished to bother themselves with can be phrased as follows: How can Romania go through a phase of reconciliation as long as the authors of the crimes perpetrated under communism are still enjoying privileges and are brazenly and unrepentantly defying their victims? And I am thinking particularly to individuals who have been signaled out by the Report as perpetrators of crimes against humanity, the members of the last Executive Political Committee under Ceaușescu who were directly involved in the murderous repression of the protesters in Bucharest or Timișoara.

Along these lines, historian Marius Oprea, then president of the Institute for the Investigation of Communism's Crimes in Romania (after November 2009, IICCMER), proposed a law according to which "the pensions of the secret police employees, who were found by court to have been involved in repression, would be reduced to the level of the pensions of unskilled labors [I want to note here that the pensions of former secret police members, generals, party leaders are some of the most generous in the country—VT] [...] We would opt for the latter because the people affected by this law are *perpetrators*, their sole occupation was not, neither under communism nor now, in the list of jobs recognized by the state. The funds obtained through this pension cut will be allocated to the victims and the survivors of the communist regime."[68] The draft advanced by Dr. Oprea was one of the recommendations of the Report in section III entitled "Legislation and Justice" (p. 637). After several years of negotiations this project was buried in the Parliament's archive because of an utter lack of political

---

[67] *Raport Final*, 620–622.
[68] Mirela Corlățan, "Pensiile securiștilor, greu de tăiat," *Cotidianul*, August 16, 2007.

will to promote it. In 2011, during my tenure as IICCMER's President of the Scientific Council, the institution's leadership attempted to promote a modified version of this legislative project, but again met with the opposition of the Ministry of Justice to sanction it.[69]

Another initiative that was blocked was the process of bringing to court around 210 individuals who had held leadership positions in various prisons during the dictatorship. They were accused that "they used the correctional program as a means of socially exterminating whole categories of people," their actions "falling into various category of criminal acts, such as first degree murder."[70] Between 2006 and 2012, IICCR and then IICCMER provided expertise to Romanian prosecutors for possible indictments for crimes perpetrated during the communist period, but the latter simply ignored this information. Only in 2013, Romanian prosecutors began investigating the possibility of legal action against communist perpetrators. Surprisingly, they used the legal category of genocide to build their cases, which is hardly tenable or inviting for positive results considering that, in Romania, the penal code's definition refers to genocide as "the destruction in its entirety or only partially of a collectivity or of national, ethnic, racial, and religious groups." Building a legal case on the ambiguous formulation "collectivity" potentially undermines the initiative itself.[71]

But maybe one of the most important breakthroughs of the post-Report years, however, was the nomination as Director of the Romanian National Archives of Dr. Dorin Dobrincu (member of the Commission, one of the authors and co-editor of the Report). Soon after

---

[69] The social-liberal government did pass a law in 2013 that forces perpetrators to pay reparations to their victims. But this can happened only after they are sentenced. Suffice to say that no communist perpetrator has been sentenced in Romania, so implicitly this law is simply a Potemkin legislative act. For more details, see Vladimir Tismaneanu, "Palme pentru victime: pensiile securiștilor și activiștilor," September 19, 2013, (http://www.contributors.ro/reactie-rapida/palme-pentru-victime-pensiile-securistilor-si-activistilor/).

[70] See Mirela Corlățan, "Torționarii comuniști cercetați penal," *Cotidianul*, May 24, 2007.

[71] For more on this issue see my article in Romanian "Călăul Vișinescu și genocidul," September 3, 2013, (http://www.contributors.ro/reactie-rapida/visinescu-si-genocidul/) and "Anticomunismul uselist: obsedantul deceniu redux," September 20 2013, (http://www.contributors.ro/politica-doctrine/anticomunismul-uselist-obsedantul-deceniu-redux/).

his confirmation, he decided to grant free access to all researchers and individuals to the entire archive of the RCP's Central Committee—another recommendation of the Commission's Report.[72] In retaliation for his bold move, several years later, in 2012, the newly instated social-liberal government dismissed him from his position. However, the opening of the Romanian archives remains in place as a lasting legacy of the Commission. Another important recommendation of the Report was implemented in November 2011. As a result of IIC-CMER's efforts, the Parliament passed law no. 198 on "Declaring 23 August as the Day for Commemorating the Victims of Fascism and Communism and the 21 December as the Day of Remembrance for the Victims of Communism in Romania."[73] Unsurprisingly, the social-liberal government formed in May 2012 and its subsequent incarnations simply ignored these days of commemoration.

President Băsescu created, on April 11, 2007, the Consultative Commission for the Analysis of the Communist Dictatorship (CCACDR), which was composed of twelve experts (I served as chair). The main function of this body was to provide the specialized knowledge for the legal initiatives promoted by the executive branch in relation to the overall effort of dealing with the communist past (e.g., lustration law; commemorations; textbooks; laws regarding the victims, survivors, and perpetrators). At the same time, the CCACDR was meant to be the academic backbone of two other important projects: the Encyclopedia of Romanian Communism and the high school textbook for the study of the communist historical experience in Romania. CCACDR struggled to implement its mandate because of lack of funding and consistent absence of governmental support. But it did successfully publish a collection of the archival documents used by the PCACDR's members in writing the Report (already two volumes have appeared with two others forthcoming).

---

[72] For more details see Cristian Vasile, "Cinci ani de la Raportul final. Despre o condamnare – nu doar simbolică – a regimului comunist," December 17, 2011, (http://www.contributors.ro/cultura/cinci-ani-de-la-raportul-final-de-spre-o-condamnare-%E2%80%93-nu-doar-simbolica-%E2%80%93-a-re-gimului-comunist/).

[73] For details on this law and other legislative initiatives by IICCMER see http://www.iiccr.ro/ro/proiecte_legislative_iiccmer/proiecte_legislative/.

The most important result of the collaboration between the CCACDR and the Institute for the Investigation of Communist Crimes (a governmental institution with a significant budget, which in November 2009 merged with the Institute for National Memory of the Romanian Exile to become IICCMER) was the first high-school textbook on the history of communism. In September 2008, the textbook was presented to the Romanian public. After almost one year of collecting feedback from teachers, historians, and from public opinion, the authors made the necessary revisions to the textbook and published a new edition in April 2009.[74] On the basis of it, the subject is currently taught on an optional basis in the last two years of high-school. Another crucial development which took place under IICCMER's umbrella, at a time when former experts and members of its Commission were part of its leadership, was article 125 of the penal code and law 27/2012. They modified the penal code and law 286/2009 concerning the penal code in relation to the statute of limitations concerning genocide, crimes against humanity, and war crimes. These can now be prosecuted regardless of the time of their commission. Furthermore, the same decision lifted the statute of limitations for homicide. Such changes to the penal code create the legal grounding for the prosecution of crimes committed during the communist era.[75] This legal breakthrough was achieved by Monica Macovei, a former Minister of Justice and current member of the European Parliament, but IICCMER assisted her through all the steps of drafting and promoting the legislative proposal.

As it should be apparent by now, after 2006, IICCR and then IICCMER to a large extent attempted to implement some of the Report's

---

[74] Dorin Dobrincu, Raluca Grosescu, Mihai Stamatescu, Liviu Pleșa, Andrei Muraru, Sorin Andreescu, *O istorie a comunismului din România. Manual pentru liceu* (București: Polirom, 2008). In 2012, IICCMER also launched an interactive website created by political scientist Raluca Grosescu that functions as a visual aid and a teaching platform: http://www.istoriacomunismului.ro/#/home.

[75] http://www.iiccr.ro/ro/presa/comunicate/comunicate_de_presa_2012/crimele_comunismului_pot_fi_in_continuare_judecate/. This legal act was reconfirmed by the Romanian Constitutional Court in December 2013. See http://www.iiccr.ro/ro/presa/comunicate/comunicate_de_presa_2013/iiccmer_saluta_decizia_curtii_constitutionale_privind_imprescriptibilitatea_faptelor_de_omor/.

recommendations and continue the work of the Commission on multiple levels (scholarly, investigations, commemoration, and education). In the absence of a museum of communism in Romania, the institution succeded in creating a series of websites that represent specific policies of the regime and some of its post-1989 consequences: an impressive collection of photos from those times (http://fototeca.iiccr.ro/); a website about Nicolae Ceaușescu's politics of reproduction (http://politicapronatalista.iiccr.ro/); one about the "Mineriade" June 1990 (http://mineriade.iiccmer.ro/); about the biographies of the nomenklatura (http://www.iiccr.ro/ro/biografiile_nomenklaturii/); on the geography of the Romanian exile (http://www.arhivaexilului.ro/); about the reeducation in Pitești penitentiary (http://www.fenomenulpitesti.ro/); and, last but not least, an education platform on the history of communism in Romania (see footnote 74). There is also a database with the detention information of many political prisoners from the communist period: http://www.iiccr.ro/ro/fise_detinuti_politici/. It functions as a valuable instrument for providing expert assistance for those (victims and their descendants) who wish to clarify or document individual contexts of repression. IICCMER has also published important monographs or edited volumes on the communist historical period, while also promoting an extensive program, at least until summer 2012, of translations of some of the most important scholarship in the comparative study of totalitarianism. In 2010, the institute launched the first Romanian international peer-review journal in communism entitled *History of Communism in Europe*. It also publishes its own Romanian language yearbook.

The main problem of IICCMER is its increased politicization, hardly an issue specific to Romania, as Timothy Snyder rightly remarks in his chapter in this volume. As the institution's executive president and the president of the Scientific Council are nominated by the prime minister, it only depends on those who hold these leadership positions to avoid the involvement of politics in the institution's programs and activity. For example, I resigned from the Scientific Council (along with all of its other thirteen members) because of the decision by the socialist prime minister, Victor Ponta, to abusively dismiss political scientist Ioan Stanomir (chair of the doctoral school of the Political Science Department at the University of Bucharest) from the position of executive president and myself from the presidentship of the Scientific Council. Within a year, IICCMER's entire leadership, structure, and activity were reshuffled for the worse. By 2013, the research activity of the institution almost came to a halt as did its publications program that promoted until 2012 a synchronization of local historiography with international debates in the field. Some of its best researchers (almost half) resigned in protest for the arbitrariness of the new management.[76] As mentioned earlier, the Institute did manage to collaborate with prosecutors in preparing the ground for legal action against communist perpetrators. But the fact that they used the accusation of genocide greatly subverts the potential of success of such initiative.

All in all, the years that have passed since the condemnation of the communist regime can be defined as a period of informational self-determination. I consider that President Băsescu's condemnation of the communist regime in Romania was a moment of civic mobilization. Generally speaking, decommunization is, in its essence, a moral, political, and intellectual process. These are the dimensions that raise challenges in contemporary Romanian society. The Commission's Report answered a fundamental necessity, characteristic of the post-authoritarian world, that of moral clarity. Without it one would multiply the cobweb of lies crushing us, the impenetrable mist that seemed to forever last. This state of moral perplexity inexorably turns into cynicism, anger, resentment and despair. One must greet President Băsescu's political will, the first post-1989 Romanian head of state that dared to begin such vital procedure of exorcizing the communist-Securitate demons. The shock of the past unveiled is inevitable. Moral-symbolic action is, according to McAdams, one of the four types of retributive justice (the others being the criminal, the noncriminal, and the rectifying aspects).[77] I would even argue that it is the most important, especially if one is to take the model of Jan Kubik's book on the influence of civic countersymbols in opposition to the hermeneutic routine inherent to a political establishment.[78]

---

[76] For more details on this evolution of IICCMER, see Francesco Zavatti, "'Historiography Has Been a Minefield': A Conversation with Vladimir Tismaneanu," *Baltic Worlds* 6 (April 2013), 10–13, and Mark Kramer, "Foreword," in Stan, *Transitional Justice in Post-Communist Romania*, xviii.

[77] McAdams, *Judging the Past*, 19–20.

[78] Jan Kubik, *The Power of Symbols Against the Symbols of Power: The Rise of Solidarity and the Fall of State Socialism in Poland* (University Park: Pennsylvania State University Press, 1994).

The Report identified many features of guilt, in relation to the communist experience, that have never before been under scrutiny. It offers a framework for shedding light upon what Karl Jaspers called "moral and metaphysical guilt"—the individual's failure to live up to his or her moral duties and the destruction of solidarity of social fabric.[79] This, in my opinion, is the angle from which one can see to the connection between the condemnation initiative and politics. In the words of Charles King, "The commission's chief tasks had to do with both morality and power: to push Romanian politicians and Romanian society into drawing a line between past and present, putting an end to nostalgia for an alleged period of greatness and independence, and embracing the country's de facto cultural pluralism and European future."[80] Such matters considered, the PCACDR was indeed a political project through which both the acknowledgment and conceptualization of the 1945 to 1989 national traumatic experience were accomplished, whilst those responsible for the existence of communism as a regime in Romania were identified.

I believe that, in Eastern Europe, we still experience a mnemonic interregnum, what Tony Judt defined as "a moment between myths." The Romanian exercise of "public use of history" was an endeavor to clarify the role of memory in history in order to specify its impact upon contemporary societal life. It was the only path left for truth-seeking under circumstances of a two-decade judicial stalemate in reference to the past. The Commission created a document where responsibility for the past was claimed and individualized. There are hardly other ways of reconstructing *Gemeinsamkeit*, that is, the social cohesion and communion destroyed by the atomization brought about in the communist regime. As I have already stated, the Report was written with analytical rigor, with compassion for the victims, and in full awareness of the trauma both incumbent in the past and in the act of remembrance itself. The Commission had to listen to what Frankfurt School philosopher Theodor W. Adorno referred to as "the voice of those who

---

[79] Karl Jaspers, *The Question of German Guilt* (New York: Fordham University Press, 2001). On communism as vengefulness and resentment see Gabriel Liiceanu, *Despre ura* (Bucuresti: Ed. Humanitas, 2007).

[80] Charles King, "Review: Remembering Romanian Communism," 722, *Slavic Review*, vol. 66, no. 4 (Winter 2007), 718–723.

cannot talk anymore."[81] The PCACDR and the comdemnation act can be premises for reconciliation, but they could not facilitate it in the absence of repentance. The condemnation of the communist regime therefore fully maintains its cathartic value because "unless the trauma is understood, there is no possibility of escaping it."[82]

The Report fixed the memory of the totalitarian experience in place and in time, it overcame the burden of the denial of memory, of institutionalized amnesia. It set the groundwork for the revolutionizing of the normative foundations of the communal history, imposing the necessary moral criteria of a democracy that wishes to militantly defend its values. The Commission's work and the intense debates surrounding it highlight one of the most vexing, yet vitally important tensions of the post-communist world: the understanding of the traumatic totalitarian past and the political, moral, and intellectual difficulties, frustrations, hopes, and anxieties involved in trying to come to grips with it.

If we attempt to situate the above discussion within a regional context, we need to go back to the legacy of the revolutions of 1989. The most important new idea brought about by these memorable events was the rethinking and the rehabilitation of citizenship. Many of the ideological struggles of post-communism have revolved around the notion of what is *civic* and how to define membership in the new communities. Both formal and informal amnesia and *hypermnesia*, after 1989, estranged the lessons of the totalitarian experience from the present, despite the fact that the former ought to be essential features of the latter's identity. The discomfiture with democratic challenges and the prevailing constitutional pluralist model is not only linked to the transition from Leninism, but to the larger problem of legitimation and the existence of competing visions of common good, of rival symbols of collective identity. Nevertheless, Eastern Europe has the example and the model of the West, where the process of democratization, of building sustainable postwar societies and transnational bonds, was fundamentally based upon coming to terms with the traumatic and guilty past. Therefore, the memory of both Auschwitz and the Gulag,

---

[81] See Theodor W. Adorno, *Modèles Critiques* (Paris: Payot, 1984), especially 97–112 and 215–219.

[82] Motzkin, "Memory of Crime," 200–205.

if remembered and taught, can go a long way to the entrenchment of the societal values and the political culture destroyed in the region by twentieth-century totalitarianisms.

In this sense, the Prague Declaration (signed by people such as the late Václav Havel, Joachim Gauck, and Vytautas Landsbergis) and the OSCE's "Resolution on Divided Europe Reunited: Promoting Human Rights and Civil Liberties in the OSCE Region in the Twenty-First Century" can be seen as the fulfillment of the second post-1989 stage of development in the region. If in the 1990s, one could argue that the former communist countries sought the main road back to democracy, in the 2000s, they have been trying to overcome self-centeredness in a united Europe. The two documents finally recognize that the new Europe is "bound together by the signs and symbols of its terrible past."[83] For example, the OSCE's resolution states that

Noting that in the twentieth century European countries experienced two major totalitarian regimes, Nazi and Stalinist, which brought about genocide, violations of human rights and freedoms, war crimes and crimes against humanity, acknowledging the uniqueness of the Holocaust [...] The OSCE Parliamentary Assembly reconfirms its united stand against all totalitarian rule from whatever ideological background [...] Urges the participating States: a. to continue research into and raise public awareness of the totalitarian legacy; b. to develop and improve educational tools, programs and activities, most notably for younger generations, on totalitarian history, human dignity, human rights and fundamental freedoms, pluralism, democracy and tolerance; [...] Expresses deep concern at the glorification of the totalitarian regimes.[84]

---

[83] Tony Judt, *Postwar: A History of Europe Since 1945* (London: Penguin Books, 2005), 831.

[84] "Vilnius declaration of the OSCE parliamentary assembly and resolutions adopted at the eighteenth annual session," (Vilnius, 29 June to 3 July 2009), http://www.oscepa.org/images/stories/documents/activities/1.Annual%20 Session/2009_Vilnius/Final_Vilnius_Declaration_ENG.pdf. The Prague Declaration and the OSCE Resolution are hardly singular. Other official, pan-European or trans-Atlantic have been made to condemn the criminality of communism/Stalinism following the example of the criminalization of fas-

The unmastered past of the twentieth century in Central and Eastern Europe prevents these countries from institutionalizing the logical connection between democracy, memory, and militancy. But, the flight from democracy will always be checked by conscientiousness about the consequences of radical evil in history. I consider that one can refashion both individual and collective identity on the basis of the negative lessons and *exempla* that national history can provide. Besides the trauma of the early Stalinist days, all the countries in the region (Romania included) had and still have to deal with "the grey veil of moral ambiguity" (Tony Judt) that was the defining feature of existing socialism. These societies and most of their members have a bad conscience in relation with the past. If we agree that *annus mirabilis* 1989 was fundamentally about the rebirth of citizenship and the reempowering of the truth, the gradual clarification of recent history will close the vicious circle of transition in East-Central Europe. Just like the West has come to terms with its trauma and guilt, the East can ultimately find the long lost consensus in similar ways. In this sense, I believe that the upheaval of 1989 would potentially accomplish its ideals along the road of Europeanization.

cism/Nazism. For example, the EU Parliament's resolution on European conscience and totalitarianism or the building of the Victims of Communism Memorial in Washington DC. The monument was dedicated by President George W. Bush on Tuesday, June 12, 2007. June 12 was chosen because it was the twentieth anniversary of President Ronald Reagan's famous Brandenburg Gate speech. See http://www.globalmuseumoncommunism.org/voc.

David Brandenberger

Promotion of a Usable Past: Official Efforts to Rewrite Russo-Soviet History, 2000–2014

For much of the Soviet period, party authorities endorsed a single, mobilizational view of USSR history that was supported not only by academia and the censor, but by official mass culture, public educational institutions, and state textbook publishing. Indeed, it was not until the fall of the Soviet Union in 1991 that the society's traditional reliance on an "official line" and a handful of prescribed textbooks gave way to a much looser system in which a variety of ideologically-diverse titles could vie with one another within a newly competitive public school textbook market. The curricular diversity of this new period was epitomized by the fact that at the turn of the twenty-first century, some 100 different history textbooks enjoyed official approval from the Ministry of Education and Science for classroom use.[1]

But as the heterogeneity of the early post-Soviet period gave way after 2000 to consolidationist tendencies under V. V. Putin and D. A. Medvedev, talk again turned to the reestablishment of a single, official mobilizational account of the Russo-Soviet past in order to

---

[1] The author is grateful to A. V. Filippov, A. B. Zubov, A. R. Diukov, M. V. Zelenov, N. A. Lomagin, and Jeffrey Hass for their contributions to this chapter. Aspects of this piece stem from David Brandenberger, "A New *Short Course*? A. V. Filippov and the Russian State's Search for a 'Usable Past,'" *Kritika* 10:4 (2009): 825–833. See the rest of the *Kritika* forum as well: Vladimir Solonari, "Normalizing Russia, Legitimizing Putin," 835–846; Boris N. Mironov, "The Fruits of a Bourgeois Education," 847–860; Elena Zubkova, "The Filippov Syndrome," 861–868. "Shkol'nye biblioteki Rossii proveriat na nalichie nelegal'nykh uchebnikov," *Nezavisimaia gazeta*, 27 April 2010, 8.

foster a broadly-felt sense of patriotism. Notable in this regard were efforts that gave rise to A. V. Filippov's controversial two-part teachers' manual, *The History of Russia* (2007, 2008)[2] and the infamous Presidential Commission to Counter Attempts to Falsify History at the Expense of Russian Interests (2009–2013). Even more important was V. V. Putin's 2013 bid to produce a single official public school history narrative by administrative command. This chapter assesses the extent to which these projects succeeded in catalyzing a new official line on the past.

The Search for a Usable Textbook

One of the least appreciated official priorities in early twenty-first century Russia was the campaign to develop and popularize a "usable past" based on the country's Soviet heritage.[3] Putin first spoke about the need for a new sense of historical perspective shortly after coming to power, connecting the issue to the broader imperative of a "national idea" to unify the country's fractious political system.[4] In the wake of

---

[2] For the Filippov text, see A. A. Danilov and A. V. Filippov (eds.), *Istoriia Rossii, 1900–1945: kniga dlia uchitelia* (Moscow: Prosveshchenie, 2008); A. V. Filippov, A. I. Utkin, and S. V. Sergeev (eds.), *Istoriia Rossii, 1945–2008: kniga dlia uchitelia* and S. V. Sergeev (Moscow: Prosveshchenie, 2008). The original text had a slightly different title when first released in 2007: A. V. Filippov, A. I. Utkin, and S. V. Sergeev (eds.), *Noveishaia istoriia Rossii, 1945–2006: kniga dlia uchitelia* (Moscow: Prosveshchenie, 2007). For the Danilov text, see A. A. Danilov, A. I. Utkin, and A. V. Filippov (eds.), *Istoriia Rossii, 1900–1945: 11 klass* (Moscow: Prosveshchenie, 2008); A. A. Danilov, A. I. Utkin, and A. V. Filippov (eds.), *Istoriia Rossii, 1945–2008: 11 klass*, (Moscow: Prosveshchenie, 2008). In 2007–2008, Filippov, a former school teacher from Saratov, was deputy director of the National Laboratory on Foreign Policy, an ostensibly independent think tank connected with N. B. Ivanov of the Russian Presidential Administration and G. O. Pavlovskii's then pro-Kremlin Fund for Effective Politics.

[3] See Van Wyck Brooks, "On Creating a Usable Past," *Dial* 64 (1918): 337–341; Henry Steele Commager, *The Search for a Usable Past and Other Essays in Historiography* (New York: Knopf, 1967), 3–27.

[4] V. Putin, *Gosudarstvo Rossiia: put' k effektivnomu gosudarstvu (o polozhenii v strane i osnovnykh napravleniiakh vnutrennei i vneshnei politiki gosudarstva)* (Moscow: Izvestiia, 2000), 11–12.

this announcement, a hodgepodge of deferential gestures to Soviet history began to make headlines—the revival of the Red Army battle flag and a sanitized version of the Stalin-era national anthem; the return of a bust of F. E. Dzerzhinskii to the militia headquarters in downtown Moscow; extensive state support and airtime for mass culture's "normalization" of the Soviet experience; and so on. Perhaps most notorious amid all this nostalgia was Putin's own announcement in his April 2005 "State of the State" message to the Federation Council that "the collapse of the USSR was greatest geopolitical catastrophe of the twentieth century."[5]

Subjected to scorn and ridicule by westernized Russian elites and foreign commentators alike, these attempts to promote a national idea appear to have been less haphazard than initially believed. The reason for such measures was quite clear: by the early 2000s, Russian-speaking society within the territory of the former RSFSR had been thoroughly disoriented by nearly fifteen years of lurid revelations about the most embarrassing aspects of the Soviet experience—something compounded by the demise of the USSR itself in 1991. And if elites in many of the USSR's former republics and client states were able to successfully leverage bids for national self-determination and economic reform on popular distaste for the communist past, Russian elites found this form of mobilization to be hampered by the historic conflation of Russian and Soviet identities.[6] Opinion polling spoke of a deeply demoralized society with little sense of collective identity or common cause.[7]

While these opinion polls revealed division and dejection, they also hinted at an enduring identification with certain accomplishments and

---

[5] "Poslanie Federal´nomu sobraniiu RF," *Rossiiskaia gazeta*, April 26, 2005, 3.

[6] The Yeltsin administration flirted with the idea of developing a "national idea" during the 1990s, especially after nearly losing the 1996 presidential election to the communists—see G. Satarov, *Rossiia v poiskakh idei: analiz pressy* (Moscow: Administratsiia Prezidenta RF, 2000). Generally, see Geoffrey Hosking, *Rulers and Victims: The Russians in the Soviet Union* (Cambridge: Harvard University Press, 2006), 400–409.

[7] Matthew Wyman, *Public Opinion in Postcommunist Russia* (London: Macmillan, 1997), esp. chaps 4–5.

values drawn from the Soviet past.[8] None of these points of consensus were particularly consistent, coherent, or interconnected—indeed, at first glance, they were quite reminiscent of Putin's chaotic pastiche of historical reputations and reliquary. But that did not preclude the possibility that this cacophony could be synthesized into something more systematic.[9] And indeed, official efforts to fashion something from this flotsam and jetsam—particularly for the public schools—were launched shortly thereafter when in 2002 then-prime minister M. M. Kas´ianov instructed the Ministry of Education and Science to solicit bids for a new patriotic textbook.[10] According to Putin, his government embarked upon this course out of a sense of frustration with the history textbooks in use in the public schools at that time. "There are virtually no educational materials," he complained later on, "that depict the contemporary history of our Fatherland in a profound and objective way, nor is there a systematic treatment of the new themes, directions and schools [of thought] that can advance major doctrines and

---

[8] Stephen White, Ian McAllister and Olga Kryshtanovskaya, "El´tsin and His Voters: Popular Support in the 1991 Russian Presidential Elections and After," *Europe-Asia Studies* 46:2 (1994): 285–303, esp. 295–298; Matthew Wyman, Stephen White, Bill Miller and Paul Heywood, "Public Opinion, Parties and Voters in the December 1993 Russian Elections," *Europe-Asia Studies* 47:4 (1995): 591–614; Wyman, *Public Opinion in Postcommunist Russia*, chaps. 4-5, 7; Vera Tolz, "Forging the Nation: National Identity and Nation Building in Post-Communist Russia," *Europe-Asia Studies* 50:6 (1998): 993–1022; and generally, L. Gudkov, *Negativnaia identichnost': Stat'i 1997–2002 godov* (Moscow: Novoe literaturnoe obozrenie/VTsIOM-A, 2004). See also Nanci Adler, "The Future of the Soviet Past Remains Unpredictable: The Resurrection of Stalinist Symbols Amidst the Exhumation of Mass Graves," *Europe-Asia Studies* 57:8 (2005): 1093–1119.

[9] Even without a more systematic approach to the Soviet past, Putin's halting rehabilitation of the Soviet period led public approval ratings for Stalin to climb from 19 percent to 53 percent between 1998 and 2003. See L. Gudkov, "Pamiat' o voine i massovaia identichnost' rossiian," *Neprikosnovennyi zapas* 2–3 (2005) (http://magazines.russ.ru/nz/2005/2/gu5.html, last accessed October 31, 2013).

[10] See, for instance, Vladimir Berlovich, "Sovremennye rossiiskie uchebniki istorii: mnogolikaia istina ili ocherednaia natsional´naia ideia," *Neprikosnovennyi zapas* 4 (2002) (http://magazines.russ.ru/nz/2002/4/brel.html, last accessed October 31, 2013).

explain contemporary events."[11] When nothing came of the 2002 competition, the presidential administration held several further rounds, soliciting submissions from A. O. Chubar'ian and other leading historians. It was in the context of one of these state-sponsored sorties in search of a usable past that Filippov and his collaborators first attracted the attention of the administration.[12]

Released between 2007 and 2008, the Filippov teacher's manuals and their auxiliary textual materials embraced many of the modern production values of the contemporary Russian textbook market. The shortcomings of these manuals received a lot of attention in the press, particularly in regard to their tendency to rehabilitate I. V. Stalin as a political visionary and empire builder.[13] Close analysis reveals this

---

[11] Although Putin blamed much of this ineffectiveness on the poorly conceptualized curriculum, he also spoke menacingly of the influence of historians who receive foreign grants and therefore "dance to the tune that's required of them." Sergei Minaev, "Da malo li chego bylo," *Vlast'* 24 (728) (June 25, 2007), 19.

[12] Oleg Kashin, "V poiskakh 'Kratkogo kursa': Avtory 'kremlevskogo' uchebnika ne nashli obshchego iuzyka s soobshchestvom istorikov," *NG—Politika* (supplement to *Nezavisimaia gazeta*), July 3, 2007, 1–2. The Filippov text was part of a larger project launched in 2006 by V. Iu. Surkov under the auspices of the Russian presidential administration. According to rumors in Moscow, Surkov aspired to release a statist textbook for the public schools but was concerned about being accused of rehabilitating the USSR. For that reason, he decided to sponsor two public school history textbooks—an accessible pro-Soviet narrative and a more bookish anti-Soviet one. Filippov was to supply the pro-Soviet text, while the anti-Soviet volume was to be edited by A. B. Zubov and A. I. Solzhenitsyn. When the latter editorial team couldn't agree on its approach, Solzhenitsyn quit the project and Zubov published his text privately as *Istoriia Rossii. XX vek. V 2-kh tomakh,* ed. A. B. Zubov, 2 vols. (Moscow: AST, 2010).

[13] The best exposé of the selectivity of Filippov's 2007 postwar text is V. Lavrov and I. Kurliandskii, "Posobie po istorii—Filippiki," *Novaia gazeta*, March 17, 2008, 12–13. Such criticism resulted in a number of cuts to the 2008 version of the manual (esp. on pp. 88–90), as well as the removal of an entire section of the chapter on Stalin from the Danilov textbook. A thorough critique of his volume on the 1900–1945 period is Irina Karatsupa, "Uchebnik Filippova: prodolzhenie posledovalo," *Uroki istorii XX vek*, October 28, 2009 (http://urokiistorii.ru/current/view/2009/10/uchebnik-filippova, last accessed October 31, 2013).

treatment of Stalin to be not only apologetic, but highly tendentious.[14] But if the Russian press largely focused on Filippov's apparent revival of the cult of personality, at least as eye-catching was his broader selectivity and indulgence in other sorts of hyperbolic revisionism.[15] Equally troubling were the manuals' partisanship and Russia-centric focus at the expense of the USSR's other republics, satellites and client states.[16]

---

[14] According to Filippov's manual on the postwar period, Stalin's leadership followed a 500-year Russian political tradition which demanded that power be concentrated in the hands of a single, autocratic ruler and his centralized administrative system (81). Stalin apparently not only embraced this governing principle, but essentially dedicated his reign to the restoration of the Russian empire (88). Prioritizing the perennial imperative of national defense, Stalin also focused on economic modernization and reform of the country's administrative command structure (86–90). Stalin was demanding, harsh and unsentimental, embracing a style of leadership that Filippov connected to Peter the Great (88). Ultimately, even Stalin's most cruel means were held to be justified by their ends, inasmuch as "their goal was the mobilization of the administrative apparatus in order to ensure its effectiveness both in the process of industrialization and, after the war, in the restoration of the economy" (87–88). According to Filippov, Stalin and the system he created deserved credit not only for reuniting the lands of the former empire, but for transforming the country into an industrial superpower capable of vanquishing the "invincible" Nazi war machine and holding its own against the US and its NATO allies during the Cold War (93). According to Filippov's critics, this approach to Stalin's various accomplishments teleologically justified even the worst excesses of the period, See Anatolii Bershtein, "Vspomnit' vse!" *Istoriia* (supplement to *Pervoe sentiabria*) 23 (839) (December 1, 2007): 24–26, 24.

[15] Postwar events as important as the civil war in western Ukraine (37), the retrenching of collective agriculture (32–33) and the anti-cosmopolitan campaign (43) were treated carelessly. Major international developments were given highly idiosyncratic readings, whether concerning the United States' "loss" of the Korean War (66), the Warsaw Pact's suppression of the 1956 Hungarian uprising (133–134), or the USSR's "victory" during the Cuban Missile Crisis (145). For a thorough accounting, see Mikhail Borisov, "My vas nauchim Rodinu liubit'," *Otechestvennye zapiski* 4 (2007): 292–298.

[16] Broader themes in postwar domestic history were also narrated in highly partisan terms, such as the role of the Russian people in the development of the former republics (218–227). Similar bias marred the discussion of international dynamics surrounding the Cold War (9–19, 56–66, 241–242), the standoff with China (136–138, 229–230) and relations with the non-aligned world (138–142). The USSR's relations with the countries of the former Warsaw Pact were treated as almost an afterthought, with agency emanating almost exclusively from Moscow (56–60, 131–138, 234–235).

Professional historians, pedagogues and critics alike found much to critique in these new publications.

Officially, Filippov's manuals—particularly the postwar volume and its auxiliary materials—were billed as a means of cultivating a mass sense of historically-informed patriotism. Content analysis, however, reveals the narrative's ideological objectives to have differed rather markedly from this agenda. Instead of emphasizing conventional, grassroots patriotism based on either an ethnic or civic conception of the nation, the manual focused on state power, self-determination and the construction of an administrative-command system. This was most visible in the volume's final chapter, which hailed Putin's formation of a successful executive team and his defeat of opposing forces—details which suggested an etatist ideological vision emplotted around the exercise of centralized, hierarchically-organized political power (the so-called *vertikal vlasti*).[17]

This impression was confirmed by the structure and periodization of the rest of the book. Ignoring Soviet historiographic traditions that mapped the history of the USSR into stages of economic development ("The USSR During the Fifth Five-Year Plan," "The New Stage in the Struggle for Communism"), Filippov also broke with post-Soviet paradigms that divide the postwar years into cultural periods (the "Thaw," "Stagnation," "Glasnost" and "Perestroika"). Instead, he endorsed a heroic "great men of history" periodization that organized the narrative around a highly personalized sense of political power. Although this focus on personality seemed at first glance to be a rather primitive choice of emplotment for professional historians to make, this paradox was later resolved by the revelation that the manuals' basic schema had originated within the presidential administration itself. Journalist Anna Kachurovskaia, for instance, quoted unnamed sources as saying that not only had the manuals been sponsored by the administration, but its authors had received explicit instructions from above on how to

---

[17] The chapter, entitled "Sovereign Democracy" (and its analog in the Danilov textbook, "Russia's New Path"), elaborates upon Surkov's thesis regarding the evolution of representative governance in the Russian historical context. See *Russkaia politicheskaia kul'tura: Vzgliad iz utopii (Lektsiia Vladislava Surkova; materialy obsuzhdeniia v "Nezavisimoi gazete")* (Moscow: Izd-vo NG, 2007); Vladislav Surkov, *Teksty 97–07: stat'i i vystupleniia* (Moscow: Evropa, 2008).

structure their narrative. "It should go approximately like this," Filippov and his collaborators were apparently told: "Stalin was good (he established the power hierarchy, although not private property); [N. S.] Khrushchev was bad (he weakened the hierarchy); Brezhnev was good for the same reasons as Stalin; [M. S.] Gorbachev and [B. N.] Yeltsin were bad (they collapsed the country, although Yeltsin did allow the development of private property); Putin is the best state manager (he strengthened the power hierarchy and private property)."[18] At first glance a childishly simplistic approach to historical analysis, this advice was actually quite reminiscent of the binary "good-bad" oppositions that Stalin demanded of a previous generation of textbook brigades working in the 1930s.[19] It also displayed the same sort of unvarnished, folksy wisdom that Putin is known for when speaking off the cuff.[20]

Ultimately then, the usable past promoted by the Filippov manuals was designed to promote the interests of the political command structure. This conservative vision of the historical process held that nothing was more important than the establishment and maintenance of state power and political hierarchy, inasmuch as only these factors could guarantee national security and domestic stability. Political leaders were evaluated according to their record of defending state interests from foreign and domestic forces that challenged Russian sovereignty, its executive power and its political centralization. More liberal

---

[18] Kachuarovskaia, "Istoricheskii pripadok."

[19] David Brandenberger, *National Bolshevism: Stalinist Mass Culture and the Formation of Modern Russian National Identity, 1931–1956* (Cambridge: Harvard University Press, 2002), chap. 3.

[20] See, for example, Putin's speech to teachers at Novo-Ogarevo in June 2007 in which he called for an end to a peculiarly Soviet sense of historical guilt: "Yes, we have had our own frightful pages of history—1937, let us not forget about that. But other countries have had even more frightful times. In any case, we never used nuclear weapons against civilians, we never poured chemicals over thousands of kilometers of territory and never bombed a small country with seven times more explosive than was used in the Great Patriotic War, as was the case with Vietnam. We also never had other dark pages, such as the Nazi experience, for instance. There's always something in the history of every state, every people. But we cannot allow others to make us feel guilty. . . . If some outsider tries to pass out grades and play teacher, this is [really] an attempt to seize administrative power." See Minaev, "Da malo li chego bylo."

governing paradigms were held to result only in hardship, frustration and tragedy, as illustrated by the historical experiences of the Khrushchev, Gorbachev and Yeltsin periods. Patriotism too was slaved to this sense of loyalty to a strong, centralized state and the etatist belief that the state was better equipped to safeguard national interests than grassroots socio-political movements, civic organizations or democracy itself.[21]

Curiously, despite predictions in the press to the contrary, the Filippov manuals and their associated textbooks and curricular materials were never awarded anything close to a monopoly over the public school history curriculum. Perhaps this was due to public outcry and criticism over their tendentiousness. Perhaps it was due to rival publishing houses' behind-the-scenes defense of their share of the lucrative textbook market. Perhaps official priorities changed within the presidential administration after Medvedev became chief executive in 2008. But even without the promised monopoly, the Filippov manuals enjoyed significant sway over the evolving public school history curriculum. Not only were they continuously republished, but they gave rise to a series of textbooks and auxiliary materials that were widely used in public schools for a number of years. And perhaps most importantly, the texts' semi-official status indirectly shaped the content and approach of competing textbooks—a process aided by the Ministry of Education and Science's simultaneous narrowing of its list of formal curricular endorsements.[22] If a general convergence of history textbook narratives had been observable in the Russian Federation since the

---

[21] This central emphasis in the text is overlooked by recent commentators, including Solonari, "Normalizing Russia, Legitimizing Putin"; Mironov, "The Fruits of a Bourgeois Education"; and David W. Benn, "The Teaching of History in Present-Day Russia," *Europe-Asia Studies* 62:1 (2010): 173–177.

[22] This conclusion is based on an unsystematic survey of textbooks available in Moscow and St. Petersburg between 2010–2013. See also Mariia Biletskaia, "Analiz pravovogo regulirovaniia i sushchestvuiushchego poriadka obespecheniia Ministerstvom obrazovaniia i nauki Rossiiskoi Federatsii povysheniia kachestva uchebnoi literatury," *Uroki istorii XX*, May 9, 2009 (http://www.urokiistorii.ru/sites/all/files/analiz.pdf, last accessed October 31, 2013).

start of Putin's presidency, the role of the Filippov materials in accelerating this process was quite palpable.[23]

The Campaign Against the "Falsification of History"

If Medvedev did not grant Filippov a formal textbook monopoly in the years following 2008, this did not deter him from making a major contribution of his own to post-Soviet Russia's search for a usable past: the Presidential Commission to Counter Attempts to Falsify History at the Expense of Russian Interests. Founded by presidential decree in 2009 in order to identify and investigate damaging distortions of the Russian historical record, the commission's launch was the source of considerable debate in the press. Some saw the commission as an organ of state censorship designed either to enforce Filippov's new semi-official historical line in the public schools or to curtail embarrassing archival research and historical publications. Others connected the initiative to the defense of the Soviet Union's World War II reputation, as the commission was unveiled in the run-up to the sixty-fifth anniversary of the allied victory. Still others linked its formation to the geopolitical need for steps to be taken to refute historical revisionism that threatened to compromise the country's interests abroad.[24] Curiously, Russian authorities demurred in the face of questions about the exact nature of the commission's mandate, stimulating further public attention and debate.

As chartered, the commission was comprised of a blue-ribbon panel of twenty-seven prominent members of the Russian political

---

[23] Ekaterina Levintova and Jim Butterfield, "History Education and Historical Remembrance in Contemporary Russia: Sources of Political Attitudes of Pro-Kremlin Youth," *Communist and Post-Communist Studies* 43 (2010): 139–166; Miguel Vázquez Liñán, "History As a Propaganda Tool in Putin's Russia," *Communist and Post-Communist Studies* 43 (2010): 167–178. For objections to this notion of convergence, see Filipp Chapkovskii, "Uchebnik istorii i ideologicheskii defitsit," *Pro et Contra* 51 (2011): 117–133.

[24] On this commission, see A. Samarina and R. Tsvetkova, "Patriotizm po ukazu: Prezident sozdal ekspertnuiu komissiiu po vyiavleniiu fal'sifikatorov istorii," *Nezavisimaia gazeta*, May 20, 2009 (http://nvo.ng.ru/history/ 2009-05-22/1_patriotism.html, last accessed October 31, 2013).

establishment and was chaired by S. E. Naryshkin, the then head of the presidential administration. Among its members were seventeen high-ranking state officials, four deputies from the State Duma, Federation Council and other representative bodies, three professional historians, two officials from the secret services, and one ministry of defense official. A consultative body, it depended on the Ministry of Education and Science for research, technical and publishing assistance and generally confined its activities to biannual hearings and public relations.[25] Such institutional weakness heightened questions about the commission's purpose and mandate from the start.

In retrospect, it seems that foreign policy concerns—particularly those arising from a series of bitter clashes between the Russian Federation and its neighbors over the history of the Soviet period—prompted the commission's creation.[26] One such conflict emerged from the Soviet secret police's massacre of nearly 22,000 Polish prisoners of war in Katyn Forest and several other locales in May 1940. Long a source of tension with Poland despite Gorbachev's and Yeltsin's historic admissions of Soviet responsibility, Katyn stood at the center of

---

[25] See, for instance, the dismissive position of Memorial chair Nikita Petrov, quoted in Vladimir Kara-Muza, "Stanet li sozdannaia pri prezidente komissiia po bor'be s fal'sifikatsiei istorii organom tsenzury dlia istoricheskoi nauki?" *Radio svoboda*, 19 May 2009 (http://www.svobodancws.ru/content/transcript/1735458.html, last accessed October 31, 2013); also John Beyrle, "Is Stalin's Ghost a Threat to Academic Freedom?" (U.S. State Department Cable, October 30, 2009), *Wikileaks* (http://wikileaks.org/cable/2009/10/09MOSCOW2688.html, last accessed October 31, 2013).

[26] That foreign policy concerns informed the mandate of the commission was obliquely confirmed by commission members S. A. Markov and A. N. Sakharov, the latter the then director of the Russian Academy of Science's Institute of Russian History. See M. Moshkin, "Kto staroe pomianet," *Vremia novostei online*, May 20, 2009 (http://www.vremya.ru/print/229467.html, last accessed October 31, 2013); O. Bychkova, "Narod protiv Komissii po protivodeistviiu fal'sifikatsii istorii," *Ekho Moskvy*, May 26, 2009 (http://www.echo.msk.ru/programs/opponent/593895-echo/, last accessed October 31, 2013). Many of these foreign policy concerns can be viewed as an unintended consequence of glasnost and the openness of the 1990s, when the Russian Federation assumed a surprisingly liberal attitude toward many of the embarrassments of the Soviet era. Since 2000, Russian officials have assumed a steadily more guarded posture in regard to subjects that might threaten national security or diplomatic priorities abroad.

a major investigation launched in 1990 by the Soviet Chief Military Prosecutor. After 1991, Russian authorities took up the investigation and slowly built a case against the Stalin-era leadership for abuse of power. Accusations of genocide were also investigated at the request of Polish authorities. In 2004, however, the Chief Military Prosecutor of the Russian Federation precipitated a full-scale diplomatic row when he executed an about-face and announced the closure of the Katyn case on the eve of the 65th commemoration of the massacre—ostensibly because all potential defendants had died and because the massacre did not conform to the international legal definition of genocide. This decision, compounded by the Russian secret services' refusal to declassify the bulk of the archival record, prompted the Polish parliament to lodge a formal protest. Descendants of the Polish victims of Katyn then appealed the decision in Russian court, petitioning for their slain relatives' posthumous political rehabilitation. The failure of this case in Russian Appeals Court in 2008 and Russian Supreme Court in 2009 led the plaintiffs to appeal their case to the European Court of Human Rights later that year, restarting the whole process and creating a host of new complications concerning jurisdiction and the declassification of state secrets.

A similar scenario emerged at about the same between Russia and Ukraine over the 1932–1933 terror famine, or Holodomor. A humanitarian catastrophe with its origins in a natural wave of crop failures, the terror famine was exacerbated by bad agricultural planning and punitive state policies designed to suppress peasant resistance to collectivization. Ultimately, it claimed the lives of at least 3–4 million Ukrainian, Russian, Cossack, and Kazakh peasants throughout the best grain-growing regions of the USSR. Relevant to this discussion is the fact that Ukrainian communities both at home and abroad have historically viewed the terror famine as having been directed mainly against their co-nationals, and that these charges have repeatedly led to international controversy for Moscow, both during and after the Cold War. After the election of V. A. Yushchenko in 2005, tensions over the terror famine mounted into a full-scale diplomatic clash between Russia and Ukraine as the Ukrainian president launched an official campaign to recognize the terror famine as an act of genocide against the Ukrainian nation. Legislation to this effect was passed in Ukraine in 2006, precipitating the trial and conviction of the Stalin-era leadership in absentia in 2009–2010. The issue of genocide was also debated in the United Nations (2003), the European Parliament (2008), and the Council of Europe (2010), although none of these bodies ultimately sided with Ukraine on the issue.

Two aspects of the Katyn and Holodomor cases appear to have threatened Russian authorities in 2009 in ways that other revelations about the Soviet past had not since 1991. First, accusations of genocide risked implicating the Soviet Union in a category of criminal activity traditionally associated with Nazi Germany—an almost unpardonable insult in the post-Soviet space. Second, a judicial finding of genocide either at home or abroad would have permanently exposed the Russian Federation to reparations lawsuits, inasmuch as this crime is not bound by any statute of limitations. Yushchenko publically denied pursing such objectives at the time, but his stance on the issue was contradicted by other Ukrainian politicians.[27]

High stakes, then, likely provided the premise for the formation of the commission on historical falsification as an official coordinating body for the refutation of criminal charges of such historic proportions. This rationale was obliquely confirmed at the commission's third meeting in September 2010, when Naryshkin and the head of the Russian Archival Agency (Rosarkhiv), A. N. Artizov, initiated calls for the declassification and release of archival documents as a means of reclaiming the initiative in certain diplomatic and legal contexts.[28] The prototype for this sort of publication was held to be *The Famine in the USSR, 1930–1934*, a glossy, full-color anthology of archival documents on the terror famine that was released by Rosarkhiv in 2009 along with a CD-ROM containing many of the same documents in English translation. This collection explicitly refuted Ukrainian claims of exceptionalism and genocide in 1932–1933, stressing the breadth of the famine's impact on Russian, Cossack, and Kazakh populations, the coercive but nonmurderous intent of the period's punitive policies, and the com-

---

[27] "Ukraina grozit potrebovat' ot Rossii kompensatsiiu za golodomor," *Izvestia*, October 27, 2008 (http://izvestia.ru/news/437989, last accessed October 31, 2013).

[28] Report of A. N. Artizov, head of the Russian State Archival Agency, at the commission's third session (September 9, 2010) (http://archives.ru/press/comission_history_artizov_070910.shtml, last accessed October 31, 2013).

plicity of Ukrainian and Kazakh Communist Party officials in the famine's development in the non-Russian republics.[29]

Release of this collection was followed in early 2010 by Rosarkhiv's website publication of a more limited group of documents on the Katyn massacre.[30] These documents confirmed the complicity of high Soviet officials in the crime, but also supported the official Russian position that the tragedy was the result of the officials' abuse of power rather than any officially sanctioned action. The collection also revealed attempts by party apparatchiks years later under Khrushchev to distort the historical record surrounding the Katyn massacre—revelations that provided a convenient explanation for the Soviet Union's half-century cover-up of the crime while reinforcing the notion that culpability within Soviet officialdom rested with renegades rather than with the state itself. An explanation developed by the Chief Military Prosecutor during the early 1990s, it was endorsed by then Prime Minister Putin in 2009 and ratified by the Russian State Duma in November 2010.

A deft use of the past to serve contemporary national interests, Rosarkhiv's publications allowed the Russian Federation to seize the upper hand in these two bitter international disputes and preclude international recognition of the genocide charges.[31] What's more, this

---

[29] *Golod v SSSR: 1930–1934*, ed. O. A. Antipova (Moscow: Federal'noe arkhivnoe agenstvo, 2009); *Famine in the USSR, 1929–1934: New Documentary Evidence / Golod v SSSR, 1929–1934: novye dokumenty*, ed. E. V. Borova (Moscow: Federal'noe arkhivnoe agenstvo, 2009) (http://www.rusarchives. ru/publication/famine/famine-ussr.pdf, last accessed last accessed October 31, 2013). For hints of the selectivity of this collection, note its failure to reproduce Stalin's famous August 11, 1932 letter to L. M. Kaganovich about "losing Ukraine" during collectivization.

[30] "Arkhivnye dokumenty po 'probleme Katyni' iz 'paketa N1'" (http://rus-archives.ru/publication/katyn/spisok.shtml, last accessed October 31, 2013).

[31] Markov asserted that the commission played a role in the Parliamentary Assembly of the Council of Europe's refusal to recognize the Holodomor as a Ukrainian genocide. See T. Krasil'nikova, "Chto udalos' sdelat' Komissii po fal'sifikatsii istorii," *Trud*, May 14, 2010 (http://www.trud.ru/article/14-05-2010/242097_chto_udalos_ sdelat_komissii_ po_falsifikatsii_istorii. html, last accessed October 31, 2013). For mention of other such projects focusing on Ukraine and the Baltics, see Artizov, "Ob itogakh raboty Federal'nogo arkhivnogo agenstva i podvedomstvennykh emu uchrezhde-

official trumping of Russia's critics abroad was accomplished with surprising media savvy, amid discussions of archival openness and the defense of the historical record against revisionism and falsification. But at least as interesting as the nature of this diplomatic coup is the fact that Rosarkhiv, a formally neutral government agency, had suddenly become quite activist in advancing the "anti-falsification" agenda nominally assigned to the commission. At first glance, this makes perfect sense, as the commission lacked the institutional resources to wage such a campaign on its own. That said, Rosarkhiv's accomplishments were clearly far more valuable to the country's image at home and abroad than the grandstanding and photo opportunities that characterized most of the commission's early public sessions. It is perhaps for this reason that the commission was quietly disbanded in early 2013, having fulfilled its purpose of drafting the historical record into the service of the state.[32]

---

niiakh za 2010 g. i zadachakh na 2011 g." (http://archives.ru/coordination/koll/doclad150311.shtml, last accessed October 31, 2013).

[32] See the comments of A. O. Chubar'ian in Iu. Kantor, "'Bez fal'sifikatsii': 'Istoricheskaia' kommissiia pri prezidente raspushchena," *Moskovskie novosti*, March 19, 2013 (http://www.mn.ru/society_history/20120319/313741427.html, last accessed October 31, 2013). Aside from its encouragement of new publishing priorities, the commission inspired a wide variety of state and nongovernmental organizations to review their activities in order to bring them into alignment with the new priorities. The commission also indirectly encouraged provincial authorities to interfere with research judged to be potentially harmful to state interests, most famously in Arkhangel´sk. On state and NGO activity, see for instance "V tseliakh patrioticheskogo vospitaniia podrastaiushchego pokoleniia..." (May 2, 2012) (http://www.archiv.nnov.ru/?id=5062&query_id=43451, last accessed October 31, 2013); and at the Fifth Plenum of the Central Council of the Russian Society of Historians and Archivists (July 20, 2010) (http://www.vestarchive.ru/iz-jizni-roia/1164.html; http://www.vestarchive.ru/iz-jizni-roia/1163.html, last accessed 31 October 2013). On the quashing of GULag-oriented research projects, see for instance "Arkhangel'skoe delo: nakanune protsessov," *Ekho Moskvy*, November 23, 2010 (http://www.echomsk.spb.ru/programmes/intervyu-v-efire-eha-peterburga/arkhangelskoe-delo.html?sphrase_id=413960, last accessed October 31, 2013).

The Search for a Usable Textbook, Renewed

The year 2012—officially dubbed the "year of Russian history"—set the stage for the resumption of discussions on the role that the past was to play in contemporary Russian society. Unsatisfied with Medvedev's campaign against historical falsification, Putin noted while campaigning for a third presidential term that public school history instruction remained inadequate. "In history textbooks," he told a forum in Kurgan, "things are described in such a way that it makes your hair stand on end."[33] Following his reelection several months later, Putin revived a nineteenth-century civic body called the Russian Historical Society in order to provide leadership and guidance for the field under Naryshkin's watchful eye.[34]

Putin returned to the subject of deficient public school instruction in February 2013 after weathering months of popular protest triggered first by his own return to the presidency and then by contested elections to the Duma. It was time, he now argued, for a single textbook to replace the existing array of competing curricular materials and thereby promote a standardized narrative on the past. This new textbook, according to Putin, "should be created in the context of a single, unified conception, within the context of the singular logic of Russian history, the interconnectedness of its stages, and respect for all of the pages of our collective past. And, of course, it is necessary to demonstrate on the basis of concrete examples that Russia's fate was created by a combination of different peoples, traditions and cultures." Aside from that, the textbook "should avoid internal contradictions and double meanings." Such a model text would finally provide the coun-

---

[33] It is unclear precisely what Putin was referring to, inasmuch as there was little variety in the 2012 textbook market. See Andrei Sidorchuk, "Proshloe v tumane: kakim budet edinyi uchebnik istorii," *Argumenty i fakty*, June 18, 2013 (http://www.aif.ru/society_education/trend/44364, last accessed October 31, 2013).

[34] Aside from Naryshkin, the Russian Historical Society included other officials formerly associated with the Commission to Counter Attempts to Falsify History including V. A. Sadovnichii, I. I. Sirosh, Markov and Artizov. See the undated press release from the Russian Academy of Sciences: http://hist-phil.ru/saity/rio/, last accessed October 31, 2013.

try with a galvanizing "national idea" to calm societal restiveness and interethnic tension and promote an all-Russian sense of patriotism and loyalty. According to Putin, responsibility for the creation of this text ought to rest with the Ministry of Education and Science, the Academy of Sciences and the new Russian Historical and Military-Historical Societies.[35]

Although Putin's populist demand for a unified patriotic curriculum found immediate support in public opinion polling,[36] it was in many other senses rather surprising. Not only did the proposal smack of an authoritarian approach to public school instruction, but many professionals questioned the merits of such a policy decision and doubted whether the construction of a single, monolithic history textbook was even possible. Putin's own experience with this issue in the past would seem to have confirmed these misgivings, as his administration had repeatedly failed to produce such a unified curriculum. Nevertheless, he pressed onward.

Shortly after Putin's statement about the need for a single history textbook, a working group was formed under the auspices of the Russian Historical Society to develop a set of standards for the new historical narrative.[37] A highly centralized project despite its nominal nongovernmental sponsorship, it produced the first draft schema of the needed two-thousand year narrative in June 2013. This outline was designed to identify key events, dates and personalities that would structure the eventual curriculum, which was now referred to as a set of texts rather than a single, monolithic one.[38] At the same time,

---

[35] "Stenograficheskii otchet o Zasedanii Soveta po mezhnational'nym otnosheniiam ot 19 fevralia 2013 g." (http://state.kremlin.ru/council/28/news/17536, last accessed October 31, 2013).

[36] "Press-vypusk №2373: 'Edinyi uchebnik istorii: Za i protiv,'" VTsIOM, August 16, 2013 (http://wciom.ru/index.php?id=459&uid=114349, last accessed October 31, 2013). Much of this popular support likely stems from the notion that a standardized curriculum would ease students' preparation for rigorous state graduation exams.

[37] "Sostav rabochei gruppy po podgotovke novogo uchebno-metodicheskogo kompleksa po otechestvennoi istorii" (rushistory.org/wp-content/uploads/2013/11/Рабочая-группа.pdf, last accessed October 31, 2013).

[38] "Istoriko-kul'turnyi standart," *Vedomosti*, June 17, 2013 (http://www.vedomosti.ru/cgi-bin/get_document.cgi/vedomosti_17-06-2013.doc?file=2013/06/17/469951_2305200889, last accessed October 31, 2013).

thirty-one controversial moments in history were identified that would require particularly careful attention during the construction and eventual instruction of the official line.[39]

At first glance, the draft schema was a surprisingly inclusive, liberal document advancing a narrative that embraced a sense of patriotism, citizenship and interethnic tolerance without presenting a purely apologetic reading of the past. The evocation of patriotic emotions was clearly a top priority, of course, but even that was apparently to be accomplished as much by attention to the tragedy of Russian history as its triumphs. What's more, while the schema prioritized the relationship between state and society, it also sought to cultivate in its readers a sense of civic engagement and the ability to distinguish between acceptable and unacceptable forms of social activism (the latter being defined as nationalism, chauvinism and other forms of extremism).[40]

Critics quickly identified a series of problems with this schema, however. Billed as a narrative for the entire breadth of Russian society, it favored centralizing tendencies at the expense of regional and non-Russian interests. And while it generally balanced a positive reading of each historical period with information on shortcomings and errors, the narrative clearly downplayed the abuse of power. This was nowhere more noteworthy than in its treatment of contemporary history, which presented a sanitized account of Putin's consolidation of political and economic power after 2000 that failed to mention issues ranging from the Second Chechen War to the roles played by opposition figures from V. A. Gusinskii and M. B. Khodorkovskii to A. A. Naval'nyi.[41] Perhaps even more worrisome was another liability of the schema that went uncritiqued in the press: like the Filippov manuals, this document's sense of patriotism was based on state-based etatism rather than a more broadly based appreciation of popular sovereignty or civil society.

Late September 2013 saw the release of a second draft of this schema that was considerably more sophisticated than its predecessor

---

[39] I. Rodin, "Vyiavleny trudnye voprosy istorii Rossii," *Nezavisimaia gazeta*, June 11, 2013 (http://www.ng.ru/politics/2013-06-11/1_history.html, last accessed October 31, 2013).

[40] "Istoriko-kul'turnyi standart," 2-3.

[41] S. Bocharova, "Istoriia Rossii oboidetsia bez Bolotnoi," *Vedomosti*, September 26, 2013 (http://www.vedomosti.ru/politics/news/16782651/istoriya-obojdetsya-bez-bolotnoj, last accessed October 31, 2013).

and that attempted to resolve many of the issues that critics had raised in the intervening months. The official list of controversial moments had been winnowed from thirty-one to twenty. Polarizing language that reflected a centralizing bias within the first draft was toned down. A greater emphasis on the negative dimensions of Russo-Soviet political history was also a bit more palpable, even in regard to Putin's presidency. But if some of the first draft's problems were corrected, others were not. Some controversial terms remained unchanged (e.g., references to the 1930s as "Stalinist Socialism"), while other tendentious choices materialized unexpectedly (e.g., the conflation of the "bourgeois" February 1917 revolution and Great October socialist revolution into the "Great Russian Revolution of 1917"). To many, the schema's simplistic, negative emplotment of the 1990s seemed instrumental, setting up an exaggerated sense of contrast with the presidencies of Putin and Medvedev in the early 2000s. And if the latter period was no longer cast in a purely positive light, its shortcomings and political restiveness were given little more than perfunctory attention. Unnoticed in the press at the time was the draft's deletion of its predecessor's endorsement of civic activism.[42]

More worrying were two other problems that likewise went unmentioned by the critics. First, like the initial draft of the schema, its second incarnation presented a patriotic vision of the past that was clearly designed to rally emotions around the state rather than society. Successful governance was characterized by the centralization of power and the maintenance of stability and order, rather than the promotion of social equality or civil rights. Second, the schema's heroes tended to be evaluated on the basis of their accomplishments rather than their methods. This meant that even if the schema included mention of various periods' false starts, mistakes and failures, it teleologically framed these details in such a way that the ends justified the excessive means used in their attainment. Indeed, the whole schema appeared to be emplotted according to a theme of tragic but ultimately justifiable sacrifice in the service of the state.

---

[42] "Kontseptsiia novogo uchebno-metodicheskogo kompleksa po otechestvennoi istorii," *Kommersant*, September 26, 2013 (http://www.kommersant.ru/docs/2013/standart.pdf, last accessed October 31, 2013).

Aside from its teleology, the schema's emplotment hinted of other malignancies as well. Putin's demand for the official line to be developed around a single, interconnected narrative without internal contradictions resulted in the construction of a storyline that subordinated every major historical event and personage to the celebration of centralization, order and stability. Digressions, false starts, dead ends, and lost causes were included in the narrative only to set up more dramatic course corrections later in the story. This overdetermined linearity ultimately reduced the past to a self-fulfilling prophecy, stripping it of internal tension, suspense and drama that can be heuristically valuable not only within the classroom, but throughout society as a whole. None of these issues were resolved when the final version of the schema was released on Halloween 2013.[43]

Conclusion

According to official plans, the schema was designed to provide the framework for a textbook competition that in 2014 would identify a central text (or set of texts) for future use in the public school history curriculum. This program stalled, however, amid continuing controversy over the schema's final form and the political drama surrounding the fall of pro-Russian Ukrainian president V. F. Yanukovych, the Russian annexation of Crimea and the emergence of a Russian-Ukrainian proxy war in the Donbass. By the fall of 2014, Russian minister of education and science D. V. Livanov was suggesting that the idea of a competition to identify a single new text had been replaced by plans to officially endorse a variety of textbooks loyal to the new schema.[44] Livanov's disclosure, however, was then called into question by

---

[43] "Kontseptsiia novogo uchebno–metodicheskogo kompleksa po otechestvennoi istorii" (October 31, 2013) (rushistory.org/wp-content/uploads/2013/11/2013.10.31-Концепция_финал.pdf, last accessed October 31, 2013).

[44] "Minobrnauki otkazalos´ ot idei vvedeniia edinogo uchebnika istorii," *RIA Novosti*, August 27, 2014 (http://ria.ru/society/20140827/1021587921.html, last accessed December 12, 2014); "Dmitrii Livanov: 'Edinyi uchebnik istorii—eto tselaia kontseptsiia," *Izvestiia*, August 27, 2014 (http://izvestia.ru/news/575874, last accessed December 12, 2014).

comments made by both Putin and Chubar'ian, which hinted that the government nevertheless remained interested in a single canonical set of texts.[45] Insofar as this chapter goes to press before the resolution of this confusing situation, it is not clear what the eventual outcome will be. Given the priority that the presidential administration has afforded to the creation of a single, official "usable past," it seems likely that the end result of this process will be further consolidation of the textbook market, either around a single text or an handful of nominally different texts based on an official narrative promoting patriotic etatism.

Even if such a formal consolidation of the textbook market does not come to pass, post-Soviet Russia's search for a usable past between 2000 and 2014 remains instructive on a number of levels. Most glaring is Putin's and Medvedev's gradual return to Soviet-style administrative methods and diktat. In some senses a coup d'ctat displacing earlier, less centralized efforts to produce a new narrative, their initiatives prioritized command and control over professionalism and disciplinary standards. Worse, the arbitrariness of this approach—particularly its demand for a single narrative devoid of internal contradiction—threatens to blunt the whole mobilizational premise of the project and produce a plodding narrative bereft of the tension, drama, and suspense that animate superior classroom pedagogy and effective storytelling within society itself.

This recourse to diktat is all the more unfortunate in light of the fact that it was never really necessary in the first place. On the eve of Putin's 2013 decision to overthrow the existing order and impose a single narrative from above, many of his fundamental objectives for history instruction in the public schools had already been realized. The semi-official Filippov texts had given a clear, articulate signal to educators and mass-market authors about what was to be considered the correct version of the usable past. They also signaled that state support would be awarded to those who followed their template and denied

---

[45] "Putin shitaet pravil'nym poiavlenie edinogo uchebnika istorii," *RIA Novosti*, August 27, 2014 (http://itar-tass.com/obschestvo/1408798, last accessed December 12, 2014); Elena Novoselova, "'Edinyi ne na shutku': pervogo aprelia budut predstavleny novye uchebniki istorii," *Rossiiskaia gazeta*, November 18, 2014 (http://www.rg.ru/2014/11/17/istoriya-site.html, last accessed December 12, 2014).

to those who didn't. And such interventions had a major effect on
the textbook market, where the vast majority of competing textbooks
was brought into rough conformity with the new official line between
2008–2012 through a combination of oblique signaling, selective
endorsement, and self-censorship.[46] Put another way, de facto hegemonic control over the public school history curriculum was accomplished years before Putin's 2013 initiative without recourse to the
administrative-command practices of the past.

---

[46] On the administrative resources, particularly those related to local school
endorsements and the massive publishing house "Prosveshchenie," see Biletskaia, "Analiz pravovogo regulirovaniia i sushchestvuiushchego poriadka
obespecheniia Ministerstvom obrazovaniia i nauki Rossiiskoi Federatsii povysheniia kachestva uchebnoi literatury;" Beyrle, "Is Stalin's Ghost a Threat
to Academic Freedom?"

Jan-Werner Müller

Germany's Two Processes of *"Coming to Terms with the Past"*— *Failures, After all?*

Germany's dealing with its two difficult pasts—the East German state socialist dictatorship and, much more important, Nazism and the Holocaust—has almost globally been considered a success, even a model for others to emulate.[1] Human rights activists and politicians from South Africa, for instance, closely studied what the Germans had done by way of trials, public commemoration and schoolbooks; and the Chinese would at one point admonish Japan that, in dealing with World War II, it should adopt the "German model." Not surprisingly perhaps, this *Modell Deutschland* was increasingly viewed with pride within Germany itself, especially, but not only, among the Left.[2] Some outside observers picked up on this peculiar form of pride—a kind of anti-nationalist nationalism—and gently mocked it: Timothy Garton

---

[1] This essay incorporates parts of a previous assessment of dealing with the East German past, "Just another *Vergangenheitsbewältigung*? The Process of Coming to Terms with the East German Past Revisited," in: *Oxford German Studies*, vol. 38 (2009), 334–344. I am grateful to Helge Heidemeyer for a background conversation at what was then the *Birthler-Behörde* in February 2009, to Karen Leeder and the audience of the Special Taylorian Lecture in Oxford in May 2009, as well as the participants in the November 2010 conference on "Remembrance, History, Justice" for comments and suggestions. Thanks also to participants in the 2011 Berlin Princeton Global Seminar on "Memory, Democracy, and Public Culture" for stimulating exchanges.

[2] See for instance Helmut Dubiel, *Niemand ist frei von der Geschichte: Die nationalsozialistische Herrschaft in den Debatten des Deutschen Bundestages* (Munich: Hanser, 1999).

Ash, for instance, spoke of *Deutsche Industrie-Normen* in "coming to terms with the past"; others crowned the Germans "world champions in remembrance."[3]

Today the picture appears to look a little different: not from the outside, where fears of a resurgent German nationalism have largely subsided, give or take the political and economic struggles about the Euro—but from the inside. Critics have charged that both "coming to terms with the Nazi past" and "overcoming the legacies of the GDR" might have been failures, after all—though for very different reasons: in the case of the former, the critics claim that Germans have essentially appropriated the victims of the Holocaust in order to feel good about their own efforts in remembrance.[4] Yes, these critics admit, the centre of Berlin prominently features the Jewish Museum, the "Topography of Terror" (devoted mainly to exploring the workings of the Gestapo), and, above all, the Holocaust Memorial, a few steps from the Brandenburg Gate.[5] But in their eyes, these are essentially tourist attractions that do not shake anyone up or make anyone think. Former Chancellor Gerhard Schröder inadvertently revealed their real meaning when he talked about a "memorial which one enjoys visiting." The cheap cafes, souvenir shops, and beer halls now surrounding the Holocaust Memo-

---

[3] There are usually two blind spots in celebrations of the supposed "German model": first, it is based on a historical situation where a country of perpetrators was completely conquered, and it might suit only post-dictatorship conditions—not post-civil war conditions. Second, de facto remembrance was preceded by forgetting or at least a widespread silence about the evil perpetrated under the Nazi regime (which is not to say that forgetting and silence were somehow historically necessary, as argued, most recently, by Christian Meier, *Das Gebot zu vergessen und die Unabweisbarkeit des Erinnerns: Vom öffentlichen Umgang mit schlimmer Vergangenheit* [Munich: Siedler, 2010]).

[4] See in particular, Ulrike Jureit and Christian Schneider, *Gefühlte Opfer: Illusionen der Vergangenheitsbewältigung* (Stuttgart: Klett-Cotta, 2010).

[5] On Berlin's new Erinnerungslandschat, see Karen E. Till, *The New Berlin: Memory, Politics, Place* (Minneapolis: University of Minnesota Press, 2005) and Brian Ladd, *The Ghosts of Berlin: Confronting German History in the Urban Landscape* (Chicago: The University of Chicago Press, 1997).

rial are all-too-appropriate within this logic. So remembrance has been set in stone—but, as Robert Musil once remarked, "there is nothing in the world as invisible as a monument." And nothing, one might be tempted to conclude, was better designed to ensure that memory no longer hurts than placing a memorial in the very middle of the new "Berlin Republic."[6]

In fact, then, the Jewish wisdom that the secret of memory is redemption—famously quoted in a speech by then President Richard von Weizsäcker in 1985—has been vindicated for the Germans, but with a perverse twist: whoever goes through the motions of remembrance, need not feel bad, let alone guilty. One enjoys visiting the Holocaust memorial not least because it makes one feel that one has done something—even if it is just getting upset about the teenagers sunbathing on the "steles" or tourists eating their sausages in what ought to be a sacred space.

How about the process of dealing with the East German past? Here critics claim that defenders of the old regime have been allowed to impose a very soft image of the dictatorship, more *Goodbye Lenin* than *The Lives of Others*.[7] This is partly because everyone is so careful not to equate socialism and National Socialism (and thereby, the charge goes, ends up downplaying the evils of state socialism). And it is partly because the Left Party—*die Linke*—which has entertained an, to say the least, ambiguous relationship to the East German past has become a real force to be reckoned with—which is to say, a force that is courted by other parties and a force that can shape political outcomes, including symbolic representations of the past, to its liking. Former East German dissident Freya Klier has prominently warned that "their networks have not dissolved, but been strategically refined. . . . The supporters of the former dictatorship . . . sit in the

---

[6] See also Wolfgang Wippermann, *Denken statt denkmalen: Gegen den Denkmalwahn der Deutschen* (Berlin: Rotbuch, 2010).

[7] See for instance, Hubertus Knabe, *Die Täter sind unter uns: Über das Schönreden der SED-Diktatur* (Berlin: List, 2008) and Uwe Müller and Grit Hartmann, *Vorwärts und Vergessen! Kader, Spitzel und Komplizen—Das gefährliche Erbe der SED-Diktatur* (Berlin: Rowohlt, 2009).

Bundestag, in the media, in schools, in manifold commissions of our democracy. . . . They are aiming at the future."[8]

Ironically, civil society is flourishing, just as political scientists wishing to promote democracy often argue is necessary for a proper consolidation of liberal-democratic regimes. Except the civil society that is flourishing is one of associations often with idealistic-sounding names (such as *Gesellschaft für Bürgerrecht und Menschenwürde e. V.*) which seem essentially devoted to rehabilitating the Stasi, to fighting for benefits for supporters of the regime, and to rather aggressive campaigning against commemorating the victims of the SED—all in the name of human rights (namely of those who see themselves on the losing side of history after 1990).[9]

---

[8] She observed "seit dem Ende der DDR ein kontinuierliches Weiterwirken ehemaliger Nomenklaturkader. Ihre Netzwerke haben sich nicht aufgelöst, sondern strategisch verfeinert. Die Stützen der untergegangenen Diktatur marschieren ja nicht nur in Gedenkstätten auf—sie sitzen im Bundestag, in den Medien, in Schulen und vielfältigen Gremien unserer Demokratie. Und sie werden nicht müde, ihren Unrechtsstaat im Nachhinein demokratisch aufzupolieren und in der öffentlichen Erinnerung zu glätten. Sie zielen auf Zukunft." Freya Klier, "Sondervotum," http://www.zeitgeschichte-online.de/portals/_rainbow/documents/pdf/sondervot_klier.pdf, last accessed May 19, 2009.

[9] The "model institution" of coming to terms with the East German past— what used to be known as the Gauck authority but then became the "Birthler-Behörde" (named after Gauck's successor as head of the authority, the East German dissident Marianne Birthler) and is now the "Jahn-Behörde" (named after its current head, a journalist—and *Bürgerrechtler*—from East Germany) has also been heavily criticized in recent years, not least after it had been revealed that the office actually kept employing a number of former Stasi-members (who, recently, had to be transferred to other administrative offices. See http://www.sueddeutsche.de/politik/bundestag-beschliesst-gesetzesaenderung-ex-stasi-mitarbeiter-muessen-jahn-behoerde-verlassen-1.1153748, last accessed October 31, 2011). In addition, the one-time model institution for dealing with an authoritarian regime's secret service has been attacked for supposedly dragging its feet in addressing the question of Stasi informers in the West (West German parliamentarians in particular), and, generally, seeming arbitrary in its decision on what kind of information to release to historians and journalists. The privileged access to the files by a number of in-house researchers has also been subject to continuous criticism.

The upshot of all this is—once more—complacency about the past, though of a different kind. In the case of the Nazi past, remembrance is about the wrong kinds of emotions and attitudes; in the case of the GDR, remembrance is about the wrong kind of memory content, so to speak, and the problem that justice might not have been done properly at all in dealing with the legacies of the dictatorship. A further result, however, appears to be plain ignorance: in 2008 a highly controversial survey showed that especially—but not only—East German school children knew shockingly little about the GDR past; a majority thought the Stasi was an intelligence service like any other; many held that the West had erected the Wall and opined that the environment had been cleaner during state socialism.[10]

These two alleged failures of Germans in dealing with their pasts are distinct. Yet in one concrete way they might actually come together, at least according to an acute observer like Perry Anderson: namely, in the urban landscape of the "new Berlin." There Anderson discerns an "ideological will to fix civic memory on images stamped by guilt or nostalgia—the element of guilt mostly coming from the West, the element of nostalgia (for the Palace of the Republic, etc.) from the East. The result is a kind of an antiquarian masochism—a clinging to what is aesthetically ugly, often because it was also morally and politically ugly, in the name of truth to history."[11] An exaggeration—and a slander of a city that tries ever so hard to combine hipness with historical consciousness? But how else, then, to be "truthful to history," in public self-representations—and in patterns of remembrance more broadly?

This essay seeks to take stock of the two processes of what the Germans call either *Vergangenheitsbewältigung* or *Aufarbeitung der Vergangenheit* (actually, the latter term has become almost completely dominant in recent years, since it supposedly suggests less of a sense of closure, mastery, and "being done with the past" in the way the for-

---

[10] Monika Deutz-Schroeder und Klaus Schroeder, *Soziales Paradies oder Stasi-Staat? Das DDR-Bild von Schülern - ein Ost-West-Vergleich* (Ernst Vögel, 2008). Pupils in East Berlin and Brandenburg knew least about the GDR; the report concluded that the more young people knew about the GDR, the more critical they tended to be. One should add that the report has been severely criticized for its methodology.

[11] Perry Anderson, *The New Old World* (London: Verso, 2009), 229.

mer does).[12] The essay's central question is whether Germans are justified in their recent tortured self-criticism. Of course, this raises the
question what ought to count as reasonable moral and empirical criteria of how processes of coming to terms with the past should unfold
and when they could be considered a "success" (to be sure, there is
something deeply problematic about the language of "success" in this
context—but then again, it would be foolish to pretend that these processes cannot go more or less well). However, rather than putting forward a full justification of criteria here, I want to develop them through
reconstructing recent debates in Germany. I will first engage with criticisms of the *Bewältigung* of the Nazi past; I shall argue that, while some
critics of the process of coming to terms with the Nazi past no doubt
are right that guilt has strangely (dialectically, some might say) turned
into pride, it is still wrong to judge that process as a whole a failure.
Second, in surveying debates both about the Nazi past and the East
German state socialist past, I want to claim that there remain indeed
curious blind spots—or, as the authors of the most trenchant critique
of *Vergangenheitsbewältigung* have put it, "illusions"; the way many of
these debates are structured and address questions of comparability
in particular, is unhelpful, to say the least. This, however, is a different point than saying that the actual process of coming to terms with
the state socialist past has been a failure; and thus, in the third, more
empirically oriented part of the essay I argue that by any reasonable
standard, the process of coming to terms with the East German past
has been a success—and especially so in comparison with the experience of other post-communist countries. 'Failure' can only be diagnosed against the background of unreasonably high expectations.

Finally, I want to stress that the dialectics of remembrance can
only be perceived as such a problem because German cultures of
remembrance are so highly developed and firmly grounded in the
country's political culture in the first place. This is not a call for self-
celebration or self-promotion—it is, I would submit, at this point simply a fact. Having said that, it is important to stress that recent critics
do have a point: there is indeed a danger of remembrance degenerat-

---

[12] To be sure, the latter term has also had its critics—Theodor W. Adorno, for
instance.

ing into a kind of routine[13]; it is the case that a moral consensus about the past is not necessarily a good sign; and it is a real peril that public memory can foster a sense of forgiveness and reconciliation—when not the memory-fixated descendants of the perpetrators, but only the victims and their descendants are in a position even to broach the topics of forgiveness and reconciliation. Countering these tendencies ought to be a conscious and ever renewed effort—without aspiring to impossible standards of self-criticism and subversion. But there is no real way to institutionalize self-subverting memory, only a conscious and reflective way of engaging with—and passing on of—institutionalized memory.

Feel-Good Remembrance?

Remembrance has to hurt.[14] This seems to be the underlying assumption of those who argue that the process of coming to terms with the Nazi past and the Holocaust has turned not so much into a spectacle as into a form of moral self-celebration for Germans—or, at least, a perverse identification with the victims (and therefore a convenient excuse for not thinking about one's links with the perpetrators). Ulrike Jureit and Christian Schneider have coined the term "counter-identification" to capture what has happened with the generation of 1968 in particular: a more or less conscious identification with the Jews against their own fathers and mothers, hence a sense of exculpation, and, finally, a new form of pride in the "success" of *Vergangenheitsbewältigung*.[15] In the model of "collective guilt" recently put forward by Bernhard Schlink, "collective guilt" has finally been overcome, because

---

[13] More needs to be said here: nobody wants "routine remembrance"—but repetition and ritualization are in an important way integral to stabilizing meanings over time. Novelty—a different memory spectacle each time—is not automatically a good thing, and not all repetition means that remembrance has to turn into "myth" or "liturgy." See also Aleida Assmann, *Der lange Schatten der Vergangenheit: Erinnerungskultur und Geschichtspolitik* (Munich: C. H. Beck, 2006), 217–234.

[14] The origin of this thought can be found in Nietzsche, of course: "Nur was nicht aufhört, weh zu tun, bleibt im Gedächtnis."

[15] Jureit and Schneider, *Gefühlte Opfer*.

all ties of solidarity with the perpetrators have been conclusively broken; the children and grandchildren and great-grandchildren of the perpetrators are safe from guilt because they engage in a permanent renunciation.[16] Paradoxically, not guilt, but innocence, has been put in stone—forever.

For critics such as Jureit and Schneider, contemporary forms of Holocaust remembrance in Germany are all about reconciliation, self-affirmation and even—again, whether consciously or unconsciously—redemption. Intellectual and, above all, emotional contradictions and any sense of ambivalence cease to be part of the picture; the nation is truly united in the identification with its victims through a shared *Gesinnungsästhetik* (an—untranslatable—combination of Max Weber's *Gesinnungsethik*—the ethics of conscience—and aesthetics). The upshot seems clear: what looks like earnest remembrance is in fact a highly sophisticated form of forgetting, not of the "facts" about the past, but about what the past should really mean in a country of perpetrators.

What could be the antidote to such a forgetting? One common answer is counter-monuments instead of monuments, "stumbling blocks" for feeling and thinking about the past, rather than props for present-day identities, let alone some form of pride (even if it is pride in "having-come-to-terms-with-the-past"). Counter-monuments question traditional conceptions of remembrance and complicate the viewer's relationship to artifacts and their supposed "messages"[17]; outstanding examples are the counter-monument by Renata Stih and Frieder Schnock at Berlin's Bayerischer Platz (called a "Denk-Installation"[18]) and the "stumbling blocks" in German (and now also other European) cities installed by the artist Gunter Demnig.[19] The point is—literally—to unsettle, as the pedestrian trips over the slightly elevated or uneven stones with information about the victims engraved on them. Remembrance, here, destabilizes, or, at the limit, subverts itself entirely.

Another common answer is "commemoration through communication." Especially with more distance to the acrimonious controver-

---

[16] Berhard Schlink, *Guilt About the Past* (Toronto: Anansi, 2010).
[17] James E. Young, *At Memory's Edge: After-Images of the Holocaust in Contemporary Art and Architecture* (London: Yale University Press, 2000).
[18] See http://www.stih-schnock.de/remembrance.html.
[19] See http://www.stolpersteine.com/.

sies of the 1980s and 1990s (such as the famous "historians' dispute" of 1986–1987 or the "Walser-Bubis-debate" of 1998), many observers have concluded that the continuous debates—including the harshest controversies—over the moral meaning of history actually constitute the real achievement of (and the key to) the success of coming-to-terms with the Nazi past.[20] For instance, it was often pointed out that the real Holocaust memorial in Berlin might not be the physical entity designed by Peter Eisenman, but the long-lasting, deeply self-searching and, not least, very painful debate which preceded its construction.[21]

There clearly is something to this thought: arguing about the past keeps memory alive in a way that "routine remembrance" does not necessarily, because it forces participants and observers of these debates to think harder about the precise moral meaning of the past. But not all arguing is productive, and, in any case, arguments and debates cannot be generated artificially, especially not from on high: states can decree commemoration, but only individual politicians and intellectuals (in the broadest sense, including professional historians and journalists) can ignite individual debates (if they are sufficiently influential or lucky); there might be "Memory Ministries" now in many countries, but there aren't (and there ought not to be) "Ministries of Public Controversies." Conversely, only the state can institutionalize self-critical commemorations; and this is hardly a trivial fact because there is always the option of doing nothing at all, or of reverting to more nation-affirming, less self-critical forms of remembrance.

It is true that, prima facie, forms of remembrance which stress ambivalence, and which provoke unexpected thoughts and feelings, are preferable to alternatives which suggest easy patterns of identification and closure. But there is no undisputed way of bringing about such kinds of remembrance, no "model" of how to make memory "cause pain." And, furthermore, there is no way we can—or, for that

---

[20] On the *Historkerstreit*, see Charles S. Maier, *The Unmasterable Past* (Cambridge, MA: Harvard University Press, 1988); on the Walser-Bubis debate, see the last chapter of my *Another Country: German Intellectuals, Unification National Identity* (London: Yale University Press, 2000).

[21] See Michael Jeisman (ed.), *Mahnmal Mitte: Eine Kontroverse* (Cologne: DuMont, 1999) and Claus Leggewie and Erik Meyer, *Ein Ort, an den man gerne geht: Das Holocaust-Mahnmal und die deutsche Geschichtspolitik nach 1989* (Munich: Hanser, 2005).

matter, should—truly know (let alone somehow measure) the inner feelings and attitudes of those taking part in commemoration. To be sure, the rhetoric of elites is precisely not just rhetoric and can give crucial clues of how a culture of public remembrance as a whole is developing. But even agonizing and ambivalence can be faked by politicians, if need be.

In any case, the critics of *Vergangenheitsbewältigung* can only make the rather subtle claims they make because they can take a certain consensus about the meaning of the Nazi past and the Holocaust for granted. As previously mentioned, not all arguments about the past are productive: the fact that some arguments about the past—such as Holocaust denial—are nonexistent or marginal is an achievement, not an illegitimate silencing, or a false form of reconciliation. Would critics really want different forms of commemoration of the Nazi past—ones that celebrate aspects of that past—so that there would be more ambivalence? Are a few neo-Nazis a good thing to reinvigorate the official culture of remembrance and demonstrate its relevance? The answer, it seems to me, clearly has to be "no."

Peculiarities of the German Debates on Coming to Terms with the Past

"Commemoration through communication," then, is not some kind of political and social-psychological panacea. It might be crucial in arriving at a morally attractive consensus about the meaning of the past— but arguably it can also hinder or, in the worst case, destroy such a consensus. This problem seems particularly acute in debates about the East German state socialist past. On the one hand, there is the much-discussed and almost unanimously endorsed aim of creating something called "inner unity" among German citizens, that is to say, a feeling of shared values and common identifications among East and West German citizens. This, one might suppose, would also require some kind of shared image of the past—*ein gemeinsames Geschichtsbild*, as it is often put. But if "commemoration through communication" is to be real, then it is far from obvious that the closure implied by a consensual *Geschichtsbild*—as opposed to ongoing communication, including harsh disagreements—is as desirable as it is often made to seem. And there is no way of resolving this tension in the abstract—all will depend on the particular questions at issue in a particular debate or particular decision (on memorials, for instance). But the tension itself is hardly ever recognized in German debates.

The general lack of what one might call meta-reflections on memory is clearly more pronounced in the discussions about dealing with the East German state socialist past: there has been a very strong focus on particular policies, or sometimes scandals—while there has been relatively little discussion about what in theory should be the prior question to be settled: which criteria and goals are appropriate for the *Aufarbeitung* of state socialism, and also which moral principles might guide both the process of *Aufarbeitung* in general, and more specific assessments of the aspects of the GDR past (both individual behaviour and more systemic features of the regime). Of course, one can object that this constitutes a very academic, or perhaps apolitical, expectation—first we ought to deliberate on reasonable criteria, and only then to argue about substantive questions. Still, what is striking is the relative paucity of a more general moral discourse, and also the relative absence of moral philosophers or legal theorists (as opposed to historians and politicians) from the debate. Relative, that is, to the historians' dispute, in which the moral philosopher Jürgen Habermas played a leading role, or the general philosophical discourse about the Third Reich's legacy (one might think of Karl-Otto Apel's contributions in this context).[22]

Another peculiarity of the German debates have been the uses (and abuses) of comparison and as well as the general assumptions about historical (and moral) comparability underlying them. Of course, it might again be seen as a form of wishful thinking that the objective historian will parachute into the middle of a debate and decree *wie es eigentlich gewesen*. The politics of memory is always also—politics. Still, as said above, conflicts over the past can be more or less productive,

---

[22] See for instance, Karl-Otto Apel, "Zurück zur Normalität? Oder können wir aus der nationalen Katastrope etwas Besonderes gelernt haben? Das Problem des (welt-)geschichtlichen Übergangs zur postkonventionellen Moral aus spezifisch deutscher Sicht," in: Forum der Philosophie Bad Homburg (ed.), *Zerstörung des moralischen Selbstbewußtseins: Chance oder Gefährdung?* (Frankfurt/Main: Suhrkamp, 1988), 91–142.

and arguably the controversies over the GDR in particular have been less so. This is true, it seems to me, in at least three respects.

Two debate-stoppers have dominated—and to a certain degree stalemated—what in the best of circumstances are likely to be highly complex conversations about the nature of the SED regime and GDR society: the concepts of totalitarianism and *Alltagsgeschichte*, or everyday history.[23] Critics of the concept of totalitarianism have argued that the East German state, despite the supposed omnipresence of the Stasi, never controlled everyday life in the total way that many theories of totalitarianism seem to suggest; those who lived in East Germany also frequently insist that they had been able to lead perfectly normal lives outside politics, as opposed to the image of a complete politicization of society and even private life. A historical diagnosis of totalitarianism thus also seems to amount to an (or perhaps, yet another) act of dispossession vis-à-vis the East Germans: it robs them of their own past.[24]

Conversely, a focus on everyday history—prominent in the last experts' commission on GDR *Aufarbeitung*, which reported in 2006— is often immediately criticized as a form of *Verharmlosung*, of softening the image of the regime, and of automatically confirming Richard Schröder's controversial claim: "Es gab ein richtiges Leben im falschen"—which is to say, one could lead a morally good life in a politically immoral context.[25]

Yet, I would submit, this is a profoundly unhelpful, provincial, and, above all, theoretically impoverished polarization of positions. On the one hand, the critique of approaches informed by the concept of totalitarianism somehow seems to assume that all theories primarily

---

[23] I am not suggesting that the debate is entirely between these two positions. There have been many attempts at more nuanced conceptual approaches, from *Fürsorgediktatur* to *durchherrschte Gesellschaft* to the—in my view highly problematic—notion of a *Konsensdiktatur*. A more helpful map of GDR memories—with distinctions among a memory of dictatorship, a memory of "arrangements" (more or less opportunistic adaptations to the regime), and a memory of progress—has been put forward in Martin Sabrow, "Die DDR erinnern," in: Martin Sabrow (ed.), *Erinnerungsorte der DDR* (Munich: Beck, 2009), 11–27.

[24] See also Geoff Eley, "The Unease of History: Settling Accounts with the East German Past," in: *History Workshop Journal* (2004), 175–201.

[25] Martin Sabrow et al. (eds.), *Wohin treibt die DDR-Erinnerung? Dokumentation einer Debatte* (Göttingen: Vandenhoeck & Ruprecht, 2007).

concerned with institutions are inherently conservative;[26] they also misunderstand the more subtle theories of totalitarianism (such as those of the French Second Left; I am thinking of Claude Lefort in particular), which do *not* take regimes at their own word in such a way that critics then can immediately conclude that a particular state-cum-party apparatus could not actually achieve making total claims on its citizens. Such more sophisticated theories suggest that totalitarianism is about a particular social imaginary, a genuinely collective aspiration, as might have been the case with Nazism (or an aspiration promoted and to some extent realized from above, as in Stalinism). To be able to show that it was possible to escape these aspirations is important, but it says in itself nothing about the particular character of the aspirations in question. Now, this does of course not mean that serious historical investigations have to conclude that theories of totalitarianism best explain what happened after the period of high Stalinism—I have serious doubts that they could. But the argument has to be on a higher theoretical level than has been the case so far, and it cannot be cut short with the claim that a historical diagnosis of a totalitarian state implies an actually totalitarian society and therefore robs East Germans of their sense that decent lives were possible. Sophisticated theories of totalitarianism or authoritarianism do no such thing.

Conversely, a focus on *lived experience*, on day-to-day negotiations with political power-holders in particular, can unlock larger characteristics of a regime, rather than just foregrounding human interest stories and thereby soften the image of any regime by insisting that there was space for some form of normality—in particular the kind of tacit social contract that came to characterize so many societies in the Eastern bloc after the period of high Stalinism[27]: political apathy in exchange for consumer goods; or, as the formula was sometimes summarized: we pretend that the regime is legitimate, and the regime pretends that we are working. Perhaps precisely because of the infor-

---

[26] On the overlapping of conservatism and institution-centred approaches and the Left and " http://www.ghi-dc.org/publications/ghipubs/bu/026/b26ja-rausch.html (last accessed May 19, 2009).

[27] Social contract is no more than a metaphor that approximates an idea of a more flexible relationship between state and society—society was obviously not free really to negotiate its side of the contract.

mal and fragile nature of this social contract, secret services were pen-etrating ever more areas of society, controlling the boundaries between apathy, cynicism, and some form of political dissent.[28] These are only sketchy thoughts, of course—put forward not to advocate a substantive historiographical position, but to suggest ways of escaping the fateful opposition of totalitarianism and everyday history, or, put with differ-ent, also frequently used categories: authoritarianism and some form of individual autonomy, or *Eigensinn*.[29]

Second, there have been repeated efforts to de-legitimize all attempts to talk of Nazism and real-existing-socialism in the same context. The charge against such talk is best summed up in the title of a book by the Berlin historian Wolfgang Wippermann: *Dämonisier-ung durch Vergleich*—in other words, the suggestion that comparisons between the GDR and the Third Reich primarily serve to demonize socialism.[30]

This, it seems to me, is a profoundly misguided approach to understanding not just the German experience. The fact is that the European twentieth century is incomprehensible without talking about varieties of dictatorship in a common context, making comparisons between them, and trying to delineate their underlying logics, social imaginaries, and public justifications (as opposed to actual practices). In particular—as the American historian Timothy Snyder has recently pointed out—the experience of Eastern Europeans who suffered (and collaborated with) the two extreme forms of dictatorship successively, and sometimes their cooperation, is incomprehensible without recog-nizing the fact that, as he put it, "in this part of Europe, comparison of the two systems was necessary in daily life, and thus banal."[31] But

---

[28] Such an approach has been most fruitfully pursued by Thomas Lindenber-ger. See for instance, Thomas Lindenberger (ed.), *Herrschaft und Eigen-Sinn in der Diktatur: Studien zur Gesellschaftsgeschichte der DDR* (Cologne: Böh-lau, 1999).

[29] I put forward an actual historiographical position—and a fleshed-out inter-pretation of totalitarianism and subsequent developments in Central and Eastern Europe—in *Contesting Democracy: Political Ideas in Twentieth-Centu-ry Europe* (London: Yale University Press, 2011).

[30] Wolfgang Wippermann: *Dämonisierung durch Vergleich: DDR und Drittes Reich* (Berlin: Rotbuch, 2009).

[31] Timothy Snyder, "The Historical Reality of Eastern Europe," *Eastern Euro-pean Politics and Society*, vol. 23 (2009), 7–12; 7.

such comparison does not have to deny that Nazism was a *Zivilisations-bruch*—a break with civilization and shared notions of humanity—in the way that dictatorship in the name of communism was not.[32] One might have widely differing views on whether something like "a common European memory" of the atrocities of the twentieth century is possible or even desirable—but mutual comprehension surely is, and in the process of striving for comprehension comparison will sooner or later have to be an issue.[33] As has been pointed out so many times— not least during the *Historikerstreit*—comparison does not mean equation or equivalence. Analytical rigour requires it in many cases; while the political and moral sensitivity of the questions inevitably raised by comparison makes it mandatory to pay especially close attention to nuances of style, tone, and context.

Having said that: it is striking how ubiquitous both historically sound as well as casual, sometimes all too casual, comparisons between National Socialism and the GDR dictatorship have been—and how few attempts there are seriously to compare post-1989 developments in Germany and other Central and Eastern European countries. This, one might have thought, for all the more or less obvious differences in context, might prima facie be a more fruitful area for comparing both the experience of dictatorship and the process of dealing with difficult pasts. What sometimes is labeled methodological nationalism—a more or less unthinking focus on one's own nation or nation-state—seems to have been at work here yet again.

---

[32] See also, Avishai Margalit, *The Ethics of Memory* (Cambridge, MA: Harvard University Press, 2002), 79. It also often overlooked that the prohibition on comparison and the moral injunction "never again" are prima facie incompatible; as Schlink put is, "future generations can be warned by the Holocaust not to do something they are about to do only if what they are about to do is somehow comparable to the Holocaust." See Schlink, *Guilt the Past*, 28.

[33] On this point, see my "On 'European Memory.' Some conceptual and normative remarks" in Małgorzata Pakier and Bo Stråth (eds.), *A European Memory? Contested Histories and Politics of Remembrance* (Oxford: Berghahn, 2010), 25–37, and Claus Leggewie, with Anne Lang, *Der Kampf um die europäische Erinnerung: Ein Schlachtfeld wird besichtigt* (Munich: Beck, 2011).

Coming to Terms with the East German Past:
A Very Brief Reassessment

As previously mentioned, criticisms of the process of coming to terms with the Nazi past have largely focused on having the wrong emotional effects and resulting in the wrong attitudes to oneself and the political collective. To be sure, there is no lack of voices who would insist that the concrete political and judicial measures in the 1950s, 1960s, and 1970s were ruefully deficient—but disputes about them (a kind of *Vergangenheitsbewältigung* of *Vergangenheitsbewältigung*) have been less frequent (though witness the recent discussion of the role of the foreign office during the Third Reich, ignited by the report of a historical commission).

The case of coming to terms with state socialism is different: here the success or failure of the concrete political and judicial measures remains very much at issue. Hence, this section will take a close look at what is nowadays mostly termed *Aufarbeitung* (a concept not usually associated with reactions to the Nazi past). I shall focus on three mains goals (or criteria) of dealing with a dictatorship and its legacies: justice, democracy-strengthening, and social cohesion (or, if one prefers, some measure of inner unity). I recognize that these goals are often (and with good reasons) said to be in conflict. But their conflict is, for the most part, an empirical question—not a normative one. Under favorable circumstances—in particular political stability and little danger of a comprehensive backsliding to authoritarianism—it is far from obvious that there have to be significant trade-offs between them. And Germany, it is hard to deny, was lucky to experience such favorable circumstances.

Justice: It would be hard to argue that compared to experiences in other Central and Eastern European countries, united Germany really failed in its attempts to establish justice: lustration and purges were comparatively intensive *and* extensive, without deteriorating into the kind of witch hunts which for instance Poland experienced a few years back; restitution, while generating much resentment and frustration, was still largely successful.[34] Compared to what *theoretically* united Germany might have been

---

[34] See also Hilary Appel, "Anti-Communist Justice and Founding the Post-Commuist Order: Lustration and Restitution in Central Europe," *East European Politics and Societies*, vol. 19 (2005), 379–405.

capable of—given the financial resources, the experienced administrative and legal personnel, and the fact that there was no real need to make concessions to former socialist political elites—the picture looks less impressive: many measures were delayed, the administration of justice was often underfunded, and the conviction rates look disappointing: 100, 000 people were subject to preliminary judicial proceedings (*Ermittlungsverfahren*). But, according to what appear as the most reliable estimates, there were only 1,021 actual prosecutions, involving 1,737 defendants (these figures exclude prosecutions for espionage), and in fact just forty people ever served time in prison for what they had done during the GDR.[35]

Above all, the administration of justice appeared to be uneven. Some *Länder* undertook comprehensive investigations of public sector employees, for instance, and saw substantial number of dismissals; others hardly any. Record keeping, classifications and even criteria for judging injustice seemed arbitrarily to vary among regions; and to this day there are no commonly accepted figures about prosecutions and their success. Prima facie, the ideals of generality and evenness associated with the rule of law make such an outcome normatively very problematic. It has to be borne in mind, though, that the ultimate problem here is German federalism and the fact that the administration of justice is also subject to party-political vagaries: in *Länder* like Mecklenburg-Vorpommern and Brandenburg, long under the control of the Social Democrats and what is now *Die Linke*, understandings of justice differed from that in, for example, Saxony, long a stronghold of the Christian democrats.[36] These facts do not remove the normative worries. But they point to a much larger conflict between the diversity inevitably brought about through federalism and the evenness demanded by the rule of law.

Bärbel Bohley famously observed: "We wanted justice, and we got the rule of law." This statement is perhaps even more profoundly true than the former leading dissident realized when she made it. Even-

---

[35] Klaus Marxen, Gerhard Werle and Petra Schäfer, *Die Strafverfolgung von DDR-Unrecht: Fakten und Zahlen* (Berlin: Stiftung zur Aufarbeitung der SED—Diktatur and Humboldt-Universität zu Berlin, 2007).

[36] Even though there has been some homogenization over time, Brandenburg, the only land without a *Stasi-Beauftragter*, eventually felt the need for such a figure and, more broadly, the *Aufarbeitung* of its own previous *Aufarbeitung* of the state socialist past. In December 2009, former dissent Ulrike Poppe was appointed to the post. See http://www.aufarbeitung.brandenburg.de (last accessed October 31, 2011).

tually members of the former regime (or those close to it), portraying themselves as victims of *Vereinigungsunrecht* (violations of the rule of law in connection with unification), made very skilled use of the *Rechtsstaat*: in particular, they appealed many of the measures taken to establish justice—especially the cutting of pensions (or what the subjects of such cuts derided as *Rentenstrafrecht*, a play on the words pension and critimal law, suggesting that pensions were illegitimately instrumentalized for political punishment). The courts, in fact, granted many of these appeals based on the right to property and the principle of equality (*Gleichheitsgrundsatz*) enshrined in the Basic Law.

In fact, the impression has taken hold that many perpetrators are today considerably better off than their victims. This is especially so because attempts to compensate victims for their suffering—and recognize dissenters for their courage—have been long delayed and rather paltry. Whoever was in opposition in the German parliament invariably called for *Ehrenpensionen* (pensions based on honor) as a sign of such recognition, but as soon as the same parties entered the government they apologized for not doing anything by pointing to supposedly empty coffers. Some measures were eventually passed in 2007, but they fell short of what victims' representatives had demanded—and they connected what was now called *Opferrente* (pensions based on victimhood, not honor) to the social status of the victims, in a way that seemed illogical, even illegitimate, from any but a financial viewpoint.

Strengthening of democracy. Has *Aufarbeitung* helped to consolidate democracy? Of course, in an ideal world, all measures of transitional justice will do so; but, empirically, the connection is far from obvious. In the case of the GDR past, many observers have remarked on the apparent failure to have a symbolically charged moment or institution to explicate the normative transition to democracy—something comparable to the Nuremberg Trials (a comparison that does not imply an equivalence of Nazism and real existing socialism, one hastens to add). The Honecker trial had precisely that potential: after all, there—for first time since the creation of the Holy Roman Empire—a German ruler was taken to court for violating the rights of his own citizens.[37] But, as is well known, the trial ended in failure. On the other hand, the conviction of Erich Mielke, the head of the Stasi, for a crime commit-

---

[37] Müller and Hartmann, *Vorwärts und Vergessen!*, 19.

ted in 1931 (the shooting of two police officers) seemed arbitrary and slightly absurd in the eyes of many of his post-1953 victims.

Overall, the focus shifted relatively early on from the political leaders, the members of the Politbüro, to the Stasi as the central symbol of oppression as well as to the history of violence at the Wall— in the so-called *Mauerschützenprozesse*. To be sure, the opening of the files remains in many ways the great success story of the past two decades—despite the more recent criticisms to which I alluded earlier in this chapter. More problematic is the fact that the concentration on the Stasi and on the Wall in a sense narrowed an understanding of the GDR as a particular kind of dictatorship and a particular kind of society. As critics have rightly argued, the Stasi—even after its official dissolution— once more served according to its infamous self-description: "the shield and sword of the party." In other words, the concentration on the Stasi diverted attention from the people who ultimately pulled the levers of power—the higher functionaries of the SED and, to some degree, the leaders of the so-called bloc parties.[38] A focus on the SED would also have revealed a quite different pattern of complicity—after all, the party alone boasted 2.5 million members; every fifth adult was associated with it. But de-Stasification was given priority over decommunization, or in fact equated with decommunization.[39]

It is telling, then, that Marianne Birthler claimed in 2009 that the SED should have been officially outlawed.[40] This clearly would have

---

[38] Telling in this regard is also the fact that in the first years of the Gauck authority three times as many people applied to see their files than actually had one. See Inga Markovits, "Selective Memory: How the Law Affects What We Remember and Forget about the Past—The Case of East Germany," *Law and Society Review*, vol. 35 (2001), 513–564.

[39] And, one might say, not without good normative reasons: after all, the Stasi was exclusively an instrument of repression (and moral corruption), unlike other institutions of the GDR that played a more ambiguous role. See Gary Bruce, "Access to Secret Police Files, Justice, and Vetting in East Germany since 1989," *German Politics and Society*, vol. 26 (2008), 82–111.

[40] Marianne Birthler, "Man hätte die SED verbieten sollen," *Frankfurter Allgemeine Zeitung*, May 216, 2009. One might also recall that the Greens in the last Volkskammer had tried to declare the Stasi a criminal association. Other parties opposed such a declaration. In general, there is something to be said for the argument that more *Aufarbeitung* should have been left to legislatures—as opposed to the courts who then de facto had to engage in a certain amount of retroactive legislation. On this point, see also Schlink, *Guilt About the Past.*

been, above all, a symbolic act, or a measure associated with what the political theorist Peter Niesen has called "negative republicanism" (as opposed to the West German doctrine of "anti-extremism"): the symbolic repudiation of one particular political experiment or experience in the past, as for instance in the 1948 Italian constitution which prohibited the reestablishment of the Fascist Party (but did not generally ban extremist parties).[41] The dominant German conception of anti-extremism or anti-totalitarianism—with its condemnation of a variety of historical phenomena and its openness to new political threats in the present—might have good normative arguments in its favor. But it might be less useful for preserving a *historically specific* understanding of oppression and other forms of politically caused suffering.

Social cohesion. Of course one can find many indicators for a continuing division between East and West Germany—and also for many divisions within East Germany itself. But, as I have already suggested—and want now to argue more explicitly—"inner unity" is not only an elusive ideal, but an inherently dubious one.[42] All political cultures are split in one way or other; conflict and not even a certain degree of social disengagement are not necessarily "pathologies," and, especially in Germany, with its long history of *Gemeinschafts*-ideologies, a desire for social *Einheit* should be viewed with a healthy dose of skepticism. To be sure, there are alarming statistics about the number of people especially—but not only—in the East who harbor serious doubts about democracy and the rule of law. But it would be very difficult to argue that these are directly the outcome of the failure of *Aufarbeitung*. Moreover, the figures in question and the general political divisions are hardly as alarming as some that can be found in other Central and Eastern European countries. The cold civil war in a country like Hungary, the rise of right-wing parties like Jobbik (also in Hungary) or the League of Polish Families, has no

---

[41] Peter Niesen, "Anti-Extremism, Negative Republicanism, Civic Society: Three Paradigms for Banning Political Parties," in Shlomo Avineri and Zeev Sternhell (eds.), *Europe's Century of Discontent: The Legacies of Fascism, Nazism and Communism* (Jerusalem: Magnes Press, 2003), 249–268.

[42] For an excellent argument against such thick social unity, see Jonathan Allen, "Balancing Justice and Social Unity: Political Theory and the Idea of a Truth and Reconciliation Commission," *University of Toronto Law Journal*, vol. 49 (1999), 315–353.

real equivalent in Germany. Obviously this is not a call for complacency about German political culture. But even the most cursory comparison suggests that political alarmism—and blaming the process of *Aufarbeitung*—are surely out of place.

What is not out of place either in Germany or elsewhere is a reminder that *Vergangenheitsbewältigung* is of course also *Gegenwartsbewältigung* as well as *Zeitgeschichtsbewältigung* (that is, coping with the present and the most recent past). While inner unity remains an impossible goal, it is important to counter attempts at creating artificial political cleavages based on false recent history. Concretely, it needs to be said time and again that the image of the West having unleashed a witch-hunt on the East in the name of *Vergangenheitsbewältigung* is fundamentally flawed: in fact the last freely elected Volkskammer (and the dissidents) wanted to make sure that justice would reign and that the files would be preserved and their content become known to victims; and it was East German prosecutors and judges who in 1990 began to hold the old elites accountable for corruption, election fraud, and abuse of office in particular.[43] It was also East German civic committees who resisted the incorporation of the Stasi archives into the Federal Archives in Koblenz that West German politicians and bureaucrats were advocating at the time. The person who came closest to preventing an open *Vergangenheitsbewältigung* in this manner was in fact Helmut Kohl.[44] *Aufarbeitung* was in one sense victors' justice—namely that of the victorious dissidents. As Wolfgang Thierse, a Vice President of the Bundestag put it, the Stasi archive was "the fruit of the 1989 fall revolution" —and also remains a symbolic expression of that revolution.[45]

---

[43] The actual *Stasi-Unterlagen-Gesetz* passed by the Bundestag in December 1991 went further than the Volkskammer proposal in allowing victims to see documents directly. On GDR *Strafverfolgung* in the last months of the state, see Marxen, Werle and Schäfer, *Die Strafverfolgung.*

[44] And the person who came closest to preventing unification and keeping the East Germans excluded or in some second-class status was, of course, Social Democrat leader Oskar Lafontaine, today one of the leaders of *Die Linke.*

[45] Quoted by Bruce, "Access," 83. To be sure, it is now certain that the Stasi materials archive will eventually be incorporated into the Federal Archives.

Conclusion

Recent criticisms of *Vergangenheitsbewältigung* seem based on largely unrealistic expectations—expectations that can only arise precisely because Germany's memory culture is so highly developed and remains in many ways an exception, as far as both the fascist and the communist past are concerned.

In particular, it is simply implausible to claim that a form of remembrance could be institutionally secured which only and permanently causes pain and stimulates self-critical thought. One might get closer to such an ideal through counter-monuments, through approaches that create intellectual and emotional stumbling blocks, rather than props for present-day identities, let alone pride—but certain intellectual and emotional outcomes cannot be guaranteed through some kind of social memory engineering. What can be guaranteed, in addition to state-sponsored forms of public remembrance, are political and legal institutions that have absorbed the lessons from the past and that perpetuate a kind of morality that can be empirically observed—unlike the emotional states of individual citizens in their efforts at remembrance.[46]

This is not to deny that memory can dialectically turn into forgetting—but in the absence of any sure way of preventing this, public remembrance supported by both the state and civil society is always preferable to its absence. "Destabilizing" only works if there is something to destabilize in the first place; one only stumbles if one wants to go somewhere; and subversion is only possible if there is some established position to subvert. One should remind oneself—and others—that in truth there is no final overcoming or mastering of the past—but there is what Schlink calls "living consciously with present-day questions and emotions that the past releases."[47]

It is also implausible to claim that compared to other Central and Eastern European post-communist countries, united Germany failed

---

[46] Schlink helpfully reminds us about the importance of institutional morality—as opposed to an exclusive emphasis on the individual or, for that matter collective, morality. See Schlink, *Guilt About the Past*.

[47] Ibid., 38.

to establish justice for victims of the GDR, or that democracy and social cohesion were deeply damaged through *Aufarbeitung*.[48] It is true that parts of *die Linke* are committed to fighting for a rosier picture of the East German regime—but the more important political fact is that Germany is still one of the few European countries without a successful populist right-wing party. This absence is least partially explained by the thorough discrediting of nationalism after Nazism and the fact that, unlike farther east, communist elites did not become corrupt *noveaux riches* (and therefore the subject of a right-wing backlash, as in Hungary, for instance). There is no guarantee that things will stay this way—but for now, it remains plausible to claim that *Aufarbeitung*, for all its blind spots and failings, has fostered an antitotalitarian consensus and been a good thing for German political culture as a whole.

---

[48] See also Stefan Troebst with Susan Baumgartl (ed.), *Postdiktatorische Geschichtskulturen im Süden und Osten Europas* (Göttingen: Wallstein, 2010).

Part Three

SEARCHING FOR CLOSURE
IN DEMOCRATIZING
SOCIETIES

Andrzej Paczkowski

Twenty-Five Years "After"— the Ambivalence of Settling Accounts with Communism: The Polish Case

On 22 April 2009, the Polish Supreme Court confirmed a sentence passed against militia functionaries who, on December 16, 1981, shot nine miners and wounded twenty-one while putting down a "Solidarity" strike at the "Wujek" mine. The platoon commander was sentenced to six years in prison and his fourteen subordinates to two-and-a-half to three years. More than twelve months later, on September 15, 2010, the same court validated a verdict (of one-and-a-half to two years) passed against two functionaries who, on May 3, 1983, participated in a police attack carried out in Warsaw, involving a church charity organization. The two individuals assaulted the persons present there at the time and then they took them in a lorry out of town and left them at night in a forest. It would be certainly worthwhile to consider the type and scale of the two crimes as well as the severity of the sentences. The most interesting fact, however, is that in the first case, the prosecutor's office began its work in 1991. In the second case, it was in 1993. In other words, the whole legal procedure lasted eighteen and seventeen years, respectively. This was a sufficiently long period for Poles born after the fall of communism to reach adulthood and an age of legal and civic maturity (e.g., voting age).

Since the above-mentioned situations could appear to be extreme, we should add that they were by no means exceptions. For example, in October 1990, the prosecutor's office initiated an investigation concerning a massacre of strikers committed in December 1970 in several towns along the Baltic coast (with several scores dead). The court trial began in 1995. The number of defendants, originally more than ten persons, continued to "shrink": some died, while others, such as General Wojciech Jaruzelski, in 1970 minister of national defense, were excluded from the proceedings due to poor health. Consequently, the verdict passed in April 2013 pertained to only three defendants: one was acquitted and two received a four-year suspended sentence.[1] In many other cases, trials have been dragging in successive instance courts for several years and not a single one ended sooner than two years. One could therefore assert with certainty that in post-communist Poland "transitional justice" is slow and thus of little effectiveness. It is not surprising that in the past it gave rise to reservations on the part of public opinion, and it continues to do so until today.

Such a rate of settling accounts with the communist *ancien régime* has been determined by several factors. Primarily, it was the fact that the system collapsed not due to violence, a sudden revolution, or a (lost) war. Systemic transformations stemmed from an agreement (negotiations) between its leaders and representatives of the opposition. The negotiating parties assumed *a priori* that the transition would be peaceful, fragmentary, and evolutionary. Consequently, they omitted the problem of "settling the accounts" with representatives of the old system. Certain members of the oppositional political elite referred to the Spanish example from 1976–1978, which, as it is well known, accepted the principle of "amnesty and amnesia." It excluded the past from the list of topics of future political controversies. The Spanish solution, conceived as a model to be emulated, was cited already in 1985 by the then imprisoned Adam Michnik.[2] In the 1970s, the dissident called for understanding the opponent although no one, including him, even imagined that the system would soon enter into a phase of agony. The "spirit" of the Round Table was preserved in subsequent years, although the crushing defeat of the communists in the partially democratic elections of June 4, 1989 accelerated changes within the country. The cabinet of Tadeusz Mazowiecki, known as the "first non-communist government in Central Europe since 1948," was actually a coalition (with the participation of the communists). If only due to this fact it did not embark upon radical undertakings. Consequently, the political police was not dissolved until April 1990, censorship was

---

[1] http://www.naszdziennik.pl/polska-kraj/30271.html.
[2] A. Michnik, *Takie czasy… Rzecz o kompromisie* (London: Aneks, 1985), 83.

liquidated in May of that year, and the heads of the two "ministers of force," who were part of General Jaruzelski's team uninterruptedly since 1981, only left the Mazowiecki cabinet at the end of June 1990.

The factor that exerted a negative impact on settling accounts with the *ancien régime* was the unwillingness of the leftist part of the opposition, influential in the cabinet, and of its intellectual establishment to pursue such a course. Its members feared that radicalization could result in the deployment of state forces and that the communists would resort to defensive measures with the backing of the army and the security troops, which remained at their disposal. It was claimed that revolutions, as assorted examples, starting with the French Revolution, demonstrated, do not lead to democracy. They rather replace one dictatorship with another. It was also feared that radicalization could enable nationalistic forces, supported by the Catholic Church, to come to power in the country. Although the Church had been previously a fervent adherent of a compromise with the communists and of evolutionary changes, anxiety about its might was rather strong among these circles. This situation led to a consolidation of contacts with the communist camp. In turn, the latter, after the self-dissolution of the communist party at the end of January 1990 and the establishment in its stead of a party that described itself as social-democratic, was, obviously, a radical opponent of any sort of accounts with the past. This attitude, however, did not stop it from loyally participating on the parliamentary forum in a systemic transformation of the economy or government. Their approach was similar to General Jaruzelski's. He, as president, did formally enjoy a rather wide range of authority, but *de facto* he did not put it to use in order not to hamper the process of post-communist transformation.

At a time when Poland was entering a period of systemic change, accompanied by strong social emotions and great expectations, there was no universal revolutionary atmosphere although it was obvious that certain forces strove toward determined initiatives. They were concentrated, however, not on the nationalist and clerical right wing, as the left wing feared, but on that part of the opposition which already postulated radical solutions earlier. The latter contested the Round Table negotiations, which it regarded as treason, and called for a boycott of elections held as a result of an agreement reached by the Jaruzelski team and the "Solidarity" *mainstream* personified by

Lech Wałęsa. The supporters of these efforts were found mainly in such organizations as "Fighting Solidarity" ("Solidarność Walcząca") and the Confederation of Independent Poland as well as among youth groups, including those with neo-anarchist inclinations. In the autumn of 1989, radical groups demanded the resignation of General Jaruzelski from the presidential office, the liquidation of the political police, the dissolution of the communist party, totally free elections, and bringing to justice the authors of martial law and those guilty of the crimes committed at the time. Ultimately, the groups in question proved incapable of influencing the course of events.

Despite the above-mentioned resistance on the part of the liberal leftist opposition and the communists, the first attempt at embarking upon settling of accounts took place relatively early. On August 2, 1989, two weeks after the election of Jaruzelski for the presidency and prior to the establishment of the Mazowiecki cabinet, the Sejm enacted a resolution about the creation of an Extraordinary Committee for Examining the Activity of the Ministry of Internal Affairs (the minister was coordinated by the security service, i.e., the political police) after December 12, 1981, from the moment of the proclamation of martial law. The Committee was to consider 122 cases of death, whose perpetrators were suspected to be Ministry functionaries. The Committee's competences were limited: it did not possess investigative rights and thus the presence of witnesses was neither obligatory nor could it conduct interrogations according to the code of penal procedure and it was deprived of access to the Ministry's archives. Nonetheless, in more than a year, the Committee was capable of ascertaining that at least eighty-eight cases called for penal procedure; it informed the prosecutor's office of its findings.[3] The inauguration of the Committee work appeared to demonstrate that despite all odds the procedure of settling accounts would assume impetus. In the spring of 1990, Lech and Jaroslaw Kaczyński created a new party, known as the Centre Agreement (Porozumienie Centrum [PC]). This new political actor proposed dismissing Jaruzelski from office, the election of Lech Wałęsa for president, the acceleration of systemic transformations, and the recognition of the responsibility of the communist party for "the wrongs and losses

---

[3] *Raport Rokity. Sprawozdanie Sejmowej Komisji Nadzwyczajnej do Zbadania Działalności MSW* (Cracow: Wydawnictwo Acana, 2005), 185.

suffered by the Polish nation." The prosecutor's office, however, acted sluggishly and in two years managed to examine only twenty-one cases indicated by the Sejm Committee.

Naturally, at the time of the inauguration of systemic transformation there were no legal institutions or regulations that could indirectly serve the cause of settling accounts with the past. This state of things gradually changed due to the enactment of a statute on rescinding the sentences passed in the years 1944–1956 and concerning conspiracy activity. At the same time, in April 1991, the Polish Parliament changed a statute in force since 1945 about the Main Commission for the Investigation of Nazi Crimes in Poland. The new body was named the Main Commission for the Prosecution of Crimes against the Polish Nation. The newly introduced term "Stalinist crimes" described crimes committed by the functionaries of the Polish (and Soviet) security apparatus before December 31, 1956. It was also recognized that the statute of limitation for crimes of this nature started not from the moment of their commitment but as of January 1, 1990, i.e., the date when it was truly possible to prosecute them. Subsequently, the chronological range of the work of the Main Commission was expanded by introducing the term "communist crimes," that is, those perpetrated by regime officials up until December 31, 1989. This allowed the inclusion as well of crimes perpetrated during the martial law period. Both categories were granted the status of "crimes against humanity" and thus were not subjected to the statute of limitations, although in 1999 the period of penalization was defined as thirty years in the case of homicide and twenty years for other felonies (starting on January 1, 1990). In this way, and despite assorted obstacles, in the course of several years there gradually emerged a legal *instrumentarium* for settling accounts with communism, although the prosecutor's office and the courts applied it hesitantly and lethargically. No more than twenty sentences were passed until the year 2000. The most significant case concerned a group of investigators working at the Ministry of Public Security from 1945–1954 (the case of Adam Humer, et al.), who were sentenced in March 1996.

In this situation, an essential step toward a legal and court settling of accounts with the communist period was the establishment, upon the basis of a statute of December 18, 1998, of the Institute of National Remembrance (Instytut Pamięci Narodowej [IPN]). This institution also encompassed the Main Commission for the Prosecution of Crimes against the Polish Nation. The same law granted prosecutors employed by IPN the right to transfer indictment acts directly to court. Previously, the Main Commission's prosecutors were *de facto* examining justices, who presented the gathered evidence to prosecutors from the general prosecutor's office and only the latter decided about the preparation (or not) of an indictment decision. This change made it possible not only to shorten the procedure but it also resulted in the emergence of a group of prosecutors specialized in investigations pertaining to communist crimes from the sometimes not so recent past. The number of procedures grew rapidly, but their effectiveness perceived by public opinion—and measured by the number of issued sentences—was not impressive. For example, in 2012, IPN prosecutors completed as many as 1,234 procedures, of which 661 concerned "communist crimes," 518 "Nazi crimes" and 55 "other crimes" (wartime or against humanity). However, they filed only ten indictment acts to court involving twelve persons and discharged as many as 944 cases (including 606 due to the nonidentification of the perpetrators).[4] In the same year, courts issued adjudications concerning twenty-eight persons previously accused by IPN prosecutors: thirteen persons were sentenced, one was acquitted, four benefitted from an amnesty (enacted already in December 1989), and ten cases were discharged due to the enforcement of the statute of limitations.[5]

Although IPN prosecutors work intensively, the documentation, which they gather is by rule, solely of historical importance. Sometimes it can become a valuable source for research into the communist (or Nazi) system of repression, but very rarely does it serve as a basis for concrete charges of a person in court. Nonetheless, each year, at least a few dozen persons were accused of having committed "communist crimes" (although "Nazi crimes" also appear, albeit rarely). Only a limited number—less than a half —among them are sentenced. The verdicts usually prescribe short prison terms and quite often the penalty is suspended because the majority of the crimes belong to less drastic categories: assault in detention, stifling a demonstration,

---

[4] *Informacja o działalności 1 stycznia 2012-31 grudnia 2012*, www.ipn.gov.pl/_data/assets/pdf-file/0010/110008/informacja o dzialalnosci. html, 131.

[5] Ibid., 143.

or malicious treatment during interrogation. The majority of the trials are "provincial" and take place in small towns and remain unnoticed, while the press at best publishes a brief note about the verdict. Only some trials gave rise to wider interest, as they became the topic of articles and polemics in the media or on television. All of this holds true for cases that pertain to such dramatic events as the massacres organized by the communist power, whether it be at the "Wujek" mine or the deaths of three demonstrators in the small town of Lubin in August 1982. The courts usually try (and sentence) direct perpetrators—lower rank functionaries and frequently the rank and file members of militia units that were sent to put down demonstrations. Very rarely does an indictment concern persons charged with "crime commissioning," ministers or directors of departments. Only a single sentence of this sort has been passed by a first instance court. Up until present, it has been impossible to deprive a judge or prosecutor of his/her immunity and thus bring to court a single person among those whom the IPN wished to accuse of "court crimes," that is, participation in passing verdicts involving political cases upon the basis of enforced confessions or forged documents.

Public opinion was most interested in accountability for the martial period. This is simultaneously an excellent example of existing political and legal barriers resulting from the "nonrevolutionary" manner of settling accounts with the past. In December 1991, on the tenth anniversary of the proclamation of martial law, when the parliamentary majority belonged to parties derived from "Solidarity" and the democratic opposition, the Sejm enacted a legislative act condemning the martial law. The document recognized the latter's introduction as illegal and commissioned that it had to be examined by the Constitutional Accountability Committee, which is the only parliamentary instance capable of filing motions for trying politicians by the State Tribunal. The Committee, however, started its work (the gathering of documents, the interrogation of witnesses, and do on) with considerable delay—not until September 1992—and had not completed it before the premature dissolution of the Parliament in the summer of 1993. New elections were won by parties that were successors to the communist party. For two more years, the Committee (with changed membership) continued to work and it amassed considerable data. In the end, the Committee decided, by a majority of votes, that the proclamation of martial law was justified and legal. In this manner, the question of trying the authors of martial law "was struck off" before it even appeared in court. Not until 2004 did IPN prosecutors revive the investigation, as they prepared a legal action against General Jaruzelski and several other persons who played the main roles in the preparation and carrying out of the martial law. The trial began in September 2008 and it was conducted at an extremely slow pace. Just as in the case of the proceedings concerning the massacre of workers committed in 1970, the number of defendants gradually decreased. In August 2011, the court suspended proceedings relating to the most important defendant (General Jaruzelski) in view of his poor health. Subsequently, only three defendants remained and the final sentence was passed in May 2013—five years after the commencement of the trial. One of the accused, General Czesław Kiszczak (in 1981, the minister of internal affairs), received a two-year sentence suspended from a total of five years, while Stanisław Kania (First Secretary of the Polish United Workers' Party until October 1981) was acquitted. In the case of the third defendant, Eugenia Kempara (in 1981, member of the Council of State), penal proceedings were discontinued. In this manner, the most awaited trial of persons fulfilling leading functions in communist Poland came to nought.

The problem with legal accountability for the martial law period consisted of the fact that both the political and media elites and, predominantly, public opinion were and continue to be strongly divided. The fall of communism was followed by numerous public opinion studies. In all cases, the majority of the respondents (from 47 percent to 54 percent) declared that the proclamation of martial law was necessary or justified, while a distinctly lower number (from 19 percent to 35 percent) assessed that it was incorrect. A relatively large group of people (from 16 percent to 27 percent) refused to answer ("difficult to say"). It follows from these studies that, as a rule, positive opinions about martial law predominated among older persons (more than 60 percent), while the "difficult to say" response prevailed among the youth.[6] Without delving into the details of the motifs to which the

---

[6] Piotr T. Kwiatkowski, *Stan wojenny w badaniach opinii publicznej w latach 1982–2003* (Szczecin: Societas Scientarium Stetinensis, 2005), 58 (results of studies conducted in 2001).

respondents referred, one could say that, as Kwiatkowski wrote, "an argument with greatest impact on the imagination" is the conviction that thanks to the introduction of martial law by local (Polish) forces it was possible to avoid an invasion by the Soviet Union and other member states of the Warsaw Pact.[7] The attitude toward martial law cannot be extrapolated into other events associated with the past, especially in particular, concrete cases of homicide. Nevertheless, this example shows that the successors of the communist party and the leftist political media or intellectual elites were not the only ones to resist radical attempts at legal-penal resolutions in relation to the communist period. Generally speaking, there is division on these issues across the entire society. At any rate, in Poland, there is no automatic social consensus for penalizing the perpetrators of all the symptoms of the evil produced by the communist regime, especially those persons who were to be held responsible for making decisions and not only those who are held accountable for their implementation.

Nor is there consensus in relation with other elements of settling accounts with communism. For instance, the Parliament lacked necessary majority to enact the so-called decommunization statute, upon which basis certain categories of communist party members and activists would be deprived of assorted rights, such as appointments to public offices or state enterprises, as was the case in the Czech Republic. True, the Sejm enacted laws condemning communism, but they did not result in direct legal consequences for individuals. A one-time verification of civil servants, judges,[8] prosecutors and professors was never carried out (it did take place in Germany, for example). The only verification (in 1990) concerned functionaries of the security apparatus of the Ministry of Internal Affairs. Naturally, there did take place an important turnover of the state administration or the diplomatic corps, but it was carried out in accordance with democratic standards.

A relatively large scope, although it too encountered certain resistance, was assumed by symbolic condemnation and public shaming. Already between 1990 and 1992, the names of thousands of streets

---

[7] Ibid., 67.

[8] Initially, it was anticipated that the judges would carry out "self-cleansing" and eliminate from among their ranks persons who had violated the principles of impartiality and independence. This never happened.

and squares, and the patrons of schools or assorted enterprises were changed. A majority of the monuments and commemorative plaques from the communist period were disbanded. Naturally, these changes did not affect cemeteries (including those of Red Army soldiers) and up to this very day the so-called alleys of men of merit in various necropolises feature at times bombastic gravestones of persons who contributed to the installation of the communist system in Poland. From time to time, there appear to be initiatives of commemorating those who had not been suitably honoured prior to 1989. As a rule, this holds true for Edward Gierek—first secretary of the communist party from 1970–1980—whom many Poles still regard as a "good administrator" while considering the period of his rule to have been one of prosperity, full employment, and social security. A majority of public holidays, still existing in 1989, disappeared without any distinctive protests. Holidays important in the communist calendar (e.g., the 7th of November—the anniversary of the Bolshevik revolution) are no longer held. Actually, the only communist holiday to have survived is May Day, although the state does not organize any formal celebrations.

Enormous changes took place in education and within the mass media. Present-day textbooks depict the period of the People's Poland, as a rule in a highly negative light. The repressive features of the system and the dependence upon the Soviet Union are signalled out. Other issues widely discussed are the ineffective economy and the choice of a wrong path for the country's modernization, the violation of human rights, censorship, or the dictatorial character of the authorities, and so on. Also in the media, the predominating image is disapproving. Upon the occasion of various anniversaries (such as the proclamation of martial law, the assassination of Rev. Jerzy Popiełuszko, or the student strikes in March 1968), the same images recur—dispersed demonstrations, tanks in city streets, empty shops or the ambiguous warm embraces of Polish and Soviet dignitaries. This characteristic *sui generis* mixture consists of brutality and scenes (queues) or objects (the Polish-produced "syrenka" car) comical from today's point of view. Ridicule has become a popular way of compromising the *ancien régime*. The authors' intention was probably to reach the young spectators who might be tired of an excess of martyrology and the lifeless figures of the indomitable heroes of the battle against "the commune." This approach, however, deprives communism of its odious traits as evil.

All these efforts, though incomplete or limited, were to a certain degree simply a continuation of the struggle waged prior to 1989 by the opposition and "Solidarity" (as well as, in a specific manner, by the Catholic Church), whose purpose was to topple (or alter) the communist system. The division into "communists" and "anti-communists"—to resort to a conventional and unavoidable generalization—was certainly not the only one to exist within Polish society, but from 1980 it played a key role. In the vocabulary of the opposition, it was described as a division into "the authorities" (the communists) and "the society" (the rest of the nation). The moment the regime collapsed, the ensuing transformation changed this division by introducing the category of "post-communists." According to certain sociologists, the division into the "'post-communists" and the "anti-communists" became a counterpart of a class division, classical for Western democracy, and it was conceived as a fundamental social division.[9] This is not to say that there were no further splits among the "anti-communists," who experienced intense ideological conflicts (and personal ones within the opposition or "Solidarity"). It did mean, however, that the basic differences of stands and views stemming from the pre-1989 period were of essential significance. The "communist successors" were tried for the crimes and faults of a defunct system, while they held positive opinions about the experiences of People's Poland. At the same time, the "anti-communists" were in favor of a more or less radical settling of accounts with the past.

Rather unexpectedly, one of the instruments used for settling accounts with the communist system was applied in an internal battle waged within the vast and differentiated "anti-communist" camp. I have in mind the policy we all know by the name of lustration, that is, the disclosure of persons who prior to 1989 were secret collaborators of the security apparatus (widely comprehended so that it would include the Intelligence and the Counter-Intelligence sections). Previous experience in other countries has shown that in the course of settling accounts with the past, which took place on an extremely wide scale after the World War II both in Germany and Italy as well as those states which had collaborationist governments (France, Hungary, and

---

[9] Mirosława Grabowska, *Podział postkomunistyczny. Społeczne podstawy polityki w Polsce po 1989 roku* (Warsaw: Scholar), 2004, 369.

Norway), the prosecution of secret collaborators was not distinguished in a general denazification, defascization or "de-Vichyzation" policy. This reality gives much food for thought. I propose as a topic worthy of a separate debate a hypothesis contending that this difference resulted probably from the fact that in totalitarian or authoritarian states, other than communist ones, collaboration with the political police, although extremely frequent, was, as a rule, spontaneous, occasional, and anonymous. In contrast, in communist states, following the Soviet example, secret collaboration was included into a system subject to a considerable degree of bureaucratization and formalization.

One way or another, in Poland, the first demands calling for the disclosure of secret collaborators were made in the spring of 1991.[10] In July that year, the Senate of the Republic passed a statute on the lustration of candidates to parliamentary seats. The law, however, was not granted legal procedure and the elections took place without the vetting a given candidate on the matter of whether s/he had been registered as a collaborator or not. The issue returned on the agenda on May 22, 1992, when the Sejm forced the minster of internal affairs to verify which of the persons fulfilling public functions (parliamentarians, high ranking civil servants, members of local governments, judges, and attorneys) had been secret collaborators. Relatively early, on the 4th of June, the minister presented a list of sixty-six such persons, including President Lech Wałęsa. The reaction was instantaneous: the President dissolved the whole cabinet and an *ad hoc* created Sejm committee recognized the minister's activity to be illegal. Nonetheless, the problem could no longer be swept under the rug.

Quite possibly, if the matter had concerned only names, even such significant ones as that of President Wałęsa, lustration would have not gained the relevance that it did. The crux of the matter consisted in the fact that lustration had been included into an extensive problem, of crucial importance not only for current politics but outright for the state as such, namely, the legitimization of the system that came into being as a result of the dissolution of communism and became known as the Third Republic. Moreover, and this is of importance for reflec-

---

[10] The most relevant studies on lustration in Poland—see: Piotr Grzelak, *Wojna o lustrację* (Warsaw: Trio, 2005) and Agnieszka Opalińska, *Lustracja w Polsce i w Niemczech* (Wrocław: Atut, 2012).

tions on settling of accounts with communism, lustration partly transferred—although, naturally, not totally—the burden of responsibility
from the functionaries and administrators of the system onto those
who struggled against it. Secret collaborators were not, as a rule, party
activists or officials of the communist state, but usually persons who
belonged to the opposition or who were sufficiently close to opposition
groups to be capable of providing "insider" information. Although the
"communist successor parties" decidedly criticized lustration undertakings, in reality they regarded them as highly useful since the debate
about and application of the law opened up a new front on the Polish
political scene, in which they were not involved directly.

Seven projects of lustration laws were submitted as a reaction
to the events of June 4, 1992,[11] but growing conflicts among the
"anti-communists" and the 1993 election victory of "the successors of
the communist party" made it impossible, for many years, to complete
the legislative procedures. Throughout this time, lustration appeared
to acquire a life of its own in the form of particular documents intend-
ing to confirm the secret collaboration of politicians or of intellectuals
with the communist police. Circulating conjectures and insinuations
were based on the enigmatic recollections of former functionaries.
At the same time, certain political milieus and experts expanded and
disseminated a thesis about the existence of a post-communist "Network" ("Układ" in Polish), which supposedly decisively influenced
Polish economic and political life after 1989 and which supposedly
was even part of the onset of systemic transformation. The "Network"
was putatively made up of leading party dignitaries ("nomenclature"),
high-ranking functionaries of the security apparatus (including the
Intelligence), and opposition and "Solidarity" activists embroiled by
them, who had become in the past secret collaborators or/and party
members.[12] In certain studies on the "Network," Vladimir Kriuchkov
was considered the true "godfather" of transformations across the
whole communist camp. He was the head of the KGB, the "patron

---

[11] By sheer accident this was the anniversary of the 1989 elections, crucial for
the initiation of the systemic transformation.

[12] The first extensive reflection on this subject: Andrzej Zybertowicz, *W uścisku tajnych służb. Upadek komunizmu i układ postnomenklaturowy* (Warszawa:
Antyk, 1993).

of the Round Table" and "animator of the constructive opposition in
Central Europe," as Jadwiga Staniszkis wrote.[13] In light of such opinions it became obvious for those who believed in them that the 1989
negotiations were conducted by the "Reds" and the "Pinks" (the left-
wing opposition) or their own "agents." It was accepted that only a
widespread and radical version of lustration would make it possible to
destroy the "Network," "a virus of sorts, whose existence within the
social organism favors the dissemination of further ailments and makes
it impossible to wage an effective battle against them."[14] In this way,
lustration was not simply a mechanism resembling the "purges" operated in postwar Western democracies, while simultaneously making
appointments for responsible posts in the administration. It became a
prospective tool for the Salvation of the State and Nation. The success of parties' successors to the communist party in the 1993 parliamentary elections seemed to confirm the conviction of some that the
"Network" not only existed but that it triumphed. The belief in the
importance of lustration for a better arrangement of the state became
increasingly universal: in 1994 it was supported by 57 percent respondents in sociological polls, while in 1997 the number rose to 76 percent.
With time, the percentage of the supporters of lustration dropped, but
never below 70 percent.[15]

After several years of political wheeling and dealing, the lustration
law was enacted in April 1997,[16] and after further political controversies (i.e., it was vetoed by the "post-communist" President Aleksander
Kwaśniewski) it was implemented as late as 1999. In contrast to the
situation in Germany or the Czech Republic, where collaboration was
confirmed upon the request of an employer by means of formal information supplied by an institution supervising the former security service archives, in Poland, each person fulfilling functions listed in the
law made a declaration in which she or he stated whether she or he
had been or had not been a secret collaborator. Such declarations were
then checked in the archives by a specially established office (known as

---

[13] Jadwiga Staniszkis, *Postkomunizm. Próba opisu* (Gdańsk: Słowo/obraz tery-
toria, 2001), 6.
[14] Zybertowicz, *W uścisku tajnych służb*, 9.
[15] Opalińska, *Lustracja*, 215.
[16] Text of the law—see, Grzelak, *Wojna o lustrację*, 227–238.

the Public Interest Spokesperson; today, the IPN Lustration Bureau). If it was discovered that such declarations were false, the case was transferred to a separate department (the so-called Lustration Court). If the latter confirmed collaboration, the decision was announced publicly and the person who made the false statement was deprived (for ten years) of all rights to public functions. The whole procedure was rather complicated and time consuming. Additionally, the Supreme Court, which considered a defendant's appeal, established extremely demanding criteria for recognizing someone as a "conscious secret collaborator" (e.g., the preservation of receipts for money received). During the first five years of the statute's implementation, out of a total of about 19,000 checked declarations, 150 motions for penalization were filed to court, of which sixty-three were judged by the court as justified.[17] Since 2007, the statute considerably expanded the list of posts affected by lustration (i.e., all persons elected to local self-governments). In 2012, the Lustration Bureau was supposed to check almost 300,000 declarations. Since in a single year the Office is capable of examining documents pertaining to a maximum of 10,000 persons, the whole procedure is almost at a standstill. Consequently, in 2012 only 136 accusations of "lustration lies" were forwarded to courts of law, and the latter sentenced a mere sixty-eight persons.[18] For all practical purposes, "lustration liars" who received court verdicts did not include individuals with a well-known past as collaborators of the secret police. For example, the court recognized Lech Wałęsa as innocent. Many celebrated members of the former opposition (Adam Michnik, Jacek Kuroń) spoke against lustration, as did the intellectual milieu formed around "Gazeta Wyborcza," the largest Polish political daily, as well as a considerable number of members of the "post-Solidarity" leftist-liberal Democratic Union or certain politicians representing the centrist Civic Platform (Platforma Obywatelska). A considerable part of the Catholic Church hierarchy also opposed lustration, or rather lustration concerning the clergy.

---

[17] www.senat.gov.pl/druk no. 1024. The majority of persons recognized as "lustration liars" were lawyers. Around 200 persons admitted in their declarations that they had been either functionaries or secret collaborators.

[18] *Informacja o działalności...*, 153.

From the viewpoint of the political struggle, the access to operational documents of the communist secret service, guaranteed in the statute of the IPN, to persons vetted by the Institute, as well as to historians and journalists, could have been even more important than lustration itself. Such documents were rendered available on a larger scale in 2004 and 2005. From that time on, they served as a basis for the disclosure of the collaboration of hundreds of persons, including members of the opposition and "Solidarity" activists as well as priests, who were the object of the special interest of the security apparatus. Taking into account the state of the preservation of these documents, which in large part were destroyed by the communists between 1989 and 1990, information about secret collaborators was frequently provided on the basis of circumstantial files and of evidence provided by unverifiable records. This in itself rendered support to the opponents of lustration and of disclosing the fact of collaboration, but it did not hamper its adherents. Alongside more or less reliable information about secret collaboration with the security apparatus, the opening of archives also offered access to protocols from the interrogations of persons detained, the contents of tapped telephone conversations or notes from secretly controlled correspondence as well as various opinions, including expert ones, concerning the opposition and the struggle waged against it. Knowledge about the secret police apparatus as such increased considerably, especially on matters pertaining to its structure, techniques, activity, or tasks created for it by the communist party leaders. A large part of this knowledge, though, was by the very force of things, directed against certain members of the former opposition.

The adherents to theories about the "Network," or those who, in more general terms, seem to fall for conspiracy theories, did not find direct proof for a conspiracy in 1989 involving the communist elite and certain members of the opposition. They did, however, try to make use of all the unclear points in the documents or unambiguous formulations for the sake of confirming their convictions. The Law and Justice Party (PiS), created by the Kaczyński brothers, declared lustration and the disclosure of documents as the prime objective of the political struggle. The Fourth Republic planned by this party was supposed to be totally free of the "Network." This battle deployed numerous arguments, one of which was to undermine the position of Lech Wałęsa as the symbol of the Round Table and the "founding father" of the Third

Republic. Some politicians, publicists, and historians, either connected with PiS or the party's sympathizers, attempted in numerous publications or documentary films to prove that the "Solidarity" leader, as a secret informer of the security service in December 1970, from the time of his arrest at the time of the strike (a fact which did take place), had been a constant lackey of the communists. Moreover, they tried to also show how while Wałęsa was President, he came to their assistance by protecting the "Network." The anti-Wałęsa campaign engaged even the Institute of National Remembrance, which published a sizeable monograph on this subject.[19] The whole liberal and leftist wing of the former "anti-communists" joined forces in the defense of the former President.

The Wałęsa *cause célèbre* is a relevant, although only an individual example of using the past for the sake of present-day political struggles. It obviously concerns predominantly the not-so-distant communist past, although the debate about the history of the Poles and Poland affects also other areas, such as Polish-Jewish relations or national myths. In Poland, settling accounts with communism, which in certain aspects has been completed (e.g., in the domain of symbols) and in others is being continued (e.g., the prosecution of "communist crimes"), has from a certain moment acquired a rather unexpected twist by providing an argument for intensifying the internal battle among the former members of the "anti-communist" camp. Those who due to their age cannot refer to personal experiences in their assessments of communism might have found themselves caught in an uncomfortable crossfire of contradictory interpretations. What has happened is an exemplification of a concentrated attempt at depriving events and persons of their importance and place in the most recent history of the country. It was ultimately a struggle to overturn the glory of people and events central for the coming into being of democratic, post-communist Poland.

---

[19] Sławomir Cenckiewicz, Piotr Gontarczyk *SB a Lech Wałęsa. Przyczynek do biografii* (Warsaw: IPN, 2008).

RALUCA GROSESCU and RALUCA URSACHI

The Romanian Revolution in Court: What Narratives about 1989?

Introduction

Trials against former leaders of a dictatorial regime are symbolic moments in the founding of a new political order. Beyond the classic functions of criminal justice (punishing the guilty, preventing similar deeds in the future and reinforcing respect for the law), these trials can also play an epistemic role in societies in transition.[1] They constitute important processes of narrative construction, understood as "storytelling" *(mise en récit)* about injustice. The selection of the relevant facts at the trial, their legal characterization, and the assignation of blame by sentencing may constitute public affirmations of an official and normative version of events,[2] which implicitly grants legitimacy to the values of the new democratic society. The Nuremberg trials or Adolf Eichmann's conviction in Jerusalem are high impact examples of the way in which criminal proceedings have modeled public awareness of mass murder.[3] Theoreticians of transitional justice believe that such trials largely contribute to the forging of a common historical memory of the recent past.[4]

---

[1] Ruti Teitel, *Transitional Justice* (New York, Oxford University Press, 2000), 49.

[2] René Remond, "L'histoire et la loi," www.diplomatie.gouv.fr/fr/IMG/pdf/LHistoireetlaLoiReneRemond-2.pdf, accessed July 31, 2011.

[3] For accounts of the narrative function and the aftermath of the Nuremberg Trials and Adolf Eichmann's conviction, see for example, Anette Wieviorka, *Le procès de Nuremberg* (Paris, Editions Liana Levi, 2006); Anette Wieviorka, *Le procès Eichmann* (Paris: Editions Complexe, 1989).

[4] Such as Teitel, *Transitional Justice.*; Marc Osiel, *Mass Atrocity, Collective Memory, and the Law* (New Brunswick : Transaction Publishers, 1997); or Jaime Malamud Goti, "Trying Violators of Human Rights," *State Crimes: Punishment or Pardon* (Aspen, CO: Justice and Society Program of the Aspen Institute, 1989).

This vision has its origins in Durkheim's theory of a collective consciousness of the values shared by the members of a society. Normally, the punishment and coercion contained in criminal law protect a set of values from whence they draw their strength, granting them a sacred aura.[5] In this view, the criminal trial is a ritual for reaffirming the common values of society and strengthening the moral sentiment. Durkheim's theory, however, is not heuristic for contemporary societies in transition, which often go through a radical refounding of their legal, political, and moral values. Thus, courts cannot restore symbolic unity in society by unilaterally putting certain values on show, but they can rather constitute a forum where various versions of the recent past confront each other.[6] In transition trials, through the diverging testimonies and scenarios that are set out, a historical narrative can emerge, drawing a picture of the overturned regime, of its crimes and of its shared guilt.[7] The verdict, in this view, signifies the validation of one or another of those versions of the recent past, as well as an expression of the identity of the new political regime. In Otto Kirchheimer's words, those trials "allow building a permanent wall, without ambiguities, between the new beginnings and the old tyranny."[8]

The epistemic function of the trials does not, however, exhaust the historiographical experience. Historians such as Henry Rousso or Richard J. Evans have shown the serious limitations of the idea of "history written by courts."[9] Even though justice and history do function within the common horizon of truth finding, the very purpose of criminal trials is different. History seeks to explain, to grant intelligibility and coherence to events, while the judiciary seeks to apply justice, assign

---

[5] David Garland, *Punishment and Modern Society* (Chicago: University of Chicago Press, 1993), 57.

[6] Osiel, *Mass Atrocity*, 42.

[7] Carlos Santiago Nino, *Radical Evil on Trial* (New Haven: Yale University Press, 1996), 147; Osiel, *Mass Atrocity*, 50.

[8] Otto Kirchheimer, *Political Justice: The Use of Legal Procedure for Political Ends* (Princeton: Princeton University Press, 1961), 308.

[9] Henry Rousso, *The Haunting Past: History, Memory and Justice in Contemporary France* (Philadelphia: University of Pennsylvania Press, 2002); Richard J. Evans, "History, Memory and the Law: The Historian as Expert Witness," *History and Theory*, nr. 4, 2002.

responsibility and mete out punishment. Judges do not seek to find what "the whole truth" was, like historians would, but only the facts that support the charges, administrated as proof within the strict limits of the procedural codes. Justice tries individuals and individual causes, while history has a permanent opening toward the collective and institutional dimension of phenomena.[10] As opposed to history, which is permanently being revised, narratives offered by courts "classify, finalize, condemn," and thus offer an official and closed version of events, a "unique and definitive history."[11]

Another vulnerability of these narratives as potential creators of common historical memory is their possible exposure to political influence. Depending on the relationship between the new power holders and the past, as well as on their ideological vision, trials may be manipulated for purposes other than those specific to justice. Trials can thus become strategies for building political legitimacy for the new power, or acts of revenge disguised as legal procedures.[12] Often times, the symbolic purpose of the trials, to "draw a line" between the old and the new regime, to mark a clean break and a new beginning, seems to be a "profoundly dishonest act," given that societies in transition bear the scars of the institutional and cultural heritage of recent past. Such symbols and rituals of rupture may often serve to hide "guilty continuities" between the leaders of the old and the new regimes, and the solid ties that unite present and past.[13] In addition, the trials can become political weapons for delegitimizing adversaries. To the extent that political aims gain precedence over the law and procedural guarantees, the epistemic function of the trials is compromised. The narrative risks becoming a form of propaganda, a political tool that acts in a Manichean and emotional manner.[14]

---

[10] Paul Ricoeur, *La mémoire, l'histoire, l'oubli* (Seuil, Paris, 2000), 420–425.

[11] Henry Rousso, "Juger le passé? Justice et histoire en France," in Florent Brayard (ed.), *Le génocide des Juifs entre procès et histoire 1943–2000* (Paris,: Editions Complexe, 2000), 283.

[12] Claus Offe, "Coming to Terms with Past Injustices," *Archives Européenes de Sociologie*, vol. 33, nr.1, 1992, 19.

[13] Ibid., 18.

[14] Rousso, *Haunting Past*, 38.

In post-communist Romania, the transitional criminal justice was concerned almost exclusively[15] with the crimes committed during the Revolution of December 1989.[16] The importance of this event as a founding moment of the new political order, as well as the open violence of repression, rendered judicial silence impossible and imposed trials of the responsible parties as a necessity.

This study analyzes the epistemic role of the trials of communist leaders involved in repression against protests in December 1989. We will examine the narratives produced by these trials and the way in which they were built. The questions we try to answer are the following: How do these narratives contribute to clarifying the events and to building a common historical memory? What values have they reinforced? To what extent have these narratives been politically instrumented?

I. A Short Presentation
of the Events of December 1989

The Romanian revolution broke out in the city of Timişoara on December 15–16,[17] when ample protests against the regime occurred. On December 17, Nicolae Ceauşescu called a meeting of the CPEx (the Political Executive Committee, the equivalent of Politburo) of

---

[15] Only four indictments referred to crimes perpetrated before this date, and only two of them resulted in convictions. For the trials against former communist leaders in Romania after 1989, see: Raluca Grosescu and Raluca Ursachi, *Justiţia penală de tranziţie de la Nurnberg la postcomunismul românesc* (Iaşi, Polirom, 2009). For transitional justice in Romania, see Lavinia Stan, *Transitional Justice in Post-Communist Romania. The Politics of Memory* (Cambridge: Cambridge University Press, 2012), and Lavinia Stan, "Romania," in Lavinia Stan, (ed.), *Transitional Justice in Eastern Europe and the Former Soviet Union: Reckoning with the Communist Past* (New York: Routledge, 2009), 128–151. See also Raluca Ursachi, *Justice de transition en Roumanie post-communiste. Usages politiques du passé*, PhD dissertation, University of Paris 1.

[16] Even if, referring to the fall of communism in Romania, the term "revolution" is contested by some analysts (see, for instance, Alex Mihai Stoenescu, *Istoria Loviturilor de Stat din România*, vol. IV, Bucharest, Rao, 2004); we will be using it in this article to refer to the events that took place in Romania between December 16 and 22, 1989, which led to the change in political regime.

[17] For the December 1989 events, see Peter Siani-Davies, *The Romanian Revolution of December 1989* (Ithaca: Cornell University Press, 2005) (Roma-

the Communist Party of Romania (PCR), which decided to repress, militarily, the protests in Timişoara. The next day, Army troops—led by generals Victor Athanasie Stănculescu and Mihai Chiţac, as well as Police (Miliţia) and Securitate troops and conscripts, acting on orders from Minister of the Interior Tudor Postelnicu and the head of the Securitate, general Iulian Vlad, intervened violently, leaving dozens dead and hundreds injured and operating numerous arrests. Allegedly on Elena Ceauşescu's personal order, forty bodies were illegally incinerated and disposed of, without informing the families.

On December 21, protests against the regime sprang up in other cities in Romania: Cluj, Braşov, Sibiu. In Bucharest, Nicolae Ceauşescu called for a popular rally of support for the Party. However, the mass of people brought in front of the Central Committee building started yelling slogans against the regime. The rally was stopped, but some of the participants regrouped in the center of the capital city, calling for the regime to be removed. That night, the authorities violently repressed the demonstrators, leaving forty-nine dead and 463 wounded.[18] Similar state-engineered bloodshed happened in other Romanian cities.

On December 22, Bucharest population took over the city center and Ceauşescu called, for one last time, a meeting of the Politburo, where he decided to intensify repression against the population. But the Minister of Defense, general Vasile Milca (probably to avoid putting the plan into practice) took his own life, and his second in command, general Victor Athanasie Stănculescu, having just returned from Timişoara, ordered Army troops back to their barracks.[19] This deci-

---

nian version, Bucharest, Humanitas, 2006); Vladimir Tismăneanu (ed.), *The Revolutions of 1989* (London: Routledge, 1999); Stelian Tănase, *Istoria căderii regimurilor comuniste. Miracolul revoluţiei* (Bucharest: Humanitas, 2009); Katherine Verdery, Gail Kligman, "Romania After Ceauşescu: Post-Communist Communism," in Ivo Banac (ed.), *Eastern Europe in Revolution* (Ithaca: Cornell University Press, 1992); Steven D. Roper, *Romania: The Unfinished Revolution* (London: Routledge, 1999); Bogdan Murgescu (co-ord.), *Revoluţia română din decembrie 1989: Istorie şi memorie* (Iaşi: Polirom, 2007); Dragoş Petrescu, *Explaining the Romanian Revolution of 1989: Culture, Structure, and Contingency* (Bucharest: Editura Enciclopedica, 2010).

[18] Sergiu Nicolaescu, *Cartea revoluţiei române din decembrie '89* (Bucharest: Editura Ion Cristoiu, 1999), 122.

[19] Siani-Davies, *The Romanian Revolution*, 135.

sion allowed the crowd to enter into Central Committee building, as Ceaușescu fled by helicopter.

At nightfall, gunshots were heard around the Central Committee building, quickly spreading over the entire city. This violence was attributed to "terrorists," alleged fanatic supporters of Nicolae Ceaușescu's regime. The Army took once again to the streets, and the people were given weapons in order to "defend the Revolution." Starting on the night of December 22, the streets of Bucharest were the stage for a plethora of uncoordinated armed forces—Army, Securitate, Miliția (police), armed civilians—who shot at each other, leaving hundreds dead and thousands injured. In that state of uncertainty and chaos, amplified by rumors spread by Romanian Television, most victims were the result of friendly fire and miscommunication. There was no functional coordination between various forces of public order, as units attacked each other, civilians confused soldiers for terrorists and the other way around.[20]

On the evening of December 22, the creation of a provisional institution of power was announced: the National Salvation Front, made up mostly of former Communist Party leaders marginalized by Ceaușescu over the last two decades (such as Ion Iliescu, Silviu Brucan, Alexandru Bârlădeanu, Dumitru Mazilu and others). Several Army officers, including the generals Victor Athanasie Stănculescu and Mihai Chițac, were included over the next few days in the new political structure.[21]

Shootings continued in the city over the next few days, their intensity decreasing only after December 25, when the Romanian Television announced that the Ceaușescus had been trialed and executed. The tally of the violence was 1,104 dead and 3,352 wounded or which 162 were killed and 1,107 wounded before December 22, while the rest of the victims (the great majority: 942 dead and 2,245 wounded) came after that date. Exactly 543 people died in Bucharest, and 561 in the rest of the country. Investigations carried out between 1990 and

---

[20] Ibid., 187.
[21] For the makeup of the NSF Committee and the role of the former *nomenklatura* in the December events, see Raluca Grosescu, "Political Regrouping of the Romanian Nomenklatura during the 1989 Revolution," *Romanian Journal of Society and Politics*, no. 1, 2004.

1994 indicated that the Army was responsible for 333 dead and 648 wounded, while the Securitate was responsible for 63 dead and 46 wounded. No responsible party has been identified for the rest of 708 dead and 2,658 wounded.[22]

December 1989 is still a controversial historical topic. The pace and amplitude of the events, the role played by the Army in the repression and then in the fall of Nicolae Ceauşescu, the role of the *nomenklatura* in forming the new power structures, the violent chaos after December 22, as well as the so-called "terrorists," who were never identified, have generated several hypotheses regarding the fall of communism in Romania. Three main types of scenarios can be discerned from narratives regarding December 1989: the "pure revolution" (accomplished through the spontaneous revolt of the population); the "coup d'état" (organized by Soviet or Hungarian secret services); and, the "diversion" (organized after December 22 by the communist elites who took power, in order to consolidate their position).[23]

Beyond such synthetic evaluations, which hardly reflect any analytic consensus, the very reconstruction of the events and the assignment of responsibilities are in themselves problematic. Alongside historians and various official investigative committees, reconstructions and interpretations of events were provided by the trials of the communist leaders involved. Throughout the transition, hundreds of persons were investigated in such trials for crimes committed in December 1989.

II. December 1989 as "Genocidal Repression"

The transitional criminal justice in post-communist Romania started in December 1989 with the speedy trial and execution of Nicolae and Elena Ceauşescu on charges of "genocide" and "undermining state power." By the end of 1990, six more political and military leaders

---

[22] The Archive of Military Prosecutor Offices with the High Court of Cassation and Justice (AMPOHCCJ), unnumbered file, "Synthesis of Aspects Resulting from Investigations Carried Out by Military Prosecutors between 1990 and 1994 regarding the Events of December 1989," 28–29.

[23] For scenarios regarding the December 1989 events, see Ruxandra Cesereanu, *Decembrie '89. Deconstrucţia unei revoluţii* (Iaşi: Polirom, 2004).

had been tried and convicted for "genocide." These trials—character-ized by spurious procedures and the building of charges based on an amalgam of accusations that could not be proven and phantasmagori-cal statements—officialized the narrative of "genocidal" repression in December 1989 perpetrated both before and after December 22 by the Securitate and "terrorists." Bolstered by the trials, the "genocide" ver-sion of events was borrowed in the public discourse by various political and civic actors, who built their legitimacy and public identity around the events of the Revolution.

On December 25, 1989, Nicolae and Elena Ceaușescu were exe-cuted by a firing squad after a secret trial that lasted 55 minutes. The trial was a mockery of juridical procedures and it ended with a sen-tence that had been decided on before hand by the new political lead-ers.[24] The trial of the Ceaușescu couple was the "political trial"[25] par excellence, in which both the judge and the defense attorney acted as accusers. The list of charges, only two pages long, accused the two dictators, without specificity or proof, of "genocide," "undermin-ing state power," "diversionary acts" and "undermining the national economy."[26] Additionally, the accusations issued by the judge included "starving the people" in the so-called rational nutrition programs, the policy of systematic razing of villages, erecting "megalomaniac build-ings," embezzling the country's riches, destroying the national culture, as well as the "willful neglect" of supplying the Army forces with "war technology worthy of modern times." These policies were invoked as evidence of a premeditated "genocide" of two decades, for "slowly but

---

[24] Silviu Brucan, *De la capitalism la socialism și retur. O biografie între două revoluții* (Bucharest: Nemira, 1998), 235.

[25] By "political trials" we understand judicial procedures in defiance of cri-minal law, with the purpose of issuing convictions that set an example and serve a political agenda, based on uncertain accusations, not proven by proper evidence. See Ron Christenson, *Political Trials: Gordian Knots in the Law* (New Brunswick, NJ: Transaction Press, 1999).

[26] The Archive of the Territorial Military Tribunal of Bucharest (ATMTB), file no. 417/2003, Reconstruction of case file 1/1989 of the Bucharest Exceptional Military Tribunal, "Indictment of December 24, 1989 of the Bucharest Military Prosecutor Directorate." The original file of the Ceaușescu trial disappeared right after December 1989, and was reconsti-tuted as late as 2003 based on copies recovered from various sources.

surely destroying the Romanian people and national minorities."[27] The court included, therefore, under the heading of "genocide," charges that reflected state policies pursued throughout Ceauşescu's rule, which involved an entire political and administrative apparatus. Such a legal interpretation was abusive. Irrespective of the brutality of the Ceauşescu regime, it was historically inappropriate and legally impossible to prove that the dictator intended to destroy the Romanian people.

Nicolae Ceauşescu was simultaneously accused for the bloody repression between December 16 and 22, 1989. "Thousands of dead" were mentioned as victims of the "genocide" ordered by the dictator in the main cities of Romania. Even though the minutes of the trial did not specify a number of victims, the judge claimed it was 64,000 dead and wounded.[28] No written evidence was submitted, and no witnesses took the stand. These charges, considered by the court "notorious and incontestable activities, which do not need to be proven," were characterized as "genocide" aiming at "the physical and psychological destruction of the entire community in our country."[29] Invoking "genocide" for the events of December 1989 is in itself inadequate, in terms of both the Romanian criminal code and of relevant international conventions.[30] The group affected by repression was a political group opposing the Ceauşescu regime, and not a "national, ethnic, racial or religious group" as mentioned in the legislation. Even though the number of victims in the Romanian revolution was considerable, invoking even a "partial destruction" of the "national group" would have been inappropriate, given that the entire nation had not taken to the streets.

The sentence states that the "genocide" of December had been prepared by recruiting and training "in secret military groups with high

---

[27] Ibid., "Sentence nr. 1 of December 25, 1989 of the Extraordinary Military Tribunal," 4, 7, 8.

[28] Domniţa Ştefănescu, "Stenograma procesului Ceauşescu," in *Cinci ani din istoria României. O cronologie a evenimentelor Decembrie 1989 —Decembrie 1994* (Bucharest: Maşina de Scris, 1995), 36.

[29] ATMTB, case file no. 417/2003, "Sentence no. 1 of 25 December, 1989, of the Extraordinary Military Tribunal," 3, 6, 8.

[30] Neither art. 357 of the Romanian criminal code, nor the *Conventioin on the Prevention and Punishment of the Crime of Genocide* (UN Resolution 230 of 9 December 1948) include in their definition of genocide political groups, only national, ethnic, racial or religious groups.

quality military technology and training, to be used [by Ceauşescu] if needed against the Romanian people." The repression was attributed not to state institutions, but to "mercenary and terrorist forces" directly subordinated to Nicolae Ceauşescu. Trial documents did not mention the involvement of the Securitate or the Miliţia. In the case of the Army, the court not only obscured its role in the repression, but presented it as a victim of the Ceauşescu regime: "Obsessed by a fear of the people, whom they hated, the two dictators, in parallel with dismantling the Romanian Army, which they did not trust, seeing it as the military arm of the people, deliberately neglected to supply it and robbed it of the possibility of training properly."[31]

The trial of Nicolae and Elena Ceauşescu, therefore, produced a false narrative on the 1989 events, presenting them as a revolt of the entire nation against the dictatorship, followed by a "genocide" ordered by the two defendants and perpetrated not by state institutions, but by obscure forces, generically referred to as "terrorists." By its hasty character and the absence of any evidence, the trial missed the opportunity to clarify the chain of command of the repression, sweeping under the rug the responsibility of the upper Party hierarchy, as well as that of the Army and the Securitate.

The convictions for "genocide" continued throughout 1990. In January, four close associates of Nicolae Ceauşescu, among them the Minister of the Interior Tudor Postelnicu, and three members of the CPEx (Emil Bobu, Ion Dincă and Manea Mănescu)[32] were accused of failing to oppose the dictator's decision to violently repress the protests, as well as of directly coordinating the repression in various cities. The charges included killing and injuring "thousands of men and women, children and youth, adults and old people, of all social strata," with the "direct intention of destroying the community which peace-

---

[31] ATMTB, case file no. 417/2003, "Sentence no. 1 of December 25, 1989 of the Extraordinary Military Tribunal," 3, 6, 8.

[32] Tudor Postelnicu—Minister of the Interior and deputy member of the CPEx; Emil Bobu—secretary of the Central Committee of the CPR in charge of cadre and organizational issues and member of the CPEx Permanent Bureau; Ion Dincă—first deputy prime minister and deputy member of the CPEx Permanent Bureau; and Manea Mănescu—member of the CPEx Permanent Bureau.

fully called for the removal of the dictatorial system."[33] The evidence submitted were the minutes of the two CPEx sessions of December 17 and 22, 1989 as well as a transcript of a teleconference on December 21, in which the accused had taken no position toward Nicolae Ceaușescu's intention of violently intervening against the protesters. The four were accused of having "participated in committing genocide by approving measures taken by the dictator, even though, in line with the prerogatives incurred by their positions, they had the possibility of preventing them."[34] Other charges were: orders given to Ministry of Interior troops, direct participation in the repression in Bucharest, Timișoara, Brașov and Sibiu, and involvement in "the theft of a large number of bodies, incinerating them and inscribing them on the list of fraudulent defectors."[35]

The charges did not cover, however, only the days preceding the flight of Ceaușescu, but also the violence from December 22 to 31, 1989. As in the case of the Ceaușescu trial, the panel of judges looked more like a punishment committee, barring the accused from speaking, declaring their guilt from the start, and invoking eccentric and baseless accusations alongside documentary evidence. One such example was the so-called "ZZ plan," or "the end of all ends," an alleged plan to poison water in the capital and destroy dams across the country in order to decimate the population of Romania.[36] The coordination of "terrorist" troops after December 22 was also mentioned in the trial, the defendants being barred from expressing any opinion on this issue.

Since capital punishment was abolished early 1990, the four defendants were sentenced to life imprisonment for "genocide," having their entire estates confiscated and being stripped of military rank. The same series of sentences also targeted General Iulian Vlad, head of the former Securitate, and general Andruța Ceaușescu, the dictator's brother and head of the School of Military Officers of the Ministry of the Interior in Băneasa. The first was accused of ordering the repression deployed by the Securitate at a national level. The second was

---

[33] AMPOHCCJ, case file no. 2/P/1990, "List of charges on January 22, 1990," 2.
[34] Ibid., 5.
[35] ATMTB, case file no. 33/1990 , "Sentence no. 2/2 February 1990," 5, 9.
[36] AMPOHCCJ, case file no. 2/P/1990, "List of charges of 22 January 1990," 5.

charged with coordinating Securitate regular troops in repressing the protests in Bucharest, as well as of killing protesters himself.[37]

These sentences continued to present the Revolution as genocidal repression. In contrast, with the Ceaușescu trial, where violence was blamed on forces extraneous to the Romanian state, the 1990 sentences pointed to the responsibility of the leadership of the Interior Ministry and the Securitate in the plight of the victims (those killed before the dictator's flight from Bucharest). However, the trials did not indicate the exact manner in which the orders were carried out and by whom, which the press at the time presented as a failure of justice:

> In our opinion, the charges were "thin," and the "discretion" of the panel in finding out details which are essential in the perpetration of the genocide, inexplicable! . . . What exactly did Bobu do in the Martyr Town [Timișoara]? Whom did he order to shoot at the protesters, and who among them ordered the Securitate to do so? What are the names of the individuals who were ordered to organize the disappearance of the dead? Who knew of this plan, aside from him [Bobu] and Dăscălescu, who, under pressure from the masses, promised to return the dead to their families? All these questions still go unanswered. Did the prosecution fail to find a single witness, even in Timișoara? Or have they failed to even try to do so? . . . The cross-examination was designed in a way that prevents us from finding out anything.[38]

The charges remained vague and imprecise, mixing facts, which could be proven (such as the order to shoot at the protesters), with fantasy scenarios (e.g., the plan ZZ or the coordination of unidentified "terrorist" troops). Extending the charges beyond December 22 insinu-

---

[37] AMPOHCCJ, case file no. 81/P/1990, "List of charges of 17 July 1990," 1–28, AMPOHCCJ, case file no. 65/P/1990, "List of charges of February 27, 1990," 1–23. General Iulian Vlad was sentenced to nine years' in prison and dishonorable discharge for complicity to genocide; Andruța Ceaușescu was sentenced to life in prison and dishonorable discharge for instigation to genocide and aggravated murder, see Domnița Ștefănescu, *Cinci ani din istoria României,* 156.

[38] Emil Munteanu "Sentința s-a pronunțat, întrebările persistă," *România Liberă,* February 6, 1990.

ated an association between "terrorists" and Securitate troops, lending credibility to the scenario of their existence. These trials had the role of distorting history,[39] not only by improperly accusing the defendants of "genocide," but also by invoking imaginary facts with no real basis. The epistemic value of the trials was compromised by a willingness to pronounce exemplary sentences, which ran against finding out what the course of events was, and against their correct legal evaluation.

The Political Instrumentation of "Genocidal Repression"

The idea that there was a "genocide" in Romania in December 1989 was taken over by various political and civic actors. In Romanian society, the term genocide had a significant posterity during transition, being used generically to describe the repression in December, thus serving as a rhetorical weapon in the political competition.

On December 25, a communiqué from the National Salvation Front announcing the execution of the Ceaușescu couple for "genocide,"[40] mentioned a death tool of 60,000 victims, a flagrant inadvertence, even though the actual documents of the trial did not report any figure. Cashing in on the general hostility of the population toward the old regime, the exaggeration of the amplitude of the repression reported by the new authorities and the evocation of "terrorists" and "genocide" against the nation had the role of securing public consensus over the execution of Nicolae Ceaușescu. It also granted legitimacy to the new power as adversary of the dictatorship and of the "generalized massacre" perpetrated by the *ancient regime*. Besides, the artisans of the process, like the president Ion Iliescu, justified the hasty execution of the dictator by evoking the military state of emergency, the need for national security and the need to stop the "terrorists,"

---

[39] For the manner in which trials can distort history, see Michael Schudson, "Dynamics of Distortion in Collective Memory," in Daniel L. Schacter, *Memory Distortion: How Minds, Brains, and Society Reconstruct the Past* (Cambridge MA: Harvard University Press, 1995).

[40] Press release of the Council of NSF, *Monitorul Oficial*, December 26, 1989, Year I, no. 3.

defined as Ceaușescu sympathizers: "It was first of all a matter of security. Because we were not sure that the two could not flee. The haste in
which this trial was carried out was a measure taken precisely to limit
suffering and loss of human life. There were still Ceaușescu sympathizers who wanted to grab power. And I think this decision was correct,
because right after the execution, the violence stopped in the capital.
It was a trial carried out under exceptional conditions, and I repeat:
I don't think it was a mistake."[41] Silviu Brucan stressed the same idea:
"The decision we made proved correct after the trial was televised.
Most terrorists immediately surrendered."[42]

The "terrorists," a veritable leitmotif of the 1989 moment, have
never been identified and are still one of the great mysteries of events
in December. Even though the National Salvation Front announced
on December 26 that it had formed extraordinary military tribunals to
prosecute "terrorist activities," none has ever been tried. Of the hundreds of people who were arrested on suspicion of "terrorist activities," only four have been brought to court for illegal possession of fire-
arms.[43] A report of the military prosecutor offices in 1994 claimed that
many "suspects" were arrested either accidentally, as a result of misunderstandings, or by following unverified denunciations.[44]

---

[41] Interview with Ion Iliescu by Raluca Grosescu, Bucharest, October 25,
2005.
[42] Interview with Silviu Brucan by Raluca Grosescu, Bucharest, January 17,
2005.
[43] AMPOHCCJ, "The Synthesis of Aspects Resulting from Investigations
Carried Out by the Military Prosecutors between 1990 and 1994 on the
Causes Regarding the Events of December 1989," 255–259.
[44] Ibid., 249–251. The military prosecutors mention many such cases: a deaf-
mute citizen was suspected of speaking foreign languages and immediately
he was thought to be a terrorist. Some people were arrested only for having
dark beards and complexions, being taken for Arab citizens (some rumors
referred to terrorists as mercenaries recruited by Ceaușescu in the Middle
East). Other people were accused only for being related to various Securitate officers or Party officials. Some people who were wounded were reported
to the police as being under the influence of illegal drugs, and immediately detained as "terrorists." Dozens of arrests, the report indicated, come
from denunciation calls made by abandoned concubines who accused their
former partners of being "terrorists." There are even cases of people being
reported as "terrorists" simply because they chased a bus or a tram, thus
seeming "agitated and suspect."

The invocation of this symbolic figure of the enemy legitimized the new political leaders as victors against the "foes of the Revolution" and as artisans of social pacification,[45] which was endangered by the specter of "genocide." In the first half of 1990, the press close to the NSF emphasized the identification of the Front with the Revolution itself, through its role in stopping the "genocide": "The Front is the emanation of our Revolution, it is our blood, our hope, our sweat, our life. It is the people itself, since it made the Revolution happen, since it put a stop to the genocide."[46] This type of discourse is emblematic of NSF leaders, who continued as late as the 2000s to present the Front as savior of the people in December 1989: "The front finalized the Revolution. It created a political platform and secured peace in society, at a time when blood was flowing on the streets of Romanian cities."[47]

In this way, the narrative of the "genocide" in December, officialized with the execution of Nicolae and Elena Ceaușescu and the prosecution of their cronies, was instrumented by the representatives of the new power into a simple equation: NSF = Peace = the People. The latter rendered powerless, at least on short term, any criticism leveled at the Front for its continuity with the new regime.[48]

The version of "genocidal repression" was also taken over by associations of victims of the Revolution, especially after 2004, when investigations into the December 1989 events were threatened by the statute of limitations,[49] and the violence post-December 22 had still not been investigated. In 2004, an association of revolutionaries called *21 Decembrie* filed a criminal suit against several political and military leaders, among whom former president Ion Iliescu, accusing them of "genocide" and "instigation to war": "Aside from Stănculescu, who

---

[45] Alexandru Gussi, *Usages du passé et démocratisation. Le rapport des partis politiques roumains à la période communiste*, PhD thesis for the Institute of Political Studies of Paris, 2007, 59.

[46] *Adevărul*, February 24, 1990.

[47] Interview with Ioan Mircea Pașcu (politician, member and ideologist of the NSF and successor parties led by Ion Iliescu) by Raluca Grosescu, Bucharest, November 15, 2005.

[48] Alexandru Gussi, *Usages du passé*, 59.

[49] Starting in 1991, the crimes of the revolution were mostly classified as murder or instigation to murder, crimes whose statute of limitations was 15 years. Therefore the investigation of these crimes was only possible before 2005. See Grosescu and Ursachi, *Justiția penală de tranziție.*, 113.

has to be prosecuted for the genocide in Timişoara, after December 22, 1989, Ion Iliescu and his acolytes instigated to war against those to shouted "Down with communism." It was a genocide against the entire people, instigation to war on a national level."[50] In 2007, the legal action was filed again, and the president of the association Teodor Mărieş said that there were witnesses willing to testify that Ion Iliescu, willfully and deliberately, took no measures to stop the violent chaos in the capital after December 22: "When Ion Iliescu returned from the Ministry of Defense, asked by the exasperated revolutionaries about the way in which bullets were flying everywhere on the night of 22–23 December, Iliescu answered: "Let them shoot, lads. We have to have some dead, that's how revolutions are like."[51] For the associations of the victims, the employment of the "genocide" accusation had a double role. On the one hand, this particular legal classification would have ensured that the crimes of the Revolution did not fall under the statute of limitations, and those responsible could be prosecuted at any time. This logic was also employed for the communist crimes committed before December 1989. As the Romanian criminal code provided a fifteen-year statute of limitation for homicide, while the crimes against humanity were not defined and punished, many former political prisoners and decommunization activists found in the "genocide" legal classification a possible, although misleading, solution for convicting human rights violations perpetrated before 1989, as the contributions by Iacob and Vasile point out in the present volume. On the other hand, this legal classification was clearly a weapon used against Ion Iliescu, in an equation robbing him of his revolutionary legitimacy: NSF/Ion Iliescu = instigation to war = enemy of the people. Lacking concrete proof, the suit filed by the association *21 Decembrie* did not result in legal proceedings.[52]

---

[50] Interview with Teodor Mărieş (President of the *21 Decembrie* Association) by Raluca Grosescu, January 17, 2007.

[51] Statement by Teodor Mărieş, *NewsPad*, May 18, 2007.

[52] By November 2011, the date this article was completed.

III. December 1989 as the Responsibility of the Party, Miliția and Securitate

In 1991, the prosecutions for "genocide" came to an end, in parallel with the normalization of the political situation and the consolidation of power by the NSF. A new stage of the transitional criminal justice, characterized by stricter observance of procedures and legal classification, started with the trials against many officials in the Communist Party, the Miliția, and the Securitate, as well as the revision of the sentences of "genocide" pronounced in 1990.

On June 4, 1990, 24 members of the CPEx were accused of "genocide." The list of charges included "the destruction of human communities, consisting of the masses of revolutionaries"[53] in December 1989. This accusation proposed an image of the repression as "planned massacre," with the intent of destroying the entire population of the insurgent cities, to "raze to the ground" Timișoara and Bucharest. The evidence was based on the minutes of the two CPEx meetings of December 17 and 22, as well as on proof of personal involvement of some of the accused in coordinating repression in various cities of the country. Victims were not called to testify. No list of their names was drawn up as evidence.

During the trial, legal classifications were changed several times, proposing different narratives on the responsibility of the accused. The court abandoned from the start the charge of "genocide" stating for the first time that, after 1989, neither the Romanian criminal code nor the international conventions allowed the repression of a political group of protesters (the December 1989 protesters) to be classified as "genocide," which definition only referred to ethnic, racial, religious or national groups.

In March 1991, the court decided that the CPEx meeting of December 17 was not politically relevant, since the decision to repress the protests in Timișoara was not made by statutory procedure, and that "the cowardly attitude toward the dictator could be condemned

---

[53] Mircea Bunea, *Praf în ochi. Procesul celor 24 1–2* (Bucharest: Scripta, 1994). "List of charges from June 4, 1990 of the General Prosecutor's Office, the Military Prosecutor Directorate," 98–99.

morally, but not legally." Consequently, the responsibility for ordering the repression between December 17 and 21 belonged solely to Nicolae Ceauşescu, not the members of the CPEx.[54] However, the CPEx meeting of December 22 was taken into consideration, the court arguing that, after the mass meeting of December 21 in Bucharest, it had become "evident" that there was, all over the country, a movement of solidarity with Timişoara. For the CPEx members who had attended that meeting, the court considered the charge of "aiding and abetting the criminal" Nicolae Ceauşescu. Also, the court considered the direct involvement of some of the defendants in the military operations in Timişoara, Târgu Mureş, and Cluj. In these cities there had been a large number of victims. But these actions were classified as "negligence in the line of duty" committed during "operations of restoring public order," with no intention of violently repressing the protests.[55] Thus, the members of the CPEx who took part in the December 17 session and who had not coordinated operations in these cities were acquitted. The others were convicted for "aiding and abetting a criminal" and "negligence in the line of duty," and given sentences of between two and five and a half years' imprisonment.[56]

This sentence created a different narrative about the Revolution than the one evoked in the previous trials. First, the charge of "genocide" was abandoned, even though the charge of "aiding and abetting" continued to make reference to "genocide" but perpetrated only by Nicolae Ceauşescu. The violence was no longer presented as willful repression against the entire nation, but as an "operation to restore public order" by the state authorities, which implicitly put into question the very legitimacy of the Revolution. Second, the role of the defendants in the repression was minimized. Invoking procedural matters, the court laid the responsibility of the military intervention from December 17 to 21 exclusively on Nicolae Ceauşescu, thus sweeping under the rug the role of the accused as decision makers in state policies. Interpreting the repression post-December 22 as simply "aiding

---

[54] ATMTB, case file no. 126/1990, "Sentence no. 11 of March 25, 1991 of the Bucharest Military Tribunal, Inferior Section," 51–58.

[55] Ibid.

[56] For the sentences issued to the members of the CPEx see Grosescu and Ursachi, *Justiţia penală de tranziţie*, 139–143.

and abetting" or "negligence in the line of duty" gave the impression that the CPEx members had no intention of using violence to repress the protesters.

After this sentence was appealed, the Military section of the Supreme Court of Justice decided, in December 1991, that even those charges were baseless, since there was no evidence to prove that the members of the CPEx had decided "expressly or tacitly" the repression of the Revolution.[57] As for the direct coordination of operations in the field, the court decided that the accused were there "in order to solve possible problems with supplies, and to provide public order and peace,"[58] thus exonerating them completely. Another argument taken into consideration by the judges was the absence of precise lists of victims, and the lack of correlation between their death and orders issued by the accused. All defendants were acquitted. This sentence meant that, aside from Ccaușescu and his four close associates who had already been convicted, no Party dignitary was considered guilty of the repression in December 1989. The court ignored any political responsibility on the part of the CPEx as a collective ruling body of the party-state, even though, according to the Constitution, it was the regime's ruling body.

The sentence was, however, contested by extraordinary appeal[59] in early 1992. The Prosecutor General of Romania underlined the decision-making position held by the members of the CPEx and the ruling role played by the Communist Party. He proposed that the accused be prosecuted for first-degree murder and as accomplices. All the defendants received sentences between eight and sixteen years in prison.[60] In 1993, the sentences for "genocide" given to the associates

---

[57] ATMTB, case file no. 126/1990, "Decision no. 53, December 12, 1991 of the Supreme Court of Justice—Military Section," 12–13, 25.

[58] Ibid., 39.

[59] According to the criminal code, the appeal in cancellation was, until 2004 when it was annulled, an extraordinary means of appeal for the General Prosecutor or the Minister of Justice against definitive decisions. In criminal matters, the appeal could be made in first entry trials due to a wrong legal classification or for improper procedure in court.

[60] ATMTB, case file no. 126/1990, "Extraordinary Appeal of the General Prosecutor of Romania,"' 8, 10; "Decision no. 37, April 20, 1992 of the Supreme Court of Justice—Seven Judge Panel," 21.

of Ceauşescu were reviewed as instigation or complicity to first-degree murder.[61]

As opposed to the convictions in 1990, which excessively politicized the charges, in defiance of the law, the first two convictions in the CPEx trial showed that the judges once again obscured the political dimension of the crimes. They framed them within a purely technical narrative. Ignoring the political significance of the facts in transitional justice, they generated a situation in which these trials lost their epistemic function.

The flagrant discrepancy between the "genocide" prosecutions in 1990 and the acquittal of the CPEx members in late 1991 for the same actions demonstrated a lack of predictability of the act of justice. It also created confusion by advancing divergent narratives of the past. As Marc Osiel shows, if the judiciary is not predictable and if it does not treat similar cases in a similar manner, it compromises not only its narrative function and role in building collective memory, but justice itself.[62]

The final conviction of the CPEx members in 1992 did however establish their responsibility for the repression before Ceauşescu fled. Reviewing the accusations of "genocide" and reclassifying their acts as murder did grant coherence to the Revolution trials and to the narratives they produced. The repression was presented as action against a political group, not against an entire nation, and the culpability was laid on the top-level Party hierarchy and the leadership of the Ministry of the Interior and the Securitate.

Blaming the Ministry of the Interior and Exonerating the Army

In parallel with the CPEx trial, Party leaders at the local level and many military men were put on trial. Between 1991 and 1994, during Ion Iliescu's first presidential term, the trials were directed mainly at

---

[61] For health or age reasons, many of the convicted were released before they carried out their sentences. Also, in 1994 and 1995 Ion Iliescu successively pardoned all the members of the CPEx who had been incarcerated, with no public justification for his decision. The last of the convicted were released from prison in September 1996.

[62] Osiel, *Mass Atrocity*, 136.

the Party and the Ministry of the Interior (which included the Miliția and Securitate) cadres, as opposed to the small number of Ministry of Defense (Army) officers. Accusations were made only in relation to events before December 22, and only to violence outside Bucharest. No action was brought in relation to the victims in Bucharest. In relation to the victims in Timișoara, Sibiu, Cluj and other cities in Romania, 198 people were prosecuted.[63]

Numerous defendants were convicted for murder, such as secretaries of the Communist Party Central Committee or Party heads at the local level, as well as officials of the Securitate and Miliția in counties and cities where violence had occurred. In many instances, the cases were sent back to prosecutors, as judges deemed the investigations incomplete. Other defendants were found guilty only of "negligence in the line of duty" or "bodily harm inflicted with melee weapons." Ion Iliescu granted amnesty to this type of acts by executive order in the first days of 1990, before any trial began.[64] The decision, which was not publicly justified in any way, was interpreted by the victims of the Revolution as a form of tacit exoneration of some of those responsible for the repression. As in the CPEx case, some of those convicted immediately benefited from the presidential pardons. The number of convictions issued between 1991 and 1994 was nevertheless significant. Exactly 132 individuals were found guilty out of 198 individual trials.[65]

The military officers brought to court were less numerous and there were no convictions. In Timișoara, Cluj, Târgu Mureș, and Bucharest, the courts decided either to acquit, or to suspend procedures. In addition, until 1996, some military officers prosecuted for

---

[63] AMPOHCCJ, "The Synthesis of Aspects Resulting from Investigations Carried Out by the Military Prosecutors between 1990 and 1994 on the Causes Regarding the Events of December 1989," 28, 36, 127.

[64] *Monitorul Oficial*, no. 2, January 5, 1990, "Law Decree no. 3 of January 4, 1990 on amnesty for crimes and pardon for certain sentences."

[65] Processing the information from 95 criminal cases results in the following statistic: of the 95 military men indicted, 51 received final sentences, 14 were acquitted, 12 cases were forwarded to the prosecutor's office for final processing, while 18 defendants were amnestied by the decree issued on January 4, 1990. At the same time, five people who were convicted were pardoned by Ion Iliescu. See Grosescu and Ursachi, *Justiția penală de tranziție*, 163–164.

actions taken during the Revolution were promoted, some reaching the rank of general.

The exoneration of the Army and the assignation of blame on the Ministry of the Interior are proven by statistics linking the number of victims caused by the two institutions and the number of people prosecuted from each. In 1994, a report by the office of the Military Prosecutor offices revealed the following figures:[66]

	Dead and wounded	Prosecuted
Interior Ministry (Miliția and Securitate)	63 dead, 46 wounded	92 officers
Ministry of National Defense (The Army)	333 dead, 648 wounded	19 officers (+26 conscripts)

Statistics showing the number of victims caused by actions by the Interior Ministry and the Ministry of Defense and the number of people from those ministries who were prosecuted[67]

These trials also involved thirty-eight members of the central and local Party apparatus.[68] Even though the Army was responsible for a much larger number of victims, as shown by investigations, Army officers were not convicted. The image that these trials created was that the bloody repression of the Revolution was almost exclusively the work of Miliția and Securitate troops. The Army appeared as backing the masses of revolutionaries. The lists of charges between 1991 and 1994 unanimously declared the "act of salvation," which the Army had done in fraternizing with the people, sweeping its repressive role under the rug.

This image served the interests of the NSF, which had been associated with the Army, granting it the role of vanquisher of the dictatorship. "Victory in the Revolution" was attributed in public discourse to the NSF (self-described as "an emanation of the will of the people") in

---

[66] The figures refer to victims identified in criminal investigations. For the rest of 765 dead and 2,658 wounded in the revolution, the responsible parties are not mentioned.

[67] AMPOHCCJ, "The Synthesis of Aspects Resulting from Investigations Carried Out by the Military Prosecutors between 1990 and 1994 on the Causes Regarding the Events of December 1989," 29, 36.

[68] Ibid., 36.

collaboration with the "glorious national Army." The two institutions thus mutually granted each other a legitimacy that was very hard to question. As Silviu Brucan put it, prosecuting military officers would have been contrary to the political interests of the NSF: "After December 1989, because of the political situation . . . the Army was the only factor of stability in this country. Therefore we could not say that some generals had been loyal to Ceaușescu, while others had been dissidents, that the Army opened fire on the crowd in Timișoara, Sibiu, Cluj, and in Bucharest on December 21—even though this is the historical truth . . .) It would have been irresponsible to open such a discussion at a time when this was the only thing we could rely on."[69]

As opposed to the Army, the most popular institution of the state,[70] the Miliția and the Securitate were hated by the population, and they could be much more easily labeled "anti-national" and associated with the violence perpetrated against the protesters. This dichotomy between the Army and the Securitate was formulated first at Ceaușescu's trial by the defense attorney turned accuser: "You dressed your Securitate officers as officers of the Ministry of National Defense to deal one more blow to the Army so it wouldn't join the people, so the people would hate the Army."[71] By the same token, criminal investigations into violence after Nicolae Ceaușescu fled, even though not resulting in prosecutions before 1996, supported the same narrative: the Securitate troops were associated with the mysterious terrorists. If the theory of the "terrorist plot" was eventually abandoned for lack of

---

[69] See Bunea, *Praf în ochi*, 163.

[70] Historically, including the communist period, the Army was for Romanians one of the symbolic pillars of the nation-building. The image of the Army as a heroic institution was systematically bolstered in school textbooks and in historiography. Starting with 1990, opinion polls show constantly that the Army was for Romanians the most trusted state institution. In 1995 and 1996, over 90 percent of the population had full confidence in the Army (*The Barometer of Public Opinion*, The Open Society Foundation, Synthesis, 1999). A poll from 2006 also showed that 77 percent of the population of Romania trusted the Army, compared to 55 percent trust in the presidency, 20 percent in political parties, and 19 percent in Parliament (*Realitatea.net*, October 22, 2006).

[71] Romulus Cristea, *Revoluția 1989* (Bucharest: România Pur și Simplu, 2006), 236.

evidence, no alternative explanation was offered for the violence continuing after December 22.

The exoneration of the Army in the 1990–1994 trials was perceived by the victims of the Revolution as a concealment of real responsibilities: "In the early 1990s, the trial in Timişoara put under accusation officers of the Miliţia and Securitate, which was a form of justice, but most of the crimes were really committed by the Army. For us it was important that the investigations run further so it would be aimed at Army generals. Such crime at a national level was simply ignored through the decisions of military prosecutor offices across the country, by their failure to investigate generals and superior officers of the Army involved in the repression."[72]

In conclusion, the trials against the military before 1994 strengthened the narrative founded with the conviction of the CPEx members, according to which the only guilty parties were the leaders of the Party and of the Interior Ministry, described as partisans of the old regime. The Army, which caused the largest number of victims, was guaranteed impunity, thus securing the image of key institution in the "revolutionary victory." After 1994, Revolution trials were interrupted, no important case was prosecuted, and public interest in this topic decreased.

IV. December 1989
and the Responsibility of the Army

The Revolution trials reopened after 1997, once the center right coalition The Democratic Convention of Romania (CDR) came to power. This process was part and parcel of the construction of a new narrative about the events in December. As opposed to the previous period, the trials proved the involvement of the Army in the repression, altering its image of "savior of the nation."

The most emblematic trial of this phase was against generals Victor Athanasie Stănculescu and Mihai Chiţac,[73] who coordinated the repres-

---

[72] Interview with Traian Orban (President of the association *Memorialul Victimelor Revoluţiei din Timişoara* [Memorial for the Victims of the Revolution in Timişoara]), by Raluca Grosescu, Timişoara, January 15, 2007.

[73] As part of the same case, general Stefan Gusa was also investigated, as head

sion in Timișoara. The trial was part of a wider series of prosecutions against Army officers, whose dossiers had been declared incomplete by courts in the early 1990s.[74] Among these, the most significant was the prosecution of the officers responsible for the victims in Cluj. We will analyze the two trials to illustrate the change in the narrative about the Revolution, which had been officialized in previous convictions.

The case of the two generals sheds light on the complex nature of events in December, and the difficult legal problems facing courts, which had to prosecute them. As heads of the armed forces (Stănculescu ranked second in the military hierarchy after the Minister), the two generals executed, between December 17 and 19, the order to repress protests in Timișoara using military ammunition, which left 72 dead and 253 wounded.[75] However, Stănculescu was also the one who ordered the troops on December 22 to go back to their barracks, thus allowing the protesters to enter the Central Committee building, which brought the Army on the side of the people. Both generals held ministerial positions in the first post-1989 governments formed by the NSF. In 1998, they were put on trial for "murder and instigation to commit first degree murder." Class action was brought by 219 wounded people and heirs of those killed, and the material damages were to be paid by the two, together with the Ministry of National Defense.[76]

The defense of the two generals mobilized arguments that were radically opposed to the discourse used in 1990–1994. The Army had presented itself as an unconditional supporter of the people against the tyranny. At their trial, however, the generals argued that the protests in December 1989 started against a "legitimate regime," which it compelled by law to defend.[77] "Recognized by the entire world, the leadership of the Romanian communist state could not become illegitimate from one day to the next," said the Ministry of Defense attorney. If Stănculescu and Chițac emphasized back in 1990 the role they played in the victory of the

---

of the communist Joint Chiefs of Staff, and associate of the NSF after 1989, but died in 1994.

[74] See Grosescu and Ursachi, *Justiția penală de tranziție*, 177.

[75] AMPOHCCJ, case file 11/P/1996, "List of charges of December 1997 for generals in reserve Victor-Atanasie Stănculescu and Mihai Chițac," 4.

[76] Marius Mioc, *Procesele revoluției din Timișoara (1989): documente istorice* (Timișoara: Artires, 2004, 241, 243.

[77] Ibid., 187–188.

Revolution by showing solidarity with the protesters, that discourse had been replaced by a diametrically opposed one, convenient for the purpose of exoneration of responsibility in repressing the protesters.

Another argument of the defense was that, as Army officers, they only carried out orders given by Nicolae Ceauşescu, head of state and commander in chief of the armed forces. The trial thus opened another significant debate: the individual responsibility of military men when faced with an order from a superior officer. The Ministry invoked the "unconditional obligation" to carry out orders as being "a fundamental principle in the functioning of the Army." The generals "had neither the obligation, nor the freedom of having normative opinions, so that, depending on their conclusions, they could have acted in any other way than that dictated by the military code in force at that time."[78] Military men "cannot be considered responsible for executing orders issued by the political power, and the entire responsibility falls on the latter," the Ministry of Defense claimed.[79] Opposed to this position, prosecutor Dan Voinea explained that a military man has an obligation to evaluate the legality of an order, claiming that use of the Army against civilians to restore public order was illegal: "The duty to carry out orders should not be seen as an absolute. Executing an order is necessary, but within limits. It is specified in military codes that an illegal order should not get executed. Not every order has to be carried out. In 1989 many officers refused to fire."[80]

The debate around the Army's actions was central in the proceedings of a trial in Cluj, where one of the defendants was General Iulian Topliceanu, head of the 4th Army Corps. This case was reopened in 1998 after the investigations had been terminated in 1992.[81] The prosecution believed that the order given to the Army to intervene had been illegal, because, according to the Constitution and other laws, the Army "could under no circumstance be used in solving problems related to domestic order (with the exception of calamities and natural

[78] Ibid., 260.

[79] Ibid.

[80] Interview with Dan Voinea by Raluca Grosescu, Bucharest, November 20, 2006.

[81] AMPOHCCJ, case file no. 217/P/ 1997, " Indictment of May 1998," 126–127.

catastrophe)." Domestic orders "were exclusively under the jurisdiction of the Miliția, Securitate troops, firefighters, border police and, to a very small extent, the patriotic guards."[82]

The court in Cluj ruled in 2003, five years from the trial's beginning, when the political power had once again passed to Ion Iliescu's party. The verdict stated that the prosecution, which had claimed that the December 1989 protests were a legitimate form of defense against a dictatorial regime, overstepped its authority. The court argued that the prosecutor's office was not authorized to present the political context, but only to bring to the legal authority's attention deeds that constitute crimes from a purely legal standpoint.[83] Thus, right from the start, the judges considered that any political responsibility on the part of military leaders was irrelevant to the case. The court offered its own interpretation of the political context: since Romania functioned as a dictatorial regime and Nicolae Ceaușescu was "vested with unlimited authority," General Topliceanu could not have resisted the order. Also in defense of the accused, the court contended that rumors during the days of the Revolution that "a foreign intervention in Romania was imminent" could create the "subjective representation" that it was the Army's duty to intervene. Subsequently, "they are not to be blamed for the decision to take the military out in the streets," but only for possible mistakes in coordinating military operations.[84] As a result, the court decided to acquit some of the defendants and to reclassify the acts of General Topliceanu in such way as to fall under the statute of limitations and thus putting an end to the trial.[85]

In the case of the two generals in Bucharest, the court did side with the prosecution. Generals Stănculescu and Chițac were sentenced, in July 1999, for instigating to first-degree murder. They were given fifteen years in jail and were stripped of their rank. [86] Material damages owed to victims and their inheritors were granted to the amount of 36 billion ROL (over 10,000,000 Euros). These were to be paid by the two

---

[82] Ibid., 20.
[83] The Archive of the High Court of Cassation and Justice of Romania (AH-CCJR), case file no. 2956/1998, "Sentința Nr. 33 din 9 aprilie 2003," 20.
[84] Ibid., 39–40.
[85] Ibid., 42.
[86] AHCCJR, "Sentința nr. 9/15 July 1999."

together with the Ministry of Defense. For the first time, an institution of the communist state was declared a responsible and ordered to pay reparations to the victims of repression.

The reaction of the Ministry was prompt. In 1999, Defense Minister Victor Babiuc (member of the Democratic Party, an offshoot of the NSF) claimed that by convicting the two generals and forcing damages on them, the entire Army would be declared guilty, denying its "savior" role in the events of December 1989. It was considered that such a trial constituted an attack against the "Army of the People," essential part of the national being: "If two generals are considered responsible, then the entire Army is considered responsible."[87] This attitude showed how the democratic Ministry of Defense made common cause with the communist one. The Minister went so far as to call for amnesty for the events of December 1989: "If amnesty can secure national peace and stability, I am in agreement with such amnesty."[88]

For prosecutor Dan Voinea, such arguments were but a way of eluding the truth and defend the criminals. He said that hiding the role played by the Army in the repression, far from creating an image of "heroes of the people," it compromises it:

> Saying that if two generals were guilty, the entire Army is guilty, Mr. Babiuc makes a great mistake, because he is discrediting a very important institution, the Army. The Army too has to be defended from criminals who may act under its aegis. We frequently find criminals in the Army, because the Army grants you power. And this power has to be measured, evaluated, controlled, and prosecuted every time it oversteps its legal bounds. Consider that in 1989 no Army unit was attacked by civilians. Therefore the Army was not acting in legitimate self-defense when it opened fire, because it was never attacked by civilians. Not only was it not attacked: civilians were shouting "The Army is with us!" The repression was unjust, and those who gave the order to open fire are guilty. The role of the Army is to defend civilians, not kill them.[89]

---

[87] *Evenimentul Zilei*, July 20, 1999.
[88] *Adevărul*, April 10, 1999.
[89] Interview with Dan Voinea, made by Raluca Grosescu, Bucharest, November 20, 2006.

The Party of Social Democracy in Romania (PDSR) led by Ion Iliescu, in the opposition at the time, took the side of the generals, claiming that the trial was political manipulation:

> The PDSR is unsettled by the sentence issued by the Supreme Court of Justice, as well by the dangerous consequences created by this precedent. In our opinion, the SCJ ruling is not justified by the events in Timişoara, in December 1989, but by the wish of certain parties in the present coalition in power to rewrite history, including with help from the judicial system, and to confirm theses proffered for years, but which have no grounding in reality. . . . The PDSR considers demeaning this gesture made by some political people in power. They turned Justice into a servant of their interests, bringing grave offense to the Army in its entirety, and to the officer corps.[90]

After the PDSR returned to power in 2000, the conviction of the two generals was overturned on procedural grounds. In 2006, when center right parties won the general elections, Stănculescu and Chiţac were sentenced again to fifteen years in prison, the sentence being declared definitive in 2008. In the same electoral cycle, the trial in Cluj resumed, and it ended with the conviction of the defendants prosecuted in 2003. The Revolution trials continued to be systematically dependent on the political interests of various parties that switched power positions. As Dan Voinea pointed out: "Political interests determined the opening of these trials during right-wing governments. For similar reasons they closed during left-wing incumbents. The political factor influenced the continuation or termination of prosecution. Political influence was one of the main causes for which criminal prosecution on the Revolution and the crimes of communism were delayed. In 2000–2004, for instance, I was removed from all these cases. My files were taken away, with no given motivation. When the regime changed, I got my files back. Once again, a political decision."[91]

---

[90] Press release by the PDSR, quoted in *Jurnalul Naţional*, July 17, 1999.
[91] Interview with Dan Voinea, made by Raluca Grosescu, Bucharest, November 20, 2006.

To summarize, the trials between 1997 and 2000 officialized the Army's responsibility towards the victims of December 1989. For the first time, a sentence involved not only individuals, but also a state institution—the Ministry of Defense, which was declared responsible party and ordered to pay damages to the victims. The trials proved the importance of their narrative function because the proceedings established the course of specific events under scrutiny. The courtroom turned into an arena where various perspectives on the nature of the December 1989 moment clashed. Put in the position to justify the role played by the Army in the repression, its commanders radically shifted the discourse they advocated in the previous years. They play the card of the "illegal" nature of the protests. In contrast, the prosecution claimed that the protests against the regime were legitimate, and that the Army's intervention was illegal. This would prove to be the final official version on the basis of the pronouncement of the verdict. Even though the act of justice was dependent on the political context, these trials proved that it was not just the Party, the Miliția, and the Securitate who were to blame. The Army shared of the blame for the victims from the days before Ceaușescu fled from Bucharest. These actions however did not have a major impact on the Army's image in Romania society. Throughout the transition period, it continued to enjoy the population's confidence, with popularity figures of over 60 to 70 percent. In 1997, 84 percent of Romanians fully trusted the Army, while, in September 1999, right after generals Stănculescu and Chițac were convicted, the percentage dropped to 65 percent.[92]

The Revolution trials did not bring justice to all the victims of the period between December 17 and 22. The responsibility for the violence in Sibiu or Brașov, in December 21, has not yet been assigned. Furthermore, the repression in Bucharest between December 21 and 22 has not been mentioned at all in any trial. In several cases, the statute of limitations came into effect, which led to the discontinuation of legal action. After 1997, certain crimes, such as abuse of official position and second degree murder or assault, could no longer be punished.

---

[92] *Barometru de Opinie Publică*, Fundația pentru o Societate Deschisă, Sinteză, 1999.

V. December 1989 as the Result of Incompetence

Most of the Revolution trials were aimed at the repression that had been ordered before 22 December, even though there were many more victims past that date. A single major criminal trial focused on the events that happened after Ceaușescu fled: the case of fifty soldiers killed on the Bucharest Otopeni Airport on the night of December 22 to 23. The prosecution's argument in this case is representative for the violent chaos that set in after December 22. The lawyers proved that the death toll was caused by the negligence of certain officers and the lack of operative coordination between the Ministry of Interior and the Ministry of Defense.

On the evening of December 22, while gunshots were making hundreds of victims in the capital, the chain of command in military operations had broken down and orders sent down the ladder through public radio and television. In this context, there were rumors that the Otopeni Airport was going to be attacked by forces loyal to the dictator. The commanders of Army and Securitate troops, without communicating between themselves, made parallel plans for defending the objective. Upon contact, Army and Securitate troops mistook each other for the expected attackers, and opened deadly fire.[93] In 2001, the trial of the Army and Securitate commanders involved in the operation resulted in prison sentences between four and eight years, and payment of damages together with the Ministry of Defense.[94]

This act of justice officialized the fact that military incompetence was one of the engines of violence, partially demolishing the theory of the "terrorist plot" after December 22. The idea was circulated as early as 1994 by military prosecutors, who pointed to the military's lack of coordination, which resulted in an authority vacuum, confusion, or accidents. These were the main sources of the violence post-December 22:[95] "The events in December caught the Army unprepared, painful

---

[93] AMPOHCCJ, case file no. 59/P/1990, "List of charges of December 17, 1993" 1–4.

[94] Ibid., "Decision nr. 1 of January 27, 2003 of the Supreme Court of Justice—Joint Sections," 18–23.

[95] AMPOHCCJ, "The Synthesis of Aspects Resulting from Investigations Carried Out by the Military Prosecutors between 1990 and 1994 on the Causes Regarding the Events of December 1989," 121, 303.

as it is to admit. . . . The vacuum of power within Army ranks . . . a polarization of authority between commanders of various branches of the armed forces . . . as well as some redundancies in exercising command functions were the background against which some nefarious sequences of events occurred, which unfortunately resulted in too many victims."[96]

This single trial, however, proved insufficient to get a clear image of the chaos produced after Nicolae Ceauşescu fled Bucharest. The absence of investigations and trials continued to leave room for the most diverse of theories, ranging from the involvement of obscure, "terrorist" forces to criminal political interests. For instance, throughout the transition, certain NSF leaders continued to talk about "terrorists," which they identified as Securitate troops or "fanatic supporters of Ceauşescu."[97] In their turn, adversaries of the NSF accuse Ion Iliescu directly of the crimes perpetrated after December 22: "When Ion Iliescu understood that the protesters would never have a communist leading the country, he created this terrorist-Securitate diversion. This was instigation to war at a national scale. The population was given weapons to fight ghosts. They were talking about the glorious Romanian Army who fought the terrorists, just to realize later that the terrorists were their colleagues."[98] The image of the Romanian Revolution thus continues to be fragmented and incomplete.

Conclusions

Examining the epistemic dimension of the Romanian Revolution trials helped us identify the narratives they put in circulation about the events of December 1989, the values they promoted, and the extent to which they were used politically during the transition. The Romanian trials were built on four narratives about the nature of the Revo-

---

[96] Ibid., 15.

[97] Silviu Brucan, *Generaţia irosită. Memorii* (Bucharest: Univers & Calistrat Hogaş, 1992), 230–232; Brucan, *De la capitalism la socialism*, 265, Ion Iliescu, *Revoluţie şi Reformă* (Bucharest: Editura Enciclopedica, 1994), 61–62.

[98] Interview with Teodor Mărieş by Raluca Grosescu, Bucharest, January 17, 2007.

lution and its violent repression. First, convictions issued during the event's immediate aftermath targeted the most visible figures of the regime. They presented the Revolution as a revolt of the entire nation and the repression against the protests as "genocide." The incriminating facts were investigated poorly or were simply made up. Their legal basis could be found neither in Romanian nor in international law. The chain of command for the repression was not identified beyond Nicolae Ceaușescu and his close associates, thus giving the impression that their trials were smokescreens concealing real investigations of the hierarchical responsibility across the entire institutional apparatus. These trials did not contribute to clarifying the events, but they misrepresented them, subsequently distorting history.

The second narrative, created by the trials between 1990 and 1994, proposed an image of repression resulting almost exclusively from the decisions and actions of the Communist Party and the Ministry of the Interior. The repression was no longer characterized as "genocide" directed against the entire nation. The idea that pushed forward was that the Revolution meant the protest of a political group. The first two CPEx sentences, however, brought up the issue of the legitimacy of the demonstrations. Their repression was presented as a simple "operation for restoring order." The acquittal of the accused was based on an interpretation of violence outside the political context. The leading role of the Communist Party in society was not taken into consideration. Nevertheless, the final conviction for "first degree murder" of CPEx members and many officials within the Ministry of the Interior clarified, from a legal standpoint, the events under investigation. The narrative that resulted was, however, fragmented. The selection of the accused almost exclusively from among the Miliția and the Securitate, as well as the exoneration of the Army in spite of the findings of criminal investigations, revealed how trials can build a history of events not only by describing facts, but also by selecting defendants.

The third narrative, created by the trials targeting Ministry of Defense officers (from 1997 onward), complemented the previous one by officially stating that the Army did bear responsibility for violence before Ceaușescu fled the capital. Even though the passage of time robbed them of much of their effectiveness, these trials generated important clarifications regarding the flow of events and the resulting guilt. For the first and only time in Romania, an institution of the communist state (the Ministry of Defense) was declared responsible alongside its leaders, and it was ordered to pay damages to the victims of repression.

With all this progress made in clarifying the facts and in spite of the large number of defendants brought before the courts along the years, the 1989 Revolution still has not been entirely clarified after more than two decades. Even though trials have gradually reconstructed the chain of decision making for the repression, they also nurtured confusion by handing out different sentences for the same deeds and based on the same body of evidence. Such unpredictability in the act of justice, proposing diverging narratives from one trial to the next, or even as part of the same case, prevents the coalescing of a common historical memory. More than that, in some cases, intentional procrastination allowed the coming into effect of the statute of limitation, making further prosecution impossible. The trials concerning the repression in cities such as Braşov and Sibiu were thrown out of court for lack of evidence. No trial whatsoever was held in relation to the military operations of December 21 in Bucharest. Also, the nature of violence after December 22 remains unclear to this day. Aside from the "terrorist" theory invoked in the trials of 1990, only the Otopeni Airport case tried to fill in this information vacuum. The latter created a fourth narrative about the Romanian Revolution: the violent chaos after Nicolae Ceauşescu fled was caused by military incompetence. This lone trial regarding the post-December 22 victims is not sufficient to institute a coherent narrative that would supersede alternative narratives.

In addition to setting an official course of events, the Revolution trials also had a normative function, in the Durkheim understanding of affirming a fundamental set of new rules for a society. The first of these was the *imagology of the Revolution,* which was presented in several registers. Initially, the Revolution was identified with the nation itself. Its legal legitimacy was a direct expression of the popular will. The first trials affirmed this identity, which made any repression illegitimate and contravening to the interest of the country. The idea of socialist legitimacy was completely brushed aside. The repression was declared "genocide," the supreme accusation of trying to destroy the entire nation, which could not have been planned by the Romanian state, but by deviant, "foreign" forces. This explains the need for scenarios such as that involving "terrorists" or the "plan ZZ" of poisoning the water. Even if these were mere fantasies born out of the fears of the moment, such scenarios were necessary to support the idea that the Revolution was the will of the people, without accusing though the Romanian state of being an oppressor of the nation. The matter of the legality of the Revolution was brought up again in the subsequent trials, first in the CPEx trial. Then it was debated in court as argument in the defense of the Army. The Revolution appeared in these narratives either as "disturbance of public peace" by "hooligan elements," or as a coup attempt devised by foreign agents. Both interpretations implied that the communist regime had been legitimate, "recognized by all countries of the world," and that defending it had been obligatory. The convictions, in the end, validated the legitimacy of the December 1989 protest and the illegal nature of the military intervention against them. The verdict therefore reset the relationship between power and civil society: the Party and its coercive apparatus did not have the right to repress political protest. Civil disobedience in the face of abusive power was thus consecrated as a fundamental value of the new society.

The trials also raised *the issue of personal responsibility* in a dictatorial system. In transitional justice, the non-democratic nature of the regime and the impossibility of opposing orders are arguments frequently invoked by the defense. In Romania they were accepted by the judges in two important trials. Acquitting the CPEx members at an initial stage obscured the leading role of the Party as decision maker in the state, describing it rather as a powerless tool in the hands of the dictator. Also, at the trial in Cluj, the first verdict argued that Nicolae Ceaușescu had supreme powers in the state, which made any resistance futile. The final sentences in these cases, as in the trial of generals Stănculescu and Chițac, reaffirmed the legal obligation to evaluate the legality and consequences of an order before executing it. Even in a dictatorship, the courts said, the military or political hierarchy cannot exempt an individual from responsibility. Post-communist justice affirmed the precedence of the liberal values of individual responsibility and the right to question an illegal and immoral order, over values of unconditional obedience and organic solidarity around the institutions of the national state.

Finally, the examination of the narratives created by these trials allows us to evaluate their politicization as weapons for granting and removing legitimacy in election campaigns. The interpretations given to the 1989 moment were a key element in defining the identity of the post-communist political and civic players. Public debates around the Revolution had a subsidiary role, namely that of stating or questioning the role which various actors held in the *ancien régime* or in its over-turning.

The cycles of trials, with their various categories of defendants and incriminating evidence, corresponded to election years. Unsurprisingly, they provided grounds for political legitimacy to the various parties that succeeded each other in power. To this effect, the execution of the Ceauşescus, the conviction of CPEx members, and those of the leader-ship of the Securitate and Miliția in the 1990–1994 trials, overlapped with the interest of the NSF in gaining legitimacy. The latter system-atically tried in early 1990s to set itself apart from Ceauşescu's elite. Simultaneously, the NSF's association with the Army and its image of representative of the nation led to exemption of the Army from its responsibility during the December events. This is how it became important that the Revolution was presented in court as a victory of the Army and the repression as the exclusive responsibility of the Min-istry of Interior. The amnesty declared by Ion Iliescu in January 1990, the systematic pardons and extraordinary appeals, which resulted in the overturning of so many convictions, showed the constant preoccu-pation on the part of the authorities with exonerating high military offi-cials. The parties who branched from the original catch-all NSF con-tinued to claim that the Army played an essential role in the victory of the Revolution. They contended that these 1997 trials, which empha-sized its responsibility, were "political trials" and "offenses brought against the Army."

At the same time, the trials held during the Democratic Conven-tion's administration officially spelled the responsibility of the Army for the repression. They proposed a narrative of events that directly weak-ened the revolutionary legitimacy of president Iliescu and the NSF, providing evidence for their complicity with the initiators of the vio-lence. Their political enemies—not just center-right parties, but many civic organizations, associations of former political prisoners and asso-ciations of victims of the Revolution—used this narrative in the elec-toral struggle, showing the guilty continuities tying Romania's present to its past.

The game of self-granted legitimacy continued in the election cycles that followed. The Revolution trials remained systematically tributary to political interests. This often broke the continuity of the investigations and disrupted the possibility for their resolution in court by stopping or restarting them, by transferring the files from one Prosecutor General to the next. The verdicts also varied depending on who was holding political power at the moment of the judicial decision. All these dependencies bring into question the predictability of the act of justice, and, more fundamentally, its effectiveness in carrying out a narrative function about the past. Even though the trials did contribute to the gradual normalization of the historical discourse on the repressions of December 1989, their epistemic role was partially compromised by the influence of the political factor on justice. The instrumentation of "genocide," the successive acquittals and convictions for the identical charges, as well as the absence of trials in relation to the events post- December 22 make it impossible even to this day to have public consensus on who bears responsibility for the victims of the Romanian revolution.

VLADIMIR PETROVIĆ

Slobodan Milošević in the Hague:
Failed Success of a Historical Trial

The death of Slobodan Milošević, on March 11, 2006, in the detention unit of the International Criminal Tribunal for the former Yugoslavia (ICTY) put an abrupt end to yet another process dubbed as "the
trial of the century." Three days later the Trial Chamber took notice
of the death of the accused, hence terminating the case IT-02-54 that
dragged on for more than four years toward its anticlimactic end. Disappointment among the interested parties was as deep as the earlier
feeling of success upon his bringing to justice. "I deeply regret the
death of Slobodan Milošević. It deprives the victims of the justice they
need and deserve . . . It is a great pity for justice that the trial will not
be completed and no verdict will be rendered," reacted ICTY's Chief
Prosecutor Carla Del Ponte.[1] Journalists went on to speculate what
the verdict might have been and the protagonists attempted to salvage
the remains of this enormous judicial venture.[2] The body of literature

---

[1] Carla Del Ponte feels "Total Defeat," Swissinfo, March 12, 2006.
[2] Roger Cohen, "To His Death in Jail, Milosevic Exalted Image of Serb Suffe-
ring," *New York Times*, March 12, 2006; Peter Ford, "How Milosevic Death
Sets Back Justice," *Christian Science Monitor*, March 13, 2006; "Milosevic
Death Precedes War Crimes Verdict," *Online News Hour*, March 13, 2006;
Joshua Rozenberg, "Trying Milosevic: What Went Wrong?" *Telegraph*, September 14, 2006; Carla Del Ponte, *Madame Prosecutor: Confrontations with
Humanity's Worst Criminals and the Culture of Impunity* (New York: Other
Press, 2008); Florence Hartmann, *Paix et châtiment, Les guerres secrètes de la
politique et de la justice* (Paris: Flammarion, 2007); Geoffrey Nice, *The Victims
of Srebrenica—Living and Dead—Deserve the Truth*, http://www.helsinki.org.
rs/doc/geoffrey%20nice%2001.doc; Geoffrey Nice, *Final Interview*, http://
www.sense-agency.com/en/stream.php?sta=3&pid=7979&kat=3.

about the trial, which grew alongside with the proceedings, was further enriched with studies dedicated to drawing lessons from its undesired outcome.[3] Difficult as it is to contest its failure, this contribution aims to demonstrate that the shadow cast by its sudden end seems darker than it actually is. What is the purpose of judging a criminal leader? Is it simply to put him behind bars or should the court aspire to reveal an extensive record of wrongdoings over which he presided? What is to be done if it proves next to impossible to do both things at the same time? The Milošević case was an attempt to answer these questions.

Milošević Trial—Chronology

- March 24, 1999: NATO campaign against Federal Republic of Yugoslavia
- May 26, 1999: Milošević indicted for war crimes on Kosovo
- June 11, 1999: Cessation of hostilities
- October 5, 2000: Milošević ousted from power
- June 28, 2001: Milošević extradited to The Hague
- June 29, 2001: Kosovo indictment amended
- July 7, 2001: Milošević pleads not guilty
- October 8, 2001: Croatian indictment
- November 22, 2001: Bosnian indictment
- February 12, 2002: Milošević trial commences
- February 25, 2004: Prosecution rests its case

---

[3] Norman Cigar, Paul Williams, *Indictment at The Hague. The Milošević Regime and Crimes of the Balkan War* (New York: New York University Press, 2002); Michael P. Scharf, William A. Schabas, *Slobodan Milošević on Trial: A Companion* (New York: Continuum, 2002); Chris Stephen, *Judgment Day. The Trial of Slobodan Milošević* (London: Atlantic Books, 2004); James Gow, Ivan Zverzhanovski, "The Milošević Trial: Purpose and Performance," *Nationalities Papers* vol. 32, no. 4 (December 2004), 897; Sabrina P. Ramet, "Martyr in His Own Mind: The Trial and Tribulations of Slobodan Milošević," *Totalitarian Movements and Political Religions* vol.5, no. 1 (Summer 2004), 113. Kari M. Osland, "The Trial of Slobodan Milošević," in Sabrina Ramet, Vjeran Pavlaković, *Serbia Since 1989* (Seattle: University of Washington Press 2007), 227–251; Gideon Boas, *The Milosevic Trial: Lessons for the Conduct of Complex International Criminal Proceedings* (Cambridge: Cambridge University Press, 2007); Judith Armatta, *Twilight of Impunity. The War Crimes Trial of Slobodan Milosevic* (Durham and London: Duke University Press, 2010); Timothy William Waters, *The Milošević Trial: An Autopsy* (Oxford: Oxford University Press, 2013).

- August 31, 2004: Defence begins its case
- March 3, 2005: Motion for Judgment of Acquittal by amici curiae
- June 16, 2005: Motion for Judgment of Acquittal denied
- March 11, 2006: The accused died

This was hardly the first time that the question was posed. "The purpose of the trial is to render justice, and nothing else," commented famously Hannah Arendt after the Eichmann trial. She was of the opinion that "even the noblest of ulterior purposes—"the making of a record of the Hitler regime which would withstand the test of history"—can only detract the law's main business: to weigh the charges brought against the accused, to render judgment, and to mete out punishment." [4] If one ascribes to her influential dictum, it is difficult to perceive the Milošević trial as anything but blunder. However, high-profiled proceedings such as this operate in a complex manner. Law, politics, history, and memory intertwined in an extraordinary media event, which symbolical aspects tend to be at least as important as their legal outcome. Hence this case deserves to be assessed against a similarly complex background, as pointed out recently by Lawrence Douglas, who convincingly contested the Arendtian creed: "No one, I believe, would deny that the primary responsibility of a criminal trial is to resolve the question of guilt in a procedurally fair manner. And certainly one must appreciate the potential tension between the core interest of justice and the concerns of didactic legality. To insist, however, as Arendt does, that the sole purpose of a trial is to render justice and nothing else, presents, I will argue, a crabbed and needlessly restrictive vision of the trial as legal form." [5]

---

[4] The book appeared as Hannah Arendt, *Eichmann in Jerusalem. A Report on the Banality of Evil* (London: Faber and Faber, 1963), 233. It was republished a number of times and translated in many languages. Arendt's views are examined in details in Steven E. Ascheim, *Hannah Arendt in Jerusalem*, (Berkeley: University of California Press, 1999). Cf. Barry Sharpe, *Modesty and Arrogance in Judgment. Hannah Arendt's Eichmann in Jerusalem*, (Westport: Praeger, 1999); Richard J. Bernstein, *Hannah Arendt and the Jewish Question* (Cambridge: Polity Press, 1996).

[5] Lawrence Douglas, *The Memory of Judgment. Making Law and History in the Trials of the Holocaust* (New Heaven/London: Yale University Press, 2001), 27. Various aspects of prominent criminal trials were thematized early on by Judith Shklar, *Legalism: Law, Morals, and Political Trials* (Cambridge, MA: Harvard University Press 1964). This approach became increasingly important in the light of the sequence of high profiled trials followed by the re-

In this sense, the real difficulty in departing from a strictly legal assessment lies in finding a convincing yardstick to review the impact of a trial. One of the possible roadmaps for such evaluation is offered by the International Criminal Tribunal for the former Yugoslavia itself. ICTY was founded by the Security Council of the United Nations in May 1993, "for the sole purpose of prosecuting persons responsible for serious violations of international humanitarian law committed in the territory of the former Yugoslavia from 1 January 1991."[6] However, over time, the Tribunal has built wider self-definition, resting on six proclaimed goals: (1) Holding leaders accountable, (2) Bringing justice to victims, (3) Giving victims a voice, (4) Establishing the facts, (5) Developing international law and (6) Strengthening the rule of law.[7] Although Slobodan Milošević was only one among 161 persons indicted by the ICTY, his trial was considered to be the peak of the Tribunal's activity and it was supposed to be its finest hour. Therefore, it makes sense to juxtapose its achievements to the above listed ambitious set of demands through which the first international criminal court after Nuremberg attempted to define the purpose of judging criminal leaders.

To begin with the issue of *accountability of leaders* and *developing international law*, with or without a verdict, Milošević will forever remain the first head of the state charged by an international court for the crimes committed during his tenure.[8] Chief Prosecutor of the ICTY

---

cent explosion of scholarship on transitional justice. Cf. Ellen Lutz, Caitlin Reiger (ed.), *Prosecuting Heads of State* (Cambridge: Cambridge University Press, 2009); Shoshana Felman, *The Juridical Unconscious: Trials and Traumas in the Twentieth Century* (Cambridge: Harvard University Press, 2002).

[6] S/RES/827 (1993), Detailed account on the establishment of the Tribunal in Rachel Kerr, *The International Criminal Tribunal for the former Yugoslavia, An Exercise in Law, Politics and Diplomacy* (Oxford: Oxford University Press, 2004).

[7] ICTY, About the ICTY, Achievements, http://www.icty.org/sid/324.

[8] It is a frequent misconception that Milošević is the first head of the state put to trial. Heads of states were fairly frequently tried on national level (Charles I, Louis XVI...). Even in Nuremberg, Admiral Karl Doenitz, Hitler's successor as President of the Third Reich was on trial. However, Milošević was the first to be indicted for crimes committed while he was acting in the capacity of the head of the state.

Louise Arbour signed and issued an indictment against him on May 26 1999, while he was well in office, waging a double war against NATO and his own citizens of Albanian ethnicity. The indictment stated that "the campaign undertaken by forces of the FRY and Serbia in Kosovo, was planned, instigated, ordered, committed, or otherwise aided and abetted by Slobodan Milošević, the President of the FRY; Milan Milutinović, the President of Serbia; Nikola Šainović, the Deputy Prime Minister of the FRY; Colonel General Dragoljub Ojdanić, the Chief of the General Staff of the VJ; and Vlajko Stojiljković, the Minister of Internal Affairs of Serbia."[9] Once the hostilities ended, due to the indictment, Milošević remained a pariah in the international community, without a possibility to repair his tarnished reputation. To be sure, in order for him to land into the ICTY's dock, it was necessary to fall out of power first. His electoral defeat and the popular uprising in Serbia in October 2000 opened up such possibility. After a protracted political crisis in the country, he was arrested and eventually transferred to The Hague on June 28, 2001.

In this respect, the very fact that Milošević stood on trial represents a breakthrough in implementation of international criminal law. As Carla Del Ponte recollects in her memoires, "this was a historic moment—the first trial of a head of state before an international tribunal."[10] The initial indictment was amended immediately upon his arrival. In October, another indictment against Milošević was raised for crimes committed in Croatia, and in November the indictment for Bosnia followed. The indictments were merged in a single trial, which commenced on February 12, 2002.

As far as the issues of *bringing justice to victims* and *giving them a voice* are concerned, strange as it might seem, those two goals could operate in a cross-purpose. The guiding concept of the prosecution was to cover the entire "crime base" and introduce as much evidence as possible, enabling both satisfaction to the victims and giving them an opportunity to testify.[11] Therefore Milošević defended against an extensive number of counts covering wide range of war crimes, crimes against humanity, and genocide charges committed between 1991 and

---

[9] ICTY, Milosevic, Initial Indictment, 38.

[10] Del Ponte, *Madame Prosecutor*, 120.

[11] Boas, *The Milosevic Trial*, 112.

1999 in Croatia, Bosnia, Herzegovina, and Kosovo. The result was a mammoth trial, in which quite a number of victims testified for the prosecution's case. However, this strategy revealed backlash potential. Milošević was a stubborn defendant, who denied the Tribunal's legality and legitimacy, therefore representing himself in the courtroom in order to further his political message. Uninterested in the legal outcome of the trial, Milošević took considerable pleasure in using cross-examination in order to abuse witnesses, who were time and again bullied by him. To take but a few examples: Agron Berisha, whose relatives were executed by Serbian police in Suva Reka, Kosovo, testified that the police "came to kill Albanian civilians, men, women and children, even pregnant women. The reason, the sole reason, was because they were Albanians." Milošević retorted: "You're an Albanian too. Berisha: Yes. Milošević: They didn't kill you."[12] Some days later, protected witness K15, victim of rape testified. Milošević started the cross-examination in a deeply offensive way: "I am sorry that this young girl was the victim of rape, of course, if it is all true, and I'm not going to ask her any questions with respect to those events. . . . As far as rape is concerned, it wasn't done certainly by the army and police but by criminals. The army and the police arrested criminals of that kind even for attempted rape."[13] Having in mind that it took considerable courage to step out and testify against the man whose supporters were, and still are scattered across security apparatus, one cannot but conclude that more could have been done to protect the dignity of the victims who testified.[14]

In the area of *establishing the facts*, although the judgment was not rendered, it needs to be noted that during the three years of the trial, an enormous record was generated. Chief Prosecutor Louis Arbour, who indicted Milošević, cautioned in 1999 that "we must determine whether it is realistic for a criminal prosecutor to undertake the task

---

[12] ICTY, Milošević trial, 26.2.2002. P.1034 http://www.icty.org/x/cases/slobodan_milosevic/trans/en/020226IT.htm.

[13] ICTY, Milošević trial, 1.3.2002, P.1384 http://www.icty.org/x/cases/slobodan_milosevic/trans/en/020301CR.htm.

[14] More about witnessing in the ICTY in Eric Stover, *The Witnesses. War Crimes and the Promise of Justice in The Hague* (Philadelphia, PA: University of Pennsylvania Press, 2005).

of a historian. History leaves room for doubt."[15] Once Milošević was in the dock, the temptation proved irresistible to Arbour's successor, Carla Del Ponte. Del Ponte loathed the idea that Milošević should have a limited, Al Capone-esque trial on the basis of selection of most provable counts, and insisted that indictments need to expose as full scope of wrongdoings as possible. At the very opening of the trial, she boldly announced: "I recognize that this trial will make history, and we would do well to approach our task in the light of history."[16] Over 1,250 exhibits—documents, photos, maps, expert reports—were presented in open court. The transcript of the trial itself amounts to 46,639 pages, which contain testimonies of nearly 400 witnesses. Prosecution tendered 930 exhibits on 85,526 pages, plus 117 video records, and produced 352 witnesses (114 viva voce, 218 testimonies in written form, 20 expert reports), whereas Milošević submitted 9,000 pages of exhibits including 50 videos and brought 40 witnesses from the list which initially amounted to 1,631.[17] Witnesses included personalities such as leader of Kosovo Albanians Ibrahim Rugova, President of Croatia Stjepan Mesić, and the last Yugoslav Prime Minister Ante Marković as well as a number of high profile international mediators who took part in solving the crises in Southeast Europe. The majority of this collection is in the public sphere. Documents which would normally be inaccessible for decades are now available for research and scrutiny, which both prompts scholarly research on the topic and influences the process of creating new indictments.[18]

Such an approach came with a high price, insofar as the management of the case was concerned. The scope of the indictment, coupled with the intent to expose the entire crime base and political intent

---

[15] Louise Arbour, *War Crimes and the Culture of Peace* (Toronto: University of Toronto Press, 2002), 35.

[16] ICTY, Milosevic trial, 10 April 2002.

[17] Cf. Human Rights Watch, Weighing the Evidence. Lessons from the Slobodan Milosevic trial, vol. 18, no 10(d), December 2006, http://www.hrw.org/sites/default/files/reports/milosevic1206webwcover.pdf; See also, Boas, *The Milosevic Trial*.

[18] Video record accessible at Milosevic Trial Public Archive, http://hague.bard.edu/. Full transcript in 45 volumes from the trial was published by Humanitarian Law Center in Belgrade: *Suđenje Slobodanu Miloševiću*, Transkripti 1–45, Fond za humanitarno pravo, Beograd 2007.

behind it resulted in a complex and hectic case presentation spanning chronologically from 1991 until 1999 and geographically from Slovenia to Kosovo. Understandably, this pace was difficult to follow, both for the judges and the interested spectators.[19] A large number of witnesses and an enormous quantity of documents had an immediate effect on the duration of the trial, which seemed never ending and convinced many that the more prudent strategy would be to expose the general pattern of criminality, followed by a selection of crimes which could be easily proven, and a credible link toward the accused. The Trial Chamber reacted by limiting the time allocated to the prosecution and significantly curbing the number of proposed witnesses.[20] Still, the complexity of the case, the decision of the accused to represent himself and frequent recesses due to the state of his health took their toll in the most dramatic way. Milošević suffered from high blood pressure, aggravated by the strains of his workload. Still, he resisted the attempts to appoint an attorney to represent him, as he viewed the trial as a political forum to address his audience in Serbia. Once his defense case commenced, it was clear that he is not interested to defend. His opening statement was filled with accusations against his former and current enemies, and the choice of his witnesses was clearly serving propaganda purposes, addressing mainly the audience back home.

The reactions of that audience are indeed the real crux of the matter, hidden under the last goal of the ICTY, *strengthening the rule of law*. It reads: "The Tribunal has influenced judiciaries in the former Yugoslavia to reform and to continue its work of trying those responsible for war crimes. The Tribunal works in partnership with domestic courts in the region—transferring its evidence, knowledge and jurisprudence—as part of its continuing efforts to strengthen the rule of law and to bring justice to victims in the former Yugoslavia." Actually, this goal deals with the ability of the court to induce a change of attitudes in the post-

---

[19] Boredom in historical trials is seldom recognized and scrutinized, yet it is commonplace. Even Rebecca West, attentive observer of the Nuremberg trials was forced to acknowledge that the courtroom was, more than occasionally, "a citadel of boredom." The length and complexity of any trial present a challenge to ones' attention, even if their historical significance is beyond any doubt, and Milošević case was no exemption.

[20] Armatta, *Twilight of Impunity*, 44–45.

war setting and primarily to break the wall of denial. This is the true symbolic battlefield of the case, and its results are rather mixed.

The history of the reactions to the Milošević trial in Serbia is complex. By the time he fell out of power, he was widely hated by his former subjects. As Erich Gordy noticed, "everyone in Serbia thinks Milošević is guilty of something."[21] However, there was no consensus over the exact nature of his guilt, nor on his extradition to The Hague. In a post-Milošević period, much of the anti-Hague discourse survived and was utilised by moderate and extreme right-wing political groups. These narratives also proved to be "the last refuge of scoundrels," who used patriotic rhetoric to paralyze proceedings and mobilize parts of Serbian society unwilling to question the legacy of the Milošević period. Stjepan Gredelj claimed that "the views of the public opinion about The Hague Tribunal are predominantly negative, since the respondents manifest a high level of agreement with some of the most widespread negative stereotypes about the institution which are increasingly placed in public."[22] The attempts of the Serbian reformist government to extradite the accused persons added to its unpopularity and led the country on the brink of *coup d'état* at least twice—in November 2001 and in March 2003. Only after the murder of Zoran Đinđić, the first democratically elected Serbian Prime Minister, who played a decisive role in Milošević's transfer to The Hague, wide governmental crackdown on organized crime changed the political landscape significantly. Practically overnight, cooperation with the ICTY became much more popular, and the state formed a specialized War Crimes Prosecutor's Office in Serbia in June 2003.[23]

---

[21] Eric Gordy, "Rating the Sloba Show. Will Justice Be Served?" *Problems of Post-Communism*; May-June 2003, vol. 50 no. 3, 53.

[22] Stjepan Gredelj, "War, Crimes, Guilt, Sanctions," in Ivana Spasic, Milan Subotic (ed.), *R/Evolution and Order. Serbia After October 2000* (Belgrade: Institute for Philosophy and Social Theory, 2001), 255. Shifts in public opinion toward war crimes were subject of repeated surveys. Cf. OESC and BCHR, *Public perception in Serbia of the ICTY and the national courts dealing with war crimes*, http://www.osce.org/publications/srb/2009/12/41942_1399_en.pdf.

[23] Republic of Serbia, Office of the War Crimes Prosecutor, http://www.tuzilastvorz.org.rs/html_trz/pocetna_eng.htm.

However, setting up of the institutional framework was no more than a precondition in the area of strengthening the rule of law. The creation of domestic war crimes offices did not lead to an immediate synergic effect.[24] National proceedings for war crimes were invariably following the bottom-up strategy, indicting low-ranked perpetrators for isolated crimes. Consequently, the audience was unable to comprehend that the proceedings in The Hague and in Belgrade deal with the same subject. Still, through this activity an indispensable channel for the internalization of the process of prosecuting war crimes was set.[25] It was a question of time when would the effects take place.

By the beginning of June 2005, the Milošević trial was viewed in Serbia with a mix of boredom and occasional sympathy for the accused, until one day, when the prosecutor Geoffrey Nice played a tape in the course of the cross-examination of Serbian police General Obrad Stevanović. The prosecutor was describing the footage: "This video, which is potentially distressing viewing and I'm only going to play very small parts of it, reveals, Mr. Stevanovic . . . that men were brought from Srebrenica in batches to this group of Scorpios to be executed and they were executed. . . . The lorry leaves. The men are eventually taken up into the hills. . . . Here they are taken up into the surrounding countryside. Two remaining not shot are untied. . . . They're untied, they move the four bodies, and then they are themselves shot, and I'll leave it there."

Milošević's witness seemed shaken: "As I am upset, I have to say that this is one of the most monstrous images I have ever seen on a screen. Of course I have never seen anything like this—live. I am astonished that you have played this video in connection with my testimony because you know full well that this has nothing to do with me

---

[24] Diana F.Orentlicher, *Shrinking the Space for Denial: The Impact of the ICTY in Serbia*, Centre for Transitional Processes, Belgrade, 2008, 69–94.

[25] Vladimir Petrović, *Gaining Trust Though Facing the Past? Prosecuting War Crimes Committed in the Former Yugoslavia in a National and International Legal Context.* CAS Working Paper Series No. 4/2011: Sofia 2011, 1–35. Shaken Order: Authority and Social Trust in Post-Communist Societies (Case Studies in Law), a project of the Centre for Advanced Study Sofia.

or the units I commanded."[26] The infamous footage was filmed by a Serbian paramilitary unit called "The Scorpions," depicting the execution of Muslim civilians in the vicinity of Srebrenica in July 1995.[27] This screening had multiple consequences, none directly related to the Milošević case. An evidentiary role of the visual record was virtually nonexistent. The prosecution screened it in a belated phase of the process, and in December 2005 the judges ruled out the possibility of admitting it as evidence. They also decided against the reopening of the case in light of new evidence, the tape being the most relevant one.[28] However, its collateral effect cannot be overemphasized. Avril McDonald, a professor of international law from Asser Institute, estimated that "it was significant at the time that it came out because a lot of people were presented with something that they might not have wanted to believe." She added that its showing in court "got exposure that it wouldn't have had, had it just simply been a regular news story."[29]

After the release of the footage, which was aired by the most important world broadcasting services, the capacity for denial in Serbia has shrunken over the night, giving space to horror and remorse, as well as contempt and whitewashing. In a matter of hours, Serbian police has identified and apprehended several persons seen on the footage. Their arrest was hailed as a "change of heart" in Serbia.[30] The video was broadcast on Serbian national television and Serbian Presi-

---

[26] ICTY, Milosevic case, Transcripts, 1.6.2005, p.40277 http://www.un.org/icty/transe54/050601IT.htm.

[27] The basic details about the handover of the tape are given in Daniel Williams, *Srebrenica video vindicates a long pursuit by Serb activist*, http://www.washingtonpost.com/wp-dyn/content/article/2005/06/24/AR2005062401501.html, accessed Decmber 1, 2006.

[28] ICTY, Cases and Judgments, The Milosevic Case, Decision on application for a limited re-opening of the Bosnia and Kosovo components of the prosecution case with confidential annex.

[29] *Judges Crack Down on Milosevic Case*, Institute for War and Peace Reporting, http://www.iwpr.net/?p=tri&s=f&o=258726&apc_state=henptri, accessed December 1, 2006.

[30] Reuters, 3.6.2005, *Srebrenica Video Sobers Serbia, Prompts Arrests*, http://www.tiscali.co.uk/news/newswire.php/news/reuters/2005/06/03/world/srebrenicavideosobersserbiabringsarrests.html, acessed December 1, 2006. Radio Free Europe, A Video Shocks Serbia, http://www.rferl.org/featuresarticle/2005/6/2DF1E167-F27F-46F3-A2B1-0548E86FCE88.html.

dent Boris Tadić gave a speech condemning the crime. The effect of the release of the Scorpions' tape strengthened optimism, best expressed through the opinion of Prosecutor Carla Del Ponte, who labeled it a turning point of the trial: "Internet will make the Scorpions' video accessible to everybody any time, with a computer mouse click, which would roll Milosevic legacy in the dust next to the Bosnian road where Scorpions killed their victims. . . . Consciously or perhaps more importantly unconsciously, Milosevic had to know that he will never be a free man again."[31]

However, after the initial local reaction, which indeed had elements of awakening from the decade-long denial, public discourse again accommodated the voices of dissent, occasionally even doubting the authenticity of the tape or relativizing its importance.[32] The Scorpions were prosecuted in Serbia, and on April 2007 they received their sentences. Two of them got twenty years, one got thirteen years, and another received five years in jail, in a highly controversial ruling.[33] Members of the Scorpions unit were sentenced by the Serbian judiciary, but their connection with the Serbian authorities was not clearly demonstrated during the proceedings. They were convicted solely for war crimes against civilian population, even though it was apparent that the victims were executed in a wide pattern of elimination of thousands of prisoners taken after the fall of Srebrenica, qualified as genocide by several judgments of the ICTY.

This legal Rashomon was bound to become even more complex, including another court—International Court of Justice (ICJ), where Bosnia and Herzegovina sued Serbia for breaking the Genocide Convention. According to the ICJ ruling from February 2007, Serbia did

---

[31] Del Ponte, *Madame Prosecutor*, 308.

[32] See Nebohsa Malic, Deaths, Lies and Videotape, http://www.antiwar.com/malic/?articleid=6275; Julija Gorin, Serbs, Lies and Videotape, Frontpage Magazine, http://www.freerepublic.com/focus/f-news/1424168/posts; Some of those critiques contain very sophisticated post-modern argumentation. The other ones, f.e. Milan Bulajic, *Srebrenica—Outline for Revision of the ICTY Judgment on Genocide*, http://guskova.ru/misc/docs/2004-may, accessed December 1, 2006.

[33] Transcript of the case is published by Humanitarian Law Centre, *Škorpioni—od zločina do pravde* (Fond za humanitarno pravo: Beograd, 2007).

so, not through committing or adding and abetting genocide, but through failure to prevent it.[34] This case was dragging from 1993, and was considered to be a Damocles' sword for the fragile post-Milošević government. This later aspect helps one better understand the rationale for the ambivalence of the Serbian public's reactions toward the Milošević case. One can now only speculate what this ruling would be had Milošević lived to hear his own verdict, as he was indicted for Srebrenica genocide as well. However, his death in spring 2006 made the clarification of the exact measure of involvement of the leadership of Serbia and Federal Republic of Yugoslavia in the Srebrenica genocide more difficult.

The dynamic afterlife of the Milošević case shows that the trial not only played, but also continues to play an important role in the process of coming to terms with the atrocious decade for the region of former Yugoslavia. Its legacy of mixed record seems to indicate that the effects of high-profile trials are neither immediate, nor fully predictable. They tend to manifest themselves long after the courtrooms emptied, as Michael Scharf, one of the first observers of the ICTY, suggested at the time of its creation: "Will an assessment of the brutal history of Yugoslavia by three judges from outside the Balkans, skilled jurists all of them but acknowledged amateurs when it comes to history and politics, help the fractured country to recover? We recall the words of former Chinese premier Chou En-Lai who, when asked whether the French Revolution had been a success, famously replied: 'It's too early to tell.'"[35] As the Milošević trial moves from the legal field to join the ongoing memory wars over his role in the Yugoslav wars, it seems that the same could be said about its success or failure. In the meanwhile, some concluding interim remarks are warranted.

---

[34] *The Application of the Convention on the Prevention and Punishment of the Crime of Genocide (Bosnia and Herzegovina v. Serbia and Montenegro)* [2007] Judgment, ICJ General List No. 91, 108, paragraph 297. http://www.icj-cij. org/docket/files/91/13685.pdf.

[35] Scharf, *Milošević on Trial*, 147.

The death of Milošević seemed a blow so serious that the Prosecutor of the ICTY Carla Del Ponte felt the need to organize a press conference to "make it clear that the Yugoslavia tribunal was something more than just the Milosevic tribunal and that its success of failure did not depend solely upon the case against Milosevic." Del Ponte's memoires also reveal the bitter taste of failure: "In many ways, on a deeper level, Milosevic's death angered me. After four years of hearings, only forty hours remained for the defense to present its case. The proceedings were likely to end in a matter of weeks. . . . Slobodan Milosevic had nothing to gain by living longer, and he had everything to lose. In death, Milosevic had escaped. He had deprived his hundreds of thousands of victims of the full degree of justice they deserved."[36] Against such background, it is understandable that the prevailing comments were highly critical of the trial's performance, focusing on what was perceived as prosecution's attempt to judge history as the most important reason for the scope, length, and ultimate procedural failure of the trial. From a strictly legal perspective, which perceives judgment as the ultimate goal of a criminal trial, the Milošević case was undoubtedly a fiasco.

However, moving from the Arendtian position on the functions of a high-profiled trial to a more contemporary understanding of its functions, the outcome is not so clear-cut. By opting for a historical trial, the prosecution was undoubtedly running a significant risk, as it became clear that such demanding approach was adding to an already unbearable strain on the management of the case. In the opening of the trial, senior prosecutor Geoffrey Nice noted: "This trial, as, again, the Prosecutor has correctly explained, will not be making findings as to history. Matters of history always leave scope for argument, for doubt between historians. But history, even distant history sometimes available to this Court through the witnesses, will have a relevance from time to time in showing what the accused thought, what those identified in indictments as his co-perpetrators thought, what his compliant supporters thought, and what was available in history to fire up the emotions."[37] In practice, this meant that the prosecution explored

---

[36] Del Ponte, *Madame Prosecutor*, 331–332.

[37] ICTY, Milosevic Trial, Prosecution's Opening Statement, February 12, 2002, 15 http://www.un.org/icty/transe54/020212IT.htm.

and presented a detailed overview of the context in which war crimes were perpetrated.

Expectedly, shielding behind history became an important cornerstone of Milošević's defense, announced in his own opening statement: "Accusations leveled against me are an unscrupulous lie and also a tireless distortion of history. . . . Scholars will be coming here, academicians, if they dare come."[38] As a consequence, the Milošević trial has drawn an impressive range of historians and social scientists, who testified in capacity of expert witnesses.[39] What followed was a set of more or less incompatible historical narratives of dubious relevance for the trial's outcome. These excurses proved to be consuming considerable time, as well as the patience of judges and spectators, adding to existing debates about usage of history in the courtroom.[40]

With some years of distance, one needs to reconcile with inherently mixed record of the Milošević trial. His unlikely appearance in front of the international court signifies a major breakthrough in the area of establishing accountability on the highest level and for eroding the impunity of state leaders. This is indeed an important development in international law. The ambitious design of the prosecution was reflected in a set of expansive indictments and it resulted in an

---

[38] ICTY, Milosevic Trial, Defense's opening statement February 14, 2002, 246, 258, http://www.un.org/icty/transe54/020214IT.htm.

[39] For the prosecution, two of the most representative historical testimonies have been given by Dr. Robert Donia and Dr. Audrie Budding. The defense called upon Serbian historians academician Čedomir Popov, professor of the University of Novi Sad and Dr. Slavenko Terzić, director of the Historical Institute, Serbian Academy of Sciences. For the submitted expert reports see *Milosevic Trial Public Archive*, Expert Report of Robert Donia, "The Assembly of Republika Srpska, 1992–1995, Highlights and Excerpts," submitted August 1, 2003, Expert Report of Audrey Budding, "Serbian Nationalism in the Twentieth Century," submitted May 29, 2002, http://hague.bard.edu/icty_info.html, accessed May 29, 2001.

[40] Cf. Richard Ashby Wilson, "Judging History: The Historical Record of the International Criminal Tribunal for the Former Yugoslavia," *Human Rights Quarterly*, vol. 27, no. 3 (2005), 908–940. Ksenija Turković, "Historians in Search for Truth About Conflicts in the Territory of Former Yugoslavia as Expert Wtinesses in Front of the ICTY," *Časopis za suvremenu povijest*, vol. 36, (2004), 41–67., Robert J Donia, "Encountering the Past: History at the Yugoslav War Crimes Tribunal," *The Journal of the International Institute*, vol. 11 (2004), http://www.umich.edu/~iinet/journal/vol11no2-3/donia.htm.

unmanageable, prolonged, and eventually aborted trial, which ultimately collapsed under its own weight. At the same time though, it has
produced a massive body of evidence, inspiring further proceedings on
both the international and national level. Had the trial been less ambitious, it could have ended with a verdict, perhaps at the expense of
other demanding goals ICTY had set for itself. Unfinished as it was,
it remained an enormous prosecutorial venture to collect and exhibit
an extensive record about individual criminal responsibility of a head
of the state in the whirlwind of a complex conflict. Milošević trial succeeded to meet that challenge, at the high cost of its own failure.

CHARLES VILLA-VICENCIO

The South African Transition: Then and Now

The South African transition from apartheid to the country's first democratically elected government in 1994 is widely acclaimed as an example of a successful political transition that avoided the predicted blood-
bath and political chaos. Some among the oppressed people of South
Africa, however, had quite unrealistic expectations of what the new age
could usher in. This has contributed, two decades later, to a wave of
disillusionment and resentment in the country, raising questions about
the viability of the soft South African transition. It also adds to the
global debate on the nature of political transitions from dictatorship
and authoritarian rule to the beginning of democracy.

Many newly founded states, which emerged in the wave of democratization that swept the globe after the collapse of the Berlin Wall in
1989, are today governed by ruling elites, tempted if not driven, to
govern with unrestrained power. This tendency of new democracies
to slide back into some of the ways of the oppressive states they have
replaced, poses the pertinent question as to how nations, comprising
what Sir Isaiah Berlin aptly defined as a "crooked timber of humanity,"
ought best to go about establishing lasting peace? University of Notre
Dame professor James McAdams argued that "if one looks over the
mountain of articles, books, and other learned treatises on the topic
of transitional justice, one cannot help but come to an uncomfortable
realization: for every argument that can be summoned in favor of doing
more to address a past wrong, we can find an equally compelling coun-

ter-argument to do less.[1] Bernard Williams, in turn, suggested it has as much to do with "moral luck" as anything else.[2]

Consideration is given in this paper to the South African breakthrough in negotiations that led to this country's first democratic elections in 1994 and the fruits of this transition, almost two decades years later. It was relatively easy to distinguish between good and evil during the days of struggle. Today it is more difficult. We discovered that not all political leaders were neither wholly Satanic nor entirely angelic. This suggests that political leaders have an ability and capacity to respond, both out of self-interest or empathy with others, to both the carrots and sticks of history. It is this that makes peace building a trade-off that reaches deep into the psyche and identity of adversaries and political opponents, as well as into the fabric of the political process that shapes the fortunes of a nation.

With this in mind, this chapter will deal with three issues that are considered crucial for a full understanding of the nature and results of the South African transition. The first is the context of the South African political settlement, culminating in the 1994 elections. The second is the nature of the South African Truth and Reconciliation Commission. And the third is the unfinished work of the South African transition.

The Context of the South African Settlement

It is easy to forget the nature of the anticipated doom that faced South Africa in the late 1980s. It is, in turn, still a bit nerve-racking to recall the tenuous and fragile nature of the negotiations between the apartheid regime and the liberation movements that came in the wake of the unbanning of political organizations and the release from prison of Nelson Mandela and other political prisoners in 1990. Suspicions intensified on both sides and violence escalated into the killing fields

---

[1] James McAdams, "Transitional Justice: The Issue That Won't Go Away." A paper delivered at a conference entitled "Twenty Years After—Dealing with the Heritage of Communism," Munk Centre for International Studies, University of Toronto, March, 2009.

[2] Bernard Williams, *Moral Luck* (Cambridge: Cambridge University Press, 1981).

of Kwa Zulu Natal and beyond, threatening to reduce the country to chaos at the very time when a settlement seemed possible.

An iconic moment came when shortly after Mandela's release from prison, he met with General Constand Viljoen, head of the South African Defense Force. "If you want to go to war," Mandela told Viljoen, "I must be honest with you and admit that we cannot stand up to you on the battlefield. We don't have the resources. It will be a long and bitter struggle, many people will die and the country may be reduced to ashes. But you must remember two things. You cannot win because of our numbers; you cannot kill us all. And you cannot win because of the international community. They will rally to our support and they will stand with us."[3] Mandela's optimism concerning the stance of the international community suggested that a turning point had been reached in South Africa—there was no turning back. Viljoen was, in turn, drawn into the settlement process, eventually bringing conservative Afrikaners into the political process.

Suffice it to say, the South African conflict drew to a climax in a historic settlement, forged essentially between black Africans and white Boers. The settlement was designed to stop an escalating war that threatened to destroy the very identity, infrastructure, and promise of a nation yet to be born. Both sides to the conflict, however, through long and tedious contacts and negotiations, came to believe that new life could still emerge out of the strife that characterized the apartheid years. At the heart of the settlement was a commitment to a conditional amnesty—which was judged by a cross-section of South African political leaders to be the only way forward. In the words of the postamble to the Interim Constitution, agreed to by both sides of the political divide, it was agreed that: "In order to advance reconciliation and reconstruction, amnesty shall be granted in respect of acts, omissions and offenses associated with political objectives and committed in the course of conflicts of the past. To this end, the Parliament under this Constitution shall adopt a law . . . providing for the mechanisms, criteria and procedures, including tribunals, if any, through which such amnesty shall be dealt with at any time after the law has been passed."

---

[3] Alister Sparks, *Tomorrow Is Another Country* (Johannesburg: Struik Book Distributors, 1994), 204.

Looking back on this process, Justice Richard Goldstone, who later became a judge in the South African Constitutional Court and subsequently held several important international positions, argued that: "The decision to opt for a Truth and Reconciliation Commission was an important compromise. If the ANC had insisted on Nuremberg-style trials for the leaders of the former apartheid government, there would have been no peaceful transition to democracy, and if the former government had insisted on a blanket amnesty then, similarly, the negotiations would have broken down. A bloody revolution sooner rather than later would have been inevitable. The Truth and Reconciliation Commission is a bridge from the old to the new."[4]

The Nature and Mandate of the Commission

The TRC was intended to be part of a larger bridge-building process designed to help the nation move from its deeply divided past to a future founded on reconciliation, the recognition of human rights, and democracy. This placed a huge responsibility on the TRC—and yet its parliamentary-defined mandate was a narrow one. It was to investigate and document *gross violations of human rights*, defined in the legislation governing the TRC as "killings, abductions, torture and severe ill-treatment." The mandate period was from May 1, 1960, when the African National Congress (ANC) and the Pan Africanist Congress (PAC) were banned and resorted to armed struggle, to the inauguration of the first democratic president on May 10, 1994.

The narrowness of the TRC's mandate needs to be understood in the context of a number of other commissions in the country, which mandates incorporated similar objectives. These included the Land Claims Court, the Constitutional Court, the Human Rights Commission, the Gender Commission, and the Youth Commission. Other violations of human rights that formed part of the apartheid past, including Bantu education and forced removals, were to be addressed and corrected through legislation and policy developed by the new government.

---

[4] Richard Goldstone, "The Hauser Lecture," New York University, January 22, 1997.

The Objectives of the Commission

The *Promotion of National Unity and Reconciliation Act* required the Commission to promote national unity and reconciliation in a sprit of understanding by:

- establishing as complete a picture as possible of the causes, nature and extent of gross violations of human rights . . . by conducting investigations and holding hearings;
- facilitating the granting of amnesty to persons who made full disclosure of all the relevant facts relating to acts associated with a political objective and which comply with the requirements of the Act;
- establishing and making known the fate or whereabouts of victims and restoring the human and civil dignity of such victims [survivors] by granting them an opportunity to relate their own accounts of the violations they suffered, and recommending reparation;
- compiling a report that provided as comprehensive an account as possible of the activities and findings of the Commission, and making recommendations to prevent the future violations of human rights.

Structure of the Commission

The Commission established a number of internal structures in order to carry out its multiple tasks—these included a team of people responsible for an extensive database that recorded the names and details of victims, perpetrators, and witnesses; a witness protection unit; an investigative unit; a research department; a legal unit; a safety and security department; a mental health unit; and a media and communications department. These structures were required to service the three major committees which constituted the Commission.

The Amnesty Committee

This body consisted of judges of the Supreme Court, who co-opted several lawyers to serve on the amnesty panels under them. The task of the committee was to consider applications for amnesty on the basis of the following conditions:

- The person applying for amnesty was required to appear personally before an Amnesty Committee hearing and make full disclosure of all relevant facts concerning the act for which he or she was seeking amnesty.
- Only members of state institutions, members and supporters of political organizations and liberation movements were eligible for amnesty.
- The actions for which applicants applied for amnesty needed to have had a political objective and to have been carried out in pursuit of the aims of their respective organizations.

The legislation governing amnesty emphasized that amnesty could not be extended to any person for any act, omission or offence committed for personal gain or out of personal malice toward someone. It required that the Amnesty Committee be guided in its decisions by the following criteria:

- the motive of the person who committed the act, omission or offense;
- the context of the act, omission, or offense;
- the legal and factual nature of the act, omission, or offense, as well as the gravity of the act, omission or offense;
- the object or objective of the act, omission, or offense;
- whether the act, omission or offense was executed in response to an order, or on behalf of, or with the approval of, the state, a political organization or liberation movement; and
- the relationship between the act, omission, or offense and the political objective pursued, and in particular the directness and proximity of the relationship and the proportionality of the act, omission, or offense to the objective pursued.

In brief, the TRC legislation offered amnesty in return for truth about South Africa's past. Those denied amnesty, or who chose not to apply for it, were subject to prosecution in terms of established criminal law. Of the 7,116 applicants, 1,167 were granted amnesty. The majority of those whose applications were refused failed to meet the criteria as set out above, while a number of applicants were deemed not to have made full disclosure on the acts in which they were involved. Others chose not to apply for amnesty, hoping their crimes would either go undetected or be ignored and some, especially in the liberation movements, argued that they were soldiers fighting a just war did not require amnesty.

Human Rights Violations Committee

A major responsibility of the Human Rights Violations Committee was to invite victims of gross violations of human rights to inform the Commission and the South African public of these violations. This task was undertaken by sending out trained statement takers to interview victims and their families in their own languages. This information was entered into a database and investigated with a view to enabling the Commission to decide whether the disclosed information was true or not. Of the 21,290 people who submitted statements to the TRC, 19,050 were found to be victims of gross violations of human rights as defined in the *Promotion of National Unity and Reconciliation Act.* A further 2,975 names were identified through the amnesty process as possible victims, although not all were ultimately found to be such in terms of the legislation governing the TRC. Because of time and other restraints the TRC could not invite all victims to give testimony in public, although approximately 2,000 of the total number of victims appeared in hearings that were held in cities, towns, and rural areas across the country.

These hearings were extensively covered on radio and television as well as in all major South African newspapers. A journalist indicated at the close of the TRC that the nation "now had TRC fatigue." He went on to say, "I cannot open the newspapers, turn on the television, or listen to the radio without being exposed to another horrific story." Perhaps that was the good news. No South African, black or white, could again either deny that atrocities had happened or say he or she did not know that they had happened. This provided a basis on which to build a new society, with a commitment to ensure that such things did not happen again.

Unlike the Amnesty Committee where public hearings were conducted according to established legal procedure, the Human Rights Violations Committee sought to create an opportunity for victims to tell their stories in a psychologically and socially secure space. Victims were not cross-examined or put under any kind of threat. In addition to seeking to establish what has been called the objective truth concerning their suffering, the Committee also sought to record the subjective truth or the way in which victims themselves perceived and remembered their violations.

On the basis of the information gained from victims and the subsequent investigations, the Human Rights Violations Committee made a formal finding as to whether or not the person could be regarded as a victim in terms of the *Promotion of National Unity and Reconciliation Act*. The information and findings were made available to the Amnesty Committee when the information was relevant to an amnesty application, as well as to the Reparations and Rehabilitation Committee for reparation purposes. The Human Rights Violations Committee had the additional responsibility to publish a brief synopsis of each of the 19,050 testimonies of those people found by the TRC to be victims of gross human rights violations.

The Human Rights Violations Committee also held institutional hearings for religious communities, the legal community, business and labor, the health sector, the media, prisons, and the armed forces. In addition, political party hearings were held within which all the major political parties and liberation movements gave testimony. The aim was to gain as complete a picture as possible of events in the mandate period of the Commission and to understand the role played—both positive and negative—by the various institutions and parties during the thirty-four years under review.

The Reparations and Rehabilitation Committee

The Reparations and Rehabilitation Committee received information concerning victims from the Amnesty and the Human Rights Violations Committees, and developed a reparations and rehabilitation policy to address the needs of those who had suffered in one way or another. Recognizing that the granting of amnesty denies victims the right to institute civil claims against perpetrators, the need for adequate reparations and rehabilitation became obvious. The government had to accept responsibility for the wellbeing of victims.

The Committee studied international law and policy on reparations and looked at reparation practices in other countries and situations. On the basis of this it established five components for reparations and rehabilitation:

- *Urgent Interim Reparation*: This was developed to meet the needs of victims in urgent need of assistance, which could range from the provision of a wheelchair to emergency support for medical, emotional or educational needs.
- *Individual Reparation Grants*: The Commission decided to make an individual reparation grant to each victim of gross violations of human rights. Having considered various formulae for deciding on the amount to be paid, it ultimately recommended a payment of up to R 23,023 per victim per annum (currently slightly over EUR 1,800), conditional on the number of dependents the victims had and whether the victims were living in a rural or urban area. This payment was to be made in six monthly instalments for a period of six years. It took the government five years to announce that the TRC's recommendation would not be implemented and that there would be a one-off payment of R 30,000 to each victim (at present rates around EUR 2,400).
- *Symbolic Reparations* plus *Legal and Administrative Interventions*: These included the issuing of death certificates; carrying out exhumations, burials and ceremonies; erecting tombstones; expunging criminal records for political activities; declarations of death where this would assist families; the renaming of streets and facilities, memorials and monuments; and instituting days of remembrance. A major development in this category of symbolic reparations is the Freedom Park presently under construction in Pretoria.
- *Community Rehabilitation:* In addition to the suffering of individuals, whole communities were often subjected to attacks and suffering that ranged from massacres to systematic abuse as a result of army and police occupation. Community reparations were in-

tended to meet the need for health and social services, education facilities, institutional reconstruction and housing.

- *Institutional Reform*: These proposals included legal, administrative and institutional measures designed to prevent the recurrence of human rights abuses.

A President's Fund, located in the Ministry of Justice, was established to meet these and other related needs, with contributions coming from the government, some foreign countries and individuals. To date the Fund continues to be underutilized. This is primarily because the fund was originally structured to meet the payment of individual reparations, although legislation is still not finalized for the fund to be used for community and other forms of reparation.

The Final Report of the Commission

The first five volumes of the Commission's Report covered the following issues: the Commission's mandate, structure, and methodology; the investigations and research undertaken by the Commission into gross violations of human rights in various institutions and structures of government as well as the liberation movements; reports of activities in the various provinces of the country in the pre-1994 dispensation; institutional hearings; and finally, various analyzes and recommendations made by the Commission to ensure that the kinds of atrocities of the past do not recur in the future. Two further volumes were completed at the conclusion of the final amnesty hearings: volume six provides a final report from the Amnesty Committee, plus comments and amendments to the earlier volumes; volume seven compromises short summaries of the testimony given by those whom the TRC found to be victims of gross violations of human rights.

On the eve of the first five volumes being handed to then President Nelson Mandela in October 1998, former President F.W. de Klerk went to the Cape High Court demanding that certain findings against him be taken out of the Report. In order to allow the Report to be released, the Commission agreed to black out the relevant page. The Commission had found that Mr. de Klerk failed to make a full disclosure regarding the violations of human rights committed by senior members of his government and the South African Police. These included the bombing of Khotso House. This finding became part of the court record and was subsequently highlighted in the media.

In turn, the ANC appealed to the court to stop the release of the TRC Report in its entirety because the Commission's criticism of the ANC's liberation struggle. The Commission had, in fact, used classic "just war" theory to distinguish between the *just cause* of the ANC's fight against apartheid and *just means*, which showed that some of the methods employed by the ANC—not least torture and killing in its detention camps in Angola and elsewhere—constituted gross violations of human rights. The irony is that these gross violations of human rights were acknowledged by the ANC itself in its submission to the Commission. The court overruled the ANC's application, allowing the TRC to hand the Report to the President and to release it to the media.

The Unfinished Work of the TRC

The goals of the South African TRC were always going to be incomplete. I offer three observations in this regard, among the many concerns that warrant debate on the South African settlement:

Investigations and Prosecutions

Two questions in this regard: first, would there have been a relatively peaceful settlement in South Africa had the architects and implementers of apartheid—senior political leaders and generals—faced the possibility of extended jail sentences? The answer is probably not—and there was no Rome Statute for South Africans to negotiate themselves around. Second, why were prosecutions against those who either failed to apply for amnesty or been denied amnesty by the TRC not investigated and where necessary instituted by the state? Briefly stated, the answer is that the state has, for a variety of reasons, lost the political will to prosecute past political offenders.

For example, consider the "Amendment of Prosecuting Policy: Prosecution of Criminal Matters Arising from the Conflicts of the Past and Which Were Committed before 11 May 2004" issued by the National Director of Public Prosecutions (NDPP) with the concurrence of the Minister of Justice and Cabinet in 2006, intended to amend section 179(5)(a) and (b) of the Constitution, pertaining to prosecutions. The proposed amendment would have:

1. Empowered the NDPP to decline to prosecute, or to offer indemnities against prosecution.
2. No longer made full disclosure a requirement, as it was in the TRC amnesty process, for indemnity against prosecution.
3. Unlike the TRC Act, it provided no measure to protect the rights of victims to be heard in response to the proposed indemnities.

In brief, the amendments to the prosecution policy opened the door to impunity. It placed South Africa in potential violation of its international law obligations. It provided perpetrators with an opportunity to escape justice without the kind of public disclosure required in the TRC. And, failed to provide victims with a legal space within which to give expression to their rights and concerns.

The International Bar Association and a number of leading South African lawyers expressed their concern at this turn of events. A coalition of South African NGOs, in turn, successfully challenged the amendment in the Constitutional Court, on the grounds that contrary to the TRC requirements, the proposed amendment on prosecutions did not require victims to be consulted prior to amnesty or indemnity being granted. Before judgment was delivered, former police minister Adriaan Vlok, former police commissioner Johan van der Merwe, and retired police officers Christoffel Smith, Gert Otto, and Johannes Van Staden received suspended sentences in a court case that lasted only a few hours, without any public disclosure concerning past atrocities.

This was followed in November 2007 by President Mbeki's "Special Dispensation for Presidential Pardon's for Political Offenses," which enjoyed the support of a presidential advisory committee chaired by the official opposition party in parliament. It sought to give the prosecutor's office the power to effect plea bargains, again without consulting victims. Once more, civil society representatives resorted to the courts, and the Constitutional Court unanimously passed judgment in favor of the civil society coalition. Without seeking to limit presidential pardons per se, the judgment stated that "given our history, victim participation in accordance with the principles and the values of the TRC was the only rational means to contribute toward national reconciliation and national unity." Responding to the judgment, on October 18, 2010, the government released the names of 149 offenders, for a total of 652 offenses including 339 murders and 200 counts of attempted murder, being considered for pardon.

Suffice it to say, while the South African settlement prioritized truth over retributive justice, the quest for truth, whether through the courts or by other means, continues. This is seen, for example, in the stance of Thembi Simelane-Nkadimeng who has spent twenty-three years trying to find out what happened to her sister, Nokuthula, who was abducted by the security police and has not been seen since. Speaking at a symposium on the tenth anniversary of the TRC, she observed: "I am favoring prosecutions now because it is the only option I have left, but if I had an option to sit down and talk [with Nokuthula's abductors] I would choose that."[5] Not all victims would necessarily make the same choice as Simelane-Nkadimeng. Her testimony is, however, in continuity with a survey conducted earlier which showed that black South Africans saw truth, acknowledgment, apology, and an opportunity for victims to relate their stories of suffering in public as important alternatives to both retribution and monetary compensation.[6] The survey, interestingly, also showed that 65 percent of blacks viewed amnesty as a price that needed to be paid in return for disclosure of the truth about the past and a peaceful transition to democratic rule whereas, interestingly, only 18 percent of white South Africans saw it as such! Seventy-three percent of whites surveyed, however, concluded that apartheid was a crime against humanity—probably partly as a result of the extent of public disclosure about the past through the TRC.

The jury will always be out on just how much truth is required for victims to achieve a measure of closure on the past. What the debate in South Africa revealed is that victims are seeking more truth – as much

---

[5] See Charles Villa-Vicencio and Fanie du Toit (eds.), *Truth and Reconciliation in South Africa: Ten Years On* (Cape Town: David Philip, 2006), 108.

[6] James L. Gibson, *Does Truth Lead to Reconciliation? Testing the Considered Assumptions of the TRC Process* (Bloomington, Indiana: Midwest Political Science Association, 2004); James L. Gibson and Helen MacDonald (eds.), *Truth—Yes, Reconciliation—Maybe: South Africans Judge the Truth and Reconciliation Process* (Cape Town: Institute for Justice and Reconciliation, 2001).

truth as possible – and some form of reparation to get a measure of closure on past suffering.

Reparations and Victim Restoration

The ruling of the South African Constitutional Court in 1996, in response to the application brought by the Azanian Peoples' Organization (AZAPO) and other victims of apartheid concerning the amnesty clause in the TRC Act, is instructive in this regard.[7] The court upheld both the criminal and civil clauses of the amnesty clause, presenting reparations as a *quid pro quo* for victims and survivors being required to surrender their right to prosecution. It further ruled that parliament was justified in adopting a wide concept of reparations, which needs to be seen in relation to other programs of reconstruction and development. The separate judgment of Justice John Didcott is particularly important in this regard. It stated that any notion of reparations at the time needed to be indecisive for the simple reason that the government was not in a position to either assess the cost of reparations or to state whether it was possible to compensate all victims of apartheid.[8] Often overlooked in the reparations debate, Didcott's words are as telling today as they were in 1996, with the nature of reparations continuing to fuel the fires of debate.

This is seen in the continuing struggle for reparations by some victims who are making demands for reparations beyond the one-off payment of R 30, 000 to each victim named by the TRC as already discussed. At the forefront of this quest for reparation is the alien tort law

---

[7] AZAPO and Others vs. The President of the RSA and Others, 1996 (8) BCLR 1015 (CC).

[8] Section 2, 32 (4) of the Interim Constitution allows that no section of the Constitution, including the postscript on amnesty, should be regarded as having less validity than any other part of the Constitution. Of the nine judges, J. Didcott provided a separate concurring judgment, suggesting there is no way for the court to assess the cost involved or whether it is impossible to compensate all victims of apartheid. Arguing that the Act allows for "some *quid pro quo* for the loss" suffered as a result of gross human rights violations, he concedes that nothing "more definite, detailed and efficacious could feasibly have been promised at this stage." His substantial argument is, however, that Section 33 (2) of the Interim Constitution allows for amnesty for vicarious liability.

cases brought before in the U.S. Court of Appeals in New York by a group of apartheid victims, in which U.S.-based multinational companies that did business in South Africa during the apartheid years were sued for damages. The court case was supported by several high-profile South Africans, including Archbishop Emeritus Desmond Tutu, the former chairperson of the TRC and most of the TRC commissioners. The South African government has, in turn, acknowledged the right of victims to sue for damages under the alien tort law, although it earlier opposed this action, which it feared could have a negative impact on foreign investments and as being a matter to be decided within the context of South African law and the TRC.

While the need for material reparations was a central ingredient of TRC legislation and practice, the TRC mandate sets the bar considerably higher than the payment of monetary or material compensation. This involves the need to "restore the human dignity" of victims, which involves more than any one-off action by the courts, the state, or any other agency can deliver. It entails the manner in which the people of South Africa today relate to one another, whether they were oppressors, victims or bystanders in the apartheid struggle. It has particular significance for the coexistence between those who today continue to live under the shadow of past oppression, those who continue to enjoy the riches of the past, and those who have managed to establish themselves within the new economic élite. In brief, at the center of the reparations debate is the creation of a political, social, and economic dispensation that enables the nation to promote the possibility of social decency, economic justice, and a participatory democracy.

Reconstruction and Development

The struggle continues for what is required for the restoration of the human dignity of victims of South Africa's past dispensation. What is clear is that there is a need for economic growth, skills development, and adequate access to decent education and job creation to enable the poor to benefit from the resources of the South African economy which are not inconsiderable.

I interviewed Govan Mbeki, a veteran liberation leader and father of President Thabo Mbeki, shortly before his death in 2001. He had spent twenty-four years in a cell adjacent to Nelson Mandela on Robben Island. I asked him what it would take to repair the damage of apartheid. His answer was decisive: "having and belonging." "For political renewal to happen," he observed, "the economy needs to be restructured in such a way that the poor and socially excluded [the victims of apartheid] begin to share in the benefits of the nation's wealth." He insisted that for this to happen, all South Africans, "both black and white . . . need to feel they are part of the new nation. Those who do not feel welcome or at home in South Africa will not work for the common good. They can also cause considerable trouble."[9]

The political strife of the past years in the ruling ANC party in South Africa is underpinned by increasing tension between government and business interests on the one hand and workers on the other, in relation to Mbeki's concerns. Teachers, health workers, and others in the public services have gone out on extended strikes in demand of better salaries. There is growing discontent concerning the current brand of black economic empowerment, which trade unions see as a crude attempt at building a middle class that marginalizes and excludes the majority of black South Africans. Unemployment has increased and the gap between the rich and poor has widened since the demise of legislated apartheid. Even where the government improved its social services, the absolute level of poverty has risen. Tax adjustments have put approximately R 60 billion into the pockets of upper income earners and corporations, while trade liberalization has seen thousands of jobs lost due to tariff cuts, important parity pricing, and bilateral trade agreements. The lifting of exchange control has, in turn, helped companies that have made their wealth through South African raw materials to move their primary listing to the London and New York stock exchanges. Whatever the benefits of this liberalization of the economy, those excluded from its benefits are resentful and increasingly angry.

In brief, the international economic debate separates those, on the one hand, who favor and benefit from globalization, technological advancement, and international finance and those, on the other hand, who are unable to lift themselves out of the exploitation associated with sweatshops, the "dark satanic mills" and the ranks of the

---

[9] Charles Villa-Vicencio, *Walk with Us and Listen: Political Reconciliation in Africa* (Washington, DC: Georgetown University Press, 2009) 95–96. Mbeki was interviewed in Cape Town in April 2000.

unemployed. These realities are tearing at the fabric of South African politics in a way not seen since the inauguration of Nelson Mandela as president of a democratic South Africa in 1994. Unless the country can increase economic growth, while ensuring that the poor are drawn from a "second" and "third" economy into the mainstream economy, the recent forms of discontent among South Africa's under-classes is likely to intensify. They will probably not materialize into a popular revolution, but they would decidedly turn into what has been called "movements of desperation" with a capacity to undermine the sense of a national well-being expectation that was unleashed with the release of Mandela from prison, the unbanning of political organizations, and the advent of democracy.

Politics is about dealing with the possible. South Africa chose to deal with its "possible" in a certain way in 1994. The challenge today involves an urgency to address the gross economic disparity that characterizes South Africa—the structures and boundaries of which were entrenched in the economy of the past and perpetuated in the present. Get this one right and the deep wounds of the past are likely to heal with a little more success.[10]

---

[10] The final version of this chapter has been submitted in 2011.

CRISTIAN VASILE

Scholarship and Public Memory: The Presidential Commission for the Analysis of the Communist Dictatorship in Romania (PCACDR)

The Presidential Commission for the Analysis of the Communist Dictatorship in Romania (PCACDR—from now on the Commission) was founded in April 2006 by President Traian Băsescu to draft a report on the crimes of the 1945–1989 period. The document would provide the basis for the official condemnation of the Romanian communist regime. The report had to investigate the institutions and methods that made the crimes and abuses of the totalitarian regime possible, as well as to document the role of communist officials in supporting and perpetuating the system.[1] Even after 1989, many communist crimes were concealed and denied. Until 2006, important communist archives, including the Communist Party archives, remained inaccessible to researchers. Historians were hindered in their efforts to study the recent past, while the victims of the communist regime could prove neither the political nature of their convictions nor the unjust manner of the confiscation of their property. This chapter will examine the cooperation within the Commission between historians and other social scientists, on the one hand, and former political prisoners, dissidents, members of the Romanian Diaspora. At the same time, I will look into the debate involving the Commission's members and other societal actors, who employed history for their ends in the pub-

---

[1] Vladimir Tismaneanu, "Democracy and Memory: Romania Confronts its Communist Past," *The Annals of American Academy of Political and Social Sciences* vol. 617, no. 1, May 2008.

lic sphere (politicians, university professors, who organized conferences harshly criticizing the report on communist system, and Romanians nostalgic for Nicolae Ceauşescu's dictatorship).

The Commission was created two years after the International Commission for the Study of the Holocaust in Romania completed its own denouncing Romanian Fascism and revealing the country's involvement in the Holocaust. In a 2005 interview, President Băsescu suggested that a report on communist crimes should be drawn up by senior historians associated with the Romanian Academy. Civil society leaders opposed this approach, pointing out that some elderly Academy historians were nationalistic and had significant track records of involvement in the communist regime's politics of culture. For instance, former chair of the Academy's History Section was mentioned in the Wiesel Commission's as a "selective denier" of the Holocaust.[2]

Sorin Ilieşiu, vice president of the Civic Alliance, an independent organization highly regarded by large sections of the domestic public sphere, called for the official condemnation of the communist regime in February 2006. He published a public appeal supported by several trade union leaders, civic organizations, and prominent intellectuals. In doing so, he resumed the efforts from the 1990s of Senator Constantin Ticu Dumitrescu, leader of the Association of Romanian Former Political Prisoners. The latter initiated Law 187/1999 on "Access to One's Own File and the Unmasking of the as a Political Police." It granted Romanians access to the files compiled by the communist secret service, the dreaded Securitate. In 2006, Dumitrescu became one of the eleven members of the Executive Committee of the National Council for the Study of the Securitate Archives.[3]

The Commission's activity cannot be understood without examining both the political struggle and the debates over the CNSAS

---

[2] Tuvia Friling, Radu Ioanid, Mihail E. Ionescu (eds.) *Final Report* (Iaşi: Polirom–International Commission on the Holocaust in Romania, 2004), 379, n. 234. http://www.inshr-ew.ro/pdf/Final_Report.pdf. Accessed on October 28, 2010.

[3] For details about CNSAS, see Lavinia Stan, "Access to Securitate Files: The Trials and Tribulations of a Romanian Law," in *East European Politics and Societies*, vol. 16, 2002, 55–90; Lavinia Stan (ed.), *Transitional Justice in Eastern Europe and Former Soviet Union: Reckoning with the Communist Past* (Oxon–New York: Routledge, 2009).

leadership. In spring 2006, Parliament renewed the mandate of the CNSAS leadership. The Democratic Party of President Băsescu then inexplicably blocked Dumitrescu's election as the Committee's chair. Dumitrescu lost the position to the Democratic Party representative Corneliu Turianu, although he was the best choice for the CNSAS presidency. After the general elections, the CNSAS faced internal crisis, and the press accused President Băsescu and the Democratic Party of having masterminded Dumitrescu's failure to grant access to some Securitate files. Moreover, journalists focused on the allegedly autocratic nature of the intelligence agencies and national security laws that Băsescu had promoted in 2005. They contrasted Băsescu's reluctance to condemn the communist dictatorship with the Liberal prime minister's readiness to establish the Institute for the Investigation of Communist Crimes in Romania. Subsequently, the Commission was created during the battle between the ruling Democratic and Liberal Parties, which both competed for the anti-communist vote.[4]

Political scientist Vladimir Tismaneanu's name appeared frequently in the discussions on the need to investigate communist repression. In 2005, in an interview with the weekly, the Social Democratic leader Mircea Geoană named the University of Maryland professor as a possible head of a commission. In an interview with President Băsescu, mentioned Tismaneanu's book (2003)[5] as a landmark in the interpretation of Romanian communism because it showed the continuity between the Stalinist regime of 1945–1964 (and its allegedly "ethnically non-Romanian" Securitate controlled by Jewish, Hungarian, and Russian agents) and Ceauşescu's regime of 1965–1989 (and its allegedly "patriotic" state security). Because Tismaneanu's writings were well-known in Romania (he received two honorary doctorates for his academic analysis of totalitarianism) and his scholarly domestic and international profile was unmatched by other Romanian scholars, Băsescu appointed Tismaneanu as chair of the Presidential

---

[4] Cristian Vasile, "The Presidential Commission for the Analysis of the Communist Dictatorship in Romania," in Lavinia Stan, Nadya Nedelsky (eds.), *Encyclopedia of Transitional Justice* (Cambridge: Cambridge University Press, 2012), 366–371.

[5] Vladimir Tismaneanu, *Stalinism for All Seasons: A Political History of Romanian Communism* (Berkeley and Los Angeles: University of California Press, 2003).

Commission. Yet, the appointment was bitterly contested, primarily by extreme right and extreme left groups supportive of virulent nationalism, both because Tismaneanu had denounced Romanian intolerance toward ethnic minorities and because he belonged to a Jewish family known for its ties to the Stalinist regime. Tismaneanu's parents were underground members of then illegal Romanian Communist Party. They fought in Spain with the International Brigades, but they never belonged to the communist leadership. In 1960 his father was expelled from the Communist Party for deviating from the official dogma.

The Commission was not a parliamentary commission backed by a wide range of political parties. With a mandate for truth exclusively, the body was academic in nature and significantly different from South Africa's Truth and Reconciliation Commission. Because it had no subpoena power to summon perpetrators and no budget of its own, its mission was limited to analyzing the communist dictatorship. The mission of the Romanian Commission was to elaborate a "scientific"— that is, objective, systematic and comprehensive—report on the communist repressive institutions, methods, and leaders responsible for human rights violations. Its name was inspired by the German parliamentary inquiry commission of 1992.

After President Băsescu's nomination, Tismaneanu was entrusted to choose twenty other Commission members, including scholars (historians like Dragoş Petrescu, Andrei Pippidi, Marius Oprea, Alexandru Zub, political scientist Levente Salat, and UCLA sociologist Gail Kligman), civil society representatives (Sorin Ilieşiu, Romulus Rusan), opinion leaders (Nicolae Manolescu, H.-R. Patapievici, Stelian Tănase), former political prisoners or dissidents such as Constantin Ticu Dumitrescu, Radu Filipescu, and highly respected members of the democratic communist-period exile—Virgil Ierunca, Monica Lovinescu, Sorin Alexandrescu, and Mihnea Berindei. I served as scientific secretary.

The non-scholar members assured moral standing and symbolic endorsement for the report. The document was drafted with the aid of thirty experts, mostly young historians (ethnic Romanians, Hungarians, and Germans). Except for the secretary, Commission members worked without compensation. Due to their collaboration with the Securitate, two Commission members—historian Sorin Antohi and Metropolitan of Banat Nicolae Corneanu—had to resign in May and December 2006, respectively. On December 18, 2006 President Băsescu endorsed the report before the Parliament and proclaimed the Romanian communist regime as "illegitimate and criminal."[6] His speech broke the judicial deadlock both in property restitution cases (e.g., the presidential speech was invoked in court the Northern Maramureş County) and in instances of wrongful condemnation in the communist period (e.g., the case of Romanian Hungarians condemned after their solidarity with the 1956 Hungarian Revolution).

A survey of post-1990 works on the historiography of communism in Romania suggests that memory has had a significant impact on historical writing. However, in some cases various anti-communists with antidemocratic stands during 1930s and 1940s—even associated with the extreme right political parties and Marshall Ion Antonescu's dictatorship[7] were praised and uncritically presented by several influential historians (mainly trained during national Stalinism[8]). In the early 1990s, one could notice the glaring absence of a clear distinction between memory and history. The situation contrasted with western theoretically informed historiographical studies which tend to locate memory as a subcategory of oral history or to ignore it.[9] After a decade this historiographical trend was diminishing and the 2004 of the International Commission for the Study of the Holocaust (Wiesel Commission) contributed to such process of reevaluating this methodological confusion.

Historians within the Commission dealing with the communist past had to confront such an overlap between memory and history as well. They tried to avoid giving preference to memory. At the same time though, the body was mandated to provide legitimate voice to the

---

[6] Traian Băsescu, *The Speech Given by the President of Romania, Traian Băsescu, on the Occasion of the Presentation of the Report by the Presidential Commission for the Analysis of the Communist Dictatorship in Romania*, available at: http://cpcadcr.presidency.ro/upload/8288_en.pdf, accessed on May 20, 2009.

[7] See Dennis Deletant, *Hitler's Forgotten Ally: Ion Antonescu and His Regime, Romania, 1941–1944* (Palgrave Macmillan: Basingstoke, 2006).

[8] On a comparative discussion of this concept, see Vladimir Tismaneanu, "What Was National Stalinism?" in Dan Stone (ed.) *The Oxford Handbook of Postwar European History* (Oxford: Oxford University Press, 2012), 462–479.

[9] Katharine Hodgkin, Susannah Radstone (eds.), *Contested Pasts: The Politics of Memory* (London-New York: Routledge, 2003), 3.

victims. Therefore, it showed empathy for the victims of communism. However, some experts of the Commission were reluctant to accept both the term (e.g., Adrian Cioflâncă, research fellow at the "A.D. Xenopol" History Institute) and the number of the victims of communist dictatorship provided by the representatives of the former political prisoners (e.g, university professor Andrei Pippidi, and Dorin Dobrincu, research fellow at the Jassy "A.D. Xenopol" History Institute).[10]

Within the Commission there were divergences between experts and the so-called "memory activists," but specific disagreements never escalated into crises. There were situations when historians were more firm regarding the communist past in comparison with memory activists, and dissidents. There were debates within the Commission between Radu Filipescu and some historians over the role of the former procommunist prime minister Petru Groza during the totalitarian regime. Radu Filipescu was jailed in the 1980s for his political involvement against the Ceaușescu regime. At the time, he distributed leaflets and therefore was arrested and indicted for propaganda against the communist system. In the context of the attempts by Radio Free Europe and various western NGOs to release him, the communist propaganda machinery launched many calumnies against Filipescu including the fact that his protection is due both to his privileged statute rooted in the Stalinist period (1948–1953) and to his family origins. Filipescu's mother was the niece of Groza, the former Romanian prime minister in (pro) communist governments. Filipescu's proposal during the sessions of the commission included empathy and understanding for Petru Groza, but the scholars rejected his suggestion to appeal to the information provided by an authorized biography of the former prime minister.[11] Just before the end of the official condemnation, Filipescu posted his resume on the Romanian Presidency website admitting that he was in a conflict of interest due to his family background, as a distant relative of Groza, and that the other members of the Commission rejected his proposal for a more lenient reading of

---

[10] Vladimir Tismaneanu, Dorin Dobrincu, Cristian Vasile (eds.), *Raport final*, (Bucharest: Humanitas, 2007), 463, n. 4.
[11] Dorin Liviu Bîtfoi, *Petru Groza. Ultimul burghez* (Bucharest: Compania, 2004).

Groza's involvement in the communist takeover and consolidation in Romania.[12]

As mentioned earlier, the Commission included also Romanian Hungarian historians. After Nikita Khrushchev's Secret Speech and during the 1956 Hungarian Revolution, Romania's intellectual milieus and other social groups made a few demonstrations of solidarity going beyond ethnic boundaries. It is true that Romanian-Hungarian latent tensions in Transylvania—also seen in the literary and academic circles—were deepened by the creation of the Hungarian Autonomous Region. They did hinder communication at critical moments, especially in 1956, when the existent communist leadership showed signs of weakness and illegitimacy. The revolutionary process in Budapest, which also questioned the one-party monopoly of power, was not used to develop a Romanian–Hungarian joint platform liable to challenge the supremacy exerted over the Romanian society by the communist party apparatus. However, several interethnic networks (i.e, Romanian-Hungarian) appeared in 1956, as their members expressed solidarity with the ideas of the Hungarian revolution. The Hungarian Catholic priest Aladár Szoboszlay led such a network which also pleaded for the creation of a Romanian-Hungarian-Austrian confederation.[13] It was discovered by the political police and as a consequence fifty-seven people were sentenced in 1958 (ten of them were executed). The history of these initiatives and groups was detailed in the Comission's Report. The juridical rehabilitation and the annulment of these sentences were hampered after 1989 because many judges and segments of the public opinion considered that the fifty-seven people were not victims of communism, but pro-Hungarian militants for the disintegration of Romania. Among those who think in such a way were also ethnic Romanian former political prisoners. This is so despite the fact that Romanians and Hungarians were jailed together, especially after the Hungarian Revolution. The old Romanian-Hungarian distrust reappeared mainly in the context of March 1990 interethnic clashes

---

[12] Radu Filipescu, "Curriculum Vitae"; http://cpcadcr.presidency.ro/upload/Radu_Filipescu.pdf; accessed on October 26, 2010.

[13] Levente Salat et al., "Situaţia minorităţilor naţionale. Maghiarii," in *Raport final*, 351.

in Târgu Mureș.[14] With all this in mind, it truly was an achievement that, after a few objections, Constantin Ticu Dumitrescu endorsed the Report, including the sections about the 1956–1958 period, which were written by Romanian Hungarian experts. In this sense, the Report brought together the traumatic experiences of Romanians and Hungarians during the communist period.

But there is an even better aftermath to this story. In 2010, the Court of Appeal of Cluj accepted the December 18, 2006 presidential message addressed to the Parliament as evidence in favor of Aladar Szoboslay's relatives claiming the annulment of their penalties and condemnations during communist period. The judges were convinced by the lawyers of the victims of the 1958 repression, who invoked the presidential discourse condemning the communist regime as illegitimate and criminal. The consequence to abiding to the verdict of the Presidential Speech is that the military communist criminal justice system in 1958 was part and parcel of the mechanisms of totalitarian power that defied both the rule of law and the separation of powers.[15] Taking into account the Court's reparatory decisions and the historiographical trends advanced by the Report, one can say that the Romanian Hungarians' memory was included officially within Romanian collective memory generating a consensual discourse. Such interethnic consensus—in contrast with the Yugoslav case, for example—aims at understanding the mechanism of pedagogy and representation necessary for a successful exit from dictatorship.

During the Commission's activity, the members and the experts also faced difficulties in obtaining access to requested archival material necessary for providing a fuller account of some of the topics analyzed. For example, in 2006, sociologist Gail Kligman and other Hungarian-Romanian experts demanded access to the archives of the National Institute for Statistics. They wanted to obtain more data on the num-

---

[14] Tom Gallagher, "Nationalism and Romanian Political Culture in the 1990s," in Duncan Light, David Phinnemore (eds.), *Post-Communist Romania: Coming to Terms with Transition*, (Basingstoke: Palgrave Macmillan, 2001), 104–126. Tom Gallagher, *Democrație și naționalism în România, 1989–1998*, (Bucharest: All, 1998).

[15] "Condamnarea unor participanți la revoluția maghiară (1956)–anulată." http://www.historia.ro/exclusiv_web/actualitate/articol/condamnarea-unor-participanti-revolutia-maghiara-1956-anulata, accessed October 29, 2010.

ber of legal and illegal abortions, socio-demographic information regarding the evolution of Transylvanian towns' population, and on the Romanianization process in the communist period. The research was hindered and blocked by the head of the Institute for Statistics probably because the topic—the nation building process—was too sensitive in the eyes of this "patriotic" official. There might have also been another reason for such a refusal. The Institute was subordinated to the prime minister and in 2006 the political dispute between the presidency and the head of the government was at its peak.[16] But beyond such failures to access some significant documents, I believe that the whole activity of the Commission represented both an attempt to symbolically build a civic nation, and a serious effort to avoid writing the history of communism only from the perspective of ethnic Romanians.

As part of the Department of Political Affairs of the Romanian Presidency, the Commission followed the internal rules of the presidency. Its leadership maintained close contact with Claudiu Săftoiu, then the presidential adviser on domestic politics. It communicated with the archives of the army and intelligence services through C. Săftoiu and Sergiu Medar, the presidential adviser on national security. The PCACDR received privileged access to some communist cadres' files preserved in the National Archives (including the documents of the Agitation and Propaganda Department of the Communist Party) and the archive of the Aiud prison, one of the harshest jails in communist times. The members and experts of the Commission had the possibility to photocopy thousands of archival documents. Some were cited in the report, while others, the most important ones, were published in two separate volumes.[17]

In November 2006, after seven months of activity and research in the National Archives, the archives of the CNSAS and of the Inte-

---

[16] Cristian Vasile, "Comisia Prezidențială pentru Analiza Dictaturii Comuniste din România și accesul la arhivele comunismului românesc," in Sergiu Musteață, Igor Cașu (eds.), *Fără termen de prescripție. Aspecte ale investigării crimelor comunismului în Europa* (Chișinău: Editura Cartier, 2011), 208–209.

[17] Mihnea Berindei, Dorin Dobrincu, Armand Goșu eds., *Istoria comunismului din România. Perioada Gheorghe Gheorghiu-Dej (1945–1965)* (Bucharest, Humanitas: 2009) and *Istoria comunismului din România. Volumul II: Documente Nicolae Ceaușescu (1965–1971)* (București: Polirom, 2012). At least another volume is scheduled in this series.

rior and Defense Ministries, the Commission completed its 660-page report, endorsed by all Commission members. The report detailed the organization and functioning of the party-state, the role of ideology, the failed de-Stalinization of 1955–1958 and 1965–1971, the emergence of national communism in the 1960s, and Ceauşescu's dynastic communism. The document was criticized for employing a broad definition of unrecognized in international law, although the term "communist genocide" was used only once, in the chapter prepared by the representatives of the former political prisoners (for more details see Bogdan C. Iacob's chapter in this volume).

Lustration was not initially on the Commission's agenda, but in the end the body agreed to recommend its adoption. Opinion polls suggested that, while only 34 percent of Romanian saw communism negatively, one in two respondents believed that lustration was necessary. This public support for lustration contradicted the lack of enthusiasm for such a measure among Commission members, who saw the communist ideology as a blueprint for totalitarian repression, but noticed the practical obstacles to pursue lustration. Some of them supported lustration other feared that the *lustrati* would successfully appeal to the European Court of Human Rights. Another recommendation asked for the publication of a history textbook on communist repression. In August 2008, a textbook for high school, written by researchers from the governmental Institute for the Investigation of the Crimes of Communism in Romania (IICCR) and two members of the Tismaneanu Commission, was published.

The Commission ended its activity in December 2006. On the 18th of that month, President Traian Băsescu endorsed the final report in front of parliament and proclaimed the Romanian communist regime as "illegitimate and criminal." To mark the occasion, his speech became an official state document, but the president retained only a handful of the report's policy recommendations. For example, he supported "the identification of legal solutions to annul politically motivated prison and forced labor sentences given in virtue of Decree no. 153/1970 on 'social parasitism,' 'anarchism,' and any other 'deviant behavior.'"[18] The decree persecuted people unsupportive of the Ceauşescu regime and the unemployed (mostly Roma population).

---

[18] Traian Băsescu, *The Speech Given by the President of Romania.*

Traian Băsescu did not endorse lustration and the ban on communist symbols, but his speech broke the judicial deadlock in several cases of politically motivated arrests and abusive property nationalization.[19]

Part of the political elite disapproved of the Commission's report. The ultra-nationalistic and anti-Semitic Greater Romania Party headed by Corneliu Vadim Tudor tried to stop the president's speech with loud, hooliganic background noise, while the Social Democratic Party, heir to the Communist Party, boycotted the parliamentary session. This was because the report revealed the extent to which both Tudor and the Social Democrat leader Ion Iliescu were involved in the communist propaganda apparatus. Iliescu was head of the Propaganda Department in the 1960s and, as the first post-communist president, he avoided an honest assessment of his communist past and the regime's censorship practices. Criticism also came from the dominant Orthodox Church hierarchy, which alleged that the report breached the (without hate and zealousness) principle in historical writing. The Holy Synod of the Romanian Orthodox Church established a commission of historians with the mission to defend the Church and its prelates accused by PCACDR.[20] The problem here was that the Report did not avoid controversial topics such as the collaboration of the Orthodox officials with the Communist Party or the discrimination of the Roma population. From this point of view, the Report expressed symbolically the separation of Church and State and it challenged the mainstream historical discourse regarding the recent ecclesiastical history. In a way the Report was questioning a traditional definition of national identity.

---

[19] Mihai Bacalu, "Raportul Tismăneanu le-a adus terenuri," *Adevarul*, October 6, 2008. Available at: http://www.adevarul.ro/articole/raportul-tismaneanu-le-a-adus-terenuri.html, accessed June 2, 2009.

[20] In 2009 the Church historians published their report; among other assertions they charged the members of the Commission of displaying a historiographical scenario similar with Novatian's heresy; George-Eugen Enache et al., "Biserica Ortodoxa Romana in anii regimului comunist. Observatii pe marginea capitolului dedicat cultelor din *Raportul final* al Comisiei Prezidentiale pentru Analiza Dictaturii Comuniste din Romania," *Studii Teologice* (Bucharest), no. 2, 2009, 7–104.

It must be stressed that at the end of the communist regime, the Romanian Orthodox Church was deeply under control in terms of personnel policy, priests' appointments, transfers and promotions—almost entirely decided by the inspectors for religious affairs (împuterniciți).[21] In each phase of the development of the regime, the Orthodox prelates managed to establish a negotiation mechanism for the Church (quite different in the 1950s in comparison with the 1980s). In the context of this cooperation, one can identify various alliances established by the orthodox hierarchy with different groups of the communist leadership. The Church used also the mechanism of negotiation with delegates for religious communities at the local level. Additionally, the corruption of the Religious Denomination Department allowed the Church to be quite present in the life of its believers.[22] At the same time though, the Church was weakened by its own corruption, by a great number of clergy with pro-fascist past who were prisoners of their own biographies, thus subjects of possible blackmail. But it is worth noticing that some of them were recuperated and rehabilitated after their imprisonment; and even joined the ecclesiastical diplomacy after the 1960s. How did the church confront its past compromises and collaboration with the communist regime? While we try to find an answer to this question it is useful to underline that the aforementioned negotiation mechanisms forged during the communist period lasted in post-1989 years. This is due to the fact that continuity with communist times was characteristic both for the Church's structures and various political bodies: government, Parliament, local and county councils, and so on. Persons compromised under the communist regime both in political life and within ecclesiastical milieus survived and maintained themselves in high positions.

A prominent example of persistence of such negotiation mechanism could be identified two years after the endorsement of the *Final*

---

[21] Special delegates supervising the Church at the local level; for details see: Anca Maria Şincan, *Of Middlemen and Intermediaries: Negotiating the State Church Relationship in Communist Romania. The Formative Years*, Ph.D. Thesis, Central European University, 2011, 116.

[22] Anca Maria Şincan, "Mecanisme de opresiune si control: Imputernicitul pentru culte," in Vladimir Tismaneanu, Dorin Dobrincu, Cristian Vasile (eds.), *Raport final*, 271–272.

Report when the Orthodox Church's lobby[23] decisively influenced the Juridical and Legal Affairs Commission of the Romanian Senate and Chamber of Deputies. In 2008, this parliamentary body adopted a political initiative regarding the change of the Law concerning both CNSAS and the access to personal files, defying the recommendations of the *Final Report*. Up until 2008, the law stipulated that every Romanian citizen (meaning also every NGO, mass media, political parties, public institution) had the right to be informed by CNSAS whether a certain person, including the Orthodox Patriarch, prelates, bishops, high clergy, had been working for the former Securitate as officer, collaborator, agent, or informant. The version of the law adopted that year by the Senate limited the right of the public by reducing the large scale process of vetting the prelates.[24] It specified only that the clergy can be verified exclusively at the demand of the representatives of their own religious denomination, meaning the leadership of their Church.[25] Somewhat predictably, until now the legal representatives of the Orthodox Church did not formulate any demand concerning the vetting of their subordinates or colleagues from the Holy Synod.[26]

Some historians considered useless the unmasking of the Orthodox prelates who collaborated with the communist regime. For example, Florin Constantiniu stated in 2005 that: "paradoxically, after the demise of communism—in some circumstances—the attacks against the Church are becoming increasingly active in comparison with the

---

[23] Professor Thomas Bremer said that after 1989 in Central and Eastern Europe "the role of religion was to change radically"; see "Religion and the Conceptual Boundary in Central and Eastern Europe: Introductory Remarks," in Thomas Bremer (ed.), *Religion and the Conceptual Boundary in Central and Eastern Europe: Encounters of Faiths* (Palgrave Macmillan: Basingstoke, 2008), 2. I would say that for Romania it is true in a greater measure the statement "the role of Orthodox hierarchy changed radically."

[24] Lucian Turcescu and Lavinia Stan, "The Romanian Orthodox Church and Democratisation: Twenty Years Later," *International Journal for the Study of the Christian Church*, vol. 10, no. 2, May 2010, 8.

[25] Legea nr. 293/2008 pentru aprobarea Ordonanței de urgență a Guvernului nr. 24/2008 privind accesul la propriul dosar și deconspirarea Securității published in *Monitorul Oficial*, Part I, No. 800, November 18, 2008.

[26] It is wise not to single out the Romanian Orthodox Church's hierarchy: with few exceptions the behavior of the other religious denominations' leadership was similar.

communist period." One year later, the same historian, with strongly nationalistic opinions, member of the Romanian Academy, who worked with Ceauşescu's brother (Ilie Ceauşescu) during the 1970s and the 1980s, also accused Vladimir Tismaneanu of denigrating the image of his own father, Leonte Tismaneanu.[27] Some of his colleagues also strongly attacked the Report for questioning Ceauşescu's independence from Moscow, as implied in his speech of August 21, 1968, condemning the Soviet invasion of Czechoslovakia. Scholars whose careers spanned over decades of communist rule felt threatened by this interpretation. In contrast, younger scholars praised the report as truthful and objective.

On April 11, 2007, President Băsescu created the twelve-member Presidential Advisory Commission for the Analysis of Communist Dictatorship in Romania, chaired by Tismaneanu, to monitor the implementation of the original Commission's recommendations. Only four of the twelve recommendations assumed by the president were implemented to date: presentation of the Final Report in the country's major university centers, the publication of the history textbook on communist dictatorship, greater transparency of and access to the archives of communist regime, and the public recognition of the sufferings endured by the former political prisoners. The plan to create in Bucharest a Museum of Communist Dictatorship, which seemed feasible at one point in 2011, collapsed. It was rejected both by the political elite and influential intellectuals, while other alternative projects came out especially after 2010. For example, there were proposals for a Museum of Totalitarianism, including both the fascist and communist experiments, and a Museum of the Communist Prison System based in Jilava penitentiary, the dreaded Fort no. 13, near Bucharest.[28]

---

[27] Florin Constantiniu, "Condamnarea comunismului: observaţii preliminare," *Dosarele Istoriei*, no. 12 (124), 2006, 4–5.

[28] For example see Ion Vianu, "Pentu un muzeu al totalitarismului," *Revista 22*, July 19, 2011; Lucia Hossu-Longin, "În viziunea Palatului Cotroceni: un muzeu al comunismului mai relaxat?!" *Observatorul Cultural*, no. 591, September 9, 2011; Vasile Ernu, "Muzeul comunismului: povestea celor din primăverii spusă celor din Ferentari," *Critic Atac*, August 31, 2011; Florin Abraham, "Muzeul Comunismului sau Muzeul Dictaturilor. Critica tendinţelor hegemonice în interpretarea trecutului," *Critic Atac*, September 1, 2011. On the curatorial proposal that was advanced

Besides producing an academic report, the Commission was mandated to pass moral judgment on the communist regime's record of lawlessness, to provide legitimate voice to the victims, and to reignite the long delayed transitional justice process. In the absence of public consultations, victims were given a "voice" by the inclusion in the Final Report (Part 3, Chapter 1, pp. 459–469)[29] of a document produced by the Association of the Former Political Prisons. One should not forget that in drafting various chapters of the Report, members and experts of the Commission relied on oral history interviews and estimates of the number of victims provided by the Sighet Memorial of the Victims of Communism. According to Tismaneanu, the Commission aimed to understand the traumatic history through an academic approach that presupposed distance from the surveyed topic and empathy for the victims.[30] This presupposed continuous efforts to balance the normative and analytical approaches. Its members believed that historians are not judges, but they cannot refrain from engaging in moral judgment when exploring crimes against humanity.

In spite of the brevity of its activities, the continuous harassment from the extreme right and extreme left media, the Commission fulfilled its task and identified the responsibility of communist leaders and institutions for the killings, abuses, and crimes of 1945–1989. In the absence of support from the government and the civil society, not all the body's recommendations have been implemented. The Commission did not enjoy the support of a broad range of political parties, but its Final Report was the first to engender a national debate on the communist regime and its crimes. It raised key questions regarding the repressive character of Romanian communism, the role of the

---

to governmental authorities by the representatives of the Institute for the Investigation of Communist Crimes and the Memory of the Romanian Exile (between March 2010 and May 2012, Vladimir Tismaneanu was the president of the Scientific Council; the present author was Scientific Director between September 2011 and May 2012) see Viviana-Roxana Iacob, "The Laboratory-Museum. Explorations for a Museum of the Communist period in Romania," *European Museum Academy*, http://www.europeanmuseumacademy.eu/4/upload/1_the_laboratory_museum.pdf, accessed December 12, 2013.

[29] *Genocidul comunist în România*, in *Raport final* cited, 459–469.

[30] See also his contribution in this volume.

secret informers, the collaboration of some prelates (mostly Orthodox) with the and the Communist Party, and the destruction of communist archives. A major challenge was that individuals linked to the
communist past—perpetrators, victims, and bystanders—were still
alive and present in the public sphere. The PCACDR was not only
a history commission[31] that aimed to disseminate a democratic re-
education of post-1989 society. It also became a pillar for supporting
the development of sites, institutions (a museum of communist dictatorship, a memorial) and processes devoted to remembering, commemorating and working through the communist past.[32] Nevertheless,
the legitimacy of the Commission and of the Final Report was consistently challenged by multiple public and political actors (for details
on this delegitimization process see Bogdan C. Iacob's chapter in this
volume). Bordering on the absurd, among those involved was a former member of the Commission, Sorin Ilieșiu, the initiator of the
civic appeal that led to the creation of the body itself. He is currently a
member of the Romanian Senate on the part of the Reformed Liberal
Party. Very recently, on December 9, 2013, Sorin Ilieșiu criticized what
he perceived as the fallacies the 2006 Report and called for a new condemnation which had to be initiated and documented by the Romanian Academy with the support of the Institute for the Investigation
of Communist Crimes and the Memory of Romanian Exile[33]. From
2006 until 2011, Ilieșiu fully and enthusiatically supported the Commission's Report. Recently, he shockingly lambasted the document's
failure to present both the profanation of the Christian faith, and the

---

[31] For analysis of the PCACDR as history commission and *not* a truth commission see Lavinia Stan, *Transitional Justice in Post-Communist Romania:
The Politics of Memory* (Cambridge/New York: Cambridge University Press,
2013), 111–135.

[32] Cf. James Mark, *The unfinished Revolution: Making Sense of the Communist
Past in Central-Eastern Europe* (New Haven and London: Yale University
Press, 2010), XII.

[33] Sorin Ilieșiu, "Apel pentru condamnarea totalitarismului comunist de către
membrii Parlamentului României, având ca fundament un raport elaborat
de Academia Română," http://www.agerpres.ro/media/index.php/comuni-
cate/item/243511-Comunicat-de-pres-Senator-PNL-Sorin-Ilieiu.html; accessed on January 6, 2013.

fact that even communist leaders contributed to the salvation of Romanian soul and being under Soviet attack.[34] This is only an example of how the process of dealing of the past in Romania and the Commission's long-term impact were compromised by increasing politicization and personal agendas as the country experienced, between 2006 and 2013, successive systemic crises and mass protests.

---

[34] Ibid.

IGOR CAŞU

Moldova under the Soviet Communist Regime: History and Memory

The history of Communism in the Republic of Moldova is arguably little-known in the West. Most of the Republic of Moldova was a part of Romania in the interwar period and it is historically, linguistically, and ethnically intertwined with that of Romania. However, one cannot ignore the status of Bessarabia as part of the Soviet Union. During the Cold War, Bessarabia was the only Soviet territory belonging historically and ethnically to a neighboring state—Communist Romania. Thus, one needs to make an extensive introduction on the nature of Soviet regime in former Moldavian SSR. One also has to answer a fundamental question that is intimately related to the mainstream discussions in the last twenty years about the Communist rule in the present day Moldova. Two seem to be the most pressing questions: Could the annexation of Bessarabia in the USSR in 1940, its reannexation in 1944 as well as subsequent Soviet policies be defined as a form of imperial rule? If so, what was specific in this story? The answers, however, cannot be separated from a more general issue: Was the Soviet Union an Empire?

The Soviet Union as Empire:
Theoretical Considerations

The nature of a given polity could be grasped more clearly in the light of the causes that brought about its end. The causes of the breakdown of the Soviet Union were manifold. Ideological crisis, economic failure, and the nationalities problem are usually invoked as main causes of the Soviet collapse. There were scholars though, such as Victor Zaslavsky, who argued that the nationalities policies and imperial character of the Soviet state were the main cause of the demise of USSR.[1] Other authors rightly distinguished between systemic crisis of the Communist regime in the Soviet Union and the crisis of Soviet federalism.[2] What is certain is that the Soviet collapse was less violent than expected, especially if we keep in mind the tradition of large-scale use of state violence during USSR's history. That was due to the fact that political secessionism from the part of national republics coincided with the desire of the leadership of the Russian Republic, personified by Yeltsin, to liquidate the Union Center as well as Gorbachev's unwillingness to use force on a large scale.

Between 1990 and 1991, at the level of perceptions, both national republics—to a lesser degree the Central Asian ones—and the Russian Republic felt they were victims of the unjust redistribution of resources and unequal system of economic exchanges. In other words, at the level of perceptions, nobody was satisfied with the situation and apparently approved the demise of the Soviet Union. At the level of objective, measurable variables, the absolute majority of Russians from Russia and from the non-Russian republics voted for the signing of the new Union Treaty in the federal referendum held in March 1991. At the same time, Baltic republics, Moldavia, Georgia, and Armenia decided to boycott the referendum, as it was anticipated that Moscow could use the vote of Russians and Russian speaking minorities as a motive to impose the signing of the new Union Treaty.[3]

The most authoritative and well documented account on the Soviet Nationalities Policy—albeit covering only the first two decades of the existence of the USSR—has been written by Terry Martin. Martin's

---

[1] Victor Zaslavsky, "Collapse of Empire—Causes: Soviet Union," in Karen Barkey and Mark von Hagen (eds.), *After Empire. Multiethnic Societies and Nation-Building: The Soviet Union and the Russian, Ottoman and Habsburg Empires* (Boulder, Co: Westview, 1997), 73–98.

[2] Andrea Graziosi, *Histoire de l'URSS* (Paris: Presse Universitaire de France, 2010), 500–501; Mark Kramer, "The Collapse of East European Communism and the Repercussion Within the Soviet Union," *Journal of Cold War Studies*, vol. 5, no. 4, 2003, 178–256; vol. 6. no. 4, 2004, 3–64.

[3] A. S. Barsenkov, A. I. Vdovin, *Istoriia Rossii, 1938-2002*, (Moscow: Aspekt, 2003), 373.

book stipulates that the Soviet Union was the first "affirmative action empire," which codified and institutionalized ethnicities, consolidating and even inventing, in some cases, alphabets for certain tribes, promoting ethnic cadres and intelligentsia in their own national territories. This was envisaged as a strategy of Lenin and Stalin to fight against and control a competing political ideology of mass mobilization—nationalism that was viewed as responsible for the liquidation of four empires after the World War I. The policy of *korenizatsiia* was promoted (Stalin called it *nationalizatsiia*) with this particular purpose in mind in the 1920s. It relied on the positive discrimination of non-Russians in order to convince them that in national terms USSR was not a continuation of the Tsarist Empire. In early 1930s, however, with the inception of the first Five-Year-Plan based on mass industrialization and collectivization and on the abandonment of NEP, *korenizatsiia* was relegated to the role of secondary policy. Instead, one could witness a slow rehabilitation of Russian Great Power nationalism, to be strengthened on the eve of World War II and especially during the war.[4]

The field of Soviet studies still lacks a detailed and minutely documented examination on the Soviet nationalities policy after 1945, at least one equal in scope and quality to Terry Martin's book on the interwar period. However, one assumes—and Martin is extrapolating in this sense—that up until the end of the Soviet Union, local nationalism and not Great Russian nationalism was perceived by Moscow as the greatest danger to the cohesion and the very existence of the USSR. This was the case at lest of Moldavian SSR as I will try to show further in this article.

Another important theoretical contribution to the study of Soviet nationalities policy has been made by Rogers Brubaker. His main argument is that the Soviet Union institutionalized nationhood, but at the same time it tried to wither away any political content of the meaning of the nation. His analysis echoes Stalin's well-worn pronouncement of socialist communities "national in form, socialist in content." Another

---

[4] David Brandenberger, "'...It Is Imperative to Advance Russian Nationalism as First Priority': Debates Within Stalinist Ideological Establishment, 1941–1945," in Ronald Suny and Terry Martin (eds.), *A State of Nations: Empire of Nations: Empire and Nation-Making in the Age of Lenin and Stalin* (New York, 2001), 275–300.

interesting and useful distinction that Brubaker makes is related to the institutionalization of two contradictory paradigms in the Soviet nationalities policy. The first was based on collective and territorial principles while the second was founded on the personal and ethno-cultural one. The former referred to the myriad of Soviet ethnicities that were offered the possibility to enjoy national rights such as schools in their language, newspapers, journals, and so on, but only within the borders of their own national territory. The latter concerned the Russians who enjoyed access and privilege to Russian schools and all other national rights in all parts of the Soviet Union, not only in the Russian Federation.[5] Even though the official policy in national Union republics was bilingualism, Russians were not supposed or expected to know the language of the titular nationality.

Mark Beissinger, one of the current authorities on ethnic mass mobilization in Soviet Union in the late 1980s to early 1990s,[6] emphasized "the pivotal role played by the Soviet state in blurring the boundary between state and empire and in pioneering forms of non-consensual control." He defined the USSR as "the most striking example of informal empire." He also insisted on the idea that one should understand "empire as claim rather as things" and even though Soviet Union did not claim to be an empire, the outcome was rather the contrary and "empire implies today illegitimate and non-consensual rule."[7]

Moldova under the Soviet Regime: What Was Specific?

How are the above mentioned theories of Soviet Union as empire relevant for the case of the Republic of Moldova (the former Moldavian Soviet Socialist Republic)? What was the character of relations between the authorities in Moscow and Chișinău and to what extent

---

[5] Rogers Brubaker, "Nationhood and the National Question in the Soviet Union and Post-Soviet Eurasia: An Institutional Account," in *Theory and Society*, vol. 23, no. 1 (February 1994), 47–78.

[6] Mark Beissinger, *Nationalist Mobilization and the Collapse of the Soviet State* (Cambridge: Cambridge University Press, 2002), 6.

[7] Mark Beissinger, "Rethinking Empire in the Wake of Soviet Collapse," in Zoltan Barany and Robert Moser (eds.), *Ethnic Politics and Post-Communism: Theories and Practice* (Ithaca: Cornell University Press, 2005), 19, 21, 25, 32.

they can be defined as imperial? At the same time, which are the difficulties of such a conceptualization?

Throughout the existence of the USSR, Soviet historiography and propaganda claimed that Russia and Moldavia had century old relations. It was stated that at least two medieval rulers of Principality of Moldavia[8]—Stephen the Great in the late fifteenth century and Dimitrie Cantemir (a personal friend of Peter the Great) in the early eighteenth century—asked for their principality to be included in Tsarist Empire. This narrative relied on a biased interpretation of the documents in which Moldavians asked for help in fighting the Ottomans. Such requests never implied the desire to unite with Russia. In 1812, after a six-year Russian-Turkish war, the Tsarist Empire occupied the Eastern part of medieval Principality of Moldavia and renamed it Bessarabia. At that time around 90 percent of the local population was ethnic Romanian.[9] This dropped to 50 percent on the eve of Bolshevik revolution due to mass colonization of the province with Russians, Ukrainians, Bulgarians, Gagauz, Germans, and Swiss. In March 1918, the local parliament *Sfatul Țării* voted for Union with Romania based on the so-called Lenin-Wilson principle of self-determination of peoples.

Throughout the interwar period, the Soviet Union did not recognized Romanian sovereignty over Bessarabia. This behavior was based on geopolitical reasons, as the USSR was interested to create a security zone for its biggest port on the Black Sea, Odessa, situated just 60 kilometers from the frontier. But they could not explicitly admit that Bessarabia was claimed based on dynastic, Tsarist criteria: that is, it had been conquered by sword by Alexander I in 1812 and the Soviet Union was the *de facto* heir of the Russian Empire. This was

---

[8] The Principality of Moldavia covered the territories from Carpathian Mountains in the West to Dniester River in the East, and from Black Sea and Danube mouths in the South to Podolia in the North.

[9] The terms Moldavian and Bessarabian refers to regional identity, not ethnic. From an ethnic point of view, historical Bessarabia and present day Republic of Moldova are inhabited by Romanians. The interchangeable use of the term Moldavians/Moldovans has been ethnicized in the Soviet period. The majority of this population self identifies as Moldavians (*Moldoveni*). See more on that in Dmitri Furman, "Moldavskie moldavane i rumynskie moldavane," *Prognosis*, no. 1, 2007, 278–315, Charles King, *Moldovans. Cultural Politics between Romania and Russia* (Stanford: Hoover Institution Press, 2001).

especially true in the 1920s, when the official Soviet paradigm about the Tsarist Empire was extremely critical of pre-revolutionary Russia and especially its policy toward non-Russians. This situation was best expressed in Lenin's famous postulate that "Tsarist Russia was the prison of peoples." This is also one of the explanations for Moscow's promotion of the *korenizatsiia* process in the first decade after the revolution. The Kremlin leadership wished to demonstrate to non-Russians that the Bolshevik regime was different from the *ancien régime*. In the case of Bessarabia, the Soviet regime invented a new formula, ideologically mixed with the ethnic one, in order to legitimize its pretentions over the territory between Prut and Dniester Rivers. After several abortive military attempts to establish control in Bessarabia, Moscow changed its tactics in mid 1920s by creating a separate Moldavian autonomous republic (MASSR) on the Ukrainian territory. Situated just across the Dniester river and Bessarabia, it comprised some 160,000 Moldavians, (i.e., ethnic Romanians), but their share in the total population of MASSR was only a third.[10] The establishment of Moldavian autonomy had first and foremost a crucial function for external consumption: to show to the world and to European Communists particularly that USSR was different from Tsarist Russia, that it was not imperialistic. It was proof that it cared about the supposed injustice made to Bessarabia and its inhabitants through their incorporation into Romania. More precisely, the idea was to demonstrate that the unification engineered by Bucharest authorities and their local stooges divided a people, as the two parts were separated by the Dniester River. In this narrative, Soviet claims over Bessarabia simply became manifestations of the USSR's will to unite a nation—the so-called Moldavian one—that supposedly was subject to the national and social yoke of the Romanian "landlords and bourgeoisie" in the interwar period.

This was the first instance when there was a direct connection between Soviet foreign policy goals and the creation of the national territory inside the Soviet Union. According to historian Terry Martin, the situation presented above was an exceptional case when "the Piedmont principle was even the primary motivation for the formation of a

---

[10]   Elena Negru, *Politica etnoculturală in RASSM, 1924–1940* (Chişinău: Editura Prut Internaţional, 2003), 17.

national republic: Moldavian ASSR." According to the same author, the Piedmont principle was nothing else than "the belief that cross-border ethnic ties could be exploited to project Soviet influence into neighboring states."[11] Ukraine itself employed the Piedmont Principle in relation to Poland and even Russia at that moment, but Kharkov [the capital of Ukraine until 1934] agreed on the formation of MASSR as it remained a territory of this Soviet republic. The new autonomous republic had its temporary capital established in Balta and, since 1929, in Tiraspol. What is more important from the point of view of the perspectives invested by Moscow in this endeavor, the founding document of MASSR dated from October 12, 1924 mentioned that the western frontier of new autonomous republic was Prut River. It included *a priori* Bessarabia and Chișinău was to become its permanent capital. The MASSR existed from 1924 to 1940. Its development is important as the national formation experiment employed in this case anticipated in great part Moscow's policy toward the Moldavian SSR, established in 1940 after the occupation of Bessarabia (and Northern Bukovina) by the Red Army. Between 1924 and 1932, the Soviet authorities tried to create a separate Moldavian language based on a local Russified vernacular in Cyrillic alphabet. Such experiment though was abandoned after it was admitted to be total failure because the local Moldavians did not recognize it as a literary standard. Subsequently, from 1932 to 1938, Stalin himself agreed to switch to Latin alphabet and make the local Moldavian as similar to Romanian as possible.[12] Among the promoters of Romanian was a Russian Bessarabian, Grigori Staryi, president of the Council of People's Commissars of MASSR. He would be shot by Stalin in October 1937 during the Great Terror. Other members of the party and state nomenklatura from the MASSR establishment, as well as writers and journalists were sent to their deaths on

---

[11] Terry Martin, *The Affirmative Action Empire. Nations and Nationalism in the Soviet Union, 1923–1939* (Ithaca and London: Cornell University Press, 2001), 274.

[12] Charles King, "The Ambivalence of Ethnicity or How the Moldovan Language Was Made," *Slavic Review*, vol. 58, no. 1, Spring, 1999, 117–142. See also his seminal book that includes a detailed analysis of the interwar experiment in MASSR: *Moldovans: Cultural Politics Between Romania and Russia* (Stanford: Hoover Institution Press, 2001).

accusations of putatively being Romanian and sometimes Polish or German spies.[13]

On June 28, 1940, the Red Army occupied Bessarabia and Northern Bukovina as a result of the Nazi-Soviet Pact of August 23, 1939. According to several articles published by *Pravda* in the aftermath of the occupation, the latter was presented as a union of MASSR and Bessarabia. There were numerous letters, including from ethnic Ukrainians living in the South and North, supporting this plan. A Moldavian-Ukrainian frontier commission chaired unofficially by Khrushchev was created in order to make the final territorial settlement. It decided to give one-half of the MASSR back to Ukraine along with a third of the territory of Bessarabia in the south and north. The basic idea invoked was that Moldavians/Romanians are a majority in these areas of Bessarabia. The argument was partially legitimate if assessed from an ethnic standpoint, but it was also true that the Romanian element was the most important ethnic group in the area, 28 percent compared to the Ukrainians, who were only 25 percent. Moreover, as various authors reported, including Russians as well as Moldavian Communist authorities in 1946, the majority of the local non-Romanian population spoke Romanian, the latter being the language of interethnic communication during the Tsarist period, too.[14] In this case, however, Khrushchev used his double authority as first secretary of the Central Committee of the Communist (Bolshevik) Party of Ukraine and secretary of CC of All-Union CP (b) SU to push for more territories for Ukraine. He tried the same with Belorussia in 1939, but the secretary of the Central Committee of the latter had direct access to Stalin, so the Ukrainian pretensions were declared void.[15] Authori-

---

[13] Elena Negru, *Politica etnoculturală in RASSM, 1924–1940*, 115–127. The complete list of the victims of Great Terror in MASSR are to be found in Ion Varta, Tatiana Varta, Igor Şarov [Sharov] (eds.), *Marea Teroare în RASSM. Documente* (Chişinău: Editura ARC, 2010), vol. I, no. 2 to 5 to be published.

[14] The Archive of the Social-Social Organizations of Moldova, former Archive of Central Committee of the Communist Party of Moldavia (AOSPRM), Fond 51, inv. 4, d. 64, f. 7–12.

[15] V. Ju. Vasil'ev, R. Ju. Podkur, H. Kuromiya, Ju. I. Shapoval, A. Weiner (eds.), *Politicheskoe rukovodstvo Ukrainy, 1938–1989* (Moscow: ROSSPEN, 2006), 65–66.

ties of the MSSR did not have the same connections with Stalin and lost out. Furthermore, the division of Bessarabia was anticipated by the contents of the Soviet ultimatum sent to Bucharest on June 26, 1940, which mentioned that Bessarabia has been populated since ancient times by a Ukrainian majority.[16] That was false, but the formula was employed deliberately in order to inculcate the idea—especially for Western audiences—that the partition of Bessarabia was a continuation of the unification of all Ukrainian inhabited territories in one Ukrainian Soviet state. It was a process that had began a year before with the annexation of Polish-ruled Galicia.

What was Moscow's policy in the province in the aftermath of the occupation? Was it resembling a colonial experiment or was it rather close to the emancipation claim of Soviet Communist propaganda? One should mention that in the first year of Soviet occupation of Bessarabia—two-thirds of it and half of the MSSR forming Moldavian Union republic in August 1940—the colonial policy was more evident and brutal than in the following decades. This was true in terms of the forceful inclusion of Bessarabia in the Soviet Union and of the imposition of Communist ideology and institutions. It also comprised the imposition of the linguistic hegemony of Russian. The process presupposed investing loyalty only to cadres from across the Dniester River as well as discriminating against the local ones. In other words, the Soviets did not trust even members of the illegal Bessarabian Communist party—no matter their ethnic background[17]—who were active on the territory of Bessarabia in the interwar period.[18] Such discrimination obviously targeted those who represented or collaborated in some way or another with interwar Romanian authorities, as well. They were suspected of being traitors to the Soviet power, at least 136 of them were shot in 1940–1941[19]. This was based on the assumption that Soviets supposedly took power in Bessarabia in early January 1918 just a few

---

[16] *Dokumenty vneshnei politiki SSSR*, vol. I, part 1 (Moscow: Mezhdunarodnye otnosheniia, 1995), 385–386.

[17] AOSPRM, F. 51, inv. 6, d. 3, ff. 62–74.

[18] That was also true of the leaders of the Communist Parties in the Baltic States. See more in Elena Zubkova, *Pribaltika i Kreml', 1940–1953* (Moscow: ROSSPEN, 2008).

[19] Igor Cașu, *Dușmanul de clasă. Represiuni politice, violență și rezistență în R(A)SS Moldovenească, 1924–1956* (Chișinău: Cartier, 2014), 132–136.

days before the Romanian army arrived at the request of the local parliament. According to Moscow's viewpoint—in contradiction to elementary international rules—the entire Bessarabian population was Soviet in terms of citizenship *ab initio* and implicitly, in 1940, so its members were considered traitors to the Soviet fatherland for paying taxes to the Romanian state, for participating in the public life as members of cultural or political organizations and so on. All these activities were regarded as counterrevolutionary and anti-Soviet.[20]

Unsurprisingly, there were three mass deportations in mid-June 1941, early July 1949, and late May 1951 that brought about the forced displacement of 60,000 persons. Among the victims of the Soviet regime one also has to count around 150,000–200,000 dead, the outcome of a mass organized famine in 1946–1947 in former Bessarabia.[21] The total number of victims of Moscow's policy in the Moldavian SSR during the Stalinist period exceeds 300,000 persons (including the victims of the 1930s in the MASSR). As to the ethnic composition of the victims, they were of various ethnic backgrounds and in this sense Communist authorities did not discriminate against any ethno-national group.[22]

In economic terms, Soviet Moldavia received usually more than other USSR republics (situated in the Western borderlands). This trend was a continuously ascending one according to the official figures up until the end of Soviet Union. In this sense, the Moldavian SSR was not discriminated against in contrast to what has been defined as a classical unjust economic relation between metropolis and colony.[23] It is also apparent from this perspective that the imperial paradigm does not apply to post-Stalinist Moldavia especially if one looks at the economic, investment rate variable as compared to the amount

---

[20] M. Semiriaga, *Tainy stalinskoi diplomatii* (Moscow: Vysshaia Shkola, 1992), 270.

[21] See A. Țăranu, I. Șișcanu (eds.), *Golod v Moldove, 1947–1947* (Chișinău: Știința, 1993), 10.

[22] See more in Igor Cașu, "Stalinist Terror in Soviet Moldavia, 1940–1953," in Kevin McDermott, Matthew Stibbe (eds.), *Stalinist Terror in Eastern Europe: Elite Purges and Mass Repression* (Manchester and New York: Manchester University Press, 2010), 39–56.

[23] *Narodnoe Khozyaistvo Moldavskoi SSR v 1984* (Chișinău: Cartea Moldovenească, 1985), 15.

received by other national peripheries of the Soviet Union. The same argument can be made if one takes into consideration the situation of the Baltic republics. Their level of consumption, quality of life, and economic development rate was higher than the all-union one, being in the top of all union republics.[24]

At a closer look, however, the efficiency of central investments in Moldavia was not as impressive as it appears at first glance. Moreover, the funds came with a very precise political agenda. According to the economist Sergiu Chircă, the overall investments in Soviet Moldavia have been rather modest if one takes in account their share per capita, which was less than the Soviet average.[25] In 1965, for instance, the Moldavian SSR was rated seventh among the fifteen union republics in terms of economic development.[26] Twenty-five years later (1990), it dropped to ninth place, being the least developed of all European Soviet republics.[27] Taking into account the higher level of the birth rate among ethnic Romanians and their progressive decrease in the total share of the population inside the MSSR, one can conclude—as in the case of other union republics—that the high investments were made in combination with an influx of cadres from the center. In other words, more Russians and Ukrainians were sent to the Moldavian SSR in parallel with allotting more money from Moscow for developing the industrial sector. In the meantime, more Moldavians, especially ethnic Romanians were encouraged to work in Russia and Ukraine.

The specificity of Moscow-Chișinău relations could be noticed also in the way the investments from the center were distributed at the regional level. For instance, the present day Transnistrian territory, which after 1940 was never an officially distinct region, received around 30 percent of the total investments allotted by Moscow to the Moldavian SSR. Such an allocation was disproportionate if one considers that this region comprised less than 10 percent of the territory

---

[24] *Osnovnye pokazateli ekonomicheskogo i sotsial'nogo razvitiia Moldavskoi SSR i soiuznykh respublik v 1988 godu* (Chișinău: Gosdepartament po statistike, 1989), 45.

[25] S. Chircă, *Regional'nye problemy protsessa sozdaniia material'no-tekhnicheskoi bazy kommunizma v SSSR* (Chișinău: Cartea Moldovenească, 1979), 65.

[26] *Voprosy Ekonomiki* no. 4, 1970, 128.

[27] Igor Cașu, *"Politica națională" în Moldova Sovietică, 1944–1989* (Chișinău: Cartdidact, 2000), 95.

and population of the republic. The districts across Dniester were inhabited by a Slavic majority—Ukrainians and Russians (more than 50 percent), while ethnic Romanians represented 40 percent and lived mainly in villages. For instance, the largest city in the area—Tiraspol—had only 17 percent of ethnic Romanians in 1989.[28]

Another aspect as to the urban-rural development in Soviet Moldavia relevant for the nationalities policy and imperial character of Soviet rule in MSSR refers to the evolution of urbanization rate of ethnic Romanians. According to the last Soviet census of 1989, their share in the total number of urban dwellers was only 25 percent. This is to say that two-thirds of Romanians lived in the rural areas, that is, in a less developed environment. In the meantime, the share of urbanized Russians was 80 percent and 45 percent of Ukrainians.[29] It still remains unclear if that low share in the total urban population was an intended part of the centrally planned nationalities policy or just a side effect of the center administered industrial enterprises, which covered about 25 percent of the total local industry in comparison with only 10 percent in the Baltic republics.[30]

What is certain is that the discrimination of local ethnic Romanian cadres was not merely a perception. In the industrial sector, for instance, at the level of managers of enterprises, Romanians were 2.3 percent in 1964, rising to only 8.6 percent twenty years later, in 1984.[31] If in the immediate postwar period the focus on arriving cadres—especially Russians and Ukrainians was somewhat justified, from the Moscow point of view, as the local cadres were lacking or could not be trusted because of their social and ideological origins—that could be hardly the case after the 1960s. The cadres that were prepared offi-

---

[28] See more on that in *Istoria Transnistriei. De la începuturi până în zilele noastre* (Chișinău: Civitas, 2005).

[29] Current archive of the Department of Statistics of the Republic of Moldova, document 07.13. 26 dated March 30, 1990.

[30] See more in Jean Radvanyi (ed.), *Les États postsoviétiques: Identités en construction, transformations politiques, trajectoires économiques* (Paris: Armand Colin, 2011).

[31] Archival data published by V. Stăvilă in "Evoluția componenței naționale a elitei politico-economice a RSSM," 1940–1991, în *Revista de Istorie a Moldovei*, nr. 4, 1996, 39.

cially for Moldavia's needs were sent to work in other republics, primarily in Russia and Ukraine.

Another factor on the basis of which one can verify the level and dynamics of Moscow's control in Soviet Moldavia is the evolution of the share of ethnic Romanians in key Communist party and government positions. In the early 1950s, the share of ethnic Romanians in the Communist nomenklatura was around 10 percent. In 1967, it increased to 42.5 percent and in 1987 it reached 54 percent.[32] The share of ethnic Romanians among the total number of communists was around 8 percent in 1950, increasing to 35 percent in 1965 and 49 percent in 1989. Simultaneously, however, the same share in government positions at the republican level increased from 38 percent to 49 percent in 1984. However, if one looks at the key positions in the party and government, the situation is far from impressive. For instance, the first ethnic Romanian from the Bessarabian part of the former Moldavian SSR to serve as First Secretary of the Central Committee of the Communist Party of Moldavia was Petru Lucinschi appointed in mid-November 1989. Before that, this position was held by Transnistrians—including ethnic Romanians but highly Russified, some of them speaking poor Romanian if at all. The position of Second Secretary of the local party organization, the individual who de facto controlled the cadres' policy at the republican level and other key domains, was always held by an ethnic Russian. The first ethnic Romanian to hold this position was Ion Guţu, appointed in 1989. This was true also in what concerns key governmental positions such as President of the Council of Ministers. The first ethnic Romanian—born in Northern Bukovina—to hold this position was Mircea Druc, elected by a democratic Supreme Soviet (parliament) in May 1990. Key ministries such as Ministry of Interior and the KGB were always headed by non-Romanians or ethnic Romanians from across the Dniester, i.e., Russified ones. The first ethnic Romanian from the Bessarabian territory to serve as Ministry of Interior was Ion Costaş, who was nominated in 1990. The first to become local chief of the KGB was Tudor Botnaru, appointed in the same year—just on the eve of the collapse of the

---

[32] V. Stăvilă, "Evoluţia componenţei naţionale a elitei politico-economice a RSSM," 1940–1991, in *Revista de Istorie a Moldovei*, nr. 4, 1996, 38, 39, 41.

Soviet Union. The latter remained subordinated to Moscow until the official collapse in December 1991.

One can identify the particularities of the Soviet Communist regime in the Moldavian case also from other points of view: the linguistic or cultural policies. Officially, there was a permanent increase starting with the 1960s of the total number of books, journals, and newspapers published in Romanian (officially called Moldavian) in Cyrillic alphabet. However, one can notice a dramatic decrease in the public use of Romanian language. That could be observed especially at the level of higher education institutions, as more and more disciplines every year switched to Russian as the language of teaching among the official Romanian groups.

The quality of the spoken language was decreasing because Russian became the main language in the mass media, higher education, and academia. Not to mention that all documents in the government and party were only in Russian. This was a permanent reality until 1989 when the first official documents in Romanian timidly made their way out of the central administration. Speaking Romanian publicly was often a sign for Communist authorities of Moldo-Romanian nationalism, especially during party meetings or meetings held at various educational institutions (this was also true, for instance, of Ukrainian language in Ukraine).[33] The Latin alphabet in the Moldavian SSR had been prohibited since 1944 as in the most part of Tsarist period. It had been replaced with the Cyrillic one, which was envisaged to serve as an identity marker and a communication barrier for the Romanians across the Prut River. Those contesting the appropriateness of employing Russian letters for an East Romance language were severely punished. In the Stalinist period they were arrested and deported to Siberia as Moldo-Romanian nationalists. After 1953, they were either socially marginalized or sent to psychiatric hospitals, as was the case of numerous citizens, among them Gheorghe David, who was sent to Dnepropetrovsk psychiatric hospital during Gorbachev's rule in 1986. Besides asking to reestablish the Latin script for "Moldavian language," David also criticized the discrimination against local cadres and the Soviet invasion in Afghanistan. It is interesting that David sent letters with the

---

[33] A.S. Barsenkov, A.I. Vdovin, *Istoriia Rossii*, 1938–2002 (Moscow: Aspekt Press, 2003), 311, 315.

same messages to Brezhnev, Andropov, and Chernenko, but only under Gorbachev was he sentenced to psychiatric treatment.[34]

Other symbolic assertions of national identity, within the officially imposed limits, were subject to KGB intervention and treated as disloyal political behavior. For instance, the simple gesture of putting flowers at the statue of the most important Romanian poet, Mihai Eminescu, in downtown Chişinău (officially he was accepted by Moscow as a Moldavian poet, too) was interpreted as a manifestation of nationalism and anti-Russian attitude.[35] The same was true about the statue of Moldavian medieval Prince Stephen the Great.[36] In 1964, Mihai Moroşan, a student from the Polytechnic Institute, initiated with colleagues from other higher education institutions a letter of protest against the removal of Stephen the Great statue from the downtown area to a marginal location. He was promptly arrested by the KGB, expelled from the Polytechnic Institute, and sentenced to two years in a correctional work camp.[37]

Romanian identity, called Moldavian throughout the Soviet period in the Moldavian SSR, was allowed only at the level of folk culture. There were folklore ensembles, national theater, and opera performing in Romanian, but almost all the movies until late 1980s were broadcasted exclusively in Russian, including those made in Chişinău by the republican movie company, Moldova-film. This was also true of almost every TV program and this contradicted flagrantly the official pretension that national republics enjoyed equal conditions to develop their own language and culture. Those who insisted on buying books from Romania, in the Latin alphabet, were harassed by the authorities. And those doubting the existence of a "Moldavian nation" in ethnical terms were severely punished. The individuals who did not question the Communist system, but just proposed the Union of former Bessara-

---

[34] The Archive of Service of Information and Security of the Republic of Moldova, former KGB, *ASISRM-KGB*, personal file of Zaharia Doncev, no. 06696, f. 243 verso; *Basarabia*, no. 9, 1990, 140–152, etc.

[35] Interview with Nicolae Cibotaru, Associate Professor in History at Moldova State Pedagogical University, March 11, 2011.

[36] AOSPRM, F. 278, inv. 8, d. 82, f. 27.

[37] Archive of the Polytechnic University (in the Soviet period it was an Institute), personal file of Mihai Moroşan, f. 31. Interview with Mihai Moroşan, March 2011.

bia and North Bukovina with Romania were condemned as nationalists. This was especially the case of the group called National Patriotic Front led by Alexandru Usatiuc and Gheorghe Ghimpu. Two other leading members of this group were arrested and sent to the Gulag plus exiled to Siberia for four to thirteen years.[38] At the same time, there are few cases when a Russian from Soviet Moldavia—albeit there are cases in Russia—was imprisoned, trialed, or at least admonished for Russian chauvinism or Great Power nationalism.[39]

Speaking about the short-term perspective in center-periphery relations in the late 1980s, it is important to stress several factors that dramatically worsened the interethnic dialogue and the relations between the republican periphery and the Kremlin center. The first factor was the promulgation of language laws in the late 1980s in Moldova, which revealed the tensions between the authorities in Chişinău and Moscow, on the one hand, and Romanian speakers and the local Russian speaking community, on the other hand. To put it differently, even though linguistic laws were among the most liberal as compared to other republics,[40] the Russian speakers perceived the establishing of Romanian language in Latin alphabet as an affront to their previous status. They claimed that their rights were violated. In fact, they were losing a privileged position. Another problem was related to some new industrial projects initiated by Moscow in Chişinău, such as building a huge computer manufacturing company of all-Union importance in the late 1980s. This also contributed to the growing tension in the center-periphery relations because it involved a mass influx of cadres from the Center. The situation fueled mass mobilization on an ethnic basis, because the new cohorts were perceived to be a threat to local interests considering that unemployment in the urban areas, especially in Chişinău, was already rampant. Another problem that was used to mobilize local masses against the center was the ecological issue; Moldova being one a notorious polygon in the Soviet Union for experimenting new chemicals in agriculture.

---

[38] ASISRM-KGB, file 017006, Usatiuc – Ghimpu, in 11 volumes.

[39] AOSPRM, F. 51, inv. 29, d. 34, f. 186–190.

[40] See, for instance, Nikolai Guboglo, *Jazyki etnicheskoi mobilizatsii* (Moscow: Vysshaia Shkola, 1998)

Out of all of these sources of conflict, the most enduring was the linguistic problem as well as the issue of interpreting the Communist past. Ethnic Romanians tended to blame the local Russians as occupiers, accusing them for transplanting Communism in Moldova. In their turn, the latter argued that they have been victims of the Communist regime too, and they did not suffer less than the Romanians. In this sense, the best answers to such questions were formulated by a Russian journalist from Moldova in 1989. Addressing her fellow Russians from Moldova, Evghenia Solomonova said:

> A lot of you would ask me: what is the guilt of the Russian people [in establishing Communism in Moldova], who have been themselves victims of Stalinist repressions and stagnation [referring basically to Brezhnev period]? [You would say that] It is about our common misfortune, not about guilt, isn't it? Dear fellow citizens! My opinion is that our sufferings could not justify us in the face of others whom we forced to share our misfortune.

She continued mentioning the realities of the Soviet nationalities policy in Moldova in order to reach her fellow Russians:

> Under the influence of the Stalinist national policy, there was a stereotype in our thinking . . . namely that we are liberators and protectors of the Moldavian people. . . . We developed the psychology of the "Big brother" who should guide, but who is not obliged to take into account, himself, the opinion of the "Smaller brother," less to learn his language, history, and culture. Such an ideology that saved us from such "details" was convenient for us because it compelled the "Smaller brother" to "mutual understanding," namely on the level that was suitable for us. The fact that we are asking now for two state languages is a proof in this sense.[41]

These words obviously hardly convinced all to whom they were addressed. The refusal of Russian speakers to accept Romanian as official language ignited the phenomenon of Transnistrian separatism, which is to be explained in itself primarily as a result of competition

---

[41] "Învăţămîntul public," 10 iunie 1989, 2.

between left-bank elites and Bessarabian ones. The former were losing their privileged connections with Moscow and thus initiated a strike and then a separatist regime in 1990. The latter survived until present and it benefited from strong Russian support, including the involvement of Kremlin's armed forces.

The Rehabilitation of the Victims of Communist Terror

The partial rehabilitation of the victims of the Communist terror commenced as early as the mid-1950s. It was only partial because the former repressed (in concentrations camps and special settlements) did not have the right to return back to their homes. However, by 1960, around 80 percent of the persons deported from Moldavian SSR returned in their republic, but few of them succeeded to settle in their former households. Their properties were expropriated and given to state or party officials. In this sense, the return of deportees was a danger for the Soviet Communist regime.[42]

After 1989, the victims of the communist regime were further rehabilitated, but their properties were never returned or they never received material and moral compensation for their suffering. The main reason was that, with the exception of the period from 1998 to 1999, post-Soviet Moldova never had, until 2009, a pro-European government. The various state leaderships feared that the full rehabilitation of the victims of communist terror would be perceived by Russia as an anti-Russian policy. The novel element brought by the post-Soviet process of rehabilitation was that not only the victims of the period 1917–1953 were the object of the new laws, but also all those who have been condemned for political crimes after Stalin's death up until the late 1980s. The Law of 1992 also included the victims of political psychiatric imprisonment, unlike similar laws adopted around the same time in Russia and Ukraine.

---

[42] For more about the rehabilitation process after Stalin in MSSR, see Igor Caşu, "The Fate of Stalinist Victims in Moldavia after 1953: Amnesty, Pardon and the Long Road to Rehabilitation," in *The Rehabilitation of the Victims of Stalinism in Eastern Europe*, ed. Kevin McDermott, Matthew Stibbe (London: Macmillan, forthcoming).

Some families, however, protested against the deportations even as they were taking place. They sent letters to communist authorities in Moscow or Chişinău. Those who had one or more family members serving in the Red Army were paid attention to. In mid-1952, eighty-seven families (389 individuals) were rehabilitated along with 108 other individuals. After Stalin's death, in July 1953, the Soviet Minister of Internal Affairs, S. N. Kruglov, suggested that the Soviet government abolish deportation decisions and liberate the deportees, including those from Soviet Moldavia. It was admitted that the deportations, especially those in 1949, disregarded the principles of socialist legality. The mass rehabilitation of deportees began after the Twentieth Congress of CPSU, in February 1956, when the new Soviet leader Nikita Khrushchev denounced Stalin's cult of personality and his terror tactics. By October 1956, 3,290 Moldavian families (6,950 persons) were released from special settlements. By 1961, most Moldavian deportees had been liberated as a result of the Supreme Soviet decree of May 19, 1958, which abolished residence restrictions for the majority of the victims of Stalinist terror. Nevertheless, the decree did grant them the right to return to their previous place of residence or to receive back their confiscated properties. The decree of January 7, 1960, abolished further restrictions of movement for other social categories. The decision whether to allow the return of the deportees or not was the prerogative of local authorities. Between 1958 and 1963, 2,033 families received permission to return to Moldova. In August 1961, the Moldavian branch of the Soviet KGB estimated that the absolute majority of deportees had returned home to their villages and cities and lived with relatives or rented private apartments. Though they had found jobs, they neglected the obligation to officially register at their place of residence (*propiska*). Most returnees did not receive their confiscated property back and thus lost forever their previous social status in Moldavian society.[43]

The full rehabilitation of the victims of Stalinist terror began on April 10, 1989, when the Council of Ministers of the Moldavian SSR annulled its decision of June 28, 1949 regarding the deportation of families of *kulaks*, former landowners, and tradesmen. Almost three

---

[43] Valeriu Pasat, Surovaia pravda istorii. *Deportatsii s territorii Moldavii '40–'50 gg.*, (Chişinău: Momentul, 1998), 370–378.

years later, on December 8, 1992, the Moldovan Parliament adopted Law 1225-XII on the Rehabilitation of Political Victims, which applied to all those deported, arrested, or executed during the Soviet rule. According to the law, survivors were entitled to a monthly pension of 200 Moldavian Lei (US $16).[44] The amendments passed on June 29, 2006 prescribed that all political victims of the Soviet period were entitled to compensation for their lost real estate. The state must compensate the victims within three years if the price of their properties did not exceed 200,000 Moldovan Lei (about US $11,000 in 2014). The compensation for more valuable properties should be paid within five years.[45] These changes did not affect compensations related to the return of agricultural land, forests, or pasture. Local authorities, not the central government, were responsible for the payment of compensations, a stipulation hindering the law's application since Moldovan local authorities generally lacked the financial resources needed for the restitution program. Thus, the Communist parliamentary majority passed this law under pressure from the opposition parties without creating the financial and institutional framework means necessary to carry out such an ambitious program.

Politics of Memory and the Victims of Communism After 1989

From 1956 to 1991, Soviet Moldova lacked a strong anti-communist opposition. There was an upsurge of anti-Soviet and anti-communist sentiments in 1956 following the secret speech of Khrushchev at the twentieth CPSU Congress. After Soviet tanks crushed the Hungarian Revolution in November 1956 and Western governments adopted a policy of noninvolvement, Moldovans decided not to oppose Soviet rule.[46] In the late 1950s and 1960s, resistance primarily took the form of protest against the Russification of the Romanian language.

---

[44] *Monitorul Oficial al Republicii Moldova*, nr. 12, 30.12.1992.
[45] *Monitorul Oficial al Republicii Moldova*, nr. 126–130, 11.08.2006.
[46] See more on that in Igor Caşu, Mark Sandle, "Discontent and Uncertainty in the Borderlands: Soviet Moldavia and the Secret Speech 1956–1957," *Europe-Asia Studies*, vol. 66, no. 4, 2014., 613–644.

There were, however, some individuals or small groups questioning the monopoly of power of the Communist Party in Moldavian SSR in particular and in the USSR as a whole.[47] During the late 1980s, Mikhail Gorbachev's glasnost and perestroika encouraged public discussions about the Stalinist terror and the fight against nationalists during the Brezhnev era. Writers and intellectuals started to touch upon the repressive aspects of the Soviet regime. Historians, a highly dogmatized stratum of intellectuals in the USSR, joined the anti-Communist and anti-Soviet writers in 1989. The newspaper *Literatura și arta* and journal *Orizontul* took the lead in reconstructing collective memory. Among the main issues discussed, related to the Soviet past, were the consequences of the Ribbentrop-Molotov Pact for Bessarabia, the Stalinist deportations, and the postwar famine of 1946–1947. The debates on these questions of repressed memory helped Moldovans to better understand their identity, encouraging them to push first for more autonomy and then for complete independence from Moscow. As in the case of the Baltic States, the resolution of the Yakovlev Commission in December 1989 on the political and juridical evaluation of the secret protocols of Molotov-Ribbentrop Pact triggered a national movement in Moldavia. The Commission was established at the First Congress of Peoples' Deputies of USSR held in May–June 1989 under the initiative of Alexander Yakovlev, one of the spiritual fathers of perestroika. The memory of Stalinist terror and the recognition on the part of the CPSU that Moscow sided with Nazi Germany in occupying the Baltic States and Bessarabia delegitimized the Soviet regime and hastened the collapse of the Soviet Union.

The Moldovan Popular Front was at the forefront of decommunization in the late 1980s and early 1990s. This organization failed to gain parliamentary majority in March 1990, winning only 25 percent of the seats. As an economic crisis developed in the country, Moldovans, regardless of their ethnicity, voted in the 1994 parliamentary elections for the Democratic Agrarian Party, which represented the former Soviet nomenklatura. As expected, this party held a nostalgic view of the Soviet past and it supported a less critical view of the Soviet

---

[47] Igor Cașu, "Political Repressions in Moldavian SSR After 1953: Towards a Typology Based on KGB files," *Dystopia. Journal of Totalitarian Ideologies and Regimes*, vol. I, no. 1–2, 2012, 89–127.

Union in the public discourse and history textbooks. Their efforts failed because cultural and educational elites organized mass rallies protesting against these initiatives and blocked them.

In the earlier 2000s, attempts to rehabilitate the Soviet past and to justify mass deportation and famine came from another party. The Communist Party, which was in power from February 2001 to August 2009, embarked on the "soft" restoration of Stalinism: the public discourse was invaded by nostalgia toward the Soviet past, with communism celebrated as the most progressive and glorious period in the history of Moldova. In 2006, history textbooks were changed to reflect a communist interpretation of the past despite the vehement protests of civil society groups like the Association of Historians and other anti-communist professional organizations. As a result, from 2006 to 2009 there unfolded a war of history textbooks, as high school teachers boycotted the new interpretation of history and continued to use the former history textbooks. From their point of view, the latter presented a European, national interpretation of the past that was not reflective of the historical narrative and mythology imposed by the Soviet Union before 1989.[48]

The Creation of the Commission for the Study and Evaluation of Totalitarian Communist Regime in the Republic of Moldova

The politics of memory played an important role during the two parliamentary campaigns of 2009. The anti-communist Liberal Party tried to gather electoral support by invoking the need to outlaw the Communist Party, claiming that communism was as criminal as National-Socialism in particular and Fascism as a whole. Another important political party of the Alliance for European Integration, the Liberal Democratic Party, was very critical of the Communist Party's reluctance to condemn communist-era crimes. It promised to restore the

---

[48] See more on that in Igor Caşu, "Nation Building in the Era of Integration: The Case of Moldova," in Konrad Jarausch, Thomas Lindenberger (eds.), *Conflicted Memories. Europeanizing Contemporary History* (New York and Oxford: Berghan Books, 2007), 237–253.

pro-Romanian and pro-European national discourse on history dominant in the 1990s. The strong appeal to the Moldovan electorate of these two parties was due to the fact their leaders represented a new generation of Moldovan politicians educated mainly in Romania and the West, with no nomenklatura past. Even the oppositional "Our Moldova Alliance," lead by former middle level nomenklatura-members, played the anti-communist card. Following the elections, these three parties, along with the Democratic Party led by Marian Lupu, formed a coalition government in September 2009. Although the Communist Party pursued a policy of rehabilitating Stalin and worshiping Lenin, during the 2009 electoral campaign it changed its attitude toward the victims of mass deportations. Sensing the loss of popular support after the violent anti-communist riots in Chişinău on April 7, 2009, the communist government allotted around thirteen million lei (one million US dollars) for reparation payments to the victims of Stalinist deportations. This was an excellent example how the politics of memory was instrumentalized for electoral purposes.

Lustration was discussed publicly in 2005 and 2006. One of the leading national weeklies, *Jurnal de Chişinău*, published around 200 interviews with local politicians and cultural personalities asking for their opinion about communism, the possibility of a lustration law, and if they collaborated with the KGB in the Soviet period. Although the majority condemned communism, only a minority supported a lustration law and some voiced no regret for their Soviet-era collaboration with the political police.

The breakthrough in the politics of memory came in January 2010 when a Presidential Commission for the Study and Evaluation of the Communist Totalitarian Regime was created by the interim President of the Republic, Mihai Ghimpu, who was also the leader of Liberal Party. The Commission included thirty members, among them historians, writers, sociologists, lawyers and linguists. As a result, the previously inaccessible archival depositories were disclosed, including that of the former KGB and the Ministry of Interior. The Commission was supposed to deliver a preliminary report by June 1, 2010, but it could not be finalized because there was no unanimity on the final version. There were two contending groups, the one represented by former Soviet official historians who played now the nationalistic card and another composed of young historians educated in Romania and in the

West who insisted on a more balanced approach, rejecting the ethnicization of the Communist repressions.

Finally, a volume covering the main contributions of the members of the Commission was published in the fall of 2011 in Chişinău.[49] It comprised the main aspects related to repressive policies of Moscow in former Moldavian SSR, including several chapters on Soviet nationalities policy and an extensive chapter on the politics of memory of Chişinău authorities after 1989. The first part of the volume includes articles written by historians and political scientists from Eastern and Central Europe, including several members of the Presidential Commission for the Analysis of the Communist Dictatorship in Romania. These scholars helped their Moldavian colleagues by generously sharing their experience in working in the Romanian archives and dealing with administrative issues related to the access to previously secret files. Several volumes of documents were also published as a result of the activity of the Commission[50] and others will be published in the years to come.

The outcomes of the Moldovan Commission for the Study and Evaluation of the Communist Totalitarian Regime in the Republic of Moldova have been summarized briefly by one of its young members, Andrei Cuşco, who holds a Ph.D. in History from Central European University:

> The Commission's effectiveness was limited by the vagueness of its mandate; the short time span of its operation; the lack of effective legal tools (subpoena powers); the limited political support for its work and the tendency of certain political forces to use it for their own purposes; and the underrepresentation of the civil society, the victims' associations, and ethnic minorities on the Commission. However, it helped to open previously inaccessible archival (including secret police) files and it increased public awareness

---

[49] Sergiu Musteaţă, Igor Caşu (eds.), *Fără termen de prescripţie. Aspecte ale investigării crimelor comuniste în Europa* (Chişinău: Cartier, 2011).

[50] For instance, Gheorghe Cojocaru (ed.), *Operatsiia IUG: Kishinev 1949* (Chişinău: Bon Office, 2010). Igor Caşu, Igor Şarov, (eds.), *Republica Moldova de la Perestroika la independenţă, 1989–1991. Documente secrete din arhiva CC al PCM* (Chişinău, Cartdidact, 2011).

of the nature and consequences of the former regime. The Commission represents only the first step in the creation of a complex and multilayered institutional structure that might eventually lead to an effective system of transitional justice in Moldova.[51]

More recently, there has been an ongoing discussion to create a similar state commission to disclose the crimes of the Antonescu regime in Bessarabia and Transnistria during the World War II. Besides the data published by the Wiesel Commission in Romania (2004), the recently opened archives in Chișinău can shed new light on the scale of the Holocaust on the territory of the present day Republic of Moldova and Ukraine.[52]

Conclusions

The specificities of the policies of the Soviet regime in the Republic of Moldova can be generally explained by the fact that Bessarabia was the only republican territory in the Soviet Union inhabited by an ethnic majority belonging to a Communist neighbor state, i.e., Romania. This reality had a considerable impact on the nature of Communist rule in the former Moldavian SSR and on the center-periphery relationship. The interaction between Moscow and Chișinău was often influenced by the state of relations between Bucharest and Moscow and vice versa, especially starting with the 1960s when Romania became a maverick state, with a strong nationalistic component.

---

[51] Andrei Cușco,"Commission for the Study and Evaluation of the Totalitarian Communist Regime in the Republic of Moldova," in Lavinia Stan, Nadya Nedelsky, (eds.), *Encyclopedia of Transitional Justice*, vol. 3 (Cambridge: Cambridge University Press, 2012), 52.

[52] One of the best accounts on the Holocaust in Bessarabia and Transnistria has been published by Moldovan historian Diana Dumitru, together with Canadian political scientist Carter Johnson. Their study was awarded the best article in Political Sciences for 2011 by the American Political Association. See Diana Dumitru, Carter Johnson, "Constructing Interethnic Conflict and Cooperation: Why Some People Harmed Jews and Others Helped Them During the Holocaust in Romania," *World Politics*, vol. 63, no. 1, January 2011, 1–42.

The politics of memory on Communism after 1989 in the Republic of Moldova have been quite ambiguous, to say the least. Sometimes the discourse of the Moldavian authorities was nostalgic toward the Communist past, especially, but not exclusively, during the government of the Party of Communists from 2001 to 2009. After 2009, however, a new democratic, pro-Romanian and pro-European alliance came to power in Chișinău. Its leadership embarked on a new policy toward the Communist past. The creation of a special State Commission for the Study and Evaluation of the Communist Totalitarian Regime in January 2010 and the subsequent opening of the archives of KGB were the main aspects of this new policy.

The problem of punishing former officials who perpetrated crimes during the Soviet regime has been not discussed widely in Moldova yet. In this sense, the politics of memory and the rehabilitation of the victims of Communism in Moldova is closer to the model followed by Russia and other post-Soviet republics than to cases on East Central Europe. However, if Moldova wants to integrate one day into the European Union, it should take into consideration that the EU shares a set of values that are contrary to the Soviet ones. This means that it should condemn the crimes committed by the communist regime and the mass terror exerted over its various ethnic groups, not only the Romanian speaking majority.

Part Four

COMPETING NARRATIVES
OF TROUBLED PASTS

JOHN CONNELLY

Coming to Terms with Catholic-Jewish Relations in the Polish Catholic Church

In this chapter I wish to propose an unusual, almost revolutionary approach to studying Catholic-Jewish relations in Poland: namely to treat the Polish Catholic Church as a theological institution, that is, a place producing ideas about religion, in particular, ideas about Jews. A central theme in these relations is of course hostility, yet it has been notoriously difficult to specify the relation between religiously based hostility and modern anti-semitism, the sort that led to the Holocaust. The Holocaust's planners after all considered themselves anti-Christian. They regarded Christianity as a Jewish faith and they tried to weaken the Catholic Church as a prelude to its full destruction. If one looks at works on anti-semitism and the Polish Catholic Church, the focus tends to be ethnically based hostility, with few references made to religious ideas.

To make matters more complicated, Catholicism goes far beyond Poland, and represents an international institution with pretensions to a teaching that is universal. Over the last sixty-five years the Church has grappled seriously with the religious roots of anti-semitism and made efforts to review its teachings about Jews. It achieved a breakthrough in the 1960s with the statements of the Second Vatican Council, one of which decried "hatred, persecutions, displays of anti-Semitism, directed against Jews at any time and by anyone." I want to ask how and whether the Polish Catholic Church has embraced those ideas.

The challenge in studying anti-semitism as something grounded in Christian faith is a challenge to all histories of ideas in the Church: if we assume that Christian teaching is a coherent body of beliefs, based in ancient texts hardly modified over centuries, then how could any event change it? The Holocaust after all could not rewrite the New Testament.[1] To put it more concretely: if Poland's Primate Cardinal August Hlond said, in 1934, that Jews were destined to suffer for killing Christ, perhaps citing Matthew 25:27 ("His blood be on us and our children"), how could his successor Cardinal Stefan Wyszyński arrive at a different conclusion twenty years later? Or take the question of "mission" to the Jews. In Matthew 28 Christ commanded his followers to baptize all nations. Yet when Benedict XVI issued a reprinted Good Friday prayer suggesting that Jews should turn to Christ in 2008 he encountered criticism. How was that possible? Even the bishop of Rome cannot rewrite Matthew's Gospel.

In what follows I hope to reverse the flow of work in the study of totalitarian regimes which have imagined modern political ideologies as "political religions." Instead, I would like to consider religion itself as an ideology, something with an interlocking set of tenets that demand commitment from the individual. Such an approach contrasts to the way we often treat religious faith, especially Christian faith, in our own context, namely as a guide to good behavior, a set of ethical precepts that can be appealed to in terms of right and wrong. Thus the belief that Jews might be suffering in history is considered ethically repugnant. But religion is not primarily about good and bad, but rather about ritual and belief. If anti-Judaism was a pillar of a Christian belief system up to World War II, then we need to treat seriously the factors that supported that belief, and ask how a pillar might be removed without upsetting the entire edifice.

---

[1] Some translators (for example in "the Good News Bible") render "the Jews" in John's Gospel as "the Jewish authorities," for example in 2:18, yet the New English Bible has this passage as "The Jews challenged Jesus: 'what sign' they asked, 'can you show for your action.'" He had just chased the money changers out of the Temple. Cited in Lucylla Pszczołowska, "Antisemitismus und religiöse Haltung, Polen und Juden" in *Gemeinsam unter einem Himmel*, *Znak* special edition (Cracow, 2000), 157.

Controversies in Catholic-Jewish Relations in Poland

One does not encounter questions such as these in some of the recent controversies in Catholic-Jewish relations in Poland. The most eminent Catholic opponent of anti-semitism was the Cracow Jesuit Stanisław Musiał who made an important intervention in 1997 with the essay "Black is Black." But the issue was simple and the piece contained next to no theological argument. Influential Gdansk prelate Henryk Jankowski had just said "we cannot tolerate a Jewish minority in the Polish government, because that makes the people afraid."[2] Jankowski, by this point infamous for such comments, made no appeal to scripture or Catholic tradition, and neither did Musiał in his refutation. The Jesuit simply noted that the Church had declared anti-semitism—hatred of Jews—a sin (just as it has declared racism sinful in general), and here was a clear case of that sin.

Argumentation at this basic level occluded deeper consideration of how Christian faith might have been a cause of the hatred. The polemic with Jankowski tended to cause people like Musiał to claim that Christianity as such had always condemned contempt for Jews. "We must remember," Musiał wrote, "that not only Hitler killed Jews in the name of his racist, pagan anti-Semitism. The 'sin of anti-Semitism' also physically killed Jews over the past centuries—a sin committed by Christians against the teaching of the Church, and against numerous decrees issued by the popes, to protect people and property that were Jewish. On March 23, 1928, the Congregation of the Holy Office in Rome issued a verdict: 'The Holy See and specifically condemns hatred of the people once chosen by God, which is colloquially called anti-semitism.'"

In fact the history was more complicated. The Vatican released this condemnation in order not to *seem* anti-Semitic in the wake of closing an association devoted to bettering relations between Christians and Jews (its name was Amici Israel). The repudiation of anti-semitism was meant to isolate and protect an "acceptable," purely religious disdain for hatred based in the belief that Jews lived under a

---

[2] *Tygodnik Powszechny*, November 16, 1997.

curse from God. In secret memoranda leading to the banning of Amici Israel, Vatican Cardinal Secretary of State, Rafael Merry del Val, dictated that the relation between Christians and Jews must be negative. "Hebraism with all its sects inspired by the Talmud continues perfidiously to oppose Christianity," he had written. Individual Jews might convert, but the Jewish people as such were damned.[3]

Other controversies that come to mind in Catholic-Jewish relations in Poland likewise do not evince deep theological reflection. Much has been written in recent years about the planting of crosses at Auschwitz as well as the resistance of nuns to abandoning a convent adjacent to the territory of the former camp, but in both cases the issue was not religion but an ethnic group's claim to territory. Poles wanted to ensure that Auschwitz was understood to be a territory where ethnic Poles had died. When John Paul II finally ordered the Carmelite nuns to move, he did not belabour scriptural references.[4] In the early years of this century the rector of All Saints Church in Warsaw tolerated a bookstore ("Księgarnia patriotyczna Artyk") selling the *Protocols of the Elders of Zion* in the cellar of his church despite calls by Catholic intellectuals to close it. He did not defend it in theological terms, but simply said the owners had repaired damage to the cellar, did not occupy consecrated space, and what they sold was not his business. His successor then closed it in 2006, not bothering with theological reasoning.

The Polish Church
and New Catholic Visions of the Jews

Preoccupied with (or failing to be preoccupied with) ethnic anti-Semitism in its own ranks, the Polish Church has failed to engage the deeper religious bases of anti-Semitism and only slowly absorbed the revolutionary changes in Catholic thinking about the Jews that took

---

[3] Hubert Wolf, *Pope and Devil: The Vatican's Archives and the Third Reich* (Cambridge MA: Harvard University Press, 2010), 105–106. In this internal opinion he also wrote that Hebraism "attempts more than ever to establish the Kingdom of Israel in opposition to Christ and his Church."

[4] The letter of April 9, 1993 is reproduced in Alan L. Berger, et al. (eds.), *The Continuing Agony: From the Carmelite Convent to the Crosses of Auschwitz* (Washington, DC: University Press of America 2004), 253–254.

place at the Second Vatican Council in the early 1960s. Such is the judgment of literary historian Lucylla Pszczołowska, who explored this problem in 1988, in an essay written for the Polish Catholic periodical *Znak*. In this piece, she paid special attention to how catechisms produced in Poland might have reflected post-Vatican II teaching on the Jews. She was first alerted to the problem in 1968, when her son told her that children at the playground were saying that Jews ought to be destroyed because they had killed Christ. Though he and his friends had attended Sunday school instruction, they had heard nothing of the new teaching of the Vatican II document *Nostra Aetate* (1965), among whose passages is the following: "True, the Jewish authorities and those who followed their lead pressed for the death of Christ; (13) still, what happened in His passion cannot be charged against all the Jews, without distinction, then alive, nor against the Jews of today."

Preceding the drafting of this statement, theologians had debated for years the passage cited above from Matthew 25, but decided that given the size of the Jewish diaspora of New Testament times, "the crowd" in Matthew could not claim to speak for all Jews of any time: "the Jews" had not killed Christ. The Church did not need to rewrite Matthew's Gospel; rather, it had to read it in a new way, a way that broke with interpretations going back centuries, to the earliest days of the church.

The Vatican II document *Nostra Aetate* emphasizes the Jewishness of Jesus, his mother, and disciples: "The Church keeps ever in mind the words of the Apostle about his kinsmen: 'theirs is the sonship and the glory and the covenants and the law and the worship and the promises; theirs are the fathers and from them is the Christ according to the flesh' (Rom. 9:4-5), the Son of the Virgin Mary. She also recalls that the Apostles, the Church's mainstay and pillars, as well as most of the early disciples who proclaimed Christ's Gospel to the world, sprang from the Jewish people."

Yet Pszczołowska found that nothing appeared about the Jewishness of Jesus in the Polish Catholic catechisms that she surveyed (published by the Loretto sisters). About Christ's mother, the catechism said only that she was "born in a land that today is called Palestine."[5]

---

[5] This has changed in a uniform catechism issued by the Vatican in 1992 (corrected in 1997) that has been translated into many languages, including Polish.

In a catechism for older children she found the following study question: "what was the reason that the Jews were angry at Jesus and condemned him to death?" The authors had ignored directives issued by the Vatican in 1975 emphasizing—in the spirit of *Nostra Aetate*—the need for care and precision in discussing the role of Jews in Christ's crucifixion.[6]

Pszczołowska praised the efforts of Catholic publishers to bring classics onto the bookshelves of People's Poland, but noted that the otherwise excellent book of the French Catholic intellectual Henri Daniel-Rops (*Holy Scripture for My Children*) contained the following: "His blood be upon us and our children: in this way the Jews assumed collective responsibility for the death of Jesus." The book was written in 1946, reflective of the failure of the Holocaust to penetrate the Catholic mind, but also of the later sea change caused by *Nostra Aetate*. Yet a Polish imprimatur was issued in 1984! She examined texts of sermons held in Warsaw churches and found similar statements: "Jesus and his disciples had to hide from the Jews," or "let us eject sins from our hearts just as Jesus threw the Jews out of the Temple."[7] A few years after Pszczółkowska wrote her study, the venerable publisher Jerzy Turowicz, a pioneer in Jewish-Catholic dialogue in Poland, wrote the following: "the overwhelming majority of Polish Catholics knows nothing at all about how deep and special is the bond connecting Christianity with the Mosaic religion."[8]

Polish Church, Universal Church and the Origins of New Thinking

Vatican II teaching resulted from reflection upon the Holocaust. If that event happened in Poland, should not Polish Catholic theology have had a central role in bringing about this new thinking? What other

---

[6] From: "Vatikanische Richtlinien und Hinweise für die Durchführung der Konzilserklärung 'Nostra aetate,' nr. 4 vom 3. Januar 1975," in *Freiburger Rundbrief*, 26 (1974), 4.

[7] Pszczolowska, "Antisemitismus," 155–156.

[8] Michał Okoński, "Żeby istniał żal: Kościół wobec Żydów," *Znak*, 541 (June 2001).

theological community would have been as traumatized? This indeed is the kind of expectation one encounters in writings of the liberal Catholic circles of the journals *Tygodnik Powszechny* and *Znak*, with their assumptions that prewar liberal intelligentsia (of the *Odrodzenie* organization) prefigured the intellectual development leading to *Nostra Aetate*. The mythology is represented in the following statement of Henryk Woźniakowski, son of Jacek, one of the leading early figures in the *Tygodnik Powszechny* circle: "Our founding fathers came from a milieu which maintained friendships with Jews, and with Jewish converts. They were probably the only Catholics of that kind during that era. They sought dialogue. Their thought foreshadowed the conclusions of Vatican II and *Nostra Aetate*."[9]

Within Poland these liberals were probably the only Catholics intensely interested in dialogue with Jews, but within Europe such contacts existed from 1946 in France, Germany, and Switzerland, in part due to the work of U.S. occupation forces, who transported American models of interfaith cooperation to Europe. A Polish council of Christians and Jews (Polska Rada Chrześcijan i Żydów) did not emerge until 1991, however, thus decades after the societies of Christian-Jewish cooperation in Western Europe.

Did the thought of the *Znak* circles foreshadow that of Vatican II? Further study would be necessary to say for sure one way or another. But it did not cause it. Polish Catholicism did not generate the reflection upon the Christian tradition and its underlying beliefs about Jews that led to the statements on the Jews of Vatican II. That energy came from German and French Catholics, strongly influenced by the work *Jesus and Israel* by the French Jew Jules Isaac. Drafts of the conciliar statement of 1965 were the work of a priest, Johannes Oesterreicher, who had been born into a Moravian Jewish family in 1904 and converted to Catholicism in 1924. The strongest voices during decisive debates in the fall of 1964 among the bishops came from North America, Germany, and France. Among the two dozen speakers figured only one Pole, Nowicki of Gdańsk, but not Wojtyła of Cracow (later Pope John Paul II).

Oesterreicher was not a strikingly original thinker but he was a gifted organizer and synthesizer. He funneled the growing consensus

---

[9] Jean-Yves Potel, *La Fin de L'innocence: La Pologne face a son passé juif* (Paris: Editions Autrement, 2009), 85.

of French and German theologians that Catholic thought on Jews must focus on Paul's letter to the Romans. As he knew from close association with the major German thinkers on the subject, this was Paul's most developed and only "prophetic" statement on the Jewish people. The Vatican II document *Nostra Aetate*, which broke with the ancient tradition of deicide, emphasized Paul's letter to the Romans to the exclusion of all other scripture as well as tradition. Father John Pawlikowski, at the forefront of Catholic-Jewish dialogue in the United States, has commented upon the magnitude of the shift: "In making their argument for a total reversal in Catholic thinking on Jews and Judaism, the bishops of the Council bypassed almost all the teachings about Jews and Judaism in Christian thought prior to Vatican II and returned to chapters 9 to 11 of Paul's Letter to the Romans where the Apostle reaffirms the continued inclusion of the Jews in the covenant after the coming of Christ even though this remains for him a "mystery" that defies complete theological explanation. In one sense, the bishops in *Nostra Aetate* were picking up where St. Paul left off in the first century."[10] Pawlikowski interprets the failure to make any reference to the letter to the Hebrews (with its claim that the old covenant was obsolete) as a sign that the bishops "judge it to be a theologically unsuitable source for thinking about the connection between Church and Jewish people in a way that is appropriate to our age."[11] In return-

---

[10] Pawlikowski ably summarized this reversal: "Since at least the second century of the common era the prevalent position in Christian thought was that Jews had been replaced in the covenantal relationship with God by the newly emergent Christian community, the 'true Israel,' because of Jewish failure to acknowledge Jesus as the expected Messiah and Jewish responsibility for his eventual death on the cross. In contrast, *Nostra Aetate* affirmed the continuity of the Jewish people in the convenantal relationship, underscored the constructive influence of the Jewish tradition on Jesus and the early Church, and said that there never was a basis in fact for the historical deicide accusation against the Jews that over the centuries was the source of their persecution and at times even death." John T. Pawlikowski, "The Search for a New Paradigm for the Christian-Jewish Relationship: A Response to Michael Signer," in John T. Pawlikowski and Hayim Goren Perelmuter (eds.), *Reinterpreting Revelation and Tradition: Jews and Christians in Conversation* (Franklin, WI: Sheed & Ward, 2000), 25.

[11] Father Pawlikowski noted in a 2005 talk what was put aside by the drafters of *Nostra Aetate*: writings on the Jews by the church fathers, papal pronouncements, citations from earlier conciliar texts, and very much scripture,

ing to Paul, they reaffirmed the continuing "inclusion of the Jews in the covenant after the coming of Christ even though this remains for him a 'mystery' that defies complete theological explanation. In one sense, the bishops in *Nostra Aetate* were picking up where St. Paul left off in the first century."[12]

The bishops could not rewrite scripture, but they could establish relative weight among contradictory bible passages. The essence of the new teaching was threefold:

1. Christians should see Jews not as cursed but as loved by God.
2. The Jews are not simply a "religion," but are as they understand themselves: a people, a community of tradition, a vocation, exiting to the end of time, as anticipated by Paul in his letter to the Romans, chapters 9–11.
3. That all humankind will one day be joined, but how exactly cannot be known. *Nostra Aetate* put this rather vaguely, citing the prophet Zephaniah: "In company with the Prophets and the same Apostle, the Church awaits that day, known to God alone, on which all peoples will address the Lord in a single voice and "serve him shoulder to shoulder" (Zeph. 3:9).

This first point is the most direct response by the Church to the legacy of the Holocaust. Whether or not Catholics directly participated in the Jews' destruction, deep down, they shared an assumption with the persecutors: Jews were fated to suffer. The Nazis said they were executing God's will and Catholics had no vocabulary with which to dissent. Notably the Pope never defended the rights to life of the Jews during the Shoah, but at best made general objection to human beings being killed "because of their nationality or race" – as he did in the fifty-sixth paragraph of his 1942 Christmas address.[13]

---

in particular the Letter to the Hebrews, for generations a source for the belief that the Old Covenant was no longer valid. See Markus Himmelbauer, "Ein neuer Geist in Kirche und Gesellschaft," http://www.jcrelations.net/de/?item=2588, accessed December 7, 2011.

[12] Pawlikowski, "The Search for a New Paradigm," 25.

[13] See "The Internal Order of States and People," at http://www.ewtn.com/library/papaldoc/p12ch42.htm, accessed December 7, 2011.

If Polish Catholics were not centrally involved in producing these new thoughts for the universal church, the year 1978 brought a major event for Polish Catholicism with the arrival at the Holy See of Karol Wojtyła, Archbishop of Cracow and now Pope John Paul II. From the early days of his papacy the Polish Pope released a series of statements and made a host of gestures toward the Jews which were registered on all sides as bold and meaningful. Best known are his simple assertions that the Jews are "older brothers in faith."[14] He frequently signaled the continuing validity of the promises made by God to Israel, for example in a 1980 speech to Jewish leaders at Mainz, when he spoke of Jews as "the people of God of the Old Covenant never revoked by God," or in 1987 in Miami, when he called the Jewish people "partners in a covenant of eternal love which was never revoked."[15]

Comments made by John Paul inspired a set of "Notes on the correct way to present Jews and Judaism in preaching and catechesis of the Roman Church," released in 1985. The Notes reflect "the permanence of Israel (while so many ancient peoples have disappeared without trace)" as "a historic fact and a sign to be interpreted within God's design." Israel remained a "chosen people, 'the pure olive on which were grafted the branches of the wild olive which are the gentiles.'" Its permanence was "accompanied by a continuous spiritual fecundity, in the rabbinical period, in the Middle Ages, and in modern times, taking its start from a patrimony which we long shared," so much so that "the faith and religious life of the Jewish people as they are professed and practiced still today, can greatly help us to understand better certain aspects of the life of the Church."[16]

---

[14] First said in his 1986 visit to the Synagogue in Rome. *Rzeczpospolita*, December 5, 2003.

[15] Cited in Mary C. Boys, "Does the Catholic Church have a Mission 'with' or 'to' Jews," *Studies in Christian-Jewish Relations*, vol. 3, no. 1 (2008), 5.

[16] The Pope's statement was made on March 6, 1982. For the text of the "Notes," released by the Vatican Commission for Religious Relations with the Jews, see http://www.vatican.va/roman_curia/pontifical_councils/chrstuni/relations-jews-docs/rc_pc_chrstuni_doc_19820306_jews-judaism_en.html, accessed November 8, 2011.

Continuing Difficulties

In controversies about the mission to the Jews, John Paul is cited by "liberal" Catholics in their arguments with traditionalists over the Good Friday prayer resuscitated by Benedict XVI in 2008: "that God our Lord should illuminate their hearts, so that they will recognize Jesus Christ, the Savior of all men." Somehow Christian-Jewish relations are never entirely free of controversy, and that has to do in part with the nature of religion as ideology, the point I began with. The most obvious continuing difficulty is that Christianity considers itself an evangelical faith, and it has always attempted to spread among all human populations, beginning with the Jews. Without (originally) Jewish Christians, there would be no Church.

But there are deeper problems that Catholicism has had difficulty confronting in the post-Holocaust period. As a form of Christianity, Catholicism is a historical faith that looks toward the transformation of the world at the end of time, the eschaton. Some readings of Christian scripture assign a particular role to the Jews at that point, indeed many Christian commentators expect Jews to turn en masse to Christ. Such visions, when alluded to, cause concern among Jewish partners in interfaith dialogue, who imagine that Christians always see them as potential Christians and never simply as Jews.

Christianity (and Catholicism) is also a faith built upon the assumption that suffering is a virtue. This repeatedly leads to misunderstandings. Iwona Irwin-Zarecka tells us that "At a Mass said there [Auschwitz] in 1987, the Bishop of Cracow delivered a sermon on the meaning of the Holocaust, a sermon perhaps best exemplifying the problems of the Church when it *does* reflect on the subject. In that sermon, the death of millions of Jews was assigned a significance paralleling that of the death of Christ, one of 'redemption' of the world." Irwin-Zarecka notes that "No one protested." That same year New York's Cardinal O'Connor said that Jewish suffering at Auschwitz 'may be an enormous gift that Judaism has given the world.'"[17] The

---

[17] "O'Connor Is Upset by Critics of Trip," *New York Times*, January 12, 1987.

following year at Mauthausen, John Paul II proclaimed that the suffering there of the Jews and Christians was a "gift to the world."[18]

Commentator George Will expressed some of the objections to this line of thinking: "Not being steeped in what O'Connor calls his 'theology of suffering' (suffering they understand; the theological coating of it is opaque), Jews may wonder if the slaughter of six million Catholics would be interpreted as an enormous gift to the world. Even if the 'theology of suffering' makes sense to people within the closed circle of such theorizing, surely the cardinal should understand how offensive it sounds to people who are outside that circle and who once were within the barbed wire of Auschwitz."[19] The author did not stop to wonder at what might cause three high officials, not hostile to Jews, to make statements like these decades after Auschwitz. Can Christians imagine suffering as nonredemptive? Fellow conservative William F. Buckley strongly dissented from George Will's point of view, saying that Will had "transformed these words into an endorsement of the Holocaust. . . . Such perverse readings of an impulsive response by a transparently good man should bear in mind that Christendom celebrates as its primary day of joy the day of the Resurrection, which could not have happened save for Christ crucified."[20]

The lesson seems to be that less is more. The text of *Nostra Aetate*, with its inspiration from the minor prophet Zephaniah, left unsaid what neither scripture nor human intelligence can specify. Similarly there is no need to specify what might have been the meaning of the Holocaust, and Cardinal O'Connor quickly withdrew his speculative statement. Recently deceased Paulist Father, Lawrence Boadt, spoke in general about the problem of evil. "We can't explain evil, why a month-old child dies," Father Boadt said. "Why does a person who's led a good life have so much suffering? We don't know."[21]

---

[18] Robert G. Weisbord, Wallace P. Sillanpoa, *The Chief Rabbi, The Pope and the Holocaust: an Era in Vatican-Jewish Relations* (New Brunswick, NJ: Transaction Publishers, 1992), 198. He included Christians in the statement. See "John Paul Cites Suffering of Jews," *New York Times*, June 26, 1988.

[19] "What Vatican Should be Told: Jerusalem None of Its Business," *Orlando Sentinel*, January 15, 1987.

[20] William Buckley, *Happy Days Were Here Again: Reflections of a Libertarian Journalist* (New York: Basic Books, 1993), 300.

[21] *Catholic Virginian* 83:22 (2008).

LEONIDAS DONSKIS

After Communism: Identity and Morality in the Baltic Countries

Eastern European countries seem locked mentally somewhere between the discovery of the intrinsic logic of capitalism characteristic of the nineteenth century and the post-Weimar Republic period. This is a period characterized by an incredibly fast economic growth and a passionate advocacy of the values of free enterprise and capitalism, accompanied by a good deal of anomie, fission of the body social, stark social contrasts, shocking degrees of corruption, a culture of poverty (to recall Oscar Lewis's term which refers to low trust, self-victimization, disbelief in social ties and networks, contempt for institutions, and so on), and cynicism.

In the Baltic region, the post-modern and post-totalitarian era proved capable of squeezing two centuries of uninterrupted European history within two decades of "transition." The Baltic States and other East-Central European countries moved from the planned economy of communism to free-market economy and global capitalism. In a way, Eastern Europe appears to have become a kind of laboratory where the speed of social change and cultural transformation could be measured and tested. In fact, the Baltic countries and their societies are far ahead of what we know as the grand historical narrative, or, plainly, predictable and moralizing history; nay, these societies are faster than history.

After the collapse of the Soviet Union, identity and morality became, in the Baltic States, core issues of political existence. One was tempted to apply to the Baltic countries the description used by Milan

Kundera in "The Tragedy of Central Europe" published in 1984[1] to characterize Central European countries: a huge variety of cultures and thought in a small area. Yet the question immediately raised was if the connection that binds Lithuanians to their neighbors, Latvia and Estonia, will be just a remembrance of common enslavement and a sense of insecurity. Will we be able to create a new Baltic regional identity, one that is both global and open and in which we can map our past and our present according to altogether different criteria?

Up to now modernity in Western Europe was supplying a theory to explain the world around us. The point is that Eastern Europe has changed the world becoming more than a theory-emanating entity. Eastern Europe is a laboratory of change and a vast area of side effects and damage inflicted by modernity on the world. As such, it still supplies empirical evidence to the West to judge the "second modernity" (according to Ulrich Beck[2]), or "liquid modernity" (as Zygmunt Bauman would have it[3]), squeezed and condensed here in less than two decades.

As Vytautas Kavolis (1930–1996), an eminent Lithuanian émigré sociologist, described the Baltic region, it appears as a laboratory of change deeply embedded in Eastern Europe, itself a boundary region of Europe. It is the laboratory where the great challenges and tensions of modernity can be tested; where the scenarios for European life in the not-too-distant future take shape.

Does the Baltic Region Exist After 1990?

What is the relationship between Lithuania and the other two Baltic nations? It differs from Latvia and Estonia in more than one way. No matter how rich in historically formed religious communities and minorities it is, Catholic Lithuania, due to its historic liaisons with

---

[1] Milan Kundera, "The Tragedy of Central Europe," translated by Edmund White, *New York Review of Books*, vol. 31, no. 7, April 26, 1984, 33–38.

[2] Ulrich Beck, *The Cosmopolitan Vision*, translated by Ciaran Cronin (Cambridge, UK: Polity Press, 2006).

[3] Zygmunt Bauman, *Liquid Modernity* (Cambridge, UK: Polity Press, 2000).

Poland and other Central and East European nations, is much more of an East-Central European nation than Lutheran Latvia and Estonia. Therefore, it would be quite misleading to assume seemingly identical paths by the Baltic States to their role and place in modern history.

Lithuania's history and its understanding would be unthinkable without taking into account countries such as Poland, Belarus, or Ukraine. Latvia is inseparable from major German and Swedish influences, and Estonia from Swedish and Danish, not to mention its close cultural ties with Finland.

Lithuania is an old polity with a strong presence in medieval and Renaissance Europe. Latvia and Estonia emerged as new political actors in the twentieth century. It was with sound reason, then, that after 1990, when Lithuania and the other two Baltic nations became independent, politicians and the media started making jokes about the unity of the three Baltic sisters. It had been achieved by them through their common experience of having once been three inmates in the same prison cell.

Small wonder, then, that this situation led Toomas Hendrik Ilves, a former foreign minister (then president) of Estonia, to describe the latter as a Nordic country, rather than a Baltic nation. In fact, once they had come into existence, the Baltic States underwent considerable political changes in the twentieth century. It is worth recalling that Finland, before the World War II, was considered a Baltic State, too. That is to say that four Baltic States existed in interwar Europe. The fact that only three entered the twenty-first century is a grimace of recent history. Yet some similarities and affinities between the Baltic States are too obvious to require emphasis. All three nations stood at the same historic crossroads after the First World War. All were linked to the fate of Russia in terms of (in)dependence and emancipation. All three existed as independent states from 1918 to 1940.

At that time, all three introduced liberal minority policies, granting a sort of personal, nonterritorial cultural autonomy to their large minorities, Lithuania to its Jewish, Latvia to German, and Estonia to German and Russian minorities. All three sought strength and inspiration in their ancient languages and cultures. All have a strong Romantic element in their historical memory and self-perception. Last but not least, all benefited from émigrés and their role in politics and culture. It suffices to mention that the presidents of all three Baltic States have been, or continue to be, émigrés, who spent much of their lives abroad and who returned to their respective countries when they restored independence after 1990: Valdas Adamkus in Lithuania, Vaira Vyke-Freiberga in Latvia, and Toomas Hendrik Ilves in Estonia. Most important, the trajectories of the Lithuanian and Baltic identity allow us to understand the history of the twentieth century better than anything else.

Yet questions arise: What will the Baltic Region be like in the twenty-first century? What will be the common denominator between Klaipeda, Riga, Tallinn, Kaliningrad, and St. Petersburg in the new epoch? Will the Baltic States come closer to the Nordic states, or will they remain a border region in which contrasting Eastern and Western European conceptions of politics and public life continue to fight it out amongst themselves? Will we able to apply to the Baltic countries that description by which Milan Kundera attempted to identify Central European countries: a huge variety of culture and thought in a small area? Will the bonds that tie us to our neighbors be just a remembrance of common enslavement and a sense of insecurity, or will we create a new Baltic regional identity, one that is both global and open and in which we can map our past and our present according to altogether different criteria?

These are some of the questions the problem of a Baltic region raises. Formulating them is no less useful and meaningful than answering them. Possibly here is where some vital experiences are tried out, experiences that larger, more influential countries have not yet had but which await them in the future. It may be that the Baltics were and still remain a laboratory where the great challenges and tensions of modernity can be tested and the scenarios for European life in the not-too-distant future take shape.

Faster than History

Interestingly enough, the "faster than history" idiom acquires a special meaning when dealing with social change in Central and Eastern Europe. The speed of time in what Czesław Miłosz and Milan Kundera, each in his own way, described as "yet another Europe" is beyond the historical, cultural, and political imaginations of Western Europeans and North Americans. After the collapse of the Soviet

Union, post-Soviet and post-Communist countries underwent considerable social and cultural change. To paraphrase the title of Kundera's novel that became one more admirable idiom to express the East-Central European sense of history and grasp of life, all this leads to the experience of the unbearable lightness of change.

What happened in Western Europe as the greatest events and civilization-shaping movements of centuries acquired a form—in Central and Eastern Europe—of mandatory and rapid economic and political programs that had to be implemented by successor states of the Soviet Union. This is to say that the new democracies had to catch up with the Western part of history to qualify for the exclusive and honorary club of Europe. Moreover, "yet another Europe" had to become even faster than history, transforming itself into a more or less recognizable collective actor of global economy and politics.

Capitalism, which had long been presented in Soviet high school textbooks as the major menace to humankind, now seems more aggressive and dynamic in post-Soviet societies than in far more moderate, timid, egalitarian, social-democratic, welfare-state-orientated, and post-capitalist Western European countries. Sweden, Finland, and the rest of the Nordic countries, for instance, can only marvel at what they perceive as a sort of old-fashioned, historically recycled, and ruthless capitalism of the Balts—or, to put it in more conventional terms, the libertarian economy of Estonia and other Baltic countries. The countries that used to symbolize to Soviet citizens the embodiment of "wild capitalism" with its overt glorification of the winners and contempt for the losers now appear to them as astonishingly communitarian, warm, and humane.

Indeed, they are pure and innocent in comparison with the "first come first served" or "grab the stolen" or "catch it all" type of mentality that paradoxically, albeit logically, blends with a sort of Marxism turned upside down. This extremely vulgar variety of economic determinism and materialism in Lithuania and other East-Central European countries barely surprises those who know quite well that the last thing one could expect to be named among priorities is the issue of culture. Although quite a few pay lip service to it without giving much consideration as to how to foster intellectual dialogue among countries, somehow almost everybody agrees there that the West has to pay for "the culture, uniqueness, and spirituality" of post-totalitarian countries.

These former-communist societies are faster than history, yet slower than a lifetime. People often complain here that their lives and careers have been ruined by this rapid social change and grand transformation. They take it as a tragedy arguing (and not without reason) that their lives, energies, and works have been wasted, if not completely spoiled. A lifetime of a human being proves insufficient to witness a thrilling and sweeping transformation of society.

Vytautas Kavolis worked out a theory of post-modernism as an attempt to reconcile what has been separated by modernity. At the same time, the idea of post-modernism served, for Kavolis, as an interpretative framework for the split between the modernist and the anti-modernist. He accorded the concept of the post-modern to the process of desovietization, too: "If desovietization, in its diversity of forms, continues relatively unhindered and does not become complacent with its own rhetoric, it has the potentiality of becoming a first-rate (that is, 'enriching') civilizational movement. If the concept of the '*post*modern' can still be retrieved from the cultists who have made it a monopoly of their own exuberance, desovietization could even be considered, in some of its cultural emphases, as 'postmodern.' (I conceive of the 'postmodern' not as antimodernist, but as the building of bridges between the 'modernist' and the 'antimodernist')."[4] Artists and humanists in Lithuania might fill many gaps and bridge some parts of human sensibility divided between disciplines and scattered across the universe of our global culture. They are ahead of many social and political processes that are on their way in Lithuania. They predict and passionately deny these processes, laugh at them, make fun of them, anticipate and critically question them. The contemporary art has become a sort of social and cultural critique in our post-modern world—yet this applies to Central and East European societies better than to anybody else.

At the same time, contemporary art and culture may prevent the spread of one more disease of our time—unlimited manipulations of public opinion shamelessly performed in the name of freedom and democracy. It can do this by calling into question everything that fails to do justice to humanity or respect human dignity. In doing so, con-

---

[4] Vytautas Kavolis, *Civilization Analysis as a Sociology of Culture* (Lewiston, NY: The Edwin Mellen Press, 1995), 166.

temporary artists and scholars would be able to find their raison d'être in our age of the divorce of words and meanings, power and politics, politeness and sensitivity—along with their efforts to help restore the damaged sociability and power of association crucial for their societies. In the twentieth century, modern artists hated the crowd intensely and spoke up in favor of the individual. Post-modern art, if properly understood, could advocate community, thus attempting reconciliation of the individual and community or society.

Whatever the speed of life and the intensity of change, our epoch can be faster than history—especially, if the latter is measured like it was a century ago. Yet it will always be slower than a lifetime of a particular human individual. The efforts within contemporary culture to reconcile the individual with him or herself, with community, society, and history would therefore come as a perfect tribute to what always remains beyond or ahead of history—values, humanity, and the miracle of human dialogue.

The Culture of Determinism

The phenomena of innocence and self-victimization are instrumental in shaping what might be termed the culture and determinism of poverty. Victimized consciousness is moved by the belief in malevolent and sinister forces of the universe—allegedly manifesting themselves through secret and elusive human agencies—that come to manipulate and dominate the world through their subversive activities immediately targeted at a single actor, the most vulnerable and fragile one. The principle of evil is permanently ascribed to the big and powerful, while reserving the principle of good exclusively for the small, vulnerable and fragile. By implication, one cannot err or sin because she/he happens to belong to a small, vulnerable and fragile group. Or vice versa, one can never be on the right side if she/he, by birth and upbringing, belong to a privileged or powerful one. This means that my human value and merit are predetermined and, subsequently, can be lightly judged by my race, gender, nationality, or class.

This sort of modern barbarity, which takes all human beings as irreversibly shaped and moved by biological or social forces with no moral or intellectual choice involved, stands powerfully behind conspiracy theory. Regrettably, modern barbarity, which deprives humanity of the sense of human fellowship and tends to replace it with the concepts of natural animosity and ever-lasting struggle between irreconcilable groups or forces, tends to surface and extend its influence beyond underground consciousness. Far from being qualified as social pathology, it assumes its status as what is supposed to be normal and even progressive.

A conspiracy theory allows no room for critical self-reflexivity and critical self-discovery. At this point, it is a mortal enemy of moral philosophy. Whereas modern political philosophy, if properly understood, is an extension of moral philosophy, the conspiracy theory's point of departure is the radical denial of theoretical reflection, critical judgment, and moral accountability. Instead, the core assumption of any conspiracy theory is that the agencies of good and evil are established once and for all, that the only distinction between good and evil is that good is powerless and condemned to suffer endlessly, while evil is all-powerful and solely motivated by the hunger for power. In this reading, infinite manipulation and unlimited power are the ultimate ends that motivate evil forces. The world is too naïve, vulnerable, and fragile to unmask the real masters and their dirty manipulations with which they keep that world in the darkness of ignorance, stupidity and self-deception—this is the revealing message conspiracy theory conveys to its adherents.

Vytautas Kavolis suggested that this phenomenon is deeply rooted in a modern system of moralization, which he termed the culture of determinism. Kavolis puts it thus:

> A modern amoral culture, in the sense that it tends to eliminate the notion of individual moral responsibility without taking collective responsibility seriously, is the *culture of determinism*. In this culture it is assumed that individuals are shaped and moved by biological or social forces in al! essentials beyond the control, or even the possibility of major choices, of individuals affected by them. The four major intellectual foci of this culture are the theory that "biology (or racial inheritance) is destiny," the belief that the human being is and should be nothing but a utility-calculating, pleasure-maximizing machine; the conviction that the individual is, in currently existing societies, only a victim of the

"oppressive," "impoverished," "devitalizing," or "traditionally constricted" social conditions of his or her existence (without the ability to become an agent of his fate and assume responsibility for her actions); and the notion that he can be helped out of such conditions solely by the "guidance of experts" who have a "rational social policy" at their disposal, in the determination of which those who are to be helped participate merely as instruments of the experts.[5]

Kavolis's concept of a modern amoral culture sheds new light on why victimized groups or societies relate to the ruling élites as patients to diagnosing and curing specialists. At the same time, it allows us an essential comprehensive point of entry: we can understand why and how victimized culture manifests itself as the culture of destiny and determinism—in contrast to the culture of freedom and choice.

This concept reveals the links between all kinds of deterministic theories, especially in the social sciences. Kavolis starts by quoting Sigmund Freud's dictum, "Biology is destiny," and then goes on to show other modes of discourse that speak out in favor of inexorable laws of racial inheritance, history, milieu, societal life, social organization, and so forth. A modern amoral culture denying individual responsibility and moral choice, or the culture of determinism in Kavolis's parlance, is a system of moralization disseminated in the modern moral imagination. Hence, we can identify what might be called natural innocence and victimization. According to this attitude, people cannot in principle control biological or social forces. On the contrary, particular individuals and even entire societies are shaped and moved by those forces. Since the world is controlled and dominated by powerful groups, clandestine international organizations, or secret agencies and their elusive experts, individuals cannot assume moral responsibility for their actions. Nor can they influence or change the state of affairs. Such an attitude is characteristic of marginalized and victimized groups, but it is equally characteristic of the kind of consciousness shaped by anti-liberal and anti-democratic regimes.

---

[5] Vytautas Kavolis, *Moralizing Cultures* (Lanham, MD: University Press of America, 1993), 48.

The Culture of Poverty

The culture of determinism is also characteristic of what Oscar Lewis described as the culture of poverty.[6] The culture of poverty is not identical to real poverty, according to Lewis, who studied for many years the trajectories of the identities of people living in the shanties of Puerto Rico and Mexico, their value orientations and evaluations of the world. There are cases, when groups living in poverty have their social networks, conspicuous cooperation and social forms (for instance, East Europe's Jews during the nineteenth century and the first half of the twentieth century or craftsmen from India). The culture of poverty manifests itself first of all in an absolute distrust of institutions and the state, unwillingness to participate in the state's life, and the conviction that everything in the world is predetermined—social roles, distribution of power, wealth and poverty.

Let us say that the culture of poverty was not characteristic of Fidel Castro's post-revolution Cuba, since the society (even the poorest layers of it) acquired its value and a sense of the meaning of life, as Lewis had noticed, in the revolution. A strong sense of fatalism, a low level of social trust, a matriarchal family, man's distancing of himself from the most important family problems—these are all characteristic of the culture of poverty. In other words, this whole anthropological complex of the culture of poverty clearly points to the fact that it is a variant of determinism.

Incidentally, Lewis has discovered that the main characteristics of the culture of poverty—isolation, disbelief in the possibility of social linkage, fatalism, distrust of everything—have been encountered even in wealthy people's thinking and worldviews. At this point, it is worth remembering that Kavolis, as early as 1996, asked rhetorically whether the culture of poverty exists in Lithuania. In fact, ample evidence shows the solid foundations that the culture of poverty has in Lithuania. As recent sociological polls suggest, a strong sense of helplessness, fatalism, and failure is accompanied by a growing hostility to liberal

---

[6] For more on this, see Oscar Lewis, "The Culture of Poverty" in Richard T. LeGates and Frederic Stout (eds.), *The City Reader* (London & New York: Routledge, 1996), 217–224.

democracy and democratic institutions. Quite a few Lithuanians would prefer an authoritarian leader to parliamentary democracy. They would favor the strong man's rule, rather than the rule of law, representation, and the division of powers. Powers of association have deteriorated considerably. Social atomization and the fragmentation of society have gone so far as to allow us to talk about new forms of cultural colonization, isolation, and marginalization. The Soviet regime seems to have transformed Lithuania into a kind of low-trust nation where disbelief in authorities and institutions threatens the fragile foundations of civil society, yet where people—oddly enough—place an enormous amount of trust in the media and TV, in particular.

This sort of explosive and destructive potential was revealed and successfully exploited by Lithuanian populists during the presidential election in 2002 and afterward. People of the older generation often feel that their lives have been spoiled, if not totally wasted. Many of them have lost their jobs and savings. Their children have left the country and settled in Ireland or Spain, whereas they have to live on a miserable pension. It is hardly possible to convince these people that Lithuania has a vibrant economy or that it is "a Baltic tiger" (as Poland's Leszek Balcerowicz once described it). Quite a large segment of Lithuanian society lives beyond the EU reality.

In fact, Lithuania has the highest suicide rate in the world—quite a sad and scary fact that might shed new light on the degree of social depression, alienation, and despair in Lithuanian society. Moreover, growing emigration has deprived the country of many young and highly qualified people. Nearly 800,000 people have left Lithuania over the past twenty years settling in the United States, Great Britain, Ireland, and Western Europe. Consequently the country has lost much of its potential, and the countryside has been deprived of some prospects for more rapid economic and social development.

The fragmentation and segmentation of Lithuanian society has reached dangerous limits and can become a threat to democracy, not to mention social cohesion and civic solidarity. During the Paksas scandal, which ended in 2004 with the impeachment of Lithuanian President Rolandas Paksas, some political commentators and politicians coined the phrase "two Lithuanias," thus dividing Lithuanian society into the "sugar-beets"—the term *runkeliai* in Lithuanian is a far from innocent word, and in this context appears as a derogatory term—

and the "élite." At this point, great uncertainty hangs over Lithuania's future. As the presidential scandal has shown, there are still all too many temptations to talk of two Lithuanias. On the one hand, there is the westward-looking and dynamic Lithuania, celebrating its dynamism and rejoicing over the accession of Lithuania to the European Union (EU) and NATO. On the other, there is the élite-abandoned, long-suffering, divided and depressed Lithuania, longing for something like the equality-in-misery it knew in the Soviet Union.

Each time it comes to an election, a certain segment of society perceives the vote as an opportunity for revenge against the much-hated and semi-mythical élite. Usually these voters of despair and revenge are described as the aforementioned "sugar-beets," although it would be naïve to reduce this problem to the depressed countryside. Quite a few Lithuanian tycoons and public figures overtly supported Rolandas Paksas and then Viktor Uspaskich, another populist politician who founded the Labor Party, made up by the graduates of the Higher Institutions of the Communist Party, former functionaries, and the *nouveaux riches*.

All of the above, though, does not explain the roots of the culture of poverty in Lithuania, especially if one bears in mind Lewis's idea that the culture of poverty does not necessarily coincide with actual poverty. At this point, most telling was the fact that 34.2 percent of Lithuanians—according to the results of a sociological poll conducted by the market analysis and research group *Rait* on December 2–5, 2004—thought that the period of 1990–2004, that is, the period of the newly-gained independence of Lithuania, was the most unfortunate period in the country's entire history. Only 29.7 percent of respondents reserved this honor for the Soviet period, and even fewer—22.7 percent—for the period under Tsarist Russia (1795–1915).[7] Small wonder, then, that many commentators shocked by this outcome jumped to conclusions diagnosing a new social disease. They suggested that Lithuania is suffering from an identity crisis, amnesia, political illiteracy, the loss of the sense of history, and, ultimately, the disappearance of national pride.

The culture of complaint coupled with the culture of poverty go so far as to depict Lithuania as an unfortunate, corrupt, cynical,

---

[7] For more on this, see http://www.rait.lt/.

predatory, amoral country devoid of justice, benevolence, fairness, and respect for human dignity, a country which does not have a future among civilized countries of the EU, and so on. Yet on a closer inspection, it appears that the main characteristics of the culture of poverty—isolation, disbelief in a possibility of social link, fatalism, distrust of everything—are stronger in Lithuania than ever. Most probably it is the high price Lithuania has to pay for an incredibly fast and drastic sociocultural change. This became especially obvious from 2009 onward, as Lithuania—and Latvia as well—suffered a dramatic slowdown of their economies accompanied by a backlash of far-right, xenophobic, homophobic, and anti-Semitic attitudes.[8] Lithuania went so far as to challenge core European values, such as human rights and civil liberties, and to question the moral validity of the EU.

On July 14, 2009 we celebrated two hundred and twenty years from the beginning of the French Revolution. One would have expected a celebration of the date trying to embrace the new reality of Europe—first and foremost, its unique and historically unprecedented solidarity. One would have thought that the day marked the reconciliation of Europe, the Old and the New—to use Donald Rumsfeld's parlance—especially in the light of the election of the Polish MEP Jerzy Buzek, the former prime minister of Poland and one of the heroes of the Solidarity movement, President of the European Parliament. A unique chance opened up to put many things behind us, including the frequent clashes of the moral and political sensibilities of the "two Europes," meaning the Old Europe's liberal and tolerant attitudes towards human diversity, and the New Europe's old-fashioned infatuations and reactive conservatism. Yet this was not to be. It would have been too good to be true.

How ironic that on that same day when the newly elected European Parliament opened its plenary session, the *Seimas*, that is, Lithuania's parliament, adopted the law which rejected, almost overnight, everything that today's Europe stands for and is all about. The new Lithuanian Law on the Protection of Minors from the Detrimental Effects of Public Information adopted on July14, 2009 struck human rights defenders and media people, both in Lithuania and in the EU,

---

[8] For more, see Leonidas Donskis, *Troubled Identity and the Modern World* (New York: Palgrave Macmillan, 2009).

as overtly homophobic and profoundly undemocratic. This law was vetoed twice by the former President of Lithuania Valdas Adamkus, yet he was overruled by the *Seimas*. In addition, the law was severely criticized by the current President of Lithuania Dalia Grybauskaitė. Moreover, the law in question has been criticized in vigorous terms by the Lithuanian media, political commentators, and several civil liberties and human rights defenders who have stressed its homophobic substance along with its dangerous political implications, such as censorship and self-censorship. Needless to say, this law had little if anything to do with the protection of children. Instead, it was against gay and lesbian citizens of the country. Whatever the case, the equation of homosexuality to physical violence and necrophilia is morally repugnant and deeply disgraceful.

Still, it was difficult to believe that the adoption of such a law was possible in an EU country at the beginning of the twenty-first century. One can take this law as an unfortunate move or as a profound misunderstanding, to say the very least. Changes to articles 310 in the penal code and 214 in the administrative code, which were debated in the *Seimas*, criminalize—with the threat of a fine, community work or imprisonment—anyone involved in the "promotion" of homosexuality in "any public space." If this is not the slide to state-sponsored homophobia and the criminalization of public self-expression by Lithuania's gay and lesbian citizens, what is it? Is it not a sad reminder of the cycle of abuse in a country that suffered isolation and humiliation for more than five decades?

This law was a disgrace, but even more so would be an attempt to obfuscate, trivialize, and, in effect, justify it. This is why a sort of déjà vu appeared on hearing how some conservative politicians in the European Parliament (EP) tried to depict the EP Resolution criticizing the law as a blow allegedly dealt by the EP to the national parliament of a sovereign country. In their understanding, the idea to ask for the Human Rights Agency's expert opinion on whether this law contradicts fundamental rights would jeopardize the independence and sovereignty of Lithuania.

If we apply double standards refusing to react to the violations of human rights within the EU, yet simultaneously engaging in verbose assaults on Russia, China, or Iran, are we not in peril of closing ranks with those profoundly undemocratic countries? What would be the dividing line between the EU and Russia if we had adopted the principle of noninterference with national parliaments on such matters as human rights?

This would signify the end of Europe the way it is now. If so much sound and fury comes defending the "holy" rights of the national parliament to criminalize diversity, are we not at risk of transforming the EU into merely an amoral trading bloc? All in all, European values, norms and solidarity prevailed, and the EP sent a powerful message reasserting the simple truth that civil liberties and human rights can never be confined to domestic affairs. They are not the property of the state, no matter how just and democratic that state might be. And they never will be so as far as the EU is concerned.

What happened to us? Did we decide to use democracy in a nonchalant and selective way, appropriating some parts that suit us while discarding what we dislike? Had it become the enthusiastic "yes" to the simplistic notion of democracy as a 50 + 1 methodology, yet the strong "no" to minorities? "Yes" to the right to practice our mainstream Lithuanian culture, national identity, and Roman Catholic faith, yet the resolute "no" to gay and lesbian rights? If so, not a single chance exists that such a selective and arbitrary concept of democracy will be ever accepted in the EU—and rightly so.

It turned out to be difficult to be independent and responsible for the social and moral order that allows every citizen to experience their sense of pride and dignity. It is hard to extend our modern political and moral sensibilities to the extent of every human being, regardless of his or her creed, faith, or gender. The simplest things, as we thought of them in the 1990s, turned out to be the most challenging ones. We have had a valuable lesson in democracy.

Intellectuals: Roles and Identities

What is the role of intellectuals in the nation- or community-building process? Some scholars of nationalism suggest that intellectuals invent traditions, work out interpretive frameworks for collective identity and self-comprehension, establish collective identities, forge political and moral vocabularies, and even shape their respective nations. At the same time, dissenting intellectuals may challenge their nations by offering an alternative vision or critique of their societies and cultures.

In the early 1990s, some Lithuanian intellectuals were quite optimistic about their social roles in society. For instance, writer Ričardas Gavelis (1950–2002), who might well be described as a caustic public intellectual and libertarian-minded critic of society and culture, responding to the journal *Metmenys* 1993 questionnaire, wrote about the role of what he termed the free intellectual in the following way:

> I nevertheless have some hope. It is precisely thanks to the fact that Lithuania dropped out of the general development [of Western culture] that we have managed to preserve a now almost extinct species—the free intellectual. Such creatures are virtually extinct in Europe, and even more so in America. There the intellectual is almost always part of some kind of academic circle. And that means that he unavoidably becomes a member of the state hierarchy, even if he teaches at a private university. Whether they like it or not, they must accommodate the rules of the academic career, of the narrow world of academia, of a narrow context of specialized reference. The era of the free intellectual—of the kind that Russell and Sartre were—has long passed in the world... . In Lithuania, for now, the true intellectual is free whether he wants it or not, because there is basically no influential academic world. For that reason, individual intellectuals have a greater influence on overall cultural development than anywhere else... . I would consider this to be a positive thing. In times of change and confusion free intellectuals are more useful than inflexible academic structures. Individuals are more flexible, more inclined to take risks, are not afraid to lose their academic positions or authority. It is my hope that free intellectuals will be the ones to launch the process of synchronizing Lithuanian and world culture.[9]

Yet quite different positions were expressed regarding the social role of the intellectual in society by Donatas Sauka, a conservative literary scholar. He wrote, as early as 1995, that Lithuanian intellectuals had forgotten their mission to preserve cultural traditions and to defend the

---

[9] Cited in Leonidas Donskis, *Loyalty, Dissent, and Betrayal: Modern Lithuania and East-Central European Moral Imagination*; pref. by Zygmunt Bauman (Amsterdam and New York: Rodopi 2005), 7.

nation. He advocated the rather well-worn paradigm of the building and defense of the nation against those who tarnished its image and international reputation. Small wonder, then, that Sauka, in doing so, also warned that "the liberals of the younger generation and their older colleagues among émigrés" threatened the injured nation. Sauka put it as follows:

> Who, then, defends society's conservative opinions—who speaks in the name of the injured nation, who expresses its historical insults, who mythologizes its rural moral reputation? Who, really? What is the point of trying out the sharpness of one's arrows when attacking a monster created by one's own imagination; but please give us a true picture of its traits, give us its first and last names! The liberals of the younger generation and their older colleagues among émigrés, who often hold condemnatory trials, do not have a concrete target which could embody the essence of such an ideology. And the target of their polemic is not too fresh—but faded ideas and moral directives, statements by the current leaders of the nation that were expressed during the euphoria of the Rebirth period.[10]

Here we have two opposing concepts of the intellectual. On the one side, Gavelis suggested a concept that depicts the intellectuals as critics of the establishment, society, and culture. On the other side, Sauka presented them as defenders of the nation's pride and prejudice. What lurks behind the critique of society and culture offered by intellectuals—loyalty or dissent? Fidelity or betrayal? Last but not least, what is the real raison d'être of modern intellectuals? Personification of conscience? Dedication to the nation and its historical injuries and moral traumas? Advocacy of individual reason and conscience? Social and cultural criticism? The politics of loyalty or the politics of dissent? The work for the sake of sustainable society? Preservation of historical memory? The defense of the nation from the attacks of liberals? The struggle against cosmopolitanism?

---

[10] Cited in Leonidas Donskis, *Identity and Freedom: Mapping Nationalism and Social Criticism in Twentieth-Century Lithuania* (London & New York: Routledge, 2002), 37.

The essence of the populist struggle against cosmopolitanism is excellently expressed by Romualdas Ozolas, a former MP and the signatory of the Independence Act: "I am a nationalist. Nationalism is the sole source of my strength. Each, according to the level of his stupidity, is free to decide what that means." The following maxim is a unique pearl of nationalist wisdom: "The cosmopolitan cannot be moral. The cosmopolitan is a-subjective; for that reason, he is incapable of imperative self-questioning."[11]

The nature of this kind of ghost-chasing is very well expressed in an introductory passage of an issue of the journal of cultural resistance *Į laisvę* (To Freedom): "A spiritual gap is growing between the sincere Lithuanian intellectual, for whom Lithuanian-ness, Lithuanian culture and the nation's interests are of the first order, and that new creature—probably a product of the Soviet period—the super-cultural-activist-intellectual, who, supposedly in the name of Western culture, offers obscene trash to television programs, books, and theatre festivals of a questionable nature. Unfortunately, together with these self-named intellectuals comes another threat to the Lithuanian nation—cosmopolitanism."[12]

Interestingly enough, one thing that has long been taken for granted in Lithuania—the idea that the real intellectual is a dedicated educator, builder, and shaper of the nation, rather than a public thinker or social and cultural critic—underwent considerable change and was put into question over the past ten years. If very few have critically questioned the idea that the intellectual is or at least ought to be instrumental in the nation-building process, things started changing around 1995. The mainstream Lithuanian nationalism was challenged by a new approach, which brought about the concept of civil society instead of the people or the nation. Some local intellectuals began increasingly associating themselves with civil society, the community-building process, and the public domain. This tendency was extremely timely and important, bearing in mind the deterioration of social links and networks, anomie, and the atomization of Lithuanian society. The Lithuanian philosopher Arvydas Šliogeris anticipated and aptly described this shift, calling into question Gavelis's enthusiasm for

---

[11] Ibid., 36.
[12] Ibid.

individual intellectuals, and placing more emphasis on the community-building instead of personal emancipation. Despite some undertones of *Kulturpessimismus*, that is, a sort of extremely harsh and exaggerated critique of Lithuanian public life, Šliogeris's standpoint sheds new light on the critical importance of public debate for society in transition. According to Šliogeris,

> Several years of independence have proven our inability to order our present *rationally*, our lack of common sense, and even any sense. What can that pitiful handful of active and thinking people—still capable of seeing the world clearly, simply, with a sober and cold eye—accomplish? Some such individuals exist, but they are powerless, because the parade is being led by the *mobile vulgus* and its idols. Is there any hope? Yes, there is, but that hope is hazy and cannot be transformed into a technical project, because in its deepest essence it is non-technical, anti-technical. My hope is all tied to the spontaneous emergence of small communities in which organic future forms of communal existence can begin to grow. However, these new forms of community can only develop somewhere beyond the boundaries of existing "organized" forms of (political, religious, economic, educational) life. The instigators of these communities must say a determined *No* to all, absolutely all, currently dominating structures of public and private life, because those structures are in fact dead and continue to exist only from habit. Democracy, freedom, prosperity, spirituality, truth, conscience, Christianity, culture, tradition—all of this has turned into ideological chatter and self-deception. If "values" and forms of existence remain as they are, it is no longer possible to breathe life back into these things. Why do I speak about the creation of new types of communities? For, after all, here remains the danger that such a newly created community will be nothing but a herd of slaves and schizophrenics ruled by paranoid and cynical Rasputins. There are already more than enough such sects in today's world. The formation of authentic communities involves enormous risk. But there is no other option, because individuals are ultimately helpless.[13]

---

[13] Cited in Donskis, *Identity and Freedom*, 9.

It is widely and rightly assumed that loyalty and betrayal are among the key concepts of the ethic of nationalism. The marriage of state and culture, which seems the essence of the congruence between political power structure and collective identity, usually offers a simple explanation of loyalty and dissent. Within such an interpretative framework of nationalism, loyalty is seen as a kind of once-and-for-all commitment of the individual to his or her nation and its historical-cultural substance, whereas betrayal is identified as a failure to commit him or herself to a common cause or as a diversion from the object of political loyalty and cultural/linguistic fidelity.

However, huge gaps exist between different patterns of nationalism. For conservative or radical nationalists, even a social and cultural critique of one's people and state can be regarded as nothing more and nothing less than treason. For their liberal counterparts, it is precisely what constitutes political awareness, civic virtue, and a conscious dedication to the people, culture, and state. Upon closer look, it appears that the concepts of loyalty, dissent, and betrayal can be instrumental in mapping the liberal and democratic facet of nationalism because they are both political and moral categories. It is impossible to analyze them without touching upon crucial issues of the twentieth and twenty-first centuries, such as political culture, liberal democracy, poverty, hatred, populism, manipulative exchanges and deliberate political manipulations, social criticism, and political commitment. The analysis of the aforementioned phenomena may reveal what it means to live in a changing society where all these things increasingly tend to become the nexus of social and political existence. History, socio-cultural dynamics, and the dialectic of identities can be properly understood only where the acceleration of the speed of change reaches its climax, and where social change becomes faster than history.

The Treason of Intellectuals or Identity Crisis?

Tomas Venclova is regarded as one of the most accomplished and noted Lithuanian humanists, and rightly so. An eminent poet, literary scholar, and translator, Venclova had long acted as a conscious and dedicated dissident opposed to the entire project of the former Soviet Union with its crimes against humanity, severe human rights violations, brutal suppression of all fundamental rights and civil liberties, and violent politics. Having spent a good part of his life in Lithuania, he was exiled to the West in 1977 where he built an academic career, eventually becoming Professor of Slavic Literatures at Yale University. Far from a conservative nationalist, Venclova has always spoken out in favor of liberal values. This could be a clue to his deeply moving and sensitive essay on the tragedy of Lithuania, the Holocaust that claimed the lives of more than 220,000 Lithuanian Jews.

The essay in question, "The Jews and the Lithuanians," written in the 1970s, made Tomas Venclova the first Lithuanian writer who showed the real scope of the tragedy, admitting the guilt and responsibility of those Lithuanians who collaborated with the Nazis and actively participated in the massacre of the Jews. Deeply embedded in the best intellectual traditions of Eastern and Central Europe, his collection of essays, *Forms of Hope*, reads like a moral map of a great European public intellectual and political thinker.[14]

Venclova made a strong and effective comeback to the public domain of Lithuania publishing, in July 2010, an elegantly written and caustic essay "It Suffocates Me Here." Wittily referring to the clash of the character Strepsiades, a staunch defender of the ancient Greek tradition, and its challenger Socrates, both depicted in Aristophanes' comedy *The Clouds*, Venclova described some of the ongoing political and moral debates in Lithuania as a backlash of parochialism and moral provincialism, and as a fear of modernity, applying harsh words and judging his country from a critical perspective. Without the shadow of a doubt, the essay became a landmark in the area of public debate. Small wonder that a dozen of angry and noisy reactions to Venclova's essay appeared over the following two months, as this piece of polemical writing dealt a blow to conservative and nationalistic writers in the country. The bitter response would not be long, though. Adding insult to injury, Venclova's critics came to describe him as an arrogant and rootless cosmopolitan. The opposing camp, the supporters of the aforementioned essay, implied that Venclova came up with a timely and principled call upon his country to take a closer look at itself at the beginning of the twenty-first century to be able to rethink its past and present.

---

[14] See Tomas Venclova, *Forms of Hope: Essays* (Riverdale-on-Hudson, NY: Sheep Meadow Press, 1999).

Furthermore, much in the spirit of Julien Benda's manifesto *La trahison des clercs* (*The Treason of Intellectuals*), Venclova's essay became an attack against those who regard the nation-state as the end in itself and against those who see the paramount mission of the intellectual as the defense of the nation-state at any price against the supposed evils of modernity and globalization. To his credit, Venclova was correct in raising this issue, because, the months before the essay's publication, Lithuanian media was peppered with a number of skeptical comments on the loss of Lithuanian identity and even of the independence after the country's accession to the EU. Some of the former political activists who fought for the country's independence in the national liberation movement *Sąjūdis* in the late 1980s had gone so far as to suggest that the EU was hardly any different from the Soviet Union. In their view, both these political formations were the gravediggers of the European peoples and of their independence and liberty.

What can be said in this regard? No matter how critical or skeptical we could be of European bureaucracy or the new managerial class that ignore local sensibilities and cultural differences, such a comparison does not merit serious attention. Yet, this new sort of rhetoric sent a clear message that part of the former political and intellectual elite of Lithuania found themselves deeply alienated from the new political reality of Europe.

In ancient Athens, writes Venclova, Socrates died for his freedom of thought, doubt, and for the right to question everything. As we learned from Socrates, uncertainty is not the enemy of a wise man and an unexamined life is not worth living. These pieces of perennial wisdom became an inescapable part of critical European thought. For Strepsiades and his modern followers, everything has to be certain and easily predictable. Therefore, one's little garden becomes more important than universal humanity. Whatever the case, says Venclova, it is Strepsiades, rather than the greatest cultural hero of Western Europe Socrates, who is alive and well in present Lithuania. According to him, to defend the pattern of identity and statehood of the nineteenth century, instead of modern moral and political sensibilities, is nothing other than a betrayal of the mission that intellectuals must carry.

The question remains quite timely and serious: What is the pattern of identity that Lithuania and two other Baltic States could maintain as a bridge between their precious cultural legacy and the world? In fact, an identity crisis is part of the search for identity. The Baltic States that surfaced to the world restoring their existence and securing their place in the political, mental and intellectual maps of the world, know it better than any other country or region on the globe.

Memory Wars

We are witnessing how a sinister tendency is increasingly getting stronger in the United States and in Europe. Politicians find themselves preoccupied with two domains that serve as a new source of inspiration: namely, privacy and history. Birth, death, and sex constitute the new frontiers on the political battlefields.

Politics is dying out nowadays if we define it as a translation of our moral and existential concerns into rational and legitimate action for the benefit of society and humanity. Instead it is becoming a set of managerial practices and skillful manipulations with public opinion. In this context, it is not unwise to assume that a swift politicization of privacy and history promises the way out of the present political and ideological vacuum. Suffice it to remember the bitter debates over abortion, euthanasia, and gay marriage over the past twenty or so years to conclude that the poor human individual continues to be regarded either as a property of the state and its institutions or, at best, as a mere instrument and hostage of a political doctrine.

There is nothing new under the sky, though. If we are to believe such incisive dystopian writers as Yevgeny Zamyatin, Aldous Huxley, and George Orwell, or groundbreaking social theorists such as Michel Foucault and Zygmunt Bauman, modernity always was, and continues to be, obsessed with how to get as much control over human body and soul as possible without physically exterminating people. The same is true with regard to society's memory and collective sentiment. As we learn from George Orwell's *1984*, history depends on who controls the archives and records. Since individuals have no other form of existence than that which is granted by the Party, personal memory has no power to create or restore history. But if memory is controlled or manufactured and updated every day, history degenerates into a justificatory and legitimizing design of power and control. Logically enough, this leads the Inner Party to assert that who controls the past controls the future and who controls the present controls the past.

If you think that it does not make sense to refer to the Orwellian world any longer, please think about the memory wars in present Europe. That Russia has already become a revisionist power is obvious. Moreover, it attempts to rewrite the history of the twentieth century by rehabilitating Stalin and depicting him as merely a wise, albeit sometimes cruel, modernizer of Russia. In this narrative, Stalin appears as just another version of the Great Modernizer of the State like Peter the Great. Needless to say, an attempt to outlaw what is regarded in Russia as historical revisionism, that is, the criminalization of any effort to put into question whether the Soviet Union with its labor camps, overtly fascist practices, and anti-Semitism (for those who have doubts about this, please do recall the Holodomor in Ukraine or the methodical extermination of Russian Jews and Jewish culture under Stalin) was any better than Nazi Germany, has its logic.

By no means is all this about the past. Already during Mikhail Gorbachev's reign, a plethora of decent and courageous Russian historians exposed the Soviet Union to have been a criminal state. Stalin was explicitly regarded as a criminal and paranoiac dictator who committed the most horrible crimes against humanity. The fact that Vladimir Putin's Russia changed the interpretation of history nearly overnight shows that everything is about the present, rather than the past. Although the denial of the Holocaust is too complex a phenomenon to be confined to legal practices and administrative measures, Germany outlawed the denial of the Holocaust out of its firm commitment never to repeat its past. Russia cynically denies its occupation and annexation of the Baltic States, as well as its numerous crimes against European nations, because it is sending a message to us that it would gladly repeat recent history, restoring the past and rehabilitating a political doctrine which Gorbachev's and Yeltsin's Russia regarded as overtly criminal and hostile to Russia itself.

Under the circumstances, one could witness an attempt by the Baltic States and the Eastern-Central European nations to work out a viable antidote to Russia's revisionism. However understandable and logical this attempt, the idea of the political and moral equivalency of Communism and National Socialism is not the most convincing way to do it. Western Europe and the United States will always take a deep exception to the claim that the Holocaust and Soviet crimes were of the same nature. Therefore, something has to be done to untie this Gordian knot of history. I propose that our politicians and public figures stop romanticizing the political forces of 1941 that tried to save the independence of the Baltic States collaborating with the Nazis. The tragedy was that our countries were "liberated" from the Nazis by the Soviets, instead of Great Britain or the United States.

All in all, only political courage and moral integrity, rather than selective interpretation of history, can end the memory wars with Russia or with the far Left of Western Europe. We cannot allow Russia to distort history spreading ugly lies about the Baltic States as crypto-fascist countries. Yet, we have to be fair and sympathetic to the Holocaust survivors, who fear, and rightly so, that a simplistic and relativistic approach to the Shoah as, supposedly, one of many Holocausts in Europe becomes a sort of obfuscation and trivialization of the tragedy. History can never be left solely to politicians, no matter whether democratic or authoritarian. It is not the property of the political doctrine or regime that it serves. History, if properly understood, is the symbolic design of our existence and moral choices we make every day. Like human privacy, our right to study and critically question history is a cornerstone of freedom.

The Strange Birth of Liberal Lithuania

The American political theorist Mark Lilla once wrote a perceptive review essay on the New Right in France, which he entitled "The Strange Birth of Liberal France."[15] This title, if slightly paraphrased, would be tailor-made to draw the attention to the adventures of liberalism in Central Europe.

In fact, we have to draw a strict dividing line here between Eastern European and Central European politics. Otherwise, we will be at the peril of missing the main point trying to understand the genesis of liberalism in Lithuania. At this point, Lithuania stands closer to the Central European pattern of post-communist politics than to that of East-

---

[15] Mark Lilla, "The Strange Birth of Liberal France," *The Wilson Quarterly* (Autumn 1994), 106–120.

ern Europe. No matter how similar the cases of endemic corruption, populism, and simplistic political reasoning in all post-Soviet countries, time flies, and Lithuania swiftly became to Moldova or Ukraine what Denmark used to be to Lithuania in the early 1990s—a model state, a benevolent patron, and nearly a rock star in public perception.

I will never forget how an Armenian colleague had once wittily explained to me the crucial difference between the logic of becoming a politician in Armenia and Ukraine. Whereas in Ukraine, he insisted with the stroke of subtle humor, you become rich and only then go to politics, things in Armenia are simple and straight: you go to politics to become rich. We would deceive ourselves by lightly assuming that we are an epoch away from this sort of politics. Much remains to be desired and even more so to be done in Lithuania to get closer to the level of the German political class; yet we deserve to be classified as a different case.

The matrix of Central European politics would shed more light on the strange birth of liberal Lithuania. What is that matrix? I would argue that it is a bipolar logic of political cleavages between the former establishment whose political offspring are still in the Soviet period, and the new one that came into existence after 1990. Whereas the former is essentially made up by the remnants of the Communist Party and therefore has a family resemblance name, be it Socialists or Social Democrats, the latter appears as a fiercely nationalistic and religious party. It is a Heimat-type party with an established moral monopoly of patriotism and local sensibility even if it claims more or less identifiable liberal ancestry (which is the case with Fidesz in Hungary).

Such a Heimat-type political lineage deeply permeated by religious and conservative value orientation is characteristic of the Homeland Union in Lithuania. In the European Parliament, this political formation is quite logically represented in the EPP—European People's Party, the largest political family dominated by German Christian Democrats. Without a shadow of a doubt, the heirs to the former communist establishment in Central Europe are embraced by the second largest political family in the EP—that is, S&D, or the Group of the Progressive Alliance of Socialists and Democrats.

What is left of the hardcore communists and radical left in the EP is the GUE/NGL (European United Left—Nordic Green Left), which is known as home for a mishmash of left-wing radicals of various shades in Europe and pious communist believers from the former Soviet bloc. Among them nobody is really shocked by figures like Alfrēds Rubiks who can defend such despots and demagogues as the late Hugo Chavez or Alexander Lukashenko in a public debate with tears in their eyes.

And where are the liberals in this matrix? This is the pivotal question. They are doomed to be somewhere in between the two trying to fish in the muddy waters of ideological and political leftovers. This is not to say, however, that genuine liberals do not exist in Lithuania or elsewhere in Central Europe. Of course, they do. Yet the problem is that due to weak traditions of liberal thought and politics in Lithuania, they are relegated to the fringes or are scattered across the spectrum where they may find themselves in other parties that claim and use the same adjective "liberal."

What happens frequently is that people who pass for liberals may well function anywhere across that same political spectrum—having been dismissed or forgotten elsewhere they become "newly discovered" liberals only due their inability to get closer to the distribution of power and prestige in other parties. Vladimir Tismaneanu once described a big part of Romanian liberals as an opportunistic and ad hoc political force; I am afraid, we could hardly avoid that same labeling.

The most difficult task is to consolidate the truly liberal electorate not only in Lithuania itself but across the UK and Europe as well. Young Lithuanians who study in British, German, Danish, Swedish, or American universities are leaning toward liberalism. Yet they are not always happy with an outdated not to say politically worn-out version of militant ideological liberalism of the nineteenth and twentieth centuries with almost no attention for today's moral and political sensibilities.

Unfortunately, such an out-of-date variety of liberalism if not libertarianism is presented in Lithuania as sensational news, which comes as an embarrassment to more sophisticated voters who would not exclude the sensitivities and values of center-left from the European and national liberal agenda. Political technocrats who parrot the vocabulary of American neoconservatives appear even more remote from inclusive liberalism able to tackle the most difficult challenges and dilemmas of our time. Therefore, it is high time to think. Otherwise, Lithuanian liberalism will be inexorably doomed to be merely a passing political fact that ceased existing without even having been properly born.

The Lithuanian Media, 1988–2013:
From Remembering to Forgetting

More than a quarter a century has passed since the year 1988 marked the beginning of the end for the former Soviet Union. The national rebirth movement of Lithuania, Sąjūdis, came into existence blazing the trail for Lithuania and other Soviet republics to freedom and independence. Gaining the momentum, consolidating symbolic power and authority, and making people believe that the time has come to change history and world politics restoring justice—all these magnificent things would have been beyond reach if the Lithuanian media had not changed the public domain almost overnight.

In fact, a happy combination of dedication, courage and passion made it possible, in the late 1980s and early 1990s, to reform and refurbish the entire public domain of Lithuania. There was no secret in this: old Soviet professionalism deeply embedded in the abyss between specialized writing and political engagement retreated, thus allowing new ways of thinking and writing to step in. Quite a few columnists in the early 1990s came from literature and art criticism. Others were new figures in the media and press with their roots in civil and political protests generated by the Sąjūdis.

Suffice it to mention some celebrity writers who influenced and even shaped the then leading dailies, weeklies, and magazines. Such noted Lithuanian writers and essayists as Jurga Ivanauskaitė (1961–2007) and the aforementioned Ričardas Gavelis (1950–2002) served as columnists for the daily *Respublika*. Incredible as it sounds, *Respublika*, especially notorious now for its anti-Semitic and homophobic editorials and slanderous writings, once was home for Ivanauskaitė's writings on society and culture, and also for Gavelis's brilliant essays.

Later Gavelis would begin working with the magazine *Veidas* whose closing section was reserved solely for his provocative, caustic, and ironic pieces. Rolandas Rastauskas, one of the most renowned essayists in Lithuania, was writing his essays exclusively for *Lietuvos rytas*. All these publications may be said to have greatly benefited from the talent of the aforementioned writers.

The late Gintaras Beresnevičius (1961–2006), a cultural historian and public intellectual who was able to easily surpass any political commentator in terms of the power and novelty of insight, was a true heir to this characteristically Lithuanian tradition of having a bright humanist capable of lending his or her talent to social analysis and political comment. He was a true heir to Gavelis. Not for a long time, alas. Ivanauskaitė, Gavelis, and Beresnevičius died very young.

What happened next was the swift deterioration of the level of public discourse. The Pandora Box was opened up. Everybody was welcome to comment online, and the debate was measured by sheer commercial success. Quality of thought and expression was not an issue anymore. Lithuanian online publications allowed and even warmly welcomed anonymous comments underneath serious essays and professional comments. These anonymous pearls of wisdom always were and continue to be full of anger, frustration, hatred, ad hominem attacks, overt anti-Semitic remarks, homophobic insinuations, and even more frequently—personal insults, poisonous darts, and toxic lies. This is the ugly face of our media, an aspect which distorted all good and novel things in Lithuanian online press that were brought about by freedom of expression and fundamental political change.

Yet medium is the message. This piece of Marshall McLuhan's creative genius and powers of anticipation strikes us as a prophecy of the twenty-first century. The idiom, form, language, political and moral sensibilities, and figures of speech—everything had gone with the wind of change overnight. Paper dailies and magazines began dying out right under our noses. The electronic portals started changing the landscape of the Lithuanian media dramatically. It was not that people lost their souls and sensitivities. Instead, Lithuania joined the twenty-first-century world. The old European world had more to lose, though. The post-communist world proved keener to change beyond recognition.

The brutality of the language, along with poor editing and undifferentiated attitudes both to professional assessments and sporadic mass opinions discouraged many gifted authors from writing political commentaries or else contributing to online publications. It was possible that ill manners and sadomasochistic language became a mask on the face of intellectual and moral void. Lack of content and political void, rather than merely an outbreak of stupidity, seems to have been the real reason behind confusion and uncertainty.

In the 1990s, Lithuania had high hopes concerning its bright future: it had a grand narrative and a self-legitimizing discourse of our return to Europe. On a closer look at our internal debates, it appears that part of our bitter disappointment springs from a radical change of roles: as Oscar Wilde would have had it, it is the horror of Ariel who sees in himself the mirror image of Caliban.

The country entered the phase of organized forgetting. Ours is an age of oblivion. Once we were struck by Milan Kundera's message in *The Unbearable Lightness of Being* that the sad news about the tragedy of Prague as seen through Teresa's photographs in Switzerland (where she and Tomas come to save their lives and future after the crushing of the velvet revolution of 1968) turned out old news. This is exactly what is happening in Lithuania. The best of our culture and thought is old news. The country and its media are sadly confined to TV reality shows, Vanity Fair, and private lives of public figures, which is just another term for showbiz figures.

This is not to say that Lithuania is incapable of good press and quality media. It is rather to suggest that the country seems to have next to nothing to remember and even less to celebrate but political scandals and the ups and downs of its political clowns.

BOGDAN C. IACOB

The Romanian Communist Past and the Entrapment of Polemics

I. The Puzzle

In September 2010, the Institute for the Investigation of Communist Crimes and the Memory of the Romanian Exile[1] published a survey on the opinions and attitudes of the Romanian population about the communist past. Among many of the rather contradictory results, the poll showed how 78 percent of the respondents answered "No" to the question "Did you personally or has a member of your family suffered because of the communist regime?" At the same time, 37 percent considered that the regime was criminal, 42 percent that it was illegitimate, and 50 percent admitted that there was repression under communist rule.[2] The importance of this information lies in the possibility to analyze the conceptual chain that plays the role of signifier in reference to the communist historical experience: repression-criminality-illegitimacy-suffering. If we wish to establish this connection on the basis of the mentioned statistics, it does not appear to function. Indeed, the first

---

[1] IICCMER is a governmental institution created in November 2009 as a result of the merger of the Institute for the Investigation of Communist Crimes in Romania (founded in 2006) to the National Institute for the Memory of the Romanian Exile (established in 2002). Its mandate is to produce scholarship on the communist regime, to find evidence on the latter's crimes, to develop education strategies on the communist period, and the develop memorialization initiatives. For more details see http://www.iiccr.ro/ro/despre_iiccr/cadrul_legal/legislatie, last accessed on October 10, 2010. The author of the present article was Secretary of IICCMER's Scientific Council between March 2010 and May 2012.

[2] IICCMER & CSOP, "Atitudini și opinii despre regimul comunist din România. Sondaj de opinie publică," September 16, 2010. For more detailed results see http://iiccmer.ro/ro/sondaje_iiccmer_csop/, last accessed May 28, 2011.

three seem to have a more general quality, while the fourth a personal, subjective one. Despite the proportionally majoritarian acceptance of the first three as descriptive labels for the communist regime in Romania, there is highly decreased identification with individual, collective, or even family suffering for the historical period in question.

This brings me to a crucial question: why do negative perceptions of the communist regime in Romania not overlap with personal affirmations of trauma? To take my query further, is there something in the discourse about the communist past at the level of public opinion that prevents (or does not lead to) the connection between communism as historical experience (based on perceptions about institutions, events, personalities, and so on) and communism as lived experience?

Before going any further, I need to first sketch the background for my analysis. As presented in Tismaneanu's and Vasile's papers, in December 2006, the Romanian President, Traian Băsescu, condemned, on the basis of a Report drafted by an international commission (Presidential Commission for the Analysis of the Communist Dictatorship in Romania—from now on "the Commission"), the communist regime as "criminal and illegitimate." The present paper mainly looks into some of the debates, from 2006 until 2012, about the contents of the Report and which focused on the significance of the act of official condemnation. In order to avoid redundancies with the texts of the two above-mentioned authors in this volume, I will side-step most of the public exchanges during 2006, most of the personal attacks against the Commission's chair, the uproar originating from the pro-communist and extreme-right circles, and the reactions of the Romanian Orthodox Church. These topics are already pertinently analyzed by Tismaneanu and Vasile.

The central argument here is that one can notice a phenomenon, which I called the entrapment of polemics that can explain why the discussions on the Romanian public sphere find it increasingly difficult to balance individual and collective memories of the communist past with scholarly assessments of the dictatorship and with the duty for *truth-telling*. My understanding of the function of "truth-telling" in reference to the Presidential Commission for the Analysis of the Communist Dictatorship in Romania (PCADCR) is based on Priscilla Hayner's characterization of essential functions fulfilled by a Truth Commission. The Romanian Commission was not identical to a Truth Commission, but it did "reveal a global truth of the broad patterns of events, and demonstrate without question the atrocities that took place and what forces were responsible." I also contend that it set the ground for going "beyond simply outlining the facts of abuse" and made "a major contribution in understanding how people and the country as a whole were affected, and what factors contributed to the violence."[3] In this interpretative context, I consider that any further commitment to truth-telling in the aftermath of the condemnation act and of the Report had to continue along this path of furthering society's understanding about the nature and consequences of the communist past.

The bias of the present paper toward discussing some of the criticism to the condemnation act and the Commission's Report does not mean that the latter two were not received positively by the public opinion, the academic community, or the general public. To my knowledge, the Report already went through at least two print runs.[4] If this is any indication of its impact, the Report successfully reached a wide audience despite being an 800-page mostly academic volume. Moreover, for almost a year most of the reactions were positive. Mainly starting with the end of 2007, critics in mass media increased their attacks and they became ever more visible through their presence in national cultural weeklies and on talk shows hosted by some of the most widely watched TV stations. These mass-media mediums also happened to be extremely vitriolic against the government in power and the president who created the Commission and condemned the communist regime. One explanation for this phenomenon is the fact that the political environment in Romania became ever more polarized, as the coalition that won the 2004 elections fell apart, as the President in office was impeached in spring 2007,[5] as new parliamentary elec-

---

[3] See Priscilla B. Hayner, *Unspeakable Truths: Facing the Challenge of Truth Commissions* (New York: Routhledge, 2002), 85.

[4] Information based on personal conversation in June 2010 with the general manager of Humanitas, the publishing house that issued the volume version of the Report.

[5] For details on Traian Băsescu's first impeachment, see Vladimir Tismaneanu and Paul Dragos-Aligica, "Roamania's Parliamentary Putsch," *Wall Street Journal*, April 20, 2007. http://www.romanianewswatch.com/2007/04/romanias-parliamentary-putsch.html, last accessed December 15, 2010. For details on the 2009 Presidential elections see "The Presidential Elections in Romania: Turning Point or Stalemate," *Papiers d'actualité/Current Affairs in Perspective*, Fondation Pierre du Bois, December 2009, no. 11, http://www.fondation-pierredubois.ch/Papiers-d-actualite/romanian-elections.html.

tions took place in 2008 and presidential ones in 2009 (won by a slim margin by the liberal democrats and, respectively, by Traian Băsescu). The Report, the Commission, and the condemnation act become collateral victims in a protracted and continuous political crisis in Romania that spilled into the cultural sphere.

I need to also mention that the critics I make reference to were not particularly relevant within academic debates. However, as their profile increased, from 2008 to 2012, their interventions against the Report and the condemnation act became part and parcel of their own legitimation on the domestic cultural sphere and market. In the present article, I will focus more on the content of their criticism than on the circumstantial determinations of it. I need though to briefly map out the institutional layout. Most of the critics I deal with have published initially (2006 to mid 2007) in marginal cultural weeklies with limited print runs (e.g., *Timpul* or *Cultura*) or in regional dailies (e.g., *Ziua de Cluj*). By the beginning of 2008, they featured prominently among the columnists of *Observator cultural*, a high-profile Romanian cultural weekly that adopted a vehement tone against President Traian Băsescu. The true coming onto the national scene of the Report's critics was the publication, the same year, of the volume *Iluzia anticomunismului*, which brought together a still heterogeneous group united by an antiestablishment discursive complex.[6] The ultimate aggregation

---

[6] Vasile Ernu et al., *Iluzia anticomunismului. Lecturi Critice ale Raportului Tismaneanu* (Chişinău: Editura Cartier, 2008). The authors were a heterogeneous group of vehement critics of intellectuals associated with the Commission (see the articles by political scientist Daniel Barbu, who ended up winning a MP mandate during the 2012 elections and was minister of culture in the liberal-socialist government; political scientist Michael Shafir, whose criticism initially focused on the Report's usage of the concept of genocide, but he later seemed to be more interested on a personal vendetta against Vladimir Tismaneanu; or Florin Abraham, at the time the scientific secretary of the think-tank of the Social Democratic Party and now its representative in the leadership of the National Council for the Study of the Archives of the Secret Police—CNSAS) or a group of younger editorialists (some are writers, others are junior academics) whose agenda was to bring into the Romanian public realm a New Left type of critique (Vasile Ernu, Costi Rogozanu, Ovidiu Țichindeleanu, Alex Cistelecan, etc.). I will not deal with this book, because most of the texts are in fact either articles published earlier in local weeklies or their arguments are identical with the authors' editorials from the written press. In my opinion, the volume is significant

of the critics of the Report that I am discussing in this paper was the creation, in September 2010, of the web platform *Criticatac.ro*, which declared that "our group's ideology is mainly leftist, but we are no ideological faction."[7] Despite such claims, I will show how these attacks against the Report and the condemnation act ultimately amounted to a campaign of self-legitimization as a New-left inspired, but simultaneously populist, alternative to the post-communist status quo.

Returning to the puzzle of this work, I argue that one can point to two possible types of explanation for it. On the one hand, in a highly charged post-December 2006 environment, in some areas of the Romanian public opinion, communism (taken here generically, both as regime, ideology, or experience) has ceased having value as a subject in itself. It rather served as a pretext to disparage persons, institutions, opinions in the present. In other words, talking about communism gave way to constructing a straw-man type of putatively state-engineered anti-communism. In this reading, the condemnation speech, the Commission, and the Report became just self-interested acts rather than a fundamental phase in the process of dealing with the communist past in Romania. According to this type of criticism, the publication of the Commission's Report basically officialized a new state ideology—anti-communism.

On the other hand, another post-December 2006 related development is the scarcity of further problematizations along the directions signaled by the Final Report. The latter document, being a collective work that encompasses multiple approaches on specific issues related to the analysis of the communist regime, it *does* offer significant directions of public debate on issues such as the role of ideology, legitimacy, the dyad victim-perpetrator, responsibility and guilt, and so on. In the context of apparent unwillingness to talk about communism (in the generic sense), such issues have not been touched upon. Even if they were raised, it merely served the purpose of constructing delegitimizing

---

mainly because it was the first big coming onto the cultural limelight of a group that basically founded its ascendency on the criticism of the Report and on the delegitimization of the Commission. This perspective can also explain why in local mass-media, and even internationally, the book was present as a *counter*-Report, when in fact the contributions were mostly glorified cultural weekly editorials.

[7] See http://www.criticatac.ro/despre-noi/, last accessed January 16, 2011.

narratives about the actors that brought them into public conversation. Furthermore, I will show how another cause of such lack of further problematization is the misreading or even simply fictitious reading of the Report.

II. Mapping the Final Report

I will first construct a conceptual map of the Report's analysis of the communist regime. Simultaneously, I will bring in some of the international and national reactions to the elements that I discuss from the Report.

Codifying the Regime

According to the Commission's document, the communist phenomenon in Romania was an avatar of the totalitarian experience, which manifested itself as a dictatorship of a Stalinist-type (from beginning to the end), while the party in power (Romanian Workers' Party/Romanian Communist Party) operated, during the period of the consolidation of its rule, a "nationalization" of its structures and of its ideology. The regime is defined as (national)-Stalinist, for it is considered to sum up both the phenomenon of "indigenization of Marxism"[8] and its inscription within the overall history of communism, that is, a local project of building socialism in one country. First and foremost, as Tismaneanu and Vasile emphasize as well, a proper reading of the Report must be based on the mandate granted to the Commission which drafted it. According to the official news statement, the Commission

> will analyze the main institutions that made possible the imposition and reproduction of the communist dictatorship, the methods that allowed for the dictatorship's abuses, crimes, and legal infringements, the flagrant violations of human rights, and the

---

[8] Katherine Verdery, *National Ideology under Socialism: Identity and Cultural Politics in Ceausescu's Romania* (Berkeley/Los Angeles/London: University of California Press, 1991), 139.

role of some political personalities in the consolidation and functioning of the communist totalitarian system in Romania. The
Commission will highlight the significance of actions of resistance, opposition, and dissidence to the communist system. The
synthetic report will examine the relationship between ideology
and communist practices in Romania.[9]

From the beginning, one can notice the Commission's focus were
institutions, methods of dictatorial rule, political personalities, and
ideology. In this context, the Report turned its attention to the Party,
(Secret) Police, and Propaganda as fundamental levers of domination
across the whole institutional and personnel spectrum of the Party-
State. At the same time, both the mandate and the Report indicate that
the essential act of rewriting history as part of truth-telling also presupposed the indication of a usable past. The past that was recuperated
was that of those who suffered or openly opposed the regime. These
were necessary stories that have often been lost during the politics of
amnesia perpetuated by various governments from 1989 until 2006.

Moreover, as Tismaneanu points out in his chapter, the Report
does not suffer from a Bitburg syndrome. That is, the Commission
did tell the story of the victims and of the opponents of the dictatorship, but the usable past it appealed to was that of those who suffered
and struggled because of their democratic beliefs.[10] In this sense, it
is normal that a post-communist state such as Romania, one with an
extremely dubious past of authoritarian temptations and democratic
failures, would legitimize itself as a democracy by gracing those who
endured great harm for defending similar values. The historical narrative of the Report is, in this context, a method of redress, a way to
restore the memory and dignity of those individuals who were exem-

---

[9] http://www.memoria.ro/marturii/perioade_istorice/dupa_1989/presedintia_
romaniei_-_comunicat_de_presa/1665/, last accessed September 5, 2011.

[10] For a synthetic discussion of the relationship between dealing with the past,
searching for usable past, regime legitimation, and national identity in East
Central Europe see Jacques Rupnik and Jan Zielonka, "Introduction: The
State of Democracy 20 Years on: Domestic and External Factors," Special
Section "Democracy in Central and Eastern Europe: The State of the Art,"
East European Politics & Societies, vol. 27, no. 1 (February 2013), 3–25.

plary for their suffering and/or opposition.[11] One of the most important personalities of the Romanian democratic exile, Monica Lovinescu (she produced and presented several cultural radio shows for Radio Free Europe before the end of the Cold War), asked after 1989: "are we all dirt and water [this is a play of words in Romania—*o apă și un pamânt*, literally translation is "all the same," n.a.]? That is, mud?"[12]

In order to properly contextualize the type of usable past sought after by the Commission, one needs to take into account the fundamental problem of collective responsibility *and* victimhood. This latter narrative had been highly influential in the years before the creation of the Commission. As a Romanian literary historian noticed, just before 2006, there had been a series of revelations about several Romanian intellectuals' or politicians' collaboration with the *Securitate* (secret police) that was aimed "not at proper and balanced disclosure, but the homogenization of guilt and suffering." The activity of the Commission came exactly on the background of this turmoil. The usable past that was brought forward also meant, to use the same author's words, "we were NOT all guilty and not all of us suffered!"[13] [capitals in original, n.a.] Or, to return to Lovinescu's (herself a member of the Commission) question: the Report was also an attempt to sift through the mud.

There are two categories of features of the regime that appear in the Commission's Report: systemic—industrialization, collectivization, single party domination, terror, international antagonism; discursive—popular community, moral-political monism, anticapital-

---

[11] On history as a method of redress see Elazar Barkan, "Historians and Historical Reconciliation," *The American Historical Review*, vol. 114, no. 4 (October 2009), 899–913 and Carolyn J. Dean, "History Writing, Numbness, and the Restoration of Dignity," *History of Human Sciences*, vol. 17, nos. 2–3 (2004), 57–96.

[12] For more details on Monica Lovinescu and the problem of usable past see Bogdan C. Iacob, "O antologie pentru neliniștea noastră," *Idei în dialog*, no. 4 (April 2009), 56–57.

[13] Ruxandra Cesereanu, "Tombola memoriei (fragment)," *Vatra*, nr. 20 (December 2010),71. For more details on the events discussed by Cesereanu, see Lavinia Stan, "The Vanishing Truth? Politics and Memory in Post-Communist Europe," *East European Quarterly*, vol. XL, no. 4 (December 2006), 383–408 and her chapter on Romania in Lavinia Stan (ed.), *Transitional Justice in Eastern Europe and the Former Soviet Union. Reckoning with the Communist Past* (New York: Routledge, 2009), 128–151.

ism, anti-intellectualism, national millenarism. Therefore the formula "totalitarian state" is used for emphasizing the radical revolutionary transformism exercised over society through policies that amounted to a Romanian version of building socialism in one country. Under the circumstances, the phrase "dictatorial state" defined the monopoly and exercise of state power by the Romanian Communist Party (RCP). Overall, the communist regime is presented, as "a bleak criminal inversion of democratic rights" and its victims are, indeed, "recast as victims of human rights violations," to use historian James Mark's formulations.[14] Indeed, the criminality of the regime was assessed, firstly, on the basis of the principle of inviolability of an individual's basic human rights. Then, as the Report underlined, the communist regime more often than not failed to abide by both the international laws and documents that it adhered to and by the various constitutions it produced throughout its existence. In the end, the criminality of the dictatorship rested on the fact that in the process of the socialist transformation of the country, it took absolute control over the right to life of its own citizens. This is the fundamental, primary level of victimization in any *Weltanscahuungstaat.*

The Commission contextualized the historical destiny of victims providing even a reassessment of the bases of interpretation of victimhood (e.g., many suffered, but not everybody because of democratic beliefs). It refused, however, to evaluate either the dictatorship or the ideology (in their Romanian embodiments) based on a putative humane or positive element of communism. As Ian Kershaw has shown, such position is based on a fallacious argument "based upon a deduction from the future (neither verifiable nor feasible) to the present, a procedure which in strict logic is not permissible."[15] The Report is an assessment of the *historical* phenomena that make up the Romanian communist experience. It would have been deeply cynical to

---

[14] James Mark, *The Unfinished Revolution: Making Sense of the Communist Past in Central-Eastern Europe* (New Haven/London: Yale University Press, 2010), 39.

[15] See Ian Kershaw's discussion of the errors in historical hypotheses at the basis of simplistic rejections of totalitarianism and of the comparison between Nazi Germany and Stalinist Soviet Union in *The Nazi Dictatorship— Problems and Perspectives of Interpretation*, fourth edition (London: Arnold Publishers, 2000), 36–38.

assert the potential positives of communist highly repressive policies only because they were directed toward a social utopia.

Legitimacy is analyzed in reference to the fluctuations of the regime and it is conceived from the standpoint of a rise and fall type of systemic development. The Final Report discusses four types of legitimation under communism. The first is that of primitive accumulation of legitimacy (breakthrough period). The communist takeover is seen as a "revolution from abroad,"[16] with a bias toward the label of "regime of occupation." The second is the sort of legitimacy built during the regime's consolidation and inclusion through infrastructural development and national turn—"simulated change."[17] The third is the phenomenon of *identitätsstifung*, that is, the socio-political and symbolic project of founding a novel identity for communism. The fourth is legitimacy as "suspension of disbelief"[18] and "compensatory."[19] Ultimately, legitimacy is perceived from the point of view of the regime's mechanisms of co-option. Or, as the former chair of the Commission would argue, in December 2010, "even during its moments of maximum liberalization, the communist regime in Romania never renounced its main instruments of domination."[20]

The Repot rejected altogether the *national* legitimacy of the communist regime for the *entire* period of its existence. As historian Charles King emphasized, this "represents the first collective attempt, however belated, by Romanians to conceptualize their own national experi-

---

[16] Jan T. Gross, *Revolution from Abroad: The Soviet Conquest of Poland's Western Ukraine and Western Belorussia* (Princeton: Princeton University Press, 2002).

[17] Michael Shafir, *Romania: Politics, Economy, and Society: Political Stagnation and Simulated Change* (London: Pinter Publishers, 1985).

[18] Stephen Kotkin, *The Magnetic Mountain: Stalinism as a Civilization* (Berkeley: University of California Press, 1997).

[19] See Martin Sabrow, "Dictatorship as Discourse. Cultural Perspectives on SED Legitimacy," in Konrad H. Jarausch (ed.), *Dictatorship as Experience: Towards a Socio-Cultural History of the GDR*, translated by Eve Duffy (New York: Berghahn Books, 2004), 195–211.

[20] Vladimir Tismăneanu, "Patru ani de la condamnarea comunismului. Autopsie sau vivisecție," *Contributors.ro*, 18 December 2010 (http://www.contributors.ro/cultura/cinci-ani-de-la-raportul-final-despre-o-condamnare-%E2%80%93-nu-doar-simbolica-%E2%80%93-a-regimului-comunist/, last accessed January 10, 2011).

ence from 1945 to 1989 and to shame those in power into leading the way."[21] It was an essential departure from the prevailing historiographical and public narratives produced after 1989. There have been constant attempts to salvage certain periods of the communist experience in Romania based on what is perceived as "the fulfillment of national ideals" or "national pride" discourses. Such attempts for normalization of the dictatorship focus either on the last years of Gheorghe Gheorghiu-Dej's rule (end of 1950s and mid-1960s), on the first decade of Ceauşescu's rule (1965–1975/7), or both. In other words, the Report, by breaking with tenets about national exceptionality of local state socialism, basically brought back into the history of local communism almost two decades of systemic evolution. In this sense, the Report is a political document because it promoted a new vision of Romania's recent history based on "revealing the subterranean aspects of the past."[22]

All in all, I think that one of the main keys to understanding the contents and approach of the Report is the imperative internalized by all the members and experts of the Commission to dispel and counter what was perceived as "the sullying continuity with the communist regime" that "is the foundation of both the constitutional and social edifice."[23] In this context, the Report, based on the Commission's mandate, became a redressive mechanism[24] and a preventive instrument against forgetting.

The members of the Commission or the Report never claimed to be the final word on the analysis of the communist dictatorship. The title *Final Report* was simply an emulation of the title of the document

---

[21] Charles King, "Remembering Romanian Communism," *Slavic Review*, vol. 66, no. 4 (Winter, 2007), 722.

[22] I am using John Torpey's distinction between *political* and *politicized* scholarly pursuit of the past. See his "Introduction: Politics and the Past" in John Torpey (ed.), *Politics and the Past: On Repairing Historical Injustice* (Lanham/Boulder/New York: Rowman and Littlefield, 2003), 27.

[23] Ioan Stanomir "Memorie şi construcţie democratică," *22*, 24 ianuarie 2008, http://www.revista22.ro/memorie-si-constructie-democratica-4263.html, last accessed August 23, 2012.

[24] On the Report as a "redressive ritual" see Alina Hogea, "Coming to Terms with the Communist Past in Romania: An Analysis of the Political and Media Discourse Concerning the Tismăneanu Report," *Studies of Transition States and Societies* vol. 2, no. 2 (November 2010), 16–30.

produced by the International Commission for the Study of the Holocaust in Romania (CSHR). But, the condemnation of the regime and
the individualization of responsibilities for its crimes and abuses have,
with the Report, a factual basis unprecedented in the monographs
about Romanian communism. In this sense, it is important to mention
a press release by the Commission, in the immediate aftermath of making the Report public on the Presidential Administration's website, on
December 21, 2006: "the condemnation of communism as a political
act fulfilled by the President of Romania does not close but it opens
the process of the clarification of historical truth, which will take a long
time and it will depend on the unrestricted access to the entirety of the
archives. In the following period, the members and the experts of the
Commission will take into consideration proposals, suggestions, and
critical remarks that could improve the text of the Report. We believe
that the current text can be bettered, our goal being to maintain an
open dialogue with academic institutions interested in this issue."[25]
Indeed, the volume version contained a restructured table of contents
and of the references, corrections of initial errors, and many other
editorial amendments. Ultimately, the Report was perceived by the
Commission as a framework of intelligibility for a regime that eliminated and brutally repressed entire social categories and engineered
a program of radical transformism based on a highly pervasive social
homogenization.

Scholarship and Empathy

Generally speaking, I would contend that the contributions in the
Report were based on an understanding of historical objectivity that
was based on "the reconstruction of the past within the limits allow-
able by the remains it has left behind."[26] On the one hand, the report
contained selected texts from the important volumes published by the

---

[25] Comunicat de Presa, 21 decembrie 2006, www.presidency.ro. On the first
page of the volume version of the Report there is another text, written by
the publisher, that expresses the similar principle of the document being a
strating point rather than an end moment.
[26] Richard J. Evans, "Introduction: Redesigning the Past: History in Political
Transitions," *Journal of Contemporary History* vol. 38 (1), 2003, 11.

members and experts of the Commission on the subjects analyzed by this body in accordance with its mandate. On the other hand, the Report also encompassed extensive sections that represented new research undergone as part of the Commission's activity. Some of these subchapters are on mass organizations, on the system of control for confessional institutions, on the profile of the secret police informer, on aspects of the collectivization process, on economic planning, on policies of social control, on the fate of national minorities during the communist dictatorship, and so on. Furthermore, sections of the Report that had been published earlier were revised and updated based on the Commission representatives' unprecedented access to archives, which had been mainly closed until that 2006. Last but not least, the Report represents scholarship that is fundamentally interdisciplinary and strongly comparative.

With this in mind, I consider that those domestic and international commentaries that claimed that the Report was just a collage of previously published texts ignored the novel scholarship that the latter comprises and they did not remark the differences (sometimes significant) between those older texts and their Report version.[27] One explanation for such evaluations, at least in terms of the local debate, is that some of those who commented on the Report are not historians or social scientists specialized on communism studies, as most were literary historians, writers, or essayists (see the following section of this chapter). A proper assessment of what is new and what is old in the Report does require an extensive knowledge of the scholarly literature published before 2006 both locally and internationally. Furthermore, I agree with the observation of one Romanian historian, who stated that "if there are subchapters, not many, where the poverty of argumentation and the scarcity of references is in contrast with the accumulation of rhetoric effects, in its essential parts, the Report brings together and systematizes, making it visible for the first time, a large quantity of information that is novel or, until recently, was scattered across vari-

---

[27] For example, see Mark, *Unfinished Revolution*, 38 or Sorin Adam Matei, "Condamnarea comunismului 2.0", *Observator Cultural*, nr. 193 (27 November-3 December 2008) http://www.observatorcultural.ro/Condamnarea-comunismului-2.0*articleID_20854-articles_details.html, last accessed December 19, 2010.

ous publications, many times unknown to the general public. After seeing the number and the origin of the archival funds used, one cannot
say that nothing changed. . . . "[28] The Report was both an end and a
beginning. It was an end because it can be considered a moment of
state of the art that brings together the scholarship existent up until
2006 and makes it accessible to wider audiences. It was a beginning
because most of the novel research was written by young scholars thus
signaling a new generation of academic literature more in tune with
methodological and theoretical discussions in the international field of
communism studies.

The Commission provided analyses of the status and meaning of
"victim" that were clustered. First there is a general conception of *victimhood*. Following Joseph V. Montville, the premise of this image is "a
history of violent, traumatic aggression and loss"; a belief in its unjust
nature; and a fear of its repetition. Therefore the nature of victimhood
is "a state of individual and collective ethic mind that occurs when the
traditional structures that provide an individual sense of security and
self-worth through membership in a group are shattered by aggressive,
violent political outsiders."[29] In the Report, this overall picture was
most strongly asserted by the section written by the Association of the
Former Political Prisoners (AFPP), who adopted the rather unfortunate formula of "the communist genocide in Romania." They simply
situated the Communist party outside of an abstract nation, thus providing a complete externalization of agency. In order to better understand the context of the position adopted by AFPP, one needs to look
into the developments prior to the formation of the Commission and
into the dynamics of the Commission itself.

In 2009, two political scientists, themselves members of the Commission, wrote that "in post-communist Romania, the particularities
of the pre-1989 regime, the nature of the Revolution, as well as the
post-1989 political developments made *amnesty impossible* and *amnesia*

---

[28] Florin Țurcanu, "Istoria comunismului și Raportul Final," http://www.re-
vista22.ro/raportul-final-al-comisiei-tismaneanu-4278.html, last accessed
October 20, 2010.

[29] Joseph Montville, "The Healing Function in Political Conflict Resolution,"
in Dennis J. D. Sandole and Hugo van der Merwe (ed.), *Conflict Resolution
Theory and Practice Integration and Application* (Manchester and New York:
Manchester University Press, 1993), 113.

undesirable.[30] (Emphasis in original) Indeed, up until 2006, the status of the memory and history of the communist past was heavily paradoxical, similar to how Maria Tumarkin, author of the important volume *Traumascapes*,[31] characterized the situation in Russia in 2011: the contrasting simultaneity of a powerful testimonial culture and the widescale rehabilitation, partially government encouraged, of the communist regime.[32] In a sense, the first phenomenon took a larger dimension particularly as a counterpoint to the latter. Under the circumstances, "the recollections of the victims that survived the Romanian Gulag emerged as the most powerful vector of memory," thus heavily influencing the representation of state socialism, historiography included.[33] Within Romanian public opinion, historians of communism do matter, but often not as much as expected, especially that some of the established historians (e.g., members of the Academy or employees of its research institutes) are rather normalizing discursive actors with a view to the past. At the same time, a higher profile, greater legitimacy, and a larger audience belong to what some members or experts of the Commission called "activists of memory." Furthermore, this second group, which many times represents and/or were victims of the regime, was also instrumental in pushing transitional justice-type of legislation (see Vasile's and Grosescu and Ursachi's chapters).[34] The creation of the Commission itself originated in a campaign initiated by a public figure who falls into this category (see Tismaneanu's chapter).

---

[30] Cristina Petrescu and Dragoş Petrescu,"Retribution, Remembering, Representation: On Romania's Incomplete Break with the Communist Past," in Gerhard Besier and Katarzyna Stokłosa (eds.), *Geschichtsbilder in den postdiktatorischen Ländern Europas: Auf der Suche nach historisch-politischen Identitäten* (Berlin, Lit Verlag, 2009), 155.

[31] Maria M. Tumarkin, *Traumascapes: The Power and Fate of Places Transformed by Tragedy* (Melbourne: Melbourne University Press, 2005).

[32] Maria M. Tumarkin, "The Long Life of Stalinism: Reflections on the Aftermath of Totalitarianism and Social Memory," *Journal of Social History* vol. 44, no. 4 (Summer 2011), 1047.

[33] Petrescu and Petrescu, *Remembering*, 156.

[34] For an extensive analysis of the role of civil society and particularly of organizations representing the victims in Romania's politics of transitional justice see Lavinia Stan, *Transitional Justice in Post-Communist Romania. The Politics of Memory* (Cambridge/New York: Cambridge University Press, 2013).

In this context, the Report was also the result of the negotiation between an academic approach and a traumatic memory interpretation of victimhood. The result was the chapter "The Communist Genocide in Romania" in the section "Repression" that some
domestic and international critics have used to unilaterally dismiss
the Commission's interpretation of regime criminality. For example,
political scientist Monica Ciobanu argued that "it is hardly possible
to accept the idea that the battery of repressive policies developed by
the regime—whether economic, demographic, or cultural—constituted
an intentional plan for the destruction of a large part of the population. This is a conceptual interpretation of the idea of genocide at its
most tendentious."[35] I do not know if "tendentious" is the best term to
describe the employment of the term by the AFPP's representatives in
the Commission. It is more a conceptual overinflation that needs to be
contextualized. Moreover, the Report's conclusions did not adopt this
formulation, preferring the conceptualization "crimes against humanity
that are not subject to the statute of limitations."[36]

The Commission's chair justified the insertion of the term "genocide" in the Report on two levels. First, Tismaneanu invoked the
impossibility of eliminating the victims' own narrative about their suffering; the latter was represented by AFPP's position. The Report itself

---

[35] Monica Ciobanu, "Criminalising the Past and Reconstructing Collective
Memory: The Romanian Truth Commission," *Europe-Asia Studies*, vol. 61,
no. 2 (March 2009), 334. Her argument on the topic relies heavily on the
interventions of political scientist Michal Shafir who was the first to criticize
the Report on the basis of the AFPP's usage of the concept of "genocide."
See Michael Shafir, "Raportul Tismaneanu: Note din public si din culi-
se," *Tribuna* no. 7 (1–15 March, 2007). The problem with the polemic on
the uses of the term was that, similarly with other exchanges presented in
this text, it was not based on dialogue. Tismaneanu tried to reply to this
criticism but, in Michael Shafir's case, the clash seemed to be motivated
by personal issues of this author with the former Chair of the Commission
rather than by the intention to debate the nature of mass murder in communist regimes. For example, see Michael Shafir, "Scrisoare (ultra)deschi-
sa," *Observator cultural* no. 382 (July 2007), http://www.observatorcultural.
ro/Scrisoare-%28ultra%29deschisa*articleID_18028-articles_details.html,
last accessed January 12, 2011.
[36] See Vladimir Tismaneanu, et al., *Comisia Prezindenţială pentru Analiza Dictaturii Comuniste din România—Raport Final* (Bucharest: Humanitas, 2007),
776.

contains a footnote (in the volume version) stating that "this chapter was written by the Association of the Former Political Prisoners and represents the voice of the victims."[37] The issue is connected to another topic that brought some tumult in the discussions about the condemnation act, namely, the number of victims. The range adopted by the Commission and by the President in his speech is very wide, from 350,000 to 2,000,000. As historian Dorin Dobrincu, Commission expert and between 2007 and 2012 director of the Romanian National Archives, has shown, most of the academics of this body had serious reservations to both the term genocide and to the number of victims proposed by the AFPP.[38] If in certain chapters, the number of victims of certain regime policies is much more precisely accounted,[39] the AFPP's section proposed the number of two million. Another footnote was added at this point that cautions on the validity of such estimation.[40] My reading of these dynamics is that the employment of the term genocide and the dissentions on the number of victims reflected less an epistemic failure in the Report and more a symptom of both the composition of the Commission and of its functioning based on consensual interaction.

The second way of discussing "genocide" in the aftermath of the publication of the Report, the volume version from 2007, was in fact much more interesting than simply clamoring about the alleged ignorance of the AFPP or the Commission in reference to the legal definition of the term. In an interview in 2007, Tismaneanu stated that the Commission used an intentionalist reading of the regime's crimes based on the ideological motivation of the building of socialism in one country, Romanian-style. From this point of view, "there

---

[37] *Raport Final,* 459.

[38] "Am nervii tari, nu sunt temător, nu mă intimidez," interview with Dorin Dobrincu by Ovidiu Şimonca, *Observator Cultural* no. 146 (24–30 January 2008), http://www.romaniaculturala.ro/articol.php?cod=9443, last accessed October 15, 2010.

[39] For example, see the Report's sections on collectivization, armed resistance, repression of religious denominations (pp. 245–288), on national minorities (pp. 332–394), on the "census of correctional population" (pp. 535–542), or the case studies about some of the harshest prisons or labor colonies in the Romanian Gulag (pp. 566–628) and the chapter on deportations (pp. 630–648).

[40] *Raport Final,* 463.

was intention for mass destruction of large social categories. If one wishes to call this politicide is his right; to me this seems to come within the range of genocide."[41] Furthermore, in an exchange with historian Adrian Cioflâncă, former Commission expert and also former expert in the CSHR, Tismaneanu cited Norman Naimark statement that "Both [Hitler and Stalin, n.a.] were dictators who killed vast numbers of people on the European continent. Both chewed up the lives of human beings in the name of a transformative vision of Utopia. Both destroyed their countries and societies, as well as vast numbers of people inside and outside their states. Both—in the end—were genocidaires."[42] In his turn, Cioflâncă replied: "I know that the temptation for the term genocide comes from the fact that this seems to indicate the most grievous crime in the hierarchy of political crimes. However, I avoid it for the case of communism, especially Romanian communism, because it signifies something else, not because the crimes of communism were not grievous enough. . . . Romania is not the Soviet Union, so we cannot find the documentary basis in order to prove a criminal policy of similar proportions as those in the USSR..."[43]

What I believe the exchange and discussion above show is that the use of the term was far from tendentious and more circumstantial, as it was based on the necessity of consensual functioning within the Commission. At the same time, a point that has not been dealt with by critics is how the policies of the regime changed the definition of victim populations. One crucial point made by the Report, the connection between social-cultural-economic transformation and the policies

---

[41] "Comunismul şi nazismul au fost enorme prostii care au îmbrăcat haina cunoaşterii absolute," interview with Vladimir Tismaneanu by Marius Vasileanu, *Adevarul literar şi artistic* no. 854, 17 January 2007, (http://www.romaniaculturala.ro/articol.php?cod=7564, last accessed October 20, 2010). For an overview of the intentionalist-functionalist debate concerning the interpretation of the Nazi regime, see Ian Kershaw, *Hitler, the Germans, and the Final Solution* (New Haven/London: Yale University Press, 2008).

[42] Norman Naimark, *Stalin's Genocides* (Princeton/Oxford: Princeton University Press, 2010), 137.

[43] For the full exchange between Tismaneanu and Cioflâncă see http://tismaneanu.wordpress.com/2010/08/29/stalinism-si-genocid/, last accessed January 17, 2011.

of coercion, excision, and extermination has not been touched upon by any of the critics of the Report. The academic representatives of the Commission were very much conscious of the difficulties of talking about genocide and genocidal policies.[44] The Report is a document that often stands on its own, but like any historical document it also requires contextualization in order to avoid unilateral or hasty judgments about it.

All things considered, the assessment of the communist regime's criminality in the Report was based upon constructing a case for the "imprescriptibility" of crimes against humanity undergone by the regime (as nexus of individuals, institutions, and methods). The Report adopted both a legal interpretation based on international jurisprudence of this concept[45] and a moral one founded on what the Commission perceived as, to use Derrida's formulation, "the irreparable, ineffaceable, irremediable, irreversible, unforgettable, irrevocable, inexpiable"[46] quality of suffering under communism in Romania. The Commission functioned on a dialogical basis and, even more importantly, independent of any political intervention. Romanian historian, Ruxanadra Cesereanu, herself a Commission expert, showed in her comparison of the PCACDR and CSHR that the former "did not include any presidential advisor, so that there was no interference

---

[44] Tismaneanu himself preferred to talk about "genocidal policies" and "sociocide" (Dan Diner) in both public interventions and in his most recent book *The Devil in History. Communism, Fascism, and Some Lessons of the Twentieth Century* (Berkeley: University of California Press, 2012).

[45] One could argue that the meaning given, in the Report, to the construction "communist regime as criminal" comes very close to the concept of "regime criminality" (*Regierungskriminalität*) that appeared during the trials of GDR leaders in early 1990s. At the time, the German Constitutional Court upheld and increased the sentences of those convicted, thus "driving home the point that even in dictatorships individuals had moral and political choices." See Jan-Werner Müller, "East Germany: Incorporation, Tainted Truth, and the Double Division," in Alexandra Barahona de Brito, Carmen González-Enríquez, and Paloma Aguilar, *The Politics of Memory Transitional Justice in Democratizing Societies* (Oxford: Oxford University Press, 2001), 260.

[46] Jacques Derrida, "The Unforgivable and the Imprescriptible," in John D. Caputo, Mark Dooley, and Michael J. Scanlon, *Questioning God* (Bloomington/Indianapolis: Indiana University Press, 2001) 31.

by the authorities in the activity of the commission," which gave it a "democratic and heterogeneous character."[47]

Victims and Co-Option

There are three practices of talking about victims in the Report: a) breaking with their objectivization by "laying bare" and deconstructing the penal categories that ordered communist practices of plucking and landscaping the human garden in Romania; b) the national community is presented as a victim with a secret guilt by stressing the ambivalence of suffering on the long term:

> the regime did not rule the country simply by means of a mechanism of despoilment of the masses. It knew how to create mechanisms of cooption too, through the manipulation of the chances opened by social mobility. . . . It compelled the population to live in a constant state of dissimulation . . . The massive membership within the Party does not reflect in any way their true beliefs. . . . Nonetheless, it is legitimate to argue that their adhesion, even purely formal, a meaningless opportunistic act, was indeed a first stage of a mechanism which, by means of multiple, successive acquiescence, of multilayered submission, caused the crystallization of a distinctive moral profile.[48]

The last discourse about the victims is the hero script. Despite accepting and emphasizing a negotiated aspect of the communist experience, the narrative about victims is both "reparational" (naming those who opposed the regime) but also "retributive" (cases of individual or group resistance against the regime are counterpoised to exemplary portraits of embodiments of party-state criminality).

Generally speaking, the Report discussed the problem of the victims predominantly from the point of view of the policies of the Party-State. Keeping with the Commission's mandate, it did not open the

---

[47] Ruxandra Cesereanu, "The Final Report on the Holocaust and the Final Report on the Communist Dictatorship in Romania," *East European Politics and Societies* vol. 22, no. 2 (2008), 271–272.

[48] *Raport Final*, 17, 19, and 600.

debate on individual/collective levels of responsibility and guilt beyond those of decision-makers involved in systemic consolidation and reproduction. One can argue that such an initiative coming from a top-down institution like the Commission would have been rather an imposition. Indeed, it seemed at the time that the main objective was focusing on "truth-telling" about the nature of the communist dictatorship, rather than providing guidance on how citizens and the society should reconcile with their private pasts. Political scientist Lavinia Stan remarked that such a phenomenon was to be expected: "When most citizens tacitly supported and suffered at the hands of the repressive regime, it is difficult, even morally questionable, to single out some victims as more deserving than the general population."[49] One can also reverse the polarity of Stan's statement. As, literary historian Caius Dobrescu stated "collective and individual introspection could not replace the analysis of the system's physiology, that is, the apparatus and the instruments (institutions, organizations, statutes, legislation, and "human resources") that made the communist dictatorship possible."[50] Indeed, the pre-2006 experience has shown that, in Romania, civic mastering of the past would not prevent forgetting in terms of the state acknowledgment of trauma during state socialism.

The clustered narrative about victims under the Communist regime generated a specific positioning of state vs. society that comes close to the *Rezistenz* paradigm. In this reading, "relative opposition was tied to intermittent or limited acceptance of the regime, the coexistence and simultaneity of conformism and non-conformism were the rule."[51] The Report identified the following modes of struggle against power: active resistance, Aesopian resistance, insubordination and deviancy, or autonomous forms of popular opinion. The members and experts of the Commission do present the communist power-agents (institutions, organizations, policies, individuals) as amounting to an

---

[49] Lavinia Stan, "Truth Commissions in Post-Communism: The Overlooked Solution? " *The Open Political Science Journal,* 2009, 2, 10.

[50] Caius Dobrescu, "'Ilegitim şi criminal,' discuţia abia începe" *Observator Cultural* no. 386, (August 200), 7, http://www.romaniaculturala.ro/articol.php?cod=4728, last accessed September 14, 2010.

[51] Hartmut Mehringer quoted in Saul Friedländer, "Réflections sur l'historisation du national-socialisme," *Vingtième Siècle. Revue d'histoire* no. 16 (October–December 1987), 50–51.

Other that victimized the population on the path to socialist transformation.

Regarding the presentation of perpetrators, the Report identified four types: those guilty for the thousands of deaths, for imprisonments, deportations, and other abuses related to the communist state repression or terror; those guilty for the annihilation of dissidence and of attacks against the opposition in exile; those guilty for the indoctrination of the population (propaganda and censorship apparatus); and, those guilty for the abuses and deaths of the immediate years after 1989, through their employment of strategic use of anarchy as a tool of political violence.[52] For a better accounting of perpetrators and individuals directly and heavily involved in the coming into power, consolidation, and reproduction of the communist regime, the Report contains a section entitled "the nomenklatura's biographies."[53] This part complements the extensive information provided by the Report's authors on those responsible for the policies and crimes of the dictatorship. In this sense, the Commission accomplished a fundamental aspect of "non-judicial truth-seeking as transitional justice," that is, naming names, identifying the "perpetrators"[54] (this term is used here in a generic sense reflective of a wide understanding of responsibility— legal, historical, moral). The "naming of names" had two functions: knowledge diffusion and public shaming. If one takes into account the subsequent absence of legal accountability regarding some of those named, one tends to agree with Lavinia Stan that the Commission delivered "dangerous truth" that frustrated the victims' increased expectations of punishment and exposed converted communist elites.[55] It is important though not to forget that the Commission's mandate did not allow it to institutionally pursue prosecution.

The most important element missing in the Report, in my opinion, is an extensive analysis of the formation, structure, and dynamic of

---

[52] For this interpretation of the violent demonstrations in the spring and summer of 1990 in Bucharest, see also John Gledhill, "States of Contention: State-Led Political Violence in Post-Socialist Romania," *East European Politics and Societies* vol. 19, no. 1 (2005), 76–104.

[53] *Raport final*, 785–807.

[54] Priscilla B. Hayner, *Unspeakable Truths: Facing the Challenge of Truth Commissions* (New York: Routledge, 2002), 14.

[55] Stan, *Transitional Justice in Post-Communist Romania*, 134.

"cognizant publics" under communism. That is, a discussion of the sections of the Romanian society that "recognized and acknowledged the bases upon which an [communist] elite made a claim to superior status" and "accepted the values that underlie that claim."[56] However, the Commission was instructed to provide an evaluation about the nature of the communist regime, rather than to thoroughly analyze the sociocultural experiment of communist modernity in Romania. Ultimately, the Report, through mapping the mechanisms (personnel, institutions, policies) upon which the regime functioned, laid the foundation for a deeper analysis of the transformation of society under the impact of such a system. In addition, one needs to keep in mind the remarks of former Czech dissident, Jiří Pehe, on one of the dangers that lay at the core of the moral distinction underlying lustration laws. He stated that this administrative measure "artificially divided society into 'bad people' and 'good people,' thus allowing people to avoid honestly and inclusively discussing the difficult issue of responsibility for the regime's injustices."[57] I think this is an underlying peril that any form of transitional justice (cultural-social or institutional-juridical) faces: official hierarchies and criteria of guilt can prevent owning one's past. In this sense, I consider that the Report, by focusing on responsibility by decision or action established a functionalist notion of guilt, thus allowing for individual and group introspection into private pasts. And consequently, it did not close the door on discussing subjective/personal responsibilities.

Social psychologist, Cristian Tileagă, correctly underlined that the Report did not discuss the "lived reality" of communism. However, I believe that it is rather forced to consider the analysis of the regime's "illegality and criminality" as mutually exclusive from "the variety of assumptions, individual and group frames of reference, situations and histories that are meaningful beyond any single description."[58] The condemnation act represented the formulation of a moral-civic threshold

---

[56] Verdery, *National Ideology*, 197.
[57] Quoted in Nadya Nedelsky, "Czechoslovakia and the Czech and Slovak Republics," in Lavinia Stan, (ed.), *Transitional Justice in Eastern Europe and the Former Soviet Union. Reckoning with the Communist Past* (New York: Routledge, 2009), 66–65.
[58] Cristian Tileagă, "Communism and the Meaning of Social Memory: Towards a Critical-Interpretive Approach," *Integrative Psychological and Behavioral Science*, vol. 46, no. 4 (2012), 487.

based on epistemic inquiry that de-normalized the communist experience. The underling argument was that life-worlds between 1945 and 1989 could not be envisioned outside the structures and practices of domination set up by the dictatorship. To employ Tileagă's formulation, the condemnation act did not draw attention to what *ought* to instead of what *could* be observed by any member of society.[59] It rather stated what *ought* not to be forgotten upon surveying what *could* communism as a lived experience offer to each and one of Romania's citizens.

One point of contention related to the image of the regime mapped out by the Report that remains, and which will prove extremely relevant in the post-December 2006 period, is that of communism as the Other. A few examples from the Report go as follows: "the imposition of a dictatorial regime totally surrendered to Moscow and hostile to national political and cultural values," "the antipatriotic nature of the communist dictatorship," "the truth is that neither Dej nor Ceaușescu showed patriotic sentiments," "the self-determination of Romanian foreign policy after 1964 was not the expression of an affirmation of a patriotic will, but has served communist leadership (first, around Gheorghe Gheorghiu-Dej, and then Nicolae Ceaușescu) in maintaining their power unaltered."[60] However, this total *Other-isation* of the regime reflected the radical break made by the Commission and by the condemnation act with either discourses that partially relegitimized some period in the Romanian communist experience or the politics of amnesia promoted by politicians and cultural/academic actors *across* the domestic public sphere. This mode of representation is not one of de-responsabilization by generalizing guilt and reifying a political system. It is rather a narrative that renounces any possibility of rehabilitating and/or normalizing the regime, its institutions, policies, and, representatives. But the challenge that remains in this interpretation is to avoid and move away from a Nuremberg reading[61] of the communist past, that is, an exclusive focus on perpetrator history.

---

[59] Cristian Tileagă, "The Social Organization of Representations of History: The Textual Accomplishment of Coming to Terms With the Past," *British Journal of Social Psychology* vol. 48, no. 1 (2009), 351.

[60] *Raport Final*, 774, 765, 773, 30.

[61] Mark Osiel, *Mass Atrocity, Collective Memory, and the Law* (New Brunswick/London: Transaction Publishers, 1997), 83.

Nevertheless, the thesis of the anti-national character of the communist dictatorship in the Report was not an attempt to negate the participation of the Romanian society in the Stalinist civilizational project. On the contrary, it was a direct confrontation of and an open acknowledgment of massive adhesion of the population to the nationally refurnished communist imaginary. Ultimately, I believe that Charles King's warning is an excellent assessment of the Report's approach: "viewing the past as the province of criminals is ultimately no more therapeutic than seeing it as the domain of Cominternists and foreigners. The question now is whether the Commission's report will be used as yet another opportunity to reject history or as a way of helping Romanians learn, at last, how to own it."[62] As we shall see in the following section, one of the fundamental fallacies of the polemics during the condemnation's aftermath was the inability to make the dialogic transition implied by the transfer of the discussion from perpetrators to owning one's past.

Anticipating a bit the discussions below, it has been argued by both members of the Commission and their favorable commentators that a fundamental function of the Report was to bring to the fore, with the endorsement of the Romanian head of state, the fundamental formulae "illegitimate" and "criminal." The Report, as one author stressed, could not in itself and by itself "change the way we understand the historical experience of communism and subsequently also change the way we understand and how we construct ourselves."[63] One critic empathically declared, at the beginning of 2012, that "the condemnation of communism did not change the public's perception over the previous regime and its effects are mostly symbolic and difficult to quantify."[64] Leaving aside the discussion on the legal, institutional, policy, and so on effects of the condemnation act (on this, see Vasile's chapter), it seems that the

---

[62] Charles King, "Remembering Romanian Communism," *Slavic Review*, vol. 66, no. 4 (Winter, 2007), 723. Also see Vladimir Tismaneanu's reply "Confronting Romania's Communist Past: A Response to Charles King," *Slavic Review*, vol. 66, no. 4 (Winter, 2007), 724–727.

[63] Dobrescu, "'Ilegitim și criminal.'"

[64] Andrei Muraru, "Primul cincinal de condamnare a comunismului: legenda merge mai departe," *Observator Cultural*, no. 611, February 2012, http://www.observatorcultural.ro/Primul-cincinal-de-condamnare-a-comunismului-legenda-merge-mai-departe*articleID_26527-articles_details.html, last accessed June 8, 2012.

last commentator, like many others, simply ignored the role of historical redress, one of the main functions of the Report. The condemnation of the communist regime set the ground for what historian Henri Rousso called "the nationalization of the task of memory,"[65] by which he meant the acknowledgement and knowledge of bad deeds by the wider society outside of the ever-dwindling circle of survivors.

III. Criticism and the Report's Aftermath

A Liberal History?

In 1996, Princeton professor of political theory, Stephen Macedo, warned that "we need to avoid making the mistake of assuming that liberal citizens—self-restrained, moderate, and reasonable—spring full-blown from the soil of private freedom."[66] I believe that this statement could be a useful starting point for evaluating the aftermath of the Report and of the condemnation act. Historian James Mark contended that the aim of both was "the legitimization of liberal democratic political development. . . . It was this vision of democracy—as the rule of law and this as shield for the individual from the abusive state—that would provide the template for the Presidential Commission's liberally framed condemnation of Communism."[67] Indeed, public declarations by both the Commission chair and of some of its experts stated that the Report was written from the standpoint of civic liberalism.[68] In other words, the Commission approached the communist alterna-

---

[65] Henry Rousso, "Justice, History, and Memory in France: Reflections on the Papon Trial," in Torpey, *Politics and the Past*, 298.

[66] Quoted in Osiel, *Mass Atrocity*, 67.

[67] Mark, *Unfinished Revolution*, 39.

[68] Vladimir Tismaneanu, "Liberalismul civic anticomunist," *Dilema Veche*, no. 117, 30 June 2007, http://dilemaveche.ro/sectiune/tema-saptamanii/articol/liberalismul-civic-anticomunist, last accessed 18 October, 2010. According to the political scientist, civic liberalism encompasses any form of democratic anticommunism (socialist, liberal, conservative, etc.). Also see Dorin Dobrincu's and Adrian Ciolfanca's interventions on civic liberalism in "Trecutul în spatele nostru ? Raportul Tismăneanu şi istoria comunismului românesc," în *Analele Ştiinţifice ale Universităţii "Al. I. Cuza" din Iaşi (serie nouă). Istorie*, tom. LII-LIII, 2006–2007, 303–331.

tive modernity as a negative exemplum that failed to construct a democratic state and society. The reports of the two Commissions (CSHR and PCACDR) fulfill the function of central narratives in the consolidation of a democratic culture where the past is always a reminder of the horrors that await when basic human rights are trampled for the sake of totalizing ideologies. In a country ravaged by authoritarianism from late 1930s into the 1990s, such public use of the past should hardly be worrisome.

In the summer of 2008, there was a glimmer of consensus on this very topic. During a roundtable entitled "Anti-communism as a Moral Duty," Vladimir Tismaneanu emphasized the importance of an antitotalitarian commitment in present Romanian society based on the lessons of the past.[69] A literary historian, Carmen Mușat, editor-in-chief of *Observator Cultural,* one of the cultural weeklies most critical of the Report, the condemnation act, and of the Commission chair, implicitly agreed with Tismaneanu in an editorial several days after the event. Echoing his intervention, she rightly argued that "both anti-communism and antifascism, in a word antitotalitarianism as an attitude of rejecting ideologies founded on the principle of exclusion and hate toward the Other . . . are moral duties in a world in which common sense and equanimity seem to be almost extinct."[70] The position "antitotalitarianism as a moral duty" was a proposal for finding a middle ground in a culture of remembrance so that, to use Claus Leggewie's phrasing, one can "ensure that those who speak of fascism cannot conceal Stalinism and vice versa."[71]

Nevertheless, the discussion on whether dealing with the past legitimizes the liberal democratic order or whether is the essence of

---

[69] For details, see Cristian Vasile, "Comunismul, o obligatie morala?" *22* (29 June 2007), http://www.revista22.ro/anticomunismul—o-obligatie-morala—3841.html, last accessed September 12, 2010.

[70] Carmen Mușat, "Antitotalitarismul ca obligație morală," *Observator Cultural,* no. 378 (June 2008), http://www.observatorcultural.ro/Antitotalitarismul-ca-obligatie-morala*articleID_17829-articles_details.html, last accessed September 12, 2010.

[71] Claus Leggewie, "A Tour of the Battleground: The Seven Circles of Pan-European Memory," *Social Research* vol. 75, no. 1, "Collective Memory and Collective Identity" (Spring 2008), 222.

"a culture of contrition"[72] essential for a post-authoritarian polity hides a fallacy of analysis that often affects the scholarship on politics of memory in Eastern Europe; and, it lies at the core of my thesis of entrapment of polemics for the Romanian case. Political scientist Lavinia Stan emphasized that "to reduce the complexity of the politics of memory to the level of recognizing it only as a manipulating tool used in the cutthroat battles waged by power-thirsty political parties or to relegate it to the grey zone of illusory and unattainable myths ignores the Eastern Europeans' need to know the truth about the communist regime, to confront their own personal history, and to obtain justice and absolution."[73] In similar fashion, in a study of new projects of lustration advanced in mid-2000s in Poland and Romania, Cynthia Horne found that the reactualization of such topic in these countries represented a way "to address the evidence and perceptions about economic, social, and political problems that have remained unresolved in the transition."[74] Even James Mark's thesis about the "unfinished revolution"[75] partially relies on similar findings. That is, *Vergangenheitsbewältigung* in East Europe is a means of sorting through the continuities and discontinuities generated by the "Leninist legacy,"[76]

---

[72] Karl Wilds, "Identity Creation and the Culture of Contrition: Recasting 'Normality' in the Berlin Republic," *German Politics*, vol. 9, no. 1, 83–102. For a wider discussion of the concept see David Art, *The Politics of the Nazi Past in Germany and Austria* (Cambridge: Cambridge University Press, 2006), 49–100.

[73] Lavinia Stan, "Introduction" in Stan, *Transitional Justice*, 4.

[74] Cynthia M. Horne, "Late Lustration Programmes in Romania and Poland: Supporting or Undermining Democratic Transitions?" *Democratization*, vol. 16, no. 2 (April 2009), 365.

[75] See Mark, *Unfinished Revolution*, xiii–xiv.

[76] For an excellent discussion about which types of "Leninist legacies" do come into play in evaluating the democratization of Eastern European countries see Grigore Pop-Eleches and Joshua A. Tucker, "Associated with the Past?: Communist Legacies and Civic Participation in Post-Communist Countries," *East European Politics & Societies* (February 27, 2013), Special Section "Democracy in Central and Eastern Europe: The State of the Art," 45–68 and Grigore Pop-Eleches, "Historical Legacies and Post-Communist Regime Change," *The Journal of Politics*, vol. 69, no. 4, (November 2007), 908–926. For an overview of how the concept has been used by political scientists dealing with the region, see Jody LaPorte and Danielle N. Lussier, "What Is the Leninist Legacy? Assessing Twenty Years of Scholarship," *Slavic Review* vol. 70, no. 3 (Fall 2011), 637–654.

the very factor which has deeply affected the various transitional trajectories of the countries in the region. Unfortunately, the criticism of the Romanian condemnation act gradually amounted, from 2007 until 2012, to the very denial of both its place in a future culture of contrition and its truth-telling function.

Cumulative Radicalization

The path to the outright rejection of the Report and of the condemnation act was one of cumulative radicalization. Initially, the Commission was criticized because it was argued that the political authority upon which it came about was invalid. In other words, President Traian Băscscu, a politician with a turbulent history in post-1989 party struggles, was presented as having a dubious communist past, "not really" believing in the condemnation act. The creation of the Commission was therefore based on political self-interest. Or, the president simply did not have the moral authority to condemn the former regime.[77] In parallel, a calumny campaign targeted the chair of the Commission. Initially these types of attacks came from extremist circles, but they eventually permeated newspapers and weeklies that claim to be democratic.[78] Once

---

[77] For a brief biography of Traian Băsescu, see Tismaneanu's contribution. For more details about his first six years in office as President, see Ronald F. Kind and Paul E. Sum (eds.), *Romania Under Băsescu: Aspirations, Achievements, and Frustrations During His First Presidential Term* (Lanham, MD: Rowan & Littlefield, 2011). For his involvement in party politics before becoming president see Dan Pavel and Iulia Huiu, *"Nu putem reuși decât împreună": O istorie analitică a convenției democratice, 1989–2000* (Iași: Polirom, 2003). For a characterization of Băsescu as a neo-populist see Michael Shafir, "From Historical to 'Dialectical' Populism: The Case of Post-Communist Romania," *Canadian Slavonic Papers / Revue Canadienne des Slavistes*, vol. 50, nos. 3–4, (September-December 2008), 425–470.

[78] An example is the left-wing cultural weekly *Cultura* (of course such "political" label should be taken with a grain of salt), which founding president is writer Augustin Buzura, former president of the Romanian Cultural Foundation (now Romanian Cultural Institute). Two young essayists later associated with the New Left Internet platform *Criticatac.ro*, Mihail Iovanel and Alex Cistelecan, published articles about Tismaneanu's writings during the communist period. The underlying argument was that the political scientist's anti-communist position was a sham in the context of his theoretical publications before 1989. They of course ignored an entire tradition of Eastern

the Report was published, critics began to question the academic legitimacy of the Commission's activity. Then, such arguments became more and more entangled into a struggle against "anti-communism as ideology." It all came together into an antiestablishment discursive complex that, for some was a way of delegitimizing Băsescu's administration,[79] while for others was a rejection of the post-communist status quo. From 2006 until 2012, the brunt of this cumulative radicalization was borne by a group of intellectuals who had either been associated with the Commission (Tismaneanu; Horia-Roman Patapievici, a philosopher, member of the Commission and, until the summer 2012, president of the Romanian Cultural Instiute, as institution that promoted both domestically and internationally the Report; Gabriel Liiceanu, a philosopher, who is also the owner of the publishing house where the volume version of the Report appeared; one of the Commission's legal experts, constitutionalist Ion Stanomir, and so on) or were supportive of it. In the end, by 2012, the Report and the condemnation act became victims of a *Kulturkampf* that was more interested in antiestablishment discourses and group affirmation than about *Vergangenheitsbewältigung*. The work of over forty experts from multiple fields of study (historians, political scientists, sociologists, philosophers, legal scholars, and so on) was basically dismissed as a "pile of irrelevant historical writing" that

---

European thinkers who developed critiques of communist regimes originally coming from Marxism. What was unsettling was that they employed quotations, discursive constructions, and ultimately critical practices similar with those of the calumny campaign against Tismaneanu during the Commission's activity and immediately after the condemnation act. For example, compare one of the most violent attacks on Tismaneanu's past by Gabriela Antoniu, "Tinerețe revoluționară—Tismaneanu, întâiul communist al țării," *Jurnalul national*, 20 December 2006 [only days after the condemnation speech, n.a.] http://jurnalul.ro/stire-politic/tinerete-revolutionara-tismaneanu-intaiul-comunist-al-tarii-5558.html, last accessed September 8, 2010 with Alex Cistelecan, "Refuzul de a uita," *Cultura*, no. 81 (July 2007) and Mihai Iovanel, "Apararea Tismaneanu," *Cultura*, no. 86 (August 2007), http://revistacultura.ro/cultura.php?articol=1707, last accessed September 8, 2010).

[79] See, for example, an article about how "the condemnation of communism can truly begin" written upon Vladimir Tismaneanu's revocation by Prime Minister Victor Ponta from the position of IICCMER's President of the Scientific Council in Mai 2012: Dorina Rusu, "Condamnarea comunismului abia acum incepe," *Spunesitu.ro*, 25 May 2012, http://spunesitu.adevarul.ro/Editorial/Condamnarea-comunismului-abia-acum-incepe-9957, last accessed June 7, 2012.

does not explain what communism *really* was. In this sense, narratives about Romanian communism turned into "the greatest lie within the public space since the great lie of communist propaganda."[80]

Writing a comprehensive account of the process described above would inevitably result in a volume. My account is more a synthetic summary of *some* of the positions adopted and *some* of the actors involved. I will not dwell on the debates about Băsescu's career and credentials in connection with the condemnation act. I think that much of the materials about his collaboration with the secret police that appeared in the Romanian mass-media relies on circumstantial or no factual proof.[81] Regarding his political agenda, he never denounced

---

[80] Ciprian Șiulea, "Anticomunism pentru eternitate," http://www.tiuk.reea. net/13/ernu_siulea.html, last accessed September 24, 2010.

[81] I would like to give two examples that are telling of how reliance on questionable or limited information can lead to guess-work rather than scholarly inquiry. The first comes from the Romanian public sphere. Historian Marius Oprea, one of the local foremost experts on the *Securitate*, Commission member, and IICCMER's president (2006–2010), published a series of articles in *Observator cultural* that announced his biography of Băsescu. After five episodes, the project seemed to fade away. The crux of the matter was that these articles would supposedly reveal the president's collaborationist communist past and ultimately his connections with the *Securitate*. Missing any relevant archival information, the series was simply a jumble of facts about Băsescu's life. In 2012, just before the referendum on the second impeachment of Băsescu, the same historian announced that he will finally publish the long awaited biography. The book was indeed distributed with the national daily *Jurnalul national*, days before the referendum. It appeared at the publishing house with the same name as the journal, which is owned by Dan Voiculescu, a notorious *Securitate* collaborator (by final court decision), the grey eminence of the anti-Băsescu opposition, one of the most important massmedia oligarchs, and one of the main actors involved in corruption cases under trial. A few weeks after the referendum, the book that announced itself to be the ultimate proof of Băsescu's illegitimacy as the authority to condemn the communist regime (among others) was completely forgotten with basically zero reactions or impact. An explanation is that similarly to the articles in *Observator cultural*, the volume was far from the smoking gun it boasted itself to be. See Marius Oprea, *Adevărata față a lui Traian Băsescu* (Bucharest: Editura Jurnalul National, 2012). The second example of poor documentation that leads to guess work is Monica Ciobanu's evaluation of the legitimacy of the accusations against Traian Băsescu. The author registered this criticism on the basis of "a suspicion that Băsescu's decision to set up the commission was not an expression of genuine commitment to addressing the

the Report despite several faux-pas reflective more of commonplace nostalgia toward his experience with communism as a lived system.[82] In fact, in October 2012, at the launch of the second volume of archival documents used by the Commission,[83] he declared that

> every new step taken in order to identify documents from the national archives or from the archives of any institution that further certify the report on the basis of which, on December 18, I condemned the communist regime as criminal and illegitimate gives me the feeling that the act of placing under the presidential authority the activity of historians, of researchers was one of the most fortunate and correct attitudes of the Presidential Administration during my two terms in office. I am not exaggerating . . . the report of condemnation of communism is above all else because there you have the explanation for many of the things that happen today.[84]

---

past, but an opportunity to settle scores with coalition partners and political opponents. There is also a suspicion that the creation of the commission was used as a means of avoiding lustration." Suspicions are hardly proof and ultimately both were invalidated. Băsescu did not settle scores with coalition partners on the basis of the condemnation of the communist regime, while the lustration law was passed by the Parliament during the liberal-democratic government, but it was invalidated by the Constitutional Court in 2010. See Ciobanu, "Criminalising the Past," 323.

[82] The most serious faux-pas in terms of statements that indirectly contradicted the Report was in June 2011 when Băsescu criticized King Michael of Hohenzollern for his allegedly "slavish behavior toward the Russians." This statement came in contrast with the sections of the Report about the king's position between 1944 and 1947 and on his forced abdication. What seems more an intervention rooted in a conflict between Băsescu and the monarchical family did shed a negative light on the condemnation act. However, he did not associate the text of the Report with his opinions at the time. For a full account of his statements on this issue see http://www.evz.ro/detalii/stiri/basescu-regele-mihai-a-fost-sluga-la-rusi-live-text-934964.html, last accessed June 5, 2012.

[83] See Mihnea Berindei et al., *Istoria Comunismului din România. Documente—Perioada Gheorghiu-Dej (1945–1989)* (Bucharest: Humanitas, 2009) and Mihnea Berindei, et al., *Istoria Comunismului din Romania. Documente—Perioada Nicolae Ceauşescu (1965–1971)* (Bucharest: Humanitas, 2012).

[84] http://www.econtext.ro/eveniment —2/politic/traian-băsescu-dintre-toate-lucrurile-realizate-in-mandatul-meu-cel-mai-important-a-fost-condamnarea-comunismului.html, last accessed December 20, 2012.

Considering the constitutional prerogatives of the President in Romania, the explanation about limited materialization into policy of the Commission's recommendations lies more with the various parliamentary majorities and governments that were in power from 2007 until present. One editorialist presciently warned in 2006, on the day of the condemnation of the communist regime, that "if the Report is followed by inaction, this will show that our political class is not ready to coexist with the truth and with its consequences."[85] Furthermore, it did not help either that the social-democrats, the largest and maybe the most important party in post-communist Romania, condemned the condemnation act and the Report *before* the presidential speech and the publication of the Commission's document. It was a preventive act by the new social-democratic leadership aimed to salvage the "historical honor" of the party's honorific president, Ion Iliescu (for two terms Romania's head of state).[86] In the end, when taking into account the attitudes of most Romanian politicians about the communist period, I agree with Ruxandra Cesereanu, who, in her article comparing

---

[85] Traian Ungureanu, "Raportul cel bun," *Cotidianul*, 18 December 2006, http://www.hotnews.ro/stiri-arhiva-1134809-raportul-cel-bun-traian-ungureanu.htm, last accessed September 12, 2010. Ungureanu will later become MP in the European Parliament, representing the liberal-democrats. Surprisingly, he was not involved, to my knowledge, in any initiative within his own party to institutionalize some of the Report's recommendations.

[86] One might argue that the social-democrats' resolution was almost inevitable if they were not able to distance themselves from their former leader's past. Iliescu appears in the report in multiple forms: as communist youth leader, head of the youth ministry involved in the repression of student movements, secretary of the agitprop, county party-secretary, possible successor of Ceaușescu, the revolutionary leader with spotty stories about the bloodshed after the Ceaușescus fled from the Romanian capital (see also Grosescu and Ursachi's chapter for more details on this last topic), and as state leader heavily involved in the miners presence in Bucharest and their violent repression of the anti-governmental protests. About the resolution, see "Congresul extraordinary PSD: 'Despre folosirea trecutului ca armă politică,'" 13 December 2006 http://www.9am.ro/stiri-revista-presei/2006-12-13/rezolutie-congresul-extraordinar-al-psd-despre-folosirea-trecutului-ca-arma-politica.html, last accessed October 5, 2010. On the Romanian social-democrats' inability to come to terms with the communist past of some of their leadership see Dan Tapalagă, "S-a limpezit lumea," *22*, 3 December 2006, http://www.revista22.ro/sa-limpezit-lumea-3334.html, last accessed August 10, 2010.

the CSHR and PCACDR, concluded that "unlike Ion Iliescu, who was viscerally opposed to the condemnation of communism, Traian Băsescu understood that he had to detach himself from his own past, and he did it officially, in the name of the Romanian people."[87]

The fundamental problem with the all out rejection of the Report was that it did not propose any alternative interpretation. There were at least two initiatives along these lines that faded into the background almost as soon as they were announced. The first was the initiative of Romanian Orthodox Church (BOR) to write a counter-Report (for more details, see Vasile's chapter). The second was a project launched, at the beginning of 2008, by Sorin Adam Matei, professor of information technology at Purdue University, "the condemnation of communism 2.0." BOR's initiative ultimately materialized, though its response was more witch-hunting for heretics rather than an academic work (see Vasile's contribution). The prospective Internet platform was never heard of soon after its announcement.[88] In both cases, the argument was that the Commission's activity was a failure and it should be countered with a truly academic study of the communist experience. But it seems that declaring the Report a scholarly fiasco was much easier than providing a comprehensive, interdisciplinary account about phenomena from 1945 to 1989.

The rejection of the Report developed along two types of inter-related directions—political and conceptual. As early as July 2006, so only three months after the creation of the Commission, Octavian Paler, a respected novelist with an important track-record of pro-democratic commitment after 1989, but with a murky communist past (in 1960s and 1970s),[89] wondered in one of the most important Romanian dailies: "How is it possible for a criminal regime to be condemned by another one, which is criminal (*de facto*) without though relying on a criminal ideology?"[90] To a certain extent, Paler was very much ahead of his time. His argument reflected both his political options (he was very critical of Traian Băsescu) and his ideological approach—a

---

[87] Cesereanu, "The Final Report," 276.

[88] Sorin Adam Matei, "Condamnarea comunismului 2.0."

[89] In the 1970s, for five years he was acting member of the Central Committee of the Romanian Communist Party.

[90] Octavian Paler, "Lupta pentru trecut," *Cotidianul*, 25 iulie 2006, http://www.9am.ro/stiri-revista-presei/2006-07-25/lupta-pentru-trecut.html, last accessed September 14, 2010.

populist, antiliberal, autochthonism that expressed his rejection of the perceived post-communist status quo. I argue below that this type of standpoint will gain significant steam in the following years.

An additional complication that fueled Paler-type criticism was the difficulty, from the beginning, of the Romanian public opinion to understand the significance of a Commission for the analysis of the past. Initially, the presidential proposal for the creation of a Commission was perceived as a ploy to side-step the condemnation of the former regime. Then the same body, after being created, was seen (as in the social-democrats pre-emptive resolution) to be an instrument against the president's political enemies. Furthermore, the activity of the Commission itself was more often than not analyzed outside the context of the international culture of contrition that developed since 1980[91] or in disconnect with previous projects of state-sponsored public use of history in Europe.[92] This type of criticism tended to conveniently forget or ignore the established practice of state commissions entrusted with dealing with the past. With very few exceptions,[93] the entire debate largely overlooked the examples of Germany, other East European countries, South Africa, or Latin America. This happened despite repeated references made by members of the Commission to these cases. The only two examples sometimes invoked were the

---

[91] Barkan, "Historians," 902.

[92] For an analysis on how the relationship between the process of Europeanization and dealing with the past in Central and Eastern Europe see John Gledhill, "Integrating the Past: Regional Integration and Historical Reckoning in Central and Eastern Europe," *Nationalities Papers*, vol. 39, no. 4 (July 2011), 481–506. Gledhill shows how the European Commission did not initiate or manage top-down remembrance programs in former communist countries. However, "the accession to the EU may have created opportunities for advocates of reckoning in CEE states to draw Europe behind their remembrance projects on an ad hoc basis." The author concludes that "there is little immediate likelihood that European integration will lead to the institutionalization of pan-European collective remembrance programs." (497).

[93] Lavinia Stan, "Comisia Tismaneanu – Repere internaționale," *Sfera politicii*, nrs. 126–127 (2007), http://www.sferapoliticii.ro/sfera/126-127/art02-stan. html, last accessed September 21, 2010 and Bogdan C. Iacob, ""Comisia Prezidențială, consensul antitotalitar și perspectiva internațională," *Observator cultural*, no. 372 (May 2007), http://www.observatorcultural.ro/Comisia-Prezidentiala-consensul-antitotalitar-si-perspectiva-internationala*articleID_17588-articles_details.html, last accessed August 25, 2010.

Institute of National Memory in Poland and the House of Terror (a museum) in Hungary. Both were uncritically presented as ideal institutions for working through the communist past in comparison to which the Commission fell short. This fact in itself proved the futility of the Romanian initiative and its *politicized* nature.

Public intellectual Andrei Pleşu correctly noticed in 2008 that "Romanians do not seem to know that the act made by our local presidency is part of a series of similar acts that took place in almost all ex-communist countries and in the plenums of the most important European institutions."[94] But only two years earlier, the same commentator reluctantly tackled the idea of an expert Commission: "one will answer me that the premise of the present commission is a negative judgment on the *ancien regime* and that its main purpose is to centralize and systematize all the existing information in order to provide 'the scientific' basis for a political act that is after all inevitable."[95] Pleşu was far from being a critic of the Commission and the Report, to the contrary. The public opinion had problems in comprehending the Commission in terms of its role, limits, significance, and function as a mechanism for analyzing the past in a post-authoritarian society.[96]

What complicated the situation further was the fact that there existed already a group of critics who, before 2006, presented the negative assessments toward the communist period as simply tools for consolidating cultural hegemony.[97] I believe that, within an increasingly

---

[94] Andrei Pleşu "Despre condamnarea comunismului," *Adevărul,* 17 September 2008, http://stiri.rol.ro/andrei-plesu-despre-condamnarea-comunismu-lui-148312.html, last accessed January 7, 2011.

[95] Andrei Pleşu, "O comisie pentru condamnarea comunismului?" *Dilema Veche,* Anul III, no.118, 28 April 2006, http://86.124.112.53/sectiune/situa-tiunea/articol/o-comisie-pentru-condamnarea-comunismului, last accessed January 7, 2011.

[96] For an early, pertinent comment about the expectations that one should have on the basis of the Commission's activity see Adrian Cioflâncă, "Regret formal," *Ziarul de Iaşi,* 10 April 2007, http://www.ziaruldeiasi.ro/editori-al/regret-formal~ni4aos.

[97] For example, Sorin Adam Matei, *Boierii minţii. Intelectuali români între grupu-rile de prestigiu şi piaţa liberă a ideilor* (Bucharest: Compania, 2004) or Ciprian Şiulea, "Anticomunismul (I-II)," *Observator Cultural,* no. 281 and no. 282, 11 and 18 August 2005, http://www.observatorcultural.ro/Anticomunismul-(I)*articleID_13710-articles_details.html, last accesed September 2, 2010.

polarizing political context, these three phenomena—populist antiliberalism, lack of international contextualization, and latent anti-anticomunism—were the premises for the ultimate unmitigated rejection of the Report and of the condemnation act.

Ideology and the Communist Past

In the aftermath of the Report's publication, leaving aside accusations of direct political instrumentalization by the President or Democratic-Liberal Party, the two elements that appeared to bind together most of the criticism I am focusing on were the problem of ideology and that of empathy. Critiques against these two conceptual approaches adopted by the Commission functioned as the basis for questioning its validity and as the starting point for making a case for unmasking an alleged cultural hegemony.

During a debate in December 2006, at the German Cultural Center in Iași (main city in Moldova), one of the Commission experts provided the following overview of this body's view of the relationship ideology-system: "[it was] a commission meant to analyze a political regime and the ways of institutionalizing an ideology. But, as it is obvious in several sections of the Report, it was also a condemnation of an ideology because, as those who read the classics of communism well know, there is a consubstantiation between ideological content and the form in which the latter institutionalized. There is no a priori good communism."[98] Or, as the Commission chair put it during a dialogue with some of the critics of the Report: "Communism was a world and in any world good things also happen, but not BECAUSE but DESPITE the totalitarian ideology."[99] (Capitals in original n.a.)

There are two explanations for this theoretical preference in the Report. First, as stated in the document's introduction, the com-

---

[98] See historian Adrian Cioflâncă's intervention in "Trecutul în spatele nostru?" 315.

[99] See Vladimir Tismaneanu's intervention in "Poporul român și comunismul: viol sau amor" Interview with Tismăneanu vs. Ernu, Rogozanu, and Șiulea by Vlad Mixich, *Hotnews.ro*, 22 December 2008, http://www.hotnews.ro/stiri-esential-5279303-poporul-roman-comunismul-viol-sau-amor-interviuri-oglinda-tismaneanu-ernu-rogozanu-siulea.htm, last accessed on October 16, 2010.

mon denominator of the Commission's members and experts was the acceptance of the concept "totalitarianism." As exemplified by the section "The Communist Regime in Romania: Historiographical Overview,"[100] the members and experts of the Commission had a rather flexible and often guarded understanding of the term. The starting point was the classic conceptualization formulated by Hannah Arendt, Zbigniew Brzezinski, and Carl Friedrich.[101] In a body made up by academics, public intellectuals, or activists of memory, one should not be surprised that a basic common denominator was sought after, especially if one takes into account the limited emancipation of historical and social studies of communism in Romania from the frameworks of classic Sovietology/Kremlinology.[102] Nevertheless, sections such as "Mass Organizations,"[103] "The Collectivization of Agriculture,"[104] "Methods of Social Control in the Ceauşescu Period,"[105] "The *Securitate* and Methods of Recruiting Informers,"[106] "Dissidence in the Communist Regime"[107] reveal a much more *participatory* understanding of totalitarian rule that significantly departed from the vision of a static and immutable polity encompassing a society defined by a generalized state of anomie.[108] This ambivalence of conceptualization is appar-

---

[100] *Raport Final*, 36–46.

[101] Ibid., ft. 27, 33.

[102] For example, historian Dorin Dobrincu, stated that throughout the writing of the Report the main imperative was "bringing to a common denominator the contrasting opinions expressed within the Commission." See his intervention in "Trecutul este in spatele nostrum?" 320.

[103] *Raport Final*, 176–198.

[104] Ibid., 238–257.

[105] Ibid., 395–436.

[106] Ibid., 505–520.

[107] Ibid., 712–738.

[108] On "participatory totalitarianism" see Stephen Kotkin, "The State—Is It Us? Memoirs, Archives, and Kremlinologists," *Russian Review*, 61 (January 2002), 35–51 and Astrid Hadin, "Stalinism as a Civilization: New Perspectives on Communist Regimes," *Political Studies Review*, 2004, vol. 2, 166–184. For communist regimes as "participatory dictatorships" see Mary Fulbrook, "Reckoning with the Past: Heroes, Victims, and Villains in the History of the German Democratic Republic," in *Rewriting the German Past—History and Identity in the New Germany*, (ed.) Reinhard Alter and Peter Monteath (Atlantic Highlands, NJ: Humanities Press, 1997), 175–96 and Mary Fulbrook, *The People's State: East German So-*

ent from the opening sentence of the Report: "Communism, which claimed to be a novel civilization, superior to the capitalist one that it vehemently lambasted, force hundreds of millions of people to live in a closed, repressive, and humiliating universe."[109]

With this in mind, I would argue that the second option for choosing a "primacy of ideology" approach was based on recent scholarship that does indeed envisage the communist experience as alternative modernity, but one essentially illiberal.[110] The points made by the two Commission representatives echo in fact Tony Judt's blunt remark: "The road to Communist hell was undoubtedly paved with good (Marxist) intentions. But so what? . . . From the point of view of the exiled, humiliated, tortured, maimed or murdered victims, of course, it's all the same."[111] Of course, historians steeped in the methodological and theoretical debates of the past decades in communism studies would prefer a post-revisionist/totalitarian approach. And such criticism would be entirely justified. But it would have been unrealistic and probably impossible to expect a sharp departure from the totalitarian paradigm within the Commission, especially if one takes into account that Romanian historical studies and social sciences are yet to fully deparochialize and delocalize themselves.

Such subtleties, however, seem to have been lost on some of the critics of the Report. Their reaction to the Commission's "primacy of

---

ciety from Hitler to Honecker (New Haven, CT and London: Yale University Press, 2005). In fact, two Commission representatives already adopted Fulbrook's conceptualization. See Petrescu and Petrescu, "Retribution, Remembering," 170. I believe that the Report's approach to totalitarianism is quite similar to Anne Applebaum's recent attempt to analyze the totalitarian nature of Central European communist regimes from the point of view of the intersection between top-down policies/decisions and (re)actions from below. Of course, this approach can be criticized for its overreliance on the dichotomy state-society. See Anne Applebaum, *Iron Curtain: The Crushing of Eastern Europe, 1944–56* (London: Allen Lane, 2012).

[109] *Raport Final*, 23.

[110] For an overview of the discussion on the relationship between communism and the problem of multiple modernities see Michael David-Fox, "Multiple Modernities vs. Neo-Traditionalism: On Recent Debates in Russian and Soviet History," *Jahrbücher für Geschichte Osteuropas*, Neue Folge, Bd. 54, H. 4 (2006), 535–555.

[111] Tony Judt, "The Longest Road to Hell," *New York Times*, December 22, 1997, A27.

ideology" choice was zero-sum: "written by a commission of intellectuals still engaged in an imagined and immature struggle with a world that they do not understand that well, the Report employs simplifications. The most serious one is the way it envisages social relations under communism. The latter is not seen as a web of intermediaries, but as a spider (Ceaușescu)[112] who took hostage an entire society."[113] This statement was made in 2007; only a year later, the same author, Sorin Adam Matei, reached a radical conclusion: the Report was "a document that in the Romanian language can only be described with a single word: superficial *(fușerit)*."[114] He would use such characterization to justify his launching of the online platform "The Condemnation of Communism 2.0," initiative pregnant with the promise of a true scholarship. But, the gap between stated intentions and actual academic production was, for this author and for similar critics of the Report, insurmountable.

Another author's criticism was similarly unforgiving with the Commission's approach: "it is one of judging communism as an ideological regime, thus not reaching the substance of the deep political, social, economic, and cultural realities that lay underneath the ideological discourse in which nobody believed anymore."[115] This expert in literary criticism would add a year later, in 2008, that "communism is understood in the Tismaneanu Report by way of ideology, but Romanian communism was, from one point on, very divergent from the ideology itself."[116] He claimed as early as August 2005 that "what

---

[112] Sorin Adam Matei's statement is contradicting another criticism, which stated that the Report granted only 23 pages on the Ceaușescu period. See Monica Ciobanu, "Criminalising the Past..." As a matter of fact, the Report neither situated Ceaușescu at the center of its explanation about the post-1960s stage of the communist experience nor did it allocate only two dozen pages to this period. This is just an example of criticisms that were based on factual errors but were then perpetuated in both public discussions and in some international scholarship on the Report.

[113] Sorin Adam Matei, "Unde mă duci bestie," *Adevărul*, 17 July 2007.

[114] Sorin Adam Matei, "Condamnarea comunismului 2.0."

[115] Ciprian Șiulea, „Tentația unui nou absolutism moral. Cu cine și de ce polemizează Vladimir Tismăneanu," *Observator Cultural* no. 379 (July 2007) http://www.observatorcultural.ro/Tentatia-unui-nou-absolutism-moral*articleID_17895-articles_details.html (last accessed on October 12, 2010).

[116] See Ciprian Șiulea's intervention in the discussion "Poporul român și comunismul."

is important is the research of real communism."[117] One gets an idea
of what he meant by such elusive formulation from an intervention
three years later: "In explaining the communist disaster, the Report
relies almost exclusively on the malefic character of the Party and of
the Securitate, while it tells very little about massive collaborationism
in sectors such as the judicial system, the army, the police, the education, and, last but not least, in the cultural sphere."[118] What he overlooked was that the judicial and cultural production system, the army
and police do figure preeminently in the Report as both loci and mechanisms of the establishment, consolidation, and reproduction of the
communist regime. Moreover, he, along with other critics, obstinately
bypassed the essential feature of state socialism—it was a Party-State,
where prophylactic control by the secret police in the post-totalitarian
phase functioned both as deterrent and inclusionary core instrument.
Any analyses of "collaborationism," ' of individual guilt/responsibility,
of compromise and co-option must first and foremost be framed and
founded on the investigation and clarification of the levers of power
and domination within the Party-State structures. And from this point
of view, the Report is utterly comprehensive. Indeed, it does not follow the *entire* evolution of the most important Party-State structures
from 1945 to 1989. It would have been doubtful though that a single
volume Report could achieve such feat in little over six months that
the Commission had at its disposal.[119] But in terms of deconstructing
the fundamental institutional and personnel layout of the communist
regime, the Report truly stands out within existing scholarship on the
Romanian case. But for most of these critics of the Commission and
Report, such emphasis on "collaborationism" was more important
than a diagnosis of communism as a regime founded on a Party-State

---

[117] Şiulea, „Anticomunismul (I)."

[118] See Şiulea's intervention in "Coordonatorii răspund întrebărilor revistei",
Observator Cultural, no. 449 (November 2008), http://www.observatorcul-
tural.ro/Coordonatorii-raspund-intrebarilor-revistei*articleID_20777-arti-
cles_details.html (last accessed on September 7, 2010).

[119] Historian Andi Michalache commonsensically diagnosed the impossibility
of an exhaustive analysis by the Commission's representatives within the
time-frame assigned: "these researchers could not produce a total history
of communism, maybe in fifty volumes in which to cite everyone, to list all
the names of the guilty. They could only present some aspects, some facts
that could amount to uncontestable evidence." See „Trecutul în spatele
nostru?," 306.

because it would become their crucial steppingstone to the argument of "anti-communism as ideology."

In December 2008, during an interview with three of the critics of the Report (the above author was among them), the interviewer asked them to give him a brief explanation on "What kept communism in power in Romania for five decades?" What I signaled as ignorance toward the layout of the regime as ideological Party-State is manifest in their answers. One interviewee simply claimed that "the Russians indirectly from one point on" maintained the communist party in power. Another provided an answer that was more sophisticated: "communism relies on several categories of very important people: those who participated directly and who believed, then the opportunists and, the greatest problem, communism rested on the many that were silent."[120] The first reply leaves aside the role of institutions, systemic development, ideological re-invention, of individual and collective identities and milieus, etc. simply appealing to a half-baked geopolitical explanation. The second reverts to the triad true believer-opportunist-bystander that is both elusive and contradicts the very thesis of 'collaborationism.' What differentiates a true believer and/or an opportunist from a perpetrator? If it is involvement in (mass) (political) murder than, are there no perpetrators after 1964? Are there degrees of collaborationism? What differentiates a collaborator from a bystander? The concept of collaborationism in itself, if applied for the communist experience, is rather forced. It presupposes the idea of 'supporting a foreign power.' Was the communist regime a 'foreign' power? Both critics failed to pertinently answer the journalist's query particularly because they ignored the dynamics, role, and possibilities of individuals in communist regimes founded on Party-States mobilized and/or routinized by way of ideology and circumscribed through a highly repressive (proactive and/or prophylactic) monopoly of violence most pervasively present in the agency of the secret police.

Because of the Commission's mandate and because of a still developing social history and everyday history of Romanian state socialism, the Report did not analyze "the motivations of social agents through the analysis of their own process of making sense and enacting

---

[120] See Șiulea's and Ernu's answers in "Poporul român și comunismul..."

interests."[121] It did not focus on "the various ways in which individuals adapted to the permanent presence of party and state domination."[122] But the Report did fulfill the function for which it was commissioned: it detailed the macro-practices that established, consolidated, and reproduced the communist system of domination—the communist dictatorship. German historian Alf Lüdtke famously argued, using the example of the GDR, that state socialist society was "durchherrscht" that is, it was "thoroughly pervaded by practices of political domination." According to him, "in a paradoxical inversion of Marx's utopian prophecy, it was rather society itself that had withered away during socialism, and not the state."[123] From this point of view, I agree with a Romanian observer's remark that the Report "stirs an anxiety about ourselves into manifestation."[124] By clarifying the macro level it opened the discussion on the role and nature of micro practices of political domination within specific individual, group, and localized contexts. Subsequently, the Report set the ground for personal and social inquiry on "the roots of moral responsibility beyond the sphere of the guilt that can be formalized."[125] Or to put it differently, the Report sketched the big picture of the regime, the ecosystem within which the habitus of the socialist citizen was structured and where it also attained a structuring nature.[126]

---

[121] Péter Apor, "The Joy of Everyday Life: Microhistory and the History of Everyday Life in the Socialist Dictatorships," *East Central Europe/ECE,* vols. 34–35, 2007–2008, part 1–2, 196.

[122] Thomas Lindenberger, "Everyday History: New Approaches to the History of the Post-War Germanies," in Christoph Kleßmann (ed.), *The Divided Past: Rewriting Post-War German History* (Oxford: Berg, 2001), 51.

[123] See Geoff Eley's discussion of the concepts of *Eigen-Sinn* and *durchherrscht* in his review article "The Unease of History: Settling Accounts with the East German Past," *History Workshop Journal,* 57 (Spring 2004), 188–192.

[124] Caius Dobrescu, "Raportul Tismăneanu: soluția de 'continuitate'," *Observator Cultural,* no. 391 (September 2007) http://www.observatorcultural.ro/Raportul-Tismaneanu-solutia-de-continuitate*articleID_18391-articles_details.html, last accessed on September 26, 2010.

[125] Ibid.

[126] I am using Ulf Brunnbauer's terminology from his article "A Promising Liaison? Social History and Anthropology in South-Eastern Europe. Opportunities and Pitfalls," *East Central Europe/ECE,* vols. 34–35, 2007–2008, part 1–2, 161–184.

The former chair of the Commission provided his own answer to the interviewer's question on the communist regime's modes of sustenance. The political scientist stated that "the regime acted in a permanent offensive against the citizens, but it knew how to also employ perverse techniques of cooption. It was not only the rule of social resentment. It was also a platform for the social mobility of those designated as the dictatorship's favorites."[127] One can still sense Tismaneanu's academic genealogy in the totalitarian school from his overall value-based assessment of social integration and self-accomplishment during communism. Nevertheless, his assertion, which echoes the overall argument made in the Report, stands out in comparison with the authors analyzed above because he took into account "the unavoidable compromises imposed by the state as the elementary prerequisites for building any kind of useful or satisfying life."[128] The Report itself discussed how, both in the early period of the communist regime and in its post-Stalinist stage, the communist leadership "knew how to also create mechanisms of co-option by taking advantage of the chances for social mobility it offered to members of some of most unprivileged groups."[129] Furthermore,

In Romania, as in most cases, the wide-reaching program of modernization launched in 1960s—that presupposed rapid industrialization simultaneous with a progressive urbanization—allowed an important section of the population to live better than it ever lived, or, better at least than during the years of Stalinism. Similar processes took place across the socialist bloc, so that, after 1960s, these regimes were able to survive on the basis of a "new social contract." . . . In contrast with repression, which caused a dichotomic split of society between executioners and victims, the control strategy based on cooption generated multiple reactions. The most representative from a quantative point of view was the one that the regime aimed at: conformism. There was, of course, a hierarchy of co-option levels within the system. . . . We can go as far as to state that the communist regime sur-

---

[127] See Tismaneanu's intervention in "Poporul român și comunismul."
[128] Eley, "The Unease of History," 118.
[129] *Raport Final*, 33.

vived for so many decades because of the tacit support, based on the mechanism of "the new social contract," of all those who accepted to live in Romania without publicly expressing their discontent against the regime.[130]

With this argument, we are far away from the Russians who brought and preserved the communist regime or from generic, de-contextualized categories of responsibility.

The Report did acknowledge difficulties of living in truth as one would become ever more integrated in the communist society, in the Party-State. Historian Geoff Eley's stressed in one of his articles on dealing with the past in Germany: "not only did the GDR's citizens have little choice about where they lived, but they were also encouraged by their West German compatriots to accept the permanence of their lot."[131] In following the principle of his argument, I would state that the favorable way in which the communist leadership was received and presented in the West at certain stages of the regime's development functioned domestically as an element of the very basis of identity-building and cooption incentives.[132] But, as Tismaneanu put it in one of his Romanian editorials, the Report firmly stated that this was an *abnormal normality*.[133] The critics of the document simply ignored that this "dictatorship of and by boundaries"[134] could not be taken at face value, as a "normal state," only because individuals and groups built their life-worlds and negotiated their coexistence with the Party-State. Simultaneously, the very fact that they achieved such system-reproductive *modus vivendi* did not instantly produced easily distinguishable hierarchies of responsability.

---

[130] Ibid., 716.

[131] Eley, "The Unease of History" 180.

[132] There is in the Report a memorable formulation about the impact of Western perceptions about the Romanian regime and its effect on the population's attitudes toward the communist regime: "the seemingly independent foreign policy within the Soviet bloc, greatly heralded for a long time by the West, transformed Ceaușescu, for an extended period, the most important 'dissident' of Romania." See *Raport Final*, 738.

[133] Vladimir Tismaneanu, "Despre cinismul ludic: Sindromul anti-anticomunismului," *Contributors.ro*, 18 May 2011, http://www.contributors.ro/politica-doctrine/3841/, last accessed June 8, 2012.

[134] Lindenberger, "Everyday History," 55.

Strategic Empathy?

The last statement takes us to another central topic advanced by both the Commission representatives and their critics—that of empathy for victims and for those that lived under communism. One of the authors who would end up simply dismissing the Report (on academic, symbolic, or institutional grounds) and the validity of the condemnation act, also preemptively declared in the summer of 2006: "All those who have suffered because of communism, in one way or another, are entitled to demand its condemnation, of its crimes, and of the authors of these crimes. Up until this point, anti-communist discourse is legitimate and necessary. It becomes illegitimate when it implicitly presupposes that this is the aspiration of the entire society and, more than this, that it can play the role of the political project that could extract Romania from the quagmire she is in."[135] In 2010, another author would be even more straightforward than the earlier like-minded critic: "the centrality of the memory of the victims and of the regime's harshness mainly plays the role of posthumously justifying any substantial form of anti-communism when the latter still made sense."[136] In November 2008, a third representative of the group that would later aggregate in the project *Iluzia anticomunismului* and on the internet platform *Criticatac.ro* sternly expressed the gist of his and colleagues' position: "We cannot swallow pathetic discourse as intellectual public legitimization. At the core of this scattered group come to life the first forms of anti-capitalist protest, pro-individual rights movements and others. One does not have to belong to the left in order to notice how poor the local social discourse is."[137] In the end, they did not simply reject anti-communism as a public discourse, but they legitimized their own political/ideological views on the basis of such rejection. For them, debating the communist experience was either a decoy for consolidating the establishment or a way to denounce the post-communist status quo. Or, to use the formulation of another critic from the group:

---

[135] Şiulea, "Anticomunism pentru eternitate."

[136] Florin Poenaru, "Anti-comunismul, mecanismul uitării," *Vatra*, no. 20-11 (2010), 34.

[137] See the intervention of Costi Rogozanu (a writer and journalist) in "Coordonatorii răspund întrebărilor revistei," *Vatra*, no. 20-11 (2010), 34.

"Instead of questioning the principles and the conditions for the possibility of such a regime [n.a. communism], the condemnation of communism declared a break for masking continuity. . . . The one which successfully applies the communist utopia of a capitalism without contradictions in reference to the relations of production, without antagonisms in the relationships among classes, without the obstacle of its own conditions of possibility, is exactly the political system of today."[138]

What the succession of the above quotes reveals is that the condemnation of the communist regime and the Report are delegitimized not because they are empathic to the victims of the past crimes. They were criticized particularly because of their role as truth-telling mechanisms that bring about state acknowledgment of crimes in the name of the victims. It seems that the authors mentioned earlier needed to obliterate such legitimacy in order to loudly claim their position as being the *only* legitimate and real social discourse in tune with the "true" will of the people. From this point of view, we come full circle to the populist, antiliberal, antiestablishment arguments employed by writer Octavian Paler against the Commission and the condemnation act: Is the present political system any better than communism in order to condemn it? What gives the "condemners" (the president, the Commission, the Report's supporters) the right to condemn? In this reading, the condemnation act became a form of political manipulation that legitimized the elite few at the expanse of the alienated many. Or, as another author from the group that is currently claiming an identity under the egis of the New Left blog *Criticatac.ro*, emphatically stated: "anti-communism . . . increased the alienation of the popular masses from a public sphere managed by intellectuals, journalists, and politicians (because nostalgia intensified as the living conditions got worse during the transition) and it compromised to a large extent the necessary work of placing the historical experience of really existing socialism within its own epistemic field."[139]

---

[138] Alex Cistelecan, "Condamnare și contaminare: Visul comunist al capitalismului," *Cultura*, no. 62, 8 March 2007, http://revistacultura.ro/cultura. php?articol=964, last accessed June 15, 2012.

[139] Ovidiu Țichindelean, "Câte ceva despre anticomunism, stânga sa și o altă stângă," *Cultura*, no. 31 (August 12, 2010), http://revistacultura.ro/blog/ 2010/08/cate-ceva-despre-anticomunism-stanga-sa-si-o-alta-stanga-o-seama-de-raspunsuri-de-la-ovidiu-tichindeleanu/, last accessed June 9, 2012.

For these critics, the only anti-communism that might work is the one that reclaimed and reused the critique from the left of state socialism. Interestingly enough, Tismaneanu himself, like many East Central European anti-communist intellectuals, comes from this tradition of Marxism turned into a left critique of communism turned into liberal political thought. Moreover, the Report rehabilitated all democratic victims of the regime, including social-democrats or individuals inspired by Marxist beliefs. To make matters worse, up until 2012, *Criticatac.ro* had yet to reclaim the antitotalitarian tradition of Romanian left-wing political thought in the past century. Despite the valid criticism that domestic anti-communist public discourse often forgets that some of the most sobering diagnoses of communist regimes came from the Left, it seems that its advocates have yet to figure out what tradition and how they are reprocessing it. The absence of which they might consider as legitimate anti-communism indicates to a certain extent more their will to assert themselves as an ideological alternative on the basis of a wider phenomenon of the revival of the New Left across Europe.[140]

The New Left-type of criticism against the condemnation act and the Report was also rooted in the attempt to safeguard the possibility of Utopia against the impact of the process of dealing with the past. Historian Geoff Eley underlined that the recourse to "a memorial language of traumatized identity easily spectacularizes suffering and injustice, so that any dramatic or large-scale experience of exceptional violence becomes implicitly privileged as the principal ground from which legitimate and effective political claims may now be filed.

---

[140] For example, the case of *Krytyka Polityczna* (*KP*) in Poland, a group that appears to be the model of *Criticatac.ro*. *KP* has already established a partnership with Dissent Magazine. For details see http://www.dissentmaga-zine.org/blog/dissentniks-in-poland and http://www.dissentmagazine.org/blog/in-poland-followed-by-shadows, last accessed June 11, 2012. However, *KP* and *Criticatac.ro* do differ in many ways: in terms of impact, quality, profile, funding, dissemination within the publish sphere. Just an example, the Romanian group's twin international publication is *The New Left Review*. For details see http://www.criticatac.ro/17014/privind-dinspre-rsrit/, last accessed June 11, 2012. On Sławomir Sierakowski, the leader of *KP*, see Marci Shore, "'A Specter Is Haunting Europe...' Dissent, Intellectuals and a New Generation" in Vladimir Tismaneanu and Bogdan C. Iacob, *The End and the Beginning. The Revolutions of 1989 and the Resurgence of History* (New York/Budapest: CEU Press, 2012), 492–493.

In the process other grounds of democratic action—positive ideals of human self-realization and social emancipation, for instance, or the mundane suffering of everyday poverty and exploitation—can become much harder to find."[141] In 2003, sociologist John Torpey made a similar statement: "my concern, however, is that the pursuit of the past by progressives during the last decade has come to replace a more vigorous and compelling idea of what such a society might be like."[142] Making an argument that resembles the positions advocated by Eley and Torpey, a member of the *Criticatac.ro* group argued in one of his articles that the condemnation act and the Report aimed at discrediting Utopia. He stated that "the biggest problem with delegitimizing the function of utopia by a large section of Romanian intellectuals rests in the fact that one cannot imagine any wide comprehensive horizon, no social project meant to overcome the imperfections of the present social order, one characterized, among others, by a strong social stratification because of the private appropriation of resources."[143] According to this standpoint, as another author emphasized, "communism, as criminal and illegitimate, plays the role of underlining and legitimating by contrast the natural, humane, noble nature of the post-December [1989] status quo."[144]

The difference however between the position of the two Romanian authors and the ideas advocated by Eley and Torpey is that the latter take for granted the phase of working through of a traumatic past. They are concerned about its preeminence in societies with established traditions of public use of history and truth-telling. Though debatable, Eley and Torpey's viewpoints have an evolutionary approach to the duty of memory and history in post-authoritarian societies. The Romanian critics preemptively dismiss the process of dealing with the past in order to safeguard a purportedly endangered possibility for a social alternative

---

[141] Geoff Eley, "The Past Under Erasure? History, Memory, and the Contemporary," *Journal of Contemporary History*, Special Issue on "At the Crossroads of Past and Present—'Contemporary' History and the Historical Discipline," July 2011, vol. 46, no. 3, 558–559.

[142] John Torpey, "The Entrepreneurs of Memory," http://www.opendemocracy.net/democracy-apologypolitics/article_907.jsp (January 21, 2003), last accessed June 10, 2012.

[143] Adrian Dohotaru, "Pentru o reabilitare a utopiei," *Vatra*, no. 20-11 (2010), 36–39.

[144] Alexandru Cistelecan, "Utopia răului mai mic," 41.

to the status quo. In a country that experienced, up until mid-2000s, to varying degrees of intensity, *state* politics of amnesia and a rather dubious social acknowledgment in reference to both the Holocaust (with the corollary of domestic passions for the extreme-right) and the crimes of the communist regime (with the corollary of the sometimes enthusiastic support for the RCP's policies), sacrificing memory work and public use of history for the sake of utopia seems to be dangerously premature. Historian Marci Shore underlined the crucial contradiction in this first-order interpretation of the communist experience in her exchange with new-left Polish philosopher Sławomir Sierakowski. Discussing the destiny of intellectuals who supported communism, she told Sierakowski: "these people I wrote about—things turned out *really, really badly* for all of them. This book [*Caviar and Ashes*, n.a.]—their story—is a tragedy." Sierakowski replied, "But I didn't read it as a tragedy! . . . I read it as a romance."[145] I believe that the rejection of the condemnation of the communist regime is Romania is similarly rooted in the fear, among younger left-wing intellectuals, that the acceptance of the Report's findings obscured the romance with social Utopia, thus barring the way for reenacting similar enchantments.

Hegemony or Populism?

This last observation is supported by the complete dismissal by these Report critics of the complex picture behind the wider reactions against the condemnation act. First and foremost, it remains unclear in their writings what is the post-1989 establishment that they are rejecting. Some of the attacks against the Commission, the New Left included, claimed that this body expressed an anti-communist hegemony over the public sphere. The aftermath of the condemnation act showed that the Commission was the manifestation of an anti-communist consensus within several sectors of the civil society that managed to catch the attention of a crucial political actor (the president). The members' dominance over purported political and ideological superstructures could hardly be proven. After the condemnation act, serious rifts developed even among the Commission's former representatives, as some members simply took a step back from the limelight,

---

[145] Marci Shore, *The Taste of Ashes: The Afterlife of Totalitarianism in Eastern Europe* (New York: Crown Publishers, 2013), 358. See also fn. 143 on p. 464.

while others became engaged in polemics that reflected political polar-izations. At the same time, the passive attitude of most members of the Romanian Parliament toward the hooliganic manifestations of the extremists during the condemnation speech was hardly a conclusive proof of the ideological dominance of anti-communism. The rather limited fulfillment of the Commission's recommendations (see Tis-maneanu's chapter) could not be counted as an indication of a strong influence that this body had over the political decision makers. Gen-erally speaking, one cannot miss the fact that, several years removed from the condemnation speech, within the society and the political sphere, there is a long way to go before the Report's narrative could be suspected of attaining hegemonic qualities.

The gradual rejection of the Report on the part of many of the Romanian Academy's members or of representatives of some univer-sity departments across the country, the vehement opposition to it by the Romanian Orthodox Church, the condemnation of the condemna-tion speech by the Social Democratic Party, the inflamed reactions of various former communist officials (who also happen to be very pres-ent in local mass media) or of extreme-right groups showed that there are an important sections of the Romanian society strongly opposed to the narrative of the Report and to the idea of confronting the com-munist past. The advocates of the so-called "anti-communist hege-mony" simply brush off this reality. To the extent that, as one author proclaimed, in Romania, the abstract hegemonic entity he called along with other critics "anti-communism" becomes "a greater farce than communism itself."[146] Along this line of thinking, philosopher Gabriel Liiceanu, for example, was presented as much worse of an influence for Romanian history and culture than one of the main authors of Nicolae Ceauşescu's personality cult, poet Adrian Paunescu.[147] Liiceanu might be a public intellectual who, across the years, did make some question-

---

[146] Ciprian Şiulea, "Anticomunismul (I)."

[147] See Caius Dobrescu, "Gabriel Liiceanu lângă Herta Müller?" *Obser-vator Cultural*, no. 544 (October 2010), http://www.observatorcultural. ro/*articleID_24327-articles_details.html and Ciprian Şiulea, "Ce rămâne după ce tragem linia," *Criticatac.ro*, (28 noiembrie 2010),(http://www.criti-catac.ro/2991/ce-ramine-dupa-ce-tragem-linia/. For an exemplary reply to this type of articles see Andrei Cornea, "Contra Caium," *22*, 12 October 2010 http://www.revista22.ro/contra-caium-9096.html. All the links have been last accessed on June 8, 2012.

able statements on matters of cultural history, but to deny his commitment to and involvement in the construction of a democratic public culture in post-1989 Romania does indeed require a certain immoderation and ahistoricism that are simply destructive for any democratic dialogue. Or, it just presupposes total oblivion toward the original topic of discussion—the process of dealing with the past—with the purpose of settling accounts in a contemporary *Kulturkampf*.

At this point I would like to return to the matter of the populist facet of some of the reactions against the condemnation act. One local author claimed that the work of the Commission sought "to 'clutter' the collective memories of the communist past, thus dislodging in the process alternative forms of memories and experiences as 'nostalgia' or 'negationism.'"[148] For him, the Report became more a symbolic document rather than an analysis of the past upon which further discussion about and understanding of the past would ensue. In this reading, "it [the publication of the Report] was the moment of transition from moral and historical condemnation to memorialization and indoctrination. . . . Once the verdict was given, any later historical research that whishes to be validated domestically must necessarily reproduce this verdict."[149] Leaving aside the ludicrous presupposition that members of the Commission control the academic field and that they would repress scholarship in different key than that of the Report, what this type of approach seems to state is the inconsistency of a burdened past that needs to be overcome. Such criticism was not interested in the justifications about a regime's criminality (crimes against humanity, massive violations of basic human rights) and illegitimacy (total absence of mechanisms of democratic accountability and of pluralism). It simply rejected the validity or relevance of the process of working through the communist past.

The critics who adopted this position often combined the claim for "hegemony of anti-communism" with "the imperative of private

---

[148] Florin Poenaru, "'Tismăneanu Report' as Autobiography. History Writing at the End of (Soviet) Modernity," *Studia UBB Sociologia*, vol. LVI, no. 2, 2011, 26.

[149] Florin Poenaru, "Nostalgie, pedagogie, umor sau despre a doua venire a anti-comunismului," http://www.criticatac.ro/2034/nostalgie-pedagogie-umor-sau-despre-a-doua-venire-a-anti-comunismului/, (last accessed May 22, 2012).

memories." As one of them more brusquely declared, "I don't need to have someone come and tell me that my life was different from how it was."[150] This is in my opinion the populist facet of the criticism against the Commission and the Report: the authors I discuss constructed a political field that opposed a fully unified—but essentially fictional—people against a small minority ("the hegemonic anti-communists"), who is placed outside the realm of authentic or legitimate representation on either matters of the past, politics, or culture. Jan Werner-Müller emphasized that "it is a hallmark of populism—and a structural one, independent of any particular national context or policy issue—that it construes an 'unhealthy coalition' between an elite that doesn't really belong and marginal groups that don't really belong either."[151] In the Romanian case, antiestablishment narratives basically equated the condemnation act and the Report (and implicitly the support for them) with marginality (cloaked as hegemony) fuelled by the putative mis-memory and misrepresentation of history.

Furthermore, as discussed throughout the present article, one of the essential tasks that followed from the condemnation act was the duty to own one's past. That is, to assess how individual or group memories can be situated within the bigger picture of communism as a political regime. Or, to use a social psychologist's formulation, after December 2006, Romanian society had to engage into a "dialogue between factual truth and diversity of opinions, individual/subjective and official remembrances. Not all members of a national community will tell the

---

[150] Ciprian Şiulea, "La ce bun expertiza," *Vatra*, no. 20-11 (2010), 33.

[151] Jan-Werner Müller, "Getting a Grip on Populism," *Dissent. A Quarterly of Politics and Culture*, September 23, 2011, (http://www.dissentmagazine.org/blog/getting-a-grip-on-populism, last accessed June 3, 2012). Müller's article offers an answer for the critique from the left that the authors, grouped under the umbrella of *Criticatac.ro*, attempt to inject in Romanian contemporary public sphere. The author of *Contesting Democracy* argues that the Left should "by all means" mobilize "to articulate a vision of society that all citizens could potentially share." But they should do it "through making political arguments and with policy proposals, not by relying on a populist imaginary." The Romanian critics' consistent failure to engage into an alternative reading of the communist past or to dwell on the Report's content in itself indicates that the group from *Criticatac.ro* is yet to overcome a populist imaginary.

same stories."[152] Historian James Mark judiciously argued that communist regimes were also "biocracies," systems in which "an individual's chances of succeeding are determined by his or her ability or readiness to construct a politically acceptable public autobiography."[153] In this context, personal stories of self-accomplishment or anti-victim stories will ran counter with the Report's narrative about systemic "illegitimacy and criminality." However, to bring in private memories of the past as counterarguments against the epistemic, analytical overview of the communist dictatorship seems at least forced, if not altogether an exercise in sacrificing scholarship for safeguarding historical subjectivities. Claiming the preeminence of a purported "naturally occurring diversity of experiences, perspectives and interpretations"[154] comes close a fetishization of private memories. There is already extensive literature on communist subjectivity that revealed how (auto)biographies were altered and reinvented at various stages of Soviet-type regimes. Furthermore, as Mark has shown, post-communism brought about its own series of rewriting of the selves.[155] In this context, how *natural* is the memory of communism as a lived system? And, should it be considered mutually exclusive from the assessment of the regime as a dictatorship that was criminal and illegitimate?

These questions bring us back to the issue of empathy. Most of the critics of the Report were bothered, as discussed earlier, by the fact that academic discourse was combined with a traumatic narrative emphatic of the victims' experience. Legal scholar Mark Osiel stressed that discursive democracy in reference with the process of dealing with past fails "when the victims claim a monopoly over the meaning of the event, brooking no disagreement over its interpretation and the reach of its relevance. It also fails to occur when partially complicit parties treat the legal condemnation of others as irrelevant to a moral assessment of their own conduct during the period."[156] As some of the quotes from the Report's critics already indicated, the hegemony of the

---

[152] Tileagă, "Communism and the Meaning," 489.

[153] Mark, *The Unfinished Revolution*, 174.

[154] Cristian Tileagă, "Communism in Retrospect: The Rhetoric of Historical Representation and Writing the Collective Memory of Recent Past," *Memory Studies* 2012 vol. 5, no. 4, 475.

[155] Mark, *The Unfinished Revolution*, 215.

[156] Osiel, *Mass Atrocity*, 150.

victims was defined exactly in terms of the impossibility to consider their experience relevant to the moral assessment of communism as a lived system. Or as one Romanian author bluntly stated, "absolutely all causes served by human beings throughout history have produced victims... "[157] Osiel went even further; he argued that the invocation of popular memory as a counter point to the past as dictatorship because of the former purported *immunity* from elite manipulation "is largely a populist shibboleth."[158] Ultimately, the great danger of delegitimizing the truth-telling work of a Commission such as the Romanian one is the denial of historical thinking. Historian Michael Geyer remarked, in an article on the role of World War II in German history, that such an act "does not do away with the past—but it is injurious to the present."[159] In other words, many Romanians own positive private memories of the communist historical experience, but to disregard the regime's mass crimes, massive violations of human rights, dictatorial rule, or disastrous social engineering would simply mean walking away from the past.

IV. Where We Are and What Comes Next?

Romanian historian Florin Țurcanu, a year after the condemnation speech, wrote in one of the most important Romanian cultural weeklies: "[for many years] the trial of communism has uselessly eclipsed the idea of a history of communism [in Romania]. It is enough to mention the seductive, but intellectually sterile forms of 'communism as parenthesis,' of communism as 'non-history' or as 'exit from national history'. . . . National history unites, history of communism divides. The history of Romanian communism brings about conflicting tensions and interpretations within the very core of collective consciousness."[160] Furthermore, the same author declared that the long-term relevance of the Report will

---

[157] Alexandru Matei, "Introducere în estetica puterii (fragmen)," *Vatra*, no. 20–11 (2010), 58.

[158] Osiel, *Mass Atrocity*, 231.

[159] Michael Geyer, "The Place of the Second World War in German Memory and History," *New German Critique*, vol. 71 (Spring–Summer, 1997), 12.

[160] Țurcanu, "Istoria comunismului."

only be confirmed by the scholarship that can be developed on the basis of the avenues of research that it opened and considering that on some disciplinary areas it basically closed a historiographical stage.

However, the present article has shown how the discussion about the Report gradually evolved from a debate on how the criminality of the regime affects individual, social, cultural, economic, or institutional assessments of communism as lived system into a polemic about a putative "anti-communist hegemony" that alienates the people and blocks alternatives to the post-1989 status quo. From this point of view, Țurcanu's judicious conclusion on the stakes of the Report's aftermath requires a caveat that was best formulated by another commentator. Historian Cristian Vasile, the scientific secretary of the Commission, taking into account the cumulative radicalization of the criticism against the condemnation act, remarked in 2011 that "the real stakes of this debate (historiographical, moral, and so on) have been blurred because of the strange discourse tied to the ever more evident affirmation of a new, young, anti-anti-communist left."[161] I would add that in the end it is not that important what sort of ideological trend is struggling for preeminence. The fundamental problem is that the process of dealing with the past becomes a victim of either temporary political polarizations or of attempts to delegitimize public actors who still advocate the importance of the lessons of the traumatic historical experience of the communist period. Critics of the Report and of the condemnation act, regardless of political coloring, gradually become ever more unwilling to engage in memory work or epistemic inquiry. Their critical endeavor ultimately foundered into political philippics against either a perceived establishment (President Băsescu's administration, various governments, or post-communism as a whole) or a section of the cultural elite, which supported the Report and the condemnation act (without being however the only group to do so).

Despite the fact that from many points of view the Commission's Report depatrimonialized historical analysis of Romanian communism

---

[161] Cristian Vasile "Cinci ani de la Raportul final. Despre condamnare—nu doar symbolică—a regimului comunist," *Contributors.ro* 17 December 2011, http://www.contributors.ro/cultura/cinci-ani-de-la-raportul-final-despre-o-condamnare-%E2%80%93-nu-doar-simbolica-%E2%80%93-a-regimului-comunist,- last accessed June 5, 2012.

(through deideologization/mythologization and reprofessionalization[162]) and denormalized the dictatorial past, many individuals, newspapers, weeklies, blogs, TV shows, and so on have seemingly decided that this collective effort could not be a starting point for further discussion and debate. It is no surprise therefore to find out from surveys that concepts such as "suffering [during communism]" have a rather limited and skewed understanding within the population. At the level of the public sphere, the complex determinants of suffering under a communist regime have yet to enter into discussion. The invention of entities, which supposedly either conceal the "truth" about suffering or overinflate it for the sake of their own symbolic profit, are preferred. In such context, the whole point of working through the past is missed.

To return to my initial puzzle, I would conclude that one of the explanations for the apparent absence of a more complex and internalized individual and/or collective working through of the communist experience in Romania is the side-tracking of the process of dealing with the past. I mean by this the fact that introspective and public debates about crucial problems related to a better understanding of the communist experience, to an expansion of knowledge on the basis of public use of history, have been gradually replaced (or eclipsed) in some sectors of the public opinion by instrumentalist obsessions. For the latter, any narrative about the past that claims to attempt a clarification by subject, theme, or concept only serves to legitimize the powers that be in present Romania and to repress alternative (but undefined and unconstructed) interpretations. In this context, from 2006 until 2012, one could notice a cumulative process of delegitimization of the condemnation of the communist regime and of the Report upon which this act was based.

Working through the communist past in Romania is suffering from a case of arrested development. Areas of the public opinion stopped assessing the past for the past's sake, using it only as a pretext to continue talking about the present. If one expected after December 2006 a boom (or at least an important increase) of collective or individual self-

---

[162] Cristina Petrescu and Dragoş Petrescu "Mastering vs. Coming to Terms with the Past: A Critical Analysis of Post-Communist Romanian Historiography" in Sorin Antohi, Balázs Trencsényi and Péter Apor (eds.), *Narratives Unbound Historical Studies in Post-Communist Eastern Europe* (Budapest/ New York: CEU Press, 2007), 311–408.

evaluations, the years that followed revealed the contrary. Current public entanglements serve for many as sole reasons to play the card of the communist past. Under the circumstances, the entrapment of polemics consists in the fact that the past owns no value in itself for it merely turned into a pun for the present. For the impatient, this could be the sign of the impossibility of a culture of contrition in Romania. For the persevering, the fate of the Report and of the condemnation act might appear as part and parcel of a protracted and bitter public discussion about the meaning of the past for Romania's present and future. If we are to look at historian Dirk Moses's analysis of the attitudes of German intellectuals toward the Nazi past, one could argue that this difficult discursive process will be essential to bringing a long-awaited political consensus about the democratic institutions of the post-communist state. Such resolution though remains in the making for many years, if one is to take into consideration both the almost paralyzing constitutional crisis in Romania during the summer–autumn of 2012[163] or vehemently antiestablishment, antiliberal, populist and sometimes anti-European discourses advanced by various, young and old, representatives of this country's public sphere.

---

[163] See *The European Commission for Democracy Through Law* (Venice Commission), Opinion no. 685/2012, December 17, 2012, http://www.venice.coe.int/webforms/documents/?pdf=CDL-AD(2012)026-e, last accessed on January 7, 2013

Nikolai Vukov

Past Intransient/Transiting Past: Remembering the Victims and the Representation of Communist Past in Bulgaria

As in most other East European countries, commemorative attention to victims of totalitarian rule held a central place in the public discourses after 1989 in Bulgaria. In the stead of the grand narrative of antifascism and partisan resistance during World War II, which was sustained in the communist period, there came to the fore long suppressed testimonies about the crimes of the regime and facts whose disclosure called for ethical and historical justice. The terror of the so-called People's Courts, the brutal treatment of the democratic opposition after 1944, the murders of political opponents, the purges and the terror of Stalinization, the crude reality of the labor camps, and so on—all these stepped out of the realms of silence and triggered public demands for a proper historical evaluation. Customarily accompanied by rigorous debates, the acts of remembrance and commemoration to the communist victims sought to respond to the newly emerging memories and to narrate about the communist times in ways that were unthinkable before—through the discourse of terror and repression, through examples of violent death and crushed fates. With them, the Bulgarian society in the first post-communist decade witnessed an increased ambiguity of mourning and a changed sensitivity to memory and sacred death. It was not the communist special dead that would have the right to "demand" commemoration as the persecuted elect, but the "other" dead—those, whom the Party itself had persecuted, imprisoned in camps, tortured and killed. While the pantheon of communist heroes was gradually crumbling, the bodies of political victims of the communist regimes emerged for public view, creating "communities of mourners"[1] and calling for proper commemoration.

Considering its enormous significance for the symbolic overturning of the communist rule and for developing an anti-communist stance in the first years after 1989, within two decades and a half this memory resource underwent a gradual exhaustion. The latter manifested in a general relativization, overshadowing by other issues of political and social pertinence, and substitution by new realms of commemorative attention. The hardships of the socio-economic transition, the whirlpools of political developments in the course of twenty-five years, the interplay between nostalgia and rejection of the recent past[2] not only led to the progressive sidestepping of references to communist crimes in public remembrance and political ceremonies, but also situated the very issue of coming to terms with the communist past on problematic grounds. In the current article, I will discuss the issue of time and temporal distance in maintaining an ethical distance to the communist past, as well as the failure to extend the sensitivity to this distance two decades and a half after the political changes. By shedding light on aspects of the public remembrance of communist victims in Bulgaria after 1989 (monuments, museum representations, public rituals, legislation, political meetings, and so on), I will address the issues of relativism in the course of time's passing, the encounter between contested notions of commemorative legitimacy, and the ethics of remembrance beyond the framework of immediate political associations.

Among the main questions to be addressed in the text are: how public commemorations reflected the penetration of politics into the sphere of collective memory and what changes they underwent in the course of two and a half decades; how this memory resource changed over time and what has been its interplay with attempts for moral judgment and historical assessment; how commemorations contributed to elaborating notions of the communist past, and what was their role in coupling these notions with relativist or revisionist readings. Draw-

---

[1] Katherine Verdery, *The Political Lives of Dead Bodies: Reburial and Postsocialist Change* (New York: Columbia University Press, 1999), 164.

[2] See for example Stefan Troebst and Ulf Brunnbauer (eds.), *Zwischen Nostalgie, Amnesie und Allergie: Erinnerung an den Kommunismus in Suedosteuropa* (Cologne: Böhlau, 2007).

ing parallels between instances of public remembrance in the first years after 1989 and the celebrations of the twentieth anniversary after the political changes, the paper will outline the new emphases that occurred in the representation of the communist period and the intransient nature of trauma beyond the vicissitudes of the post-communist transition.

Looking Back in Anger:
The First Post-Communist Years

The attention to the victims of the communist regime started almost immediately after November 10, 1989 in Bulgaria. Within days after the overturn of the head of state Todor Zhivkov, claims to shed light on the persecutions and crimes committed by the communist regime and to disclose the truth about its victims were raised. Already until the end of 1989, detailed data about people who died in communist repressions were disclosed to the public and, despite the political contestations that emerged, it exercised an enormous political and psychological effect for the Bulgarian society at the time. In the stead of the dissolving pantheon of the special dead of the communist period (partisans, communists, and Soviet army soldiers), a set of personalities and events that were previously unknown to the wide public came forth to social awareness and turned into a focus of media presentations and political debates. Already toward the end of the *ancien régime*, the communist party itself demonstrated an intention to admit about having committed crimes. It claimed to take responsibility for the lives it ruined. However, this was an admission not about the labor camps and the numerous arrested and killed during the regime's existence, but, almost exclusively about the members of the Party who had suffered and perished during the Stalinization period or after. Among the first ones who were conmemorated along these lines were the victims of the communist purges in the late 1940s. Of particular significance was the case of Traicho Kostov and his comrades, who were sentenced to death in the show trials and were surrounded by due silence for decades on, limited solely to the label of "mistakes in the years of the personality cult." Aside from special decisions of the Communist party for their rehabilitation and proposals for naming streets and public institutions after him, Traicho Kostov and his comrades became a target of intensive exploration. It resulted in the publication of the trials' proceedings, memoirs, documents and monographs about their lives.[3] However, by admitting the crime committed against Kostov and his comrades after 1989, and by publicly embracing the garment of repentance, the communist party aimed to save face while keeping silent about crimes on other victims —non-Party members and less known cases. Yet, by pointing at victims coming from its own ranks, the Party actually sought to confess guilt without endangering the aura of communist ideas.

The cases in which the Party manifested an intention to repent (and here we can refer exclusively to examples similar to the one of Traicho Kostov) were far from being the sole ones that stirred the public attention in the first post-communist years. Parallel to the reemerging remembrance of the victims of the intra-party purges, the other main realm of public interest were the repressions against the democratic opposition after 1944 and the murders of the main political figures that opposed the establishment of the communist regime.[4] The focus fell upon the leaders of the agricultural union (e.g., Nikola Petkov, G. M. Dimitrov, and their collaborators), who were the most prominent representatives of the political opposition in the first years after 1945; as well as on members of other smaller formations in the interwar and war periods. Information about their persecution and imprisonment, about the trials or sentences without trials, about incarceration, execution, or forceful emigration—all these were disclosed in avalanche-like form during the first months after 1989, turning the previous concealment of the crimes into an accusation in itself.

---

[3] Boris Hristov, *Izpitanieto. Spomeni za protsesa i sadbata na Traicho Kostov i negovata grupa* (Sofia: Universitetsko izdatelstvo Sv. Kliment Ohridski, 1995); Petar Yapov, *Traicho Kostov i Nikola Geshev: Sadebnite procesi prez 1942 i 1949 g.* (Sofia: IK Iztok Zapad 2003); Georgi Chankov, *Ravnosmetkata* (Sofia: IK Hristo Botev, 2000); Georgi Chankov, *Ravnosmetkata v dokumenti, spomeni, statii, intervyuta, pisma* (Sofia: IK Hristo Botev, 2001).

[4] Zhoro Tsvetkov, *Sadat nad opozitsionnite lideri* (Sofia: Kupesa, 1991; Georgi M. Dimitrov, *Prisada sreshtu komunizma 1949–1972. Statii, rechi i izkazvania* (Sofia: IK Tsanko Tserkovski, 1991); Nikola D. Petkov, *Predsmartnite pisma na Nikola D. Petkov do Georgi Dimitrov i Vassil Kolarov, 19 avgust–22 septemvri 1947* (Sofia: Universitetsko izdatelstvo Sv. Kliment Ohridski, 1992).

In parallel to similar communist takeovers across the region, in the spring of 1945, the Bulgarian communist party undertook mass persecution of political opponents and succeeded to split existing political parties. As a result of the crushing of the opposition, thousands of political opponents were killed, tens of thousands were interned and scattered around the country, and many people found emigration as the only way of survival. On August 16, 1947, the leader of the opposition, Nikola Petkov, was sentenced to death and hanged, which virtually marked the ultimate establishment of single-party rule in the country. The remembrance of these events and the honoring of the opposition leaders were at the core of public attention in the first years after 1989, finding expression in various political activities and artistic forms. While many of the towns and villages in the country had the names of these leaders reflected in streets, squares, and public institutions, a set of literary and theater forms were prepared to recreate the drama of these events and to stir public awareness about the forceful ways of introducing communism in the country.

No less appalling were the disclosures about the dimensions of the so called "Red terror" in the first postwar years. After Soviet troops entered into Bulgarian territory in August and September 1944, several thousand people (according to some estimations reaching twenty and even thirty thousand) were killed at the direct order of Georgi Dimitrov from the Moscow Bureau and of the local leadership of the communist party. The victims were of different professional and social background—policemen, mayors, teachers, clerks, industrialists, lawyers, doctors, priests, journalists, and so on. Many of these victims disappeared without a trace and investigation about their fate was not taken up until the end of the communist rule. The main perpetrators of these murders were the 8,000 criminals, who were released from jail on September 9, 1944. It had been claimed that they were political prisoners, albeit the large majority of them were sentenced for criminal acts. Until the end of 1944, they swamped the country in repressions and murders. Their victims (state officials, priests, members of the intelligentsia, ordinary people) were buried in mass graves, which discovery and unearthing took place only after 1989. The violence in the country did not cease with the end of the terror of the first postwar months. Soon after the war, around 2,000 Bulgarian officers were persecuted upon their return from the war front. The proletarian dictatorship included also the nationalization of private property, the collectivization of agricultural lands, the exercising of total political control on cultural and religious activities, the confiscation of church properties—all of these accompanied with due persecution of individuals and groups of the population.

Seeking to fulfill an information void about these events, within the first years after 1989, a series of previously inaccessible archival materials were disclosed and published: on the establishment of the communist power and the activities of the Fatherland Front;[5] on the antireligious propaganda and the religious persecution in the first years of the People's power;[6] on secret documents of the Comintern and undisclosed conversations between Bulgarian and Soviet authorities;[7] on the involvement of historians, journalists, and writers in the political and social changes after 1944, and so on. Made possible by the liberalized access to state and party archives after 1989, these collections of documentary materials were an opportunity to shed light on taboos of the pervious years. More importantly, these specialized publications found their abundant reflection in the pages of newspapers and journals, triggering a wave of recollections, witness testimonies and memoirs about the crimes of the communist period. This phenomenon helped supplanting information beyond the relative lack of archival evidence and it revealed a significant focus on personal recollections and familial testimonies in the reconstruction of historical events.

Another topic that captivated public attention were the victims of the People's Court and the fate of the ministers and military officials who took key state positions in the period between 1941 and 1944. While some were trialed and executed, others were taken for investi-

---

[5] See for example, Lyubomir Ognyanov, (ed.), *Borbi i chistki v BKP (1948–1953). Dokumenti i materiali* (Sofia: Glavno upravlenie na arhivite, 2001); Zdravko Dafinov, *Pod diktaturata na proletariata (1944–1956). Spomeni, dnevnitsi, pisma* (Sofia: IK Rodina, 1998).

[6] Gavril Belovezhdov, *Stradanieto ne e etiket—to e dostoinstvo. Dokumenti ot sadebnite protsesi sreshtu katolicheskata tsarkva v Balgaria prez 50-te godini na 20-ti vek* (Sofia: Universitetsko izdatelstvo Sv. Kliment Ohridski, 2001); Daniela Kalkandjieva, *Balgarskata pravoslavna tsarkva i darzhavata, 1944–1953* (Sofia: Albatros, 1997).

[7] Angel Vekov, *Stalin i Balgarskiat komunizam. Iz sekretnite ruski i balgarski arhivi. Protokoli, Stenogrami. Dnevnitsi. Pisma* (Sofia: Damyan Yakov, 2002).

gations to the Soviet Union and many disappeared without a trace. Between December 1944 and April 1945, the People's Court stated as its purpose the punishment of those culpable for Bulgaria's participation in World War II. It involved state prosecutors to whom the party affiliation, not the juridical preparedness was of key importance. The first supreme committee of the People's Court dealt with the legal cases against the regents, prime ministers, and ministers in governments of the war years, as well as fifty-one court counselors. The second committee targeted 129 representatives at the National Assembly and other civil and military officials. Illegal from its inception, the "court" tried more than 11,000 people and issued 9,155 sentences, 2,730 of which were death sentences, and 1,305 were lifelong imprisonment. About 1,500 people were sentenced posthumously—in fact, most of them were killed during the red terror and the sentences therefore aimed to legalize these crimes postfactum. On February 1, 1945, death sentences were issued for the three regents (Prince Kiril Preslavski, Professor Bogdan Filov, and General Nikola Mihov), twenty-two ministers, sixty-seven Parliamentary representatives, forty-seven army generals and colonels. The sentenced were executed on the same day. Most of their relatives were resettled in different parts of the country and were persecuted as "enemies of the people." It was only after 1989 when details about the trials of state officials in service during the World War II were disclosed and presented in several systematic historiographic studies.[8] Aside from them, the media of the first postcommunist years abounded with testimonies and reflections about the court and its victims. Most of the public protests against the communist party drew heavily on these sentences in order to represent symbolically the nature of the previous regime.

Another particularly sensitive realm of commemorative focus in the first years after 1989 was related to the communist labor camps and the interment of political opponents and ordinary people. Created in December 1944—in the midst of the ongoing terror in the coun-

---

[8] Nikolay Poppetrov, Polya Meshkova, and Dinyu Sharlanov, *Balgarskata gilotina. Taynite mehanizmi na Narodnia sad* (Sofia: Agentsia Demokratsia, 1994); Petar Semerdjiev, *Narodniat sad v Balgaria, 1944–1945* (Blagoevgrad: Makedonia Press, 1998); Tasho v. Tashev, *Ministrite v Balgaria, 1879–1999* (Sofia: Akademichno izdatelstvo Prof. Marin Drinov, 1999).

try, the labor camps were a destination of exile and imprisonment for around 220,000 people. Most of them were sent there without trial, or on the basis of unfounded or exaggerated accusations of being enemies to the communist state. The camps functioned intensively until 1962 and were scattered in different locations of the country. The most notorious ones were those of Belene, Lovech, Skravena, Bogdanov Dol, and so on. Albeit officially closed in 1962, some of the camps continued to exist into the late 1980s. For example, they became destinations for arrested and interned Bulgarian Turks who protested against the violent change of their names. While previously the information about the almost fifty camps that existed in Bulgaria was limited to mere awareness of their existence, details about the rules of their functioning were expectedly not accessible. The voices of the victims, the memories about those who did not survive, the conditions of torture and humiliation erupted after the fall of the regime and turned into a major tool for its delegitimation. Already in the first years after 1989, memoirs of political prisoners and camp interns were published[9] together with studies about individual camps.[10] General overviews with witness sources and documentary materials about life in the camps appeared in Bulgarian and in foreign languages.[11] An interesting example of the first post-communist years was the slogan with the map of

---

[9] Hristo Brazitsov, *3000 noshti v zatvora* (Sofia: Universitetsko izdatelstvo "Sv. Kliment Ohridski," 1991); Konstantin Kostov, *Zatvornik K-89* (Sofia: Universitetsko izdatelstvo Sv. Kliment Ohridski, 1992); Stefan Tanev, *Otvoreni pisma. Spomeni i izpovedi na glavnia redaktor na vestnik "Utro," pisani v Tsentralnia zatvor* (Sofia: Universitetsko izdatelstvo Sv. Kliment Ohridski, 1994).

[10] Georgi N. Vassilev, *Ostrov "Persin." Pozorat na Balgaria* (Sofia: Universitetsko izdatelstvo "Sv. Kliment Ohridski," 1995); Stefan Bochev, *Belene, Skazanie za kontslagerna Balgaria* (Sofia: Nauka i Izkustvo, 1999).

[11] Ekaterina Boncheva (ed.), *Balgarskiat Gulag: svideteli. Sbornik dokumentalni razkazi za kontslagerite v Balgaria* (Sofia: Izdanie na Vestnik Demokratsia, 1991); Penka Stoyanova and Emil Iliev, *Politicheski opasni litsa—vadvoryavania, trudova mobilizatsia, izselvania sled 1944 g.* (Sofia: Universitetsko izdatelstvo Sv. Kliment Ohridski, 1991); Petko Ogoyski, *Zapiski po balgarskite stradaniya, 1944–1989, tom 1–3* (Sofia: Fenomen, 1995); Tzvetan Todorov (ed.), *Au nom de peuple. Témoignes sur les camps communists* (Paris: Editions de l'Aube, 1992); Todorov, Tz. (ed.), *Voices from the Gulag: Life and Death in Communist Bulgaria* (University Park, PA: Pennsylvania State University Press, 1999).

Bulgaria covered by human skulls at places where labor camps existed. Created by the Union of Democratic Forces before the first democratic elections in 1990, the slogan gained enormous popularity and—despite producing, on the long-term, a negative reaction and withdrawal of the support for the anti-communist opposition, it is still remembered as a major symbol of the first post-communist decade.

Another dramatic episode in the first years after 1944 that came to the fore of public awareness were the attempts for a forceful "self-identification" of the population living in the area of the Pirin Mountain in the census of 1946. The pressure on more than 300,000 people to identify themselves as "Macedonians" led to protests. Around one hundred people were killed, several thousands were resettled, and widespread terror fell upon the region. This case was among the few examples of overt opposition against the communist power and it involved around one hundred secret organizations with nine voluntary troops that fought state authorities. The only real armed resistance against the regime was the one of the so-called *goryani* [people of the mountains] in 1945–1949. In response to generalized repression in the country, around thirty voluntary armed troops were formed. Fifty more came from neighboring Greece and Turkey. The overall number of *goryani* was around 1,800. They had a varied professional and social background, involving peasants, nationalists, former communists, former policemen, anarchists, and so on. In the fights with the regime, around 1,200 found their death, most of them actually shot without trial. It was again only after 1989 when the public could talk about these dramatic events and when memory accounts and archival evidence could shed light on this episode of the early communist years.

The release of abundant information about repressions in the decades of communist rule opened a commemorative gap that needed to be filled in urgently with relevant initiatives. Already in the first two years after the fall of the communist regime, demands were raised for commemorating the victims of totalitarianism—not only in terms of information about their fates during public meetings and protests, but also through monuments and memorials. The first memory resource that was utilized in this respect was related to the events of the so-called *Vazroditelen protses* [Revival process] of the mid-1980s, when the communist state organized a campaign to forcefully rename the Bulgarian Muslims with Slavic names, thus causing their mass emigration from the country.[12] In 1992, the first monument to the victims of totalitarianism in the period of 1944–1989 was built in the town of Momchilgrad in Southeast Bulgaria. Initially thought to be a monument to the *Vazroditelen protses*, it also listed the names of several opposition victims from the late 1940s. The unveiling of the monument took place on December 27—the day when eight years earlier the last victims of the renaming campaign had died. A commemoration prayer was read and wreaths were placed on behalf of the Parliament, the President, the Confederation of Labor "Podkrepa," social organizations, schools, municipalities and political parties. A minute of silence was taken as a sign of respect to the memory of people from the region who had died in communist camps and prisons.

In the years that followed, several other monuments to the victims of the *Vazroditelen protses* were built in other towns of the country, for example, Gorna Oryahovitsa and Aytos. There were also initiatives to raise monuments to the victims of the communist labor camps. In 1995, at the initiative of "Podkrepa" Trade Union Confederation and the Union of the Repressed, funds were collected for building a monument to the victims of the death camp in Lovech. The memorial complex included seven human figures and twelve columns and a cross—symbolizing the twelve apostles and Christ. In 1996, a monument to the victims of communism was constructed in Plovdiv in the yard of "Vassil Levski" school, near the place where several people were killed. At the initiative of "Rayna knyaginya" foundation, a memorial sign to those murdered after 1944 was created at their common grave. A monument to six young peasantist activists, victims of the communist regime, was unveiled near Lyubimets in 1998. A memorial plaque to seven Bulgarian officers and soldiers who were shot without a trial on September 12, 1944 by partisan guerilla troops was unveiled in Haskovo in 1999.

Until the end of the 1990s monuments to the victims of the communist repressions were placed in most of the large towns in Bulgaria, forming thus a trend that affected the memorial spaces in most town

---

[12] See for example, Boncho Asenov, *Vazroditelniyat protses i Darzhavna sigurnost* (Sofia: izd. avt., 1996); Mihail Gruev and Aleksey Kalyonski, *Vazroditelniyat protses: myusyulmanskite obshtnosti i komunisticheskiyat rezhim* (Sofia: Universitetsko izdatelstvo Sv. Kliment Ohridski, 2008).

centers in the country. In 1999, a memorial to the victims of the communist terror was built near Yambol, at the location where ten people were killed without trial by local communists. In 2000, the construction of a monument to the victims of communism in Bulgaria in the center of Pazardzhik began. "Sveti Georgi Pobedonosets" Foundation suggested to the municipality to raise a monument to the local priests killed after 1944 in Plovdiv. At the initiative of "Nikola Petkov" Agricultural Union, a monument to the repressed was constructed in Plovdiv, and in 2000, a monument to the victims of communism—a cross between two pillars, was unveiled in Perushtitsa. Chapels and memorial walls dedicated to the victims of totalitarianism were raised in Vidin and Sofia. Many of those monuments were based on religious imagery and stressed theological aspects of martyrdom. The chapel, the cross, and the tortured human figure were widely used in the anti-totalitarian memorial forms and symbolically equated the victims with Christ's suffering. Largely aiming to commemorate people who perished by the hands of the regime, they were expressions of a refusal "to bind meanings across dissimilar historical epochs" and of a new approach to the dead—"victims" rather than "heroes," mortal and vulnerable rather than undefeatable.

The remembrance of the victims of the totalitarian rule inscribed collective memory with images of torture and guilt and "rewrote the soul" of the national community with multiple recollections and versatile positions on commemoration. The rigid dividing line between whom to commemorate and how to commemorate, made it impossible for the symbolic loss to encompass the entire national community. The difficulty rested mostly in the outlining of the two groups—the repressed (both living and dead) and those who alleged their affiliation with the socialist ideas. While the former demonstrated their memory as heavily burdened with pain, threat and suffering, the latter insisted on the inherently noble character of the socialist credo and refused to be seen as related to persecutors and oppressors. The "visual recovery of the repressed past"[13] posed a challenge to the consolidation of collective identities around commonly embraced narratives—of national, historical, or cultural nature. In light of the encounter between the

---

[13] Beverly James, *Imagining Postcommunism: Visual Narratives of Hungary's 1956 Revolution* (College Station: Texas A&M University Press, 2005), 5.

different forms of commemoration and of the lack of negotiation between them, Bulgaria's post-communist coming to terms with the past revealed itself as problematic, uneasy, and (at least during the first decade after the political changes) hardly possible at all.

Authenticating the Past and Relativizing Its Meanings

With the creation of memorial forms and the development of respective commemorative ceremonies around them, Bulgarian society not only honored the memory of people, who were previously denied public recognition, but also manifested a turn in its self-representation as exercising a moral and ethical distance to the communist period. However, aside from the political and moral implications of such commemorative acts, the claims concerning the remembrance of the regime's victims touched closely on issues of historicity and data verification: to uncover the "factual nature" of these suppositions meant to certify that the past "had actually happened like that." It is important to point out, however, that most of the disclosed information was shocking enough for a society where the closed and centralized circle of information that existed before generated suspicion regarding the credibility of information that was not officially sanctioned. Overcoming the silence cast on events and figures from communist times was frequently approached with reservation, mistrust, and denial. These feelings had to be fought back by unveiling a range of evidence-based materials. At the face of explicit accounts about the scale and rigorousness of the crimes, there were suppositions about putative exaggeration in such reports, about possibly forged evidence and deceitful testimonies. Such reservations and denials needed to be approached by acts and strategies that confirmed that it was not a matter of coining "facts" that aimed to defeat the previous ideology, but was rather an issue of "undeniable" reality, which the society had to pay due attention. Reports about the waves of repressions; survivors' and witnesses' accounts; photo documentation of labor camps, tortured bodies, and death spots; biographic accounts about people persecuted by the regime; testimonies of émigrés from abroad—all these complemented and mutually supported each other. They were recurrent in various narrative and media forms, in political speeches and ritual occasions. Each of them testified to the fact that the regime's crimes did not result merely from political contestations, but it was based on actual events that took place in the past. All these materials had to convey the message that the violations of human rights was the most prominent factor in evaluating the period before 1989. It was the element on the basis of which the political and social life during communist times had to be analyzed. In such a way, while on the one hand, they sought to confirm facts considered to be beyond political judgments, on the other, they enforced the political call for justice, responsibility, and justified claims of public legitimacy.

The efforts for revealing and recreating such facts in the first post-communist years were, however, systematically obstructed by representatives of the previous regime and by the networks of state security and public institutions that functioned in favor of the political power before 1989. Very often, the investigations about guilt and responsibility for the crimes entered a vicious circle of inadequate and outdated legal regulations, putting thus the various claims for perpetrators' punishment into a continuous roundabout without an ultimate result. Among the first challenges that were encountered was the difficulty to secure sufficient evidence to prove the actual commitment of the crimes. A large amount of the documentation was not preserved, being intentionally destroyed or carefully concealed by the authorized institutions. Access to archival information was systematically denied. With the case of the labor camps for example, out of at least forty-five labor camps for regime's opponents, detailed documentation was preserved for only the last two that remained in function—Lovech and Skravena. The systematic obstacles to get access even to existing data about the crimes of the communist rule furthermore complicated the unearthing of necessary facts.

A notorious case in this respect was the secret operation for destroying the files of collaborators to the communist State Security system. Undertaken in January 1990—less than three months after the fall of the regime, the operation resulted in the destruction of almost half of the existing files. Although subsequently there was a legal procedure against the figures who commanded this operation, the destruction of evidence was irreversible and it put most future explorations on shaky grounds. The repercussions of this act and the continued speculations about the identities of those who were involved in the secret police (some of whom

bore direct responsibility for the policies and crimes of the regime) res-
onate in Bulgaria even today. Although in later years, the specialized
Commission for investigating the files of collaborators to the communist
secret police managed to publicize extensive reports about agents infil-
trated in various public institutions (army, university system, banking,
and so on), the suppositions about the "real" dimensions of this infiltra-
tion will always persist.

No less complicated was the problem of demanding legal responsibility and sentences for the perpetrators of crimes. For some of them
(such as those of the People's Court and the establishment of the communist power) it never actually turned into an issue, but was largely
limited to rehabilitating the victims in these events. For others, such
as the case of the labor camps, the attempt to achieve legal accountability was obstructed by statute of limitations for the murder of two
or more people, which was twenty years. In 1990, an amendment was
passed in the Parliament to extend it to thirty-five years, but it did not
refer explicitly to crimes that had already been committed and could
thus have no practical implication. A striking point is that, in spite of
the numerous testimonies that were found and reported, firm evidence
was collected for only about fourteen murders in the labor camps. Even
in these cases the attempts to put on trial those who were responsible
did not result in actual sentences. Proper juridical response was not
ensured for almost any acts of criminal nature that predated the political changes of 1989. Perpetrators from the previous regime remained
largely untouchable by the post-communit legal system. Despite recurrent calls for accountability for repressions and the broken human lives
during commemorative events, the issue of the responsibility of people
directly involved as functionaries with the previous regime is obliterated
and relativized with the claim that nothing actually could be proven.

In fact, this last interpretation gradually took prevalence in Bulgarian society at large. Although nowadays most of the instances testifying
about the regime's crimes are no longer denied and rejected, whenever
the case more closely approached, reservations spring forth and the
discussion turns to a shifting ground. The impossibility to measure the
"exact" number of victims and those persecuted, the difficulty to measure suffering and to identify, in the context of repression, who, when,
for what reasons, and by whom, facilitated the avoidance of the topic
and its gradual neglect. During the first years after 1989, the remem-

brance of the communist victims posed a sharp dividing line between the opponents of the regime and those who alleged their affiliation with socialist ideas. After the end of the 1990s, when this distinction was gradually blurred, the memory of the victims was to a lesser extent a fighting ground for political contestation. While in the 1990s the disclosure of facts about the regime's crimes encountered the danger of exaggeration and bias, in the second post-communist decade this memory resource was progressively relativized and also threatened by revisionist approaches. With the increasing temporal distance from the period before 1989, the issue of remembering communist victims was gradually overcome by other themes of political and social pertinence, and has entered the realm of relative neglect—both on political and general public levels. Although it preserved its position as a reference point in public ceremonies, its representation was mostly of customary and unavoidable character—one testifying to the withering of the commemorative potential, and to its transiting relevance in the representation of the communist past.

It is interesting to note, however, that toward the end of 1990s, a wide range of state institutions, political parties, and public organizations took part and manifested their engagement with the commemoration of the victims of the communist regime. During commemorations, the presence of state representatives was largely perceived as mandatory, and the participation of political parties' members—as indispensable in taking a moral stance against the communist period. Despite such demonstrative engagement, the presence in these ceremonies did not surpass the mere pronouncement of standardized statements against the repressive character of the communist regime, which seemed to bear the marks of a ceremonial obligation. These formal declarations were merely labels and they would not be extended through concrete steps. In none of the numerous sites where crimes were perpetratred can one find a museum that would sustain the visual message with a narrative and documentary account. References to communist rule continue to be absent from exhibitions in national and regional history museums in the country. The situation is striking also in view of the fact that until today the representation of the period in school textbooks and overviews of national history continues to be characterized by summary statements and formulaic pronouncements, hardly affording a deeper interpretative involvement.

In contrast to the enhanced attention to the recent past in the years that immediately followed the communist rule, the second decade and a half after 1989 revealed rather a state of indifference to what was before and a high level of disengagement from what are sometimes interpreted as "overpoliticized" aspects of memory. Whereas in the first years after 1989 the reconstruction of the communist past was done in the context of heightened public sensitivity and at the cost of ruptures and unbridgeable debates, nowadays, the publicly embraced denouncement of the communist rule as a totalitarian one has led to a prevailing restraint from approaching it through the lens of limited freedoms, persecution, and trauma. Together with the challenges that it brought in economic, social and demographic perspectives, the transition opened a stance for approaching the communist period along the lines of nostalgia and relativism. In the background of the now entranched commemorative rituals and references to the victims of the communist regime, the presence of the communist past in recent years is increasingly limited to nostalgic reminders—in advertisements, media, films, songs, and so on. It may not be a surprise in this respect that the most widespread historiographic form of the second post-communist decade turned out to be the memoirs and autobiographic accounts by communist officials.[14] They took it on as a personal obligation to share their recollections about the development of the country under their rule, trying to explain the motifs of their political decisions, or fighting with the proposed interpretations after 1989. Memoirs were published by some of the former military officials and participants in the partisan movement of the 1940s (some of whom were active memorialists before 1989 too),[15] by prominent journalists and intellectuals, historians and diplomats, or by people who had worked closely with the figures in power.[16] Under-

---

[14] See for example, Todor Zhivkov, *Sreshtu nyakoi lazhi* (Sofia: Delfin press, 1993); Stanko Todorov, *Do varhovete na vlastta. Politicheski memoari* (Sofia: IK "Hristo Botev," 1995); Ornyan Doynov, *Spomeni* (Sofia: IK "Trud," 2002).

[15] Slavcho Transki, *Nevazmozhni istini* (Sofia: IK "Slavika-RM," 1994); Atanas Semerdjiev, *Prezhivyanoto ne podlezhi na obzhalvane* (Sofia: IK "Trud," 1999); Dimo Stankov, *Sled dalgo malchanie. 42 godini v balgarskoto razuznavane* (Sofia: IK "Hristo Botev," 2001).

[16] Vladimir Topencharov, *Bessove na moeto vreme* (Sofia: Bulvest-2000, 1993); Hristo Radevski, *Razgovor sas sebe si. Nepublikuvan dnevnik* (Sofia: IK "Za-

standably, in these memoirs, the issues of repressions, persecutions, and violations of human rights were elegantly avoided, or, when occurring, were justified either by a "lack" of actual knowledge, or by accusations about victim's sabotage actions against the communist state.

An indicator of the shifting grounds in the memory about the communist victims and the communist period in general is the state of September 9, the day when communist Bulgaria celebrated the victory against fascism. Already in the first years after 1989, a range of labels were attached to this date, exposing a wide array of its possible interpretations: the beginning of the totalitarian period in Bulgaria, the end of Bulgarian independence, the day of "occupation" by Soviet troops, and the day of joining the "evil empire." In rejection to the previous propaganda framing of the event as a "triumph" of the antifascist resistance and a day of "liberation," this date was declared already in early 1990s as one of national mourning, of enslavement, shame and national disunity. To counteract such interpretations, a position was formulated by the political left not to dishonor the memory of the dead in the antifascist resistance and not to disregard their noble mission in opposing the spread of fascism in Europe. This clash of approaches opened the grand debate about Bulgarian fascism and antifascism, and the different opinions about the actual role of partisans and antifascists in the course of World War II, as well as in the first postwar years. Thus, on the one side there were the rejections of the putative equivalence between communism and Nazism and protests against historical revisionism, on the other, there was the insistence not to forget the perished in the first communist years and constant emphasis on the waves of repressions that followed September 9, 1944.

The clash of interpretations about that date led to regular battles during the 1990s between groups from the left that joined together veterans and socialist youth in festive celebrations, and groups of the democratic opposition that commemorated the victims of totalitarianism in Bulgaria. Whereas for the former, flowers and wreaths were placed on that date at monuments to the partisan movement antifas-

---

hari Stoyanov," 2000); Ivan Venedikov, *Poznayte gi po delata im. Balgarskata inteligentsia v moite spomeni* (Sofia: IK "Hristo Botev," 1993); Ilcho Dimitrov, *Vsichko teche... Spomeni* (Sofia: Tilia, 2000); Emil Aleksandrov, *Kultura i lichna vlast. Az rabotih s Lyudmila Zhivkova* (Sofia: Slantse, 1991).

cist resistance, for the latter, solemn processions were held to recently created monuments of the totalitarian victims and candles were lit in silence for their memory. The contest and physical encounters between the two groups left an undeniable mark on the memory of September 9 in the 1990s. After 2001, this dynamic was further complicated with the increasing involvement of nationalist and radical right groups, who chose September 9 as the day for their main political manifestations. The latter were especially visible in the celebrations of the sixtieth anniversary of the event, which was pompously staged by the ruling government of the socialist party and by the Bulgarian President Georgi Parvanov (former leader of the socialist party) as an anniversary of the victory over fascism. Largely as a reaction to this, the refusal of nationalist groups and formations of the radical right to accept the propagated "all-national character of the fight against fascism" resulted in the overall disclaiming of September 9 as a day holding any "national" significance. Beyond the anti-communist mode that it maintained, the nationalistic interpretion of the event and of the postwar period in general drew on the interpretation of communist victims outside their historical and moral contexts, as they became solely as losses suffered by the nation. This interpretation simultanneously attributed attention to the suffering of individuals and groups during the totalitarian rule and dissolved their commemoration within a series of other nationally colored events. Sometimes the victims of communism were merged with supporters of authoritarian rule during World War II.

A notable step toward finding common ground for interpreting September 9 in recent years was the proposal made by the Bulgarian President in 2009 to declare the date as a "day of forgiveness and national reconciliation." His major arguments were in fact again relativizing ones: that it was not very clear who the victims were both prior and after the establishment of communist rule; that there were no reliable grounds to distinguish between victims and perpetrators, so it was not possible to achieve legitimate historical interpretation; that after a certain passage of time such distinctions did not matter much, therefore time actually helped to reach a distance and evaluative disengagement. The proposal and its arguments clearly pursued the relativization of the communist crimes and their gradual absolution with the passage of time. The latter was particularly problematic if one takes into consideration the absence of public repentance about the victims of totalitarian rule on behalf of the party that has been a direct heir of the political system before 1989—the socialists. One should keep in mind that although in 2000 the Bulgarian Parliament accepted a law for proclaiming the communist regime in Bulgaria as criminal, since then no admittance of responsibility was expressed among members of the socialist party. On the contrary, the celebration of September 9 was hailed as one of the brightest days in modern Bulgarian history. From such a viewpoint, the search for political reconciliation was obviously yet another step to reduce the poignant content of this "victory day" and to avoid the claims of historical and legal accountability for what came in its aftermath.

The gradual displacement of the memory about regime's victims from the public evaluation of the communist period was well expressed also in the celebrations of the twentieth anniversary of the regime's fall on November 10. This day, for the Bulgarian population was accompanied with an overall confusion of what to celebrate and how to celebrate. Following a continuous avoidance of the anniversary and a lack of interest in marking the day when the communist party made a desperate attempt to save its power by replacing its general secretary, in the end, the Bulgarian society followed the pattern of other East European countries and swiftly organized artistic happenings to mark the event. Aside from being a direct replica to the celebrations in Berlin, the artificial wall that was built in the center of the Bulgarian capital yet again confirmed the discarding of the commemorative references and the new emphases in the representation of the communist past along the lines of irony, entertainment, and festive happening. The latter was particularly well outlined in the web forums and Internet discussions. They had become the main arena of sharing views on the communist years over the past years. Yet, in parallel to the changed means of communication, other factors (e.g., generational differences or different life experiences) exercised an impact on the interpretation of the "recent" past. In the first post-communist years, the need to remember encountered a diversity of approaches for alternative recollection. But as we increasingly moved away from the pre-1989 period, the act of rememberance was engulfed by quicksands, which often made the very idea of "remembrance" problematic. The distinctions did not follow anymore the dividing line of "positive" or "negative," left- or right-wing evaluation of the past. They rather reflected the presence or absence of shared experience in those years, or the availability or lack of memory about that period. The new generations for whom the communist times have been nothing else but times preceding their lives accelerate the shift from a "memory of communism," to a "memory about communism," and then to memory that may even have no direct relationship to communism as a reference. In such a situation, the remembrance of communist times is unavoidably marked by the trap of emptiness, despite the gradual institutionalization of memory cultures and demonstrative political stances about the period in question.

Conclusion

I would like to emphasize that the remembrance of the victims of the communist rule oscillates nowadays between revisionist claims and politics of neglect. This phenomenon is indicative for the reworking of the problematic past in the period of the post-communist "transition." Whereas in the early 1990s, commemorative acts testified to the entering of the victim's memory in public memory and in the political discourse. It also reflected its transformative potential after decades of silence. Gradually however, this memory began to illustrate the penetration of politics in public commemorations, and the increasing disengagement of Bulgarian society from what was seen as memory's politicization. Having played a key role in creating a discourse of detachment from the pre-1989 years, remembrance ultimately fell prey to the nostalgic revision of communist decades and to discourses flirting with the reengagement with a period that failed to receive a systematic historical representation until today. After two decades and a half of attempts for moral judgment and historical assessment, the memory resource about the crimes of the communist regime increasingly led to formulaic, relativist, or revisionist readings. In the process, the ethics of remembrance were subordinated to memory's political appropriations. The avoidance of traumatic references to the communist past and the revisionist tendencies in its representation opened however a new gap in the negotiation between individual and collective memories that are yet to be ossified. It is this tension and the accumulating attempts of revisiting the period from a plethora of angles and representations, which, in my view, would maintain "the intransient nature" of the communist past beyond the ever expanding temporal distance.

We would certainly not be able to reduce the issue of the gradual relativization of communist crimes only to the increasing temporal distance after 1989, the same way as memory of the victims cannot be the sole lens to assess the changed attitudes to the communist period. The variations in political reactions against attempts to restore practices from those times; the expansive debates on overcoming the heritage of communism; the continuation of opening of secret files of collaborators with the secret police, and so on—all indicate a steady process of reassessing the period before 1989 and the attempts to come (somehow) to terms with the past— albeit not necessarily involving the issue of justice. Not surprisingly, parallel to this process, one can witness the softening of the critical stance concerning the communist period and a reduction of the transformational praxis mainly to time—as healing wounds and bringing reconciliation. But, in order to have an idea of such transformations, one needs to have a notion of the evolution of a certain ethos. With respect to communist crimes, this ethos have not yet undergone the necessary change. This is due because of the missing repentance on the left-wing supporters regarding crimes before 1989. Another cause is lack of legal accountability because of the invocation of the statute of limitations. This way responsibility is entirely absent. The passing of time has not played much in favor of the truth about these crimes and their ongoing neglect is yet another confirmation of the present state of things.

List of Contirbutors

David BRANDENBERGER is Associate Professor of History and International Studies at University of Richmond. Among his publications are *National Bolshevism: Stalinist Mass Culture and the Formation of Modern Russian National Identity, 1931–1956* (Harvard, 2002) and *Propaganda State in Crisis: Soviet Ideology, Indoctrination and Terror under Stalin, 1928–1941* (Yale, 2011).

Igor CAŞU is Associate Professor at the State University of Moldova and director of Center for the Study of Totalitarianism. Among his publications are: *Duşmanul de clasă. Represiuni politice, violenţă şi rezistenţă în R(A)SS Moldovenească, 1924–1956* (Cartier, 2014) and "Stalinist Terror in Soviet Moldavia, 1940–1953" in Kevin McDermott and Matthew Stibbe (eds.), *Stalinist Terror in Eastern Europe* (Manchester University Press, 2010).

Daniel CHIROT is Herbert J. Ellison Professor of Russian and Eurasian Studies at Henry M. Jackson School, University of Washington. Among his publications are: the co-authored book (with Scott L. Montgomery), *The Shape of the New: Four Big Ideas and How They Made the Modern World* (Princeton University Press, 2015) and the co-edited volume (with Gi-Wook Shin and Daniel Sneider), *Confronting Memories of World II: Recriminations and Reconciliations in Europe and Asia* (University of Washington Press, 2014).

John CONNELLY is Professor at University of California at Berkeley and director of the Institute of Slavic, East European, and Eurasian Studies. Among his publications are *From Enemy to Brother: The Revolution in Catholic Teaching on the Jews* (Harvard University Press, 2012) and the co-edited volume (with Michael Grüttner) *Universities under Dictatorship* (State College: Pennsylvania State University Press, 2005).

Leonidas DONSKIS is Professor of Politics and Senior Fellow at Vytautas Magnus University in Kaunas, Lithuania. Among his publications are: co-author (with Zygmunt Bauman) of *Moral Blindness: The Loss of Sensitivity in Liquid Modernity* (Polity, 2013), and author of *Modernity in Crisis: A Dialogue on the Culture of Belonging* (Palgrave, 2011).

Raluca GROSESCU is Associate Research Fellow at the Department of History (University of Exeter). Among her publications are *Les communistes dans l'après-communisme. Trajectoires de conversion politique de la nomenklatura roumaine après 1989* (Michel Houdiard, 2010) and the co-edited volume (with Agata Fijalkowski) *Transitional Criminal Justice in Post-Dictatorial and Post-Conflict Societies* (Intersentia, 2015).

Alexandru GUSSI is Lecturer at University of Bucharest. Among his publications are: *La Roumanie face à son passe communiste. Mémoires et cultures politiques* (l'Harmattan, 2011) and "The Ex-communist's Policy of Forgetting in Romania after 1990", *Studia Politica- Romanian Political Science Review*, vol. IX, no. 2/2009, 273–290.

Jeffrey HERF is Distinguished University Professor at University of Maryland (College Park). Among his publications are: *Nazi Propaganda for the Arab World* (Yale University Press, 2009) and *The Jewish Enemy: Nazi Propaganda During World War II and the Holocaust* (Harvard University Press, 2006).

Bogdan C. IACOB is Post-doctoral Fellow at New Europe College in Bucharest. He is co-editor (with Vladimir Tismaneanu) of *The End and the Beginning: The Revolutions of 1989 and the Resurgence of History* (CEU Press, 2012) and author of "Is It Transnational? A New Perspective in the Study of Communism," *East Central Europe*, vol. 40, no.1 (2013), 114–139.

Eric LANGENBACHER is Associate Teaching Professor and Director of the Senior Honors Program in the Department of Government (Georgetown University). Among his publications are: *The Merkel Republic: The 2013 Bundestag Election and its Consequences* (edited volume, Berghahn Books, forthcoming 2015) and *Dynamics of Memory and Identity in Contemporary Europe* (co-edited with Ruth Wittlinger and Bill Niven, Berghahn Books, 2013).

Jan WERNER MÜLLER is Professor of Politics at Princeton University. Among his publications are: *Contesting Democracy: Political Ideas in Twentieth-Century Europe* (Yale University Press, 2011) and *Constitutional Patriotism* (Princeton University Press, 2007).

Eusebio MUJAL-LÉON is Professor at Georgetown University where he is also director of the Cuba XXI Project. Among his publications are: "Survival, Adaptation and Uncertainty—The Case of Cuba," *Journal of International Affairs* (Fall/Winter 2011) Vol. 65, No. 1, 149–168 and "Spanish Foreign Policy and EU-Cuba Relations 1982-2010" in Gabriel Castro and Jesús de Miguel (eds), *Spain in America* (Madrid: Fundación ENDESA, 2010), 489–515.

Andrzej PACZKOWSKI Is Professor at the Political Institute of Polish Academy of Sciences. Among his publications are: *Revolution and Counterrevolution in Poland, 1980-1989* (University of Rochester Press, 2015) and *The Spring Will be Ours* (Pennsylvania State University Press, 2003).

Vladimir PETROVIĆ is senior researcher at the Institute of Contemporary History in Belgrade and visiting scholar at Brudnick Center on Violence and Conflict (Northeastern University). Among his publications are: "Power(lessness) of Atrocity Images. Visual Evidence of War Crimes in the former Yugoslavia," *International Journal for Transitional Justice* 2015/3 and "A Crack in the Wall of Denial. Scorpion Srebrenica Footage in and out of the Courtroom," in Dubravka Zarkov and Marlies Glasius (eds), *Narratives of Justice in and Out of the Courtroom* (Springer 2014), 89–110.

Timothy SNYDER is Bird White Housum Professor of History at Yale University. Among his recent publications are: *Black Earth: The Holocaust as History and Warning* (Tim Duggan Books, Crown Publishing, 2015) and *Bloodlands: Eastern Europe Between Hitler and Stalin* (Basic Books, 2010).

Vladimir TISMANEANU is Professor of Politics at University of Maryland (College Park) and director of the Center for the Study of Post-communist Societies. Among his publications are: *The Devil in History. Communism, Fascism, and Some Lessons of the Twentieth Century* (University of California Press, 2012) and *Promises of 1968. Crisis, Illusion, and Utopia* (edited volume, CEU Press, 2011).

Raluca URSACHI has a Ph.D. from Université Paris 1 Pantheon Sorbonne. Among her publications are: co-author with Raluca Grosescu of the volume *Justiţia penală de tranziţie. De la Nuremberg la postcomunismul românesc* (Polirom, 2009) and "Transitional Criminal Justice in Post-Communist Romania" in Thede Kahl and Larisa Schippel (eds.), *Kilometer Null: politische Transformation und gesellschaftliche Entwicklungen in Rumänien seit 1989* (Frank & Timme, 2011), 405–422.

Cristian VASILE is Senior Researcher at "Nicolae Iorga" History Institute of the Romanian Academy. Among his most recent publications are: *Viaţa intelectuală şi artistică în primul deceniu al regimului Ceauşescu. 1965–1974* (Humanitas, 2015) and *Politicile culturale comuniste în timpul regimului Gheorghiu-Dej* (Humanitas, 2011).

Charles VILLA-VICENCIO is Visiting Professor in the Conflict Resolution Program (Georgetown University) and Emeritus Professor at the University of Cape Town. Among his publications are: *Looking Back, Reaching Forward: Reflections on the Truth and Reconciliation Commission of South Africa* (co-edited with Wilhelm Verwoerd, Zed Books, 2000), and *The Provocations of Amnesty: Memory, Justice, and Impunity* (co-edited with Erik Doxtader, New Africa Books, 2003).

Nikolai VUKOV is Associate Professor at the Institute of Ethnology and Folklore Studies with Ethnographic Museum (Bulgarian Academy of Sciences). Among his publications are: *Witnesses of Stone: Monuments and Architectures of the Red Bulgaria, 1944–1989* (co-authored with L. Ponchiroli, Mantova, 2011) and "From the 'Thirst for Change' and 'Hunger for Truth' to a 'Revolution that Hardly Happened': Public Protests and Reconstructions of the Past in Bulgaria in the 1990s" in Kevin McDermott and Matthew Stibbe (eds.), *The 1989 Revolutions in Central and Eastern Europe. From Communism to Pluralism* (Manchester University Press, 2013), 253–270.

Index